Byles on Bills of Exchange and Cheques

AUSTRALIA
Law Book Co.
Sydney

CANADA and USA
Carswell
Toronto

HONG KONG
Sweet & Maxwell Asia

NEW ZEALAND
Brookers
Wellington

SINGAPORE and MALAYSIA
Sweet & Maxwell Asia
Singapore and Kuala Lumpur

Byles on Bills of Exchange and Cheques

Twenty-seventh Edition

by

NICHOLAS ELLIOTT, Q.C.

and

JOHN ODGERS

and

JONATHAN MARK PHILLIPS

all of 3 Verulam Buildings, Barristers

 Sweet & Maxwell
A THOMSON COMPANY

2002

Published in 2002 by
Sweet & Maxwell Limited of
100 Avenue Road London NW3 3PF
http://www/sweetandmaxwell.co.uk
Typeset by Interactive Sciences Ltd, Gloucester
Printed in England by MPG Books Ltd, Bodmin, Cornwall

First published in 1829 as *Byles on Bills of Exchange*

A CIP catalogue record for this book is available from the British Library

ISBN 0421 456000

No natural forests were destroyed to make this product, only farmed timber
was used and re-planted

ISBN 0-421-45600-0

9 780421 456006

PREFACE TO THE 27th EDITION OF BYLES

With the arrival of the new millennium comes a new edition of Byles, whose first edition was published in 1829. As the century has changed so have those responsible for this edition. From the 21st edition in 1955 onwards one or both of the editorial team of Maurice Megrah and Frank Ryder had undertaken the editorial task.

The change of editorial team, the developments in the law during the thirteen years since the last edition and the changes to the Rules of Court, have meant that many Chapters have undergone major revisions. At the same time we have taken the opportunity to excise a fair amount of historical material setting out the law relating to bills prior to the passing of the 1882 Act. The most significant change in the law has been the introduction, by the Cheques Act 1992, of non-transferable cheques. Within the United Kingdom cheques are now almost invariably issued in "account payee" form to take advantage of this Act. Cheques were always a somewhat distinct species of bill of exchange, with a body of law largely separate from that of other bills; however, the fact that nowadays most cheques are never issued in a negotiable form widens that distinction still further. It is for that reason that the opportunity has been taken to adopt, what some might regard as the heretical step, of changing the title to that of *"Byles on Bills of Exchange and Cheques"*.

As in previous editions, the sections of the 1882 Act are not dealt with in strict order, unlike Chalmers & Guest on Bills of Exchange. The order of the main divisions of the book has been retained but much within has been amended. In particular, Part II of the book, "Cheques", has been expanded and substantially rewritten. Chapter 21 now deals with "account payee" cheques under the Cheques Act 1992 and also with the 1996 legislation permitting the presentation for payment of cheque details by electronic or other means. The same chapter now contains a section on travellers cheques, which although not true cheques are a related class of instrument. In Chapters 22 and 23 we have tried to clarify the sources of liability of paying and collecting banks and draw attention to the importance of money laundering legislation.

Similarly Part V "Practice and Procedure" has been re-written to take into account the very substantial changes in matters of procedure and evidence, particularly following the introduction in England and Wales of the Civil Procedure Rules. Previous editions have contained a wealth of authority bearing little relation to modern conditions or practice. A delicate balance has been sought between relevance and accessibility to practitioners, and the retention of material which remains of value. Chapter 29, dealing with Limitation has been largely re-structured and updated.

Chapter 25 on the Conflict of Laws has also been heavily revised and re-ordered. The treatment of defects of title (in Chapter 18) and failure of consideration (in Chapter 19) is largely new. Chapter 32 which deals with the recovery of payments made under a mistake is entirely new, and replaces the short section on this subject which appeared in Chapter 13 of earlier editions.

Less radical changes have been made throughout the book, not only to update it in the light of developments in the law, but in an effort to modernise the style and presentation.

We hope that the changes introduced make this edition somewhat easier to use to those unfamiliar with bills and notes, although we are all too conscious that there is yet further room for improvement.

As is so commonly the case we cannot pass up the opportunity of expressing our thanks for the patience shown by our Publishers and, no less importantly, our respective wives. The law is stated as at October 1, 2001.

3 VB   NE
Gray's Inn   JO
October 2001   JMP

Contents

Part Six

Appendices

TABLE OF CASES

As regards Dominion cases, only one report may be given, but it is not therefore to be presumed that any particular case is not reported elsewhere.

TABLE OF STATUTES

TABLE OF STATUTORY INSTRUMENTS

PART ONE

CHAPTER 1

NATURE, PURPOSE AND DEFINITION

Introduction

IT would appear that bills of exchange have been known to exist in England **1–01** since the time of Edward IV, having been introduced through trade with the continent.[1] At first, the use of bills seems to have been confined to foreign bills between English and foreign merchants; it subsequently extended to domestic bills between traders, and thereafter to all persons, whether traders or not.

In 1882 the law relating to bills of exchange, cheques and promissory notes **1–02** as it had developed was codified in the Bills of Exchange Act 1882 ("the 1882 Act"), which still primarily governs the position today.

At one time bills were one of the principal means of settling debts, as well **1–03** as a form of currency and a method of providing short-term finance. Their significance has substantially diminished over the last half century. As observed by Dr (now Professor) Shea in his report to the Jack Committee:

> "There is a tendency (outside banking circles) to dismiss bills and notes (other than cheques) as unimportant. The use of bills, notes and indeed cheques as a means of payment has substantially decreased over the last few decades. However within the context of international transactions bills and notes continue to be utilised and are still important."[2]

Equally the use of cheques has diminished considerably with the increase in the use of credit and switch cards, and with the advent of digital cash and electronic banking.

Purpose

However bills still feature in international trade regularly. Not only are they **1–04** a means whereby the buyer of goods in one country makes payment to the seller of goods in another, but they are used as a means of financing the transaction or obtaining credit. By this means the seller of goods receives payment as soon as the goods are shipped and the buyer of the goods defers payment until he receives the goods. In the typical example where payment under the export contract is by way of letter of credit, a sight bill or time bill (being a bill of exchange) will be one of the documents required to be presented by the beneficiary under the terms of the credit in order to obtain payment. A cheque is a special form of bill of exchange, being drawn on a banker payable on demand, and is normally intended for the immediate

---

[1] The origin and history of bills and other negotiable instruments are traced by Lord Cockburn C.J. in his judgment in *Goodwin v. Roberts* (1875) L.R.10 Ex. at pp. 346–358.

[2] See para. 2.1, Appendix A (Report on Negotiable Instruments) to the *Banking Services: Law and Practice Report* by the Review Committee (1989) Cm 622.

discharge of a single debt. More often than not a promissory note is a continuing security for a debt. Bills and cheques are orders to pay; promissory notes are promises to pay.

Nomenclature

1–05   The definition of a bill is set out below.[3] Essential to any consideration of issues arising in relation to bills of exchange, notes and cheques is an understanding of the nomenclature used. Section 2 of the 1882 Act contains an interpretation of the terms used. However by way of introduction it is necessary to go beyond the terms set out in that section. Many of the words or phrases used are dealt in greater depth in the relevant chapter applicable to the section of the 1882 Act.

"Bill" and "Note": Bill means a bill of exchange and note means a promissory note.[4]

"Parties": Although not referred to in the 1882 Act, commonly reference can be found to a person being a party to a bill. The principal parties to a bill are the drawer, the drawee/acceptor, the payee, the holder, the indorser and the indorsee. The requirements as to each of these parties and their rights and obligations are central to the law relating to bills and other negotiable instruments. The subsequent chapters deal with these matters in detail.

"Drawer": The drawer is the person who draws the bill, *i.e.* is responsible for the drawing and signing of the instrument addressed to another (the drawee) instructing him to make payment; his signature on the face of the bill is essential.

"Drawee": The drawee is the person to whom a bill is addressed and who is ordered to perform payment.

"Acceptor": The acceptor is the drawee who, by signing the bill, has undertaken to pay the bill.

"Payee": The payee is the person named in the instrument to whom or to whose order payment is to be made.

"Bearer": The bearer is the person in possession of a bill or note which is payable to bearer.[5]

"Holder": The holder means the payee or indorsee of a bill or note who is in possession of it, or the bearer of it,[6] if the instrument is payable to bearer; the 1882 Act also refers to a "holder in due course" and a "holder for value".[7]

"Indorser": The indorser is the former holder of a bill or note who has indorsed it, by affixing his signature and transferring it to another.

"Indorsee": The indorsee means the transferee of a bill or note, who has the rights under the 1882 Act in respect of a bill or note by virtue of an indorsement.[8]

---

[3] *Post* para. 1–09.
[4] Section 2.
[5] Section 2.
[6] Section 2.
[7] *Post* paras 18–01 *et seq.*
[8] See *Midland Bank Ltd v. Harris* [1963] 1 W.L.R. 1021, at 1024 and *post* para. 18–48.

"Indorsement": means an indorsement (being the signature on the bill or note by the indorser) completed with delivery.[9]

"Maker": The maker of a promissory note is the person who, since there is no drawee, corresponds with the drawer of a bill.

"Delivery": means the transfer of possession [of a bill or note], actual or constructive, from one person to another.[10]

"Issue": means the first delivery of a bill or note, complete in form to a person who takes it as holder.

Negotiability

Until the passing of the Cheques Act 1992 affected the position, bills, cheques and promissory notes were negotiable instruments. That is to say they could be transferred by mere delivery, or by indorsement and delivery, from one person to another, so as to pass a complete title free of the equities to a transferee who takes bona fide and for value, and with the right in the transferee to sue in his own name all parties to the instrument. In these respects, negotiable instruments differ from any other contract, but they are not a single contract, embodying as many contracts as there are parties. The characteristic of negotiability is still at the heart of bills and notes, and for that reason they are commonly referred to as "negotiable instruments". Cheques were equally categorised as negotiable instruments, but since the passing of the Cheques Act 1992, within the United Kingdom, cheques are now usually issued, in practice, in non-negotiable form.[11]

1–06

The statutory framework

As already set out above the basis of the law of negotiable instruments in the United Kingdom is the Bills of Exchange Act 1882 ("the 1882 Act"), which has been adopted as the basis of the law in the United States of America and the former British Dominions, as well as in other countries which are, or were, members of the British Commonwealth of Nations. The 1882 Act contains special sections (ss.76–82) relating to cheques. In addition, there are the Cheques Act 1957 and the Cheques Act 1992. The former was passed in order to eliminate the necessity for indorsement of cheques and other orders to pay. The latter was passed in order to facilitate the issuing of cheques by the customers of banks in a form whereby they could not be validly transferred to parties other than the named payee. This measure was introduced in order to reduce cheque fraud.

1–07

Other jurisdictions

There are wide differences between the laws of the United Kingdom on the one hand and, on the other hand, those of the Continent of Europe, certain South American countries and Japan, whose laws are founded on the League

1–08

---

[9] Section 2 and *post* para. 9–04.
[10] Section 2.
[11] *Post* paras 21–31 *et seq.*

of Nations Conventions Numbers 3313 and 3314 (Uniform Law and Conflicts of Law) relating to bills of exchange and promissory notes, dated June 7, 1930, and Numbers 3316 and 3317 (Uniform Law and Conflicts of Law), relating to cheques, dated March 31, 1931.[12]

Definition of a bill of exchange

1–09   A bill of exchange is defined in section 3 of the 1882 Act as follows:

3.—(1) A bill of exchange is an unconditional order in writing, addressed by one person to another, signed by the person giving it, requiring the person to whom it is addressed to pay on demand or at a fixed or determinable future time a sum[13] certain in money to or to the order of a specified person, or to bearer.

Section 3 of the 1882 Act further provides that:

(2) An instrument which does not comply with these conditions, or which orders any act to be done in addition to the payment of money, is not a bill of exchange.

An example of an instrument failing to meet the requirements of section 3 arose in *Korea Exchange Bank v. Debenhams (Central Buying) Ltd*,[14] where the draft was drawn " . . . at 90 days D/A . . . pay . . . ". The draft was held by the Court of Appeal not to be a bill as it showed no maturity date either expressly or by determination. However in a similar case the courts have indicated a willingness to give effect to an instrument if at all possible. In *Hong Kong & Shanghai Banking Corporation Ltd v. G.D. Trade Co. Ltd*[15] the Court of Appeal observed:

> "[a bill] is a document in use in hundreds of commercial transactions and, in the case of an instrument which has been drawn as a bill with the plain intention that it should take effect as such, the court should lean in favour of a construction which upholds its validity as a bill where that is reasonably possible".[16]

Section 3 of the 1882 Act goes on to provide that:

(3) An order to pay out of a particular fund is not unconditional within the meaning of this section; but an unqualified order to pay, coupled with (a) an indication of a particular fund out of which the drawee is to reimburse himself or a particular account to be debited with the amount,

---

[12] The countries signing the above Conventions and the extent to which they have been ratified are given in League of Nations Treaty Series, Vol. CXLIII, 1933–34, pp. 257, 317, 355 and 407.

[13] See *post*, para. 2–16, s.11 of the 1882 Act—definition of "determinable future time".

[14] [1979] 1 Lloyd's Rep. 548, CA.

[15] [1998] C.L.C. 238; see also *Novaknit S.A. v. Kumar Bros International Ltd* [1998] Lloyd's Rep. Banking 287.

[16] At 242.

or (b) a statement of the transaction which gives rise to the bill, is unconditional.

Form

No precise form of words is essential to the validity of a bill of exchange, **1–10** but it must comply substantially with the definition in section 3(1), particularly that it be an unconditional order. The order to pay need be in no particular form; any expression amounting to an order[17] or direction is sufficient. The word "pay" is not indispensable; any synonymous or equivalent expression, such as "credit in cash" will suffice.[18]

Parties

The person giving the order to pay and signing the bill is called the **1–11** "drawer", the person to whom the bill is addressed the "drawee" and the person named in the instrument to whom or to whose order payment is to be made, the "payee". When the payee signs on the back of a bill he is called in that capacity an indorser; if a person not already a party to a bill signs on the back he is a stranger (s.56) and incurs the liabilities of an indorser.

When the "drawee" has undertaken to pay the bill he is called the "acceptor". Such an undertaking cannot be verbal only, but the drawee's mere signature on the bill without additional words is sufficient.[19] As opposed to the drawing of a bill, the acceptance may be conditional.[20]

The essential feature in a bill of exchange is the signature of the drawer on the face of the bill; in its absence an acceptance by the drawee is inoperative and the instrument cannot be treated as a promissory note of the acceptor.[21]

---

[17] *Morice v. Lee* (1725) 8 Mod. 262. It must import an absolute intention that the money shall at all events be paid, not merely authorise its payment; see *Hamilton v. Spottiswoode* (1849) 4 Ex. 200. In France "il vous plaira payer" seems to be a common formula adopted in drawing a bill. The employment of mere terms of courtesy must not go so far as to take from the document its imperative character. Thus an instrument which ran, "Mr. Little, please to let the bearer have seven pounds, and place it to my account, and you will oblige your humble servant R. Slackford", was held not to be a bill, since it did not purport to be a demand made by a party having a right to call on the other to pay, the fair meaning being, "you will oblige me by doing it" (*Little v. Slackford* (1828) 1 Mood. & M. 171). In the earlier case, however, of *Ruff v. Webb* (1794) 1 Esp. 129, an instrument in the following form: "Mr Nelson will much oblige Mr. Webb by paying to J. Ruff, or order, twenty guineas on his account", was held to be a bill; see also *Russell v. Powell* (1845) 14 M. & W. 418.

[18] *Ellison v. Collingridge* (1850) 9 C.B. 570. "I promise to pay or cause to be paid" is a good note, the alternative expression importing the same thing (*Lovell v. Hill* (1833) 6 C. & P. 238).

[19] See 1882 Act, s.17(1), (2), and *post*, para. 10–01.

[20] See *post*, para. 10–05, and 1882 Act, s.19. According to the Uniform Law on Bills of Exchange and Promissory Notes (Convention No. 3313, Geneva, June 7, 1930), a bill of exchange must conform to a given pattern, it must contain an unconditional order to pay a determinate sum of money, include the term "bill of exchange" in the language in which the bill is drawn, the names of the persons who are to pay and to whom or to whose order payment is to be made, the time and place of payment and the date and place where the bill is issued. It must bear the signature of the issuer (drawer) (Article 1).

[21] See *post*, para. 2–06 and as to inchoate instruments, 1882 Act, s.20, paras 4–01 *et seq*.

An instrument drawn by A upon B, requiring him to pay to the order of C a certain sum at a certain time "without acceptance" is still a bill of exchange.[22]

The legal effect of drawing a bill payable to a third person is a contract by the drawer to pay the payee, his order, or the bearer, as the case may be, conditionally on the drawee's failing to do so. The effect of accepting a bill, or making a note, is an absolute contract, on the part of the acceptor of the one, or maker of the other, to pay the payee, his order, or the bearer as the instrument may require.

When the payee signs on the back of a bill he is called in that capacity an indorser; if a person not already a party to a bill signs on the back he is a stranger (s.56) and incurs the liabilities of an indorser. The effect of indorsing is a conditional contract, on the part of the indorser, to pay the immediate or any succeeding indorsee, or bearer, in case of the default of the acceptor or maker.

Payment upon a contingency

1–12   In order to be a bill, the instrument must not be payable on a contingency. By section 11:

> **"An instrument expressed to be payable on a contingency is not a bill, and the happening of the event does not cure the defect."**[23]

Bill as chattel

1–13   For almost all purposes, bills are included within the general words "*goods and chattels*", or either of them, and may be the subject of reputed ownership or fraudulent transfer[24] or conversion; " . . . there might appear some difficulty that a bank, which paid part of what it owed to its customer to some other person not authorised to receive it, had converted its customer's chattels, but a series of decisions binding on this court, culminating in *Morisons*'s case[25] and *Underwood*'s case[26] surmounted the difficulty by treating the conversion as of the chattel, the piece of paper, the cheque under which the money was collected, and the value of the chattel converted as the money received under it."[27]

The Judgments Act 1838, s.12, renders money, bank notes, cheques, bills, promissory notes and other securities for money liable to be taken in execution.[28] The money and bank notes are to be handed over by the sheriff to the

---

[22] It may be so described in an indictment for forgery, *Miller v. Thomson* (1841) 3 M. & G. 576; *R. v. Kinnear* (1838) 2 Moo. & R. 117.

[23] *Post*, paras 2–02 and 2–18.

[24] *Ryall v. Rolle* (1749) 1 Atk. 165; *Bullock v. Dodds* (1819) 2 B. & Ald. 258; *Hornblower v. Proud* (1819) 2 B. & Ald. 327; *Cumming v. Bailey* (1830) 6 Bing. 363; *Edwards v. Cooper* (1847) 11 Q.B. 33.

[25] [1914] 3 K.B. 356.

[26] [1924] 1 K.B. 775.

[27] *Per* Scrutton L.J. in *Lloyds Bank Ltd v. Chartered Bank of India, Australia and China* [1929] 1 K.B. 40.

[28] *Watts v. Jefferyes* (1851) 3 Mac. & G. 422; *cf. Johnson v. Pickering* [1908] 1 K.B. 1, where the judgment debtor died before execution.

execution creditor, and the sheriff, on receiving a sufficient indemnity, is to sue on the cheques, bills and other securities in his own name.

Assignability

Historically contractual rights, being "choses in action", could not be **1–14** assigned at common law. One of the exceptions developed in relation to this general rule was that the holder of a bill of exchange could assign as part of the *Law Merchant*. Equity and statute intervened to make assignments of contractual rights and choses in action assignable.[29]

All the contracts arising on a bill of exchange are simple contracts, but they differ in the eyes of the common law from other simple contacts. First, no notice of the transfer need be given; secondly, consideration will be presumed till the contrary appears[30] and such consideration may be past;[31] thirdly, usually in the case of assignment the assignee takes subject to the equities, but in the case of a "holder on due course" of a bill the position is otherwise. Moreover the liability of any party may be discharged in the event of renunciation by the holder, without consideration.[32] Bills are excluded from the Contracts (Rights of Third Parties) Act 1999,[33] since third parties already have rights which are governed by the 1882 Act.

As a matter of practice the assignability of cheques has been restricted by the Cheques Act 1992.[34]

Bill not an assignment

In England, though not in Scotland, the drawee is not liable to the holder **1–15** until he accepts, for the 1882 Act provides:

53.—(1) A bill of itself does not operate as an assignment of funds in the hands of the drawee[35] available for the payment thereof, and the drawee of a bill who does not accept as required by this Act is not liable on the instrument. This subsection shall not extend to Scotland.

(2) [Subject to Section 75A of this Act], in Scotland, where the drawee of a bill has in his hands funds available for the payment thereof, the bill operates as an assignment of the sum for which it is drawn in favour of the holder, from the time when the bill is presented to the drawee.[36]

---

[29] Law of Property Act 1925,s.136.

[30] Section 30(2).

[31] Section 27(1)(b).

[32] *Post* para. 14–08.

[33] Section 6(1) of the 1999 Act, which came into force fully on May 11, 2000.

[34] *Post* paras 21–35 *et seq.*

[35] Or of funds belonging to the acceptor in the hands of the acceptor's bank, at which the bill is accepted payable (*Auchteroni & Co. v. Midland Bank* [1928] 2 K.B. 294, 297).

[36] In Scots law the assignment to be effectual must be intimated to the drawee by presentment of the bill (Thomson, 3rd ed., p. 105); see *British Linen Co. v. Carruthers* (1883) 10 R. 923 for the case of a cheque. Such presentment need not, however, be in accordance with the provisions of the 1882 Act (Hamilton, *Bills* (1904), p. 116 and Gloag and Henderson, *Law of Scotland* (7th ed., 1968). Section 20 of the Trustee Savings Banks Act 1969 formerly enacting that s.53(2) of the Bills of Exchange Act 1882 "shall not have effect in relation to funds being savings account deposits or special investments of a person at a trustee savings bank", was repealed by s.36(2) of the Trustee Savings Banks Act 1976.

This section applies to cheques also.

A purchased a bill from B & Co. in America, drawn by B & Co. on K in London, and on the face of the bill there was a direction "to charge the same on account of cheese per 'Britannic' and lard per 'Greece' as advised". On the same day B & Co. wrote to K a letter of advice, enclosing bills of lading for the cheese and lard, and informing him that they had drawn on him for the amount in favour of A. K subsequently refused to accept the bill, and it was held that A was not entitled to any charge on the proceeds of the sale of the goods, since the direction on the face of the bill did not operate as an equitable assignment, nor did the letter of advice create a specific appropriation of the remittances to meet the bill in favour of B & Co. of which the benefit might have been transferred to A by the direction on the bill.[37]

An assignment of book debts includes a bill handed to a banker for discount, but not actually discounted at the time of the assignment.[38]

In England the holder of an unpaid cheque has no equitable claim on the drawee-banker,[39] but a cheque issued and accepted on the strength of a cheque card binds the bank on the latter's representation.[40]

A bill or promissory note may, in some cases, be a declaration of trust.[41]

Stamp duties

1–16   As from February 1, 1971, the duties on bills of exchange and receipts were abolished and today the Stamp Acts are of no significance in relation to bills of exchange and notes.[42]

---

[37] *Brown, Shipley & Co. v. Kough* (1885) 29 Ch.D. 848, unfavourably commenting on *Frith v. Forbes* (1862) 4 De G.F. & J. 409; *cf. Robey and Co.'s Perseverance Iron Works v. Ollier* (1872) L.R. 7 Ch. 195. For examples of good equitable assignments, see *Ranken v. Alfaro* (1877) 5 Ch. 786; *Lutscher v. Comptoir D'Escompte de Paris* (1876) 1 Q.B.D. 709. For an example of the assignment of the proceeds of a note, see *Tyrrell v. Murphy* (1913) 30 O.L.R. 235.

[38] *Dawson v. Isle* [1906] 1 Ch. 633, following *Re Stevens* [1886] W.N. 110, 116; as to the priority of a debenture containing a charge on book debts over proceeds of bills assigned to a third party, see *Siebe Gorman & Co. Ltd v. Barclays Bank Ltd* [1979] 2 Lloyd's Rep. 142.

[39] *Hopkinson v. Forster* (1874) L.R. 19 Eq. 283; *Bank of Louisiana v. Bank of New Orleans* (1873) L.R. 6 H.L. 352; *Schroeder v. Central Bank of London Ltd.* In the United States of America, s.3–409 of the Uniform Commercial Code provides similarly: "A check or other draft does not of itself operate as an assignment of any funds in the hands of the drawee available for its payment, and the drawee is not liable on the instrument until he accepts it." By s.3–411, "certification of a check is acceptance"; the same applies on the Continent of Europe (*e.g.* see Escarra, *Droit Commercial* (1952), para. 1239).

[40] See *post*, para. 21–99.

[41] *Murray v. Glasse* (1854) 23 L.J. Ch. 126.

[42] Finance Act 1970, s.32., as noted by Saville J. in *G & H Montage GmbH v. Irvani* [1988] 1 W.L.R. 1285 at p. 1293; and, as regards bank notes, Finance Act 1972, s.126.

CHAPTER 2

FORM OF BILLS AND NOTES

Unconditional order

A BILL of exchange must be an unconditional order (1882 Act, s.3), though **2–01** the acceptor may make his acceptance conditional (1882 Act, s.19). On the other hand the drawer and indorsers may qualify in any way they please their contingent liability (1882 Act, s.16(1)), though the payee or indorsee may choose not to take the bill under those terms. In a promissory note the promise must be to pay absolutely and at all events (1882 Act, s.83 (1)). Where an instrument is on the face of it conditional, it is not a promissory note. So, for example, where an instrument ran, "At 12 months I promise to pay A and B £500, to be held by them as collateral security for any moneys now owing to them by J. M., which they may be unable to recover on realising the securities they now hold and others which may be placed in their hands by him", it is no promissory note.[1] Payment must not depend upon a contingency; for, as was observed by Lord Kenyon,[2] "It would perplex the commercial transactions of mankind, if paper securities of this kind were issued out into the world, encumbered with conditions and contingencies, and if the persons to whom they were offered in negotiation were obliged to inquire when these uncertain events would probably be reduced to a certainty." Besides, the recognition of conditional promissory notes would make a variety of conditional promises in writing valid, without evidence of consideration, and thus materially infringe on an established and salutary rule of law.[3]

An instrument in the form of a cheque but which carries a condition such as a receipt to be signed by the payee, which is a condition of payment, may operate as an equitable assignment.

Instruments payable on contingency

11 ... An instrument expressed to be payable on a contingency is not a **2–02** **bill, and the happening of the event does not cure the defect.**[4]

The following are examples of instruments held not to be negotiable instruments as being payable upon a contingency. A note to this effect: "We promise to pay A B £116 11s. value received, on the death of George Hindshaw, provided he leaves either of us sufficient to pay the said sum, or if

---

[1] *Robins v. May* (1839) 11 A. & E. 213. As to pledges of collateral security not invalidating notes, see s.83(3), *post*, para. 24–16.

[2] *Carlos v. Fancourt* (1794) 5 T.R. 482, 485, applied in *Ross v. Empire Construction and Investment Co.* [1932] 1 W.W.R. 714. So a condition as to signing a form of receipt may invalidate a cheque as such (*Bavins v. London and South Western Bank* (1900) 81 L.T. 655).

[3] See *Pearson v. Garrett* (1693) 4 Mod. 242.

[4] *cf. Hill v. Halford* (1801) 2 B. & P. 413; *post*, para. 2–18.

we shall be otherwise able to pay it."[5] A written engagement to pay a certain sum so many days after the defendant's marriage, for he may never marry[6]; an order payable, "Provided the terms mentioned in certain letters, written by the drawer, were complied with"[7]; a note promising to pay, "On the sale or produce immediately when sold, of the White Hart, St. Albans, Herts, and the goods, etc., value received"[8]; an instrument in the following terms: "Borrowed and received of A the sum of £200 in three drafts by B dated as under, payable to us on C, which we promise to pay the said A, with interest," and specifying the drafts which fell due at a future date, since, as Lord Ellenborough observed, "There can be no doubt that the money was not payable immediately, and that it was not to be paid at all, unless the drafts were honoured"[9]; an instrument in the form of a bill drawn payable "90 days after sight, or when realised", since the latter alternative makes the sum payable on a contingency[10]; an order to pay at 30 days after the arrival of the ship Paragon at Calcutta[11]; a promise to pay the sum of £50, by instalments, but no instalment to be payable after the payee's death.[12]

A bill containing an arbitration clause is not a "valid" bill.[13]

Payment out of particular fund

2–03   A bill or note must not be made payable out of a particular fund, for the fund may prove insufficient. As regards the source from which a bill or note is made payable the 1882 Act provides:

3.—(3) An order to pay out of a particular fund is not unconditional within the meaning of this section; but an unqualified order to pay, coupled with (a) an indication of a particular fund out of which the drawee is to reimburse himself or of a particular account to be debited with the amount, or (b) a statement of the transaction which gives rise to the bill, is unconditional.[14]

Thus where a bill directed the payment of money out of funds in the hands of the drawee belonging to the owners of the D mines, it was held to be

[5] *Roberts v. Peake* (1757) 1 Burr. 323.
[6] *Beardesley v. Baldwin* (1741) 2 Stra. 1151; and see *Pearson v. Garrett, supra.*
[7] *Kingston v. Long* (1785) Bayley, 6th ed., p. 16.
[8] *Hill v. Halford* (1801) 2 B. & P. 413, where it was averred that before action brought the White Hart and the goods were sold; *Thomson v. Huggins* (1896) 23 O.A.R. 191; *Gardiner v. Muir* [1917] 3 W.W.R. 1080.
[9] *Williamson v. Bennett* (1810) 2 Camp. 417. Where an instrument was given for an executed consideration, *viz.* for damages ascertained by consent, held a good note (*Shenton v. James* (1843) 5 Q.B. 199). Where the instrument was on its face a mere additional security and no money was payable at all events, *secus* (*Drury v. Macaulay* (1846) 16 M. & W. 146).
[10] *Alexander v. Thomas* (1851) 16 Q.B. 333.
[11] *Palmer v. Pratt* (1824) 2 Bing 185.
[12] *Worley v. Harrison* (1835) 5 Nev. & M. 173.
[13] *Per* Lord Wilberforce in *Nova (Jersey) Knit Ltd v. Kammgarn Spinnerei G.m.b.H.* [1977] 1 W.L.R. 713, 716.
[14] See *Shaw v. Shaw* (1896) 13 Cape S.C. 81; *Van Zyl v. Swanepoel* (1913) 4 C.P.D. 244.

invalid.[15] An order from the owner of a ship to the charterer to pay money on account of freight is no bill, for the future existence and amount of any debt due for freight are subject to a contingency.[16] On the other hand, the statement of a particular fund in a bill of exchange will not vitiate it if introduced merely as a direction to the drawee how to reimburse himself or show the particular account to be debited. Thus a bill directing the drawee to pay J.S. £9 10s., "as my quarterly half pay",[17] or a note promising to pay £25, "being a portion of a value as under, deposited in security for the payment thereof"[18] is not an order or promise to pay out of a particular fund, but merely contains a direction to the drawee how to reimburse himself or an indication of the particular account to be debited. In the same way a direction to charge the amount of the bill to certain specified bales of cotton merely indicates the particular account to be debited with the amount and does not make the bill conditional.[19] A statement of the transaction which gives rise to the bill explains why the bill is drawn and is merely an expansion of the common phrase "value received", as to which see section 3(4), *post*, para. 2–10. Hence, an instrument in the following terms: "Please pay to Messrs. X or order £600, on account of moneys advanced by me for the S. & F. Co." is valid as a bill.[20]

Where a bill is presented with a memorandum to the effect that the presenter holds a bill of lading, which turned out to be forged, and the plaintiff accepted the bill, it was held that there was no guarantee regarding the bill of lading and that the money could not be recovered.[21]

Writing and printing

Bills of exchange, and promissory notes are usually, but it would seem not necessarily, written on paper. It is conceived that they might be written on parchment, linen, cloth, leather, or any other convenient substitute for paper, not being a metallic substance. By section 9 of the Coinage Act 1971, no piece of gold, silver, or any other metal shall be made or issued, except by the Mint, as a coin or token for money, or as purporting that the holder thereof is entitled to demand any value denoted thereon.[22] Bills may be written in any language,   **2–04**

---

[15] *Jenney v. Herle* (1723) 2 Ld. Raym. 1361; *Josselyn v. L'Acier* (1715) 10 Mod. 294; *Dawkes v. De Loraine* (1771) 2 W.Bl. 782.

[16] *Banbury v. Lisset* (1744) 2 Stra. 1211.

[17] *Macleod v. Snee* (1726) 2 Ld. Raym. 1881.

[18] *Haussouillier v. Hartsinck* (1798) 7 T.R. 733.

[19] *Guaranty Trust Co. of New York v. Hannay & Co.* [1918] 2 K.B. 623, 635; [1918] 23 Com.Cas. 399 and the American cases there cited, applied in *Commonwealth Bank of Australia v. Rosenhain & Co.* [1922] Vict. L.R. 155, where a bill had written at its head "documents against acceptance", and was held unconditional. In *Rosenhain v. Commonwealth Bank of Australia* (1922) 31 C.L.R. 46, it was doubted whether these words prevented the instrument from being unconditional, but the point was not decided. See also *Korea Exchange Bank v. Debenhams (Central Buying) Ltd* [1979] 1 Lloyd's Rep. 548.

[20] *Griffin v. Weatherby* (1868) L.R. 3 Q.B. 753, followed in *Peacocke & Co. v. Williams* (1909) 28 N.Z.L.R. 354, and distinguished in *Brick and Potteries Co. v. Doornfontein Hebrew Congregation* (1907) 5 T.H. 183. Bills having on their face "hold for arrival of goods" were held to be unconditional: *Union Bank of Canada v. Antoniou* (1920) 61 S.C.R. 253; 2 W.W.R. 746.

[21] *Leather v. Simpson* (1871) L.R. 11 Eq. 398, applied in *Guaranty Trust Co. of New York v. Hannay & Co. (supra)*; *Baxter v. Chapman* (1873) 29 L.T. 642.

[22] See also *post*, para. 24–14.

and in any form of words, so long as section 3 of the 1882 Act is complied with. A bill or note or any other contract may be printed or written and may be written in pencil as well as in ink. "There is", says Abbot C.J., "no authority for saying, that where the law requires a contract to be in writing, that writing must be in ink . . . I am of opinion that an indorsement on a bill of exchange may be by writing in pencil. There is not any great danger that our decision will induce individuals to adopt such a mode of writing in preference to that in general use. The imperfection of this mode of writing, its being so subject to obliteration, and the impossibility of proving it when it is obliterated, will prevent its being generally adopted."[23]

By section 5 and Schedule I of the Interpretation Act 1978, the references to "writing" in any Act anterior or subsequent thereto shall, unless the contrary intention appears, include references to printing, lithography, photography and other modes of representing or reproducing words in a visible form. By section 2 of the 1882 Act "written" includes printed and "writing" includes print.

An undertaking to pay created by way of electronic message does not constitute a bill of exchange, since it is not "in writing", but in essence a series of electronic impulses.[24]

The Electronic Communications Act 2000 received the Royal Assent on May 25, 2000. Section 8 of the Act empowers the appropriate Minister to modify the provisions of any enactment so as to facilitate the use of electronic communications. At present there are no proposals to introduce electronic bills of exchange.[25] There are problems inherent in seeking to achieve by way of electronic means, the legal effect of a paper bill of exchange. The physical piece of paper lies at the heart of the 19th century philosophy of the negotiability and transfer of bills. Any proposal to introduce an electronic instrument would require a fundamental departure from the 1882 Act as it exists at present.

Signature

2–05   No one can be liable on a bill of exchange unless he has signed it or it is signed by someone with his authority.[26] "Signature" is not defined.[27] Unless, however, the "signature" is in the generally recognised form, the necessity arises of proving its authenticity.

[23] *Geary v. Physic* (1826) 5 B. & C. 234.
[24] Payment, of course, can be made by the electronic transfer of funds: see in particular the description in Chapters 17 and 19 Paget's Law of Banking (12th ed., 2001) and Brindle and Cox, *Law of Bank Payments* (2nd ed. 1999).
[25] In The Report of the Review Committee on Banking Services: Law and Practice (1989 CM.622 ("the Jack Report"), consideration was given to instruments in electronic or "dematerialised" form (see paras 8.33 to 8.38). Their recommendations have not been adopted.
[26] See *post*, paras 7–01 *et seq.*
[27] In the case of *Ex p. Birmingham Banking Co.* (1886) L.R. 3 Ch. 651, 654, the Court was of opinion that liquidators in a voluntary winding up might accept a bill by impressing a printed mark thereon. The question of the legality of such a mode of signing a negotiable instrument does not appear to have been considered in any other case. In France a decision of the Chambre Commerciale de la Cour de Cassation of June 27, 1961, was against facsimile signatures on the ground that a written signature was an essential condition of the validity of a bill of exchange (*Banque*, January 1962, consultation du Professor J. Hamel).

In *Importers Ltd v. Westminster Bank Ltd*, MacKinnon J. expressed surprise at evidence to the effect that pencil indorsements were often seen.[28] Whether the signature may be by initials is open to question. The 1882 Act (s.2) would seem to permit a mechanically produced signature, but in *Goodman v. J. Eban Ltd*,[29] a case concerning the signature, by means of a stamp, to a solicitor's bill of costs, Denning L.J., in a dissentient judgment, at 562, seemed to doubt whether a bill of exchange or a cheque could be signed by means of a rubber stamp. The difference between such a stamp and a mark seemed to him to lie in the fact that a mark by a person who cannot write is a signature, whereas a rubber stamp denotes "the thoughtless impression of an automaton in contrast to the reasoned attention of a sensible person". He went on: "Has anyone ever supposed that a man can sign a bill of exchange by means of a rubber stamp?"

Two years later Denning L.J. referred to the earlier decision and said: "It has been held in this court that a private person can sign a document by impressing a rubber stamp with his own facsimile signature on it . . . but it has not yet been held that a company can sign by its printed name affixed with a rubber stamp."[30]

Banks normally require an indemnity before they will permit the use of facsimile signatures for the drawing of cheques.

The signature or indorsement of negotiable instruments may be by a mark, providing there is evidence that the person signing by mark habitually so signs.[31]

The forgery of a signature on a bill is not a signature at all; it is a nullity.[32]

In 1998 the E.U. issued a draft Directive, the stated aim of which was "ensuring the proper functioning of the Internal Market in the field of electronic signatures by creating a harmonised and appropriate legal framework for the use of electronic signatures within the European Community and establishing a set of criteria which form the basis for legal recognition of electronic signatures". The Electronic Communications Act 2000 implements the Directive within the United Kingdom. Under the Act electronic signatures

---

[28] [1927] 1 K.B. 869, 874.

[29] *Goodman v. J. Eban Ltd* [1954] 1 Q.B. 550; as to typewritten signatures, see *McBeath's Trustees v. McBeath*, 1955 S.C. 471.

[30] *Lazarus Estates Ltd v. Beasley* [1956] 1 Q.B. 702.

[31] *George v. Surrey* (1830) M. & M. 516 where such a signature was only admitted with some hesitation (the only English case apparently as far as negotiable instruments are concerned); *Re Blewitt* (1880) 5 P.D. 116, related to initials in the margin of a will opposite interlineations which were held valid. In America such a signature to a negotiable instrument has been held valid (*Merchant's Bank v. Spicer* (1831) 6 Wend. 443; *Palmer v. Stephens* (1845) 1 Denio (N.Y.) 471); 80 C.J.S.; Daniel (5th ed., 1903), s.94. Uniform Commercial Code, s.1–201(39): " 'signed', includes any symbol executed or adopted by a party with present intention to authenticate a writing". See also *Brown v. Butcher's Bank* (1844) 6 Hill (N.Y.) 443, and *Willoughby v. Moulton* (1866) 47 New Hamp.Rep. 205; and *Bretch v. White* (Okla.) 67 P. (2d) 945; U.C.C., s.3–401(2): "A signature is made by use of any name including any trade or assumed name, upon an instrument, or by any work or mark used in lieu of a written signature." Under South African law a witness is required to such a signature (*Philips v. Mroquoza* (1905) 22 Cape S.C. 49; 15 C.T.R. 97 and see Cowen, 4th ed., 1966, 130). Where a signature is by mark it is not necessary to prove that the person so signing cannot write (*Baker v. Dening* (1838) 8 A. & E. 94; *Hanse v. Jordan* (1909) 19 C.T.R. 530), in which case a mark was admitted though the defendant could write.

[32] See *post* para. 20–33.

will be admissible as evidence of authenticity (though not conclusive). However it is suggested that electronic signatures will play no part in relation to bills of exchange, so long as they are confined to physical pieces of paper.[33] The recognition of electronic signatures provided for in Section 7(1) of the Act is referable to those instances where the signature is incorporated into or associated with a particular electronic communication or particular electronic data; a bill is not such a communication or data.

Signature of drawer essential

2–06   The drawer's signature is essential to the validity of a bill; without it no action can be maintained against the acceptor, either as such or as the maker of a note.[34] An instrument signed by the drawer as such is, though unaccepted by the drawee, a complete and regular bill *quoad* a holder in due course within the meaning of section 29(1).[35]

The signature of the drawer or maker of a bill or note is usually subscribed in the bottom-right-hand corner; but it is sufficient if written in any other part. In the case of a promissory note where the note was in the handwriting of the maker, it was held sufficient if his name occurred in any part of it, as "I, J.S., promise to pay."[36]

No other act beyond payment of money can be required

2–07   Bills and notes must not order or promise, in addition to the payment of money, the performance of some other act. Section 3(2) of the 1882 Act provides that an instrument which orders any act to be done in addition to the payment of money is not a bill. Thus a note which, in addition to the payment of money, promises to deliver up horses and a wharf,[37] or agrees to give a real security, is not a note.[38] Nor can a bill or note be in the alternative, as to pay a sum of money, or render A B to prison.[39]

---

[33] For a fuller description of electronic signatures, see Chapter 7, Warne & Elliott, *Banking Litigation* (1999).

[34] *McCall v. Taylor* (1865) 34 L.J.C.P. 365; *Mason v. Lack* (1929) 140 L.T. 696; *cf. Stoessiger v. South Eastern Ry* (1854) 3 E. & B. 549; *Goldsmid v. Hampton* (1858) 5 C.B. (N.S.) 94. The indorsement by the drawer of a bill to his order does not remedy the absence of his signature as drawer (*South Wales Coal Board v. Underwood* (1899) 15 T.L.R. 157; *cf. Mander v. Evans and Rose* (1888) 5 T.L.R. 75 *post*, para. 17–118).

[35] See *National Park Bank v. Berggren* (1914) 110 L.T. 907. Where the acceptance is for good consideration, the drawer's name may be inserted subsequently, as after the acceptor's death (*Carter v. White* (1833) 25 Ch.D. 666).

[36] *Taylor v. Dobbins* (1720) 1 Stra. 399.

[37] *Martin v. Chauntry* (1747) 2 Stra. 1271; see also *Moor v. Vanlute* (1714) Buller, N.P., 7th ed., p. 272b; *Travis v. Forbes* (1907) 41 N.S.R. 226.

[38] *Follett v. Moore* (1849) 19 L.J. Exch. 6; but it is otherwise where the note recited that a real security had already been given (*Fancourt v. Thorne* (1846) 9 Q.B. 312). A statement in a note equivalent merely to "value received" will not invalidate it (*Dixon v. Nuttall* (1834) 1 Cr.M. & R. 307).

[39] *Smith v. Boheme* (1724) Gilbert, *Cases Law and Equity* (1760), p. 93, cited 2 Ld. Raym. 1396.

Evidence of agreement

If the instrument is defective as a bill or note, it still may be evidence of an agreement.[40]   **2–08**

Ambiguous instruments

In general, where an instrument is made in terms so ambiguous that it is doubtful whether it be a bill of exchange or a promissory note, the holder may treat it as either at his option.[41]   **2–09**

Thus, where for goods sold and delivered the defendant gave the plaintiff an instrument in the following form:

£44: 11s. 5d   London, August 5, 1826.

Three months after date I promise to pay Mr. John Bury, or order, forty-four pounds eleven shillings and five pence, value received.

J. B. Grutherot,   John Bury
  35 Montague Place,
    Bedford Square.

and Grutherot's name was written across the instrument as an acceptance, with Bury's name on the back as an indorsement, it was held that the plaintiff might treat the defendant Bury either as a drawer of a bill or maker of a promissory note, and therefore was not bound to give him notice of dishonour.[42]

So where an instrument was in the following form:

October 21, 1804.
Two months after date pay to the order of John Jenkins, £78: 11s., value received.

Thomas Stephens

At Messrs. John Morson & Co.

Lord Ellenborough held that it was properly a bill of exchange, but that perhaps it might have been treated as a promissory note, at the option of the holder.[43]

The Courts have more recently indicated that they would lean in favour of a construction which upholds its validity as a bill where that is reasonably possible.[44]

---

[40] See *Smith v. Nightingale* (1818) 2 Stark. 375.

[41] *Peto v. Reynolds* (1854) 9 Exch. 410; *Armfield v. Allport* (1857) 27 L.J. Exch. 42; *Fielder v. Marshall* (1861) 30 L.J.C.P. 158; see now, s.5(2), *post*, para. 24–5.

[42] *Edis v. Bury* (1827) 6 B. & C. 433; also *Lloyd v. Oliver* (1852) 18 Q.B. 471.

[43] *Shuttleworth v. Stevens* (1808) 1 Camp. 407; *Allan v. Mawson* (1814) 4 Camp. 115; *Gray v. Milner* (1819) 8 Taunt. 739; *R. v. Hunter* (1823) Russ. & Ry. 511; *Armfield v. Allport* (1857) 27 L.J.Ex. 42.

[44] *Hong Kong & Shanghai Banking Corporation v. G. D. Trade Co. Ltd* [1998] C.L.C. 238 at 242.

TIME OF PAYMENT

Date

2–10 It is proper, though not necessary, to superscribe the name of the place where a bill or note is drawn, or made; so, too, a bill or note should always be dated, though a date is not in general essential to its validity,[45] since the 1882 Act provides that:

3.—(4) A bill is not invalid by reason—

 (a) **That it is not dated;**

 (b) **That it does not specify the value given, or that any value has been given therefor**[46]**;**

 (c) **That it does not specify the place where it is drawn or the place where it is payable.**[47]

If there is no date, it will be considered to be dated as of the time at which it was drawn, or rather, it is suggested, at which it was issued,[48] but a holder may, by section 20, fill in the date.[49]

Ante-dating, post-dating or on Sunday

2–11 It is also provided that:

13.—(2) A bill is not invalid by reason only that it is ante-dated or post-dated, or that it bears date on a Sunday.[50]

This provision applies to cheques as well as to bills. A banker is not entitled to pay a post-dated cheque before the date it bears.[51]

---

[45] The Geneva Convention provides, in Art. 2, that an instrument in which the date of issue is not mentioned is invalid.

[46] As to value, see *post*, paras 19–01 *et seq.*

[47] As to place, see *post*, para. 12–09.

[48] *De la Courtier v. Bellamy* (1680) 2 Show. 422; *Hague v. French* (1802) 3 B. & P. 173; *Giles v. Bourne* (1817) 6 M. & S. 73. Parol evidence is admissible to show that a written contract, which has no date, was not intended to operate from its delivery, but from a future uncertain period (*Davis v. Jones* (1856) 25 L.J.C.P. 91). By the Code, s.9(3), in the case of a bill expressed to be payable with interest, but which is issued undated, the interest runs from date of issue; see *post*, p. 409.

[49] *Post*, para. 4–01.

[50] *Pasmore v. North* (1811) 13 East 517. The Sunday Observance Act 1677, forbidding Sunday trading, was in force until repealed by the Statute Law (Repeals) Act 1969, but a bill drawn on a Sunday was not void under that Act (*Begbie v. Levi* (1830) 1 C. & J. 180; *North Western Life Assurance Co. v. Kushnir* [1922] 1 W.W.R. (Can.) 692); and see *Roiloswin Investments Ltd v. Chromolit Portugal Cutelarias e Produtos Metalicos S.A.R.L.* [1970] 1 W.L.R. 912.

[51] Post-dated cheques are fully discussed in Chapter 21, see *post* paras 21–14 *et seq.*

Omission of date in bill payable after date

The 1882 Act provides as follows for the case of the issue of an undated bill **2–12** payable at a fixed period after date, or for the case of a bill payable at a fixed period after sight where the acceptance is undated:

12. Where a bill expressed to be payable at a fixed period after date is issued undated, or where the acceptance of a bill payable at a fixed period after sight is undated, any holder may insert therein the true date of issue or acceptance, and the bill shall be payable accordingly.

Provided that (1) where the holder in good faith and by mistake inserts a wrong date, and (2) in every case where a wrong date is inserted, if the bill subsequently comes into the hands of a holder in due course the bill shall not be avoided thereby, but shall operate and be payable as if the date so inserted had been the true date.[52]

The date which the section allows to be inserted is the date of issue or acceptance. Consequently, where the date from which the bill is to run is fixed by agreement, irrespective of the date of its issue or sight, *e.g.* "90 days from the 26th November", the section does not apply as between immediate parties if a wrong date is inserted in good faith and by mistake.[53]

Presumption as to date

The date on a bill is presumed to be the true date till the contrary be proved, **2–13** as provided by the 1882 Act:

13.—(1) Where a bill or an acceptance or any indorsement on a bill is dated, the date shall, unless the contrary be proved, be deemed to be the true date of the drawing, acceptance, or indorsement, as the case may be.[54]

Misdescription of the date of a bill in an agreement is immaterial if the bill were in existence and present, for *praesentia corporis tollit errorem nominis*.[55]

---

[52] By s.20, a holder would be empowered to fill in the date of any undated bill; see *post*, para. 4–01.

[53] *Foster v. Driscoll* [1929] 1 K.B. 470, 495 (Scrutton L.J.).

[54] *Roberts v. Bethell* (1852) 12 C.B. 788; *Anderson v. Weston* (1840) 6 Bing. N.C. 296; *Smith v. Battens* (1834) 1 Mood. & R. 341; *Obbard v. Betham* (1830) Mood. & M. 483; 486; *Taylor v. Kinlock* (1816) 1 Stark 175. *Aliter*, where an IOU was tendered by assignees of a bankrupt as evidence of a petitioning creditor's debt (*Wright v. Lainson* (1837) 2 M. & W. 739). The date on a bill or note is not sufficient evidence of the date of the acceptance or of the indorsement, as distinct from that of the drawing and the making, to support a petitioning creditor's debt (*Cowie v. Harris* (1827) 1 Mood. & M. 141; *Rose v. Rowcroft* (1815) 4 Camp. 245). The date is a material part of a bill or note and any alteration without consent of the parties liable thereon by s.64 avoids the instrument; see *post*, para. 20–01.

[55] *Way v. Hearne* (1862) 32 L.J.C.P. 34, 40 (the presence of the substance removes the nominal error).

Date of maturity

2–14   The time for payment is usually stated in the beginning of the order to pay as " . . . days after sight" or "after date" or "on"; but if no time is expressed, the instrument will be payable on demand.[56]

On demand

2–15   **10.—(1) A bill is payable on demand:**

    (a) Which is expressed to be payable on demand, or at sight, or on presentation; or

    (b) In which no time for payment is expressed.[57]

It is submitted that (b) applies only if the instrument displays no intention to the contrary,[58] that it cannot apply if the instrument on the face of it shows an attempt to give a maturity date. To apply the subsection (b) would be to validate the instrument in favour of the party responsible for the weakness in the instrument.

(2) Where a bill is accepted or indorsed when it is overdue, it shall as regards the acceptor who so accepts, or any indorser who so indorses it, be deemed a bill payable on demand.

A bill or note must be payable either on demand, or else at a fixed or determinable future time. There is no limitation as to the length of time. "If a bill of exchange be made payable at never so distant day, if it be a day that must come, it is no objection to the bill."[59]

At a future time

2–16   **11. A bill is payable at a determinable future time within the meaning of this Act, which is expressed to be payable—**

    (1) At a fixed period after date or sight.[60]

    (2) On or at a fixed period after the occurrence of a specified event which is certain to happen, though the time of happening may be uncertain.

An instrument expressed to be payable on a contingency is not a bill, and the happening of the event does not cure the defect.

---

[56] As to overdue bills, see *post,* para. 17–33.

[57] See *Whitlock v. Underwood* (1823), 2 B. & C. 157, 107 E.R. 342. It has been held in Canada that where no time for payment is expressed parol evidence of a memorandum on the note fixing a due date as agreed on by the parties is admissible: *Polanuk v. Osterberg* [1919] 1 W.W.R. 394, where a memorandum fixing the date was held not to be part of the instrument.

[58] See *Korea Exchange Bank v. Debenhams (Central Buying) Ltd* [1979] 1 Lloyd's Rep. 100, CA.

[59] *Colehan v. Cooke* (1742) Willes 393 (Willes C.J.).

[60] Contrast *Gaudet v. Corneau* [1936] 1 D.L.R. 764 (payable "after 12 months after date"; it would seemingly be different if the word "after" were added by mistake).

A promissory note payable "on or before" a given date was held by a majority of the Court of Appeal in *Williamson v. Rider*[61] not to be within the requirements of this section. In a dissenting judgment Ormerod L.J. expressed the view that the bill is payable at a fixed or determinable future time, *viz.*, the date mentioned, even though the person primarily liable is given the right to pay earlier. In the recent case of *Claydon v. Bradley*[62] the Court of Appeal referred sympathetically to this dissenting judgment, but stated that it was bound by its earlier decision. Thus, Dillon L.J. stated at 525:

> "In the present case the time for payment was bound to arrive; the money was payable on 1 July, 1983 if it had not been repaid, at the option of the payer before. Nonetheless, we are bound by the decision of the majority in *Williamson v. Rider*."

It is submitted therefore that the minority view of Ormrod L.J. in *Williamson v. Rider* is to be preferred, although the majority view will prevail unless and until that decision is reversed by the House of Lords. Payment before maturity does not discharge the bill; though the acceptor or other person liable may pay earlier, he must if he so wishes seek out the holder and the latter can expect nothing and can do nothing if the person liable does not.

A bill or note cannot be drawn payable "after sight" simply (as distinguished from "at sight", which by section 10 is equivalent to "on demand"); it must specify the period after sight at the end of which it is to become payable in order to comply with the definition in section 11.

The expression "after sight" on a bill of exchange means after acceptance, or protest for non-acceptance, and not after a mere private exhibition to the drawee, for the sight must appear in a legal way.[63] But if a note is made after sight, the expression merely imports that payment is not to be demanded till it has been again exhibited to the maker[64]; for a note being incapable of acceptance, the word "sight" must, on a note, bear a different meaning from the same word on a bill.

Commonly bills are drawn "at 90 days D/A", "at 90 days D/A sight", or "90 days acceptance" or some variation of such expressions. In each instance

---

[61] *Williamson v. Rider* [1963] 1 Q.B. 89; Ormerod L.J.'s view was adopted by the Supreme Court of Canada in *John Burrows Ltd v. Subsurface Surveys Ltd* (1968) 68 D.L.R. (2D) 354 in preference to the majority decision in *Williamson v. Rider* and to *Crouch v. Credit Foncier* (1873) L.R. 8 Q.B. 374, which applied *Dagger v. Shepherd* [1946] 1 All E.R. 133, and is given effect in the Uniform Commercial Code, s.3–109, and in *Creative Press v. Harman* [1973] I.R. 313.

[62] [1987] 1 W.L.R. 521. The Court decided that the note in this case was at all events merely a receipt and not a promissory note following *Akbar Khan v. Altar Singh* [1936] 2 All E.R. 545, in which it was held that a particular document setting out the terms on which an advance was repayable was merely a deposit receipt and not a promissory note, although that decision concerned stamp duty and the Indian Negotiable Instruments Act which defined a promissory note as an unconditional undertaking signed by the maker.

[63] Marius (ed. 1656) 19, cited by Lord Kenyon in *Campbell v. French* (1795) 6 T.R. 200, 212. So in America it has been held that after sight means after acceptance, and not after mere presentment (*Mitchell v. De Grand* (1817) 1 Mason 76; 17 Fed.Cas. 494, 496). By s.12(4) of the Cape Act 19 of 1893, where a bill is payable at a fixed period after sight, time runs from the date of acceptance or from the date of noting or protest, if the bill be noted for non-acceptance or non-delivery. The same applies in Canada (s.45, Bills of Exchange Act 1890).

[64] *Holmes v. Kerrison* (1810) 2 Taunt. 323; *Study v. Henderson* (1821) 4 B. & Ald. 592; *Sutton v. Toomer* (1827) 7 B. & C. 416, 418; *Dixon v. Nuttall* (1834) 1 Cr.M. & R. 307.

whether or not the instrument constitutes a bill is a matter of construction of the particular instrument.[65]

An instrument in bill form drawn "At 90 days D/A pay" is not payable at a fixed or determinable future time.[66] An instrument construed as bearing the words "At 90 days after acceptance/sight" was a bill, since it provided for payment 90 days after an identified date, the date of sight. It has been observed, *obiter*, that bills payable "60 days from shipment" and "60 days from the first presentation of documents" might satisfy the requirements of s.11 (2) of the 1882 Act.[67]

A point still open to argument is whether an instrument which is defective as drawn as to the time of payment, can be cured on acceptance, where the form of acceptance is certain and unconditional. In both *Hong Kong & Shanghai v. G. D. Trade* and *Novaknit v. Kumar* the respective Courts of Appeal were inclined to the view that a defect in the instrument as originally drawn could be cured by an unequivocal acceptance of payment on a date certain, but found it unnecessary to decide the point.

Usance

2-17 At one time foreign bills were sometimes drawn at one, two, or more usances, or, as it was sometimes expressed, at single, double, treble, or half-usance. Usance signified the usage of the countries, between which bills were drawn, with respect to the time of payment. The practice of so drawing bills has largely fallen into disuse at the present day. However, it is still quite common to encounter the term "usance bill of exchange" which now simply means a bill which is payable after a period of delay[68]; the delay until maturity being the "usance period" of the bill. The Geneva Convention, Art. 33, provides that:

> "A bill of exchange may be drawn payable at sight; at a fixed period after sight; at a fixed period after date; at a fixed date. Bills of exchange at other maturities and payable by instalments are null and void."

This does not accord with the law of England and Wales.[69]

Uncertain

2-18 It is not material that the time when the event may happen is uncertain, provided that it must happen at some time or other, since the 1882 Act provides that:

11. A bill is payable at a determinable future time within the meaning of this Act which is expressed to be payable—

---

[65] *Korea Exchange Bank v. Debenhams (Central Buying) Ltd* [1979] 1 Lloyd's Rep. 548, *Hong Kong & Shanghai Banking Corp Ltd v. G. D. Trade Co. Ltd* [1998] C.L.C. 238, *Novaknit Hellas S.A. v. Kumar Bros International* [1998] 2 Lloyd's Rep. (Banking) 287.

[66] See *Korea Exchange (supra)*.

[67] See *Novaknit (supra)*.

[68] *Power Curber v. National Bank of Kuwait* [1981] 1 W.L.R. 1233, 1237.

[69] See section 11 of the 1882 Act, below.

(2) On or at a fixed period after the occurrence of a specified event which is certain to happen, though the time of happening may be uncertain.

An instrument expressed to be payable on a contingency is not a bill, and the happening of the event does not cure the defect.[70]

Thus a note payable on the death of A B, or of the maker, is good.[71] So, a note payable when a King's ship shall be paid off, has been held to be a good note, the Court of Error observing, "The paying off of the ship is a thing of a public nature."[72] So, too, a note payable to a minor when he should come of age, specifying the date when that was to be, is payable certainly and at all events, and is a good note.[73] But it is permissible to doubt whether similar decisions would be reached today. A note will not be void as payable on a contingency if it is certainly payable, and the uncertainty is only as to the persons who may have a right to enforce it under particular circumstances.[74] A promissory note payable with interest 12 months after notice is not to be considered as payable on a contingency, and is, consequently, valid.[75]

Place of payment

A bill is not invalid by reason "that it does not specify the place where it   **2–19** is drawn or the place where it is payable" (s.3(4)(c)).

If the drawer intends that the bill shall be payable at a particular place, he may insert such a direction, and the drawer himself cannot be charged, unless the bill has been presented at the place where he has made it payable.[76] Equally so, a note may be made payable at a particular place by the maker, and presentment for payment there will be necessary to charge him, but, unlike a qualified acceptance, the note need not be expressed to be payable at such place "only and not elsewhere".[77]

Notes of the Bank of England are payable only at the head office of the Bank in London, unless specially made payable also at some other place.[78]

SUM CERTAIN

According to the definition of a bill of exchange within section 3(1) of the   **2–20** 1882 Act, a bill of exchange must be for a "sum certain" in money. The sum

---

[70] cf. Hill v. Halford, supra.
[71] Colehan v. Cooke (1742) Willes 393; Roffey v. Greenwell (1839) 10 A. & E. 222.
[72] Andrews v. Franklin (1716) 1 Stra. 24; Evans v. Underwood (1749) 1 Wils. 262.
[73] Goss v. Nelson (1757) 1 Burr. 226.
[74] Richards v. Richards (1831) 2 B. & Ad. 447, 454, 455.
[75] Clayton v. Gosling (1826) 5 B. & C. 360.
[76] 1882 Act, s.45(4), post, paras 12–08 to 12–09. The 1882 Act repeals but substantially re-enacts (s.19) the provisions of the Act of 1821 regulating acceptances. Thus even if the drawer inserts a direction as to the place of payment, it will still be a general acceptance so as to charge the acceptor, unless the acceptor in his acceptance expressly states that the bill is to be paid at the place indicated "only and not elsewhere": see Bank Polski v. Mulder [1942] 1 K.B. 497.
[77] s.87(1), post, paras 12–14 and 24–11. The Act of 1821 did not apply to notes, nor do the provisions of the 1882 Act, s.19, apply thereto: s.89(3)(b).
[78] Currency and Bank Notes Act 1954, s.3.

certain must appear on the face of the instrument.[79] As to this the 1882 Act provides that:

9.—(1) The sum payable by a bill is a sum certain within the meaning of this Act although it is required to be paid—

(a) **With interest.**[80]

(b) **By stated instalments.**

(c) **By stated instalments, with a provision that upon default in payment of any instalment the whole shall become due.**

(d) **According to an indicated rate of exchange or according to a rate of exchange to be ascertained as directed by the bill.**

A bill or note can only be payable in money *in specie* or legal currency; therefore a promise to pay in three good East India bonds is not a promissory note.[81] Where, therefore, part of the sum agreed to be paid is not in fact, by the terms of the instrument, to be paid, but to be treated as set off, that will invalidate it as a note.[82] The sum must be certain, not susceptible of contingent or indefinite additions.[83] Therefore, in the case of *Rosenhain v. Commonwealth Bank of Australia* (1922) 31 C.L.R. 46 (reversing the decision of the Supreme Court of Victoria [1922] V.L.R. 155), a bill drawn "with interest at the rate of 8 per cent. per annum until arrival of payment in London to cover" was held not to be for a sum certain. And, where an instrument promised to pay J S the sum of £65 with lawful interest for the same, and all other sums which should be due to him, Lord Ellenborough held that it was not a promissory note, even for the £65, but that it required stamping as an agreement.[84] Nor must the sum payable be subject to indefinite or contingent

---

[79] *Lamberton v. Aiken* (1899) 37 S.L.R. 138.

[80] s.9 means no more than that a "certain" sum may be made up partly of principal and partly of interest. *Lamberton v. Aiken* (1899) 37 S.L.R. 138 (instrument to pay specific sum "together with any interest that may accrue thereon" not a note within the statute). A sum certain must appear on the face of the instrument.

[81] Buller, N.P. (7th ed., 1817), p. 272b. The same was held of Bank of England notes before the latter were legal tender (*Ex p. Imeson* (1815) 2 Rose 225, applied in *Lamb v. Somerville* (1909) 29 N.Z.L.R. 138). Neither the acceptor of a bill nor the maker of a note can undertake to pay otherwise than in money; *McDonald v. Belcher* [1904] A.C. 429, PC, in which an instrument provided for "interest in gold duty at $16 per oz."; and see s.17(2)(b), *post*, para. 10–01, and s.83(1), *post*, para. 24–01.

[82] *Davies v. Wilkinson* (1839) 10 A. & E. 98; see also *Standard Bank v. Marais* (1895) 12 S.C. 342, where a note provided that the amount due was to be deducted from another note due between the same parties; *Standard Trusts Co. v. La Valley* [1931] 4 D.L.R. 634 where the obligation might be discharged by the rendering of services.

[83] *Standard Bank of Canada v. Wildey* (1919) 19 S.R. 384; *Temple Terrace Assets Co. v. Whynot* [1934] 1 D.L.R. 124.

[84] *Smith v. Nightingale* (1818) 2 Stark. 375; *Bolton v. Dugdale* (1833) 4 B. & Ad. 619 (promise to pay debt with interest at 5 per cent and "the demands of the sick club at H. in part interest and the remaining stock and interest to be paid on demand", not a sum certain); *Leeds v. Lancashire* (1809) 2 Camp. 205. In *Steel v. Bradfield* (1812) 4 Taunt. 227, the note appeared to be open to the objection—which was not, however, taken—that it was not for a sum certain.

deductions. Thus, where the defendant promised to pay £400 to the representatives of J S, first deducting thereout any interest or money J S might owe to the defendant, it was held no promissory note.[85]

The sum payable is still a sum certain even though interest is payable, provided the interest rate is ascertainable; thus if interest was to be charged at the rate chargeable to "most credit-worthy customers", that would not be sufficiently certain.[86]

Equally the period for which interest is to run must be certain. By section 9(3) of the 1882 Act where a bill is expressed to be payable with interest, interest runs from the date of the bill, unless the contrary is provided, and if the bill is undated from the issue of the bill. However where "interest from date of advance" was expressed on the bill it was held to make the sum payable not certain,[87] because it depended upon extrinsic facts.

An instance of (d) is to be found in bills drawn in the United Kingdom on South Africa and Australia, in which the order to pay contains some such words as "exchange as per indorsement", the rate of exchange appropriate to the tenor of the bill being written either on the face or the back of the bill, with the amount in currency stated against the sterling figure on the front. Sometimes the clause is augmented by the words "plus stamps" or, again, "plus charges and stamps". In this last case the instrument is not a bill because, the charges being unknown, the bill is not for a sum certain.[88]

The sum for which a bill is made payable is usually written in the body of the bill in words at length, the better to prevent alteration; and in respect of any difference between the sum in the body and the sum superscribed, the 1882 Act provides:

9.—(2) Where the sum payable is expressed in words and also in figures, and there is a discrepancy between the two, the sum denoted by the words is the amount payable.[89]

---

[85] *Barlow v. Broadhurst* (1820) 4 Moo.P.C. 471; *Ayrey v. Fearnsides* (1838) 4 M. & W. 168. So, too, where outside assistance is required to ascertain the amount due (*National Bank of Australasia v. McArthur* (1902) 23 Natal L.R. 279); see also *Wingrove v. Goodchild* (1892) 6 H.C.G. 164; *Macdonald Co. v. Dahl* (1919) 2 W.W.R. 156 (Sask.).

[86] *Bank of Montreal v. Dezcam Industries Ltd* [1983] 5 W.W.W. 178.

[87] *Macleod Savings and Credit Union Bank Ltd v. Perret* (1978) 91 D.L.R. (3d) 612.

[88] *Tropic Plastic Packaging Industry v. Standard Bank of South Africa Ltd* (1969) 4 S.A.L.R. 108.

[89] The rule is the same in the United State (U.C.C., s.3–118(c)), Canada (s.28(2)), Australia (s.14(2)), New Zealand (s.9(2)), South Africa (s.7(2)), India (s.18), and all countries which have adopted the Geneva Convention (see Art. 6). There is nothing in the 1882 Act, nor, it is believed, in any foreign Act requiring the amount to be stated both in words and figures. But should this practically universal method be departed from and the amount be stated, both in the margin and in the body, entirely in words or entirely in figures, the obvious objection thereto would be difficulty of dealing with any question of discrepancy, since s.9(2) would not cover such a case. In any case, whether written in words or figures, the amount in the body of the bill is the amount to prevail. The superscription is a mere index or summary of the contents; see *Garrard v. Lewis* (1882) 10 Q.B.D. 30, 33 (Bowen L.J.); in the United Kingdom, the cheque would be dishonoured marked "words & figures differ"; but where the amount is small and only the smaller sum is claimed the cheque may sometimes be paid (Questions on Banking Practice (10th ed., 1965), No. 465). The Geneva Convention provides that the smaller sum is payable.

When the figures express a larger sum than the words, evidence to show that the difference arose from an accidental omission of words is inadmissible.[90] An omission in the body may be aided by the superscription.[91] An inaccurate but intelligible statement of the sum payable will not vitiate. Thus an order, or promise, to pay so many "pound" instead of "pounds", is a good bill or note.[92] A bill for "twenty-five, seventeen shillings and three" was held to be a bill for £25 17s. 3d.[93]

A bill, like a cheque, may now be drawn for any sum of money, large or small.[94]

As regards promissory notes, however, it should be noted that the following legislative restriction is still in force. Section 3 of the Bank Notes Act 1826 prohibits, under a penalty of £20, the issue by any person, in England, of any note payable to bearer on demand for less than £5. Section 7 prohibits the stamping of such notes, and section 10 requires every note payable to bearer on demand for less than £20 to be made payable at the place of issue.

These provisions are, of course, primarily aimed at the issue of bank notes, but are in terms wide enough to apply to the paper of private individuals. They do not apply to the issue of bank notes for £1 by the Bank of England.[95]

Under the provisions of the Decimal Currency Act 1969 bills of exchange and promissory notes are to be payable in shillings and pence.

Value received

2–21 The words "value received" are not essential to the form of a bill:

3.—(4) A bill is not invalid by reason—

(b) that it does not specify the value given, or that any value has been given therefor.[96]

The words "value received" are ambiguous where the bill is drawn payable to a third person; for they may mean either value received by the drawer from the payee, or by the acceptor from the drawer. But the first is the more

---

[90] *Saunderson v. Piper* (1839) 5 Bing. N.C. 425. In *G & H Montage G.m.b.H. v. Irvani* [1988] 1 W.L.R. 1285, [1990] 1 W.L.R. 667 (CA), the correct amount had been completed in figures but the text omitted the word "thousand"; the Court found that the proper law applicable was German; although German law had a provision equivalent to s.9(2) Saville J. admitted evidence that there was a mistake together with expert evidence as to German law to the effect that the defendant should not be entitled to take advantage of the mistake; the finding was upheld on appeal.

[91] *R. v. Elliott* (1777) 1 Leach 175; *Heeney v. Addy* [1910] 2 I.R. 688.

[92] *R. v. Post* (1806) Russ. & Ry. 101.

[93] *Phipps v. Tanner* (1833) 5 C. & P. 488.

[94] The 1882 Act finally repeals (Sched. II) both 48 Geo. 3, c.88, which rendered void all negotiable bills or notes for less than 20s., and 17 Geo. 3, c.88, which rendered void all negotiable bills or notes for less than 20s., and 17 Geo. 3, c.30, which rendered void (unless they complied with certain regulations) and bills and notes between 20s. and £5.

[95] Currency and Bank Notes Act 1954. See *post*, para. 24–13.

[96] Formerly it was otherwise (*Cramlington v. Evans* (1688) 1 Show 5), but the principle contained in the 1882 Act was long ago acknowledged; see *Poplewell v. Wilson* (1719) 1 Stra. 264; *Macleod v. Snee* (1726) 2 Ld. Raym. 1481.

probable interpretation; for it is more natural "that the party who draws the bill should inform the drawee of a fact which he does not know, than of one of which he must be well aware".[97]

If, however, the bill is drawn payable to the drawer's own order the words "value received" must mean received by the acceptor of the drawer.'Value received" in a note means received by the maker or the payee.[98]

Account on which bill drawn

The account upon which a bill is drawn need not be specified by the **2–22** drawer.[99]

---

[97] *Grant v. De Costa* (1815) 3 M. & S. 351 (Lord Ellenborough C.J.).

[98] *Clayton v. Gosling* (1826) 5 B. & C. 360, 361.

[99] As where the defendants had agreed to accept bills on receiving invoices and bills of lading on cargoes on three ships, and the bill was drawn without specifying the ship (*Laing v. Barclay* (1823) 1 B. & C. 398).

CHAPTER 3

PAYEE AND DRAWEE

3–01 THE common law rule was that where a bill or note was not payable to bearer, the payee or, if it is specially indorsed, the indorsee, should be named or otherwise indicated therein with reasonable certainty, so that he could not be confused with another person of the same name. Also, at common law, the rule was that the payee or indorsee should be a person who is capable of being ascertained at the time the instrument is made.[1] The common law rules were somewhat modified by the 1882 Act.

Name misspelt

3–02 The 1882 Act provides as follows for cases of misdescription of the payee or indorsee:

32.—(4) Where, in a bill payable to order, the payee or indorsee is wrongly designated, or his name is misspelt, he may indorse the bill as therein described, adding, if he thinks fit, his proper signature.

If the person indorsing makes a mistake in his signature, the property in the instrument will yet pass.[2]

Cheques made payable to a limited company may misdescribe the payee. In the case of large businesses, it was the practice to use a rubber stamp bearing a number of descriptions and to place an impression from it above the signature of the person actually indorsing on the company's behalf. This is a valid indorsement and, where the intention is clear, it is immaterial that the misdescription is the similar name of an allied company.[3]

Certainty as to payee

3–03 **7.—(1) Where a bill is not payable to bearer, the payee must be named or otherwise indicated therein with reasonable certainty.**

---

[1] "To make a promissory note there must be a payee ascertained by name or designation" (*Cowie v. Stirling* (1856) 6 E. & B. 333, 337 (Jervis C.J.). Where an instrument promised to pay a sum of money into a bank but no payee's name was included it was held not to be a note (*Obermeyer v. Baumann* [1911] T.P.D. 79). At common law a bill payable to the holder of an office for the time was bad (*Yates v. Nash* (1860) 30 L.J.C.P. 306). So, too, a note payable in the alternative to one of two, or one of several, payees, as not being an unconditional promise (*Blackenhagen v. Blundell* (1819) 2 B. & Ald. 417, distinguished in *Watson v. Evans* (1863) 32 L.J. Ex. 137, where a note payable to three payees or to their order, or the major part of them, was held good).

[2] *cf. Leonard v. Wilson* (1834) 2 Cr. & M. 589; and see Hart, Banking (4th ed., 1931), p. 391; also *Arab Bank Ltd v. Ross* [1952] 2 Q.B. 216.

[3] *Bird & Co. (London) Ltd v. Thomas Cook & Son Ltd* (1937) 156 L.T. 415.

This may seem to conflict with section 3(1), for an instrument drawn payable to "the order of XYZ" is within the latter section but contrary to section 7(1). It may be that the apparent contradiction is eliminated as soon as XYZ indorses in favour of his "order". Presumably, the instrument cannot be sued upon until that happens.

(2) **A bill may be made payable to two or more payees, jointly, or it may be made payable in the alternative to one or two, or one or some of several payees. A bill may also be made payable to the holder of an office for the time being.**

If the bill gets into the hands of someone other than the intended payee, unless it is payable to bearer, he can neither acquire nor convey a title. A bill was drawn on the defendant payable to Henry Davis; it got into the hands of another Henry Davis than the one in whose favour it was drawn, was accepted by the defendant, and by the wrong Henry Davis was indorsed to the plaintiff. Evidence was admitted to show that the indorsement was not made by the real payee, and it was held that the indorsement of his own name by Henry Davis was, in these circumstances, a forgery, which (*dissentiente* Lord Kenyon) could convey no title to the plaintiff.[4] Where the name is misspelt parole evidence is admissible to show that the plaintiff was intended.[5] A note in the form: "£15 5s. balance due to A.C, I am still indebted and do promise to pay,"[6] or "Received of A B £100, which I promise to pay on demand, with lawful interest,"[7] sufficiently designates the payee. Where a note is payable to A B and there are two persons so named, father and son, the presumption is that the father is the payee, but this may be rebutted by evidence.[8]

Fictitious payee

7.—(3) Where the payee is a fictitious or non-existing person the bill may be treated as payable to bearer.   3–04

In the case of a bill made payable to a fictitious payee, a genuine indorsement is impossible, and consequently, unless it can be treated as a bearer bill, a holder for value, even though he takes it in the belief that the indorsement is genuine, will be unable to enforce it. At one time the holder was held entitled to treat the bill as a bearer bill only where the acceptor, at the time of acceptance, knew that the payee was fictitious.[9] If, however, the money to meet the bill had come into the acceptor's hands, the holder could sue him for money had and received.[10] In *Phillips v. im Thurn*,[11] which was a case of acceptance for honour, the Court (which included Byles J.), though deciding

---

[4] *Mead v. Young* (1790) 4 T.R. 28.
[5] *Willis v. Barrett* (1816) 2 Stark. 29.
[6] *Chadwick v. Allen* (1925) 2 Stra. 706.
[7] *Green v. Davies* (1825) 4 B. & C. 235.
[8] *Sweeting v. Fowler* (1815) 1 Stark. 106; *Stebbing v. Spicer* (1849) 19 L.J.C.P. 24, and cases there cited.
[9] *Gibson v. Minet* (1791) 1 H.Bl. 569. As to what might constitute evidence of such knowledge on the acceptor's part, see *Gibson v. Hunter* (1794) 2 H.Bl. 288.
[10] *Bennet v. Farnell* (1807) 1 Camp. 129, and see note thereto.
[11] (1866) L.R. 1 C.P. 463.

the case as one of estoppel, was prepared to treat the bill as a bearer bill, though the acceptor for honour did not know at the time of the acceptance for honour that the payee was fictitious.

Whether or not the acceptor or other party liable on the bill is aware of the fictitious character of the payee is now immaterial.

The subject has been discussed at great length in the important case of *Bank of England v. Vagliano*,[12] where the facts were that Vagliano, in London, had a correspondent, Vucina, in Odessa, who on many previous occasions had drawn good trade bills on Vagliano, payable to the order of C. Petridi & Co., a foreign firm trading in Constantinople. Glyka, Vagliano's clerk, forged certain instruments purporting to be bills drawn on Vagliano by Vucina in favour of C. Petridi & Co. He obtained Vagliano's genuine acceptance thereon, and, after forging the indorsement of C. Petridi & Co., obtained payment from the Bank of England in the name of Maratis, a fictitious indorsee. The point in dispute was whether the Bank could debit their customer Vagliano's account with the amount of these acceptances—in other words, whether the Bank was entitled to treat the bills as payable to bearer.[13] In the House of Lords, Lord Halsbury c. thought the documents were not bills at all, but that Vagliano's conduct might have estopped him from denying their quality as such, and so from denying the application of section 7(3).[14] Lord Selborne also was of opinion that the Bank was entitled to judgment apart from section 7(3); but, assuming that subsection to apply to a case where the payees were not fictitious persons, that the knowledge of the acceptor was immaterial.[15] Lords Herschell and Watson thought the import of the subsection to be that a bill might be treated as payable to bearer in all cases where the person designated as payee on the face of it was either non-existing, or, being in existence, had not and never was intended to have any right to its contents, his name being inserted only by way of pretence.[16] The contention that the common law cases established that the acceptor was not bound, unless he knew the payee to be fictitious, was disposed of at length by Lord Herschell.[17] In the result the decision of the Court of Appeal was overruled and the Bank was held entitled to debit the bills to Vagliano's account (Lords Field and Bramwell dissenting on the ground that, to quote from the headnote, "a banker cannot charge his customer with the amount of a bill paid to a person who had no right of action against the customer, the acceptor; that the payee was not fictitious or non-existent and that the documents could not be

---

[12] [1891] A.C. 107.

[13] In the Court of Appeal in *Vagliano v. Bank of England* (1889) 23 Q.B.D. 243 the case was almost wholly argued in reference to s.7(3), and the Court held that Petridi & Co. were not fictitious persons within that section, and that "ficitious" meant fictitious to the knowledge of the person sought to be charged on the bill. In the House of Lords the negligence of each party was strongly relied on, Vagliano not having discovered that bills to a huge amount, which represented no commercial transactions, were being drawn on him, and the bank having paid these sums across the counter to a stranger. For a further instance of an existing person being held to be a fictitious payee, see *Fok Cheon Shing Investment Co. Ltd v. Bank of Nova Scotia* (1981) 123 D.L.R. 3d 416 Can.

[14] [1891] A.C. 107, 116, 120.

[15] *ibid.* at 122

[16] *ibid.* at 132, 152, 153. The same view was expressed, but with greater elaboration, by Lord Halsbury C. at 121, 122.

[17] *ibid.* at 144–147.

treated as bills payable to bearer within section 7(3) of the Act; that the conduct of the parties did not entitle the bank to debit the acceptor . . . ").[18]

In the later case of *Clutton v. Attenborough*[19] less difficulty arose; there the plaintiffs' clerk induced them by fraud to draw cheques in favour of one George Brett for alleged work and materials. There was, in fact, no such person, and no such consideration had been furnished to the plaintiffs. The clerk indorsed the cheques in the name of George Brett, and the defendants gave him value for them in good faith. It was held too clear for argument that the cheques were payable to a "non-existing person", and so, by section 7(3), to bearer. A further contention by the plaintiffs that there had been no "issue" of the cheques was also decided against them. Both *Vagliano's case* and that of *Clutton v. Attenborough* were considered and distinguished in *Vinden v. Hughes*.[20] In this case cheques were drawn by the plaintiffs in favour of actual customers of theirs, the plaintiffs being induced to do so by the fraudulent representation of a clerk in their employ, though at the time there were no sums then due to these customers from the plaintiffs, except in the case of one cheque, the amount of which was paid into court. The clerk subsequently forged the indorsements on these cheques and negotiated them with the defendants. Warrington J. distinguished the case from that of *Clutton v. Attenborough* on the ground that there the Court had only to consider whether the payee was "a non-existing person", while in the case under consideration the point was whether the payee was "a fictitious person". Reference was made at length to the observations of Lord Herschell in *Vagliano's case* as to the meaning to be attached to the words "fictitious person",[21] and the conclusion was drawn that, since the names of the payee had not been inserted as a mere pretence, the payees were not fictitious persons, and the plaintiffs therefore were entitled to judgment.

This decision was approved in the case of *North and South Wales Bank v. Macbeth*,[22] where the House of Lords, affirming the Court of Appeal and Bray J. below, decided that a cheque which the plaintiff, the respondent on appeal, was induced by the fraudulent representations of a man named White to draw in favour of one Kerr was not payable to bearer. White represented to the respondent that he had agreed to purchase certain shares from Kerr for £11,250, and induced him, in connection with some business transactions in which they were mutually engaged, to draw a cheque for that amount in favour of Kerr or order. Kerr was not, in fact, the owner of any such shares,

---

[18] At 140 Lord Bramwell said that s.7(3) was enacted for the benefit of the holder, who is embarrassed by the difficulty of there being no actual existing payee.

[19] [1897] A.C. 90.

[20] [1905] 1 K.B. 795, approved in *Goldman v. Cox* (1924) 40 T.L.R. 744.

[21] See [1891] A.C. 107, 153, where the observations of Lord Herschell are summed up as follows: "I have arrived at the conclusion that, whenever the name inserted as that of the payee is so inserted by way of pretence merely, without any intention that payment shall only be made in conformity therewith, the payee is a fictitious person within the meaning of the statute, whether the name be that of an existing person or of one who has no existence, and that the bill may, in each case, be treated by a lawful holder as payable to bearer." These observations were followed in *City Bank v. Rowan* (1893) 14 N.S.W.L.R. 127; *Rutherford Copper Mining Co. v. Ogier* (1905) 1 Tasmania L.R. 162.

[22] [1908] A.C. 137, followed in *Town and County Advance Co. v. Provincial Bank of Ireland* [1917] 2 I.R. 421; see also *Royal Bank of Canada v. Concrete Column Clamps* [1977] 74 W.L.R. (3d) 26.

nor does he appear to have been in any way aware of the transaction. White, on getting possession of the cheque, forged Kerr's indorsement thereon and paid it into his account with the appellant bank, who duly received the amount thereof from the respondent's bank.[23]

The House of Lords approved the view taken by the Court of Appeal, where it was considered that, with reference to a cheque payable to order, the explanation of the expression "fictitious person" in section 7(3) involves an investigation into the mind of the drawer when drawing the cheque; and that if the drawer intended that the existing person whom he designated as payee should receive the money, such payee is not a fictitious person within the subsection. It was accordingly held that the respondent was entitled to succeed. He had intended Kerr should receive the money, and Kerr was not a non-existent person, two grounds on which the case was distinguishable from *Vagliano's case* and that of *Clutton v. Attenborough*.[24]

The result of the case appears to be that in determining whether a payee is fictitious or not, the intention of the drawer of the bill is decisive.[25] If he inserted the name as a mere pretence, to give colour to the instrument, the payee is fictitious, notwithstanding that he in fact exists[26]; he is just as much a fictitious person as Richard I in *Ivanhoe*. If, on the other hand, the drawer intended his named payee to receive his money, the payee is not fictitious, notwithstanding the fact that the drawer was deceived into drawing the instrument by a third person who intended to misappropriate the instrument, and to further his intention fraudulently represented to the drawer, contrary to the fact, that the payee was entitled to the sum specified in the instrument. Though the transaction is in fact fictitious, the drawer believes it to be real.[27] The drawer is intending to write history, not romance.

In the case of a non-existing person the intention of the drawer is immaterial. If the payee is in fact not a real person, the subsection applies even though

---

[23] For a reason that does not appear the bank was unable, though the cheque was crossed, to rely on the protection afforded by s.82 of the 1882 Act; see *Macbeth v. North and South Wales Bank* [1906] 2 K.B. 718, 723, following and approving *Vinden v. Hughes* [1905] 1 K.B. 795.

[24] In the case of *London Life Assurance Co. v. Molson's Bank* (1904) 8 O.L.R. 238, where the facts were indistinguishable from those in Vinden v. Hughes [1905] 1 K.B. 795, and in *North and South Wales Bank v. Macbeth, supra*, it should be noted that the Ontario Court of Appeal held that the cheques were payable to bearer. The distinction between such a case and one where the payees were never intended by the drawer to receive the money was not overlooked, but it was considered not to afford sufficient ground for refusing to follow the decision in *Vagliano's Case*. There being no corresponding provision in the Canadian Bills of Exchange Act to s.60 of the Code, the bank would have been otherwise without a defence as against the plaintiffs, their customers; see Falconbridge, *Banking and Bills of Exchange* (7th ed., 1969), p. 482.

[25] It has been held in America that the intent of the drawer of a cheque in inserting the name of a payee is the sole test of whether the payee is a fictitious person (*Snyder v. Corn Exchange Nat. Bank* (1908) 221 Penn. Rep. 599, 606, where the decision in the *Vagliano case* is referred to; and the later cases cited in Beutel's *Brannan*, 7th ed., 1948, p. 324). s.3–111 of the Uniform Commercial Code sets out what instruments are payable to bearer; the section contains no reference to fictitious payees, which is now in s.3–405 dealing with indorsements by imposters.

[26] *Bank of England v. Vagliano* [1891] A.C. 107; see also *Edinburgh Ballarat Gold Quartz Mine Co. v. Sydney* (1891) 7 T.L.R. 656.

[27] *North and South Wales Bank v. Macbeth* [1908] A.C. 137.

the drawer believed him to be a real person and intended him to receive payment under the instrument.[28]

Pay "cash"

Sometimes a cheque is used for the purpose of ordering payment in favour **3–05** of an impersonal account. No payee is named, but in place of a payee's name some word indicating the purpose for which the cheque is drawn, such as "cash" or "wages" or "office", is inserted, so that the cheque reads "Pay cash" or "Pay wages" or "Pay office". Such an instrument is in practice paid either over the counter or through the clearing.[29] Strictly speaking, however, it is not a cheque within the meaning of section 73 of the 1882 Act (see *post*, para. 21–06). An impersonal word such as "cash" is not a specified person: the document is not payable either to a specified person or to bearer and does not satisfy section 7(1), which requires that there must be a payee. If the printed words "or order", are added, then being inconsistent with the drawer's apparent intention, they must be neglected in favour of the written word "cash". The document, therefore, may be a good direction to the banker to pay the sum specified to bearer, in which case his banker would be entitled to honour it without requiring an indorsement from anyone.[30] The intention that payment be made to bearer can normally be true only where the instrument is entrusted for encashment to a representative of the drawer known to the drawee-banker and it is submitted that the latter would pay anyone else at his peril. Such an anomalous instrument is even more anomalous when it bears a crossing and yet is presented for payment over the counter and not by a bank (as the crossing requires).[31] The bank would be safe in paying the bearer only if it were satisfied that this was the drawer's intention.[32]

An instrument running "We promise to pay on demand £500," containing no payee's name, or any statement that it was payable to bearer, which has handed over by the defendant to the plaintiff's agent with the intention that it should operate as a promissory note, was held to bind the defendant, the Court treating the instrument as in effect payable to bearer.[33] Where a bill was drawn "pay to—order" and was indorsed by the defendant, the drawer, to the plaintiff, but the blank in the bill was never filled in, it was held to be equivalent to a bill drawn "payable to my order", that is, the order of the

---

[28] *Clutton v. Attenborough* [1897] A.C. 90.

[29] *Questions on Banking Practice* (the Institute of Bankers, 10th ed., 1965), No. 545; and see *Cole v. Milsome* [1951] 1 All E.R. 311. In the United States' Uniform Commercial Code, s.3–111 makes payable an instrument which, by its terms, is payable to "(c) cash" or the order of " 'cash', or any other indication which does not purport to designate a specific payee".

[30] *North and South Insurance Corporation v. National Provincial Bank* [1936] 1 K.B. 328, in which Branson J. on the facts before him said, at 336: " . . . we have a direction to pay cash—by "cash" he meant an order to pay some impersonal account which cannot indorse the document. See also *Cole v. Milsome* [1951] 1 All E.R. 311; *Orbit Mining & Trading Co. Ltd v. Westminster Bank Ltd* [1963] 1 Q.B. 794 (CA); *Judmaier v. Standard Bank of Canada* [1927] 1 W.W.R. 270, where such a document was held to be a bearer cheque.

[31] See paras 21–23 and 21–29.

[32] And see Questions on Banking Practice (19th ed., 1965), Nos. 377, 378.

[33] *Daun v. Sherwood* (1895) 11 T.L.R. 211; *cf. Gibson v. Minet* (1791) 1 H.Bl. 569, 608.

drawer, and to be a perfect bill when indorsed by him.[34] But a bill payable to "—or order" is not, it seems, a good bill, for want of a payee.[35]

To order of drawer or drawee

3–06   The drawer may make a bill payable to his own order or to that of the drawee, since the 1882 Act provides that:

5.—(1) A bill may be drawn payable to, or to the order of, the drawer; or it may be drawn payable to, or to the order of, the drawee.

Where it is drawn in favour of the drawer it becomes payable to bearer as soon as the drawer indorses in blank; the same applies to the drawee. Where the drawee is a banker he is entitled either to debit the drawer's account or to negotiate the bill further.

A cheque expressed "Pay self or order" falls within s.5(1).

To several payees or indorsees

3–07   The 1882 Act provides for the case of several payees or indorsees that:

32.—(3) Where a bill is payable to the order of two or more payees or indorsees who are not partners all must indorse, unless the one indorsing has authority to indorse for the others.[36]

If one of the payees indorses for himself alone, it is only an authority to the person to whom he indorses it to receive the amount due to him.[37]

THE DRAWEE

3–08   As regards the direction of the bill to the drawee the 1882 Act provides:

6.—(1) The drawee must be named or otherwise indicated in a bill with reasonable certainty.

A bill of exchange, being in its original a letter, should be properly addressed to the drawee.[38] Where a bill was made payable "at No. 1, Wilmot Street, opposite the Lamb, Bethnal Green, London", without mentioning the

---

[34] *Chamberlain v. Young and Tower* [1893] 2 Q.B. 206.

[35] *R. v. Randall* (1811) Russ. & Ry. 195; *R. v. Richards* (1811) *ibid.* 193. In *Chamberlain v. Young and Tower, supra,* and in *North and South Insurance Corporation v. National Provincial Bank* [1936] 1 K.B. 328, the Court declined to give an opinion on this point. A note payable to "ship Fortune or bearer" is payable to bearer simply (*Grant v. Vaughan* (1764) 3 Burr. 1516).

[36] *Carvick v. Vickery* (1783) 2 Dougl. 653. As there may be alternative payees (s.7, *ante*, paras 3–03 *et seq.*), so presumably there may be alternative indorsees (s.34(3), *post*, para. 9–11), in which case the indorsement of either office should suffice, if good in other respects.

[37] *Heilbut v. Nevill* (1869) L.R. 4 C.P. 354, 356 (Willes J.).

[38] *Peto v. Reynolds* (1854) 9 Exch. 410; *Mason v. Lack* (1929) 45 T.L.R. 363; 140 L.T. 696. See also *McPherson v. Johnston* (1894) 3 B.C.R. 465.

drawee's name, and the defendant accepted it, he was not allowed to make the objection.[39] A bill cannot be addressed to one man and accepted by another, for (except in cases of acceptance for honour)[40] only the drawee can accept a bill.[41]

6.—(2) A bill may be addressed to two or more drawees whether they are partners or not, but an order addressed to two drawees in the alternative or to two or more drawees in succession is not a bill of exchange.

Alternative drawers must be distinguished from a referee in case of need under section 15.[42]

Drawer and drawee same person

A man may draw a bill on himself, since the 1882 Act provides: **3–09**

5.—(2) Where in a bill drawer and drawee are the same person, or where the drawee is a fictitious person or a person not having capacity to contract, the holder may treat the instrument, at his option, either as a bill of exchange or as a promissory note.[43]

Thus a bill drawn by a banking company in one place on the same banking company in another place may be treated as a note.[44]

Where a bill is addressed by the drawer to himself it cannot be accepted by a third party though sent to him by the drawer.[45]

An instrument which directs the drawee to pay without acceptance is nevertheless a bill of exchange.[46]

A note written by the creditor to his debtor at the foot of the creditor's account, requesting the debtor to pay that account to the creditor's agent, has been held not a bill of exchange or an order for the payment of money within the Stamp Act.[47]

---

[39] *Gray v. Milner* (1819) 8 Taunt. 739. This decision goes to the edge of the law—see *post* para. 10–02.

[40] See para. 10–11.

[41] *Davis v. Clarke* (1844) 13 L.J.Q.D. 305; Code, s.17.

[42] See *post*, para. 10–02.

[43] *Starke v. Cheesman* (1699) Carthew 509; *Dehers v. Harriot* (1691) 1 Show. 163; *Robinson v. Bland* (1760) 2 Burr. 1077; *Roach v. Ostler* (1827) 1 Man. & R. 120; and *London City and Midland Bank v. Gordon* [1902] 1 K.B. 242. As to fictitious drawee, see *Smith v. Bellamy* (1817) 2 Stark. 223. For the case of a note made payable to the maker, see *post*, para. 24–05.

[44] *Miller v. Thomson* (1841) 3 M. & G. 576; *Re British Trade Corporation* [1932] 2 Ch. 1, in which a document was drawn by the corporation on itself, both Greer and Romer L.JJ. held that the instrument was neither a bill nor a promissory note. Romer L.J. said that s.5 "means . . . that where there is a document in the form of a bill of exchange but which is not . . . the holder may . . . treat it . . . as being what it is not . . . namely, a promissory note".

[45] *Davis v. Clarke* (1844) 13 L.J.Q.B. 305; see also *Block v. Bell* (1831) 1 Moo. & R. 149.

[46] *R. v. Kinnear* (1838) 2 Moo. & R. 117; *Miller v. Thomson, supra*; *National Park Bank v. Berggren* (1914) 110 L.T. 907.

[47] *Norris v. Solomon* (1840) 2 Moo. & R. 266.

CHAPTER 4

INCHOATE INSTRUMENTS

4–01   AN inchoate instrument is not a bill of exchange or a promissory note. Thus, where an acceptance is written upon an instrument in the form of a bill which does not contain the name of a drawer or payee and is addressed to no one, the instrument is neither a bill nor a note.[1] It may, however, be completed in accordance with the conditions of section 20 (*post*) and, if the instrument then purports to be addressed to the acceptor, it is valid as a bill.[2] If the name of *the drawee* is not inserted, but the instrument is otherwise completed and accepted, it is valid as a promissory note made by the acceptor.[3]

The omission of the payee's name, as well as that of any other material particular, may be remedied by the holder who is empowered to fill up the omission in the case of all inchoate and blank instruments under the following provisions of the 1882 Act:

20.—(1) Where a simple signature on a blank paper is delivered by the signer in order that it may be converted into a bill, it operates as a prima facie authority to fill up as a complete bill for any amount, using the signature for that of the drawer, or the acceptor, or an indorser; and, in like manner, when a bill is wanting in any material particular,[4] the person in possession of it has prima facie authority to fill up the omission in any way he thinks fit.

(2) In order that any such instrument when completed may be enforceable against any person who became a party thereto prior to its completion, it must be filled up within a reasonable time, and strictly in accordance with the authority given.[5] Reasonable time for this purpose is a question of fact.

Provided that if any such instrument after completion is negotiated to a holder in due course it shall be valid and effectual for all purposes in his hands, and he may enforce it as if it had been filled up within a reasonable time and strictly in accordance with the authority given.

In *Glenie v. Bruce Smith*, Fletcher Moulton L.J. said[6]: "The logical order of

---

[1] *McCall v. Taylor* (1865) 34 L.J.C.P. 365; *Haseldine v. Winstanley* [1936] 2 K.B. 101; *Britannia Electric Lamp Works Ltd v. Mandler (D.) & Co.* [1939] 2 K.B. 129.

[2] *Haseldine v. Winstanley, supra.*

[3] *Mason v. Lack* (1929) 140 L.T. 696; *Haseldine v. Winstanley, supra.*

[4] Such as a place of payment, *Automobile Finance Co. of Australia v. Law* (1933) 49 C.L.R. 1.

[5] See the comment of Fletcher Moulton L.J. in *Lloyds Bank Ltd v. Cooke* [1907] 1 K.B. 794, 805, CA.

[6] [1908] 1 K.B. 263, 267.

operations with regard to a bill is, no doubt, that the bill should be first filled up, then that it should be signed by the drawer, then that it should be accepted, then that it should be negotiated and then that it should be indorsed by the persons who become successively holders; but it is common knowledge that parties very often vary, in a most substantial manner, the logical order of those proceedings, and section 20 of the Bills of Exchange Act is intended to deal with those cases."

Signer not liable without delivery

In the case of a blank signature or inchoate instrument, delivery by the **4–02** signer is essential. Thus A gave his blank acceptance on stamped paper to B, authorising him to fill in his own name as drawer, but B returned the acceptance unaltered to A. It was subsequently stolen from A, and C, without authority, filled in his own name as drawer and negotiated the instrument. The plaintiff, an indorsee for value without notice, was held not entitled to recover thereon.[7] Where the defendant signed his name on a blank, (stamped) piece of paper and entrusted it to someone with authority to fill it up as a promissory note for a certain sum and the instrument was completed for a larger amount he was estopped from denying the validity for the full amount of the note.[8]

Effect of completion

A bill which is incomplete at the time of issue is to be treated, when **4–03** completed in accordance with this section, as though it had never been defective at all. Thus N, who had agreed to finance a purchase of goods by A from M, indorsed certain bills drawn by M upon A, payable to the order of M, and handed them over to M in exchange for delivery orders. The bills when handed to M were wanting in a material particular within the meaning of the section by reason of the absence of any indorsement by M above the indorsement of N. M was held to have implied authority to indorse the bills as payee above the indorsement of N, and when this was done, the bills became retrospectively enforceable.[9]

But where the date on a cheque was filled in by the payee some 18 months after its delivery to him undated, and the drawee bank refused to pay, it was

---

[7] *Baxendale v. Bennett* (1878) 3 Q.B.D. 525; and see also *Smith v. Prosser* [1907] 2 K.B. 735. It is otherwise where the instrument was stolen when in a complete state, see *Ingham v. Primrose* (1859) 7 C.B. (N.S.), in which the instrument was torn in two as if for safe transmission; valid in hands of bona fide holder for value without notice, *post*, para. 18–05; but see *Tighe v. Jorgensen* (1912) 22 W.L.R. (Can.) 621 (Alta.); 3 W.W.R. 623, in which a dishonoured cheque returned to drawer was held no longer a negotiable instrument and the plaintiff could not enforce it.

[8] *Lloyds Bank Ltd v. Cooke* [1907] 1 K.B. 794, *post*, para. 18–04, a case of common law estoppel (*per* Collins M.R.).

[9] *McDonald (Gerald) & Co. v. Nash & Co.*, [1924] A.C. 625, applying *Glenie v. Bruce Smith* [1908] K.B. 263, and *Re Gooch* [1921] 2 K.B. 593, and distinguishing *Steele v. M'Kinley* (1880) 5 App.Cas. 754; see also *Ben Baron and Partners v. Henderson* [1959] (3) S.A.L.R. 188, *G & H Montage G.m.b.h. v. Irvani* [1988] 1 W.L.R. 1285

held that the bank was under no liability, that the reasonable time within which the instrument could be completed "had long since elapsed".[10]

Authority to complete

4-04   The authority to complete the bill is not limited to the person to whom it was delivered; any holder is empowered to fill up the omission.[11] Since, however, the authority to fill it up is only a prima facie authority, the holder who takes an incomplete instrument and subsequently completes it is in the same position as the person to whom it was originally delivered and cannot rely upon his own bona fides if it is in fact filled up without authority.[12]

Mistake in completion

4-05   A mere mistake in completing the bill is not fatal to its validity. Thus, where an acceptance is placed upon a document in the form of a bill addressed to nobody, and the bill, when completed, by mistake purports to be addressed to the payee, the mistake may be corrected, and the name of the addressee altered by substituting that of the acceptor.[13] Similarly, if the payee, when intending to complete a bill already indorsed by a third person, places his indorsement inadvertently below the indorsement already on the bill, his inadvertence does not nullify the intention of the parties or alter the rights which they would otherwise have had.[14]

Negotiation to holder in due course

4-06   An instrument which has been completed without authority can only be enforced against the giver of the authority if it falls within the proviso of section 20(2). To entitle a person to the benefit of the proviso, two conditions must have been fulfilled, namely, (1) the instrument must have been completed before it was negotiated to him—"The defence of purchaser for valuable consideration without notice, by one who takes from another without inquiry an instrument signed in blank by a third party, and then himself fills up the blanks, appears to us to be altogether untenable"[15]—and (2) he must be

---

[10] *Per* Macnaghten J. in *Griffiths v. Dalton* [1940] 2 K.B. 264.

[11] *Faulks v. Atkins* (1893) 10 T.L.R. 178. It was vainly contended in *Crutchley v. Clarence* (1813) 2 M. & S. 90, and *Schultz v. Astley* (1836) 2 Bing.N.C. 544, that a bill could only be filled up by one of the original parties. As to what will constitute evidence of authority, see also *Crutchly v. Mann* (1814) 5 Taunt. 529; *Awde v. Dixon* (1851) 6 Ex. 869.

[12] *Hogarth v. Latham* (1878) 3 Q.B.D. 643, applied in *Oakley v. Boulton, Maynard & Co.* (1888) 5 T.L.R. 60; *Watkins v. Lamb* (1901) 85 L.T. 483; *Awde v. Dixon, supra; cf.* generally *Russel v. Longstaffe* (1780) 2 Doug 514; *Attwood v. Griffin* (1826) Ry. & M. 425; and see *Demers v. Leveille* (1913) 44 Q.S.C. 61; *Kunst v. Abbot* [1923] N.Z.L.R. 1072; *contra, Bacon v. Decarie* (1908) Q.R. 34 S.C. 103.

[13] *Haseldine v. Winstanley* [1936] 2 K.B. 101.

[14] *National Sales Corporation v. Bernardi* [1931] 2 K.B. 188, applied in *McCall Bros Ltd v. Hargreaves* [1932] 2 K.B. 423 and in *Lombard Banking Ltd v. Central Garage & Engineering Co. Ltd* [1963] 1 Q.B. 220. As to such bills, see *post,* para. 17–18.

[15] Court of Appeal, in *France v. Clark* (1884) 26 Ch.D. 257, 262.

a holder in due course, or in other words there must be nothing in the transaction to put him on inquiry.[16]

The payee cannot be a holder in due course (see *post*, p. 218) and is not protected by the proviso, even though the instrument does not come to his hands until after it has been completed. Thus A, wishing to borrow from B the sum of £15, gave to B his signature in blank upon paper stamped with a stamp sufficient to cover £30. B, in breach of his authority, completed the instrument by making it a note for £30, payable to C, and obtained from C, in exchange for it, £30, which he misappropriated. Though C had no knowledge of B's want of authority, he was held disentitled to recover, on the ground that the note was not "negotiated" to him, as the word is understood in the proviso to the subsection.[17]

"We do not think that the word 'completion' as used in this proviso includes delivery. It is the form of the instrument which is being referred to . . . But even if the bill could not be said to be completed unless delivered to someone, here it was delivered to the plaintiff and if what happened on his giving his cheque for it and becoming the holder for value is negotiating it to a holder in due course, it may, we think, be said to be 'negotiated after completion'."[18]

The payee, however, though not protected by the proviso, is entitled to enforce the instrument if, on the facts, a case of estoppel is raised against the person who gave the blank signature.[19] The estoppel only exists where the blank signature was placed in the hands of the person to whom it was first delivered for the purpose of being completed as a negotiable instrument. If it was handed to such person as custodian only for safe keeping, the signer having no present intention that it should be completed and used, there is no estoppel and the signer is not liable upon the instrument, even to bona fide holder for value.[20]

It has been stated that for the principle of estoppel to arise, the instrument must be a negotiable instrument.[21] However that statement can no longer be regarded as correct. In *United Dominion Trust Ltd v. Western* it was observed

---

[16] See again *France v. Clark* (1884) 26 Ch.D. 257; *Guildford Trust Ltd v. Goss* (1927) 136 L.T. 725, where the fact that the instrument (a cheque) was post-dated was held in the circumstances not to be sufficient to put the plaintiffs upon inquiry; see also *Morgan's Ltd v. Hesketh* (1890) 6 T.L.R. 162; it is submitted that the delay (18 months) in *Griffiths v. Dalton* [1940] 2 K.B. 264 might well, in view of the purpose for which cheques are ordinarily issued, be such as to put a holder on inquiry.

[17] *Herdman v. Wheeler* [1902] 1 K.B. 361, distinguished in *Lloyds Bank Ltd v. Cooke* [1907] 1 K.B. 794.

[18] *Herdman v. Wheeler* [1902] 1 K.B. 361, *per* Channell J. at 371.

[19] *France v. Clark* (1884) 26 Ch.D. 257, 262; *Lloyds Bank Ltd v. Cooke* [1907] 1 K.B. 794, followed in *Lilly v. Farrar* (1908) 17 Q.R.B.R. 554 and *Burns v. Forman*, 1953 (2) S.A. 226, 229 (see Cowen, 164–165); but distinguished in *Wilson & Meeson v. Pickering* [1946] K.B. 422; [1946] 1 All E.R. 394. The holder must be for value (*Paine v. Bevan* (1914) 110 L.T. 933). As to the estoppels binding a person who has accepted in blank, see s.54, *post*, para. 17–06, and *cf. London and South Western Bank v. Wentworth* (1880) 5 Ex.D. 96.

[20] *Smith v. Prosser* [1907] 2 K.B. 735, distinguished in *Guildford Trust Ltd v. Goss, supra. Smith v. Prosser, supra*, has been frequently followed in Canada: see *Hubbert v. Home Bank* (1910) 20 O.L.R. 651; *Ray v. Willson* (1911) 45 Can.S.C.R. 401, and the cases cited in Falconbridge (7th ed., 1969) p. 538; Maclaren (6th ed., 1940), p. 100; distinguished in *Imperial Bank of Canada v. Dennis* (1925) 57 O.L.R. 203; *Campbell v. Bourque* (1914) 24 Man.R. 242; see also *Sair v. Warren* [1917] 2 W.W.R. 265.

[21] *Wilson & Meeson v. Pickering* [1946] K.B. 422 at 427.

that the doctrine of estoppel by negligence does not apply only to negotiable instruments.[22]

Where there is authority to fill up a blank acceptance or cheque for a certain sum, it is forgery to fill it up for a larger sum.[23]

Promissory notes

4–07   **84. A promissory note is inchoate and incomplete until delivery thereof to the payee or bearer.**[24]

---

[22] [1976] QB 513 at 521–522.

[23] *R. v. Minter Hart* (1834) 7 C. & P. 652; *R. v. Bateman* (1845) 1 Cox C.C. 186; *R. v. Wilson* (1848) 1 Den. 284; *R. v. Richardson* (1860) 2 F. & F. 343, and s.9 (1)(d) of the Forgery and Counterfeiting Act 1981.

[24] See *post*, para. 24–09.

CHAPTER 5

INLAND AND FOREIGN BILLS AND NOTES, BILLS IN A SET AND COPIES

THE 1882 Act draws a distinction between "inland" and "foreign" bills. The **5–01** importance of this distinction lies in the requirements as to protesting. The essential difference between a foreign bill and an inland bill is that all foreign bills must be protested on dishonour, whether for non-acceptance or non-payment, whereas it is not necessary to protest an inland bill.[1]

4.—(1) An inland bill is a bill which is or on the face of it purports to be (a) both drawn and payable within the British Islands, or (b) drawn within the British Islands upon some person resident therein. Any other bill is a foreign bill.

For the purposes of this Act "British Islands" mean any part of the United Kingdom of Great Britain and Ireland, the islands of Man, Guernsey, Jersey, Alderney, and Sark, and the islands adjacent to any of them being part of the dominions of Her Majesty.[2]

(2) Unless the contrary appears on the face of the bill, the holder may treat it as an inland bill.

Whilst it is not necessary to protest an inland bill or one that on the face of it purports to be an inland bill, in order to preserve the rights of recourse against the drawer or indorser, where such a party is resident abroad, it is sensible to do so. The step of protesting may preserve rights against that party in the country where he is resident.

In contrast to bills, a foreign promissory which is dishonoured not need be protested.[3] However the distinction between an inland note and a foreign note is maintained.

83.—(4) A note which is, or on the face of it purports to be, both made and payable within the British Islands is an inland note. Any other note is a foreign note.

[1] See s.51 of the 1882 Act.

[2] This definition of the "British Islands" is substantially the same as that in the Interpretation Act 1978 Schedule I; the Orkney and Shetland Islands and the Inner and Outer Hebrides. The islands are therefore within the United Kingdom for the purpose of s.4. By virtue of S.R. & O. 1923, No. 405 (made under s.6 of the Irish Free State (Consequential Provisions) Act 1922), any reference in any enactment passed before the establishment of the Irish Free State to the "United Kingdom" or "Great Britain and Ireland" or the "British Islands" or "Ireland", shall be construed as exclusive of the Irish Free State. It would thus seem that a bill drawn in the Republic of Ireland payable in the United Kingdom is a foreign bill, in spite of the fact that the Ireland Act 1949 provides that the Republic of Ireland shall not be a foreign country. On the other hand, a bill drawn in the United Kingdom on the Republic of Ireland may be an inland bill.

[3] See s.89(4).

The words "or on the face of it purports to be", seem intended to cover the common case of a cheque in fact drawn abroad, but (owing to the use of the ordinary printed cheque form) purporting to be drawn within the British Islands. It was long ago held that a bill drawn payable in London on a foreign drawee, and accepted payable as drawn, *viz.*, in London, was an inland bill.[4]

BILL IN A SET

5–02   In international trade transactions foreign bills on London are sometimes drawn in parts, each part being numbered (*e.g.* the "First", "Second" "Bill of Exchange") and containing a reference to the other; the separate parts then constitute one bill.[5] Within this country bills in a set are rarely, if ever, used. The first of exchange comes forward by airmail (usually with one set of documents) and the second of exchange either by sea mail or a later air-mail. The 1882 Act contains the following provisions:

71.—(1) Where a bill is drawn in a set,[6] each part of the set being numbered, and containing a reference to the other parts, the whole of the parts constitute one bill.[7]

(2) Where the holder of a set indorses two or more parts to different persons, he is liable on every such part, and every indorser subsequent to him is liable on the part he has himself indorsed as if the said parts were separate bills.[8]

(3) Where two or more parts of a set are negotiated to different holders in due course, the holder whose title first accrues is as between such holders deemed the true owner of the bill; but nothing in this subsection shall affect the rights of the person who in due course accepts or pays the part first presented to him.[9]

(4) The acceptance may be written on any part, and it must be written on one part only.

[4] *Amner v. Clark* (1835) 2 Cr.M. & R. 468. In *Griffin v. Weatherby* (1868) L.R. 3 Q.B. 753, a bill drawn in the Isle of Man was considered a foreign bill under the Stamp Act. In *Heywood v. Pickering* (1874) L.R. 9 Q.B. 428, it was said to be customary to treat cheques on Jersey banks as foreign cheques, but such a custom could not be raised since the passing of the 1882 Act in any case where it was material whether the cheque was inland or foreign.

[5] Bills are drawn in a set to obviate the risk of loss, especially where they are sent overseas.

[6] For the United States, see Part 8, s.3–801, of the Uniform Code, 1962 Official Text; for Australasia, s.76 of the Bills of Exchange Act 1909–1973 and Weaver and Craigie (1975), pp. 318, 319; for New Zealand, s.71; for Canada, ss.158, 159 and Falconbridge (7th ed., 1969), pp. 823, 824; for South Africa, s.69 and Cowen and Gering (4th ed., 1966), pp. 80, 81.

[7] See *Société Générale v. Metropolitan Bank* (1873) 27 L.T. 849; *Davison v. Robertson* (1815) 3 Dow H.L. 218.

[8] See *post* para. 5–03, note 16.

[9] *Holdsworth v. Hunter* (1830) 10 B. & C. 449; *Perreira v. Jopp* (1793) *ibid.* 450, note. The right of the true owner to have all the parts, as suggested by Bayley J. in *Holdsworth v. Hunter*, *supra*, at 454, now appears to depend on whether any other parts have been separately accepted or indorsed, for if so he runs no risk of losing his remedy by such parts remaining in other hands, since they are separate bills. Where the plaintiffs gave value for unaccepted seconds, they were held entitled to recover the amount of their advances thereon from the holders of the accepted first, who had made no advance and were treated by the Court as having assented to hold the first on behalf of the plaintiffs (*Société Générale v. Agopian* (1895) 11 T.L.R. 244).

If the drawee accepts more than one part, and such accepted parts get into the hands of different holders in due course, he is liable on every such part as if it were a separate bill.[10]

(5) Where the acceptor of a bill drawn in a set pays it without requiring the part bearing his acceptance to be delivered up to him, and that part at maturity is outstanding in the hands of a holder in due course, he is liable to the holder thereof.

(6) Subject to the preceding rules, where any one part of a bill drawn in a set is discharged by payment or otherwise, the whole bill is discharged.[11]

Each part usually contains a condition that it shall continue payable only so long as the others remain unpaid. The following is a common form of bill in a set of two, the usual number:

No.—.   London, January 1, 1972
£100

Three months after sight of this our First of Exchange, the second of the same tenor and the date not being paid, pay to—or order the sum of one hundred pounds value received.

                                              (Sd.) A.D.

To X Y,
    Toronto.

One may be forwarded for acceptance while the other is delivered to the indorsee, thus relieving him from the necessity of forwarding his part for acceptance, but giving him the indorser's security immediately, and diminishing the chances of losing the bill. Every transferor is bound to hand over to his transferee all the parts of the bill in his possession, and he may even be liable to hand them over to a subsequent transferee, if he has them still in his possession, but not otherwise.[12]

The whole set but one bill

Though by section 71(6),[13] the discharge of any one part discharges the whole set, yet a contract to deliver up to the acceptor a bill in a set is not performed till all parts (not destroyed) are delivered up; for the acceptor would have no answer to any claim of a bona fide holder on any outstanding part that might have been accepted.[14]   **5–03**

---

[10] *Holdsworth v. Hunter, supra.*

[11] The bill will be wholly discharged, except such parts as, being either separately accepted or indorsed to separate persons, are treated as separate bills and still current (subss. (2) and (4)), or except where, on payment, the acceptor does not procure back his acceptance (subs. (5)).

[12] *Pinard v. Klockmann* (1863) 32 L.J.Q.B. 82, where the defendants indorsed a first of exchange, the only part received by them, to the plaintiff, who lost it and it was held that no action was maintainable to compel them to hand over or procure the other parts.

[13] *supra.*

[14] *Kearney v. West Granada Mining Co.* (1856) 1 H. & N. 412.

A firm, who were both payees and acceptors of a foreign bill in three parts, indorsed one part to a creditor to remain in his hands till some other security was given for it, and then indorsed another part of the same bill for value to a third person. They afterwards gave the first indorsee the proposed security, and took back the first part of the bill from him. Held, that the holder of the second part was not precluded from recovering against the firm; first, because the substitution of the security for the first part was not a payment; and, secondly, because the firm were, as between themselves and the second indorsee, estopped from disputing the regularity of their acceptance and indorsement of the second part.[15] In an action by the holders against the indorser of a bill at eight days in a set of two, the second of exchange had been fraudulently altered to one at 80 days after the defendant's indorsement, two spurious parts, a first and a second, being also fabricated so as to complete two apparent sets at eight and 80 days respectively. Both the real and the spurious second were held by the plaintiffs. It was held that they were not entitled to recover, the only real indorsement of the defendant's held by the plaintiffs being that of the second, materially altered after indorsement.[16]

Copies

5–04   Copies of bills are not, it is believed, much used in this country. A protest may be made on the copy of a lost bill.[17] But, abroad, when a bill is not drawn in sets, it is sometimes the practice to negotiate a copy, while the original is forwarded to a distance for acceptance.[18]

In such a case, the person who circulates the copy should transcribe the body of the bill, and all the indorsements, including his own, literally; and he should write, "Copy: the original being with ... " If he should omit to state that a bill is a copy, or to write his own indorsement *after* the word *copy*, he may become liable on the copy as on an original.

As to lost bills and notes generally, see *post*, Chapter 30.

---

[15] *Holdsworth v. Hunter* (1830) 10 B. & C. 499. Both parts having been accepted, there would clearly now be no defence, whether the substitution of the security was regarded as a payment or not; see s.71(4).

[16] *Société Générale v. Metropolitan Bank* (1873) 27 L.T. 849. So far as observations in the case suggest that an indorser is not bound to pay a dishonoured set until all parts bearing his indorsement are delivered up to him or accounted for, it would not appear to be law at the present day in view of s.71(6), as the payment of one part discharges the whole, except as regards the indorser, where he has indorsed the several parts to separate indorsees, to each of whom, as on a separate bill, he remains liable; see Bovill C.J. at 854. The parts in the above case were both indorsed and delivered by the defendants to the same person. It has, indeed, been stated in the 16th and previous editions of this book that it is conceived that an indorser is not bound to pay any one part, unless every part bearing his indorsement be delivered up to him, and the passage to this effect was cited by Bovill C.J. from a former edition (see 27 L.T. 854); but where the parts are indorsed to the same indorsee, the payment of one part discharges the bill (s.71(6)), so that the indorser could have no interest in claiming the outstanding parts; whereas if he indorsed to separate indorsees, he would remain liable to them, and could have no right to the possession of any parts outstanding in their hands (s.71(2)).

[17] *Dehers v. Harriot* (1691) 1 Show. 163; the 1882 Act, s.51(8).

[18] *cf.* Goirand, *French Commercial Law* (2nd ed.) p. 185; see also Lescot et Robiot, *Les Effets de Commerce* (1953), p. 260; and Arts 67 & 68 of the Geneva Convention.

Substitutions

A drawer to whom a negotiated part has come back with many indorse- **5–05** ments on it, may substitute a new part without such indorsements. The holder of such a substituted part may be deprived of his remedy against the acceptor by the intermediate act of the drawer.[19]

---

[19] *Ralli v. Dennistoun* (1851) 6 Exch. 483.

CHAPTER 6

CAPACITY

Capacity of parties

6–01 THE capacity of any person or corporation to incur liability as a party to a bill is dealt with by the 1882 Act as follows:

22.—(1) Capacity to incur liability as a party to a bill is co-extensive with capacity to contract.

Provided that nothing in this section shall enable a corporation to make itself liable as drawer, acceptor, or indorser of a bill unless it is competent to it so to do under the law for the time being in force relating to corporations.

(2) Where a bill is drawn or indorsed by an infant, minor, or corporation having no capacity or power to incur liability on a bill, the drawing or indorsement entitles the holder to receive payment of the bill, and to enforce it against any other party thereto.

The words "any other party" in subsection (2) must mean any party other than the one lacking capacity. Thus, corporations having no capacity to incur liability, and minors, may convey title and liability, though not originate it[1]; therefore, if the signature of such a corporation or of a minor is found on a bill in any such capacity, the bill is not invalidated as regards the other parties to the instrument *inter se*.

It is to be observed that subsection (2) does not deal with the case of the acceptance of a bill by a party having no capacity to incur liability. But if a bill were accepted or a note made by a person having no capacity to incur liability, and were subsequently indorsed by the payee, the latter would be estopped under section 55(2)(c) from denying that at the time of his indorsement the instrument was a valid and subsisting instrument. The drawer, it is true, is not estopped from denying the genuineness of the acceptor's signature, but it is submitted that he cannot set up the incapacity or want of authority of his own drawee.

Corporations and companies

6–02 The proviso contained in s.22(1) makes it plain that nothing in the 1882 Act determines the extent to which a corporation can make itself liable on a negotiable instrument. As one might expect the position is governed by the law applicable to companies and corporations for the time being in force.

[1] *cf. Smith v. Johnson* (1858) 3 H. & N. 222; *Merchants' Bank Canada v. McLeod* (1910) 15 B.C.R. 290; 14 W.L.R. 461; *Freeman v. Bank of Montreal* (1912) 5 D.L.R. 418; 26 O.L.R. 451.

The position at common law was that without a special power, express or implied, a corporation could not make, accept, draw or indorse bills or notes. Such power was implied in the case of a company incorporated for the purposes of trade, the very object of which requires that it should exercise this privilege.[2] It was presumed that any corporation or company has implied power to issue cheques in the ordinary course of its business.[3] However a non-trading corporation had to have an express power to enter into such transactions, or the corporation's memorandum had to be sufficiently widely drawn so as to encompass such acts. If a company entered into a transaction that was *ultra vires*, then such a transaction was void.

However in relation to companies incorporated under the Companies Act 1985 (as amended), so far as third parties are concerned the *ultra vires* principle has largely been abolished by the substituted s.35 of that Act.[4] In effect a third party need not concern himself with the capacity of the company to enter into the transaction.

Contracts under seal

Corporations in general do not require to execute contracts by seal provided the contract is signed by any person acting with authority.[5] More specifically, companies formed under the Companies Act 1985 no longer need to have a seal and may contract either under seal, or by any person acting under the company's authority.[6] Generally, as to corporations where the matter is of a trivial nature, or where the corporation is created for a particular purpose, and the contract is entered into in the ordinary course of its business, a seal is not required. It appears to have been doubtful at common law whether an instrument under the seal of a corporation could be a negotiable instrument; an instrument, for example, in the form of a promissory note, if under seal, was a covenant, and not a promise; and a covenant to pay money was not negotiable by the custom of merchants.[7] The doubt, however, has been removed by the following provision of the 1882 Act:

6–03

91.—(2) In the case of a corporation, where, by this Act, any instrument or writing is required to be signed, it is sufficient if the instrument or writing be sealed with the corporate seal.

But nothing in this section shall be construed as requiring the bill or note of a corporation to be under seal.

[2] Providing that there is no infringement of the exclusive privileges granted to the Bank of England (*Broughton v. Manchester Waterworks Co.* (1819) 3 B. & Ald. 1;). Express power may be given, in the case of limited companies, by their memorandum of association or the power may be implied (*Re Peruvian Rys* (1867) L.R. 2 Ch.App. 617, where no express power referring to bills and notes was given in the memorandum, but the actual power conferred was held to be extensive enough in its terms to authorise the issue of negotiable instruments). See also Paget, *Law of Banking* (11th ed., 1996), pp. 139 *et seq.*
[3] Paget, *Law of Banking* (11th ed., 1996), p. 142.
[4] Section 35 was substituted by s.108 of the Companies Act 1989, which governs any act by a company after February 4, 1991.
[5] Corporate Bodies' Contracts Act 1960, s.1(1).
[6] Companies Act 1985, s.36.
[7] *Crouch v. Credit Foncier* (1873) L.R. 8 Q.B. 374, 382, 384 (Blackburn J.).

And in fact, it need not. By section 37 of the Companies Act 1985, it is provided that

"A bill of exchange or promissory note is deemed to have been made, accepted or endorsed on behalf of a company, if made, accepted or endorsed in the name of, or by or on behalf or on account of, the company by any person acting under its authority."

The section does not specifically relate to cheques, but it is clear that they must be within it.[8]

Personal liability of directors and officers

6–04   By section 349(1)(c) of the Companies Act 1985 it is provided that the name of the company shall be mentioned in legible characters in all bills of exchange, promissory notes, indorsements, cheques, and orders for money purporting to be signed by or on behalf of the company.

By section 349(4) any officer of a company, or person on its behalf, who signs or authorises to be signed on behalf of the company any such instrument wherein its name is not so mentioned, is liable to a fine and is further made personally liable to the holder, unless the instrument is duly paid by the company.[9] To comply with the statutory provision, the full and exact name of the company must be placed on the instrument. However generally accepted abbreviations may be used ("Ltd" for "Limited" and "plc" for "public limited company").[10]

In order to avoid liability, various arguments have been advanced on behalf of directors signing such instruments incorrectly.

In *Durham Fancy Goods Ltd v. Michael Jackson (Fancy Goods) Ltd and Another*[11] the plaintiff drew a bill on the first defendant but addressed to them as M. Jackson (Fancy Goods) Ltd with a place for the acceptance in the same form, which the second defendant signed. The bill was dishonoured by the company. The plaintiffs sued Michael Jackson, contending that he had committed an offence under section 108 of the Companies Act 1948.[12] Donaldson J. held that he was liable to the plaintiffs but they could not enforce that

---

[8] Paget, *Law of Banking, op. cit.*, pp. 142–143c. A closely similar provision to s.37 is to be found in s.28 of the Industrial and Provident Societies Act 1965 and s.5(6)(c) requires that the society's registered name shall be mentioned in legible characters in "all bills of exchange, promissory notes, indorsements, cheques and orders for money" purporting to be signed by or on behalf of the society.

[9] *Atkins v. Wardle* (1889) 58 L.J.Q.B. 377; affirmed on appeal, 5, T.L.R. 734. An addition of anything to the proper name of the company will render the directors personally liable (*Nassau Steam Press v. Tyler* (1894) 70 L.T. 376, distinguished in *Dermatine Co. Ltd v. Ashworth* (1905) 21 T.L.R. 510, where the word "limited" was accidentally omitted, as also in *Union Bank of Canada v. Tattersall* [1920] 2 W.W.R. 497). The word "limited" may be abbreviated to "Ltd" (*Stacey & Co. v. Wallis* (1912) 106 L.T. 544; *Thompson v. Big Cities Realty Co.* (1910) 21 O.L.R. 394); and ss.26 and 27 of the Companies Act. In *Scottish & Newcastle Breweries v. Blair* (1967) S.L.T. 72 the Court of Session held that there must be strict compliance with s.108.

[10] See ss.26(3) and 27 of the Companies Act 1985.

[11] [1968] 2 Lloyd's Rep. 98. See also *British Airways Board v. Parish* [1979] 2 Lloyd's Rep. 361 and *Maxform S.p.A. v. Mariani and Goodville Ltd* [1979] 2 Lloyd's Rep. 385 and [1981] 2 Lloyd's Rep. 54, CA.

[12] The precursor of s.349.

liability, on the grounds of estoppel, as they were themselves responsible for the mis-spelling of the first defendant's name. The defence of estoppel, though, failed where the party suing the director on the instrument was not responsible for the misdescription of the company's name.[13]

The company's trade name will not suffice for that of its actual name. In *Maxform S.p.A. v. Mariani and Goodville Ltd*[14] the first defendant had merely signed his name without qualification to bills drawn on the second defendant by their registered trade name. Although Mariani could not be held liable as drawee yet, looking at the bill as a whole, he purported to sign on behalf of the drawee and was accordingly liable, the Court of Appeal remarking that the Court had to look at the bill as a whole.

It was argued by the defendant in *British Airways v. Parish*[15] that the liability of someone signing a cheque contrary to s.108(4) of the Companies Act 1948 is analogous to the liability of a surety. The Court of Appeal declined to accept this; in the words of Megaw L.J.,

" . . . once the position arises, in a case under s.108(4) [now s.349(4)], that the cheque has not been *duly* paid, the personal liability of the officer of the company . . . comes into existence at that date"

and cannot be affected thereafter.

A director cannot seek to avoid personal liability by having the instrument rectified. In *Blum v. OCP Repartition SA*,[16] the Court refused to grant rectification.

Signing on behalf of a company

Whether a facsimile signature is effective to bind a company was doubted **6–05** by Denning L.J., who said: "it has not yet been held that a company can sign by its printed name affixed with a rubber stamp".[17]

Although the name of the company must appear, it is unnecessary to state in express terms that the signature is on behalf of or by the authority of the company.[18] In *Stacey v. Wallis*, Scrutton J. held *obiter* that the terms of the then equivalent of section 349(1)(c) of the Companies Act 1985, were sufficiently met if the name of the company was properly given as addressee.[19] In

---

[13] *Lindholst & Co. A/S v. Fowler* [1988] B.C.L.C. 166; *Rafsanjan Pistachio Producers v. Reiss* [1990] B.C.L.C. 352.

[14] [1981] 2 Lloyd's Rep. 54 CA; see also *Banque de l'Indochine v. Euroseas Group Finance Co. Ltd* [1981] Com.L.R. 77; [1981] 3 All E.R. 198, deciding that "& Co." was the same as "company", and applying the dictum of Scrutton, J. in *Stacey v. Wallace* (1912) 106 L.T., 544, 547.

[15] [1979] 2 Lloyd's Rep. 361.

[16] [1988] F.L.R. 229; [1988] B.C.L.C. 170.

[17] *Lazarus Estates v. Beasley* [1956] 1 Q.B. 702, 710.

[18] *Okell v. Charles* (1876) 34 L.T. 822 (Jessel M.R. and Kelly C.B.) (bill on company, accepted J. Macdonald, Rob Charles, "Directors of Great Snowdon Mountain Copper Mining Co. Ltd").

[19] (1912) 106 L.T. 544; see also *Penrose v. Martyr* (1958) E.B. & E. 499, where the name in the address was incorrect; and *Hendon v. Adelman* (1973) 117 S.J. 631, *per* Mackenna J. who held that where a cheque was signed on behalf of L. & R. Agencies omitted the ampersand, there was a failure to comply with s.108(1)(c) of the Companies Act 1948 and thus the directors signing were personally liable under s.108(4)(b). The use of the ampersand instead of "and" was held not negligence in *Kilburn & others v. Coop Centre Credit Union Ltd* [1972] 33 D.L.R. 233.

practice, the person affixing the name of the company usually includes his own signature and official description for the purpose of indicating by whom the instrument was in fact signed. The further question then arises whether the signature is in a representative capacity only (see *post*, para. 7–06), or whether it imposes a personal liability upon the person actually signing the instrument. If the personal signature is qualified by a statement that it is for or on account of the company, no personal liability on the instrument attaches to the person so signing.[20] No express qualification of the signature is, however, necessary where the company is in fact bound and the form of the instrument shows that the company alone intended to be bound.[21] On the other hand, if the instrument is otherwise sufficient to impose a personal liability upon the person signing it, he will be liable upon it, unless the signature is expressly qualified.[22]

When the directors of a company are empowered by the articles of association to authorise the managing director to draw bills on its behalf, the company is bound to a holder in due course by a bill drawn by the managing director and purporting to be drawn on its behalf, though in fact the directors have never authorised him to do so, since the holder is entitled to assume that the bill is properly drawn on behalf of the company.[23] At the same time the

[20] *Lindus v. Melrose* (1858) 27 L.J.Ex. 326; *Alexander v. Sizer* (1869) L.R. 4 Ex. 102.

[21] *Chapman v. Smethurst* [1909] 1 K.B. 927, where the defendant was held not to be personally liable upon a promissory note in the following form: "Six months after date I promise to pay," etc., "J. H. Smethurst's Laundry and Dye Works Ltd, J. H. Smethurst, Managing Director" followed in *Kettle v. Dunster & Wakefield* (1927) 43 T.L.R. 770; *Britannia Electric Lamp Works Ltd v. Mandler* (D.) & Co. [1939] 2 K.B. 129 and *Etlin v. Asseltyne* (1962) 32 D.L.R. (2d) 489. See also *Fairchild v. Ferguson* (1892) 21 S.C.R. 484; *Canada Paper Co. v. Gazette Publishing Co.* (1893) 32 N.B.R. 369; *Northern Electric Co. v. Kasow* (1914) 20 W.L.R. (Can.) 582; *Amalgamated Handwork Manufacturers Co. v. Cole* [1935] V.L.R. 103, in which last case it was held that personal liability was excluded where they signed under "cover" of the addition of the company's name; *H. B. Etlin v. Asseltyne* (1962) 32 D.L.R. (2d) 489 (defendants signed beneath printed name of company; held ambiguous and therefore extrinsic evidence admitted to show the capacity in which the signatory signed); considered in *Bondina Ltd v. Rollaway Shower Blinds Ltd* [1986] 1 A.E.R. 564; *Alliston Creamery v. Grosdanoff and Tracy* (1962) 34 D.L.R. (2d) 189.

[22] *Dutton v. Marsh* (1871) L.R. 6 Q.B. 361, where four directors of a company who signed their names to a note as "We, the directors of the Isle of Man Slate Co. Ltd, do promise to pay J.D. £1,600 with interest at 6 per cent. for value received," and at one corner the company's seal was affixed, were held personally liable, since no statement was included to the effect that they signed on behalf of the company. This case was followed in *Loczka v. Ruthenian Farmers' Co.* [1922] 2 W.W.R. 782; see also *Union Bank of Canada v. Cross* (1909) 12 W.L.R. 539; *Elliot v. Bax-Ironside* [1925] 2 K.B. 301 (followed and applied in *Kettle v. Dunster & Wakefield, supra*), where a bill accepted by a limited company bore an indorsement containing the name of the company followed by the signatures of two directors, who were held personally liable; *Brebner v. Henderson*, 1925 S.C. 643, where the defendants were held personally liable on a promissory note in the following terms: "Four months after date, we promise to pay," etc. "A B director, C D Secretary, The Fraserburgh Empire Ltd"; *Kettle v. Dunster* (1927) 43 T.L.R. 770; *cf. Schaffer v. Tubby Smith & Co.* (1924) 1 W.W.R. 213.

[23] *Dey v. Pullinger Engineering Co.* [1921] 1 K.B. 77, following *Re Land Credit Co. of Ireland* (1869) L.R. 4 Ch.App. 460, *Royal British Bank v. Turquand* (1856) 6 E. & B. 327; *Mahony v. East Holyford Mining Co.* (1875) L.R. 7 H.L. 869; *County of Gloucester Bank v. Rudry Merthyr Colliery Co.* [1895] 1 Ch. 629; *Biggerstaff v. Rowlatt's Wharf* [1896] 2 Ch. 93, and dissenting from *Premier Industrial Bank v. Carlton Co.* [1909] 1 K.B. 106; see also *Bank of Hamilton v. Mutual Fruit Co.* [1921] 1 W.W.R. 727; *Canadian Bank of Commerce v. Rogers* (1911) 23 O.L.R. 109. Where there was in fact no by-law, resolution or other act defining the powers of the managing director, but the company had previously paid similar notes made in their name by such director, the company was held liable (*Imperial Bank v. Farmers' Trading Co.* (1901) 13 Man. L.R. 412).

person purporting to sign on behalf of the company must be acting within his ostensible authority. But a person cannot rely on ostensible authority if he has no knowledge of the articles from which it derives.[24] If he is not a person who might properly be authorised, the existence of a power of delegation in the articles does not affect the position; the bill is a forgery, and does not bind the company.[25] The cases, which are not easy to reconcile, are reviewed by the Court of Appeal in *Freeman & Lockyer v. Buckhurst Park Properties (Mangal) Ltd.*[26]

Since a bill can only be accepted (except for honour) by the person on whom it is drawn, a person, not in fact a director, who accepted as "manager" a bill drawn on the directors of a company was held not to be personally liable.[27] But where two directors and the secretary of a company, incorporated under local Acts without power to accept bills, accepted for the company in their own names a bill drawn on the company, they were held personally liable on the implied representation of authority, though not liable on the bill itself, since the bill was drawn on the company, which alone could accept it.[28] Where the instrument is manifestly irregular on its face even a bona fide holder can acquire no title thereto, as where a cheque was drawn in fraud of a railway company by three directors, though not describing themselves as such, and counter-signed by the secretary, and the only mention of the company's name was contained in the stamp impressed on the face of the cheque, it was held that no person had a right to take such an instrument as an instrument issued by the company.[29]

Company in liquidation

Under the Insolvency Act 1986 the liquidator of a company is empowered to draw, accept, make and indorse bills and notes in the name and on behalf of the company.[30] More than one liquidator may be appointed[31]; their appointment should declare whether any act is to be done by all or any one or more   **6–06**

---

[24] See *Rama Corporation Ltd v. Proved Tin & General Investments Ltd* [1952] 2 Q.B. 147, in which *Houghton v. Nothard, Lowe & Wills Ltd* was followed; *British Thomson-Houston v. Federated European Bank Ltd* [1932] 2 K.B. 176, CA was not followed, and *Mahony v. East Holyford Mining Co.* was distinguished.

[25] *Kreditbank Cassel v. Schenkers* [1927] 1 K.B. 826; *cf. Liggett (Liverpool) v. Barclays Bank* [1928] 1 K.B. 48, where the defendants were put on inquiry; and see Paget, *Law of Banking* (11th ed., 1996, pp. 142 *et seq.*).

[26] [1964] 2 Q.B. 480, especially Diplock L.J. at 500.

[27] *Bult v. Morrell* (1840) 12 A. & E. 745.

[28] *West London Bank v. Kitson* (1883) 12 Q.B.D. 157, distinguishing *Beattie v. Ebury* (1874) L.R. 7 H.L. 102, where a mere direction given by the directors of a company to a bank how cheques should be drawn for the company was held not to impose a personal liability on the directors as regards an overdraft allowed the company by the bank. In *Eastwood v. Bain* (1858) 28 L.J.Ex. 74, it was held that directors could not be personally liable on a bill which they had improperly authorised the secretary to accept on behalf of a company. Assuming that there had been a false representation and the plaintiff had proved damage, they might have been liable for such damage. There is no liability on such implied representation of authority where the plaintiff fails to prove that he had suffered damage thereby.

[29] *Serrell v. Derbyshire Ry* (1850) 9 C.B. 811.

[30] See ss.165 and 167, and para. 9 of Sched. 4 of the I.A. 1986.

[31] Section 231 Insolvency Act 1986.

of them. Similarly an administrator[32] and an administrative receiver[33] of a company have power to draw bills etc.

Power to issue negotiable securities

6–07   Previous editions of this book have addressed at length the question of whether English companies could issue negotiable securities. There has been no question for more than a century that corporations can issue negotiable instruments.[34]

Banking companies

6–08   It is provided in the 1882 Act that:

97.—(3) Nothing in this Act or in any repeal effected thereby shall affect:—
(b) the provisions of the Companies Act 1862, or Acts amending it, or any Act relating to joint stock banks or companies;
(c) the provisions of any Act relating to or confirming the privileges of the Bank of England or the Bank of Ireland respectively.

The capacity of corporations and banking companies to make, draw or accept negotiable instruments is still subject to the provisions of the Bank Charter Act 1844, and the other statutes passed for protecting the privileges of the Bank of England. The only remaining restriction on the issue of negotiable instruments by banks and other corporations is that they may not issue in England or Wales a bill or note payable to bearer on demand[35]; bank drafts are not payable to bearer, and if they were to do so would probably infringe s.11 of the 1844 Act. The Bank of England has a monopoly of note issue.[36]

Minors

6–09   An infant is a person who has not attained full age, since 1969 the age of 18.[37] By section 12 of the Family Law Reform Act 1969 a person who is not 18 years old may be described as a minor instead of an infant.

Formerly there were statutory provisions relating to infants' contracts, which were contained in the Infants Relief Act 1874 and the Betting and Loans (Infants) Act 1892. The Minor's Contracts Act 1987 disapplied the provisions contained in those two statutes, so that the position is governed by the common law. In general contracts entered into by infants were voidable at the option of the infant, although contracts for necessaries are binding.

---

[32] Section 14 and Sched. 1, para. 10 of the Insolvency Act 1986.
[33] Section 42 and Sched. 1 of I.A. 1986.
[34] Those interested in this arcane learning are referred to the previous editions.
[35] Section 11 of the 1844 Act.
[36] Currency and Bank Notes Act 1954; Halsbury, *Laws of England* (4th ed.), Vol. 4 (1987) re-issue p. 455.
[37] Family Law Reform Act 1969, s.1.

It has long been clear that an infant is not liable on his bill or note.[38] Where the bill or note is given in respect of necessaries supplied, the liability of the infant is upon the consideration and not upon the instrument.[39] Thus, if the person who supplied the necessaries indorses the instrument to another, the indorsee cannot sue or present a bankruptcy petition against the infant, founded on the debt alleged to be due to him as indorsee.[40]

Under section 2 of the Infants Relief Act 1874, a person was not liable to a holder on a bill signed by him after majority in consideration of a debt contracted as an infant, or in ratification of a promise to repay made when an infant.[41] With the repeal of this section, such a person will be liable on a bill, cheque or note. Until 1987 an instrument given in pursuance of an agreement made by a person after coming of age to pay any money which represents, or was agreed to be paid in respect of, a loan contracted during infancy was absolutely void, except in so far as it was in respect of a new advance.[42] However since the repeal of the Betting and Loans (Infants) Act 1892, such an instrument is enforceable.

If an infant, by representing himself to be of age, obtains credit from another, and gives a bill as security, he is not estopped, by reason of the representation, from denying liability on the bill.[43]

A person of full age, who accepts a bill, drawn while he was an infant, is liable thereon[44] but a bill, drawn, indorsed or accepted in blank by an infant, and filled up without his express consent after he is of full age, does not, it is submitted, bind him.[45]

If an infant is a party, jointly with an adult, to a negotiable instrument, the owner may sue the adult alone, without taking notice of the infant.[46]

---

[38] So held as long ago as 1689 in *Williams v. Harrison*, Carthew Rep. 160, through *quaere* in this case if the bill had been drawn for necessaries.

[39] The same principle applies in the case of contracts held to be for the infant's benefit; see *Aroney v. Christianus* (1914) 15 N.S.W.S.R. 118, but contrast *Manufacturers' Life Insurance Co. v. King* (1869) 9 Q.S.C. 236, where the infant was held liable on the instrument, as he pleaded, but did not prove, lesion (damage).

[40] *Re Soltykoff, ex p. Margrett* [1891] 1 Q.B. 413 and cases there cited; *cf. Bateman v. Kingston* (1880) 6 Ir.L.R. 328. If the necessaries are actually supplied, then under s.2 of the Sale of Goods Act 1893 the infant is bound to pay a reasonable price therefor.

[41] *Smith v. King* [1892] 2 Q.B. 543; in which the plaintiff took the bill with notice; *quaere*, whether notice necessary to deprive him of right to recover; see also *ex p. Kibble* (1875) L.R. 10 Ch. 373; *Fairchild v. Lowes* (1892) 8 Man.R. 527; as for bona fide transferee for value without notice, see *Belfast Banking Co. v. Doherty* (1879) 4 L.R.Ir. 124.

[42] Betting and Loans (Infants) Act 1892, s.5.

[43] *Bartlett v. Wells* (1862) 1 B. & S. 836; *Bateman v. Kingston, supra*. The latter case seems, however, open to doubt: *Levene v. Brougham*, in which the Court of Appeal held that an equitable liability resulting from a fraud did not mean that the contract would be enforced, but that some other remedy would be given. It did not amount to an estoppel: (1909) 25 T.L.R. 265. Nor is the infant liable on the fraudulent misrepresentation: see *Leslie Ltd v. Sheill* [1914] 3 K.B. 607, distinguishing *Ex p. Unity Bank* (1858) 3 De G. & J. 63 and *Ex p. Jones* (1881) 18 Ch.D 109. An infant's cheque may be met by the drawee bank (*Freeman v. Bank of Montreal* (1912) 5 D.L.R. 418; Paget, *Law of Banking* (1996, 11th ed.), p. 148).

[44] *Stevens v. Jackson* (1815) 4 Camp. 164.

[45] *cf. Hunt v. Massey* (1834) 5 B. & Ad. 902.

[46] *Burgess v. Merrill* (1812) 4 Taunt. 468; *Park v. Pullisky* (1911) 16 W.L.R. (Can.) 457. So, too, where an infant is a joint maker with an adult of a note (*Wauthier v. Wilson* (1912) 28 T.L.R. 239; see also *Pearson v. Calder* (1916) 35 O.L.R. 534).

An infant drawing and indorsing bills may convey a title to the indorsee, so
that the indorsee can sue the acceptor and all other parties, except the infant
himself.[47]

An infant may sue on a bill by his next friend.[48]

Persons under undue influence

6–10   The exercise of undue influence over persons of full age giving bills, notes
or other negotiable securities, affords ground for the interference of the Court,
which will not allow the securities to be enforced, unless they are in the hands
of a holder in due course, and will, if necessary, order them to be set aside.[49]
This jurisdiction is not confined to the case of guardian and ward, but applies
wherever there exists between the parties a relationship or connection constituting anything like a trust or guardianship, or conferring authority, control
or influence. Certain relationships as a matter of law raise the presumption that
undue influence has been exercised, for example solicitor and client, medical
advisor and patient[50] and extends to ministers of religion of any persuasion. In
these cases the Court will not suffer any such securities to be enforced, unless
satisfied that they were given freely and voluntarily, and independently of any
influence over the giver, except, in the case of negotiable securities, in favour
of a holder in due course or a holder making title through one.

It has never been part of the equitable doctrine that husband and wife stand
in fiduciary relationship to each other, so as to raise the presumption that the
husband might have influence on the wife.[51] Whether or not there has been in
a particular case is a question of fact.

Where the claimant has, either directly or through his agent,[52] knowledge of
the facts constituting the undue influence, he cannot recover upon negotiable
instruments so given, and where the defendant signing under undue influence
has done so without consideration the claimant can recover nothing.[53]

To the extent to which a person signing a bill under undue influence has
received consideration, he may be liable to repay the amount so advanced with
interest at the legal rate.[54]

Where a bill is given under undue influence and is in the hands of a holder,
the burden of proving himself a holder in due course, or a transferee from one,
is cast upon him.[55] Should he discharge that onus, he would be entitled to

[47] The 1882 Act, s.22(2); see *ante*, para. 6–01; *Taylor v. Croker* (1802) 4 Esp. 186; *Nightingale
v. Withington*, 15 Mass. American Rep. 272 (1818); and see *Grey v. Cooper* (1782) 3 Doug. 65;
Drayton v. Dale (1823) 2 B. & C. 293, 299, 301; *Smith v. Johnson* (1858) 3 H. & N. 222.
[48] *Warwick v. Bruce* (1813) 2 M. & Sel. 205.
[49] *Archer v. Hudson* (1846) 15 L.J.Ch. 211; *Maitland v. Irving* (1846) 16 L.J.Ch. 95; see also
Espey v. Lake (1853) 22 L.J.Ch. 336; *Lewis Furniture Co. v. Campbell* (1911) 21 Man. 390.
[50] See *Barclays Bank v. O'Brien* [1994] 1 A.C. 180, at 189.
[51] *Howes v. Bishop* [1909] 2 K.B. 390; see also *Bank of Montreal v. Stuart* [1911] A.C. 120,
approving *Nedby v. Nedby* (1852) 5 De G. & Sm. 377; *Mackenzie v. Royal Bank of Canada* [1934]
A.C. 468. As to the contractual position of a married woman, see *post*, para. 6–13.
[52] *Archer v. Hudson, supra.*
[53] *Maitland v. Irving, supra*; *Maitland v. Backhouse* (1847) 16 Sim. 58.
[54] *Aylesford v. Morris* (1873) L.R. 8 Ch. 484.
[55] If the bill is in the hands of the original payee, the onus of proof is not shifted, but remains
upon the person alleging undue influence (*Talbot v. Von Boris* [1911] 1 K.B. 854).

recover the full amount payable under the bill, otherwise only the consideration, if any, received by the party charged, with interest.[56]

Persons of unsound mind

It is now no answer to an action on a bill or note to plead insanity, unless   **6–11**
the defendant also pleads and proves that the person with whom he contracted
"knew he was so insane as not to be capable of understanding what he was
about".[57] Thus mental incapacity is no defence against a holder in due
course.

If a defendant proves that the first issue of a bill or note was procured by
an immediate party taking advantage of his mental incapacity, the onus of
proving that value has subsequently been given in good faith for the instrument is presumably shifted to the holder under section 30(2).[58]

Where it is shown that the defendant, as the result of senile degeneration,
was incapable of understanding the true nature and effect of the transaction for
which she gave her cheque, and that the plaintiff was aware of her condition,
it was held that he could not recover from her.[59] Indeed any transaction which
"shocks the conscience of the Court" will be set aside under the doctrine of
unconscionability.[60]

Drunkenness

The same rule prevails in regard to a person contracting when so drunk as   **6–12**
not to know what he was about when he made the promise.[61] Yet, though he
is not liable on the express contract embodied in his signature and indorsement of a bill or note, he may be liable on an implied contract, as when his
signature or indorsement is given for a good consideration supplied to him,
such as necessaries, which he has accepted and kept.[62] The contract of a
drunken man, being voidable only, and not void, may be ratified when he
becomes sober.[63]

---

[56] *Aylesford v. Morris* (1873) L.R. 8 Ch. 585, 495 (Lord Selborne C.); *Lyon v. Home* (1868)
L.R. 6 Eq. 655, 681. The 1882 Act, s.30(2), does not expressly advert to bills given under undue
influence, but the general word "illegality" may cover such a case. A holder of a bill given under
duress is obliged to prove that, after the duress, value was in good faith given for the bill; he can
then recover. Similarly, where a bill has been given under undue influence, a holder discharging
the like onus is entitled to recover, for undue influence can no more be a defence against a holder
in due course or a transferee from one, than duress is. In no case is it suggested that a holder in
due course is prejudiced by the fact of a bill having been given under undue influence. But a payee
cannot be a holder in due course, see *R.E. Jones Ltd v. Waring & Gillow Ltd* [1926] A.C. 670.
[57] *Imperial Loan Co. v. Stone* [1892] 1 Q.B. 599.
[58] But *quaere* whether proof that a note was given without consideration is enough to place on
the holder the burden of proving that he is the holder in due course: see *Alloway v. Hutchinson*
(1898) 6 Terr. 425; *Molson's Bank v. Stearns* (1905) 6 O.W.R. 667; *Bank of Toronto v. Stillman*
(1930) 65 O.L.R. 375; 3 D.L.R. 838.
[59] *Manches v. Trimborn* (1946) 115 L.J.K.B. 305.
[60] See generally *Snell's Principle of Equity* (28 ed.) p. 545; *Credit Lyonnais NV v. Burch* [1997]
1 A.E.R. 144.
[61] *Molton v. Camroux* (1849) 4 Ex. 17; *Essakow v. Galbraith* [1917] O.P.D. (S. Africa) 53.
[62] *Matthews v. Baxter* (1873) L.R. 8 Ex. 17; *Essakow v. Galbraith* [1917] O.P.D. (S. Africa)
53.
[63] *Mathews v. Baxter* (1873) L.R. 8 Ex. 132. It is otherwise in *Natal* (*Goodman v. Pritchard*
(1907) 28 N.L.R. 231).

Married women

6–13   A married woman is capable of binding herself by contract and is liable on
a bill like any other person. A wife cannot by accepting in her own name a bill
drawn on her husband bind him, as the acceptance must now be in the name
of the drawee.[64]

Where a married woman signs a bill or note at the request of her husband,
this fact alone does not cast on the husband, or on the person who is suing the
wife, the onus of disproving an allegation of undue influence.[65] It has yet to
be seen whether the doctrine of constructive notice, established in *Barclays
Bank v. O'Brien*,[66] has any part to play in relation to a bill or cheque given by
a wife in settlement of her husband's indebtedness or that of his company,
where the husband has exercised undue influence. It is suggested that, in
relation to ordinary transactions, were a bill or cheque drawn by the wife to
be provided to discharge such indebtedness, a third party, taking such an
instrument, would not be affected by the husband's alleged wrongful act.
However it is considered that circumstances may well arise where a third
party taking payment from a wife has knowledge of such facts as to put him
on inquiry; if that third party thereafter failed to take reasonable steps to
ensure that the instrument was provided free from the undue influence of the
husband, then payment under the bill or cheque would not be enforceable
against the wife by the third party.

Enemy Aliens

6–14   A contract in favour of an alien enemy, not residing in this country by the
Queen's licence, is void at law and in equity. Hence a bill drawn by an alien
enemy on a British subject in England, and indorsed to a British subject
abroad, cannot be enforced even after the restoration of peace.[67] There is no
such breach of duty in not paying at maturity bills drawn before the outbreak
of war by someone who at their maturity was an alien enemy, and thus interest
on the debt is not recoverable except from the date of the declaration of
peace.[68]

Still less can payment of a bill, even though drawn and accepted previous
to the outbreak of war and indorsed to neutrals in a foreign country, be
enforced during the continuance of the war.[69]

---

[64] In view of the 1882 Act s.17, *Lindus v. Bradwell* (1848) 5 C.B. 583 cannot now be relied
on.

[65] *Howes v. Bishop* [1909] 2 K.B. 390; *Sanguinetti v. Messiter* (1885) 2 T.L.R. 135; *Talbot v.
Von Boris* [1911] 1 K.B. 854.

[66] [1994] 1 A.C. 180.

[67] *Willison v. Patteson* (1817) 7 Taunt. 439; *Brandon v. Nesbitt* (1794) 6 T.R. 23; see also *post*,
para. 19–25, as to illegal consideration.

[68] *Biedermann v. Allhausen* (1921) 37 T.L.R. 662, followed in *N.V. Ledeboter and Van der
Held's Textielhandel v. Hibbert* [1947] 1 K.B. 964.

[69] *Weld v. Fruhling and Goschen* (1916) 32 T.L.R. 469; *cf. Wilson v. Regosine Co.* (1915) 31
T.L.R. 264.

CHAPTER 7

LIABILITY ON A BILL

SIGNATURE on a bill, note or cheque is essential to liability: **7–01**

23. No person is liable as drawer, indorser, or acceptor of a bill who has not signed it as such[1]: provided that
(1) where a person signs a bill in a trade or assumed name, he is liable thereon as if he had signed it in his own name:
(2) the signature of the name of a firm is equivalent to the signature by the person so signing of the names of all persons liable as partners in that firm.

And further by:

91.—(1) where by this Act, any instrument or writing is required to be signed by any person, it is not necessary that he should sign it with his own hand, but it is sufficient if his signature is written thereon by some other person by or under his authority.

A person whose signature does not appear upon the instrument cannot be sued upon it.[2] The signature must, however, be intended to be a signature to a negotiable instrument. If, owing to the fraud of a third person, the nature of the instrument is misrepresented, so that the person affixing his signature does not know that he is signing a negotiable instrument, but believes that he is signing a document of a different character, he is not bound by the instrument, since his mind did not accompany his signature; he never intended to sign, and therefore in contemplation of law never did sign, a negotiable instrument.[3] The misrepresentation must, too, relate to the nature of the contract: a misrepresentation as to its effect does not absolve the signer from liability.[4]

---

[1] As to signature, see *ante*, para. 2–05; as to the position of a transferor by delivery, see *post*, para. 17–21, s.58; and as to partnerships, *post*, para. 7–14.
[2] *Leadbitter v. Farrow* (1816) 5 M. & S. 345; *Ex p. Rayner* (1868) 17 W.R. 64.
[3] *Foster v. Mackinnon* (1869) L.R. 4 C.P. 704, 711, in which the essential features of the doctrine of *non est factum* are expressed by Byles J.—see Lord Pearson in *Saunders (Executrix of the Estate of Rose Maud Gallie) v. Anglia Building Society* [1971] A.C. 1004, 1035; *Lewis v. Clay* (1898) 67 L.J.Q.B. 224; see also *Cote v. Brunelle* (1916) Q.R. 51 C.S. 35; *Alloway v. Hrabi* (1904) 14 Man.L.R. 627; *Commercial Finance Corpn v. Thomas* (1925) 29 O.W.N. 148; *Royal Bank of Canada v. Wannamaker* (1929) 4 D.L.R. 999; and *cf. American Engine Co. v. Tourond* (1910) 19 Man. 660; *Banque J. Cartier v. Lalonde* (1901) Q.R. 20 S.C. 43; *Dunshea v. Kesteven* [1922] N.Z.L.R. 1036.
[4] *Howatson v. Webb* [1908] 1 Ch. 1; *cf. Duncan Fox & Co. v. North and South Wales Bank* (1880) 6 App.Cas. 1; see also *Krige v. Willemse* (1908) 25 S.C. 43; *Siffman v. Kriel* (1909) T.S. 538. As to an acceptance given under a mistake of fact, see *Ayres v. Moore* [1940] 1 K.B. 278.

Further, the signer must not be guilty of negligence, otherwise he will be estopped from denying the validity of his signature as against a holder in due course.[5]

The 1882 Act does not attempt to define "signature".[6] Prima facie, to prevent confusion the signature of the acceptor should correspond with the name of the drawee as written on the bill by the drawer, the acceptor adding his right name, if he wishes; equally an indorsee, under a special indorsement, should himself indorse in the name specified in the indorsement.[7] In the past bankers declined to accept the indorsement of the payee or an indorsee on an order cheque which did not correspond with the payee's or indorser's name as given in the body of the cheque, and there is plenty of authority for their doing so.[8] Following upon the Cheques Act 1957, indorsement is not necessary. However as a result of the Cheques Act 1992 most banks issue their customers with crossed cheques marked "Account Payee". Consequently banks will not credit the proceeds of such a cheque to anyone other than the named payee, and thus do not require an indoresement. In those cases where banks still call for indorsement such indorsement must necessarily, it would seem, be regular.[9]

AGENTS

7–02   An agent is considered as a mere instrument; therefore, infants and other persons labouring under disabilities may be agents. A mere agent cannot delegate his authority unless specially authorised to do so.[10]

No particular form of appointment is necessary to enable an agent to draw, indorse, accept or make bills or notes, so as to charge his principal; he may be specially appointed for this purpose or derive his power from general or implied authority. The ostensible authority should not exceed the actual authority, for if the principal's representations or acts give to the agent the appearance of an authority larger than the agent actually possesses, the principal may be bound by such of the agent's acts as, although beyond the agent's actual authority, are still within the ostensible or apparent authority.

General authorities to transact business, and to receive and discharge debts, do not confer upon an agent the power of accepting or indorsing bills, so as

---

[5] *Foster v. Mackinnon, supra,* where a new trial was ordered on the question of negligence. This qualification was confined to the case of negotiable instruments (*Carlisle and Cumberland Banking Co. v. Bragg* [1911] 1 K.B. 489, 497, but this decision was held by the House of Lords in *Gallie v. Lee* [1971] A.C. 1004, HL to be wrong).

[6] *Ante*, para. 2–05.

[7] See *post*, para. 9–08.

[8] See, in particular, *Arab Bank Ltd v. Ross* [1952] 2 Q.B. 216, Denning L.J., at 227.

[9] *Post*, para. 22–48.

[10] *Combe's Case* (1614) 9 Co.Rep. 75; *Pallisser v. Ord* (1724) Bunb. 166. But an authority to indorse may be an authority to indorse by the hand of another in the agent's presence (*Lord v. Hall* (1849) 19 L.J.C.P. 47; see also *Ex p. Sutton* (1788) 2 Cox 84).

to charge his principal.[11] Special authorities to accept or indorse are construed strictly.[12] Any person taking a bill, purporting to be accepted by procuration, knows that he has not got the security of the acceptor's signature, but that of the party professing to act in pursuance of the authority conferred on him by his principal. A person taking such a bill should therefore insist on the production of the authority. A B, who carried on business on his own account, and also in partnership, gave a power of attorney to certain persons, including his wife, to do certain acts on his behalf, and a further power to his wife alone to accept bills drawn by his agents, for him and on his behalf. C D, one of his partners, who was also his agent, drew a bill on him in respect of his partnership debts, and this bill A B's wife accepted *per pro*. It was held that the first power did not warrant the acceptance, that the second power only authorised acceptances *per pro* of the defendant in his individual capacity and of bills drawn by his agents as such, whereas the bill in question was drawn by C D as partner.[13] An authority to indorse bills remitted to the principal gives no power to indorse a bill which the principal could not have indorsed without a fraud, and such an indorsement conveys no title even to a holder in due course.[14] It would be otherwise had the principal himself indorsed.[15] An authority to draw cheques probably carries no implied authority to draw post-dated cheques.[16]

Subsequent recognition of an agent's acts is equivalent to previous authority, provided that the agent, when he acted, assumed to act as agent.[17]

When authority may be inferred

An authority is often implied from circumstances, as where the agent has formerly been in the habit of drawing, accepting or indorsing for his principal, and his principal has recognised his acts. Thus, to an action against an acceptor of a bill, the defence was that the drawer had forged the acceptor's signature, in answer to which it was proved that the defendant had previously   **7–03**

---

[11] *Hogg v. Snaith* (1808) 1 Taunt. 347; *Hay v. Goldsmid* (1804) 2 Smith 79; *Murray v. East India Co.* (1821) 5 B. & Ald. 204; and see *Howard v. Baillie* (1796) 2 H.Bla. 618; *Gardner v. Baillie* (1796) 6 T.R. 591; *Kilgour v. Finlyson* (1789) 1 H.Bla. 156; *Esdaile v. La Nauze* (1835) 1 Y. & Col. 394; *Re Cunningham & Co.* (1887) 36 Ch.D. 532; *Odell v. Cormack* (1887) 18 Q.B.D. 223. But where an agent managed a business and acted ostensibly as principal, it was held that he could bind his principal by accepting a bill, even though expressly forbidden so to do (*Edmunds v. Bushell* (1865) L.R. 1 Q.B. 97). As to the authority of the master of a ship to draw bills, see *Pocahontas Fuel Co. v. Ambatielos* (1922) 27 Com.Cas. 148, 153.

[12] *Morison v. Kemp* (1912) 29 T.L.R. 70; *Haine v. Pattrick* [1917] Transvaal P. 110; *cf. Jacobs v. Morris* [1902] 1 Ch. 816; *Australian Bank of Commerce v. Perel* [1926] A.C. 737; as regards cheques, see *Reckitt v. Barnett, Pembroke & Slater* [1929] A.C. 176; and *Midland Bank v. Reckitt* [1933] A.C. 1, applied in *Sniderman v. McGarry* (1966) 60 D.L.R. (2d) 404.

[13] *Attwood v. Munnings* (1827) 7 B. & C. 278; see *Bank of Bengal v. Fagan* (1849) 7 Moo.P.C.C. 61, 67.

[14] *Fearn v. Filicia* (1844) 14 L.J.C.P. 15.

[15] *ibid.* at 16 (Tindal C.J.).

[16] See *Bank of Africa v. Houlder Bros* (1906) 23 S.C. 570; *cf. Gobelar v. Cockcroft*, 1906 E.D.C. 109.

[17] *Ancona v. Marks* (1862) 31 L.J.Exch. 163; *Bank of Montreal v. Dominion Gresham Guarantee and Casualty Co.* [1930] A.C. 659. As to ratifying an unauthorised signature not amounting to a forgery, see the 1882 Act, s.24, *post*, para. 20–31.

paid such acceptances; and this was held to be an adoption by the defendant of the acceptance, whereby he made himself liable to the payment of it.[18]

'It may be admitted", says Tindal C.J., "that an authority to draw does not import in itself an authority to indorse bills; but still the evidence of such authority to draw is not to be withheld from the jury, who are to determine, on the whole of the evidence, whether such authority to indorse exists or not." Where, therefore, the defendants had in repeated instances recognised the authority of their confidential clerk to draw bills and cheques by procuration for them, and on three occasions the clerk had indorsed bills by procuration for them, on one of which occasions, at least, the defendants must have known of the indorsement, while on the other two they had received the money obtained by the indorsement, it was held that a jury was warranted in inferring that the clerk had a general authority to indorse.[19]

The acceptance of a bill drawn by procuration is an admission of the agent's authority to draw, but no admission of his authority to indorse, though the indorsement were on the bill at the time of acceptance, for the acceptor need look only to the handwriting of the drawer, whose signature alone he is precluded from disputing.[20]

Pledging by agent

7–04   An agent, who receives a bill for the purpose of getting it discounted, has no right to pawn it for a sum smaller than the amount of the bill minus the discount, for his employer may by the pawnee's detention of the bill, or by his change of residence, or by its further negotiation, be prevented from raising on the bill its full value, and yet exposed to pay its full amount to a subsequent holder in due course.

Bill brokers

7–05   According to the general law, a bill broker, who receives a bill merely for the purpose of procuring it to be discounted for his customer, has no right to mix it with bills of his other customers, and to pledge the whole mass as a security for an advance of money; for the consequence of this would in many cases be that the bill of one customer might be detained for a loss arising from the dishonoured bills of other customers. Still less has the bill broker a right to deposit bills, which are received merely for the purpose of discount, as a

---

[18] *Barber v. Gingell* (1800) 3 Esp. 60. If there is proof of general authority an admission of liability on another bill is confirmatory of it. There is a great distinction between authorising another bill to be drawn and admitting a liability on another bill so drawn; the former is evidence of a general authority to accept bills, the latter may well be confirmatory of proof of general authority (*Llewellyn v. Winkworth* (1845) 13 M. & W. 598, 599 (Parke B.), distinguishing *Cash v. Taylor* (1830) 8 L.J.(O.S.) K.B. 262). But paying on one forged signature is no estoppel in the case of a second forged signature, even where the plaintiff, though *not* to the knowledge of the defendant, has been the holder of the first bill (*Morris v. Bethel* (1869) L.R. 5 C.P. 47; *Liquidators of Union Bank v. Beit* (1892) 9 Cape S.C. 109) See also *Brown v. Westminster Bank Ltd* [1964] 2 Lloyd's Rep. 187.

[19] *Prescott v. Flinn* (1832) 9 Bing. 19.

[20] *Robinson v. Yarrow* (1817) 7 Taunt. 455, citing *Smith v. Chester* (1787) 1 T.R. 654; the 1882 Act, s.54(2)(b); see *post*, para. 17–06.

security or part security for money previously due from him.[21] But the usage of a particular district may enlarge the authority of a bill broker, and give him a right to pledge the bills of different customers in one mass.[22] Historically such was the usage of bill brokers in the City of London.[23]

In *Sheffield v. London Joint Stock Bank*,[24] it was, however, held that in the case of a moneylender dealing with his customer's securities, no such usage was binding upon a customer unless it was shown that the customer had notice of it and was proved to have dealt with the moneylender on the footing of it. Subsequently, in *London Joint Stock Bank v. Simmons*[25] it was pointed out that the decision in *Sheffield v. London Joint Stock Bank* depended upon its own peculiar circumstances; and the rule laid down in *Foster v. Pearson*, that it was not unusual or unreasonable for bill brokers in the City of London to raise money for their employers by pledging the bills of different proprietors for one advance, was distinctly upheld and applied to the case of a pledge of securities en bloc by a stockholder.[26]

Personal liability of agent

26.—(1) Where a person signs a bill as drawer, indorser, or acceptor, and adds words to his signature, indicating that he signs for or on behalf of a principal, or in a representative character, he is not personally liable thereon; but the mere addition to his signature of words describing him as an agent, or as filling a representative character, does not exempt him from personal liability.

(2) In determining whether a signature on a bill is that of the principal or that of the agent by whose hand it is written, the construction most favourable to the validity of the instrument shall be adopted.[27]

7–06

An agent will therefore be personally liable to third persons on his drawing, indorsing or accepting, unless he either signs his principal's name only, or expressly states in writing his ministerial character,[28] and that he signs only in that character: "unless", to use the words of Lord Ellenborough, "he states

---

[21] *Haynes v. Foster* (1833) 2 Cr. & M. 237.

[22] *Foster v. Pearson* (1835) 1 Cr.M. & R. 849.

[23] A bill broker is not a person known to the law with certain prescribed duties, but his employment is one which depends entirely on the course of dealing. His duties may vary in different parts of the country, and their extent is a question of fact to be determined by the usage and course of dealing in the particular place (*Foster v. Pearson, supra*).

[24] (1888) 13 App.Cas. 333.

[25] [1892] A.C. 201; followed in *Fuller v. Glyn, Mills & Co.* [1914] 2 K.B. 168.

[26] The practice was again upheld in the case of *Bentinck v. London Joint Stock Bank* [1893] 2 Ch.D. 120; see also *Fuller v. Glyn, Mills & Co.* [1914] 2 K.B. 168.

[27] For instance, a bill cannot be accepted (except for honour) by any other person than the drawee; *cf. Nicholls v. Diamond* (1835) 9 Ex. 154, 157 in which a bill was addressed to the defendant in his personal capacity, to "J.D., purser, West Downs Mining Co.," and accepted "J.D., *per proc.* West Downs Mining Co." *Held* that he was personally liable, having no right to accept on behalf of the firm. Code, ss.6, 17 and 65(1). Hence the presumption most favourable to the instrument would be, in the case of acceptance by agency, that the signature was that of the principal, as otherwise the acceptance would be void. But the agent may be personally liable, possibly under s.56, or on the implied warranty of authority. See also *Rolfe Lubbell & Co. v. Keith and Greenwood* [1979] 2 Lloyd's Rep. 75.

[28] *Slingsby v. District Bank* [1932] 1 K.B. 544, 547 (Scrutton L.J.).

upon the face of the bill that he subscribes it for another; unless he says plainly, 'I am the mere scribe'."[29] The circumstances in which a person makes it plain must be seen in the light of modern practice, where banks issue pre-printed cheques bearing the name of the drawer company.[30]

Where the defendant, agent of a banker, drew the following bill: "Pay to the order of A B £50, value received, which place to the account of the Durham Bank, as advised," and subscribed his own name, it was held that the defendant was personally answerable, and he alone, though the plaintiff, the payee, knew that he was only agent.[31] A bill for £200 was drawn upon the defendant by the description of "Mr. H. Bishop, Cashier of the York Buildings Company, at their house in Winchester Street, London"; and the bill directed him to place the £200 to the account of the company. The letter of advice from the drawer of the bill was sent to the company, and by their direction the defendant accepted it, in this form: "Accepted, June 13th 1732, per H. Bishop." He was held responsible, the Court considering the addition to his name as merely descriptive, the order to place the sum to the account of the company as a direction how to reimburse himself, and the letter of advice inadmissible to superadd to the terms of the bill, as against the plaintiff, an indorsee.[32] And a bill directed to WC for value received in machinery supplied to the adventurers in Hayter and Holme Moore Mines, and accepted as follows: "Accepted for the companies, payable at the Union Bank, etc., W.C. Purser," was held to create a personal liability.[33] A bill drawn on a limited company was accepted in the following terms: "Accepted payable at the W. Bank, A B and C D, Directors, Fashions Fair Exhibitions, Ltd" The drawer of the bill made it a condition of his doing the work for which the bill was drawn that the bill should be indorsed by the directors as well as accepted by the company, and the bill was accordingly indorsed by A B and C D as follows: "Fashion Fair Exhibitions, Ltd, A B and C D, Directors." The directors were held personally liable as indorsers on the ground that if the indorsement was to be treated as the indorsement of the company, it gave no greater validity to the bill than was already contained in the acceptance, and therefore the construction that it was the personal indorsement of the directors was to be adopted.[34] The majority of the Court also held that as the directors'

---

[29] *Leadbitter v. Farrow* (1816) 5 M. & S. 345; *Sowerby v. Butcher* (1834) 2 Cr. & M. 368; *Boyd v. Mortimer* (1899) 30 O.R. 290; *Kannemeyer v. Lubbe* [1921] C.P.D. 647. Cited with approval in *Rafsanjan Pistachio v. Reiss* [1990] B.C.L.C. 352 at 355. Where the word "witness" followed the signature of a party signing as an aval, it was rejected as surplusage (*Nicholson v. McKale* (1912) 5 W.L.R. 237).

[30] See *Bondina Ltd v. Rollaway Shower Blinds Ltd* [1986] 1 A.E.R. 564.

[31] *Leadbitter v. Farrow, supra*; *Goupy v. Harden* (1816) 7 Taunt. 159, *Rafansanjan v. Reiss, supra*.

[32] *Thomas v. Bishop* (1734) 2 Stra. 955; *Rew v. Pettet* (1834) 1 A. & E. 196.

[33] *Mare v. Charles* (1856) 25 L.J.Q.B. 119, as to which see now Falconbridge (7th ed., 1969), p. 600, where it is said that "this decision should no longer govern. It was not followed in a similar case Quebec"—*Smith v. Mason* (1911) Que.S.C. 75. Where a master of a ship drew on his owners a bill in payment of coal supplied and in discharge of disbursements, and added the words, "for which I hold my vessel, owners, and freight responsible", he was held personally liable on the bill on its dishonour by them (*The Elmville, Ceylon Coaling Co. v. Goodrich* [1904] P. 319.

[34] *Elliot v. Bax-Ironside* [1925] 2 K.B. 301, followed in *Kettle v. Dunster* (1927) 138 L.T. 158. In the former, Bankes L.J. said that it was permissible, in construing an indorsement, to take into consideration the circumstances in which it was made.

signatures did not in terms say that they were indorsing on behalf of the company, the word "directors" added to their signatures was a word of description only and did not exempt them from liability.[35]

In *Bondina Ltd v. Rollaway Shower Blinds Ltd*[36] it was held that a director who signed a cheque with the pre-printed name of the company on it without any description, had an arguable defence to a claim for summary judgment. It was held that, with the modern form of cheque with the pre-printed name of the company, the signature of a director is merely affixed as indicating the person by whom the name of the company was affixed or as otherwise validating the making of the instrument on behalf of the company.[37]

Persons filling official positions

If persons who fill official positions as churchwardens, overseers, surveyors, commissioners, managers of banks, agents and secretaries to companies, and the like, give bills or notes on which they describe themselves in their official capacity, they are nevertheless personally liable.[38] This personal liability is now dependant on the provisions of section 26(1) of the 1882 Act above set out. Where two directors of a limited company drew a cheque on behalf of the company, adding to their respective signatures the word "director", they were held personally liable, the fact that the cheque was stamped near the top with the name of the company not being sufficient to show that the defendants in fact signed in a representative character within the meaning of section 26.[39] *In Maxform S.p.A. v. Mariani and Goodville Ltd*[40] the Court of Appeal held that section 26(2) was concerned to ensure that the Court looks at the bill as a whole. The object is to make the bill valid if it is possible to make it valid. These bills were drawn on Italdesign the registered trading name of Goodville Ltd and signed by Mariani, who although not liable as acceptor (since he was not the drawee) was held liable as purporting to act for the drawee. On the other hand, where an acceptance in the name of a company was signed by the managing director and the instrument was further indorsed by the managing director in his own name only without any words of description, section 26 has no application to the indorsement, which cannot be treated as the indorsement of the company.[41]

The signature must, of course, be on behalf of a body that is itself a legal entity with power to contract by bill or note. Thus where a note was signed by the defendants "in the name and on behalf of the Reformed Presbyterian Church, Stranraer", they were held personally liable, it being impossible to

7–07

---

[35] See *ante*, para. 6–05.
[36] *Supra*.
[37] See [1986] 1 All E.R. 564 at p. 566, applying *Chapman v. Smethurst* [1909] 1 K.B. 927; see also *H. B. Etlin Co. Ltd v. Asselstyne* (1962) 34 D.L.R. 191.
[38] *Bottomly v. Fisher* (1862) 1 H. & C. 211; *Price v. Taylor* (1860) 29 L.J.Ex. 331; *Eaton v. Bell* (1821) 5 B. & Ald. 34; *Forwood Bros & Co. v. Mathews* (1893) 10 T.L.R. 138.
[39] *Landes v. Marcus* (1909) 25 T.L.R. 478, following *Dutton v. Marsh* (1871) L.R. 6 Q.B. 361 see also *ante*, para. 6–05.
[40] [1981] 2 Lloyd's Rep. 54, CA.
[41] *Britannia Electric Lamp Works Ltd v. Mandler* (D.) & Co. [1939] 2 K.B. 129; and see *Scottish & Newcastle Breweries v. Blair* (1967) S.L.T. 72.

suggest that a congregation could, as such, be debtors on a promissory note.[42] So, too, in an earlier case, where a parish vestry wished to borrow money but could not bind itself in that capacity, and the church-wardens and overseer signed notes on its behalf, adding to their signatures the words "church wardens" and "overseer" they were held personally liable.[43]

Procuration signatures

7–08   As regards signatures by procuration the 1882 Act provides:

25. A signature by procuration operates as notice that the agent has but a limited authority to sign, and the principal is only bound by such signature if the agent in so signing was acting within the actual limits of his authority.[44]

"Signature by procuration" is not defined. It obviously includes a signature affixed pursuant to a procuration or a power of attorney but it is not clear whether the section similarly relates to lesser forms of representative signature such as "for", "for and on behalf of" and "for account of".

In the 1882 Act the section falls between section 24, which speaks, *inter alia*, of unauthorised signatures and section 26, which concerns signatures for and on behalf of a principal or in a representative character. If section 25 had been intended to apply to all representative signatures, there would have been no need to refer to signatures by procuration and, accordingly, it is permissible to assume that some special authority was intended. This view has from time to time been accepted. According to Paget,[45] in *McDonald v. Nash*,[46] Scrutton L.J. approved the judgment of Pigot C.B. in *O'Reilly v. Richardson*,[47] in which the Chief Baron distinguished a form of signature showing a special and limited authority such as *per pro* or "under power of attorney" from cases of a general authority such as "A *per* B". Both Rowlatt J. and Atkin L.J. in *Stewart v. Westminster Bank Ltd*,[48] appeared to accept the distinction. The former asserted that a limited company could sign only through a natural person signing his own name as the company's agent, but the Court of Appeal declined to express an opinion on the point, though they were considering a company signature. It has been suggested[49] that Rowlatt J. thought that the

---

[42] *M'Meekin v. Easton* (1889) 16 R. 363, where the note was given previous to 1882 and the provisions of the 1882 Act were not cited; see also *Cooper v. McDonald* (1909) 19 Man.L.R. 1 (trade union); *Crane v. Lavoie* (1912) 4 D.L.R. 175; 2 W.W.R. 429; 21 W.L.R. 313; 22 Man R. 330 (company not yet informed); *Austin v. Hober* [1917] 3 W.W.R. (Can.) 994 (officer of unincorporated association).

[43] *Rew v. Pettet* (1834) 1 A. & E. 196. A parish council is now a body corporate by s.172 of the Local Government Act 1972, but can only borrow money by way of mortgage (s.196(1)), and not by bill or note.

[44] *The National Bank of Scotland Ltd v. Dewhurst, The Gonchar and The Izgar* (1896) 1 Com.Cas. 318; see also *Addaicappa Chetty v. Thomas Cook (Bankers) Ltd* (1932) 31 Ceylon N.L.R. 443; and Falconbridge (7th ed., 1969), Ch. 45.

[45] (11th ed. 1996) pp. 392.

[46] [1922] W.N. 272.

[47] (1865) 17 I.C.L.R. 74.

[48] [1926] W.N. 126 and 271; see Paget (11th ed., 1996), p. 392.

[49] *ibid.* at p. 279.

term "by procuration" in section 25, must be limited to agency on behalf of a natural person, but the report does not bear this out, and it is doubtful whether the section is so limited. On the contrary, it is the more likely that section 25 relates to procuration signatures whether affixed on behalf of a company or an individual.

It clearly applies in the case of a procuration signature which purports to transfer a bill; the transferee is put upon inquiry as to the authority of the signatory. A person taking a cheque indorsed *per pro* without knowing anything of the indorser does so at his peril.[50] But the cases in which the section has been in question have generally been cases affecting a collecting banker. In particular in relation to the protection afforded to a collecting banker provided by what was section 82 of the 1882 Act (now contained and amended in section 4 of the Cheques Act 1957).

In the case of *Morison v. London County and Westminster Bank Ltd*,[51] section 25 had been treated by Lord Reading C.J. as giving the drawer a defence, even against a holder in due course, if the agent in signing had exceeded his authority, but as conferring no right to recover the proceeds. Buckley L.J. said that the section went to the validity of the instrument and did not deal with rights arising in respect of the disposition of the proceeds—'In considering, therefore, section 82 as a defence, I think section 25 may be left out of consideration." Phillimore L.J. thought that the section was without relevance to section 82.

This must surely be the case, for the collection of cheques would be impracticable if the collecting banker had to concern himself with procuration indorsements, except in the case where he wished to establish his own right in the instrument. Today, however, the Cheques Act 1957, in so far as it permits the elimination of indorsements, avoids the difficulty, except where the instrument is negotiated.[52]

The cases of *Reckitt v. Barnett, Pembroke and Slater*[53] and *Midland Bank Ltd v. Reckitt*,[54] both concerned signatures affixed pursuant to a power of attorney. In the second, Lord Atkin, commenting on the statement of Lord Reading in the *Morison* case, said that:

> "If the words used were meant to mark off a definite period within which alone the section affects legal rights I see no ground for such a distinction. The effect of the statute is to give notice of limited authority on the face of the document, and this operates as and when the document is negotiated or delivered. The legal consequence of such notice may be to prevent the holder who obtains payment from supporting his right to have received payment. The case of *Reckitt v. Barnett, Pembroke and Slater* is a good instance. The rights in respect of a bill after payment are no doubt matters of special consideration; but whether before or after payment the fact that the bill contains on the face of it notice of limited authority to place on it the particular signature continues to be a fact affecting *pro tanto* the rights of the parties both before and after payment."

[50] *Employers' Liability Assurance Corporation v. Skipper & East* (1877) 4 T.L.R. 55, *per* Manisty J.: but, as far as can be judged from the report the indorsements were not procuration indorsements in the strict sense.
[51] [1914] 3 K.B. 356.
[52] Since the Cheques Act 1992 cheques will be negotiated far less than previously.
[53] [1929] A.C. 176.
[54] [1933] A.C. 1, 16.

If a right of recovery exists, it may be based upon grounds arising independently of the section, such as, for instance, knowledge on the part of the receiver of the money that the instrument was being used to liquidate the agent's private debt.[55]

Production of an agent's authority

7–09   If an offer to accept is made by an agent, the holder may and should require the production of his authority, and if satisfactory authority is not produced, may treat the bill as dishonoured. Where a person takes an acceptance purporting to be by procuration, he "ought to exercise due caution, for he must take it upon the credit of the party who assumes the authority to accept, and it would be only reasonable prudence to require the production of that authority".[56] The apparent authority is, however, the real authority; therefore, if the agent has in fact authority, his abuse of it does not affect a bona fide holder for value. Thus, where an agent had authority to make contracts for sale and purchase and, incidental thereto, had authority to indorse bills but not to borrow money on behalf of the company, and he indorsed two bills *per pro* in the company's name, discounting them with a banker and applying the loan to his own purposes, it was held that his abuse of his authority did not disentitle the banker to recover from the company on the bills. In *Bryant, Powis & Co. v. Banque du Peuple*,[57] the Privy Council thought that the law regarding abuse by an attorney of his trust and authority as not affecting bona fide holders for value was well stated in the New York Court of Appeal in President of the *Westfield Bank v. Cornen*[58] in the following terms:

> "Whenever the very act of the agent is authorised by the terms of the power, that is, whenever by comparing the act done by the agent with the words of the power, the act is in itself warranted by the terms used, such act is binding on the constituent as to all persons dealing in good faith with the agent; such persons are not bound to inquire into facts *aliunde*. The apparent authority is the real authority."

But where the plaintiff as holder clearly has notice of the agent's limited authority, and so cannot recover on the instrument if the agent has acted outside his authority, yet if the money obtained by the instrument has in fact found its way into the principal's possession and has been employed for his benefit, it will be money received by him to the plaintiff's use, even though the principal was unaware of the transaction.[59]

---

[55] *Reckitt v. Barnett, Pembroke and Slater Ltd* [1929] A.C. 176, following *John v. Dodwell* [1918] A.C. 563; *Reckitt v. Nunburnholme* (1929) 45 T.L.R. 629; *cf. Corporation Agencies v. Home Bank of Canada* [1927] A.C. 318; and see *Nelson v. Larholt* [1948] 1 K.B. 339.

[56] *Attwood v. Munnings* (1827) 7 B. & C. 278, 283 (Bayley J.); *Alexander v. Mackenzie* (1848) 6 C.B. 766; *Stagg v. Elliott* (1862) 31 L.J.C.P. 260; *National Bank of Scotland v. Dewhurst* (1896) 1 Com.Cas. 318; *Morison v. Kemp* (1912) 29 T.L.R. 70; *Hayes v. Standard Bank of Canada* (1928) 2 D.L.R. 898; 62 O.L.R. 186.

[57] [1893] A.C. 170; see also *Hambro v. Burnand* [1904] 2 K.B. 10; *Gompertz v. Cook* (1903) 20 T.L.R. 106; *Bank of Africa v. Houlder Bros* (1906) 23 S.C. 570, applying *Hambro v. Burnand*, *supra*; *Liggett (Liverpool) v. Barclays Bank* [1928] 1 K.B. 48.

[58] 37 N.Y.R. (10 Tiff.) 322.

[59] *Reid v. Rigby & Co.* [1894] 2 Q.B. 40, following *Marsh v. Keating* (1834) 1 Bing.N.C. 198, discussed in *Jacobs v. Morris* [1902] 1 Ch. 816. Clearly this is so where the holder has no knowledge of the agent's want of authority (*Bannatyne v. MacIver* [1906] 1 K.B. 103).

Warranty of authority

A signature in a representative capacity merely relieves the agent from **7–10** liability on the instrument. By the act of signature the agent represents to the holder that he has the principal's authority to sign and that his signature accordingly is binding upon his principal. If, therefore, the principal is not bound, owing to the absence or excess of authority, the agent will be liable in damages to the holder, whether the representation is fraudulent[60] or innocent.[61]

Rights of agent against third party

If a man holds a bill or note as agent for another, and the circumstances are **7–11** such that the principal cannot recover, the infirmity of the principal's title infects the agent's title, and the agent cannot recover. [62]

Liability of agent to his principal

If an agent, employed to present a bill, fails to make a due presentment, or **7–12** to give due notice of dishonour, he is liable to an action at the suit of his principal, who may recover nominal damages, though he has sustained no actual loss.[63]

Agent cannot receive bills in payment

The basic rule is that an agent who has authority to take cash in payment **7–13** has thereby no authority to take bills[64]; nor has he authority to take payment by cheque payable to his principal[65]; but he may take payment by a cheque made payable to himself, if it is capable of being cashed on the spot, since it is equivalent to cash.[66] Business practice has changed over the years, and the rule must be seen in the light of the principle as to the authority of agents, *viz.* agents are normally authorised to do whatever is usual in the course of business. Although there is no authority, the practice of an agent accepting a

---

[60] *Polhill v. Walter* (1832) 3 B. & Ad. 114; *Bank of Ottawa v. Harty* (1906) 12 O.L.R. 218; *Crane v. Lavoie* (1912) 4 D.L.R. 175; 22 Man.R. 330.

[61] *West London Commercial Bank v. Kitson* (1883) 12 Q.B.D. 157, *per* A. L. Smith J.

[62] *Currie v. Misa* (1875) L.R. 10 Ex. 153, 164; *ibid.* (1876) 1 App.Cas. 554, 570 (Lord Hatherley); *M'Lean v. Clydesdale Banking Co.* (1883) 9 App.Cas. 95, 114 (Lord Watson); also the American case of *Swift v. Tyson*, 1842) 16 Peters 1, 21 (Story J.).

[63] *Van Wart v. Woolley* (1824) 3 B. & C. 439; *Bank of Van Diemen's Land v. Bank of Victoria* (1871) L.R. 3 P.C. 526.

[64] *Sykes v. Giles* (1839) 5 M. & W. 645; *Williams v. Evans* (1866) L.R. 1 Q.B. 352; or payment clogged by a condition (*Bank of Scotland v. Dominion Bank, Toronto* [1891] A.C. 592.

[65] *Pape v. Westacott* [1894] 1 Q.B. 272.

[66] *International Sponge Importers Ltd v. Watt* [1911] A.C. 279, 289, in which the plaintiffs' statement of account contained the intimation "Terms 21/2 per cent. disc. for prompt cash", which may have misled the defendants. *Bradford & Sons v. Price Bros* (1923) 129 L.T. 408; *Clay Hill Brick and Tile Co. v. Rawlings* (1938) 159 L.T. 482.

cheque in payment would be likely to be recognised today as an agent acting in the ordinary course of business.[67]

PARTNERS

7–14   **23.—(2) The signature of the name of a firm is equivalent to the signature by the person so signing of the names of all persons liable as partners in that firm.**

A bill or cheque in the firm's name will usually bind all the partners. In *Ringham v. Hackett & Another*[68] cheque was drawn on a partnership account by the signature of one partner under the printed name of the partnership. It was presented by the payee to the drawee bank although it was crossed. It was held by the Court of Appeal that the case came within section 23(2) of the Act and that the firm and all partners were bound; further that the cheque had been duly presented for payment within the rules of section 45.

The rights and liabilities of partners, *inter se* are regulated by the partnership deed or agreement and, subject thereto, by the Partnership Act 1890.[69]

In some deeds and agreements of partnerships there is a stipulation that one partner shall not draw, indorse or accept bills without the consent of his co-partner; the consequence of a violation of this stipulation is, *as between the partners*, to create a right of action at the suit of the injured partner against the partner violating it, and to protect the former against bills improperly drawn, indorsed or accepted, and in the hands of a holder *with notice*.

The rights and liabilities of partners, both actual and ostensible, as between the firm and the world, in respect of bills and notes, depend upon whether the partnership is a *trade* partnership or not, since the law presumes that each partner *in trade*[70] is entrusted by his co-partners with a general authority in all partnership affairs. "Bill" obviously includes cheque and payment of a cheque may be countermanded by any partner, unless the partnership mandate provides otherwise.

Each partner, therefore, by accepting or making, drawing, or indorsing, negotiable instruments *in the name of the firm*, and for its usual business, binds the firm[71] (unless those dealing with him knew that he had no authority, or were not aware that he was a partner),[72] whether he sign the name of the

---

[67] See *Bowstead & Reynolds on Agency*, 16th ed, para 3–022.

[68] (1980) 10 L.D.A.B. 206, and (1980)124 S.J. 201 applied in *Central Motors (Birmingham) v. P.A. & S.N.P. Wadsworth (trading as Pensagain)* [1983] C.L.Y. 6, in which it was held, applying the ordinary principles of agency and partnership, that a cheque so drawn was sufficient to bind all members of the partnership.

[69] And the Limited Partnerships Act 1907.

[70] See *post*, para. 7–17.

[71] *Lane v. Williams* (1692) 2 Vern. 277; *Bank of Australasia v. Breillat* (1847) 6 Moo. P.C. 152, 194. See also *Ringham v. Hackett and Another, The Times*, February 9, 1980, above.

[72] Partnership Act 1890, ss.5 and 6. It is specially provided by s.6 that any general rule of law relating to the execution of negotiable instruments is not thereby affected.

firm, or sign by procuration.[73] But it is a strict rule that the name of the firm must be used, otherwise an action cannot be maintained against the firm, as where a partner has signed his own name only, though the proceeds were in fact applied to partnership purposes,[74] unless the name of the signing partner is also the name of the firm. In the latter case, where the partner so signing carries on no separate business, it lies on the other partners to show that the name was signed as that of the individual partner and not of the firm. But, if this is proved, then it is immaterial that the holder of the bill so accepted did, in fact, take it as the bill of the partnership, of whomsoever it might consist.[75] Where one of the partners indorsed the name of the firm on fictitious bills, and the proceeds were applied to partnership purposes, the firm was held liable.[76]

A partner cannot bind his co-partner by the several obligations of a joint and *several* note,[77] but such a note would not be void as a joint note[78] (or the separate note of the signatory),[79] for a partner, it seems, may bind his co-partner by a joint note, provided that the note is in the hands of a holder in due course even though actually made for other than partnership purposes and therefore in violation of the partnership articles, and that the nature of the partnership business was such that the partner could bind the firm by note.[80]

The firm is not liable where the signing partner varies the style of the firm, unless there is some evidence of assent by the firm to the variation, or unless the name used, though inaccurately, yet substantially describes the firm.[81] Therefore, where a firm consisted of John Blurton and Charles Habershon, who carried on business under the firm of John Blurton, it was held that the firm was not bound by an *indorsement* by one partner who had written John Blurton & Co.[82] Further, one partner cannot bind another by signing the true names of both instead of the firm name. But an authority to sign "in the names of Seymour and Ayres" will cover a signature by one of them of the names

---

[73] Where, however, the partner signs in his own name only, which is not also the name of the firm, it could not now be contended that the firm was liable: see the cases cited in *Lindley & Banks on Partnership* (17th ed., 1995), pp. 369 *et seq*; and Code, s.23. In *Mason v. Rumsey* (1808) 1 Camp. 384 and *Jenkins v. Morris* (1847) 16 M. & W. 877, it was held that the signature of the partner was in fact superfluous, since (in the then state of the law) the mere word "accepted" written on the bill was sufficient to constitute an acceptance by the partnership. The partner so accepting is, however, individually liable (*Owen v. Van Ulster* (1850) 10 C.B. 318).

[74] *Sifkin v. Walker* (1809) 2 Camp. 308; *Ex p. Emly* (1811) 1 Rose 61; *Emly v. Lye* (1812) 15 East 7; *Nicholson v. Ricketts* (1860) 29 L.J.Q.B. 55; *Re Adansonia Fibre Co.* (1874) L.R. 9 Ch. 635.

[75] *Yorkshire Banking Co. v. Beatson* (1880) 5 C.P.D. 109, citing *Ex p. Bolitho* (1817) 1 Buck 100, and *Furze v. Sharwood* (1841) 2 Q.B. 388; and see *South Carolina Bank v. Case* (1828) 8 B. & C. 427.

[76] *Thicknesse v. Bromilow* (1832) 2 C. & J. 425.

[77] *Perring v. Hone* (1826) 4 Bing. 28.

[78] *Maclae v. Sutherland* (1854) 3 E. & B. 1.

[79] See *Elliot v. Davis* (1800) 2 Bos. & P. 338; *Gillow v. Lillie* (1835) 1 Bing.N.C. 695.

[80] cf. *Cross v. Cheshire* (1851) 21 L.J. Exch. 3; Act of 1890, s.5.

[81] *Williamson v. Johnson* (1823) 1 B. & C. 146. It is a question of fact whether the variation in the style of the firm goes so far that the person so signing must be taken to have issued the instrument on his own account (*Faith v. Richmond* (1940) 11 A. & E. 339).

[82] *Kirk v. Blurton* (1841) 9 M. & W. 284. This case has, however, been much commented on; see *Forbes v. Marshall* (1855) 11 Ex. 166, 176, 180; *Stephens v. Reynolds* (1860) 5 N. & H. 513, 517; *Maclae v. Sutherland* (1854) 3 E. & B. 1, 36; *Odell v. Cormack* (1887) 19 Q.B.D. 223.

"Thomas Seymour, Sarah Ayres", those being, in fact, the names of the partners, and there being no definite firm name.[83]

Where two firms carried on business under the same firm name and a bill was drawn in the common name of both firms, a defendant was not allowed to say that, though his co-partners were members of both firms, he was a member of one firm only, and that the bill was in fact drawn by a firm of which he was not a member.[84] Where, in a like case, a bill was indorsed by the firm to which the defendant did belong, in payment of a debt contracted by the other firm, in fraud of the defendant, he was held to be liable.[85]

Limited partnerships

7–15   Where an acceptance is signed in the name of a limited partnership by the sole general partner, his signature is equivalent to his own signature, since he is the party liable on the acceptance under section 4(2) of the Limited Partnerships Act 1907. He is therefore personally liable.[86]

Non-trading partnership

7–16   Partners not in trade cannot bind each other by bills, except by express authority; thus a person who wishes to enforce payment of a bill must show that the signatory had authority. There is no authoritative decision as to what constitutes a non-trading partnership.

A solicitor, who is partner with another, has not from that relation alone power to bind his co-partner by a bill or note[87]; nor have partners carrying on business as brokers by getting orders on commission and dividing the expenses.[88] On the other hand it is submitted that a partner of a non-trading firm may bind the firm by cheque, if the cheque is not post-dated and is issued in the firm name for purposes of the firm business.[89]

It has been held that, as the drawing or accepting of bills is not in general necessary in a farming or mining concern, bills accepted by one of the partners in such a concern without express authority do not bind the firm.[90]

---

[83] *Norton v. Seymour* (1847) 3 C.B. 792. In the unreported case of *Sheppard v. Dry* (1840) Norwich, *coram* Parke B. (Affirmed in Q.B.), where the defendants never traded under the firm of Dry & Co., but only under the firm of Dry and Everett, it was held that the defendant Everett was not bound by a bill accepted by Dry, but not for partnership purposes, in the name of Dry & Co.

[84] *Baker v. Charlton* (1791) 1 Peake 111, see Lindley & Banks, *Partnership* (17th ed. 1995) paras 12–182 to 12–183 and note 58, in which it is stated that this case cannot now be relied on; *M'Nair v. Fleming* (1812) 3 Dow at 229.

[85] *Swan v. Steele* (1806) 7 East 210.

[86] *Re Barnard* [1932] Ch. 269.

[87] *Hedley v. Bainbridge* (1842) 3 Q.B. 316; *Forster v. Mackreth* (1867) L.R. 2 Ex. 163 (post-dated cheque); *Garland v. Jacomb* (1873) L.R. 8 Ex. 216.

[88] *Yates v. Dalton* (1858) 28 L.J. Exch. 69.

[89] See *Forster v. Mackreth* (1867) L.R. 2 Ex. 163; *Laws v. Rand* (1857) 3 C.B.(N.S.) 442; *Backhouse v. Charlton* (1878) 8 Ch.D. 444. In the 26th edition, the editors expressed the view that a post-dated cheque would not be binding; this view is questionable.

[90] *Greenslade v. Dower* (1828) 7 B. & C. 635; *Dickinson v. Valpy* (1829) 10 B. & C. 128. But a mining company may be regarded as a trading company (*Brown v. Kidger* (1858) 3 H. & N. 853, 859, where the partner had full power to accept, draw, etc., bills, but solely for partnership purposes).

The business of an auctioneer is not necessarily a trade, but, if the partnership deed contemplates the purchase and sale of goods and property as part of the business of the partnership, and if, moreover, the deed contemplates the drawing or accepting of bills in the course of the partnership business, a firm of auctioneers may be liable on a bill accepted by a partner in respect of a partnership transaction.[91]

Trading partnership

Where a partner in a trading partnership, or in a non-trading partnership **7–17** with express authority to draw bills, etc., pledges the partnership credit on a negotiable security for his own private advantage, his co-partners are liable to a holder who has given value without notice.

But if the party taking a bill or note of the firm knew, at the time, that it was given without the consent of the other partners, *he* cannot claim against them.[92]

Articles of agreement between the partners in a trading partnership that no one partner shall draw, accept or negotiate bills of exchange will not protect the firm against bills drawn, accepted or indorsed in violation of the agreement if the holder had, at the time of taking the bill, no notice of the stipulation, and can show that he gave value. But if notice of such agreement can be established as against the holder, or if, in the absence of such agreement between the partners, the other partners have given him notice that they will not be responsible for bills circulated by their co-partner, the firm cannot be held liable. That would remain the position even though the bill was given in the course of partnership transactions.[93]

If the defendants show that the bill was circulated in violation of partnership articles, they will thereby put the claimant to prove that he, or someone under whom he claims, gave value in good faith for it subsequently to the fraud.[94]

Changes in constitution of firm

If a new partner is introduced into a firm, an acceptance by the old partners **7–18** for an old debt in the name of the new firm will not, in the hands of the party taking it and cognisant of the facts, bind the new partner.[95]

Where bills have been accepted by a firm and, before maturity, one of the partners retires in favour of a new partner on the terms that the new firm is to

---

[91] *Wheatley v. Smithers* [1907] 2 K.B. 684, CA; *cf.* generally *Larue v. Molson's Bank* (1918) Q.R. 28 Q.B. 203.

[92] Partnership Act 1890, s.5; *Arden v. Sharpe* (1792) 2 Esp. 524; *Ex p. Darlington Joint Stock Bank* (1864) 4 De G.J. & S. 581; *Heilbut v. Nevill* (1870) L.R. 5 C.P. 478; *Garland v. Jacomb* (1873) L.R. 8 Ex. 216; *Hogarth v. Latham* (1878) L.R. 3 Q.B.D. 643.

[93] *Gallway v. Mathew and Smithson* (1808) 10 East 264.

[94] *Grant v. Hawkes* (1817), cited Chitty, *Bills*, 11th ed., p. 40; *Hogg v. Skeen* (1865) 34 L.J.C.P. 153, distinguishing *Musgrave v. Drake* (1843) 5 Q.B. 185. Under the CPR the defendant should plead that the acceptance was obtained by fraud and that the plaintiff had notice thereof or gave no value, as the case may be, and thereby shift the onus of proof on to the plaintiff under s.30(2) of the 1882 Act.

[95] *Shirreff v. Wilks* (1800) 1 East 48.

take over the liabilities of the old firm, the retiring partner is not released from
liability on the bills in the absence of an agreement to that effect between the
holder, the new firm and himself; and the fact that the holder has first proved
in the bankruptcy of the new firm does not preclude him from recovering the
balance remaining due upon the bills from the retiring partner.[96]

Security

7–19   The taking a joint security for a separate debt raises a presumption that the
creditor who took it knew that it was given without the concurrence of the
other partners.[97] If there existed fraud and collusion between the partner and
his creditor, the bill is void in the hands of the fraudulent holder against the
partnership.[98] But securities which may be unavailing against the firm, when
in the hands of the party privy to the transaction, will nevertheless bind them
when in the hands of an innocent indorsee for value.[99] In such a case,
however, on proof by the defendant of the security being tainted with fraud in
its inception, it lies on the plaintiff to show that he gave value in good
faith.[1]

The taking security from one of several partners, who are already the
plaintiff's debtors, as parties to a bill or note otherwise, will, in general,
discharge the other co-partners.[2] But where one of three partners, after a
dissolution of partnership, undertook to pay a particular partnership debt on
two bills of exchange, and that was communicated to the holder, who consented to take the separate notes of the one partner for the amount, strictly
reserving his right against all three, and retained possession of the original
bills, it was held that, the separate notes having proved unproductive, he might
still resort to his remedy against the other partners; and that the taking under
these circumstances the separate notes, and even afterwards renewing them
several times successively, did not amount to satisfaction of the joint debt.[3]

---

[96] *Prince de Bearn v. Compagnie d'Assurances La Federale de Zurich* (1937) 42 Com. Cas.
189.

[97] *Levieson v. Lane* (1862) 32 L.J.C.P. 10, followed in *Pickup v. Northern Bank* (1909) 18
Man.R. 675; *Ex p. Darlington Bank, supra.* If a bill be signed by a partner partly for a partnership
debt and partly for a private debt, that does not disentitle the holder, apart from fraud, to sue upon
it to the extent for which there was authority (*Elliston v. Deacon* (1866) L.R. 2 C.P. 20, 21).
Where it is manifest to the person advancing the money that it is upon the separate account and
so against good faith, it lies on him to show that the partner had in fact authority to bind the
partnership (*Ex p. Bonbonus* (1803) 8 Ves. 540, 542). And see the cases cited in *Lindley & Banks
on Partnership* (17th ed., 1995), p. 361, note 94 . See further, the Partnership Act 1890, s.7,
which reads: "Where one partner pledges the credit of the firm for a purpose apparently not
connected with the firm's ordinary course of business, the firm is not bound unless he is in fact
specially authorised by the other partners; but this section does not affect any personal liability
incurred by an individual partner."

[98] *Wells v. Masterman* (1799) 2 Esp. 731; *Greene v. Deakin* (1818) 2 Stark. 347; *Ex p. Goulding*
(1826) 2 G. & J. 118.

[99] *Wells v. Masterman, supra.*

[1] *Hogg v. Skeen* (1865) 34 L.J.C.P. 153; Code s.30(2).

[2] *Thompson v. Percival* (1834) 5 B. & Ad. 925, distinguishing *Evans v. Drummond* (1801) 4
Esp. 89.

[3] *Bedford v. Deakin* (1818) 2 B. & Ald. 210; *Schwartz v. Bielschowsky* (1911) 21 Man.L.R.
310.

Ratification

Where the circumstances were such that the partner had no power to bind **7–20** the firm by a bill, subsequent recognition of the act will be equivalent to previous authority.[4] A partner who signs a bill in fraud of his partners may be guilty of forgery under section 1 of the Forgery and Counterfeiting Act 1981.[5]

Dormant and nominal partners

A dormant partner, whose name does not appear, is bound by bills drawn, **7–21** accepted or indorsed by his co-partners *in the name of the firm*, and not only when the bills are negotiated for the benefit of the firm, but when they are given by one of the partners for his own private debt, provided that the holder was not aware of the circumstance[6]: for credit is given to the firm generally of whomsoever it may consist.

But where a man agreed to become a dormant partner in a firm, and the secret partnership was to commence from a time past, and after the stipulated time for the commencement of the partnership, but before the actual agreement, the members of the firm had negotiated a bill in the name of the firm, and applied the proceeds to their own benefit, the incoming partner, though a partner by relation at the time the bill was negotiated, was held not liable. He could not be charged on the ground of interest, for he derived no benefit from the bill, nor on the ground of credit having been given to him, for he was no member of the firm at the time; nor on the ground of having ratified the acts of his co-partners, for there can be no ratification where there was no assumed authority.[7]

Though a man really has no interest in a firm, yet if he suffers himself to be held out to the world as a member of it, he thereby authorises those *to whom he has been so held out* to treat him as a contracting party; for as they cannot know whether his interest is merely apparent or real, they would be injured and defrauded if they could not charge him as a partner.[8]

Dissolution of partnership

After a dissolution, the ex-partners no longer have power to bind each other **7–22** by bills or notes to persons aware of the dissolution except so far as may be

---

[4] The 1882 Act, s.24.

[5] *R. v. Holden* [1912] 1 K.B. 483., a case decided under s.24 of the Forgery Act 1861, now repealed.

[6] *Lloyd v. Ashby* (1831) 2 B. & Ad. 23; *Swan v. Steele* (1806) 7 East 210; *Wintle v. Crowther* (1831) 1 Cr. & J. 316.

[7] *Vere v. Ashby* (1829) 10 B. & C. 288, where the dormant partner was in fact held liable on two other bills, negotiated after the commencement of the partnership, the plaintiffs having no knowledge that the proceeds were not to be applied to partnership purposes. This case was distinguished in *Battely v. Lewis* (1840) 1 M. & G. 155.

[8] *cf.* Act of 1890, s.14. To make a man liable as a nominal partner he must have been held out as such *to the plaintiff* (*Dickinson v. Valpy* (1829) 10 B. & C. 128, 141 (Parke B.); *Gurney v. Evans* (1858) 3 N. & N. 122).

necessary to wind up the affairs of the partnership, and to complete transactions begun but unfinished at the time of the dissolution.[9] But notwithstanding a valid dissolution of an ostensible partnership by an agreement between the partners, still as between the firm and the world the authority of the ex-partners to bind each other by bills, notes or other contracts, within the scope of the former partnership, continues till due notice be given.[10]

The ex-partners are not safe against any of the persons whose names are on a bill of exchange, unless notice be given to each. After a dissolution, one of the ex-partners accepted a bill in the name of the firm; the payee had no notice of the dissolution, but the indorsee had. It was held that, though the indorsee had notice of the dissolution, he could recover on the bill against the firm, because the payee had no notice and the indorsee had a right to stand on the payee's title.[11]

When bankers had dissolved partnership and the name of one who ceased to be a partner was dropped from the firm's cheque, the change in their printed cheque was, as against a person who was an old customer, but had drawn a cheque in the new form, held sufficient notice of the dissolution.[12]

Where a bill had been accepted by an ex-partner in the name of the firm, in favour of an attorney who had a year before prepared a draft of a deed of dissolution between the partners, which deed it did not appear had ever been executed, Lord Ellenborough held, that if the attorney would insist on the continuance of the partnership, it lay on him to show that the intentions to dissolve had been abandoned.[13]

After a dissolution, and due notice thereof, the ex-partners become tenants in common of the partnership effects, and their authority as mutual agents is at an end, except for pending transactions and the winding-up. One ex-partner cannot, therefore, indorse in the name of the firm a bill which belonged to the firm, but all must join,[14] though the ex-partner indorsing have authority to settle the partnership affairs. "I even doubt much", says Lord Kenyon, "if an indorsement was actually made on a bill or note before the dissolution, but the bill or note was not sent into the world until afterwards, that such indorsement would be valid."[15]

But a statement by the ex-partner that he had left the assets and securities in the hands of the continuing partner, and that he had no objection to his using the partnership name, is evidence from which a jury may infer an authority to indorse.[16] An authority to indorse may be inferred, though the

---

[9] cf. Act of 1890, s.38; *Heath v. Sansom* (1832) 4 B. & Ad. 172.

[10] As to notice, see Partnership Act 1890, s.36.

[11] *Rooth v. Quin* (1819) 7 Price 193.

[12] *Barfoot v. Goodall* (1811) 3 Camp. 147. (Lord Ellenborough C.J.).

[13] *Paterson v. Zachariah* (1815) 1 Stark. 71.

[14] *Abel v. Sutton* (1800) 3 Esp. 108; *Kilgour v. Finlyson* (1789) 1 H.Bl. 156; *Ex p. Central Bank of London* [1892] 2 Q.B. 633. In the case of *Lewis v. Reilly* (1841) 1 Q.B. 349; where two partners drew a bill payable to the order of the firm and then dissolved partnership and one of the partners subsequently in fraud of his co-partner indorsed the bill in the name of the dissolved partnership to the plaintiff, who knew of the dissolution, it was held that the plaintiff could yet recover on the bill against the defrauded partner, since the plaintiff was himself ignorant of the fraud. The case, however, requires reconsideration; see Lindley and Banks, *Partnership* (17th ed, 1995) p. 403 ; see also s.38, Act of 1890.

[15] *Abel v. Sutton, supra,* n. 11 at p. 118.

[16] *Smith v. Winter* (1838) 4 M. & W. 454; see also s.38, Act of 1890.

written agreement of dissolution contains no such authority. But an authority to the continuing partner "to wind up the business" will not enable him to indorse the securities of the late firm[17]; both ex-partners ought therefore to indorse, for that is the proper mode of indorsing by persons who are not partners.[18] It is now clear that, where the outgoing partner suffers his name to continue to appear as partner, he is not liable on the new firm's acceptances in the old name to customers who had no dealings with the original firm; for proof of notice in the Gazette is a defence against such new customers[19]; and, even apart from this, the mere consent of the retiring partner to the use of his name by the new firm will not be evidence of his holding himself out as a partner therein so as to render himself liable on its acceptances.[20]

Bankruptcy of partners

Bankruptcy being a dissolution, an indorsement of a bill, the property of the partnership, by two out of three partners after the two partners had committed an act of bankruptcy confers no title on the indorsee if the indorsee is cognisant of the facts; but it is otherwise where the indorsee is unaware of the act of bankruptcy.[21]   **7–23**

Separate bills given by different partners for the same debt will both bind the firm if they are in the hands of holders in due course.[22]

EXECUTORS AND ADMINISTRATORS

The executor of a deceased party to a bill or note has, in general, the same rights and liabilities as his testator. "The executors of every person", says Lord Macclesfield, "are implied in himself and bound without naming."[23]   **7–24**

Therefore, if a bill is indorsed to a man who is dead, by a person ignorant of his death, that will be an indorsement to the personal representative of the deceased.[24] On the death of the holder of a bill or note, his executors or administrators may indorse[25] and an indorsement by the executors or administrators is for all purposes as effectual as an indorsement by the deceased.[26]

---

[17] *ibid.*

[18] *Carwick v. Vickery* (1783) 2 Doug. 653n.

[19] Act of 1890, s.36(2); and *cf. Newsome v. Coles* (1811) 2 Camp. 617. In *Williams v. Keats* (1817) 2 Stark. 290, the holder, though a bona fide one, does not appear to have been a customer of the old firm, and consequently the direction of Lord Ellenborough C.J. that proof of notice of dissolution in the Gazette was not enough, cannot now be relied on, even if it was then good law.

[20] *Ex p. Central Bank of London* [1892] 2 Q.B. 633. If the holder had dealt with the old firm, and had no notice of the dissolution, the outgoing partner would be liable (*ibid.*, at p. 637 (Lord Esher M.R.); Act of 1890, s.36(1)).

[21] *Thomason v. Frere* (1808) 10 East 418; *Lacy v. Woolcott* (1823) 2 D. & R. 458; and *cf.* Act of 1890, ss.14, 38. As regards effect of dissolution by death, see s.9 of Act of 1890.

[22] See *Davison v. Robertson* (1815) 3 Dow 218.

[23] *Hyde v. Skinner* (1723) 2 P. Wms. 196.

[24] *Murray v. East India Company* (1821) 5 B. & Ald. 204, 216.

[25] *Stone v. Rawlinson* (1745) Willes' Rep. 559.

[26] *Watkins v. Maule* (1820) 2 Jac. & W. 237, 243; as regards presentment for acceptance where the drawee is dead, see the 1882 Act, s.41(1)(c), *post*, para. 11–05; as regards presentment for payment, see *ibid.*, s.45(7), *post*, para. 12–13; and as regards notice of dishonour, see *ibid.* s.49(9), *post*, para. 15–23.

A probate, being a judicial act of the Family Division, is conclusive as to the validity and contents of the will, and the title of the executor; and, as long as it remains unrepealed, cannot be impeached in the other courts. Therefore a voluntary payment to an executor, who has obtained probate of a forged will, is a discharge to the debtor, notwithstanding that the probate is afterwards declared null.[27]

Bills of exchange are to be paid in the course of administration as simple contract debts.

If a creditor holding a negotiable instrument, e.g. a promissory note, appoints the person liable on the instrument his executor, the effect of the appointment is to extinguish the debt; at common law the debt is discharged by release at the date of the creditor's death, "because a debt is a right to sue and the executor cannot sue himself", whilst in equity the debt is discharged by payment at the date of probate.[28] The executor is regarded as having paid the debt to himself and therefore, in equity, it becomes general assets for the payment of the testator's debts and legacies.[29]

On the other hand, the taking out letters of administration by a debtor to his creditor has always been held to be merely a suspension of the legal remedies as between the parties; for being the act of the law, and not the act of the intestate, it is not extinguishment of the debt, since the action will revive when the affairs of the intestate and of the administrator are no longer in the hands of the same person.[30]

If a note or a bill is made or indorsed to an executor as executor, he may sue on it in his representative capacity, and join claims on promises to the testator[31]; and a note given to the administrator for a debt due to the testator, but unpaid at the death of such administrator, passes to the administrator de bonis non[32]; though a payment of the amount of the instrument to the administrator of the executor, instead of to the administrator de bonis non, might in some circumstances be good.[33] It is now settled that where the money when recovered is assets (that is to say, liable to the payment of debts and

[27] Allen v. Dundas (1789) 3 T.R. 125.
[28] Jenkins v. Jenkins [1928] 2 K.B. 501.
[29] Jenkins v. Jenkins, supra; Williams, Mortimer & Sunnucks, Executors, Administrators and Probate (18th ed., 2000, p. 690). Even in equity it might be a release where, on the facts, there was no reason why he should be held liable (Strong v. Bird (1874) L.R. 18 Eq. 315; distinguished in Bonham v. Bonham (1920) 48 O.L.R. 434). By s.61 of the 1882 Act it is provided that when the acceptor is or becomes the holder of the bill at or after maturity, in his own right, the bill is discharged and the words "in his own right" would appear to negative the common law rule as to executors (Freakley v. Fox (1829) 9 B. & C. 130; 109 E.R.). This section, it is to be noted, deals only with the case of the acceptor (or maker). Apart from this section, however, the general application of equitable principles would prevent the merger of the executor in a party already liable on the bill from now operating as a release. Conversely, at common law, a debtor's appointment of his creditor to be executor is no release unless there be assets (Lowe v. Peskett (1855) 16 C.B. 500, 503).
[30] Needham's Case (1610) 4 Co.Rep. 409; Williams, Mortimer & Sunnucks, Executors, Administrators and Probate (18th ed., 2000, p. 660).
[31] King v. Thom (1786) 1 T.R. 487. He may sue on the bill, or on the consideration (Aspinall v. Wake (1833) 10 Bing. 51, 55).
[32] Catherwood v. Chabaud (1823) 1 B. & C. 150; cf. Court v. Partridge (1818) 5 Price 412, confirmed in error, 7 Price 591.
[33] Barker v. Talcot (1687) 1 Vern. 474, where the original administrator had received part of the debt, and taken a note for the rest, and the acceptance of the note was held such an alteration of the property as to vest it in him, and therefore in his administrator.

legacies), the executor may declare for it in his representative capacity, and join counts on promises to his testator.[34] Thus to counts on a bill or note given to his testator, he might join a count for money paid by himself as executor,[35] or count for goods sold by himself,[36] or for works done by himself.[37]

An executor cannot complete his testator's indorsement by delivering the instrument.[38]

Executors and administrators, like agents, may be personally liable on making, drawing, indorsing, or accepting negotiable instruments, even though they describe themselves as such, unless they expressly confine their promise to paying out of the estate, or otherwise negative personal liability.[39]

---

[34] *Cowell v. Watts* (1805) 6 East 405, 409; *Heath v. Chilton* (1844) 12 M. & W. 632, 637; *Abbott v. Parfitt* (1871) L.R. 6 Q.B. 346, 349; Williams, Mortimer & Sunnucks, *Executors, Administrators and Probate* (18th ed., 2000, p. 887).

[35] *Ord v. Fenwick* (1802) 3 East 104. The estate must be solvent (*Webster v. Spencer* (1820) 3 B. & Ald. 360, 365).

[36] *Cowell v. Watts, supra.*

[37] *Marshall v. Broadhurst* (1831) 1 C. & J. 403; *Edwards v. Grace* (1836) 2 M. & W. 190.

[38] *Bromage v. Lloyd* (1847) 1 Exch. 32. But where the defendant had given the deceased a blank acceptance it was held that the administratrix might fill in her own name as drawer (*Scard v. Jackson* (1875) 34 L.T. 65).

[39] The 1882 Act, ss.26 and 31(5); *Childs v. Monins* (1821) 2 Brod. & Bing. 460; *Liverpool Borough Bank v. Walker* (1859) 4 De G. & J. 24.

CHAPTER 8

TRANSFER AND NEGOTIATION

8–01   IT was previously stated that all bills, notes and cheques were prima facie transferable and negotiable in origin. That remains the position as regards bills and notes but the negotiability of cheques have been affected by the Cheques Act 1992.[1] Equally a bill of exchange can be deprived of negotiability and transferability by superimposition on the instrument. On a bill of exchange, which is not susceptible to crossing, the use of the term will render the instrument non-transferable.[2]

Since the Code contains provisions governing the rights of third parties in relation to bills, notes and cheques they are expressly exempted from The Contracts (Rights of Third Parties) Act 1999.[3]

Neither transfer nor negotiation is defined in the 1882 Act, but the meaning of the former is indicated in the definition of "Delivery" in section 2 to mean "transfer of possession, actual or constructive, from one person to another". Transfer is thus either a physical act or what may be called an attornment by the transferor in favour of his transferee. Negotiability, on the other hand, entails a transfer which carries consequences that do not follow mere transfer.

Negotiability

8–02   The 1882 Act does not define negotiable or negotiability, presumably because the terms "bill" and "note" connoted negotiability at the time the 1882 Act was passed. "It may therefore be laid down as a safe rule that when an instrument is by the custom of the trade transferable, like cash, by delivery, and is also capable of being sued upon by the person holding it *pro tempore*, then it is entitled to the name of a negotiable instrument, and the property in it passes to a bona fide transferee for value, though the transfer may not have taken place in market overt. But that if either of the above requisites be wanting, *i.e.* if it be either not accustomably transferable, or, though it be accustomably transferable, yet, if its nature be such as to render it incapable of being put in suit by the party holding it *pro tempore*, it is not a negotiable instrument, nor will delivery of it pass the property of it to a vendee, however bona fide, if the transferor himself has not a good title to it, and the transfer be made out of market overt."[4]

---

[1] See *post* para. 21–35.
[2] *Hibernian Bank v. Gysin and Hanson* [1939] 1 K.B. 483.
[3] See s.6(1) of the 1999 Act.
[4] See the notes to *Miller v. Race* (1758) 1 Smith L.C. (13th ed., 1929), pp. 452, 533; approved in *Crouch v. Credit Foncier* (1873) L.R. 8 Q.B. 374.

The terms "transferable" and "negotiable" are hopelessly mixed up in the Act and in the judgment in *National Bank v. Silke*.[5] "Negotiable" is first used in section 8 of the 1882 Act, in which there is implied a distinction between "transferable" and "negotiable":

8.—(1) When a bill contains words prohibiting transfer, or indicating an intention that it should not be transferable, it is valid as between the parties thereto, but is not negotiable.

Negotiation of a bill, according to section 31(1) of the 1882 Act, takes place:

31.—(1) . . . when it is transferred from one person to another in such a manner as to constitute the transferee the holder of the bill.

In the case of a bill to bearer, negotiation is by mere delivery; if the bill is to order, it is negotiated by indorsement and delivery.[6] In *Jones v. Waring & Gillow*[7] the House of Lords (Viscount Cave L.C.) held that the transfer of a bill to the payee was not a negotiation within the meaning of section 31.

There is no element of value to distinguish clearly transfer from negotiation, except that mere delivery of an order bill without indorsement cannot amount to negotiation.[8] The term "negotiable" is applied to an instrument, which is capable of being negotiated. It is the term used colloquially (and in law)[9] to describe an instrument which is transferable by mere delivery, or by indorsement and delivery, free from the equities, so as to give an absolute title to a transferee who takes in good faith and for value; such transferee has, further, the right to sue on the instrument in his own name.[10]

Clearly, negotiation entails transfer and a negotiable instrument must be capable of transfer; and, ordinarily, a bill which is transferable is likely to be negotiable. In other words, transferability is only a facet of negotiability.

The question thus arises as to what words are sufficient to prohibit transfer or to indicate an intention that a bill should not be transferable,[11] and this involves an inquiry as to what bills may be made non-transferable. The answer to the question is not free from difficulty. In *National Bank v. Silke*,[12] the Court inclined to the opinion that, under section 8, there were three classes of bills, namely: bills not negotiable, bills payable to order, and bills payable to bearer, and that bills payable to order or to bearer could not be made non-transferable. The instrument in that case, however, was a cheque, which was crossed with the words "account payee", and the actual decision was that the words of the crossing did not clearly and without ambiguity prohibit transfer or indicate an

---

[5] [1891] 1 Q.B. 435.
[6] s.31(2)(3).
[7] [1926] A.C. 670.
[8] But see s.31(4) and *Walters v. Neary* (1904) 21 T.L.R. 146.
[9] See note 2, *ante*.
[10] See Willes J. in *Whistler v. Forster* (1863) 32 L.J.C.P. 161.
[11] As to restrictive indorsements prohibiting further transfer, see the 1882 Act, s.35, *post*, paras 18–51 *et seq*.
[12] [1891] 1 Q.B. 435.

intention that the cheque should not be transferable. Consequently, the expressions of opinion upon the interpretation of section 8 were dicta only.

The question was again raised in the case of *Hibernian Bank v. Gysin & Hanson*,[13] which concerned a bill as opposed to a cheque. The bill in question was a three months' bill made payable to the order of a specified person "only" and crossed "not negotiable". The plaintiffs claimed as indorsees and holders for value, and the acceptors, to whom the payees were indebted in a sum exceeding the amount of the bill, repudiated liability on the ground that the bill was not transferable. The case thus directly involved the correct interpretation of section 8. In the court of first instance[14] no particular importance was attached to the word "only", and the judgment was based upon the meaning of the words "not negotiable", which clearly could not bear the same as in the case of a cheque. Lewis J., after discussing and declining to follow the dicta in *National Bank v. Silke*,[15] pointed out that on the face of the bill it was expressly stated that it was not to be transferred or negotiated and that no stronger or clearer words could be used to say that the bill was not to be negotiable. Accordingly, he rejected the contention that a bill payable to order could never be not negotiable and held that the bill was not negotiable and, consequently that the plaintiffs could not recover.

The Court of Appeal,[16] in affirming Lewis J.'s decision, was of opinion that there was no acceptance of the bill except upon the basis that it was not negotiable, the words "not negotiable" governing the whole tenor of the instrument and indicating an intention that it should not be transferable. It, therefore, was not a bill payable to order within the meaning of the Code and could not be transferred to the plaintiffs in such a manner as to constitute them the holders of it entitled to sue upon it. The words "to the order of" the payee "only" were to be read subject to the words "not negotiable", and could be given effect to by limiting them to a case in which the order was merely for money to be paid to someone as agent for the payees and no more.

This, again, would seem to point to a confusion between "transferable" and "negotiable". It is submitted that the dicta in National *Bank v. Silke*,[17] correctly expressed the law. A bill of exchange (other than a cheque) and a cheque, which does not bear the "not negotiable" crossing, cannot be non-transferable or non-negotiable unless drawn payable to a payee "only" or transfer is restricted in some other way. It is obvious (even if section 8(1) of the 1882 Act was not explicit in this respect) that an instrument that is not transferable cannot in any circumstances be negotiable, but the reverse is not necessarily true. This view receives support from section 36(1) also. Crossing applies only to cheques, and the words "not negotiable" are applied by the 1882 Act for use in conjunction with a crossing.[18] By all rules of interpretation

[13] [1939] 1 K.B. 483.
[14] [1938] 2 K.B. 384.
[15] [1891] 1 Q.B. 435.
[16] [1939] 1 K.B. 483.
[17] [1891] 1 Q.B. 435, apparently approved in *Standard Bank of Africa Ltd v. Sham Magazine Centre* (1977) (1) S.A. 484, (AD) which denied *Dungarvin Trust (Pty) Ltd v. Import Refrigeration Co. (Pty) Ltd* (1971) (4) S.A. 300 (W.) and *Rhostar (Pvt.) Ltd v. Netherlands Bank of Rhodesia* (1972) (2) S.A. 703 (R.).
[18] s.77(4).

such words can, in relation to bills (other than cheques) have no similar meaning to that which they have in regard to cheques; if they are to be given any meaning at all in relation to bills they can only express an intention on the part of the drawer (unlike the "not negotiable" crossing, only the drawer can add them) that the instrument is not to be transferred. The *Hibernian Bank*[19] case could, it is submitted, have been decided on the basis of the fact that the bill was drawn in favour of a payee "only", without involving the question of the effect of the words "not negotiable". In spite of its wording, which was clearly conflicting, the bill was not payable to order; the word "only" overrode the normal "to the order of" and the words "not negotiable" were superfluous not only because of the word "only" but also because of the form of the instrument.

Negotiable bills

Section 36(1) of the 1882 Act provides that:

8–03

36.—(1) Where a bill is negotiable in its origin it continues to be negotiable until it has been (a) restrictively indorsed or (b) discharged by payment or otherwise.[20]

The words "in its origin" must mean "when issued". If at that time the bill bore words prohibiting transfer, it was never negotiable and, as no one but the drawer would be entitled to add such words, the bill, if negotiable in its origin, must, apart from section 36(1)(a), remain so. Any attempt by anyone other than the drawer to render the instrument non-transferable would amount to a material alteration within the meaning of section 64. There is no means within the 1882 Act for drawing a bill that is not a cheque in such a way as to make the title of a transferee dependant upon that of his transferor, as is the case under section 81; nor is there any need, for the position which led to the inclusion of section 81 or its predecessor does not exist in the case of a bill that is not a cheque. To add the words "not negotiable", therefore, is merely to render the bill non-transferable, but the same purpose is achieved by drawing it payable to the payee only.

A restrictive indorsement does not prohibit further transfer of the instrument,[21] but the instrument is not a negotiable instrument if it contains words prohibiting transfer or indicating an intention that it should not be transferable.[22] The 1882 Act does not supply any form for a restrictive drawing or making, but presumably words sufficing for a restrictive indorsement[23] may be employed.

8.—(2) A negotiable bill may be payable either to order or to bearer.

---

[19] [1939] 1 K.B. 483.
[20] The transferability of cheques is now governed by the Cheques Act 1992, *post* para. 21–35.
[21] s.35(3), *post*, para. 18–52.
[22] s.8(1), *ante*, para. 8–02.
[23] s.35(1), *post*, para. 18–51.

(3) A bill is payable to bearer which is expressed to be so payable, or on which the only or last indorsement is an indorsement in blank.

(4) A bill is payable to order which is expressed to be so payable, or which is expressed to be payable to a particular person, and does not contain words prohibiting transfer or indicating an intention that it should not be transferable.

(5) Where a bill, either originally or by indorsement, is expressed to be payable to the order of a specified person, and not to him or his order, it is nevertheless payable to him or his order at his option.

If the bill is made payable to the payee or bearer, the payee may transfer the bill to a third party by merely delivering it into his hands, and such third party then stands in the same situation with regard to the acceptor as the original payee did. Further, since the passing of the 1882 Act, a bill drawn payable to order becomes payable to bearer by a subsequent indorsement in blank; but should it afterwards be specially indorsed, it would require the signature of the special indorsee to negotiate it, whereas at common law a special indorsement following a blank one, left the bill negotiable by mere delivery, all parties being liable thereon up to and including the indorser in blank, but as against the special indorser, title had to be made through his indorsee.[24]

Previous to the passing of the 1882 Act, the word "order" or "bearer" was necessary to make an instrument negotiable. The indorser of a note which did not contain such words was held liable on his indorsement to the indorsee, but such indorsement could not render the original maker liable,[25] for in order to render the drawer or maker liable, there must be authority on the instrument to indorse.[26] Since every indorser is in the nature of a new drawer[27] it seems to have been considered by the Court of Common Pleas that the first drawing exhausted the stamp, and that the indorsee could not acquire a right, without a new stamp, which could not by law be impressed.[28] Today, the instrument remains negotiable even though "order" or "bearer" is struck out on its face.[29]

---

[24] Chitty, *Bills* (11th ed), pp. 173 and 174 and the cases there cited.

[25] See *Plimley v. Westley* (1835) 1 Hodges 324, 325 (Tindal C.J.); *Gwinnell v. Herbert* (1836) 5 A. & E. 436, 441 (Patterson J.).

[26] *Plimley v. Westley, supra.* The subject seems quite uncovered by modern authority, presumably because at the present day a bill or note, to be really not transferable, must be so drawn—as for instance, "pay A only"—as to make any attempt subsequently to transfer it a practical impossibility.

[27] *Lake v. Hales* (1736) 25 E.R. 791; *Penny v. Innes* (1834) 1 Cr. M. & R. 439, 441; *cf.* also *Burmester v. Hogarth* (1843) 11 M. & W. 97; *Allen v. Walker* (1837) 2 M. & W. 317. The passage in the test was cited with approval in *Lebel v. Tucker* (1867) L.R. 3 Q.B. 77, 81. As regards a promissory note, it has been held that the indorser of a note does not stand in the situation of a maker relatively to his indorsee (*Gwinnell v. Herbert, supra*). For though every indorser of a bill may be treated, without inconvenience, as a new drawer (for in that character he still requires notice of dishonour), yet an indorser of a note cannot be treated as a maker of the note, without altering his situation for the worse, and depriving him of the right to notice of dishonour. The 1882 Act, s.89 (2) provides that "the first indorser of a note shall be deemed to correspond with the drawer of an accepted bill payable to drawer's order".

[28] *Plimley v. Westley, supra.* Today, there is no stamp on bills of exchange.

[29] Formerly it was not so: *Smith v. Kendal* (1794) 6 T.R. 123; *R. v. Box* (1815) 6 Taunt. 325. Though not negotiable, it was still a valid instrument.

The words to his order or to bearer, if omitted by mistake, might be afterwards inserted, without vitiating the instrument either at common law, under the Stamp Act or under the provisions relating to alteration.[30]

Whether a bill or note is negotiable or not is a question of law.[31] In *Swan v. North British Australasian Co.*[32] Byles J. said:

> "The arguments drawn from negotiable instruments appear altogether inapplicable. The object of the law merchant, as to bills or notes made or become payable to bearer, is to secure their circulation as money; thereupon honest acquisition confers title. To this despotic but necessary principle the ordinary rules of the common law are made to bend. The misapplication of a genuine signature written across a slip of stamped paper (which transaction being a forgery would in ordinary cases convey no title) may give a good title to any sum fraudulently inscribed within the limits of the stamp, and in America, where there are no stamp laws, to any sum whatsoever."

Negotiability by estoppel

This is a loose expression applied to an instrument which is neither a bill **8–04** of exchange nor a promissory note, but which because of the way in which it is drawn carries the implied promise of the issuer to pay the amount for which it is drawn to the bearer or presenter of it. In his Law of Negotiable Securities,[33] Willis J. expressed the view that:

> "Title by estoppel is what men mean when they speak of negotiability by estoppel, but title by estoppel is a different thing altogether from negotiability . . . "

There is not much case decision on the subject and the chief ones are all from the nineteenth century—*Goodwin v. Robarts*[34]; *Easton v. London Joint Stock Bank*[35] and *Colonial Bank v. Cady and Williams.*[36] The point is put in various ways. In the last of these Lord Herschell expressed the principle as follows:

> "If the owner of a chose in action clothes a third party with apparent ownership and right of disposition of it, he is estopped from asserting his title as against a person to whom such third party has disposed of it, and who received it in good faith and for value."

Lord Cairns spoke of scrip which "virtually represented that the paper would pass from hand to hand and that anyone who became bona fide the holder might claim for his own benefit the fulfilment of its terms" from the

---

[30] *Kershaw v. Cox* (1800) 3 Esp. 246; *Byrom v. Thompson* (1830) 11 A. & E. 31; but see the 1882 Act, s.3.

[31] *Grant v. Vaughan* (1764) 3 Burr. 1516, 1524.

[32] (1863) 2 H. & C. 175, 184.

[33] 5th ed., 1930, p. 13.

[34] (1876) 1 App.Cas. 476, *per* Lord Cairns at 489.

[35] (1886) 34 Ch.D. 95, *per* Bowen L.J. at 113–114.

[36] (1890) 15 App.Cas. 267, *per* Lord Herschell at 285.

issuer. The scrip, he said, would be a representation that, if taken in good faith and for value, "the person taking it would stand to all intents and purposes in the place of the previous holder". And the principle thus enunciated was the basis of Bowen L.J.'s judgment.

None of these cases was concerned with an instrument in the form of a bill of exchange and therefore fell outside the Bills of Exchange Act 1882.

The expression "negotiable by estoppel" can only mean that the instrument to which it refers contains a representation upon which anyone in possession may claim against the party making the representation. The law appears to be the same in Canada: "the instrument is negotiable by virtue of the estoppel resulting from its own representation".[37]

Non-transferable cheques

8–05   At one time the transferability of a cheque had to be taken away by express words such as "Pay D only".[38]

On June 16th, 1992 the Cheques Act 1992 came into force. This Act has fundamentally affected the transferability and negotiability of cheques.[39]

Dividend warrants

8–06   As regards dividend warrants, the 1882 Act, specially provides:

97.—(3) Nothing in this Act or in any repeal effected thereby shall affect—

(d) The validity of any usage relating to dividend warrants, or the indorsements thereof.

Dividend warrants issued under the provisions of the National Debt (Conversion) Act 1888 are, by section 30(5), to be deemed cheques within the meaning of the 1882 Act.[40]

---

[37] *Re Bennett, Provincial Treasurer v. Bennett* [1936] 2 D.L.R. 291; see also *Arrow Transfer Co. Ltd v. Royal Bank of Canada* (1971) 19 D.L.R. (3d) 420.

[38] See *Chandler v. Portland Edmonton Cement Co. Ltd* (1917) 33 D.L.R. 302 where a promissory not made payable to "A.E.Chandler only" was held to be not negotiable although the debt represented by it was assignable.

[39] See Chapter 21, *infra*.

[40] In *Partridge v. Bank of England* (1846) 9 Q.B. 396, dividend warrants of the Bank of England were held, in spite of custom to the contrary, not to be negotiable, since they did not contain the word "order" or "bearer". If dividend warrants at the present day are in the form of cheques within the provisions of the 1882 Act, s.8 would not apply to instruments similar to those in *Partridge v. Bank of England*, and so get over the difficulty. Dividend warrants which are not, owing to their form, cheques within the 1882 Act are only within s.97(3)(d), and, without proof of usage, are not necessarily negotiable. It is believed that at the present day dividend warrants are in the great majority of cases drawn payable to order.

Among instruments held, on the other hand, not to be negotiable are bankers' deposit notes,[41] bankers' receipt for bonds deposited for negotiation,[42] money orders and postal orders,[43] and letters of credit, as distinguished from circular notes.[44]

Consumer Credit Act 1974

The above Act repeals the Moneylenders Acts of 1900 and 1927. In   **8–07** addition to replacing sections 1 and 10 of those Acts respectively, which dealt with harsh and unconscionable transactions, by a new provision (s.137) enabling the Court to reopen extortionate credit bargains (whether in relation to "regulated agreements" or not) it imposes considerable restriction on the use of negotiable instruments in connection with regulated agreements.

The practice which the Act was designed to restrict was the right of a holder to enforce a bill against a debtor, hirer, or surety (as defined by the Act)[45] in circumstances where such a person had a good defence or counterclaim, in whole or in part, to any claim on the underlying contract with the creditor[46] or owner.[47]

The Act therefore restricts the enforcement of security, where the taking thereof is permitted, so as to prevent the creditor or owner, directly or indirectly, from benefiting to an extent greater than would be the case if the security were not provided.[48] In other words the Act is designed to prevent the evasion of various of its provisions by the taking of security. The holder of a bill, the use of which is permitted, *i.e.* one which is non-negotiable within the meaning of section 8(1) of the 1882 Act, may find the extent to which he can enforce his security severely restricted.

The Consumer Credit Act 1974 affects the use of bills in three different ways, namely, as to:

(1) Their form and content

(2) Their negotiability and effect

(3) The ability of the Court to set them aside.

(1) Form and Content

Section 189 of the Act defines "security" in relation to an actual or   **8–08** prospective consumer credit or consumer hire agreement, or any linked

---

[41] *Pearce v. Creswick* (1843) 2 Hare 286, in which the Vice-Chancellor, at 298, said: "The defendants do not pretend that the receipts were transferable in the sense that the holder was entitled to demand payment. They do not set up any usage or custom of such a kind, but they merely insist that it is, in the course of business, the practice of the bank to pay the amount of the receipts to any respectable party presenting them." *Clegg v. Baretta* (1887) 56 L.T. 775. See today certificates of deposit—*quaere* negotiable by custom (*post*, para. 24–15).
[42] *Beauclerk v. Greaves* (1886) 2 T.L.R. 837.
[43] See *post*, p. 326.
[44] *Orr v. Union Bank of Scotland* (1854) 1 Macq.H.L. (Sc.) 513.
[45] CCA, s.189.
[46] CCA, s.189.
[47] CCA, s.189.
[48] CCA, s.113.

transaction[49] as "a mortgage, charge, pledge, bond, debenture, indemnity, guarantee, bill, note or other right provided by the debtor or hirer, or at his request (express or implied), to secure the carrying out of obligations of the debtor or hirer under the agreement".

A bill or promissory note when so provided is thus a security within the meaning of the Act.

The section further defines "surety" to mean "the person by whom any security is provided . . . "

Section 105 of the Act prescribes the form and content of securities

Form and content of securities

8–09   **105.—(1) Any security provided in relation to a regulated agreement shall be expressed in writing.**

(2) Regulations may prescribe the form and content of documents ("security instruments") to be made in compliance with subsection (1).

(3) Regulations under subsection (2) may in particular—

(a) **require specified information to be included in the prescribed manner in documents, and other specified material to be excluded;**

(b) **contain requirements to ensure that specified information is clearly brought to the attention of the surety, and that one part of a document is not given insufficient or excessive prominence compared with another.**

(4) A security instrument is not properly executed unless—

(a) **a document in the prescribed form, itself containing all the prescribed terms and conforming to regulations under subsection (2), is signed in the prescribed manner by or on behalf of the surety, and**

(b) **the document embodies all the terms of the security, other than implied terms, and**

(c) **the document, when presented or sent for the purpose of being signed on or on behalf of the surety, is in such state that its terms are readily legible, and**

(d) **when the document is presented or sent for the purpose of being signed by or on behalf of the surety there is also presented or sent a copy of the document.**

(5) A security instrument is not properly executed unless—

---

[49] CCA, s.19.

(a) where the security is provided after, or at the time when, the regulated agreement is made, a copy of the executed agreement, together with a copy of any other document referred in it, is given the surety at the time the security is provided, or

(b) where the security is provided before the regulated agreement is made, a copy of the executed agreement, together with a copy of any other document referred to in it, is given to the surety within seven days after the regulated agreement is made.

(6) Subsection (1) does not apply to a security provided by the debtor or hirer.

(7) If—

(a) in contravention of subsection (1) a security is not expressed in writing, or

(b) a security instrument is properly executed, the security, so far as provided in relation to a regulated agreement, is enforceable against the surety on an order of the court only.

(8) If an application for an order under subsection (7) is dismissed (except on technical grounds only) section 106 (ineffective securities) shall apply to the security.

(9) Regulations under section 60(1) shall include provision requiring documents embodying regulated agreements also to embody any security provided in relation to a regulated agreement by the debtor or hirer.

It will be noted that by virtue of subsection (6), subsection (1) does not apply where the security has been provided by the debtor or hirer. The section will however apply to all bills, where they can be used without contravening section 123, *e.g.* non-negotiable instruments within the meaning of section 8(1) of the Bills of Exchange Act 1882, when provided by anyone other than the debtor or hirer.

Any bill so drawn to secure the obligations of a debtor or hirer under a regulated agreement will therefore have to comply with the requirements of subsections 4(b), (c) and (d) and 5(a) and (b). Failure to comply with these requirements will render the security enforceable against the surety on an order of the Court only.[50] If the Court refuses to grant an enforcement order, except on technical grounds only[51] by section 106 of the Act the security shall be of no effect.

The consequence of this section makes the taking of security from anyone other than the debtor or hirer under a regulated agreement commercially unattractive as the creditor under the regulated agreement will have to ensure not only that he prepares and sends a copy of the bill to the surety, but that he

[50] s.105(7) and see s.127(1)(b).
[51] CCA, s.189(5).

also sends, at the appropriate time, copies of the regulated agreement and of any other document referred to in it, to the surety.

(2) Negotiability and Effect

8–10   The restrictions on the use of negotiable instruments and the consequences for their improper use are contained in the following sections of the Consumer Credit Act 1974.

Restrictions on taking and negotiating instruments

8–11   **123.—(1) A creditor or owner shall not take a negotiable instrument, other than a bank note or cheque, in discharge of any sum payable—**

(a) by the debtor or hirer under a regulated agreement, or

(b) by any person as surety in relation to the agreement.

(2) The creditor or owner shall not negotiate a cheque taken by him in discharge of a sum payable as mentioned in subsection (1) except to a banker (within the meaning of the Bills of Exchange Act 1882).

(3) The creditor or owner shall not take a negotiable instrument as security for the discharge of any sum payable as mentioned in subsection (1).

(4) A person takes a negotiable instrument as security for the discharge of a sum if the sum is intended to be paid in some other way, and the negotiable instrument is to be presented for payment only if the sum is not paid in that way.

(5) This section does not apply where the regulated agreement is a non-commercial agreement.

(6) The Secretary of State may by order provide that this section shall not apply where the regulated agreement has a connection with a country outside the United Kingdom.

Consequences of breach of s.123

8–12   **124.—(1) After any contravention of section 123 has occurred in relation to a sum payable as mentioned in section 123(1)(a), the agreement under which the sum is payable is enforceable against the debtor or hirer on an order of the court only.**

(2) After any contravention of section 123 has occurred in relation to a sum payable by any surety, the security is enforceable on an order of the court only.

(3) Where an application for an order under subsection (2) is dismissed (except on technical grounds only) section 106 shall apply to the security.

These sections refer only to negotiable instruments. Any instrument, which is not negotiable, is thus outside their scope. Section 31 of the 1882 Act defines negotiation and section 8(1) states "when a bill contains words prohibiting the transfer, or indicating an intention that it should not be transferable, it is valid as between the parties thereto, but is not negotiable". It is however thought that an instrument made payable to "X only" would fall within section 8(1).

Section 123[52] of the Act thus prohibits the taking of a negotiable instrument other than a bank note or cheque in discharge of the obligations of the debtor or hirer under a regulated agreement or a surety therefor. Subsection (2) restricts the negotiability of a cheque taken by the creditor or owner in discharge of such sums to anyone other than a banker within the meaning of the 1882 Act. Subsection (3) prohibits the taking of a negotiable instrument (including a cheque) as security for the discharge of such sums as are mentioned in subsection (1). Subsection (4) defines the circumstances in which a person takes a negotiable instrument as security. And subsections (5) and (6) exempt certain agreements from the operation of the section.[53]

Transfers of bills otherwise than by negotiation, for example by charge or assignment, are not prohibited. A transferee who takes otherwise than by negotiation can not be a holder and takes subject to equities. Such transfers are excluded as they are outside the mischief against which section 123 is aimed.

Section 123 of the Act does not define "cheque", which presumably has the same definition as section 73 of the 1882 Act.[54] It is an open question whether a post-dated cheque falls within the ambit of section 123. It can be argued that a post-dated cheque is not a cheque as defined by the 1882 Act, since it is not yet payable, and thus not payable on demand and is not payable at a fixed or determinable future time.[55] However commentators on the Consumer Credit Act argue that a post-dated cheque would be treated as a cheque for the purposes of the section.[56]

By virtue of section 124 if there has been any contravention of section 123 in relation to the sums payable under section 123(1)(a), *i.e.* payments made by a debtor or hirer to the creditor or owner in discharge of sums payable under a regulated agreement, then the agreement under which the sum is payable is enforceable against the debtor or hirer only after an order of the Court.[57] If there has been any contravention in relation to a sum payable by the surety the security is only enforceable in the same manner. If an application to the Court for an enforcement order in relation to any sums payable by any surety is refused except on technical grounds[58] then the security is of no effect. It is

[52] See note 6.

[53] Non-Commercial agreement is defined in section 189 of the Consumer Credit Act 1974. The Consumer Credit (Negotiable Instruments) (Exemption) Order (1984 S.I. 1984 No. 435) exempts consumer hire agreements, made in the course of a hirer's business, which have a connection with any country outside the U.K. In addition, by virtue of the Consumer Credit (Exempt Agreements) No. 2 Order 1985 (S.I. 1985 No. 754) Art. 5, certain consumer credit agreements having a connection with a country outside the U.K. are outside the regulation of the Act altogether.

[54] See *infra*, para. 21–04.

[55] See *infra*, paras 21–14 *et seq.*

[56] See the Encyclopaedia of Consumer Credit Law, Vol. 1, p. 2115.

[57] CCA, s.127.

[58] CCA, s.189(5).

further important to note the further restrictions placed upon the enforcement of securities in general by virtue of section 113.

The net result of sections 123 and 124 therefore is that whereas a cheque may be taken in payment of a debtor's, hirer's or surety's obligation in relation to a regulated agreement provided the cheque is negotiated only to a banker,[59] no negotiable instrument (including a cheque) may be taken as security. If any contravention takes place either the regulated agreement or the security, or both, as the case may be, will be enforceable only on an order of the Court.

The position of a holder in due course is preserved by section 125.

Holders in due course

8–13   **125.—(1) A person who takes a negotiable instrument in contravention of section 123(1) or (3) is not a holder in due course, and is not entitled to enforce the instrument.**

(2) Where a person negotiates a cheque in contravention of section 123(2), his doing so constitutes a defect in his title within the meaning of the Bills of Exchange Act 1882.

(3) If a person mentioned in section 123(1)(a) or (b) ("the protected person") becomes liable to a holder in due course of an instrument taken from the protected person in contravention of section 123(1) or (3), or taken from the protected person and negotiated in contravention of section 123(2), the creditor or owner shall indemnify the protected person in respect of that liability.

(4) Nothing in this Act affects the rights of the holder in due course of any negotiable instrument.

This section prevents a person who takes a negotiable instrument in contravention of section 123(1) or (3) from becoming a holder in due course and from enforcing the instrument.

By virtue of subsection (2) a person who negotiates a cheque in contravention of section 123(2) his doing so constitutes a defect in title within the meaning of section 29 of the 1882 Act. It is however to be noted that a person who negotiates an instrument in contravention of section 123(1) or (3) his doing so does not constitute a defect in title.

The result therefore is that a person to whom an instrument is negotiated, as opposed to the creditor or owner who takes the instrument, in contravention of section 123(1) or (3) becomes a holder in due course and his rights are protected. By virtue of section 125(2) a person to whom a bill is negotiated in contravention of section 123(2) whilst prima facie being deemed to be a holder in due course by virtue of section 30(2) of the 1882 Act may lose his status and rights as a holder in due course if the person liable on the bill proves that, at the time of its negotiation, the holder knew it had been negotiated in contravention of section 123(2).

[59] See s.2 Cheques Act 1957.

It must be emphasised, however, that by section 125(4) it is expressly stipulated that "Nothing in this Act affects the rights of the holder in due course of any negotiable instrument." It follows that such rights are unaffected by the provisions of section 113.

If a debtor, hirer or surety, (*i.e.* persons mentioned in section 123(1)(a) or (b)) becomes liable to a holder in due course then he becomes entitled to the benefit of the statutory indemnity against the creditor or owner given by section 125(3).

Where, despite the obstacles created by the above sections, a creditor or owner is in possession of a bill which he can enforce, whether on an order of the Court or not, he will not be able to do so unless a default notice has been served on the debtor or hirer under section 84. Such a notice must comply with the regulations made under section 88 and a copy thereof served on the surety by virtue of section 111(1).

(3) Setting Aside by The Court

This topic is dealt with in Chapter 19, para. 19–17, under the heading "The   **8–14** Consumer Credit Act 1974."

CHAPTER 9

MODES AND REQUISITES OF TRANSFER

9–01 A BILL or note is transferred by delivery or by indorsement and delivery. If it is not payable to bearer or has not become so payable by indorsement in blank, the transfer is incomplete in the sense that indorsement is necessary to give the transferee a better title than the transferor himself may have.[1] A distinction must be drawn between the first transfer from the drawer or maker to the first holder and subsequent transfers. The first transfer is called the "issue" of the bill or note, and is thus defined in the 1882 Act:

2. "Issue" means the first delivery of a bill or note, complete in form to a person who takes it as a holder.

"Delivery" means transfer of possession, actual or constructive, from one person to another.

The authorities show that the issuing of a document of title or negotiable instrument is not of itself the subject of any general duty. The drawer or acceptor of a bill owes no such duty to the public at large.[2]

The first delivery is essential to complete the contract,[3] but the first transferee, the payee, though a holder, is not a holder in due course, because the transfer to him is not a negotiation.[4] Where the bill is drawn in favour of the drawer, his indorsee is the first transferee.

A bill may in certain circumstances be re-issued.[5]

DELIVERY

9–02   Delivery is always necessary to complete the contract on a bill or note, for the 1882 Act provides:

21.—(1) Every contract on a bill, whether it be the drawer's, the acceptor's, or an indorser's, is incomplete and revocable, until delivery of the instrument in order to give effect thereto.

Provided that where an acceptance is written on a bill, and the drawee gives notice to or according to the directions of the person entitled to the bill that he has accepted it, the acceptance then becomes complete and irrevocable.[6]

---

[1] Section 31(4).

[2] Devlin J., speaking in *Heskell v. Continental Express Ltd* [1950] 1 All E.R. 1033, 1042, of the issue of a fraudulent document of title, a bill of lading; and see *Scholfield v. Londesborough* [1896] A.C. 514.

[3] Section 21(1).

[4] See *Jones (R.E.) Ltd v. Waring & Gillow Ltd* [1926] A.C. 670, *post*, p. 218.

[5] Section 37, *post*, para. 13–16.

[6] *Cox v. Troy* (1822) 5 B. & Ald. 474; *Chapman v. Cottrell* (1865) 34 L.J. Ex. 186.

(2) As between immediate parties, and as regards a remote party other than a holder in due course, the delivery—

(a) In order to be effectual must be made either by or under the authority of the party drawing, accepting, or indorsing, as the case may be:

(b) may be shown to have been conditional or for a special purpose only, and not for the purpose of transferring the property in the bill.[7]

But if the bill be in the hands of a holder in due course a valid delivery of the bill by all parties prior to him so as to make them liable to him is conclusively presumed.[8]

(3) Where a bill is no longer in the possession of a party who has signed it as drawer, acceptor, or indorser, a valid and unconditional delivery by him is presumed until the contrary is proved.[9]

The requirement for delivery was reiterated by Waller J. in *Citibank N.A. v. Brown Shipley*,[10] where he described an instrument as being inchoate," the instrument only becomes a valid instrument on delivery".

In that case there was a delivery of a banker's draft from an issuing bank in favour of a receiving bank with the authority of the issuing bank. Although the authority was induced by the fraud of a third party, the issue of the instrument established a contract, albeit a voidable contract. For delivery to be effective it must be either by or under the authority of the party drawing etc.[11] Waller J. held that the fact delivery was by means of the fraudster did not affect the formation of the contract because the fraudster was a mere conduit through whom title did not have to pass for there to be an effective contract.

Constructive delivery, or delivery to the agent or servant of the intended transferee, is equally binding.[12] Thus where A specially indorsed certain bills to B, sealed them up in a parcel, and left them in charge with his own servant to be given to the postman, it was held that the special indorsement did not transfer the property in the bills till delivery, and that delivery to the servant was not sufficient, though it would have been otherwise had the delivery been made to the postman.[13]

---

[7] *Pike v. Street* (1828) M. & M. 226; *Bell v. Ingestre* (1848) 12 Q.B. 317; see also *post*, Chapter 28, oral agreements, and cases there cited.

[8] In *New Jersey Mortgage and Investment Co. v. Dorsey*, 158 Atl. (2d) 712, where an inchoate note had never, in the opinion of the Court, been delivered, it was held that, provided the maker had not been negligent, not even a holder in due course could recover.

[9] *Baxendale v. Bennett* (1878) 3 Q.B.D. 525; *Surrey Asset Finance Ltd v. National Westminster Bank Ltd* [2000] Times L.R. 30.11.00.

[10] [1991] 2 A.E.R. 690, at 699.

[11] Section 21(2) of the 1882 Act.

[12] *Adams v. Jones* (1840) 12 A. & E. 455; *Brind v. Hampshire* (1836) 1 M. & W. 365.

[13] *R. v. Lambton* (1818) 5 Price 428; but this case seems inconsistent with cases cited in note 12, *infra*.

Where a bill, note or cheque is sent by post in payment of a debt, the posting of the instrument is not a delivery to the creditor[14] unless he has expressly or impliedly authorised such method. The loss falls therefore upon the sender unless the creditor has authorised or requested payment in this way.[15] As set out in section 21(2)(b) of the 1882 Act, delivery of an instrument can be shown to be conditional; however once the condition is fulfilled delivery is complete and the instrument is treated as having been issued or negotiated, as the case may be.[16]

Where A and B carried on business in partnership and, being indebted to C, A, who acted as C's agent, with the concurrence of B, indorsed a bill in the name of the firm, and placed it amongst the securities which he held for C, but no communication of the fact was made to C, it was held to be a good indorsement by the firm to C.[17]

NEGOTIATION

9–03   A distinction must be made between transfer and negotiation.

31.—(1) A bill is negotiated when it is transferred from one person to another in such a manner as to constitute the transferee the holder of the bill.

(2) A bill payable to bearer is negotiated by delivery.

(3) A bill payable to order is negotiated by the indorsement of the holder completed by delivery.

Sub-section (1) would seem to fit the case of a payee. He is the first transferee of the bill and the first holder and if he gives value for the bill under the conditions set out in section 29 he should be a holder in due course; but the decision of the House of Lords in *Jones v. Waring & Gillow*[18] is to the contrary on the ground that the bill is never negotiated to the payee; it may perhaps also be argued that the bill is not a bill capable of transfer until it bears the name of the payee, but a bill drawn "pay to . . . order" is a bill payable to my order.[19]

---

[14] *Baker v. Lipton* (1899) 15 T.L.R. 436; *Pennington v. Crossley* (1897) 77 L.T. 43; *Luttges v. Sherwood* (1895) 11 T.L.R. 233; *Shamey v. Canadian Bank of Commerce* (1919) Q.R. 58 S.C. 444; *Acraman v. South Australian Gas Co.* [1910] S.A.L.R. 59. *Miss Sam (Sales) Ltd v. River Island Clothing Ltd*, New Law Journal 25.3.94.

[15] *Thirlwall v. Great Northern Ry* [1910] 2 K.B. 509; *Norman v. Ricketts* (1886) 3 T.L.R. 182; *Re Deveze* (1873) L.R. 9 Ch. 27, 32; *Warwicke v. Noakes* (1791) 1 Peake 98; *Channon v. English, Scottish and Australian Bank* 1918) 18 S.R.N.S.W. 30; *Tetley v. Marlborough Education Board* (1909) 29 N.Z.L.R. 721. A request for a "remittance" is an authority to pay by sending money through the post in the ordinary way money is so remitted (*Mitchell-Henry v. Norwich Union Life Insurance Society* [1918] 2 K.B. 67).

[16] See *Clifford Chance v. Silver* [1992] 2 B.L.R. 11.

[17] *Lysaght v. Bryant* (1850) 9 C.B. 46.

[18] [1926] A.C. 670.

[19] See *Chamberlain v. Young and Tower* [1893] 2 Q.B. 206.

The holder of a bill being the payee or indorsee who is in possession of it or the bearer thereof,[20] the giving of value is clearly not an essential constituent of the term "negotiated" as here understood. In commercial language a transfer is a negotiation only where the transferee gives value.

In the case of an order bill, the payee's indorsement is necessary only where the bill is negotiated. The payee is always entitled to have the bill paid to himself, in which case there is no negotiation,[21] and therefore no indorsement is required. In practice, however, until the passing of the Cheques Act 1957, the payee usually wrote his name on the back of the bill before presenting it for payment or handing it to his banker for collection; he still does so in the case of a bill that is not a cheque. Though this was commonly called an indorsement, it was not an indorsement in the strict sense of the term, but operated as a receipt.[22] For negotiation, therefore, indorsement is still required unless the bill is payable to bearer either in its origin or by indorsement in blank.

Presentment for acceptance is not a negotiation.[23]

Where the holder of a bill payable to his order transfers it for value without indorsing it the transferee does not become the holder, since he is not the payee or indorsee of the instrument.[24] However such a transferee gets such title as the transferor had and can call for the indorsement by the transferor.[25]

INDORSEMENT

2. By section 2 of the 1882 Act, "Indorsement" means an indorsement completed by delivery. "Delivery" means transfer of possession, actual or constructive, from one person to another.   **9–04**

The requisites of a valid indorsement are thus stated by the 1882 Act:

32. An indorsement in order to operate as a negotiation must comply with the following conditions, namely—

(1) It must be written on the bill itself and be signed by the indorser. The simple signature of the indorser on the bill, without additional words, is sufficient.

An indorsement written on an allonge, or on a "copy" of a bill issued or negotiated in a country where "copies" are recognised, is deemed to be written on the bill itself.[26]

Subject to two exceptions an indorsement must be on the bill itself.

---

[20] Section 2.

[21] *Jones (R.E.) Ltd v. Waring & Gillow Ltd* [1926] A.C. 670.

[22] *Keene v. Beard* (1860) 8 C.B. (N.S.) 372 (Byles J.), approved in *McDonald (Gerald) & Co. v. Nash* [1924] A.C. 625.

[23] *Sharples v. Rickhard* (1857) 2 H. & N. 57.

[24] See s.2 of the 1882 Act.

[25] See s.31(4) of the 1882 Act and *post*, para. 18–49.

[26] The mark of a person who cannot write is a sufficient endorsement (*George v. Surrey* (1830) M. & M. 516); see *ante*, para. 2–05.

In *K.H.R. Financings Ltd v. Jackson*,[27] the note formed part of a larger document and the indorsement was on the back of the sheet, but not backing on to the note. The Sheriff Principal held the indorsement valid: "the purpose of the provision is to enable a bill to operate as a negotiable instrument by ensuring that one piece of paper contains all the writing constituting the obligations of the bill and the names of the parties to it".

The two exceptions are, first, in the case of an allogne.[28] Secondly on a copy of a bill, but in the restricted circumstances where a bill is drawn or negotiated in a country where copies are recognised.

The signature must be that of the payee or special indorsee as designated in the instrument or special indorsement, as the case may be.

In *Arab Bank v. Ross*,[29] Denning L.J. suggested that there were three aspects in which indorsements must be considered: (a) their regularity for purposes of section 29 (holder in due course); (b) their capacity for passing title; and (c) their capacity for imposing liability. An irregular indorsement may pass a valid title,[30] though where the name is wrongly designated, the payee or indorsee may indorse as described, adding his proper signature if he wishes.[31] In certain cases, the instrument may be drawn in the form "Pay A B *per* X", sometimes used where dividends are collected by a banker for his customer; less frequently, when an agent is intended to receive the money for his principal. The intention is that payment is to be made to A B, but only by the instrumentality of X, who alone is to receive and give a discharge for the money, but in a representative capacity as agent or trustee of the principal, for whose benefit the money is to be applied.[32] In this case, the indorsement should correspond with the description of the payee in the instrument. The correct indorsement, therefore, is "A B *per* X", and an indorsement by the agent in his own name is irregular.[33]

Allonge

9–05   It is almost invariable for an indorsement to be on the back of a bill or note; it may equally well be on the face[34] but, since there is no legal limit to the number of indorsements, there may be no room to write them all on the bill itself; the supernumerary indorsements may, therefore, as above provided, be written on a slip of paper annexed to the bill, called an "allonge", or partly on both. An allonge is thenceforth part of the bill. Allonges are rarely, if ever, met

[27] 1977 S.L.T. (Sh.Ct.) 6.

[28] See *post*, para. 9–05.

[29] [1952] 2 Q.B. 216, in which the word "Co." was omitted from the indorsements. In Canada, a cheque drawn in favour of a limited company, the word "limited" being omitted, may be validly indorsed in the proper name of the company (*Union Bank v. Tattersall* (1920) 52 D.L.R. 409).

[30] Denning L.J. in *Arab Bank Ltd v. Ross* [1952] 2 Q.B. 226, 227.

[31] 1882 Act, s.32(4), *ante*, para. 3–03, *post*, para. 9–08.

[32] See *Bute v. Barclays Bank Ltd* [1955] 1 Q.B. 202.

[33] *Slingsby v. District Bank* [1931] 2 K.B. 588, 595 (Wright J.); [1932] 1 K.B. 544; see Paget, *Law of Banking* (11th ed.), p. 391.

[34] *R. v. Bigg* (1716) 1 Stra. 18; *Ex p. Yates* (1857) 27 L.J.Bk. 9; *Tapley v. Paquet* (1910) Q.R. 38 S.C. 292; *Gorrie v. Whitfield* (1920) 58 D.L.R. 326; *Simonin v. Philion* [1922] 66 D.L.R. 673; *Boisvert v. Lavallee* (1935) Q.B. 73 S.C. 30. But a person who places his signature on a promissory note below that of the maker without indicating that he is not signing as maker is liable as a maker (*Triggs v. English* [1924] 4 D.L.R. 937).

within this country in contrast to countries where the Geneva Convention No. 3313 of June 7, 1930, has been adopted.[35]

Partial indorsement

An indorsement cannot be partial, since the 1882 Act requires that: **9–06**

32.—(2) It must be an indorsement of the entire bill. A partial indorsement, that is to say, an indorsement which purports to transfer to the indorsee a part only of the amount payable, or which purports to transfer the bill to two or more indorsees severally does not operate as a negotiation of the bill.[36]

A bill or note cannot be indorsed for part of the sum remaining due to the indorser upon it, if the limitation of the sum for which it is indorsed appears on the instrument itself. Such an indorsement is not warranted by the custom of merchants, and would be attended with this inconvenience to the prior parties, that it would subject them to a plurality of actions.[37] It is conceived that the effect of such an indorsement, when attempted, is to give the indorsee a lien on the bill, but not to transfer a right of action, except in the indorser's name.[38]

But if a bill or note is indorsed or delivered for a part of the sum due on it, and the limitation of the transfer does not appear on the instrument, the transferee is entitled to sue the acceptor or marker for the whole amount of the bill or note, and is a trustee of the surplus for the person entitled to the remainder of the money.[39]

Where there was a part payment by the drawer to the indorsee it was held that the latter could recover only the balance from the acceptor notwithstanding that the indorsement purported to be for the whole amount.[40]

There can, however, be a partial acceptance,[41] in which case an indorsement of the bill so accepted for part of the sum would doubtless be good.

---

[35] Art. 13.

[36] See Falconbridge (7th ed., 1969), p. 645; Canadian Code, s.62; see Uniform Commercial Code (U.S.), s.3–202.

[37] *Hawkins v. Cardy* (1699) 1 Ld.Raym. 360 S. 32(2) expressly uses the phrase "purports", hence a bill or note payable by instalments cannot be indorsed for one or more only of the instalments if that appears on the indorsement.

[38] This seems to be the American view; *cf.* Daniel (5th ed.), para. 668; and Uniform Commercial Code, s.3–202; Brannan (1948), 603. Such an indorsement does not, by s.32(2), operate as a negotiation, still a man having a lien is, by s.27(3) of the 1882 Act, a holder for value *pro tanto*.

[39] *Reid v. Furnival* (1833) 1 Cr. & M. 538; *Johnson v. Kennion* (1765) 2 Wils. 262. See, in this connection, *Barclays Bank Ltd v. Aschaffenburger Zellstoppwerke A.G* [1967] 1 Lloyd's Rep. 387.

[40] *Bacon v. Searles* (1788) 1 H.Bla. 88, doubting *Johnson v. Kennion, supra*. It is clear, from s.32(2), that an indorsement must now be for the entire bill, and no indorsement for the residue, as was said by Gould J. in *Johnson v. Kennion*, to be allowable where the drawer had part paid, would be good.

[41] *Post*, para. 10–06.

Several payees or indorsees

9–07   32.—(3) Where a bill is payable to the order of two or more payees or indorsees who are not partners all must indorse, unless the one indorsing has authority to indorse for the others.[42]

If one of the payees indorses for himself alone, it is only an authority to the person to whom he indorses it to receive the amount due to him.[43]

Misspelt payee or indorsee

9–08   32.—(4). Where, in a bill payable to order, the payee or indorsee is wrongly designated, or his name is misspelt, he may indorse the bill as therein described, adding, if he think fit, his proper signature.

If the person indorsing makes a mistake in his signature, the property in the instrument will still pass.[44]

Cheques made payable to a limited company may misdescribe the payee. In the case of large businesses, it used to be the practice to use a rubber stamp containing a number of descriptions and to place an impression from it above the signature of the person actually indorsing on the company's behalf. This is a valid indorsement and, where the intention is clear, it is immaterial that the misdescription is the similar name of an allied company.[45] Since the Cheques Act, 1957, such indorsements are rare.

Order of indorsements

9–09   32.—(5) Where there are two or more indorsements on a bill, each indorsement is deemed to have been made in the order in which it appears on the bill, until the contrary is proved.

But this may be rebutted by evidence, as where successive indorsers of a note were allowed to show that as between themselves, they were not principal and surety, but co-sureties.[46]

Sometimes difficulty has arisen where a stranger to a bill indorses for the purpose of "backing" it, especially, perhaps, where this is done before the bill is complete. In such a case, the position depends upon the intention of the parties.[47]

---

[42] *Carvick v. Vickery* (1783) 2 Dougl. 653. As there may be alternative payees (s.7, *ante*, para. 3–03), so presumably there may be alternative indorsees (s.34(3), *post*, para. 9–11), in which case the indorsement of either office should suffice, if good in other respects.

[43] *Heilbut v. Nevill* (1869) L.R. 4 C.P. 354, 356 (Willes J.).

[44] *cf. Leonard v. Wilson* (1834) 2 Cr. & M. 589; *Arab Bank v. Ross* [1952] 2 Q.B. 216.

[45] *Bird & Co. (London) Ltd v. Thomas Cook & Sons Ltd* (1937) 156 L.T. 415.

[46] *Macdonald v. Whitfield* (1833) 8 App.Cas. 733; *Vallee v. Talbot* (1892) 1 Q.R.C.S. 223; see also *Godsell v. Lloyd* (1911) 27 T.L.R. 383; *Steacy v. Stayner* (1904) 7 O.L.R. 684; *Lacombe v. Labonte* (1920) 59 Q.R.S.C. 17 and see *Yeoman Credit Ltd v. Gregory* [1963] 1 W.L.R. 343.

[47] 1882 Act, s.56, *post*, para. 17–13.

Date of indorsement

36.—(4) Except where an indorsement bears date after the maturity of the bill, every negotiation is prima facie deemed to have been effected before the bill was overdue.[48] **9–10**

Form of indorsement

Indorsements may be of two kinds; no particular form of words is essential to any indorsement. **9–11**

32.—(6) An indorsement may be made in blank or special. It may also contain terms making it restrictive.[49]

34.—(1) An indorsement in blank specifies no indorsee and a bill so indorsed becomes payable to bearer.[50]

An indorsement in blank is made by the mere signature of the indorser on the bill, usually and properly, though not necessarily, on the back thereof.[51] "An indorsement in blank", said Lord Ellenborough, "conveys a joint right of action to as many as agree in suing on the bill."[52] Therefore, where three persons separately indorsed a bill for the accommodation of the drawer, which was afterwards dishonoured and returned to them, and they paid the amount among them, it was held that they might bring a joint action against a previous indorser.[53] But where a bill of exchange was, by the direction of the payee, indorsed in blank, and delivered to A, B & Co., who were bankers, on the account of the estate of an insolvent, which was vested in trustees for the benefit of his creditors, Lord Ellenborough held, that A and B, two of the members of this firm, and also trustees, could not, conjointly with another trustee who was not a member of the firm, maintain an action against the indorser, without some evidence of the transfer of the bill by the firm to them, as trustees, by delivery or otherwise.[54]

34.—(2) A special indorsement specifies the person to whom, or to whose order, the bill is to be payable.

Thus a special indorsement by A B is in the form: "Pay C D, A B" or "Pay C D, or order. A B." The signature of the indorser being subscribed to the direction, its effect in both cases is to make the instrument payable to C D or his order only; and accordingly C D cannot transfer it otherwise than by

---

[48] *Lewis v. Parker* (1836) 4 A. & E. 838; *Parkin v. Moon* (1836) 7 C. & P. 408. As to an instrument payable on demand, *cf. Cripps. v. Davis* (1843) 12 M. & W. 159, 165.

[49] See s.35, *post*, para. 18–51.

[50] *cf. Peacock v. Rhodes* (1781) 2 Doug. 633.

[51] *Ante*, para. 9–04.

[52] *Ord v. Portal* (1812) 3 Camp 239.

[53] *Low v. Copestake* (1828) 3 C. & P. 300.

[54] *Machall v. Kinnear* (1816) 1 Stark. 499.

indorsement.[55] The omission of the words "or order" is not material any more than in the case of the original payee.[56] Indeed it is provided generally by the 1882 Act:

34.—(3) The provisions of this Act relating to a payee apply with the necessary modifications to an indorsee under a special indorsement.

Unlike the drawing, which, by section 3(1),[57] must be unconditional, but like the acceptance.[58] the indorsement may be conditional, since the 1882 Act provides that:

33. Where a bill purports to be indorsed conditionally the condition may be disregarded by the payer, and payment to the indorsee is valid whether the condition has been fulfilled or not.

This section alters the law, for formerly where a bill was accepted after having been conditionally indorsed, and was paid in disregard of the condition, the acceptor was held liable to pay again on the fulfilment of the condition.[59] It seems that a bill or note cannot be indorsed with a condition that, in a certain event, the indorsee shall not have the power to indorse.[60]

Conversion of a blank into a special indorsement

9–12   An indorsement in blank may be converted into a special indorsement and the 1882 Act provides:

34.—(4) When a bill has been indorsed in blank, any holder may convert the blank indorsement into a special indorsement by writing above the indorser's signature a direction to pay the bill to or to the order of himself or some other person.

If a bill, indorsed in blank, was afterwards specially indorsed, it was formerly as against the acceptor, the drawer, the payee, the blank and all previous indorsers, payable to bearer; though, as against the special indorser himself, title must have been made through his indorsee.[61]

When a holder converts a blank indorsement into a special one in favour of a stranger, he incurs no liability as indorser.[62] If the holder turns a blank

---

[55] For an example of an insufficient indorsement by a bank, see *Herderson v. Armstrong* (1916) Q.R. 50 S.C. 535.

[56] The law as regards the indorsee was so settled long before 1882; see *More v. Manning* (1718) 1 Comyns R. 311; *Acheson v. Fountain* (1722) 1 Stra. 557; *Edie v. East India Co.* (1761) 2 Burr. 1216; *Cunliffe v. Whitehead* (1837) 3 Bing.N.C. 828; *Gay v. Lander* (1848) 17 L.J.C.P. 286.

[57] *Ante*, para. 1–09.

[58] Section 19(2)(a), *post*, para. 10–05.

[59] *Robertson v. Kensington* (1811) 4 Taunt. 30.

[60] *Soares v. Glyn* (1845) 14 L.J.Q.B. 313. Therefore an indorsement may be conditional or restrictive, but not conditionally restrictive.

[61] *Smith v. Clarke* (1794) 1 Peake 295; *Walker v. Macdonald* (1848) 17 L.J.Ex. 377, see *ante*, para. 8–03.

[62] *Vincent v. Horlock* (1808) 1 Camp. 442. By the 1882 Act, s.23, no person is liable as drawer, indorser or acceptor of a bill who has not signed it as such; see *ante*, para. 7–01.

indorsement into a special one in his own favour, that is an election to take the bill or note as indorsee, and he cannot afterwards be considered as merely servant or assignee of the indorsee.[63]

Indorsement in representative capacity

31.—(5) Where any person is under obligation to indorse a bill in a representative capacity, he may indorse the bill in such terms as to negative personal liability.

9–13

Executors or administrators having to indorse may stipulate to pay out of the estate only ("so far as assets only" is believed to be a common form of doing so) or in any other manner may expressly negative their personal liability.[64]

---

[63] *Clerk v. Pigot* (1699) 12 Mod. 193; but he must be careful not to add anything further which may amount to a material alteration of the bill; *cf. Hirschfeld v. Smith* (1866) L.R. 1 C.P. 340.

[64] See *ante*, para. 7–24.

CHAPTER 10

ACCEPTANCE

10–01 THE definition and requisites of acceptance are set out in section 17 of the 1882 Act:

17.—(1) The acceptance[1] of a bill is the signification by the drawee[2] of his assent to the order of the drawer.

(2) An acceptance is invalid unless it complies with the following conditions, namely:

(a) **It must be written on the bill and be signed by the drawee. The mere signature of the drawee without additional words is sufficient.**

(b) **It must not express that the drawee will perform his promise by any other means than the payment of money.**

The acceptance of a bill is, therefore, in plain terms, a written engagement to pay the bill when due, in money and by no other means.[3] A verbal or implied acceptance is not valid.

In England the drawee of a bill is not liable until he has accepted the bill.[4]

In relation to cheques a bank does not usually accept a cheque and consequently does not incur a personal liability to the payee.[5]

Having accepted the bill the party, previously named the drawee, thereafter is called the acceptor. By accepting the bill the drawee/acceptor undertakes to pay the amount due on the bill at maturity[6]

In order for a bill to be accepted it must be presented to the drawee; acceptance cannot be presumed nor, ordinarily, can there be "deemed acceptance".[7]

---

[1] Unless the context otherwise requires, the word "acceptance" in the 1882 Act means an acceptance completed by delivery or notification (s.2).

[2] As to drawee, see *ante*, para. 3–08.

[3] An acceptance to pay by another bill is no acceptance (*Russell v. Phillips* (1850) 14 Q.B. 891); an acceptance in the form: "Accepted payable at National Bank of Greece, St. Mary Axe, from External account . . . " was not a promise to pay by "other means than the payment of money" (*Banca Popolare di Novara v. John Livanos & Sons Ltd* [1965] 2 Lloyd's Rep 149).

[4] See s.53 of the 1882 Act, and *post* para. 17–02.

[5] The bank though may be in breach of mandate to its customer, the drawer of the cheque.

[6] See Ch. 17.

[7] See *Man v. Miyazaki* [1991] 1 Ll.Rep. 154.

The usual mode of accepting a bill is to write the word "accepted" and to subscribe the drawee's name.[8] The signature of the drawee on the bill is now the only essential requisite.[9]

An instrument, which is not accepted, still constitutes a bill. There must always be a drawer, a payee and a drawee but an unaccepted bill is a negotiable instrument and enforceable by the holder against the drawer and any prior indorsers. The provisions as to acceptance do not apply to promissory notes.[10]

Who may accept

6.—(1) The drawee must be named or otherwise indicated in a bill with reasonable certainty.[11]   **10–02**

A bill can only be accepted by the drawee: a stranger may not accept, except for honour.[12] Where, therefore, a bill was drawn on the directors of a company, a person, not a director, who accepted as manager was held not to be personally liable.[13] Where indeed the bill was not addressed to anyone, but only indicated the place of payment, the person who accepted was held liable as having admitted himself to be the party pointed out by the place of payment.[14] But this decision goes to the verge of the law.[15]

Where the name of the drawee is the established trade name of a company, the signature of a director of the company will be treated as acceptance by the company.[16] Section 26(2) of the 1882 Act provides that in determining whether a signature on a bill is that of a principal or that of an agent the construction most favourable to the validity of the instrument shall be adopted.

If the drawee is fictitious or incompetent to contract, as, for example, by reason of infancy,[17] the bill may be treated as dishonoured by non-acceptance.

---

[8] For forms of acceptance, see *Encyclopaedia of Forms and Precedents*, (5th ed.) Vol 4, para. 642 *et seq.*

[9] As to the meaning of the term "signature", see *ante*, para. 2–05.

[10] Section 89(3) of the 1882 Act.

[11] See *ante*, para. 3–08; *Davis v. Clarke* (1844) 13 L.J.Q.B. 305. A mere error of description, the drawee and acceptor being admittedly the same person, will not affect the validity of the acceptance (*Dermatine Co. v. Ashworth* (1905) 21 T.L.R. 510).

[12] *Polhill v. Walter* (1832) 3 B. & Ad. 114; *Eastwood v. Bain* (1858) 28 L.J.Ex. 74; *Rabkin and Hoffman v. National Bank of South Africa* (1915) 6 C.P.D. 545; see also the 1882 Act, s.65(1), *post*, para. 10–11. The marking of a cheque is not an acceptance in this country or within the Indian Negotiable Instruments Act 1881 (*Bank of Baroda v. Punjab National Bank* [1944] A.C. 176).

[13] *Bule v. Morrell* (1840) 12 A. & E. 745.

[14] *Gray v. Milner* (1819) 8 Taunt. 739.

[15] See *Davis v. Clarke, ante*, at 31 (Patterson J.); *Peto v. Reynolds* (1954) 9 Ex. 410, 416 (Martin B.). A bill addressed not to a drawee, but to an address might, otherwise than by naming, indicate the drawee within s.6(1).

[16] See *Maxform Spa v. Mariana* [1979] 2 Ll. Rep 385, affirmed [1981] 2 Ll. Rep. 54; *Lindholst & Co. v. Fowler* [1988] B.C.L.C. 166.

[17] The 1882 Act, s.41(2)(a), *post*, para. 11–05. The holder may also treat it as a note, in which case the drawer will, as maker, not be entitled to notice of dishonour (ss.5(2), 52(3), and 89).

If a bill is drawn upon several persons not in partnership, it should be accepted by all,[18] and, if not, may be treated as dishonoured.[19] Acceptance will, however, be binding upon such of them as do accept.[20]

There cannot be two or more separate acceptors of the same bill not jointly responsible. This is illustrated by a decision prior to the 1882 Act, *Jackson v. Hudson*.[21] The plaintiff refused to supply one Irving with goods, unless the defendant would become his surety. The defendant agreed to do it. Goods to the value of £157 were accordingly sold by the plaintiff to Irving. For the amount the plaintiff drew on Irving, and the bill was accepted both by Irving and the defendant, each writing his name on it. Lord Ellenborough observed: "If you had declared that, in consequence of the plaintiff selling the goods to Irving, the defendant undertook that the bill should be paid, you might have fixed him by this evidence. But I know of no custom or usage of merchants according to which, if a bill be drawn upon one man, it may be accepted by two; the acceptance of the defendant is contrary to the usage and custom of merchants. A bill must be accepted by the drawee, or, failing him, by someone for the honour of the drawer. There cannot be a series of acceptors. The defendant's undertaking is clearly collateral, and ought to have been declared upon as such."[22]

Although there can be no other acceptor after a general acceptance of the drawee, it was formerly stated that a man might supra protest accept for the honour of the drawer a bill already accepted supra protest for the honour of an indorser.[23]

Time for acceptance

10–03   As to the time at which a bill may be accepted, the 1882 Act provides:

18. A bill may be accepted:
(1) Before it has been signed by the drawer, or while otherwise incomplete:
(2) When it is overdue, or after it has been dishonoured by a previous refusal to accept, or by non-payment:
(3) When a bill payable after sight is dishonoured by non-acceptance and the drawee subsequently accepts it, the holder, in the absence of any

---

[18] By s.23, no person is liable as drawer, indorser or acceptor who has not signed as such. As to the liability of partners inter se, *see ante*, paras 7–14 *et seq.*

[19] By s.19(2)(e), para. 10–09 *post*, the acceptance of one or more of the drawees but not all is a qualified acceptance, and by s.44 (1), the holder may treat a qualified acceptance as dishonour of the bill.

[20] Bayley (6th ed.), p. 58; *cf. Owen v. Van Uster* (1850) 10 C.B. 318, followed in *McDougall v. McLean* (1893) 1 Terr.L.R. 450; *Nicholls v. Diamond* (1853) 9 Exch. 154.

[21] *Infra.*

[22] *Jackson v. Hudson* (1810) 2 Camp. 447; the 1882 Act, ss.6, 56. Where a bill was drawn on a firm in the firm name, and a partner added his own name to such acceptance, he was held not to be personally liable thereon (*Re Barnard* (1886) 32 Ch.D. 447).

[23] Beawes (ed. 1813), Vol. 1, para. 42. There are no express words in s.65 supporting this view.

different agreement, is entitled to have the bill accepted as of the date of first presentment to the drawee for acceptance.

Subsection (1): until the drawer's name is inserted, however, the instrument is not a bill of exchange.[24] As we have seen, the signature of a drawer, maker, or indorser on blank stamped paper, delivered to be filled up as a negotiable instrument, bound them respectively; so an acceptance, written on the paper before the bill is made, and delivered by the acceptor, charged the acceptor to the extent warranted by the stamp.[25] An acceptance for value, before the bill is filled up, is irrevocable.[26] Notice that the acceptance was in blank should put the holder on inquiry.[27]

Subsection (2): this provides that a bill may be accepted after it has matured. A bill accepted when overdue is, by section 10(2), deemed to be payable on demand, so far as the acceptor and any indorser is concerned .[28]

Subsection (3): as to the date of acceptance of a bill payable after sight which has been previously dishonoured by non-acceptance but is subsequently accepted, the holder is put in the position as if the acceptance occurred when first presented for acceptance, absent any agreement to the contrary.

As already stated, the date on the bill or note, or of the acceptance, making, or indorsement thereon, is prima facie the true date[29] and where the acceptance is not dated, the presumption is that it was accepted before maturity, and within a reasonable time of its date.[30]

TYPES OF ACCEPTANCE

19.—(1) An acceptance is either (a) general, or (b) qualified.   10–04

(2) A general acceptance assents without qualification to the order of the drawer. A qualified acceptance in express terms varies the effect of the bill as drawn.

By section 44(1) the holder may refuse to take a qualified acceptance, and may treat the bill as dishonoured by non-acceptance.[31]

---

[24] See also *ante*, para. 2–06; nor when completed as a bill will completion relate back to the time when the acceptance was written on it (*Ex p. Hayward* (1871) L.R. 6 Ch. 546; *McDonald (Gerald) & Co. v. Nash & Co.* [1924] A.C. 625, 652 (Lord Sumner).

[25] See s.20, *ante*, para. 4–01, and cases there dealt with at length. There is today no stamp duty on bills, notes and cheques.

[26] See the 1882 Act, s.21(1), proviso.

[27] *Hatch v. Searles* (1854) 2 Sm. & G. 147 (giving a blank acceptance is only prima facie evidence of authority to fill up); *Hogarth v. Latham* (1878) 3 Q.B.D. 643, 647, *per* Bramwell B., acceptance by one partner without authority of another.

[28] *Mutford v. Walcot* (1700) 1 Ld.Rym. 574; *Christie v. Peart* (1841) 7 M. & W. 491; see *post*, para. 17–33.

[29] s.13(1), *ante*, para. 2–12.

[30] *Roberts v. Bethell* (1852) 12 C.B. 778.

[31] See *post*, para. 10–10.

Once a bill is accepted generally, presentment for payment is not necessary to render the acceptor liable.[32] The position will be otherwise if the term of a qualified acceptance requires presentment.[33]

Prima facie, in cases of doubt, an acceptance is to be construed as a general rather than a qualified acceptance.[34] Any alteration in any acceptance contrary to the tenor of the bill as drawn must be in the clearest language.[35]

The 1882 Act recognises five sorts of qualified acceptance.[36] The view has, however, been expressed that this list is not exhaustive, and that there may be other cases of qualified acceptances.[37] The consequences flowing from a qualified acceptance are dealt with in section 44 of the 1882 Act.[38]

Conditional acceptance

10–05   **19.—(2) . . . In particular an acceptance is qualified which is:**

(a) conditional, that is to say, which makes payment by the acceptor dependent on the fulfilment of a condition therein stated:

Whether an acceptance be conditional or not is a question of law.[39] Acceptance, "to pay as remitted for,"[40] "to pay when in cash for the cargo of the ship Thetis",[41] "to pay when goods consigned to him (the drawee) were sold",[42] have respectively been held to be conditional acceptances. The words "accepted payable on giving up a bill of lading" constitute a conditional acceptance, but not a further condition to the acceptor's liability, that the bill of lading shall be given up on the day of the maturity of the bill, for under these circumstances it is not necessary to present the bill on the precise day on which it is due.[43]

---

[32] Section 52(1) of the 1882 Act.

[33] Section 52(2) of the 1882 Act.

[34] Bills were drawn in Dutch florins on a London firm, payable in Amsterdam; it was held that the acceptances were general (*Bank Polski v. Mulder* [1942] 1 K.B. 497); see s.19(2)(c), *post*, para. 10–07, as to acceptance to pay at a particular place only. This case is almost anticipated in precise terms by *Ex p. Hayward* (1887) 3 T.L.R. 687, *per* Mackinnon L.J.

[35] *Decroix v. Meyer* (1890) 25 Q.B.D. 343, 347, approved in *Canadian Bank of Commerce v. B.C. Interior Sales* (1957) 9 D.L.R. (2d) 363; *Fanshaw v. Peet* (1857) 2 H. & N. 1, 4 (Martin B). In *Decroix v. Meyer*, the words "in favour of F. (the drawer) only" were written above the acceptance, but were held not to qualify the acceptance, meaning that the acceptance is of a bill of which Flipo is the drawer or payee (Lord Esher M.R.); it might have been otherwise if the words had been "payable to F. only"; *ibid.*, at 358 (Bowen L.J.); in *Meyer v. Decroix* [1891] A.C. 520, the House of Lords by a majority of three to two held that the acceptance was a general acceptance of a negotiable bill (Lord Herschell was of opinion that the words as written were clearly not part of the acceptance).

[36] s.19(2)(a)–(e).

[37] *Decroix v. Meyer, ante*, at 100 (Lord Esher M.R.) who further seems to be of opinion that there could be a "restrictive acceptance", if properly worded, just as there can be restrictive indorsements and drawings, ss.8 and 35, but that the drawee has no right to alter the tenor of the bill itself; see at 347).

[38] *Post* para. 10–10.

[39] *Sproat v. Mathews* (1786) 1 T.R. 182.

[40] *Banbury v. Lissett* (1744) 2 Str. 1211.

[41] *Julian v. Shobrooke* (1753) 2 Wils. 9.

[42] *Smith v. Abbot* (1741) 2 Str. 1152.

[43] *Smith v. Vertue* (1860 30 L.J.C.P. 56, applied in *Humphreys v. Taylor* [1921] N.Z.L.R. 343.

Since a bill, which has been accepted, does not ordinarily need to be presented to the acceptor for payment, a stipulation requiring such presentment would constitute a conditional bill.

Partial acceptance

A partial acceptance is thus defined: **10–06**

19.—(2)(b) partial, that is to say, an acceptance to pay part only of the amount for which the bill is drawn:

Where a drawee accepted for £100 a bill drawn for £127, it was held a good acceptance *pro tanto* within the custom of merchants.[44]

Local acceptance

19.—(2)(c) local, that is to say, an acceptance to pay only at a particular specified place: **10–07**
An acceptance to pay at a particular place is a general acceptance, unless it expressly states that the bill is to be paid there only and not elsewhere.

A bill is often by the acceptor made payable at a banker's.[45] But the relation of banker and customer does not of itself impose upon a banker the duty of paying his customer's acceptances. If a banker undertakes this duty it must be pursuant to some special agreement, express or implied. In paying his customer's acceptances the banker incurs certain risks, since he has no recourse against his customer if he pays on a genuine bill to a person appearing to be the holder, but who in fact claims through or under a forged instrument.[46] If the customer of a banker accepts a bill and makes it payable at the bank, that fact is, however, of itself sufficient authority to the banker to apply the customer's funds in paying the bill.[47]

In the case of a bill accepted payable at a banker's, though money has been remitted by the acceptor to the banker for the express purpose of paying the bill, the banker is not liable to the holder in an action for money had and received, unless he has assented to hold the money for the purpose for which it was remitted.[48] But where there is anything in the conduct or situation of the

[44] *Wegersloffe v. Keene* (1719) 1 Str. 214.
[45] This is a general acceptance (*Ex p. Hayward* (1887) 3 T.L.R. 687).
[46] See *Bank of England v. Vagliano* [1891] A.C. 107, 157, where Lord MacNaughten pointed out that it would in practice be impossible for bankers to comply with a suggestion made in *Robarts v. Tucker* (1851) 16 Q.B. 560, that they should defer payment until satisfied the genuineness of the indorsements. In the case of a cheque, or of any draft or order drawn upon a banker payable on demand, the paying banker is fully protected by the 1882 Act, ss.60 and 80, s.19 of the Stamp Act 1853 and s.1 of the Cheques Act 1957, see *post*, paras 22–33 *et seq.*
[47] *Kymer v. Laurie* (1849) 18 L.J.Q.B. 218; see also *Trustee Evans Estate v. Natal Bank* (1907) 28 Natal L.R. 106. A similar principle is suggested by s.3–121 of the Uniform Commercial Code, by which the instrument is rendered an order to the bank.
[48] *Williams v. Everette* (1811) 14 East 582; *Yates v. Bell* (1820) 3 B. & Ald. 643; *Wedlake v. Hurley* (1830) 1 C. & J. 83; *Auchteroni & Co. v. Midland Bank* [1928] 2 K.B. 294. See also Uniform Commercial Code, s.3–121.

banker, which amounts to an assent to hold the remittance upon trust to discharge the bill, he is liable to the holder.[49]

Qualified as to time

10–08   Fourthly, as to acceptances qualified as to time, that is to say, acceptances which promise to pay at a different time from that at which a bill is drawn:

> **19.—(2) . . . In particular an acceptance is qualified which is—**
> **(d) qualified as to time:**

A bill was accepted in the form "accepted on the condition of its being 'renewed' till 28th November, 1844". This was held to be an acceptance qualified as to time on which the holder might insist against the acceptor, and that the word "renewed" might be read to mean an extension of the time when the bill was to become payable.[50] An acceptance, which unnecessarily and inaccurately states the time of maturity, is not a varying acceptance.[51]

Qualified as to parties

10–09   Fifthly, as to acceptances qualified as to the parties, that is to say:

> **19.—(2)(e) the acceptance of some one or more of the drawees, but not of all.**

If the drawees are partners "in trade", one has prima facie authority to accept for all.[52]

Holder not bound to take qualified acceptance

10–10   **44.—(1) The holder of a bill may refuse to take a qualified acceptance, and if he does not obtain an unqualified acceptance may treat the bill as dishonoured by non-acceptance.**

If, however, the holder takes a qualified acceptance, he should obtain the assent of prior parties, for:

44.—(2) Where a qualified acceptance is taken, and the drawer or an indorser has not expressly or impliedly authorised the holder to take a qualified acceptance, or does not subsequently assent thereto, such drawer or indorser is discharged from his liability on the bill.
The provisions of this subsection do not apply to a partial acceptance, whereof due notice has been given. Where a foreign bill has been accepted as to part, it must be protested as to the balance.

---

[49] *De Bernales v. Fuller* (1810) 14 East 590n., commented on in *Yates v. Bell, ante.*
[50] *Russell v. Phillips* (1850) 14 Q.B. 891.
[51] *Fanshawe v. Peet* (1857) 2 H. & N. 1.
[52] See *ante*, para. 7–17.

(3) When the drawer or indorser of a bill receives notice of a qualified acceptance, and does not within a reasonable time express his dissent to the holder he shall be deemed to have assented thereto.[53]

This section of the 1882 Act does not appear to have been considered in recent authorities. Where there is a qualified acceptance, which has not been authorised by the drawer and indorser nor assented to, the effect of such an acceptance is to release them from further liability on the instrument. There is no indication in the manner in which notice of a qualified acceptance is to be communicated to the drawer or an indorser. It is suggested that no formal step has to be taken, although if formal notice is given the advantage will be that actual notice can be established more easily.[54] Equally there is no guidance as to what constitutes "a reasonable time" for the purposes of section 44(3) of the 1882 Act.[55]

Where it is doubtful whether an acceptance is conditional or not, the election of the holder to protest the bill for non-acceptance will preclude him from recovering from the acceptor.[56]

Acceptance supra protest or for honour

The exception to the rule that a bill can only be accepted by the drawee is where there is an acceptance supra protest or for honour.   **10–11**

65.—(1) Where a bill of exchange has been protested for dishonour by non-acceptance, or protested for better security,[57] and is not overdue, any person, not being a party already liable thereon, may, with the consent of the holder, intervene and accept the bill supra protest, for the honour of any party liable thereon, or for the honour of the person for whose account the bill is drawn.

(2) A bill may be accepted for honour for part only of the sum for which it is drawn.

(3) An acceptance for honour supra protest in order to be valid must—

(a) be written on the bill, and indicate that it is an acceptance for honour:

(b) to be signed by the acceptor for honour.

(4) Where an acceptance for honour does not expressly state for whose honour it is made, it is deemed to be an acceptance for the honour of the drawer.

---

[53] *Sebag v. Abitol* (1816) 4 M. & S. 462, 466. Outside Anglo-American law the only form of qualified acceptance admitted is a partial acceptance and this the holder is bound to take, protesting for the residue. On the other hand, it would seem that the acceptor remains bound within the limits of his acceptance—Geneva Convention, Art. 26.

[54] *Chalmers & Guest on Bills of Exchange*, 14th ed., includes a form of notice in Appendix A, Notice 5.

[55] Contrast s.40(3) of the 1882 Act.

[56] *cf. Sproat v. Mathews* (1786) 1 T.R. 182; *Bentinck v. Dorrien* (1805) 6 East 199.

[57] See s.51(5), *post*, para. 16–19.

(5) Where a bill payable after sight is accepted for honour, its maturity is calculated from the date of the noting for non-acceptance, and not from the date of the acceptance for honour.[58]

Where the requirements of section 65 of the 1882 Act are met anyone, not already liable on the bill,[59] may intervene and accept the bill for honour, thereby preserving the credit of the bill until it matures. Absent an acceptance the antecedent parties become immediately liable. By signing the bill the acceptor for honour undertakes to pay the bill himself if the original drawee dishonours the bill on presentment for payment, provided it is protested.

Protest has always been necessary in order to found an acceptance for honour.[60]

The method of accepting supra protest is said to be as follows, *viz.* the acceptor supra protest must personally appear before a notary public, with witness, and declare that he accepts such protested bill in honour of the drawer or indorser, as the case may be, and that he will satisfy the same at the appointed time. This declaration is known as the "act of honour", and must be written at the foot of the protest.[61] The 1882 Act is silent as to the necessity of this declaration, though in previous editions it has been stated that it is undoubtedly required by the law merchant.[62]

The actual acceptance, which should be written on the bill after the preparation of the act of honour, or simultaneously therewith, should run as follows: "Accepted 'supra protest' for the honour of the drawer (or of C.D. the indorser) 31st May, 1930, A. B."[63] In accordance with subsection (3)(a) above, the acceptance must clearly indicate that it is an acceptance for honour, therefore an acceptance running "Accepted supra protest, A. B." is legally sufficient though it does not state on whose behalf the acceptance is given.

The drawee himself, though he may refuse to accept the bill generally, may yet accept it supra protest for the honour of the drawer or of an indorser.[64] The 1882 Act does not appear to provide for more than one acceptance for honour on a bill; thus the principle formerly maintained that a bill which had been already accepted for the honour of a later indorser could be again accepted supra protest for the honour of the drawer[65] cannot now be relied on. In no case is the holder obliged to take an acceptance for honour.[66]

---

[58] Subsection (5) alters the common law rule as laid down in *Williams v. Germaine* (1827) 7 B. & C. 468.

[59] Thus it would appear the drawee can accept for honour.

[60] *Vandewall v. Tyrell* (1827) Mood. & M. 87; *Geralopulo v. Wieler* (1851) 20 L.J.P.C. 105; As to protest and noting, see *post*, paras 16–01 *et seq.*

[61] See forms, Brooks' *Notary* (9th ed., 1939), pp. 265 *et seq.*

[62] Section 97(2) of the 1882 Act provides that the law merchant shall continue to apply, unless inconsistent with the 1882 Act. In the case of payment supra protest the payment must, by s.68(3), *post*, para. 13–28, always be attested by an act of honour. But, inasmuch as a similar requirement is not to be found in s.65(3), it may be doubtful how far the rule of the law merchant is, under s.97(2), to be regarded as consistent with the express provisions of the 1882 Act.

[63] See Brooks' *Notary* (9th ed), 1939), p. 96.

[64] Beawes (6th ed.), p. 568, para. 33.

[65] See also *Mitford v. Walcot* (1700) 12 Mod. 410.

[66] Beawes, p. 569, para. 42.

Referee in case of need

Though there cannot be alternative or successive drawees, yet the drawer or   **10–12**
an indorser may insert in the bill the name of a person to whom the holder may
resort if the bill be dishonoured by non-acceptance or non-payment, as
provided by the 1882 Act:

**15. The drawer of a bill and any indorser may insert therein the name
of a person to whom the holder may resort in case of need, that is to say,
in case the bill is dishonoured by non-acceptance or non-payment. Such
person is called the referee in case of need. It is in the option of the holder
to resort to the referee in case of need or not as he may think fit.**

It has been suggested that it may have been necessary in some cases to
present to the case of need in England, in order to charge a foreign drawer or
indorser in his own country; this is clearly altered by the section.[67]

Section 67 provides that[68] before presentment for payment is made to the
referee in case of need, the bill must be protested for non-payment. The 1882
Act does not in terms provide for protest for non-acceptance where the bill is
presented for acceptance to the referee in case of need; but presumably protest
for non-acceptance would be required under section 65.

In practice the archaic use of a referee in case of need is extinct.

---

[67] See Chalmers, *Digest of Bills of Exchange* (13th ed., 1964), 39.
[68] See *post*, para. 12–24.

CHAPTER 11

DUTIES OF HOLDER AS TO ACCEPTANCE

11–01   SECTIONS 39–44 of the 1882 Act deal with the duties of the holder as to acceptance; the rules as to presentment for payment are dealt with in the next Chapter.

Presentment

11–02   It is in all cases advisable for the holder of an unaccepted bill to present it for acceptance without delay for, in the case of acceptance, he obtains the additional security of the acceptor and, if acceptance be refused, the antecedent parties become liable immediately. It is advisable, too, on the drawer's account for, by receiving early advice of dishonour, he may be better able to get his effects out of the drawee's hands.

But presentment for acceptance is not always necessary. The 1882 Act stipulates that presentment is necessary in three instances:

39.—(1) Where a bill is payable after sight, presentment for acceptance is necessary in order to fix the maturity of the instrument.

(2) Where a bill expressly stipulates that it shall be presented for acceptance, or where a bill is drawn payable elsewhere than at the residence or place of business of the drawee, it must be presented for acceptance before it can be presented for payment.

(3) In no other case is presentment for acceptance necessary in order to render liable any party to the bill.

The need for a bill payable after sight to be presented for acceptance is obvious; until presentment the date of maturity of the bill remains unfixed.

It is, perhaps, strange that in the cases other than the three set out in subsections (1) and (2), there is no requirement that a bill be presented for acceptance, for it is in the interest of all parties that the security of the acceptor's signature should be obtained. Of course, the essential thing is to fix the date of maturity, which is already fixed in a bill payable at a given period after date; but such a bill would seem to be in no different case in this respect from any other that requires presentment for acceptance.

However, it has been said that it is incumbent on a holder who is a mere agent,[1] and on the payee,[2] when expressly directed by the drawer so to do, to present the bill for acceptance as soon as possible; and that, for loss arising from the neglect, the payee must be responsible, and the agent must answer to his principal.

---

[1] Chitty (11th ed.), p. 194; see also *Bank of Van Diemen's Land v. Bank of Victoria* (1871) L.R. 3 P.C. 526.

[2] Thompson, *Bills* (3rd ed.), p. 276; see also Pothier, *Contrat de Change*, para. 128.

In the case of a bill payable at so many days' sight, the expression "after sight" is dealt with in the 1882 Act, at section 14(3), as follows:

> **"Where a bill is payable at a fixed period after sight, the time begins to run from the date of the acceptance if the bill be accepted, and from the date of noting or protest if the bill be noted or protested for non-acceptance, or for non-delivery."**

In the case of a note payable after sight, the note must again be exhibited to the maker.[3]

Bill coming forward late

39.—(4) Where the holder of a bill, drawn payable elsewhere than at the place of business or residence of the drawee, has not time, with the exercise of reasonable diligence, to present the bill for acceptance before presenting it for payment on the day that it falls due, the delay caused by presenting the bill for acceptance before presenting it for payment is excused, and does not discharge the drawer and indorsers.   11–03

This provision is said to have settled a moot point and to have been a possible alteration of the law.[4] The provision is necessary in order to cater for the provision contained in section 39(2) of the 1882 Act, which requires such a bill to be presented for payment.

Time for presenting bill after sight

40.—(1) Subject to the provisions of this Act,[5] when a bill payable after sight is negotiated, the holder must either present it for acceptance or negotiate it within a reasonable time.   11–04
(2) If he does not do so, the drawer and all indorsers prior to that holder are discharged.
(3) In determining what is a reasonable time within the meaning of this section, regard shall be had to the nature of the bill, the usage of trade with respect to similar bills, and the facts of the particular case.

Since the maturity of a bill payable after sight is only fixed upon presentment for acceptance it is in the interests of the drawer and prior indorsers that presentment be made within a reasonable time. Accordingly, except where one of the excuses for non-presentment is applicable,[6] the holder of such a bill should present it for acceptance or negotiate it within a reasonable time.

---

[3] *cf. Holmes v. Kerrison* (1810) 2 Taunt. 323.
[4] Chalmers & Guest (14th ed., 1991), p. 347.
[5] The other provisions referred to in s.40(1) seem to be those relating to excuse of presentment; see s.41(2); *Muilman v. D'Eguino* (1795) 2 H.Bl. 565; *Ramchurn Mullick v. Luchmeechund Radkissen* (1854) 9 Moore P.C. 46. As noted, *post*, para. 21–87, note 47, the doctrine of reasonable time in reference to negotiable instruments is quite unknown outside English and American law (s.3–503, Uniform Commercial Code). See also Geneva Convention, Ch. III.
[6] See s.41(2) of the 1882 Act; *post*, para. 11–06.

Section 40(3) of the 1882 Act sets out matters to which regard is to be had in determining what is a reasonable time. There have not been any recent authorities, which have examined this sub-section. The cases referred to below are all of considerable antiquity, and should be approached with that in mind; modern means of communications may have resulted in a different outcome.

Plaintiff, on Friday 9, at Windsor, 20 miles from London, received a bill on London, at one month after sight, for £100. There was no post on Saturday. It was presented on the Tuesday. The jury thought it was presented within a reasonable time, and the Court concurred.[7]

A bill drawn by bankers in the country on their correspondents in London, payable after sight, was indorsed to the traveller of the plaintiffs. He transmitted it to the plaintiffs after the interval of a week, and they, two days afterwards, transmitted it for acceptance. Before it was presented to the drawees, the drawer had become bankrupt; the drawees, consequently, refused to accept. Had the bill been sent by the traveller to the plaintiffs, his employers, as soon as he received it, they would have been able to get it accepted before the bankruptcy. "This is", says Lord Tenterden, "a mixed question of law and fact; and, in expressing my own opinion, I do not wish at all to withdraw the case from the jury . . . Whatever strictness may be required with respect to common bills of exchange payable after sight, it does not seem unreasonable to treat bills of this nature, drawn by bankers on their correspondents, as not requiring immediate presentment, but as being retainable by the holders for the purpose of using them, within a moderate time (for indefinite delay, of course, cannot be allowed), as part of the circulating medium of the country." The jury concurred with his Lordship, that the delay was not unreasonable.[8]

Where the purchaser of a bill on Rio de Janeiro, at 60 days' sight, the exchange being against him, kept it nearly five months, and the drawee failed before presentment, it was held that the delay was not unreasonable. Tindal C.J., in charging the jury, said that they were to determine whether there had been unreasonable delay on the part of the plaintiff, the holder of the bill, in sending it forward for acceptance or putting it into circulation; and that, in order to arrive at a proper determination of that question, they were to take into consideration the situation and interests not of the drawer only, or of the holder only, but of both. On a rule for a new trial the Court, in discharging it, approved this direction, observing that no other rule could be laid down than that the bill must be forwarded within a reasonable time under all the circumstances of the case, and that there must be no unreasonable or improper delay.[9]

It is no laches to put a foreign bill, payable after sight, into circulation before acceptance and to keep it circulating without acceptance so long as the convenience of the successive holders requires.[10] But where a bill, payable 90 days after sight, was drawn in duplicate on August 12, in Newfoundland, and

[7] *Fry v. Hill* (1817) 7 Taunt. 397.
[8] *Shute v. Robins* (1828) M. & M. 133.
[9] *Mellish v. Rawdon* (1832) 9 Bing. 416.
[10] *Groupy v. Harden* (1816) 7 Taunt. 159.

not presented for acceptance in London until November 16, and no circumstances were proved to excuse the delay, it was held unreasonable, the Court laying some stress on the fact that the bill was drawn in a set.[11]

Rules as to presentment

41.—(1) A bill is duly presented for acceptance, which is presented in accordance with the following rules: 11–05

(a) **The presentment must be made by or on behalf of the holder to the drawee or to some person authorised to accept or refuse acceptance on his behalf at a reasonable hour on a business day[12] and before the bill is overdue.**

There must be proof that presentation has been made to the actual drawee (or to his accredited agent), not to a person who merely refused to accept but who did not represent himself to be the drawee.[13] In the case of bankers it is well established that presentment must be made during business (*viz.* banking) hours, but in other cases the presentment must be made at a reasonable hour.[14] Presentment at a house of business must be made during times of business at such reasonable hours as a man is bound to attend.[15]

Further, the 1882 Act provides for presentment in special cases as follows:

41.—(1)(b) Where a bill is addressed to two or more drawees, who are not partners, presentment must be made to them all, unless one has authority to accept for all, then presentment may be made to him only.

In the case of such a bill the acceptance of one drawee would constitute a qualified acceptance.[16]

(c) **Where the drawee is dead, presentment may be made to his personal representative.**

In the case of the drawee's death the holder may, by section 41(2)(a), dispense with presentment.

---

[11] *Straker v. Graham* (1839) 4 M. & W. 721.

[12] For non-business days, see *post,* para. 12–07, s.92.

[13] *Cheek v. Roper* (1804) 5 Esp. 175. Presentment for acceptance generally must be personal, as distinguished from presentment for payment, which must be local; see Chalmers & Guest (14th ed.), p. 351; but see also Daniel (5th ed.), para. 589.

[14] *cf. Wilkins v. Jadis* (1831) 2 B. & Ad. 188, 189 (Tindal C.J.); see also *Parker v. Gordon* (1806) 7 East 385.

[15] *cf. Elford v. Teed* (1813) 1 M. & S. 28, 29. In America it is held that business hours, except for bankers, range through the whole of the day down to the hours of rest in the evening. It matters not, indeed, at what hour presentment is made, provided that an answer be given by an authorised person, but presentment is a mere nullity if made at an unreasonable hour and no such answer be given; *cf.* Daniel (5th ed.), para. 464, a; Brannan, pp. 1000, 1259.

[16] Section 19(2)(e) of the 1882 Act.

If the holder is dead and the executor has not yet proved the will, the executor is nevertheless apparently bound to present the bill when presentable[17]; for his title to his testator's property is derived exclusively from the will, and vests in him from the moment of the testator's death.[18] But as the title of an administrator is derived wholly from the Family Division of the High Court, and he has none till the letters of administration are granted, he would probably be excused by impossibility.

(d) Where the drawee is bankrupt, presentment may be made to him or to his trustee.

In this case also, by section 41(2)(a), presentment on the holder's part is purely optional.

Presentment may be made by post, as provided by the 1882 Act:

(e) Where authorised by agreement or usage, a presentment through the post office is sufficient.

Presentment for acceptance excused

11–06   Presentment for acceptance when otherwise necessary[19] is only excused in the following cases:

41.—(2) Presentment in accordance with these rules is excused, and a bill may be treated as dishonoured by non-acceptance—

(a) **where the drawee is dead or bankrupt, or is a fictitious person or a person not having capacity to contract by bill;**

(b) **where, after the exercise of reasonable diligence, such presentment cannot be effected;**

(c) **where, although the presentment has been irregular, acceptance has been refused on some other ground.**

(3) The fact that the holder has reason to believe that the bill, on presentment, will be dishonoured does not excuse presentment.

The section uses the word "excused", as do sections 46(1), 47(1) and 50(1); sections 46(2), 50(2) and 51(9) use the words "dispensed with". It would seem that the two expressions, though possibly of different meanings generally speaking, are in these contexts interchangeable.

---

[17] cf. *Williams Mortimer & Sunnucks, Executors, Administrators and Probate* (18th ed., 2000), p. 890. Delay in making presentment for payment is excused under s.46(1), *post*, para. 12–16, when it is caused by circumstances beyond the control of the holder and not imputable to his default. Equally so, under s.50(1), *post*, para. 15–30, is delay in giving notice of dishonour.

[18] *Woolley v. Clark* (1822) 5 B. & Ald. 744.

[19] *Ante*, para. 11–02.

If the drawee has absconded, the bill may be treated at once as dis-honoured,[20] but not merely if his house is closed, and the holder makes no further attempt to find him.[21]

Dishonour by non-acceptance

The drawee is entitled to time for deliberation whether he will accept or not, **11–07** as is impliedly allowed by the 1882 Act in the following section:

42. When a bill is duly presented for acceptance and is not accepted within the customary time, the person presenting it must treat it as dishonoured by non-acceptance. If he do not, the holder shall lose his right of recourse against the drawer and indorsers.

It seems that the drawee may demand 24 hours for this purpose and that the holder will be justified in leaving the bill with him for that period,[22] unless, in the interim, he either accepts or declares his resolution not to accept.[23] If more than 24 hours be given, the holder ought to inform the antecedent parties of it.[24]

If the owner of a bill who left it for acceptance, by his negligence enabled a stranger to give such a description of it as to obtain it from the drawee, without negligence on the drawee's part, the owner could not maintain trover for it against the drawee.[25]

43.—(1) A bill is dishonoured by non-acceptance—

(a) when it is duly presented for acceptance, and such an acceptance as is prescribed by this Act is refused or cannot be obtained; or

(b) when presentment for acceptance is excused and the bill is not accepted.

(2) Subject to the provisions of this Act, when a bill is dishonoured by non-acceptance, an immediate right of recourse against the drawer and

---

[20] *Anon.* (1695) 1 Ld. Rym. 743.

[21] *Collins v. Butler* (1738) 2 Stra. 1087. In this case, it is true, the maker of the note had gone away the previous month. Whether "reasonable diligence" has been used appears to be a question of fact for the jury; *cf. Batemen v. Joseph* (1810) 12 East 433.

[22] Marius 15; Com.Dig.Mrch.F. 6. In *Bellasis v. Hester* (1698) 1 Ld.Raym. 280, 281, Treby C.J. stated that on presentment for acceptance the drawee has allowed him by law the whole day to view the bill. The 24 hours' rule was directly approved by the Court in *Bank of Van Diemen's Land v. Bank of Victoria* (1871) L.R. 3 P.C. 526, 543. Proof of what is customary may differ from proof of what is reasonable; still it may be doubted whether in practice the expression "customary time" in s.42 will affect the 24 hours' rule. In South Africa, in the case of "ordinary trade bills", the drawer "is entitled to a customary period of 24 hours . . . " (Cowen (1966) 299). The position in Australia would seem to be the same as in the United Kingdom (Riley, (1953) 141).

[23] Bayley (6th ed.), p. 228. The Uniform Commercial Code, s.3–506, provides that; "Accep-tance may be deferred without dishonour until the close of the next business day followings presentment."

[24] *Ingram v. Forster* (1805) 2 Smith 242.

[25] *Morrison v. Buchanan* (1833) 6 C. & P. 18.

indorsers accrues to the holder, and no presentment for payment is necessary.

The other provisions referred to in sub-section (2) would seem to be (i) section 15, as to a reference in case of need, resort to whom is optional on the holder's part, (ii) sections 65–68, as to acceptance supra protest or for honour; and (iii) sections 48 and 51, as to notice of dishonour and protest. As regards the last of those the holder's right of recourse against the drawer and indorser is conditional upon giving notice of dishonour and, where necessary, protesting.

Qualified acceptance

11–08   The holder has a right to expect an absolute or general acceptance, and may treat the bill as dishonoured if he do not obtain one. Still he may, if he please, take a qualified acceptance.[26]

---

[26] As to qualified acceptances, see the 1882 Act, ss.19 and 44.

CHAPTER 12

PRESENTMENT FOR PAYMENT

THE rules as to presentment for payment are contained, principally, in **12–01** Sections 45 and 46 of the 1882 Act. Section 74A–74C of the 1882 Act[1] introduced special provisions as to cheques.

In relation to presentment for payment of bills it is essential to distinguish between the position of the acceptor, on the one hand, and the position of the drawers and indorsers, on the other.

The Acceptor

When a bill is accepted generally the acceptor is not entitled to presentment **12–02** for payment, nor is it necessary to present the bill for payment to render the acceptor liable, for it is provided in the 1882 Act:

52.—(1) When a bill is accepted generally presentment for payment is not necessary in order to render the acceptor liable.[2]

So, too, it is not necessary in the case of the maker of a note,[3] unless the note is, in the body of it, made payable at a particular place. The action itself is sufficient demand, and that though the instrument is payable on demand.[4]

Nevertheless, it is usual to present a bill to the acceptor for payment.

52.—(2) When by the terms of a qualified acceptance presentment for payment is required, the acceptor, in the absence of an express stipulation to that effect, is not discharged by the omission to present the bill for payment on the day that it matures. However it may be argued that such a bill must be so presented in order for the holder's right of action against the acceptor to accrue.[5]

The stipulation must expressly require presentment for payment on the date that the bill matures. Hence, in the case of an acceptance to pay only at a particular place, though the bill must be presented for payment at that place,[6]

---

[1] Enacted by the Deregulation (Bills of Exchange) Order 1996 (S.I. 1996 No. 2993), which introduced additional means of presenting cheques, including truncation, for cheques drawn after November 28, 1996; *post*, para. 21–82.

[2] As to qualified acceptances, see s.19, *ante*, paras 10–04 *et seq.*

[3] Section 87 (1), set out *post*, para. 24–11.

[4] *Rumball v. Ball* (1711) 10 Mod. 38; *Norton v. Ellam* (1837) 2 M. & W. 461; *Guaranty Trust Co. of New York v. Hannay* [1918] 2 K.B. 623, CA.

[5] See *Chitty on Contracts*, Vol. II (28th ed.) p. 221.

[6] *Halstead v. Skelton* (1843) 5 Q.B. 86.

non-presentment on the day when the bill becomes due does not discharge the acceptor.[7]

The Drawer and Indoser

12–03   Unless presentment be specially excused, a bill or note must be presented for payment in order to render the drawer and indorsers liable, since the 1882 Act provides:

45. Subject to the provisions[8] of this Act a bill must be duly presented for payment. If it be not so presented the drawer and indorsers shall be discharged.[9]

The holder does not, by presenting a bill for payment, warrant its genuineness.[10]

TIME FOR PRESENTMENT

12–04   In relation to when a bill is to be presented for payment, a distinction is drawn between bills not payable on demand, on the one hand, and bills payable on demand.

Bills not payable on demand

12–05   As regards bills not payable on demand, presentment in order to be valid must comply with the provisions as to the time for presentment:

45. A bill is duly presented for payment which is presented in accordance with the following rules—
(1) Where the bill is not payable on demand, presentment must be made on the day it falls due.[11]

Date of maturity

12–06   **14.—Where a bill is not payable on demand the day on which it falls due is determined as follows:**

---

[7] *Smith v. Vertue* (1860) 30 L.J.C.P. 56, 60.

[8] The other provisions seem to be those in s.46, paras 12–18 *et seq.*, *post*, relating to excuse of presentment, delay, etc. For the special provisions relating to the drawer of a cheque, see s.74, *post*, paras 21–73 *et seq.*

[9] This discharge extends also to free the parties from their liability on the consideration; *cf. Soward v. Palmer* (1818) 8 Taunt. 277, where the failure to present a bill was held an answer to an action on a note for a larger sum, in lieu of which the bill was given.

[10] *Greenwood v. Martins Bank* [1933] A.C. 51, 60 (Lord Tomlin), citing *East India Co. v. Triton* (1824) 3 B. & C. 280, 289, 291 and *Guaranty Trust Co. of New York v. Hannay* [1918] 2 K.B. 623, 632; as to pension warrants of the colonial customs service, see *Gowers v. Lloyds and National Provincial Foreign Bank Ltd* [1938] 1 All E.R. 766.

[11] See *Yeoman Credit Ltd v. Gregory* [1963] 1 W.L.R. 343.

(1) The bill is due and payable in all cases on the last day of the time of payment as fixed by the bill or, if that is a non-business day, on the succeeding business day.

This subsection was substituted by the Banking and Financial Dealings Act 1971, s.3(2),[12] which did away with "days of grace".

The date of maturity is calculated in accordance with the following:

14.—(2) Where a bill is payable at a fixed period after date, after sight or after the happening of a specified event, the time of payment is determined by excluding the day from which the time is to begin to run and by including the day of payment.

(3) Where a bill is payable at a fixed period after sight, the time begins to run from the date of the acceptance if the bill be accepted, and from the date of noting or protest if the bill be noted or protested for non-acceptance, or for non-delivery.[13]

A note payable at a certain period after sight is payable at that period after presentment for sight.[14] In the case of an acceptance for honour of a bill payable after sight, time runs, under section 65(5),[15] from the date of noting for non-acceptance, and not from that of the acceptance for honour.[16]

As to the meaning of the term "month" in a bill it is provided:

14.—(4) The term "month" in a bill means calendar month.[17]

Bills payable on demand

As regards a bill payable on demand,[18] the time within which it must be presented for payment is as follows: **12–07**

45.—(2) Where the bill is payable on demand, then, subject to the provisions of this Act, presentment must be made within a reasonable time after its issue in order to render the drawer liable, and within a reasonable time after its indorsement, in order to render the indorser liable.

In determining what is a reasonable time, regard shall be had to the nature of the bill, the usage of trade with regard to similar bills, and the facts of the particular case.

---

[12] *Post*, Appendix 1.

[13] *Campbell v. French* (1795) 6 T.R. 200.

[14] *Sturdy v. Henderson* (1821) 4 B. & Ald. 592.

[15] *Ante*, para. 10–11.

[16] It was otherwise at common law (*Williams v. Germaine* (1872) 7 B. & C. 468).

[17] As to case of "usance", see *ante*, para. 2–17. When usance is a month, half usance is always 15 days, notwithstanding the unequal length of the months (Marius, p. 93).

[18] As to bills payable on demand, see s.10, *ante*, para. 2–15.

Bills on demand other than cheques[19] are not common, but may be drawn payable at sight under documentary credits. The position of the *drawer* of a cheque is regulated by section 74;[20] the above subsection would avail to protect the rights of an *indorser*.

As regards promissory notes payable on demand it is provided as follows:[21]

86.—(1) Where a note payable on demand has been indorsed, it must be presented for payment within a reasonable time of the indorsement. If it be not so presented the indorser is discharged.

(2) In determining what is a reasonable time, regard shall be had to the nature of the instrument, the usage of trade, and the facts of the particular case.

Business and non-business days

Business day

12–08   Presentment, in order to be valid, must, in accordance with the above provisions, be made on a business day. Every day, other than those specifically dealt with in the following provision of the 1882 Act, is a business day:

92. Where, by this Act, the time limited for doing any act or thing is less than three days, in reckoning time, non-business days are excluded. "Non-business days" for the purposes of this Act mean:

(a) Sunday, Good Friday, Christmas Day:

(b) A bank holiday under the Bank Holidays Act 1871, or Acts amending it:

(c) A day appointed by Royal proclamation as a public fast or thanksgiving day.

Any other day is a business day.[22]

Saturday is a non-business day in this country.[23]

---

[19] See *King & Boyd v. Porter* [1925] N.I. 103, CA, in which it was stated that s.45 cannot apply to cheques and Moor L.J. referred with approval to Coleridge C.J. in *R. v. Clarence* [1888] 22 Q.B.D. 23, 65, to the effect that: "If the apparent logical construction (of a statute) leads to results which it is impossible to believe that those who framed or those who passed the statute contemplated, and from which one's own judgment recoils, there is in my opinion good reason for believing that the construction which leads to such results cannot be the true construction"; and see *post*, para. 21–87.

[20] *Post*, para. 21–87.

[21] For detailed treatment of this section, see *post*, paras 24–10 *et seq*.

[22] A statute may specifically provide an exception; thus the Decimal Currency Act 1969 enacted that February 11, 12, and 13, 1971, should be non-business days for the purposes of the Bills of Exchange Act 1882.

[23] The Uniform Commercial Code, s.3–503 comment that s.85 of the Negotiable Instruments Law is intended to make allowance for the increasing practice of closing banks or businesses on Saturday or other days of the week.

Non-business day

Under the 1882 Act, non-business days are defined by section 92. This **12–09** section is amended, and enlarged so as to cover the Saturday closing of banks by section 3(1) and section 4(4) of the Banking and Financial Dealings Act 1971 as follows:

3.—(1) Section 92 of the Bills of Exchange Act 1882 (which, in a case in which the time limited by that Act for doing any act or thing is less than three days, excludes non-business days from the reckoning of that time, and defines such days for the purposes of the Act) shall have effect as if paragraph (a) of the definition of non-business days, "Saturday" were inserted immediately before "Sunday".

4.—(4) Accordingly in section 92 of the Bills of Exchange Act 1882, in the definition of "non-business days", for the words "the Bank Holidays Act 1871 or Acts amending it" in paragraph (b) there shall be substituted the words "the Banking and Financial Dealings Act 1971", and there shall be added a new paragraph (d):

"(d) a day declared by an order under section 2 of the Banking and Financial Dealings Act 1971 to be a non-business day."

PLACE OF PRESENTMENT

Section 45(3)–(8) of the 1882 Act set out the rules governing the place of **12–10** presentment of bills; in relation to cheques these provisions are supplemented by section 74A–B.[24]

45.—(3) Presentment must be made by the holder or by some person authorised to receive payment on his behalf at a reasonable hour on a business day, at the proper place as hereinafter defined, either to the person designated by the bill as payer, or to some person authorised to pay or refuse payment on his behalf if with the exercise of reasonable diligence such person can there be found.

Presentment for payment should be made during the usual hours of business and, if at a banker's, within banking hours.[25] Presentment must, it has been stated, be made at such reasonable hours as a man is bound to attend.[26] A presentment at a place of residence, as distinguished from a place of business,

[24] Inserted by the Deregulation (Bills of Exchange) Order 1996, S.I.1996, No. 2993; see *post*, paras 21–80 to 21–86.

[25] *Parker v. Gordon* (1806) 7 East 385; *Elford v. Teed* (1813) 1 M. & S. 28; *cf.* also *Jameson v. Swinton* (1810) 2 Taunt. 224; *Whitaker v. Bank of England* (1835) 1 Cr.M. & R. 744.

[26] *Elford v. Teed.* See also para. 11–05, (presentment for acceptance). A presentment for payment at a place of business between six and seven in the evening has been held good (*Morgan v. Davison* (1815) 1 Stark. 114); and one at 8 p.m., at the drawee's place of residence (*Barclay v. Bailey* (1810) 2 Campl. 527); but *quaere* whether it would be equally good at so late an hour at a place of business.

may, it would seem, be made up to the hours of rest in the evening.[27] If made at the proper time it is immaterial that there be no person within to return an answer.[28] The party presenting should be ready and authorised to receive the money, and has no right (at least, unless usage require it) to impose on the drawee any trouble or risk in remitting the money elsewhere.[29]

Presentment for payment at the right place is as important, in order to charge the antecedent parties, as presentment at the right time.

45.—(4) A bill is presented at the proper place:
(a) Where a place of presentment is specified in the bill and the bill is there presented.

As has already been stated, by the 1882 Act, section 19(2)(c), an acceptor may qualify his acceptance by making it payable at a particular specified place, but it will nevertheless be a general acceptance as against him, so that presentment at the place named, or indeed anywhere, will not be necessary to charge him, unless the acceptance state that the bill is to be payable there and not elsewhere.[30]

However as regards the drawer or an indorser, presentment must be at the place specified in the bill, whether it is specified by the drawer or the acceptor, or such drawer or indorser will be discharged.[31] Thus, if the bill is made payable at a banker's, a presentment must be made there in order to charge the drawer and indorsers.[32] If the bill is accepted payable at a banker's, which banker happens to become the holder at its maturity, that fact alone amounts to presentment, and no other proof is necessary.[33] If a bill is made payable in

---

[27] See *Barclay v. Bailey, supra; Triggs v. Newham* (1825) 10 Moo.C.P. 249; Daniel (5th ed.), para. 603.

[28] *Wilkins v. Jadis* (1831) 2 B. & Ad. 188; s.45(4), *post*, p. 128.

[29] *cf. Bailey v. Bodenham* (1864) 33 L.J.C.P. 252.

[30] See *ante*, para. 10–07; and s.52(2), *ante*, para. 12–02.

[31] *Beirnstein v. Usher* (1895) 11 T.L.R. 356, in which the bill was drawn payable at 14 Picton Place, Swansea, the office of the defendants and was indorsed by the defendants to the plaintiff. It was presented to the acceptor personally not at Picton Place. It was held that s.19 applied only to the acceptance and not to an action between indorsee and indorser and therefore, by s.45, the defendants were discharged. Such had been the law even before 1 & 2 Geo. 4, c. 78, was enacted (*Gibb v. Mather* (1832) 8 Bing. 214, 220; *Saul v. Jones* (1858) 28 L.J.Q.B. 37); and see *Bank Polski v. Mulder* [1942] 1 K.B. 497; see also *Yeoman Credit Ltd v. Gregory* [1963] 1 W.L.R. 343.

[32] *Saunderson v. Judge* (1795) 2 H.Bl. 509. Presentment at the Clearing House has been held equivalent thereto (*Reynolds v. Chettle* (1881) 2 Camp. 596), but in view of the decision in *Barclays Bank plc v. Bank of England* [1985] 1 All E.R. 385 [1985] F.L.R. 209, in which Bingham J. acting as a judicial arbitrator declined to follow *Reynolds v. Chettle* and decided that only actual presentment at the drawee bank would suffice to discharge the collecting banker's duty as to presentment, this has now been thrown open to doubt. Where a bill was accepted payable at a particular bank, the laches of the holder in not presenting it until some time after it had become due, the bank meantime having failed, was held at common law to discharge the acceptor, the case being considered identical with that of a cheque (*Rhodes v. Gent*) (1821) 5 B. & Ald. 244); but the 1882 Act does not appear to allow a discharge now under these circumstances, s.74 applying only to cheques. Where a note was made payable at the office of a solicitor, who also acted on behalf of the holder, and the solicitor accordingly presented the note to himself, it was held a valid presentment (*Schentke v. Goddard* (1902) 19 S.C. 488). Failure to return an unpaid term in accordance with Clearing House Rules may amount to payment: *Reidell v. Commercial Bank of Australia* (1931) V.L.R. 382.

[33] *Bailey v. Porter* (1845) 14 M. & W. 44; *Saunderson v. Judge, supra*.

a particular town, a presentment at all the banking houses there will suffice.[34]

In *Ringham v. Hackett*[35] a crossed cheque was presented by the payee to the bank on which it was drawn. It was held to have been presented at the proper place within the subsection,[36] Lawton L.J. said:

"The provisions as to crossed cheques . . . were intended to protect the bank and its customer; they had no impact on the payee. If the latter presented the cheque in person he might not get his money but it was no less a presentment for that reason."

As set out earlier the presentation of cheques is now supplemented by sections 74A–74B of the 1882 Act;[37] however the provisions are restricted to cheques only and do not extend to other instruments referred to in section 4(2) of the Cheques Act 1957.

When no place of payment specified

45.—(4) A bill is presented at the proper place: 12–11

(b) Where no place of payment is specified, but the address of the drawee or acceptor is given in the bill, and the bill is there presented.

If a particular house is pointed out by the bill as the acceptor's residence, a presentment to any inmate,[38] or, if the house is shut up, at the door will suffice.[39] In the case of a note bearing the maker's address, presentment to the maker elsewhere is sufficient to charge an indorser, unless the note is in terms made payable at such address.[40] It is otherwise in the case of a bill; if the bill specifies the acceptor's address, presentment elsewhere is bad as against an indorser.

---

[34] *Hardy v. Woodroofe* (1818) 2 Stark. 319.

[35] (1980) 10 L.D.A.B. 206

[36] *Ringham v. Hackett and Another* (1980) 10 L.D.A.B. 206. There are two aspects of interest. A cheque was drawn on a partnership bank account. It bore the "printed name" of the partnership (as presumably is the case almost always with personalised cheques) together with the signature of a partner. It was a crossed cheque but was presented by the payee to the bank on which it was drawn. Payment was of course refused. The other partner was sued by the payee and succeeded in obtaining judgment.

Now it has to be remembered that a cheque is a bill of exchange as well as being the item causing an obligation to arise under the banker-customer contract when it is presented. Because it is a bill of exchange section 23(2) of the 1882 Act is applicable, which reads as follows:

"The signature of the name of a firm is equivalent to the signature by the person so signing, of the names of all persons liable as partners in that firm."

This meant that the other partner was liable on the cheque as drawer. This was irrespective of the mandate to the bank which could have required two signatures. Again, in order to sue on a bill of exchange it is necessary to provide due presentation. By Section 45(3) of the Act, due presentment was held to have been made—at the proper place, etc. This is despite the fact that the cheque was crossed and that the bank would have been liable to the true owner if it had been stolen or to the customer if loss had ensued to him as a result of the payment.

[37] See para. 12–01 and *post* paras 21–80—21–86.

[38] *Buxton v. Jones* (1840) 1 M. & G. 83.

[39] *Hine v. Allely* (1833) 4 B. & Ad. 624.

[40] Section 87(3); see *post*, pp. 129, 344.

When no address given on instrument

12–12   When the bill not only specifies no place of payment, but gives no address, the bill or note must be presented as follows:

> **45.—(4) A bill is presented at the proper place:**
> **(c) Where no place of payment is specified and no address given, and the bill is presented at the drawee's or acceptor's place of business if known, and if not, at his ordinary residence if known.**
>
> **(d) In any other case if presented to the drawee or acceptor wherever he can be found, or if presented at his last known place of business or residence.**

In previous editions of this book the view was expressed that, because of the development of the clearing house system, section 45(4)(a), (b), (c) and (d) of the 1882 Act, whilst still effective, only concerned bills other than cheques and clean bills of exchange (*i.e.* bills unaccompanied by the commercial documents). Thus presentment through the clearing house system itself was said to be sufficient to satisfy the requirements of section 45 of the 1882 Act.

In *Barclays Bank plc v. Bank of England*[41] Bingham J. determined, in the course of an arbitration, that the presenting bank's obligation to its customer was only discharged when the cheque, dealt with through the clearing house system, was delivered to the branch of the paying bank. He emphasised that by section 45 of the 1882 Act the drawer of a cheque has a clear statutory right to be discharged if the cheque was not duly presented to him or his branch of the paying bank for payment. The usage and practice of bankers could not abrogate this right, where the drawer was not a party to the arrangement.

The views previously expressed can no longer be regarded as correct. However, subsequent to Bingham J.'s judgment, Parliament intervened to give statutory recognition to the clearing house system by the introduction of section 74A–74B of the 1882 Act.[42]

In America there is some authority for treating as good a demand in the street of the acceptor in person, if not objected to in point of form, at least where the acceptor has no place of business, but United Kingdom law in such a case requires presentment at the ordinary residence of the acceptor if known, and only where the place of residence cannot be discovered is presentment to the acceptor, wherever he can be found, good.[43]

---

[41] [1995] 1 A.E.R. 385; Bingham J.'s award contains a useful description as to the operation of the clearing house; see also Brindle & Cox, *Law of Bankers Payments'* (2nd ed.), p. 373 *et seq.*

[42] See *post* paras 21–80 to 21–86.

[43] See Daniel (7th ed.), para. 705; Uniform Commercial Code, s.3–504, which provides *inter alia*, for presentment "through a clearing-house", which "means that the presentment is not made when the demand reaches the clearing-house, but when it reaches the obligor", *Sparks v. Hamilton* (1920) 47 O.L.R. 55, 64. For Canada, see Falconbridge (7th ed., 1969), p. 695.

No authorised person in attendance

45.—(5) Where a bill is presented at the proper place, and after the   **12–13**
exercise of reasonable diligence no person authorised to pay or refuse
payment can be found there, no further presentment to the drawee or
acceptor is required.[44]

It has been held that, during reasonable business hours, it is the duty of a
merchant to take care that a proper person be in attendance at his place of
business.[45]

Personal demand

A personal demand on the drawee, or acceptor, or maker, is not in general   **12–14**
necessary,[46] but in the case of several acceptors who are not partners, it is
provided that:

45.—(6) Where a bill is drawn upon, or accepted by two or more
persons who are not partners, and no place of payment is specified,
presentment must be made to them all.

Death of drawee or acceptor

45.—(7) Where the drawee or acceptor of a bill is dead, and no place   **12–15**
of payment is specified, presentment must be made to a personal repre-
sentative, if such there be, and with the exercise of reasonable diligence he
can be found.

This case is, therefore, unlike that of presentment for acceptance, since on
the death of the drawee presentment for acceptance is, by section 41(2)(a),
excused.

Place of presentment of note

As regards the presentment of a promissory note for payment, and in   **12–16**
particular, where the note is made payable at a named place by the maker, the
1882 Act specially provides as follows:[47]

87.—(1) Where a promissory note is in the body of it made payable at
a particular place, it must be presented for payment at that place in order
to render the maker liable. In any other case, presentment for payment is
not necessary in order to render the maker liable.

---

[44] *Wilkins v. Jadis* (1831) 2 B. & Ad. 188.
[45] *Crosse v. Smith* (1813) 1 M. & S. 545, 554. As to reasonable business hours, see *ante*,
para. 12–10.
[46] *Cromwell v. Hynson* (1796) 2 Esp. 511; *Brown v. McDermott* (1805) 5 Esp. 265.
[47] For detailed treatment of this section, see *post*, para. 24–11.

(2) Presentment for payment is necessary in order to render the indorser of a note liable.

(3) Where a note is in the body of it made payable at a particular place, presentment at that place is necessary in order to render an indorser liable; but when a place of payment is indicated by way of memorandum only, presentment at that place is sufficient to render the indorser liable, but a presentment to the maker elsewhere, if sufficient in other respects, shall also suffice.

Presentment by post

12–17   **45.—(8) Where authorised by agreement or usage a presentment through the post office is sufficient.**

The section applies to cheques as well as bills and presentment of a cheque may be made by post.[48] The United States Uniform Commercial Code provides, in section 3–504, for such presentment, "in which event the time of presentment is determined by the time of the receipt of the mail."

PRESENTMENT EXCUSED

Delay and dispensation

12–18   The 1882 Act provides for presentment for payment to be excused in one set of circumstances and for such presentment to be dispensed with in five instances. Since in general presentment for payment is not necessary in order to render the acceptor liable,[49] these cases are principally of relevance where it is sought to make the drawer or indorser liable on the bill.

Delay in making presentment or neglect to present may be excused:[50]

46.—(1) Delay in making presentment for payment is excused when the delay is caused by circumstances beyond the control of the holder, and not imputable to his default, misconduct, or negligence. When the cause of delay ceases to operate presentment must be made with reasonable diligence.

By section 47 a bill is dishonoured by non-payment when presentment is excused and the bill is overdue and unpaid; and an immediate right of recourse against the drawer and indorsers accrues to the holder. In view of this it would seem that the normal consequences of dishonour, such as the giving of notice of dishonour, noting, etc. must follow in spite of the fact that section 46 requires presentment for payment with reasonable diligence once the cause of delay ceases to operate. In other words the actual date of presentment does not

---

[48] Presentment for acceptance may be by post (the 1882 Act, s.41(1)(e)); *ante*, para. 11–05.
[49] See s.52(1) and *ante* para. 12–02.
[50] See in this connection *Hamilton Finance Co. Ltd v. Coverley Westray Walbaum & Tosetti Ltd and Portland Finance Co. Ltd* [1969] 1 Lloyd's Rep. 53, 72.

determine the time in which these consequential requirements are to be performed.

Thus delay in presentment has been excused when the place where the bill was made payable was, at the date of maturity, in a state of siege.[51]

Presentment for payment excused

The five instances where presentment for payment is dispensed with are set **12–19**
in section 46(2) of the 1882 Act.

46.—(2) Presentment for payment is dispensed with:

(a) Where, after the exercise of reasonable diligence presentment, as required by this Act, cannot be effected.
    The fact that the holder has reason to believe that the bill will, on presentment, be dishonoured, does not dispense with the necessity for presentment.

This is the first section using the term "dispensed with"; the others are sections 50(2) and 51(9). Sections 41(2), 46(1), 47(1) and 50(1) speak of some duty of the holder being "excused". It is submitted that the two expressions are interchangeable in the present connection.

It has been held that it is not sufficient to prove that the acceptor's or maker's house was closed, but that the holder must go further and show that he had inquired after the acceptor or attempted to find him.[52] An allegation in a statement of claim that bankers, who had issued notes, declined to pay any such notes owing to the failure of the bank, has been held insufficient if there be no further allegation that the notes sued on had in fact been presented for payment.[53] The mere knowledge of an indorser that the instrument will not be met at maturity is not sufficient to excuse presentment in order to charge him[54] nor will a declaration by the acceptor before the maturity of the bill that he will not pay the amount thereof, though made in the drawer's presence, dispense with presentment to the acceptor, or notice of dishonour to the drawer.[55]

---

[51] *Patience v. Townley* (1805) 2 Smith 223. By the Bills of Exchange Act 1914, the presentment of bills payable outside the British Islands was excused if the delay was caused, directly or indirectly, by circumstances arising out of the 1914–18 War.

[52] *Collins v. Butler* (1738) 2 Str. 1087; see also *Sands v. Clarke* (1849) 19 L.J.C.P. 84. In *Hine v. Allely* (1833) 4 B. & Ad. 624, there was in fact a presentment at the empty house, but there was none in the two former cases. Where a cheque was drawn on Amsterdam which was in German occupation, it was held that the holder was relieved from the obligation to present, since such presentment had been rendered impossible (*Cornelius v. Banque Franco-Serbe* [1942] 1 K.B. 29).

[53] *Bowes v. Howe* (1813) 5 Taunt. 30. If instead of being presented, the notes had been returned in due time to the person from whom they had been received, that might possibly, it has been stated, be considered equivalent to presentment; see *Rogers v. Langford* (1833) 1 Cr. & M. 637, 641. Such a course was directly approved in *Turner v. Stones* (1843) 1 D. & L. 122. The return must be within a reasonable time (*Camidge v. Allenby* (1827) 6 B. & C. 373); or notice be given (*Robson v. Oliver* (1847) 10 Q.B. 704).

[54] *Nicholson v. Gouthit* (1796) 2 H.Bl. 610; see *Esdaile v. Sowerby* (1809) 11 East 114; *Lafitte v. Slatter* (1830) 6 Bing. 623 (Notice of dishonour).

[55] *Ex p. Bignold* (1836) 1 Deac. 712.

Drawee a fictitious person

12-20   Presentment is dispensed with:

46.—(2) (b) Where the drawee is a fictitious person.

In this case the provisions relating to presentment for acceptance[56] and to presentment for payment are identical, since presentment is excused in both cases.

Dispensation as regards the drawer

12-21   Presentment is dispensed with:

46.—(2)(c) As regards the drawer where the drawee or acceptor is not bound, as between himself and the drawer, to accept or pay the bill, and the drawer has no reason to believe that the bill would be paid if presented.

If the drawer has no effects in the hands of the drawee at the time of the drawing and at the time of the maturity of the bill he is not entitled to demand presentment.[57] But, there is a distinction between this provision and the corresponding provision in section 50(2)(c),[58] dispensing with notice of dishonour. The drawer is not entitled to notice of dishonour if the drawee or acceptor, as between himself and the drawer, is under no obligation to pay. On the other hand, to entitle the drawer to have the bill presented, the existence of an obligation to pay is not essential. Thus, where the holder was informed by the drawee that he had no effects of the drawer's in his hands, but that they would probably be supplied, and the drawer subsequently informed the holder that he would endeavour to provide effects, the drawer was held entitled to presentment.[59]

As regards the indorser

12-22   Presentment is also dispensed with:

46.—(2)(d) As regards an indorser, where the bill was accepted or made for the accommodation of that indorser, and he has no reason to expect that the bill would be paid if presented.

As in the case of the drawer, the right of the indorser to require presentment for payment, as distinguished from notice of dishonour, is dependent on his

---

[56] s.41(2)(a), *ante*, para. 11–06.
[57] *Terry v. Parker* (1837) 6 A. & E. 502; *Wirth v. Austin* (1875) L.R. 10 C.P. 689 (cheque); see also *Saule v. Jones* 1 E. & E. 59.
[58] *Post*, para. 15–34.
[59] *Prideaux v. Collier* (1817) 2 Stark. 57. Where an order was, to the knowledge of the holders, given by the drawers to the drawees not to pay the bill if presented, it was held that notice of dishonour was thereby excused, but otherwise as to presentment for payment (*Hill v. Heap* (1823) Dow. & Ry.N.P. 57).

reasonable expectation that the bill will be met, where the bill is for his accommodation. Otherwise, apart from this question of reasonable expectation, notice of dishonour is more freely excused under the provisions of section 50(2)(c) and (d)[60] than is presentment for payment under the above provisions.

Waiver of presentment

Presentment may be excused: **12–23**

46.—(2)(e) By waiver of presentment, express or implied.

There may be an express waiver by stipulation inserted in the bill—see section 16(2).[61]

An implied waiver would be gathered from the conduct of the party, as when a man with notice of the failure or undue delay in presentment[62] promises to pay the bill, or makes or promises to make a partial payment on account.[63] The defendant's part payment or promise to pay, after the bill or note is due, is prima facie evidence of presentment.[64] In *Barclays Bank v. Bank of England*,[65] an arbitration award of Bingham J., it was argued that bank customers who drew cheques impliedly waived the need for presentment of the cheques at the drawee branch, such that presentment took place at the clearing house. Bingham J., as arbitrator, held that in order to establish a waiver it must be shown (1) that the participating banks had expressly or impliedly agreed to treat delivery at the clearing house as equivalent to presentment and (2) that the customer knew of and expressly or impliedly assented to this arrangement. Neither of those requirements was fulfilled. In particular, only the strongest evidence of assent by the drawer would have sufficed to deprive the customer of his statutory right under section 45 of the 1882 Act to due presentment.

Neglect to present does not discharge a man who guarantees the due payment of a bill or note;[66] and where a man became guarantor for the vendee

---

[60] *Post*, para. 15–42.

[61] *Post*, para. 17–29.

[62] No waiver is to be implied in the absence of notice (*Keith v. Burke* (1885) Cab. & E. 551, where the drawer who did not know that the bill had not been presented wrote a letter admitting liability).

[63] *Vaughan v. Fuller* (1746) 2 Stra. 1246; *Hopley v. Dufresne* (1812) 15 East 275; *Hodge v. Fillis* (1813) 3 Camp. 462, 465. Where a note was not presented for payment and the maker stated in cross-examination that he would not have paid even if it had been presented, such statement was held not to constitute a waiver (*De Beer v. Kaschula* [1917] E.D.L. 258). Part payment after due (*Netherlands Bank v. Scholchauer* [1903] 1 T.S. 180), or payment of interest (*Newman v. Browne* [1925] 1 D.L.R. 676) acts as waiver.

[64] *Lundie v. Robertson* (1806) 7 East 231; *Greenway v. Hindley* (1814) 4 Camp. 52; *Croxon v. Worthen* (1839) 5 M. & W. 5.

[65] [1985] 1 All E.R. 385:

[66] *Hitchock v. Humfrey* (1843) 5 M. & G. 559; *Walton v. Maskell* (1844) 14 L.J. Ex. 54. Nor is a guarantor entitled in general to notice of dishonour; but when by custom it is usual to guarantee, instead of indorsing bills, the party guaranteeing is, as regards his rights against the acceptor, in much the same position as an indorser (*Ex p. Bishop* (1880) 15 Ch.D. 400); and consequently may well be entitled to expect due presentment, and perhaps, too, notice of dishonour.

of goods, who accepted a bill for the amount and then became bankrupt, the notorious insolvency of the vendee was held to excuse the drawer's presentment, so as to enable him to charge the guarantor without, unless it could be shown that the bill would have been paid if duly presented, though it would have been otherwise in an action on the bill.[67]

Presentment for payment supra protest

12–24   A bill which in accordance with the provisions of section 65[68] has been accepted supra protest, or contains the name of a referee in case of need,[69] must be presented for payment in accordance with the following provisions:

67.—(1) Where a dishonoured bill has been accepted for honour supra protest, or contains a reference in case of need, it must be protested for non-payment before it is presented for payment to the acceptor for honour, or referee in case of need.

(2) Where the address of the acceptor for honour is in the same place where the bill is protested for non-payment, the bill must be presented to him not later than the day following its maturity; and where the address of the acceptor for honour is in some place other than the place where it was protested for non-payment, the bill must be forwarded not later than the day following its maturity for presentment to him.

(3) Delay in presentment or non-presentment is excused by any circumstance which would excuse delay in presentment for payment or non-presentment for payment.

Dishonour by non-payment

12–25   Where a bill is duly met by the acceptor, being the party principally liable on a bill, the bill is discharged.[70] Section 47 of the 1882 Act sets out when a bill is dishonoured for non-payment and the consequences.

47.—(1) A bill is dishonoured by non-payment (a) when it is duly presented for payment and payment is refused or cannot be obtained, or (b) when presentment is excused and the bill is overdue and unpaid.

Strictly payment in this context is in money (*i.e.* legal tender), unless otherwise agreed; although commonly settlement is made between banks by the cash equivalent being credited to the holder's account. However payment cannot be met by the provision of a cheque or draft, unless the holder consents. Furthermore there must be payment in full.

---

[67] *Warrington v. Furbor* (1807) 8 East 242; *Smith v. Bank of New South Wales* (1872) L.R. 4 P.C. 194.

[68] See *ante*, para. 10–11.

[69] Section 15, *ante*, para. 10–12.

[70] See Chs. 13 and 14, *post*.

The holder's rights consequent upon a bill being dishonoured for non-payment are as follows:

(2) Subject to the provisions of this Act,[71] when a bill is dishonoured by non-payment, an immediate right of recourse against the drawer and indorsers accrues to the holder.

A right of recourse does not mean an immediate right of action.[72] The right accruing to the holder is the entitlement to give the drawer and indorsers notice of dishonour.[73] The holder's right of action against the drawer and indorsers arises once notice of dishonour has been received (or is excused[74]); and where appropriate any necessary protesting of the bill.[75]

---

[71] The other provisions seems to be ss.48 and 51 as to notice of dishonour and protest necessary to preserve that right or recourse; and s.15 and ss.65–68 as to a referee in case of need, and acceptance and payment for honour.

[72] *Kennedy v. Thomas* [1894] 2 Q.B. 759, *per* Davey L.J., p. 765: "In my opinion, s.47 means only that the holder of the bill may, immediately upon payment being refused by the acceptor, give notice to the drawer and the indorsers, telling them that he shall hold them liable upon it. But they, as well as the acceptor, still have the whole of the last day of grace in which to pay the bill, and, if it is not paid before the end of that day, the holder's right of action against them becomes complete." See also *Gelmini v. Moriggia* [1913] 2 K.B. 549, *per* Channell J., p. 552: " . . . in all cases of contract the person who has to pay has the whole of the day upon which payment is due in which to pay".

[73] See *post* paras 15–01 *et seq.*

[74] See *post* paras 15–30 *et seq.*

[75] See *post* paras 16–01 *et seq.*

CHAPTER 13

DISCHARGE—I

13–01   THE 1882 Act, itself, sets out five instances where a bill is discharged:

(1) Section 59(1)—Payment in due course;

(2) Section 61—Where the acceptor of a bill is, at maturity, the holder;

(3) Section 62—Where the holder renounces his rights;

(4) Section 63—Where the bill is cancelled by the holder;

(5) Section 68(5)—Where a bill has been paid for honour.

13–02   However since the 1882 Act expressly preserves the rules as to the common law and law merchant[1] the rights of the holder against parties to a bill may be satisfied or affected in other ways. In addition section 64(1) of the 1882 Act provides that where a bill is materially altered without the assent of all parties, the bill is avoided except as against the party responsible for the alteration and subsequent indorsers.[2]

This chapter focuses upon payment and consequently deals with Section 59(1) and 68(5) of the 1882 Act. Chapter 14 (*post*) addresses other instances of discharge.

PAYMENT IN DUE COURSE

13–03   In relation to payment the 1882 Act provides as follows:

59.—(1) A bill is discharged by payment in due course by or on behalf of the drawee or acceptor.

"Payment in due course" means payment made at or after the maturity of the bill to the holder thereof in good faith and without notice that his title to the bill is defective.[3]

What amounts to payment

13–04   Section 3(1) of the 1882 Act stipulates that what is to be paid is a sum certain in money. A plea of payment of a bill should be supported by proof of payment in money, and not merely by proof of a satisfaction of it by an agreement.[4] If payment otherwise than in money is alleged, it must be proved

---

[1] See s.97(2).

[2] See Ch. 20, *post*, para. 20–2.

[3] See "holder" defined, s.2. As to defects in title, see s.29(2), *post*, para. 18–22.

[4] *Morley v. Culverwell* (1840) 7 M. & W. 174, 183 (Parke B.); see s.83(1) of the 1882 Act for promissory notes, *post*, para. 24–01.

that the party to whom such payment was made elected to treat a payment in that form as equivalent to a payment in money.[5] Thus if bonds are accepted in payment, the payment is good though they prove to be valueless.[6] A cheque is normally conditional payment, the debt reviving on its dishonour.[7]

A set-off does not amount to payment, unless it is mutually agreed that one **13–05** demand shall be set off against the other; such an agreement amounts to payment.[8] Credit given to the holder of a bill by the party ultimately liable is tantamount to payment.[9] Where a banker takes from a customer and his surety a promissory note, intended to secure a running balance, and makes advances on the faith of the note, it is not discharged by subsequent unappropriated repayments made by the customer to the banker, but still continues as a security for the existing balance.[10]

There are circumstances in which a legacy by a debtor to his creditor, of **13–06** equal or greater amount than the debt, will be considered a satisfaction of the debt. But a legacy to the holder of a negotiable bill or note can never be considered as a satisfaction of the debt, on that instrument. For a legacy is a satisfaction when it may be presumed to have been the intention of the testator that it should so operate; but that cannot be presumed when, from the assignable nature of the debt the testator could not tell whether or not the legatee was at the time of the bequest his creditor.[11]

To whom should payment be made

Payment should be made to the holder of the bill; the holder being the payee **13–07** or indorsee of a bill who is in possession of it, or the bearer thereof.[12] Payment to any other party is no discharge to the acceptor, unless the money paid finds its way into the holder's hands, and the holder has treated it as received in liquidation of the bill. A drew bills upon the defendant, which the defendant accepted; A then indorsed them to the plaintiffs, his bankers, who entered them to the credit of his account, and at maturity presented them to the defendant for payment and they were dishonoured. The plaintiffs then debited A with the amount, but did not return him the bills. A few days afterwards the defendant paid the amount to A; A still continued his banking account with the plaintiffs, and at different times paid in more money than was sufficient to cover the amount of the bills and all the preceding items which stood above it in the account, though there was always a balance against him larger than the amount of the bills. A failed, and the plaintiffs proved for the whole of their balance under his commission. They then brought this action on the bill against the defendant, the acceptor. Best C.J. held that, on the principle

[5] cf. Camidge v. Allenby (1827) 6 B. & C. 373; Lichfield Union Guardians v. Green (1857) 26 L.J. Ex. 140.

[6] Schroder's Case (1870) L.R. 11 Eq. 131.

[7] See Ch. 31, post, para. 31–01.

[8] Callander v. Howard (1850) 19 L.J.C.P. 312.

[9] Atkins v. Owen (1834) 4 Nev. & M. 123; Bell v. Buckley (1856) 11 Exch. 631.

[10] Pease v. Hirst (1829) 10 B. & C. 122. For an instance where a promissory note is given in respect of the banking account of a partnership where the business is transferred to a limited company, see Bank of Nova Scotia v. Radocsay (1981) 3 O.R. (2d) 785 Can.

[11] Carr v. Eastabrooke (1797) 3 Ves. 561.

[12] See s.2(1) of the 1882 Act.

established in *Clayton's case*,[13] the payment to A would not of itself have discharged the defendant, the plaintiffs having been at that time the holders, and entitled to the amount of the bills, but that the ground on which the defendant was discharged was that the plaintiffs not only entered the bills to the debit of A but treated them as having been paid.[14]

Payment to wrongful holder

13–08   In some cases payment to a wrongful holder is protected; in others it is not. Thus, if a bill or note, payable to bearer either originally or by indorsement in blank, is lost or stolen, a bona fide holder for value without notice may compel payment.[15] Not only is the payment to such a holder protected, but payment to the thief or finder himself will discharge the maker or acceptor,[16] provided that such payment was not made with the knowledge or suspicion of the infirmity of the holder's title, or under circumstances which might reasonably awaken the suspicions of a prudent man. "We may lay it down as a broad general principle that whatever one or two innocent persons must suffer by the acts of a third, he who has enabled such third person to occasion the loss must sustain it."[17] And supposing the equity of the loser and payer precisely equal, there is no reason why the law should interpose to shift the injury from one innocent man to another. But, if such payment is made in suspicious circumstances, or without reasonable caution, or out of the usual course of business, it will not as between all parties and for all purposes discharge the payer.[18] Payment before the bill or note is due or long after it is due or, in case of a cheque, long after it is drawn, or where marks of cancellation are on the instrument, are examples of payment out of the usual course of business.

13–09   Therefore, though a cheque be really drawn by a banker's customer, but torn in pieces before circulation by the drawer, with intention of destroying it, and a stranger, picking up the pieces, pastes them together, and presents the cheque soiled and so joined together to the banker, and he pays it, the banker cannot charge his customer with his payment, for the instrument was cancelled, and carried with it reasonable notice that it had been cancelled.[19] On the other hand, it is not out of the usual course of business for a banker, as

---

[13] *Clayton's case* (1816) 1 Mer. 572.

[14] *Field v. Carr* (1828) 5 Bing. 13. Where money is paid into a bank on the joint account of persons not partners in trade, the bankers are not discharged by the payment to one of those persons of the amount of a cheque drawn by him without the authority of the others (*Innes v. Stephenson* (1831) 1 Mood. & R. 145); but see the case of one executor forging the signature of another and obtaining payment, though the Court found that the bank obtained no discharge: *Brewer v. Westminster Bank Ltd* [1952] 2 All E.R. 650. But where one of three assignees in bankruptcy absconded, the Court ordered the bank to honour the cheques of the other two (*Ex p. Hunter* (1816) 2 Rose 363). And *cf. Midland Bank Ltd v. Harris* [1963] 1 W.L.R. 1021 as to return of dishonoured cheque to the customer for whom collected; and *Westminster Bank Ltd v. Zang* [1966] A.C. 182. See however, *Catlin v. Cyprus Finance Corporation* [1983] 1 All E.R. 809 not following *Brewer v. Westminster Bank*.

[15] The conviction of the thief does not divest the title of the holder in due course (*Chichester v. Hill* (1882) 52 L.J.Q.B. 160); see *post*, para. 18–20.

[16] *Smith v. Sheppard* (1776) cited Chitty (11th ed.), p. 278.

[17] *Lickbarrow v. Mason* (1787) 2 T.R. 63, 70.

[18] It has been suggested that more caution is required of a discounter than of a payer (*Snow v. Peacock* (1825) 2 C. & P. 215, 221 (Best C.J.); *sed quaere*).

[19] *Scholey v. Ramsbottom* (1810) 2 Camp. 485.

agent for a customer, to pay an instrument payable to bearer, such as a bill indorsed in blank over the counter, even though the instrument is for a large sum. Such presentment, though unusual, is nevertheless by the law merchant due presentment sufficient to require the banker to pay, in the absence of very special circumstances of suspicion, as where, possibly, presentment is by a tramp, postman or office boy.[20] Consequently, the instrument is discharged by the payment and no action is maintainable by the true owner of the instrument against the banker since he paid it in good faith and without notice of any defect in title and in accordance with the law merchant.[21]

If the bill or note is not payable to bearer, but transferable by indorsement only, and is paid to a party whose title is made through the forged instrument, the payer is not discharged unless the case falls within section 60 or section 80 of the 1882 Act, section 19 of the Stamp Act 1853 or section 1 of the Cheques Act 1957.[22]   **13–10**

A bill is not discharged and finally extinguished, until paid by or on behalf of the acceptor; nor a note until paid by or on behalf of the maker.   **13–11**

Payment by drawer or indorser

Payment by the drawer or indorser does not operate as a discharge. The reason for this is because payment by such parties is of a secondary liability and thus the bill must remain live so as to permit them to exercise their rights of recourse to or against the party primarily liable. The 1882 Act provides: **13–12**

59.—(2) Subject to the provisions hereinafter contained, when a bill is paid by the drawer or an indorser it is not discharged[23] but

(a) **Where a bill payable to, or to the order of, a third party is paid by the drawer, the drawer may enforce payment thereof against the acceptor, but may not reissue the bill.**

(b) **Where a bill is paid by an indorser, or where a bill payable to drawer's order is paid by the drawer, the party paying it is remitted to his former rights as regards the acceptor or antecedent parties, and he may, if he thinks fit, strike out his own and subsequent indorsements, and again negotiate the bill.**

Hence, it is no defence to an action by the holder against the acceptor that the holder has been paid by the drawer.[24]

---

[20] See *per* Wright J. in *Auchteroni & Company v. Midland Bank Ltd* [1928] 2 K.B. 294, 304.

[21] *Auchteroni & Co. v. Midland Bank*, *supra* at 294.

[22] See *post*, paras 22–33 *et seq.* In *Banque de l'Indo Chine et de la Suez S.A. v. J. H. Rayner (Mincing Lane) Ltd* [1983] Q.B. 711, payment under a letter of credit made under reserve was held reversible if the contingency envisaged came about.

[23] For the provisions hereinafter contained, see subs. (3), *post*, para. 13–19.

[24] *Brown, Janson & Co. v. Cama & Co.* (1890) 6 T.L.R. 250, in which the plaintiffs, who had discounted the bill, debited it to the account of the drawer upon dishonour, but retained the bill. The argument of the defendant that *Clayton's case* applied and that the drawer's debt had been paid by subsequent payments to his account with the plaintiffs was denied.

Payment before maturity

13–13   If a bill or note is paid before it is due and is afterwards indorsed over, it is a valid security in the hands of a bona fide indorsee. "I agree", says Lord Ellenborough, "that a bill paid at maturity cannot be reissued, and that no action can afterwards be maintained upon it by a subsequent indorsee. A payment before it becomes due, however, I think, does not extinguish it any more than if it were merely discounted. A contrary doctrine would add a new clog to the circulation of bills and notes; for it would be impossible to know whether there had not been an anticipated payment of them. It is the duty of bankers to make some memorandum on bills and notes which have been paid; but if they do not, the holders of such securities cannot be affected by a payment made before they are due."[25]

Striking out indorsements

13–14   The claimant may strike out an intervening indorsement which is not necessary to his title, even after the bill has been produced in evidence and the objection taken;[26] thus in Canada it has been held that an indorsement to a bank for collection may be struck out.[27] An indorsement struck out by mistake will not affect the rights of the parties.[28]

Payment or transfer?

13–15   A question sometimes arises whether a bill has been paid or transferred. Though the holder gives to a person taking up the bill a general receipt, importing that he has received payment, evidence is admissible to show that the person taking up the bill paid the money, not as agent for the acceptor or drawer, but as indorsee.[29]

Reissue of bill

13–16   Until a bill or note has been paid in due course as provided for by section 59(1),[30] it may be reissued as provided for by section 59(2). As to reissue, the 1882 Act further provides that:

37. Where a bill is negotiated back to the drawer, or to a prior indorser or to the acceptor, such party may, subject to the provisions of this Act, reissue and further negotiate the bill, but he is not entitled to enforce

---

[25] *Burbridge v. Manners* (1812) 3 Camp. 193, 195; *Attenborough v. Mackenzie* (1856) 25 L.J. Exch. 244.

[26] *Mayer v. Jadis* (1833) 1 Moo. & R. 247.

[27] *Rat Portage Lumber Co. v. Margulius* (1914) 16 D.L.R. 477; 15 D.L.R. 577; *Johnson v. L'Heureux* (1914) 27 W.L.R. 21; see also *Roos v. De Wit* [1927] O.P.D. 301.

[28] *Wilkinson v. Johnson* (1834) 3 B. & Co. 428.

[29] *Graves v. Key* (1832) 3 B. & Ad. 313. There is no obligation on the party paying to inform the holder in what capacity he pays (*Pollard v. Ogden* (1853) 2 E. & B. 459).

[30] *Ante*, para. 13–01.

payment of the bill against any intervening party to whom he was previously liable.[31]

Reissue to previous indorser

If a bill is reindorsed to a previous indorser he has, in general, no remedy **13–17** against the intermediate parties, for they would have their remedy over against him, and the result of the actions would be to place the parties in precisely the same situation as before any action at all.[32] But where a holder has previously indorsed, and the subsequent intermediate indorser has no right of action or remedy on that previous indorsement against the holder, there are cases in which the holder may sue the intermediate indorser.[33] It is advisable, where the claim is doubtful, to state all the indorsements and claim as first indorsee and alternatively as indorsee by reindorsement.

Part payment

It was once an unsettled question whether payment in part or in full by the **13–18** drawer to the holder would discharge the acceptor *pro tanto*, or whether the holder might, nevertheless, recover the whole amount from the acceptor, and hold the equivalent of the amount received from the drawer as money received of the acceptor to the drawer's use.[34] Section 59(2) expressly provides for the case of payment in full by a drawer or indorser, but does not deal with the case of part payment. In the event, however, of a bill remaining in the hands of a holder after a payment in part or in full by the drawer or an indorser, there can now be little doubt but that the holder can sue the acceptor for the entire amount, holding in trust for the party who has so paid the amount of his payment,[35] and any defence or set-off open to the acceptor against the party who has so paid is available against the holder.[36] The party paying may, it

---

[31] *Hubbard v. Jackson* (1827) 4 Bing. 390. The other provisions seem to be ss.59 to 64; and see *Jade International Steel Stahl und Eisen GmbH & Co. KG v. Robert Nicholas (Steels) Ltd* [1978] 3 W.L.R. 39.

[32] *Bishop v. Hayward* (1791) 4 T.R. 470; *Britten v. Webb* (1824) 2 B. & C. 483. The passage in the text was approved in *Wilkinson v. Unwin* (1881) 7 Q.B.D. 636.

[33] *Wilders v. Stevens* (1846) 15 L.J.Exch. 108; *Williams v. Clarke* (1847) 16 M. & M. 834; *Smith v. Marsack* (1848) 18 L.J.C.P. 65; *Morris v. Walker* (1850) 19 L.J.Q.B. 400, followed in *Watson v. Harvey* (1894) 10 Man.R. 641 and *Wells v. McCarthy* (1895) *ibid.* 639; *Wilkinson v. Unwin, supra,* followed in *Glenie v. Bruce Smith,* as reported [1907] 2 K.B. 507 (cited in *McCall v. Hargreaves* [1932] 2 K.B. 423, 430, "the bills must be regarded as indorsed by the plaintiffs to the defendant and reindorsed by him to them", *per* Goddard J.); *Re Gooch* [1921] 2 K.B. 593; see also *Holmes v. Durkee* (1883) Cab. & E. 23.

[34] In *Johnson v. Kennion* (1765) 2 Wils. 262, recognised in *Walwyn v. St. Quintin* (1797) 1 B. & P. 652, it was held that the holder was entitled to recover the whole amount; but in *Bacon v. Searles* (1788) 1 H.Bl. 88, it was considered that he could recover only the difference; see also *Hemming v. Brook* (1841) Car. & M. 57.

[35] *Jones v. Broadhurst* (1850) 9 C.B. 173, overruling on this point *Bacon v. Searles, supra*; and see *Cook v. Lister* (1863) 32 L.J.C.P. 121, 127 (Willes J.): *Agra and Masterman's Bank v. Leighton* (1866) L.R. 2 Ex. 56; *Morrison v. Margolius and Hamilton* (1914) 28 W.L.R. 508; and see s.52(4), *Barclays Bank Ltd v. Aschaffenburger Zellstoffwerke A.G.* [1967] 1 Lloyd's Rep. 387.

[36] *Thornton v. Maynard* (1875) L.R. 10 C.P. 695.

seems, leave the bill in the hands of the holder that he may take action thereon.[37]

Payment by party accommodated

13–19   A special exception to the general rule is made by the 1882 Act in the case of accommodation bills. An accommodation bill is discharged as follows:

59.—(3) Where an accommodation bill is paid in due course by the party accommodated the bill is discharged.

If a bill is paid when due by the person ultimately liable upon it, the party accommodated, it has done its work and is no longer a negotiable instrument.[38]

Payment by other persons

13–20   Payment to the creditor by a stranger of the amount of the bill must be made for and on account of the debt and with the prior authority or subsequent ratification of the debtor.[39] Payment by a stranger of the amount of a bill to the bankers at whose house the bill is made payable by the acceptor, the party obtaining possession of the bill for a collateral purpose of his own, is not a payment by the acceptor.[40]

Time for payment

13–21   The acceptor has the whole of the day on which the bill becomes due to make payment.[41] If in the course of that day the acceptor refuses payment, which refusal entitles the holder to give notice of dishonour, but subsequently, on the same day, makes payment, the payment is good, and the notice of dishonour becomes of no avail.[42]

---

[37] *Williams v. James* (1850) 19 L.J.Q.B. 445. The party paying in full may, of course, demand delivery of the bill up to him under s.52(4), *post*. Where an indorser paid the holder part of the amount of the bill, it was held that he might recover the same from the acceptor as money paid to his use (*Pownal v. Ferrand* (1827) 6 B. & C. 439).

[38] *Lazarus v. Cowie* (1842) 3 Q.B. 459, hence the party accommodated cannot sue the acceptor (*Solomon v. Davis* (1883) 1 Cab. & E. 83). For a definition of an accommodation party, see s.28(1), *post*, para. 19–38. Where a note payable on demand was given as security for a debt owing by the maker, and on payment of that debt the note was redelivered to the maker, it was held that the maker could not subsequently reissue the note (*Bartrum v. Caddy* (1838) 9 A. & E. 275; *Meakins v. Martin* (1895) Q.R. 8 S.C. 522).

[39] *Belshaw v. Bush* (1851) 11 C.B. 191; *Kemp v. Balls* (1854) 10 Ex. 607; *Simpson v. Eggington* (1855) 10 Ex. 845; *Re Rowe* [1904] 2 K.B. 483. The assent of the debtor ought, it has been stated, to be presumed (*Cook v. Lister* (1863) 32 L.J.C.P. 121, 127). The payment may be ratified by pleading payment (*Walter v. James* (1871) L.R. 6 Ex. 124, 127).

[40] *Deacon v. Stodhart* (1841) 2 M. & G. 317; *Thomas v. Fenton* (1847) 5 D. & L. 28.

[41] As to the date of maturity of a bill, see *ante*, para. 2–14.

[42] *Hartley v. Case* (1825) 1 C. & P. 555. At that date no action lay until the days of grace had expired (*Wells v. Giles* (1836) 2 Gale 209; *Kennedy v. Thomas* [1894] 2 Q.B. 759 approving the passage in the text); see the Banking and Financial Dealings Act 1971, s.3(2) which abolished days of grace.

Subsequent tender

In the past it has been said that a plea of tender[43] by the acceptor after the   **13–22**
day of payment is insufficient.[44] However that would appear to be no longer
the case under the CPR. In the notes to Part 16, Rule 5 it is stated that the
defence of tender may be raised to any money claim, whether or not a
specified amount is claimed. In order to avail himself of the defence the
defendant must make a payment into court of the amount which was tendered.[45] In the glossary to the CPR the defence of tender before claim is
defined as follows:

> "A defence that, before the claimant started proceedings, the defendant uncondition-
> ally offered to the claimant the amount due or, if no specified amount is claimed, an
> amount sufficient to satisfy the claim."

However, it is suggested that for the defence of tender to be operative the
appropriate amount would have to be tendered and in a form which amounted
to actual payment. Under section 57(1) of the 1882 Act the holder is entitled
to recover not merely the amount of the bill, but interest from the date of
demand, or maturity, whichever is applicable, together with the expenses of
noting and, where necessary, protesting.[46] For there to be a proper tender such
amounts would have to be unconditionally offered in money or its equivalent.[47] A payment after action brought will not prevent the holder from
proceeding for his costs.[48]

Payment before maturity

A payment before maturity does not, by the 1882 Act, discharge a bill.[49]   **13–23**
Payment in due course is made referable to payment "at or after maturity".
The payment of a bill by the acceptor or drawee prior to maturity operates
merely as purchase or discount, and it remains in a negotiable state.[50]

Delivery up

If the bill be paid, the payer has a right to insist on its being delivered up   **13–24**
to him in accordance with the following provision:

**52.—(4) Where the holder of a bill presents it for payment, he shall
exhibit the bill to the person from whom he demands payment, and when**

---

[43] In *Beaumont v. Greathead* (1846) 2 C.B. 494, it appears to have been held that a party to
whom payment of a note had been made some time after maturity was not necessarily entitled to
nominal damages for the detention of the money.

[44] *Hume v. Peploe* (1807) 8 East 168.

[45] See Part 37, Rule 3 of the CPR.

[46] See further Ch. 16.

[47] In this context the proffering of another bill or cheque would not be sufficient.

[48] *Toms v. Powell* (1806) 7 East 536. See Part 45.1 CPR for a parties entitlement to fixed
costs.

[49] *Ante*, para. 13–01.

[50] See *Burridge v. Manners* (1812) 3 Camp. 193 at 195.

the bill is paid the holder shall forthwith deliver it up to the party paying it.[51]

In general the subsection applies to cheques[52] and promissory notes,[53] although in practice most banks do not return cheques to their customers. Where a cheque is presented through electronic means pursuant to section 74A of the 1882 Act,[54] the requirements of section 52(4) are expressly disapplied by section 74C of the 1882 Act.[55]

Receipt on payment

13–25   A receipt on the back of a bill imports, prima facie, that it has been paid by the acceptor.[56] In relation to cheques, the Cheques Act 1957, as amended, provides in section 3, that:

"(1) An unindorsed cheque which appears to have been paid by the banker on whom it is drawn is evidence of the receipt of the payee of the sum payable by the cheque.

(2) For the purposes of subsection (1) above, a copy of a cheque to which that subsection applies is evidence of the cheque if—

(a) the copy is made by the banker in whose possession the cheque is after presentment and,

(b) it is certified by him to be a true copy of the original."[57]

The consequence of subsection 3(2) of the 1957 Act is that banks do not have to retain physically those cheques which they have paid; in practice they maintain microfiche copies of such cheques and the added subsection gives statutory recognition to this practice.

When payment is to be deemed complete

13–26   Money laid down on the counter by a banker's cashier in payment of a cheque cannot be recovered back by action, though it was handed over under a misapprehension of the state of the drawer's account; still less can it be taken back by force from the party receiving it.[58] A banker's counter is in the

---

[51] *Alexander v. Strong* (1842) 9 M. & W. 733; *Cornes v. Taylor* (1854) 10 Ex. 441. But where the bill or note is not negotiable the party paying cannot refuse to pay it until it is delivered up (*Wain v. Bailey* (1839) 10 A. & E. 616).

[52] Section 73.

[53] Section 89(1).

[54] Inserted by the Deregulation (Bills Of Exchange) Order 1996, S.I. 1996 No. 2993, art 4.

[55] See note 51 above.

[56] *Scholey v. Walsby* (1791) 1 Peake 34, 35; *Graves v. Key* (1832) 3 B. & Ad. 313, 318.

[57] The existing provision was renumbered as s.(1) and s.(2) added by the Deregulation (Bills of Exchange) Order 1996, S.I. 1996 No. 2993, art. 5.

[58] *Chambers v. Miller* (1862) 32 L.J.C.P. 30. A cheque given by one bank to another for the aggregate amount of acceptances payable at it on a given day is not provisional, and if a bill that has not been provided for is included in the amount of the cheque, the payment must stand (*Pollard v. Bank of England* (1871) L.R. 6 Q.B. 623).

nature of a neutral table, provided for the use of both banker and customer. As soon as the money is laid down by the banker upon the customer's side of the counter to be taken up by the receiver, the payment is complete.[59]

PAYMENT FOR HONOUR

A bill may be paid for honour supra protest[60]

Payment for honour is rarely encountered in practice in modern times. **13–27** Anyone may make payment for honour as provided by the 1882 Act:

68.—(1) Where a bill has been protested for non-payment, any person may intervene and pay it supra protest for the honour of any party liable thereon, or for the honour of the person for whose account the bill is drawn.

A distinction is to be noted between this subsection and subsection (1) of section 65,[61] since, in accordance with the latter provision, a bill can only be accepted for honour by a person not already liable thereon. There is no similar limitation in the case of payment for honour. Any party to a bill, whether drawer, drawee, payee, referee in case of need, or any stranger with or without a previous request from the party for whose honour he pays, may intervene and pay supra protest.

Further, it is provided that:

68.—(2) Where two or more persons offer to pay a bill for the honour of different parties, the person whose payment will discharge most parties to the bill shall have the preference.

Attestation

In order not to operate as a voluntary payment the 1882 Act requires a **13–28** notarial act of honour:

68.—(3) Payment for honour supra protest, in order to operate as such and not as a mere voluntary payment, must be attested by a notarial act

[59] *Chambers v. Miller, supra.* Where the money was seized by the sheriff under an execution before the payee could take it up from the bank counter, it was held a good seizure (*Hall v. Hatch* (1901) 3 O.L.R. 147). Where a "banker's payment", *i.e.* an order by one bank to another to pay the drawer (through the clearing house), was returned by the payee bank to the bank giving it, on a representation that it was given in error, and was never converted into cash, such payment was held not to have discharged the bill (*London Banking Co. v. Horsnail* (1898) 14 T.L.R. 266; 3 Com.Cas. 105). For the time for the completion of payment with reference to the transfer of money, see *The Brimnes* (1975) 1 Q.B. 929; *Delbrueck & Co. v. Barclays Bank International Ltd* [1976] 2 Lloyd's Rep. 341 (*sub nom. Momm v. Barclays Bank Ltd*); *The Laconia* [1977] 1 Lloyd's Rep. 315; *The Chikuma* [1981] 1 All E.R. 652. *Chambers v. Miller* is the subject of explanation and variation in *Barclays Bank Ltd v. Simms, Son & Cooke (Southern) Ltd and Another* [1980] Q.B. 677.

[60] As regards acceptance for honour supra protest, see s.65, *ante*, para. 10–11, and presentment for payment for honour supra protest, s.67, *ante*, para. 12–21.

[61] *Ante*, para. 10–11.

of honour which may be appended to the protest or form an extension of it.

(4) The notarial act of honour must be founded on a declaration made by the payer for honour, or his agent in that behalf, declaring his intention to pay the bill for honour, and for whose honour he pays.

Hence there cannot be a payment for honour, even by a referee in case of need, without protest and the notarial declaration appended to it, and a would-be payer for honour failing to comply with these formalities would be simply in the position of an indorsee of an overdue or dishonoured bill to which all defects of title affecting it at maturity attach as against him.[62]

Consequences of payment for honour

13–29   Where a bill has been paid for honour, all parties subsequent to the party for whose honour it is paid are discharged.[63] The payer for honour, though, succeeds to the rights and duties of the holder as regards the party for whose honour he pays it. So, for example, if the bill is paid for the honour of the acceptor, the payer for honour can sue the acceptor but the drawer and indorsers are discharged.

---

[62] cf. Ex p. Wyld (1860) 30 L.J. Bk. 10, 13, commenting on Mertens v. Winnington (1794) 1 Esp. 113. For the form of the notarial act of honour, see Brookes' Notary (9th ed., 1939), pp. 255, 265.

[63] S.68(5).

CHAPTER 14

DISCHARGE—II

PAYMENT in due course is, as we have seen,[1] a discharge of the bill or note; **14–01** but at common law the rights of the holder against the acceptor or maker and other parties may be satisfied, extinguished, suspended, or released in other ways beside payment. In addition the 1882 Act contains further provisions that relate to the discharge of an instrument.

Acceptor holder at maturity

A bill is discharged if the acceptor becomes the holder thereof in his own **14–02** right at maturity, since the 1882 Act provides that:

61. When the acceptor of a bill is or becomes the holder of it at or after its maturity, in his own right, the bill is discharged.

The rule is a reflection of the principle that where the rights and liabilities under a contract become vested in the same party, the contract is discharged, since a party cannot sue himself.[2]

On the other hand, a transfer to the acceptor before maturity does not operate as a discharge of the bill, since there cannot be payment by anticipation.[3] If a party pays it before maturity he purchases it, and is in the same situation as if he had discounted it.[4] Discounting the bill is not equivalent to paying it, and if it is transferred to the acceptor he may therefore reissue it, and the drawer and indorsers may become liable to a subsequent holder even with notice.[5]

Common law and law merchant

The rules of the common law, including the law merchant, are, in the **14–03** absence of express provisions to the contrary in the 1882 Act, applicable as heretofore, since it is provided:

97.—(2) The rules of common law including the law merchant, save in so far as they are inconsistent with the express provisions of this Act, shall continue to apply to bills of exchange, promissory notes, and cheques.

[1] See Ch. 13, *ante*, para. 13–1.
[2] See *Chitty on Contracts*, Vol. 1 (25th ed), para. 26–004.
[3] *Burbridge v. Manners* (1812) 3 Camp. 193 at 194.
[4] *Morley v. Culverwell* (1840) 7 M. & W. 174, 182 (Parke B.).
[5] *Harmer v. Steele* (1849) 4 Ex. 1, 13; *Attenborough v. Mackenzie* (1856) 25 L.J. Ex. 244, approving *Morley v. Culverwell* (*supra*); see discounting distinguished from moneylending in *De Villiers v. Roux* [1916] C.P.D. 295. It has been said that in the case of an acceptance for the accommodation of the drawer, the drawer is in the position of the acceptor with regard to the reissue of the bill after payment by the drawer at maturity (*Lazarus v. Cowie* (1842) 3 Q.B. 459); but see *Jewell v. Parr* (1853) 13 C.B. 909.

Satisfaction

14–04   A simple contract may be discharged before breach, without a release and
without satisfaction.[6] But after breach, unless there is a release under seal,
there must be satisfaction.[7] Accord without satisfaction is no plea, and no
action lies on an accord.[8] The accord must be binding in law and, therefore,
either made under seal or supported by consideration.[9]

A satisfaction must be beneficial to the plaintiff.[10] The benefit must be of
a kind which might in law be a good and valuable consideration for any other
sort of agreement not under seal.[11]

Payment by the debtor himself of a sum smaller than the debt is no
satisfaction,[12] unless it is paid at a date earlier than the due date of the whole.[13]
"But a promise to accept a smaller sum in discharge of a larger sum, if acted
upon, is binding notwithstanding the absence of consideration."[14] But it has
been held that a negotiable security may operate, if so given and taken, in
satisfaction of a debt of greater amount, since it is satisfaction in another form,
and the Court will not examine whether satisfaction in some other form be
reasonable, if it be satisfied that the parties in fact came to such agreement.
Moreover, the instrument, being negotiable, may be more advantageous than
the original debt, which was not negotiable.[15] Where a cheque is tendered in
settlement of a claim for a larger amount, it may be retained by the payee as
payment on account. The mere retention of the cheque is not conclusive
evidence of an accord and satisfaction. It is a question of fact, in any case,
whether such a cheque has been retained by the creditor as a payment on
account, or as an accord and satisfaction.[16]

Although a contract by the defendant himself to pay a smaller sum can be
no satisfaction, unless it is negotiable, yet a contract by a third person to do

---

[6] *Dobson v. Espie* (1857) 26 L.J.Ex. 240, where Bramwell J. cites the above passage.

[7] *Foster v. Dawber* (1851) 6 Ex 839. As regards the special provisions relating to bills and
notes, see s.62, *post*, para. 14–08.

[8] *Lynn v. Bruce* (1794) 2 H.Bl. 317, unless another person is party to it (*Henderson v. Stobart*
(1850) 5 Ex. 99).

[9] *Per* Winn L.J. in *D. & C. Builders Ltd v. Rees* [1966] 2 Q.B. 617, 632; *Pinnel's Case* (1602)
5 Co.Rep. 117a applied; and see Cheshire, Fifoot and Furmston, *Law of Contract* (11th ed. 1986)
pp. 551–552.

[10] *Cumber v. Wane* (1718) 1 Stra. 426; 1 Smith L.C., 13th ed., p. 373.

[11] *Foakes v. Beer* (1884) 9 App.Cas. 605, 614 (Lord Selbourne C.).

[12] *Cumber v. Wane, supra; Foakes v. Beer, supra.*

[13] *Smith v. Trowsdale* (1854) 3 E. & B. 83.

[14] *Per* Denning J, in *Central London Property Trust Ltd v. High Trees House Ltd* [1947] 1 K.B.
130, 135; and see *Combe v. Combe* [1951] 2 K.B. 215.

[15] *Sibree v. Tripp* (1846) 15 M. & W. 23, distinguished in *D. & C. Builders Ltd v. Rees* [1966]
2 Q.B. 617. *Goddard v. O'Brien* (1882) 9 Q.B.D. 37, distinguished in *Hirachand Punamchand v.
Temple* [1911] 2 K.B. 330, was not followed in *D. & C. Builders Ltd v. Rees* [1966] 2 Q.B.
617.

[16] *Day v. McLea* (1889) 22 Q.B.D. 610; *Bidder v. Bridges* (1887) 37 Ch.D. 406; *Ackroyd v.
Smithies* (1885) 54 L.T. 130. There appears to be no reason why the sender of a cheque offered
in settlement should not post-date the cheque, and intimate that, unless he hears previous to the
date of the cheque that it is accepted in full settlement, he will stop the cheque. For facts not
constituting an intention to take a cheque by way of accord and satisfaction, see *Nathan v. Ogdens
Ltd* (1905) 93 L.T. 553, affirmed in CA 94 L.T. 126; *Rigg v. Forest* [1913] C.P.D. 350; for the law
in Canada of accord and satisfaction see *Marr's Marine Ltd v. Rosetown Chrysler Plymouth Ltd*
[1976] D.L.R. (3d) 497.

so may be.[17] Thus the taking of a bill from one of the two partners may operate as a satisfaction of the joint debt; for the sole liability of one person may, in some instances, be more advantageous than his liability jointly with another.[18] So also a payment of a smaller sum by a third person not bound by the contract has been held to be a discharge of the whole debt.[19]

Payment of a smaller sum may be a satisfaction, where that smaller sum is the result of an account stated, including cross-demands.[20]

Where a bill or note, on which some person other that the debtor is liable, is expressly given and "accepted"[21] in "full satisfaction and discharge", the liability of the debtor of the original debt will not revive on the dishonour of the substituted instrument.[22] But if it is taken generally on account, or in renewal, the original liability of the debtor revives on its dishonour.[23]

Payment by cheque is conditional payment only, even if acknowledged by the creditor to be in full settlement.[24] The debt revives on the dishonour of the cheque.

Extinguishment or merger

The taking of a coextensive security of a higher nature for a bill or note **14–05** merges the remedy on the inferior instrument. But it must be strictly coextensive. Thus, if a note is joint and several, a deed by one of the makers is not a discharge of the other's promise;[25] nor where the note is in favour of two payees and further security is in favour of one only.[26] If, moreover, the new security recognises the bill or note as still existing it is not extinguished.[27]

A bill indorsed in blank to one of several acceptors, and in his hands when due, cannot be afterwards transferred,[28] so as to confer on the transferee a remedy against any of the acceptors; for there has been that which is an equivalent to the performance of the contract.

Judgment recovered on a bill or note is an extinguishment of the original debt, but not a satisfaction,[29] as between the claimant and the defendant. But judgment, without actual satisfaction, is no extinguishment, as between the claimant and other parties not jointly liable with the original defendant, whether those parties are prior or subsequent to the defendant.[30] Nor is it an

---

[17] *Henderson v. Stobart* (1850) 5 Ex. 99; *Bidder v. Bridges, supra.*

[18] *Thompson v. Percival* (1834) 5 B. & Ad. 925.

[19] *Welby v. Drake* (1825) 1 C. & P. 557; *Hirachand Punamchand v. Temple* [1911] 2 K.B. 330.

[20] *Smith v. Page* (1846) 15 M. & W. 683; *Perry v. Attwood* (1856) 25 L.J.Q.B. 408.

[21] *Hardman v. Bellhouse* (1842) 9 M. & W. 596.

[22] *Sard v. Rhodes* (1836) 1 M. & W. 153.

[23] *cf. Stedman v. Gooch* (1793) 1 Esp. 4, 5; *Kearslake v. Morgan* (1794) 5 T.R. 513, 518, citing Mansfield C.J.; see also *post*, para. 31–01.

[24] *Re Romer and Haslam* [1893] 2 Q.B. 286, 296.

[25] *Ansell v. Baker* (1850) 15 Q.B. 20. *Quaere* as to the effect when the note is joint only; see *King v. Hoare* (1844) 13 M. & W. 494, 496; *Bell v. Banks* (1841) 3 M. & G. 258, 267; *Sharpe v. Gibbs* (1864) 16 C.B. (N.S.) 527.

[26] *Twopenny v. Young* (1824) 3 B. & C. 208.

[27] *ibid.*

[28] *Harmer v. Steele* (1849) 4 Ex. 1, 14; see also the 1882 Act, s.61, *ante*, para. 14–02.

[29] *Drake v. Mitchell* (1803) 3 East 351; *cf. Cruickshank v. Ewington* (1905) 24 N.L.Z.R. 957.

[30] Bayley (6th ed.), p. 335; *Claxton v. Swift* (1685) 2 Show. 441.

extinguishment, as between a party prior to the claimant, to whom the claimant after the judgment returns the bill, and the defendant.[31]

Where one of several joint contractors has given his separate collateral security in respect of the same debt, judgment against him thereon, without satisfaction, is no extinguishment of the joint contract;[32] so also judgment against a joint and several promisor without satisfaction is no extinguishment of the joint promise.[33]

Nor does the issuing of execution against the person or goods of one party to a bill extinguish the plaintiff's remedy against other parties.

Waiving a *fieri facias* against the acceptor has been held to be no bar to execution against the drawer, against whom judgment had also been obtained, for the rule that giving an indulgence discharges the surety does not apply after judgment.[34]

Taking security of a higher nature, such as a deed, though it extinguishes the simple contract debt on the bill, as between the parties to the substitution, has no effect on the liability of the other distinct parties to the bill,[35] providing that it does not give time so as to prejudice the condition of sureties.

Suspension[36]

14–06   If a bill or note is taken on account of a debt and nothing is said at the time, the legal effect of the transaction is that the original debt still remains, but the remedy for it is suspended till maturity of the instrument in the hands of the creditor.[37] This effect of giving the bill has also been described as a conditional payment.[38] It is an exception, but not a solitary one, to the general rule of law that a right of action once suspended by act of the parties is gone for ever.[39] The action for the original debt is equally suspended if the bill or note

---

[31] *Tarleton v. Allhusen* (1834) 2 A. & E. 32, where A, payee of a bill accepted by T, indorsed the bill to B, who recovered against T, but without execution. A took up the bill, and afterwards took a mortgage from T for its amount, but without satisfaction. Held, that this did not constitute payment of the bill by T to A.

[32] *Drake v. Mitchell* (1803) 3 East 351; *Wegg-Prosser v. Evans* [1895] 1 Q.B. 108 (over-ruling *Camberfort v. Chapman* (1887) 19 Q.B.D. 229); *Roycroft v. Uglum* [1922] 1 W.W.R. 78.

[33] *King v. Hoare* (1844) 13 M. & W. 494; *Kendall v. Hamilton* (1879) 4 App.Cas. 504.

[34] *Pole v. Ford* (1816) 2 Chit. 125; *Bray v. Manson* (1841) 8 M. & W. 668.

[35] Bayley (6th ed.), p. 334; Bac.Ab., Extinguishment, D.; *Ansell v. Baker* (1850) 15 Q.B. 20.

[36] As to conditional payment, see *post*, para. 31–01, and see *Royal Securities Corpn v. Montreal Trust Co.* (1966) 59 D.L.R. (2d) 666, Ontario High Ct; *Crockford Club Ltd v. Mehta* [1992] 1 W.L.R. 355 at 360.

[37] *Allen v. Royal Bank of Canada* (1926) 134 L.T. 194, 196, citing with approval the passage in the text; *Kearslake v. Morgan* (1794) 5 T.R. 513; *Stedman v. Gooch* (1793) 1 Esp. 1, 5; and even when the obligation is of a higher nature, as that of rent due, the taking of a bill for the amount may be some evidence of an agreement to suspend the remedy by distress (*Palmer v. Bramley* [1895] 2 Q.B. 405, citing *Baker v. Walker* (1845) 14 M. & W. 465, where Parke B. said that from taking a promissory note, payable at a certain time, for a judgment debt must be inferred an agreement to suspend the remedy during the currency of the note); but see *Palmer v. Bramley, supra*, distinguished in *Re Defries Ltd* [1909] 2 Ch. 423. If payment of a cheque is stopped, the debt instantly revives as though it had never been given (*Cohen v. Hale* (1878) 3 Q.B.D. 371); *cf. Elliott v. Crutchley* [1903] 2 K.B. 476; *Russell v. Hellaby* [1922] N.Z.L.R. 186.

[38] *Belshaw v. Bush* (1851) 11 C.B. 191, 205; *Homes v. Smith* [2000] Ll. Rep (Banking) 139 at p. 143.

[39] *Ford v. Beech* (1848) 11 Q.B. 852 at 867.

is given by a stranger[40] or if it is outstanding in the hands of a transferee after dishonour, at the date of the commencement of the action, though it is in possession of the creditor at the date of trial.[41]

Where a bill is renewed, holding the original bill and taking the substituted one operates as a suspension of the debt till the substituted bill is paid at maturity.[42] Although the second bill for the principal sum should be paid, the plaintiff may recover interest due on the original bill at the time when the second was given, by bringing an action on the original bill, unless it appears that the second bill was intended to operate as a renewal, or satisfaction of the whole of the former bill.[43] If the second bill be discharged by an alteration, an action may be brought on the first.[44]

A covenant not to sue for a limited time will not suspend the right of action, but will only create a right to sue for the breach of covenant[45] no more will a subsequent, or even a contemporaneous, but collateral, agreement on good consideration not to sue for a limited time on a bill or note.[46]

Release

Performance of outstanding contractual obligations can be discharged by deed of release.[47] Being a deed, no consideration is essential to its validity.   **14–07**

A release, whether before or after the maturity of the bill, is good *as between the parties*, although the releasor is not at the time of the release the holder of the bill.[48]

But a release of a drawee before acceptance is inoperative.[49]

A release *by* one of several joint creditors is a release by all; and a release *to* one of several joint contractors is in law a release of all.[50] Therefore a release of one of two joint acceptors or joint indorsers is a release to both.

---

[40] *Allen v. Royal Bank of Canada, supra*; *Belshaw v. Bush, supra*.

[41] *Davis v. Reilly* [1898] 1 Q.B. 1; *Re A Debtor* [1908] 1 K.B. 344, followed in *Nathan v. Green* [1921] V.L.R. 121, and distinguished in *Re Duncan and Abbott* [1919] N.Z.L.R. 97.

[42] *Kendrick v. Lomax* (1832) 2 C. & J. 405; see *Ex. p. Barclay* (1802) 7 Ves. 596; *Bishop v. Rowe* (1815) 3 M. & S. 362; *Dillon v. Rimmer* (1822) 1 Bing. 100; *Re London and Birmingham Bank* (1865) 34 L.J. Ch. 418; *Royal Bank v. Hogg* (1930) 2 D.L.R. 488.

[43] *Lumley v. Musgrave* (1837) 4 Bing. N.C. 9; *Lumley v. Hudson* (1837) 4 Bing. N.C. 15. A renewed bill is, strictly speaking, between the same parties and for the same amount, the time of payment only being varied; but in *Barber v. Mackrell* (1892) 68 L.T. 29, the liability of a guarantor was held to extend to one that might with more propriety be called a substituted bill for the same debt.

[44] *Sloman v. Cox* (1834) 1 Cr.M. & R. 471.

[45] *Thimbleby v. Barron* (1838) 3 M. & W. 210, 216.

[46] *Ford v. Beech* (1848) 11 Q.B. 852; *Webb v. Spicer* (1849) 13 Q.B. 894; *Moss v. Hall* (1850) 5 Ex. 46, 50; *Salmon v. Webb* (1852) 3 H.L. Cas. 510; *Flight v. Gray* (1857) 3 C.B. (N.S.) 320.

[47] Section 1 of the Law of Property (Miscellaneous Provisions) Act 1989 abolished the need for a seal where the deed is executed by an individual.

[48] *Scott v. Lifford* (1808) 1 Camp. 246, 248.

[49] *Drage v. Netter* (1695) 1 Ld.Raym. 65; *Hartley v. Manton* (1843) 5 Q.B. 247; 263; and see *Ashton v. Freestun* (1840) 2 M. & G. 1.

[50] *cf.* Co.Litt., s.376. A verbal release of one of joint makers of a note is inoperative (*Goodman v. Armstrong* (1926) 47 N.P.D. 452), unless the note is delivered up (*Edwards v. Walters* [1896] 2 Ch. 157 (CA), 170, 171). See also s.3 Civil Liability (Contribution) Act 1978 and note thereon "Judgment recovered" Halsbury's Statutes (4th. ed.) Vol. 13, p. 537.

A release of one of several joint debtors, who are *severally*, as well as *jointly*, liable, is equally a release to all, for judgment and execution against one would have been a discharge to all.[51]

But it has been held that a release to parties jointly liable may in some cases be restrained by the terms of the instrument,[52] and may be construed as a covenant not to sue where such a construction is necessary to carry out the paramount intention of the deed.[53] But it cannot be defeated by a mere parol agreement.[54]

A covenant not to sue amounts in law to a release.[55] But though it may be pleaded as a release by the party to whom it is given, it does not so far operate as to discharge another person jointly liable.[56] Nor will a covenant not to sue, given by one of two joint creditors, operate as a release.[57]

The release of a debt is a release of the right to hold any securities that may have been given for the debt.[58]

Renunciation

14–08   The 1882 Act contains the following provisions in reference to the renunciation by the holder of his rights on a bill or note:

62.—(1) When the holder of a bill at or after its maturity absolutely and unconditionally renounces his rights against the acceptor the bill is discharged.[59]

The renunciation must be in writing, unless the bill is delivered up to the acceptor.[60]

(2) The liabilities of any party to a bill may in like manner be renounced by the holder before, at, or after its maturity; but nothing in

---

[51] Co.Litt. 232a; *Nicholson v. Revill* (1836) 4 A. & E. 675; distinguished in *Cardwell v. Smith* (1886) 2 T.L.R. 779; *cf. Jenkins v. Jenkins* [1928] 2 K.B. 501. This rule applies as much as to a judgment debt as to any other obligation (*Re E.W.A.* [1901] 2 K.B. 642).

[52] *Price v. Barker* (1855) 4 E. & B. 760; *Henderson v. Stobart* (1850) 5 Ex. 99.

[53] *Solly v. Forbes* (1820) 2 Brod. & B. 38; *Willis v. De Castro* (1858) 27 L.J.C.P. 243.

[54] *Brooks v. Stuart* (1839) 9 A. & E. 854; *Cocks v. Nash* (1832) 9 Bing. 341. Indeed, the most general and sweeping words of release may be qualified and restrained by the recital (*Payler v. Homersham* (1815) 4 M. & S. 423; *Simmons v. Johnson* (1832) 3 B. & Ad. 175).

[55] Com.Dig., tit. Release 5th ed., Vol. VII, p. 222.

[56] *Dean v. Newhall* (1799) 8 T.R. 168; *Hutton v. Eyre* (1815) 6 Taunt. 289; *Price v. Barker, supra.*

[57] *Walmesley v. Cooper* (1839) 11 A. & E. 216.

[58] *Cowper v. Green* (1841) 7 M. & W. 633.

[59] But if the holder expressly reserves his rights against the other parties, the acceptor, though exonerated by the holder, remains liable to the other parties (*Muir v. Crawford* (1875) L.R. 2 Sc. & Div. 456, followed in *Jones & Co. v. Whitaker* (1887) 3 T.L.R. 723).

[60] *Rimalt v. Cartwright* [1924] W.N. 229, CA; (1925) 132 L.T. 40, 42, CA. Referring to s.62 in the L.T. Rep. Scrutton L.J. said: "This is an action on a bill of exchange and the law affecting bills of exchange differs in many ways from the law affecting other contracts. In those cases evidence may be given of collateral agreements which will put an end to the liability of the parties in the original agreement, but if the original agreement is a bill of exchange, it can only be renounced by the holder if the renunciation is in writing, or the bill is cancelled by delivery up to the person liable as acceptor. The bill of exchange in the present case is still in the possession of the holder, and there has been no written agreement under which he has renounced his rights on the bill." The return of a dishonoured bill to the drawer does not affect the rights of the holder (*Cohen & Co. v. Werner & Co.* (1891) 8 T.L.R. 11).

this section shall affect the rights of a holder in due course without notice of the renunciation.[61]

It is a general rule of law that a simple contract may, "before breach", be waived or discharged without a deed, and without consideration; but after breach there can be no discharge, except by deed, or upon sufficient consideration.[62] To this rule it has been repeatedly held[63] that contracts on bills of exchange form an exception, and that the liability of the acceptor or other party, remote or immediate, though complete, may be discharged by an express renunciation of his claim on the part of the holder, without consideration. An express and complete renunciation by the holder of his claim on any party to the bill is therefore according to the law merchant equivalent to a release under seal. This seems at first sight to violate a fundamental rule, but the reason may be that the distinction between a release under seal and a release not under seal is quite unknown in most foreign countries.[64] And as it would be highly inconvenient to introduce nice distinctions and nice questions of international law, all the contracts on a foreign bill, though negotiated or made in England, and all the contracts on an inland bill, depending as they do on the same law merchant, may be so released. Such a relaxation of the general rule in the case of bills of exchange is not unreasonable on another ground. The money due at the maturity of a bill of exchange is in practice expected to be paid immediately, and in many cases with remedies over in favour of the debtor. Parties liable, who are expressly told that recourse will not, in any event, be had to them, are almost sure, in consequence, to alter their conduct and position.[65]

The cases at common law, with but few exceptions,[66] are not cases of a renunciation in writing or of the bill having been delivered up to the acceptor, and cannot therefore now be relied on. The renunciation "in writing" now required by the 1882 Act must be in itself a record of the renunciation, not a mere memorandum or note of the renunciation, or of an intention or desire to renounce.[67] Where the instrument is delivered up, delivery within the section does not include delivery to a devisee of the acceptor or maker, but delivery to the personal representatives would, it seems, be good.[68]

---

[61] *Dod v. Edwards* (1827) 2 C. & P. 602.

[62] See *ante*, para. 14–04.

[63] *cf. Foster v. Dawber* (1851) 6 Ex. 839, 851.

[64] See *per* Parke B. in *Foster v. Dawber, supra*, 852.

[65] The law seems to be now so settled in accordance with prior decisions, and with the law of France and other countries, where the distinction between simple contracts and contracts under seal is unknown; *cf.* Pothier, para. 176, sub tit. Contrat de Change.

[66] *cf. Cartwright v. Williams* (1818) 2 Stark. 340; *De la Torre v. Barclay* (1814) 1 Stark. 7. A renunciation, conditional on an affidavit being sworn that the acceptor's signature was a forgery, was held to become binding on the affidavit being sworn, though it was false (*Stevens v. Thacker* (1793) 1 Peake 249).

[67] *Re George* (1890) 44 Ch.D. 627, 632, where the Court declined to determine whether the renunciation must further be signed by the holder; see also *Dickinson v. Lucas* (1909) 101 L.T. 27.

[68] *Edwards v. Walters* [1896] 2 Ch. 157, where, as also in *Re George, supra*, the point was taken that before maturity of a bill a renunciation may be by parol, as at common law. But s.62(2) provides that the liabilities of any party to a bill, including therefore an acceptor or maker, may in like manner (*viz.* in writing) be renounced before its maturity: this seems to exclude the common law rule.

Subsection (2) refers to the "liabilities of any party" being renounced by the holder (as opposed to the renunciation of the holder's rights under subsection (1)). It is not clear why subsection (2) is in negative form and speaks of renunciation of liabilities, rather than waiver of the rights, against any party. The renunciation must be "in like manner" to that set out in subsection (1). The question which this difference in wording raises is whether the return of the bill to any other party is a waiver of rights against that party and indeed against all other parties, for an action cannot be brought without possession of the bill. There is a hint in the judgment of Megaw J. in *Midland Bank Ltd v. Harris*,[69] that this is not so, but the point was not argued. In that case, it was sought to establish a waiver arising from the return of a dishonoured cheque to the customer for whom it was being collected and the debiting of the amount of the cheque to his account. In *Westminster Bank Ltd v. Zang*[70] a dishonoured cheque was returned by the Bank to the holder in order that he might sue, and later delivered back to the Bank, the holder having abandoned his action. The Court of Appeal seemed to think that by handing the bill back the Bank lost its lien.

Cancellation

14–09   In addition to the renunciation by the holder of his rights against any party to a bill or note, a party's liability on a bill or note, or the bill or note itself, may be discharged by cancellation as provided for by the following section of the 1882 Act:

63.—(1) Where a bill is intentionally cancelled by the holder or his agent, and the cancellation is apparent thereon, the bill is discharged.

(2) In like manner any party liable on a bill may be discharged by the intentional cancellation of his signature by the holder or his agent. In such case any indorser who would have had a right of recourse against the party whose signature is cancelled, is also discharged.

In general, subsequent parties, from whom payment is enforced when the bill is dishonoured, have a right of recourse against prior parties; hence, in general, cancellation of the acceptance frees the drawer and all indorsers; cancellation of the drawer's signature, all the indorsers; and cancellation of an indorser's signature, all subsequent indorsers; cancellation of the acceptance is therefore virtually a cancellation of the bill; hence, perhaps, the drawer is not mentioned as discharged in sub-section (2), but only the indorsers. But in a bill accepted for the accommodation of the drawer, *quaere* if he would be discharged by cancellation of the acceptor's signature, though the indorsers

---

[69] [1963] 1 W.L.R. 1021. In *Cohn v. Werner* (1891) 8 T.L.R. 1, it was held that the "mere sending of the bill to the drawer and taking it back did not alter the rights of the parties"; the report is brief and the statute seems not to have been cited; see also Westminster *Bank Ltd v. Zang* [1965] 2 W.L.R. 824.

[70] [1966] A.C. 182, 202, 205, 211.

would be; and if the bill was accepted for the accommodation of the payee, cancellation of the drawer's signature would not free the payee, the first indorser, for he would have no right of recourse against the drawer.

Cancellation by mistake

63.—(3) A cancellation made unintentionally, or under a mistake, or without the authority of the holder is inoperative; but where a bill or any signature thereon appears to have been cancelled the burden of proof lies on the party who alleges that the cancellation was made unintentionally, or under a mistake, or without authority.[71]

It has been held that a cancellation by the acceptor before issue of a bill by tearing it into two pieces, the pieces being picked up in his presence and subsequently joined together so that the appearance was consistent with the bill's having been torn for purposes of safe transmission, is no answer to a claim by a holder in due course if the cancellation is not apparent.[72]

Where an acceptance has been cancelled by mistake, it is the usage in the City of London to return the bill with the words "cancelled in error" written on it.[73]

The proper and safe mode of cancelling is to draw the pen through the name, so as to leave it legible.[74]

If a banker, with whom a bill is made payable by the acceptor, cancels the acceptance by mistake, without any want of due care, and returns the bill defaced, refusing to pay it, he does not thereby necessarily incur any legal liability; but if in so doing he is guilty of want of due care, an action may lie against him at the suit of the holder for the special damage sustained by the cancellation of the bill.[75] Where a bank, as agent for the holders of a bill, without authority agreed to take payment, after dishonour of the bill, without

---

[71] *Warwick v. Rogers* (1843) 5 M. & G. 340, approved in *Prince v. Oriental Bank Corporation* (1878) 3 App.Cas. 325; *Raper v. Birkbeck* (1812) 15 East 17; *Royal Bank of Canada v. Allen* [1919] 3 W.W.R. (Can.) 1063; *cf. Sweeting v. Halse* (1829) 9 B. & C. 365; *Dominion Bank v. Anderson* (1888) 15 R. (Ct. of Sess.) 408. Where A gave B a cheque for £2,500, as collateral security for S's acceptance of bills drawn on him by A, the cancellation of those acceptances, though it discharged A's liability on the bill, did not discharge his liability on the cheque (*Yglesias v. Mercantile Bank of River Plate* (1877) 3 C.P.D. 60).

[72] *Ingham v. Primrose* (1859) 7 C.B. (N.S.) 82; in which case also it was "gravely" doubted whether the reconstruction of the mutilated bill with intent to defraud constituted a forgery. But see *Baxendale v. Bennett* (1878) 3 Q.B.D. 525, 532; and Vaughan Williams L.J. in *Smith v. Prosser* [1907] 2 K.B. 735, 746 to the effect that *Ingham v. Primrose* (and *Young v. Grote* (1827) 4 Bing. 253) had ceased to be law. *Young v. Grote* has been "rehabilitated" by the House of Lords in *London Joint Stock Bank Ltd v. Macmillan and Arthur* [1918] A.C. 777, which was approved and followed in *Tai Hing Cotton Mill Ltd v. Liu Chong Hing Banks Ltd* [1986] A.C. 80.

[73] A cancellation induced by a statement in fact false, though not so to the knowledge of the person making it, will be inoperative (*Scholefield v. Templer* (1859) 4 De G. J. 429); see also *Matthews v. Marsh* (1903) 5 O.L.R. 540.

[74] *Wilkinson v. Johnson* (1824) 3 B. & C. 428; *Ingham v. Primrose, supra.*

[75] *Novelli v. Rossi* (1831) 2 B. & Ad. 757; *Warwick v. Rogers* (1843) 5 M. & G. 340; and see *Prince v. Oriental Bank Corporation* (1878) 3 App.Cas. 325 (P.C.).

interest and expenses, and allowed the acceptor to cancel his signature, which cancellation was held bad as without authority, the bank was held liable to the holders for the amount of the bill and the costs of an abortive action thereon against the acceptor, who had become bankrupt, and against whom, by reason of the cancellation, the holders had not been able to proceed summarily.[76]

---

[76] *Bank of Scotland v. Dominion Bank of Toronto* [1891] A.C. 592.

CHAPTER 15

DISHONOUR—NOTICE

IN preceding Chapters, the duties of the holder of a bill to present it for **15–01** acceptance[1] and to present it for payment[2] have been set out. If the instrument is not accepted on presentation or not met, when presented for payment, then in order to preserve the liability of the drawer and indorsers, the holder or someone on his behalf must give notice of dishonour in accordance with the requirements of the 1882 Act. Failure to give such notice, unless otherwise excused, results in the party, to whom such notice should have been given, being discharged. The object of notice is inform the party, to whom notice is given, that the holder or or the party giving notice looks to him for payment. The rationale being that, where the bill has not been accepted or paid, the drawer or indorser will be prejudiced if no such notice is given.[3] There is no need, though, for the drawer or indorser to show prejudice, since the requirement to give notice "is an absolute one".[4] It should be noted that, where a bill has been accepted, there is no requirement to give notice of dishonour to the acceptor upon dishonour.[5]

The requirements as to notice of dishonour, including excuses for non-notice or delay in giving notice are dealt with in this Chapter; the requirements as to noting and protesting are dealt with in Chapter 16.

The necessity for giving notice of dishonour is set out in the 1882 Act as **15–02** follows:

48. Subject to the provisions of this Act,[6] when a bill has been dishonoured by non-acceptance or by non-payment, notice of dishonour must be given to the drawer and each indorser, and any drawer or indorser to whom such notice is not given is discharged; Provided that—

(1) Where a bill is dishonoured by non-acceptance, and notice of dishonour is not given, the rights of a holder in due course subsequent to the omission shall not be prejudiced by the omission.

(2) Where a bill is dishonoured by non-acceptance, and due notice of dishonour is given, it shall not be necessary to give notice of a subsequent dishonour by non-payment unless the bill shall in the meantime have been accepted.

---

[1] Ch. 11.
[2] Ch. 12.
[3] See further at para. 15–13.
[4] See *Chalmers and Guest on Bills of Exchange* (14th ed., 1991) p. 387.
[5] See s.52(3) *post*, para. 15–26.
[6] The other provisions seem to be those in s.49(15), and s.50, relating to delay in, or excuse of, notice. By s.89 these provisions apply to promissory notes.

Though it may not be necessary to present a bill for acceptance,[7] yet if it is presented, and acceptance is refused, notice of dishonour must be given.[8] Where, however, there has been refusal to accept, but no notice has been given, the omission to give such notice is, as provided above, no defence against a person subsequently becoming the holder of the instrument in such circumstances as to constitute him a holder in due course.[9]

Form of notice

15–03   No particular form of notice is required, since the 1882 Act provides:

49. Notice of dishonour in order to be valid and effectual must be given in accordance with the following rules—
(5) The notice may be given in writing or by personal communication, and may be given in any terms which sufficiently identify the bill, and intimate that the bill has been dishonoured by non-acceptance or non-payment.
(7) A written notice need not be signed, and an insufficient written notice may be supplemented and validated by verbal communication. A mis-description of the bill shall not vitiate the notice unless the party to whom the notice is given is in fact misled thereby.

Notice does not mean mere knowledge, but actual notification, for a man who can be clearly shown to have known beforehand that the bill would be dishonoured is nevertheless entitled to notice.[10] But all that is necessary to apprise the party liable of the dishonour is the giving of a notice which (i) so describes the instrument that the party to whom the notice is sent is not in fact misled thereby, and (ii) intimates that the bill has been dishonoured by non-acceptance or non-payment.[11]

The notice must not so misdescribe the instrument that the defendant may be led to confuse it with some other; but if there are more bills than one to which the notice may apply, it lies on the defendant to prove that fact.[12] If a

---

[7] See *ante*, para. 10–01.

[8] *Blesard v. Hirst* (1770) 5 Burr. 2670, 2672; *Goodall v. Dolley* (1787) 1 T.R. 712. Art. 45 of the Geneva Convention provides for the giving of notice of dishonour by non-acceptance or non-payment.

[9] *Dunn v. O'Keeffe* (1816) 5 M. & S. 282, distinguishing *Roscow v. Hardy* (1810) 12 East 434.

[10] See *Burgh v. Legge* (1839) 5 M. & W. 418; *Caunt v. Thompson* (1849) 18 L.J.C.P. 125, 127.

[11] The 1882 Act gives no ground for supposing that a notice by a person other than the holder of a bill, but having authority to give notice on the latter's behalf, need intimate that the party addressed is looked to for payment, though this was formerly thought necessary; *cf. East v. Smith* (1847) 16 L.J.Q.B. 292. As to oral notices, see *Housego v. Cowne* (1837) 2 M. & W. 348; *Metcalfe v. Richardson* (1852) 11 C.B. 1011. As to an unsigned notice, see *Maxwell v. Brain* (1864) 10 L.T. 301, where the unsigned notice, which was sent by a bank, was in fact written on the bank's addressed paper. For mere return of a bill operating as notice of dishonour, see s.49(6); *post*, para. 15–04.

[12] *Shelton v. Braithwaite* (1841) 7 M. & W. 436.

bill is improperly called a note it is no objection,[13] nor if the characters of drawer and acceptor of a bill are transposed.[14] In short, that a misdescription, which does not mislead, is immaterial[15] is now the rule of law, as well as of convenience and justice.

As to what words will sufficiently intimate that the bill has been dishonoured, it was formerly held that a demand of payment,[16] and even a letter to an indorser from the holder's attorneys saying that a bill for £683 drawn by A upon B had been placed in their hands with directions to sue unless the bill was paid, did not sufficiently convey the dishonour of the bill.[17] But this latter decision has been the subject of judicial regret, and there has been no disposition to extend it. An intimation that A's acceptance is unpaid and requesting payment of the amount, or immediate attention to the matter, has been repeatedly held to be a sufficient notice.[18]

The notice of dishonour need not state on whose behalf payment is applied for, nor where the bill is lying,[19] and a mis-description of the place where the bill is lying is immaterial,[20] unless, perhaps, a tender were made there.

If the notice, by mistake, mis-describes the party giving it, by representing that it is given by or on behalf of A, when in reality it is given by or on behalf of B, it is nevertheless good. But the party who receives the notice is to be placed in the same position as if the notice had really been given by A, and is at liberty to raise any inability in A to give notice; as, for example, that A had been discharged by laches or had no right of action on the bill.[21]

The following form was drawn out by the author as applicable to the case of a holder giving notice to an indorser:

"1, Fleet Street, London.   Sept. 26, 1842.

Sir,

I hereby give you notice that the bill of exchange dated 22nd ult., drawn by A B of—on C D of—for £100, payable one month after date to A B or his order, and indorsed by you, has been duly presented for payment, but was dishonoured and is unpaid. I request you to pay me the amount thereof."

---

[13] *Stockman v. Parr* (1843) 11 M. & W. 809. The converse case arose in *Messenger v. Southey* (1840) 1 M. & G. 76, where the notice was held bad as not sufficiently intimating presentment to and dishonour by the maker, and the misdescription was not dealt with in the judgment. Since *Furze v. Sharwood* (1841) 2 Q.B. 388, no notice has been held bad on the ground of form.

[14] *Mellersh v. Rippen* (1852) 7 Exch. 578.

[15] *Bromage v. Vaughan* (1846) 9 Q.B. 608; *Harpham v. Child* (1859) 1 F. & F. 652. In *Beauchamp v. Cash* (1822) Dow. & Ry.N.P. 3, Abbott C.J. thought a notice to an indorser that a "bill drawn by you", etc. was extremely likely to mislead, and was bad. It must now appear that the party was in fact misled.

[16] *Hartley v. Case* (1825) 1 C. & P. 555.

[17] *Solarte v. Palmer* (1823) 1 Bing. N.C. 194.

[18] *Bailey v. Porter* (1845) 14 M. & W. 44; *Everard v. Watson* (1853) 1 E. & B. 801; *Paul v. Joel* (1859) 4 H. & N. 355; *Counsell v. Livingston* (1902) 4 O.L.R. 340; *Standard Bank of South Africa v. Winder* [1920] W.L.D. 102; *Nees v. Botting* [1928] N.Z.L.R. 209; Little reliance can now be placed on earlier cases, which are virtually overruled, yet it is certainly desirable that the notice should request the attention of the person to whom it is addressed, and not merely state that the acceptance is unpaid. The words must now "sufficiently" and not, as said in *Solarte v. Palmer,* *supra*, by "necessary implication", convey the fact of dishonour.

[19] *Woodthorpe v. Lawes* (1836) 2 M. & W. 109.

[20] *Rowlands v. Springett* (1845) 14 L.J.Ex. 227.

[21] *Harrison v. Ruscoe* (1846) 115 L.J.Ex. 110.

Such a notice may easily be altered and adapted to circumstances;[22] in case of a foreign bill it is proper to add the words "and has been duly protested" after the word "dishonoured".

It is not necessary that a copy of the protest should accompany notice of the dishonour of a foreign bill.[23] But a copy or some other information of the protest should be sent, if the party to whom notice is transmitted resides abroad.[24]

Return of bill may be notice

15–04   A particular form of notice is deemed sufficient, for the 1882 Act provides:

49.—(6) The return of a dishonoured bill to the drawer or an indorser is, in point of form, deemed a sufficient notice of dishonour.[25]

The usual practice of collecting bankers would seem to be to return the bill or cheque to their own customer. If, however, the instrument is made, or has become, payable to bearer, the customer is not within the subsection, unless indorsement for collection is sufficient to constitute him an indorser within it.[26] The return of the bill to the payee-indorser (so that it was not in the plaintiff's possession at the time the writ was issued) was fatal to the plaintiff's case in *Lloyds Bank Ltd v. Dolphin*.[27]

Mode of transmitting notice

15–05   The most common and the safest mode of giving notice is by post, since this method is expressly recognised by the 1882 Act in the following subsection:

49.—(15) Where a notice of dishonour is duly addressed and posted, the sender is deemed to have given due notice of dishonour, notwithstanding any miscarriage by the post office.[28]

For the section to apply there must be evidence that the notice was posted. Where a witness said that the letter, containing notice of dishonour, was put on a table to be carried to the post office, and that by the course of business all letters deposited on this table were carried to the post office by a porter, but the porter was not called and there was no evidence as to what had become of the letter after it had been put on the table, Lord Ellenborough said: "You must

---

[22] The issue of a writ on the day of dishonour is not sufficient notice (*Commercial Bank of Manitoba v. Allan* (1894) 10 Man. 330).

[23] *Goodman v. Harvey* (1836) 4 A. & E. 870.

[24] *Robins v. Gibson* (1813) 1 M. & S. 288, 289; see also *post*, para. 16–19.

[25] The rights of the parties are not altered by the return of the bill (*Cohn & Co. v. Werner & Co.* (1891) 8 T.L.R. 11).

[26] Paget, *Law of Banking* (11th ed., 1996), p. 411.

[27] *The Times*, December 2, 1920; (1920) 3 Legal Decisions Affecting Bankers, 230.

[28] *Woodcock v. Houldsworth* (1846) 16 L.J.Ex. 49; *Mackay v. Judkins* (1858) 1 F. & F. 208.

go further; some evidence must be given that the letter was taken from the table in the counting-house and put into the post office. Had you called the porter and he said that, although he had no recollection of the letter in question, he invariably carried to the post office all the letters found upon the table, this might have done, but I cannot hold this general evidence of the course of business, in the plaintiffs' counting-house, to be sufficient."[29] The postmarks in town or country, proved to be such, are evidence that the letters, on which they are, were in the office to which those marks belong, at the time of the dates of such marks.[30] But they are not conclusive evidence.[31]

Though there is a general post, the holder may send notice by a special messenger[32] but if the notice is not communicated by the special messenger until after the day when it would have been conveyed by the post, it is insufficient.[33]

Although notice by post is expressly provided for, there would appear to be no reason why notice should not be given by telex or fax. At present it is suggested that notice sent by email would not suffice. Communication by electronic means does not satisfy the requirement as to writing (consisting merely of a series of electronic impulses), nor would constitute personal communication within s.49(5) of the 1882 Act. It is suggested, though, that there is no reason why the Government should not exercise its powers under s.8 of the Electronic Communications Act 2000, so as to allow notice of dishonour to be given by electronic means;[34] the objections that exist in relation to electronic bills[35] do not apply in relation to the giving of notice.

In the case of a foreign bill, although it was once held sufficient to send notice by the first mail or regular ship bound for the place to which it was to be sent[36] it is very doubtful that the decision would be reached today where airmail is available.

It is not sufficient for the letter containing the notice to be directed generally to a person at a large town; as, for example to "Mr. Haynes, Bristol[37]," without specifying in what part of it he resides, except where the person to whom the letter is sent is the drawer of the bill, and has dated it in an equally

---

[29] *Hetherington v. Kemp* (1815) 4 Camp. 194; *Hawkes v. Salter* (1828) 4 Bing. 715. Where the messenger is dead, see *Rowlands v. De Vecchi* (1882) Cab. & E. 10.

[30] *Kent v. Lowen* (1808) 1 Camp. 177; *Fletcher v. Braddyl* (1821) 3 Stark. 64; *R. v. Plumer* (1814) Russ. & Ry. 264; *R. v. Watson* (1808) 1 Camp. 215; *Butler v. Mountgarret* (1859) 7 H.L.C. 633, 646.

[31] *Stocken v. Collin* (1841) 7 M. & W. 515.

[32] *Bancroft v. Hall* (1816) Holt's N.P.C. 476; at least where the parties live in the same place (*Crosse v. Smith* (1813) 1 M. & S. 545, 554, citing *Goldsmith v. Bland* (1800, Bayley (6th ed.), p. 276)). But now by the 1882 Act, s.49(12)(b), *post*, para. 15–07, where the parties reside in different places, the post appears to be the only authorised means of communication, and a question might arise if a private messenger were employed, who in fact arrived later than a latter by post would have done.

[33] *Darbishire v. Parker* (1805) 6 East. 3.

[34] Recommendation 36 in Appendix N to the Banking Services: Law and Practice Report Review Committee, included a recommendation that electronic means might be used as a means of giving notice of dishonour.

[35] See *ante*, para. 2–05.

[36] *Mailman v. D'Eguino* (1795) 2 H.Bl. 565, 570. As to the validity of this decision see *Fleming v. McLeod* (1907) 39 Can.S.C.R. 290, 306.

[37] *Walter v. Haynes* (1824) Ry. & M. 149.

general manner.[38] If the notice to the drawer arrives too late, through misdirection, it is for the Court to say whether the holder used due diligence to discover the drawer's address.[39] If the notice miscarries from the indistinctness of the drawer's handwriting on the bill, he will not be discharged.[40]

Where notice should be given

15–06   The 1882 Act does not specify at what place notice of dishonour should be given. A notice of dishonour should be sent to the place of business or the residence of the party for whom it is designed, but if he has a place of business, the holder has fulfilled his duty if he sends the notice there; he need not send it also to the place of residence.[41]

If a party, whose name is on a bill, directs a notice to be sent to him when absent at a place some distance from his residence, so that its transmission there, and thereafter to the prior parties, will occupy more time than if the notice had passed through the ordinary place of residence, a notice to him at the substituted and more distant place will, it seems, not only be a good notice as against him, but also a good notice as against prior parties.[42]

A message sent to a counting-house within the usual hours of business has been held sufficient, though no person is in attendance. Thus, where the holder sent to a counting-house, and the messenger knocked at the outer door on two successive days, making noise sufficient to be heard by persons within, Lord Ellenborough said: "The counting-house is a place where all appointments respecting the business, and all notices, should be addressed; and it is the duty of the merchant to take care that a proper person be in attendance. It has, however, been argued, that notice in writing left at the counting-house, or put into the post, was necessary, but the law does not require it, and with whom was it to be left? Putting a letter into the post is only one mode of giving notice; but, where both parties are residing in the same town, sending a clerk is a more regular and less exceptional mode."[43] But the mere act of going and knocking at the door will not sustain an allegation of actual notice, though it may enlarge the time necessary for giving it, or in some circumstances be evidence of a dispensation.[44] A message left with the wife of a private person at his dwelling-house has been held sufficient.[45]

---

[38] *Mann v. Moors* (1825) Ry. & M. 249; *Clarke v. Sharpe* (1838) 3 M. & W. 166; *La Banque D'Hochelaga v. Hanson* (1917) Q.R. 53 S.C. 266. S.103 of the Canadian Act specifically provides that a notice sent to the "customary address or place of residence or at the place of which such bill is dated" shall be sufficient. In the United States this is not so; see Uniform Commercial Code, ss.3–508 and 3–510.

[39] *Siggers v. Brown* (1836) 1 Moo. & R. 520.

[40] *Hewitt v. Thompson* (1836) 1 Moo. & R. 543; *cf. Brock & Patterson v. Crockett* [1923] 56 N.S.R. 132.

[41] *Berridge v. Fitzgerald* (1869) L.R. 4 Q.B. 639, distinguished in *Du Plessis v. Bagley* [1906] T.S. 367.

[42] *Shelton v. Braithwaite* (1841) 8 M. & W. 252.

[43] *Crosse v. Smith* (1813) 1 M. & S. 545, 554; *Bancroft v. Hall* (1816) N.P.C. 476.

[44] *Allen v. Edmundson* (1848) 2 Exch. 719. If the facts show that notice was dispensed with, they should be pleaded; prior to the CPR it was stated that if the facts show that delay was excused they will be admissible under an averment of "due notice" given on a subsequent day, and need not be expressly alleged. Now see Bullen and Leake (14th ed., 2001), p. 125.

[45] *Housego v. Cowne* (1837) 2 M. & W. 348.

In the case of a company, notice served on or sent to the company's registered office would also be sufficient.[46]

TIME FOR GIVING NOTICE

When notice should be given

As to the time when notice of dishonour should be given, the 1882 Act provides that: **15–07**

49.—(12) The notice may be given as soon as the bill is dishonoured and must be given within a reasonable time thereafter.[47]

In the absence of special circumstances notice is not deemed to have been given within a reasonable time, unless:

(a) where the person giving and the person to receive notice reside in the same place, the notice is given or sent off in time to reach the latter on the day after the dishonour of the bill.[48]
(b) Where the person giving and the person to receive notice reside in different places, the notice is sent off on the day after the dishonour of the bill, if there be a post at a convenient hour on that day, and if there be no such post on that day then by the next post thereafter.

What is a reasonable time is a question of law depending on the facts of each particular case.[49] It may be necessary to see at what time of a particular day a bill is dishonoured, as if what is in question is a sequence of events happening on the same day, in which case the law pays regard to parts of a day.[50] A notice is not bad merely because it was posted before the due date of the bill: it was good unless it was received by the person to whom it was addressed before the bill was dishonoured. It is "given" when it is received. A notice prepared before the due date, but dated as of the due date and posted the day before but reaching the addressee on the due date but after the bill was dishonoured, was held good.[51]

---

[46] See s.275(1) of the Companies Act 1985.

[47] The Uniform Commercial Code, s.3–508(2) provides that "Any necessary notice must be given by a bank before its midnight dead-line and by any other person before midnight on the third business day after dishonour or receipt of dishonour."

[48] For example Upper Brook St. and Seething Lane, London, were held to be in the same place for purposes of the subsection (*Hamilton Finance Co. Ltd v. Coverley Westray Walbaum & Tosetti Ltd and Portland Finance Co. Ltd* [1969] 1 Lloyd's Rep. 53). In *Extension Investments v. Ampro* (1961) 3 S.A. 429 (citing *African Credit v. Esakov* (1938) T.P.D. 4) the City of Johannesburg was held to be one place.

[49] In *Tindal v. Brown* (1786) 1 T.R. 167, the Court treated the question of reasonable time as one of law for this purpose, upon the facts being found by the jury, and this view was apparently approved in *Darbishire v. Parker* (1805) 6 East 3, though Lord Kenyon twice refused to acknowledge its authority (see cases referred to in notes, 6 East. pp. 14–17), considering the question to be for the jury; *cf.* also *Hirschfeld v. Smith* (1866) L.R. 1 C.P. 340, 351; *Gladwell v. Turner* (1870) L.R. 5 Ex. 59, 61. What are special circumstances excusing delay would appear to be a question for the Court; *cf. Lindo v. Unsworth* (1811) 2 Camp. 602; and, on the facts being found, reasonable time is now entirely for the Court, not for the jury, to decide.

[50] Per Lord Cross in *Eaglehill Ltd v. J. Needham Builders Ltd* [1973] A.C. 992, 1010, HL, citing *Clarke v. Bradlaugh* (1881) 8 Q.B.D. 63 and *Re North* [1895] 2 Q.B. 264.

[51] *Eaglehill Ltd v. J. Needham Builders Ltd* [1973] A.C. 992, HL.

For the purposes of what constitutes a reasonable time the 1882 Act draws a distinction between the position where the parties live in the same place and where they live in different places. The rationale behind this distinction is not spelt out, and with the speed of modern communications might be considered redundant. In the context of considering the meaning of "in the same place", Mocatta J. pointed to the fact that the determining factor was whether it would be reasonable to send notice by hand rather than rely on the general post.[52]

Where the parties live in the same place

15–08   In the case where the parties live in the same place, as in London,[53] it will not be sufficient notice, in the absence of special circumstances, if the letter containing the notice is put into the post the day after the dishonour, unless it is posted in time to be delivered the same day. "The holder of a bill of exchange", says Lord Ellenborough,[54] "is not *omissis omnibus aliis negotiis* to devote himself to giving notices of its dishonour. It is enough if this be done with reasonable expedition. If you limit a man to the fractional part of a day, it will come to a question how swiftly the notice can be conveyed a man and horse must be employed and you will have a race against time. But here a day has been lost. The plaintiff had notice himself on the Monday, and does not give notice to his indorser till the Wednesday. If a party has an entire day, he must send off his letter conveying the notice within post-time of that day. The plaintiff only wrote the letter to Aylett (*viz.* a prior indorser) on the Tuesday. It might as well have continued in his writing-desk on the Tuesday night, as lie at the post office." A bill was accepted payable at one bank and later the acceptor informed the holder that he had made fresh arrangements with another bank, to which the bill should be presented. It was presented to the first bank and dishonoured and then to the second bank and again dishonoured, and only then was notice of dishonour given. It was held to be too late. In the same case it was said that if the notice is dated the day of dishonour there is no need to prove that it was written after the actual dishonour.[55] A person who puts the letter into the post office on the day when it ought to be received must show affirmatively that it was posted in time to be received on that day.[56] The post-mark is not conclusive evidence of the time when a letter is posted.[57]

---

[52] see *Hamilton Finance C. Ltd (supra)* at 73.

[53] The expression "same town or place" has been held not necessarily to include two places joined together by a continuous line of houses (*Casey v. Rose* (1900) 82 L.T. 616 (excise licence)). On the other hand, in the case of London, at least for the purposes of giving notice, all places within the London postal district would probably be regarded as within the same place. See *Hamilton Finance Co. Ltd v. Coverley Westray Walbaum & Tosetti Ltd and Portland Finance Co. Ltd* [1969] 1 Lloyd's Rep. 53, 73. This would appear to be the American view of the point (Norton, *Bills* (3rd ed.), p. 386).

[54] *Smith v. Mullett* (1809) 2 Camp. 208.

[55] *Yeoman Credit Ltd v. Gregory* [1963] 1 W.L.R. 343.

[56] *Fowler v. Hendon* (1834) 4 Tryw. 1002.

[57] *Stocken v. Collin* (1841) 7 M. & W. 515; see also *ante*, para. 15–05.

This question received the attention of Mocatta J. in the *Hamilton Finance Co. case*.[58] The learned judge reviewed the cases in relation to the particular facts before him and gave judgment in the following terms:

"In Byles on Bills of Exchange, 22nd ed. (1965), at p. 153, note 43, the view is expressed that in the case of London, at least for the purposes of giving notice, all places within the London postal district (whatever exactly that means) would probably be regarded as within the same place. The same suggestion is made in Chalmers on Bills of Exchange, 13th ed. (1964), at p. 161. As regards reported cases I was referred to only two upon this matter. The earliest was *McGregor v. Carr* (1886) 2 T.L.R. 757, in which Mr. Justice Cave is reported as having said: 'Chiswick is not the same place as London', to which Counsel answered: 'It is the same postal district'. Mr. Justice Cave thereupon said that that was very different. These remarks were *arguendo* and *obiter* since the special provisions of section 49(13) were held to apply. The second case was *Extension Investments (Pty.) Ltd v. Ampro Holdings (Pty.) Ltd and Others* (1961) 3 S.A.L.R. 429. There it was decided that for the purpose of section 47 of the Transvaal Proclamation, No. 11 of 1902, which seems to have been in the same terms as section 49(12) of the Bills of Exchange Act 1882, two addresses in the city of Johannesburg were 'in the same place'. One address was in central Johannesburg and the other in a central suburb of Johannesburg. The learned judge, after referring to an earlier decision of the Full Court that the City of Johannesburg was one place, said (*ibid.*, at p. 430):
'. . . I see no reason to differ from this view even if I were entitled to do so. It is true that cities have grown in size since the date of the Statute under consideration, but at the same time the speed of communication has increased and efficiency of postal services has, or is supposed to have, improved. I can see no logical reason why a small town should be considered to be one place and the larger city not. I leave out of account outlying suburbs which may possibly not correctly be regarded as part of the city or town. This problem does not arise in the present case.'
I do not feel that I get much assistance from either of the text-books or from the first of the two authorities; the second would seem slightly to support the first defendants' argument that I am here dealing with two addresses 'in the same place'. If I am to answer this question as one of fact as a Jury might, I would find that the two addresses, a modest bus or tube journey apart, both in the central area of London, are 'in the same place'. I would, however, wish to find some rationale on which the distinctions between section 49(12)(a) and (b) are based. A little, but not much, help is to be derived from *Smith v. Mullett*, (1809) 2 Camp. 207; 170 E.R. and *Hilton v. Fairclough*, (1811) 2 Camp. 633; 170 E.R. 1276. It will be noticed that sub-paragraph (a) makes no mention of the past (*sic*.), whereas sub-paragraph (b) does. From this it would appear that if the two addresses on other grounds would seem to be 'in the same place', the determining factor is whether it would in all the circumstances be reasonable to send the notice by hand than rely upon the general post. In view of the importance of giving due notice of dishonour, and the relative cheapness of delivery by hand between the two addresses, this factor in the present case to my mind supports what I have called the Jury view. I accordingly hold that Upper Brook Street, W.1, and Seething Lane, E.C.3, are 'in the same place' for the purposes of section 49(12)(a) of the Bills of Exchange Act 1882."

Where parties live in different places

Where the parties do not live in the same place, and the post does not go out **15–09** on the next day, notice need not be posted until the day after, or the next post day. Thus, where the plaintiff received intelligence of the dishonour on

[58] [1969] 1 Lloyd's Rep. 53, 73.

Thursday morning, at nine o'clock, though the post did not go out till nine o'clock at night, and no bag was made up on the Friday, but the plaintiff wrote on Saturday, notice was held to have been sent in time.[59] As provided by the 1882 Act, only a post going out at a convenient hour need be regarded. Where a bill was dishonoured on a Saturday, it was held that notice need not be sent by a post going out at 9.30 on Monday morning, and, there being no post on Monday night, it was sufficient if sent by the 9.30 post on Tuesday morning.[60] Where notice was received on a Sunday, it was held that it need not be transmitted by the midday post on Monday, for the party has the entire day in which to send on the notice.[61]

The provisions of section 49(12) only apply "in the absence of special circumstances". Thus it has been held that any festival, on which a man is forbidden by his religion to transact any secular affairs (for the law merchant respects the religion of different people), is not to be reckoned in computing the time within which notice of dishonour should be given.[62] Similarly, in the case of a bill drawn by a master of a ship on the owners which was dishonoured on a Saturday, the holders, on receiving notice of dishonour on the following Monday from the bank, with whom the bill had been deposited for collection, instituted inquiries as to the exact address of the drawer. After ascertaining that the ship had arrived in the Tyne, further inquiries were made, but without result, for a more definite address, and notice was eventually sent off by registered post on the Thursday addressed to the master of the ship at Newcastle-on-Tyne, which duly reached the drawer. In these circumstances, it was held that there had been no unreasonable delay in giving notice.[63]

It has been doubted whether, seeing that the acceptor of an inland bill has, in the case of other debts, the whole of the day on which the bill falls due to pay it, notice of non-payment can be given until the day after.[64] But it is now settled that notice may be given at any time after demand on the day the bill becomes due. "The other party", observes Lord Ellenborough, "cannot complain at the extraordinary diligence used to give him information."[65] Further, the expression employed by the 1882 Act, section 49(12) is that notice may be given "as soon as the bill is dishonoured", and this includes any definite refusal of payment on the late of maturity.[66]

Notice of dishonour may be given on the same day, though there is no actual refusal if the house where the bill is payable is shut up and no one is there.[67]

[59] *Geill v. Jeremy* (1827) M. & M. 61.
[60] *Hawkes v. Salter* (1828) 4 Bing. 715.
[61] *Bray v. Hadwen* (1816) 5 M. & S. 68. There is no liability on a party receiving notice on a Sunday to deal with it on that day (*Wright v. Shawcross* (1819) 2 B. & Ald. 501n). There is nothing in the 1882 Act to invalidate a notice sent or received on a "non-business day"; it is simply within the option of the person bound to give notice whether he ignore such day or not.
[62] *Lindo v. Unsworth* (1811) 2 Camp. 602.
[63] *The Elmville* [1904] P. 319.
[64] *Leftley v. Mills* (1791) 4 T.R. 170.
[65] *Burbridge v. Manners* (1812) 3 Camp. 193; *Ex p. Moline* (1812) 19 Ves. 216.
[66] *Kennedy v. Thomas* [1894] 2 Q.B. 759. A refusal to honour on the last day, which is not positive but indicates an expectation that an acceptor may have funds later in the day, does not justify a notice of dishonour (*Hartley v. Case* (1925) 1 C. & P. 555, 556).
[67] *Hine v. Allely* (1833) 4 B. & Ad. 624.

Transmission to antecedent parties

The time within which a party receiving notice must transmit it to ante-   **15–10**
cedent parties is as follows:

49.—(14) Where a party to a bill receives due notice of dishonour, he has after the receipt of such notice the same period of time for giving notice to antecedent parties that the holder has after the dishonour.[68]

Thus if an indorser of a bill receives notice of dishonour from the holder of a bill, in accordance with the requirements of the 1882 Act, that indorser has in turn to give notice of dishonour within time provided by s.49(12), to any prior indorser or the drawer. Section 49(1) provides that a notice must be given by or on behalf of "an indorser who, at the time of giving it, is himself liable on the bill".[69] If proper notice of dishonour has not been give to an indorser, not only is there no need for that indorser to give notice to any prior notice but any such notice will be of no effect.

Bill in hands of agent

Where a bill is in the hands of an agent at the time when it is dishonoured,   **15–11**
the agent may give notice of dishonour either to the parties liable on the bill or to his principal. This subsection, set out below, has particular application where a collecting bank acts on behalf of the holder of a bill in presenting it for acceptance or payment.

49.—(13) Where a bill when dishonoured is in the hands of an agent, he may either himself give notice to the parties liable on the bill, or he nay give notice to his principal. If he gives notice to his principal, he must do so within the same time as if he were the holder, and the principal upon receipt of such notice has himself the same time for giving notice as if the agent had been an independent holder.[70]

Thus, where the holder of a bill employed an attorney to give notice to an indorser, and the attorney wrote to another professional man, requesting him to ascertain the indorser's residence, and received answer to his letter, conveying the desired information, on the 16th of the month, which information he communicated to his principal on the 17th, and on the 18th forwarded the letter containing the notice of dishonour, it was held sufficient, "If", says Lord Tenterden, "the letter (containing the notice) had been sent to the principal, he would have been bound to give notice on the next day, but it having been sent to the agent, he was not bound to give notice on the following day. A banker who holds a bill for a customer is not bound to give notice of dishonour on the day on which the bill is dishonoured. He has another day, and upon the same

---

[68] *Geill v. Jeremy* (1827) M. & M. 61.
[69] See *post*, para. 15–13.
[70] *Robson v. Bennett* (1810) 2 Taunt. 388; *Langdale v. Trimmer* (1812) 15 East 291; *Bray v. Hadwen* (1816) 5 M. & S. 68. As to notice given by an agent, see s.49(2), *post*. para. 15–14.

principle, I think the attorney in this case was entitled, by law, to be allowed a day to consult his client".[71] With respect to the giving of notice, agents are treated as if they were holders.[72]

Where notice is received earlier than it need have been, the recipient is not entitled to add the time saved to that given to him by the section.[73] Where a bill passes through several branch banks of the same establishment, each branch may be considered as a distinct holder entitled to receive and transmit notices as such.[74] Where a notice was sent by mistake to the wrong branch, and, on the discovery of the mistake, the notice was repeated by telegram sent off on the following day to the proper branch, the telegram being in fact received as soon as the written notice would have been received had it been properly addressed, the notice so sent was held to be a good notice.[75]

Bills payable at bank B in Porthcawl were sent by bank W in London to bank B for payment, but were dishonoured. Bank B notified bank W on the day of dishonour and returned the bills at the same time. Bank W informed the plaintiff holder-indorsers on the day on which they, bank W, received the notice from bank B, *i.e.* on the day after dishonour. The plaintiffs did not advise the defendants on the day on which they themselves received notice of dishonour but waited until the bills were again in their hands which, it appears, was two days after they had first been notified by bank W. It would seem clear that the plaintiffs received due notice when they first heard from bank W; notice may be given by personal communication.[76] By subsection 14, a party who has received due notice has the same time after receipt for giving notice as the holder has after dishonour. By subsection 12(b), the parties not residing in the same place, the notice must be sent off the day after dishonour (or, presumably, the receipt of notice) or, if there is no convenient post, by the next post thereafter. It would seem to follow that notice in this case was given late but it was held that this was not so, there being special circumstances which exempted the plaintiffs from the timetables of rules (12) and (13). It was further held that the oral or telephonic communication of bank W was a warning of what was in the post and not the substantive notice; "notice in the circumstances of this case was the principal's receipt from the bank of the bill marked 'refer to acceptor' ".[77]

The special circumstances suggested by the plaintiffs (it is not clear if it was accepted by the Court) lay in the mode of presentation, whereby dishonour took place when neither the holders nor agents knew of it on the day of

---

[71] *Firth v. Thrush* (1828) 8 B. & C. 387. The view expressed by Kindersley V.-C., in *Re Leeds Banking Co.* (1865) L.R. 1 Eq. 1, to the effect that the law does not allow an additional day for communication from the holder's agent to the holder, appears now to be expressly overruled by the 1882 Act.

[72] *Fielding v. Corry* [1898] 1 Q.B. 268, 272, in which notice was sent by the presenting bank to the wrong branch of the transmitting bank; matter rectified by telegram and held good.

[73] *Yeoman Credit Ltd v. Gregory* [1963] 1 W.L.R. 343, 355.

[74] *Clode v. Bayley* (1843) 12 M. & W. 51.

[75] *Fielding v. Corry* [1898] 1 Q.B. 268, where Collins L.J. dissented, regarding the notice to the wrong bank as immaterial, and that by telegram, as bad in law, since it had been dispatched too late. The decision appears to go to the length of saying that notice is good if it reaches the party to whom it is addressed on the same day as a notice posted on the proper day would have reached him; for that the two branches were separate have been settled long before.

[76] Subs. (5).

[77] *Lombard Banking Ltd v. Central Garage and Engineering Co. Ltd* [1963] 1 Q.B. 220.

dishonour. It is not clear why the mode of presentation was unusual or special for purposes of section 49 of the 1882 Act, and it is submitted that there were no special circumstances.

Burden of proof

It lies on the claimant to show that notice was given in due time and before action brought. In an action by the indorsee against an indorser of a bill of exchange, a witness stated that, either two or three days after the dishonour of the bill, notice was given by letter to the defendant; notice in two days being in time, but notice on the third too late. Lord Ellenborough: "The witness says two or three days, but the third day would be too late. It lies upon you to show that notice was given in due time, and I cannot go upon probable evidence without positive proof of the fact. Nor can I infer due notice from the non-production of the letter; the only consequence is, that you may give parol evidence of it. The *onus probandi* lies upon the plaintiff, and, since he has not proved due notice, he must be called."[78] So it lies on the claimant to show that notice was given and received before action brought. Therefore, where the notice was given and the action brought on the same day, the plaintiff was non-suited, because he did not show by affirmative evidence that the notice was received before the writ issued.[79]

15–12

OTHER REQUIREMENTS

By whom should notice be given

The 1882 Act requires, for a notice to be valid and effectual, that:

15–13

49.—(1) The notice must be given by or on behalf of the holder, or by or on behalf of an indorser who, at the time of giving it, is himself liable on the bill.

The object of notice is twofold: first, to apprise the party to whom it is addressed of the dishonour and, second, to inform him that the holder, or party giving the notice, looks to him for payment. Hence it follows that notice can only be given by some party to the instrument, though he need not be the actual holder of the bill at the time,[80] but that a stranger is incompetent to give it.[81] Since the 1882 Act provides that any indorser who gives notice must himself be liable at the time on the bill, it is clear that even a party to the bill, who has been already discharged by delay, or who could not in any event sue, is incompetent to give notice. But a prior indorser who has himself received

---

[78] *Lawson v. Sherwood* (1816) 1 Stark. 314, where the plaintiffs were in fact non-suited; and see *Eaglehill Ltd v. J. Needham Builders Ltd* [1973] A.C. 992, HL.

[79] *Castrique v. Bernabo* (1844) 14 L.J.Q.B. 3, as to which see Lord Cross of Chelsea in *Eaglehill Ltd J. Needham Builders Ltd* [1973] A.C. 992, 1006.

[80] *Chapman v. Keane* (1835) 3 A. & E. 193; *Harrison v. Ruscoe* (1846) 15 L.J.Ex. 110; *Lysaght v. Bryant* (1850) 9 C.B. 46.

[81] *Stewart v. Kennett* (1809) 2 Camp. 177.

due notice may transmit it, and notice so transmitted will enure in favour of the holder as against the party to whom it is sent[82] even though the person transmitting the notice had no certain knowledge of the fact of dishonour.[83]

Notice given by an agent

15–14   A notice of dishonour given by an agent is valid and effectual:

49.—(2) Notice of dishonour may be given by an agent either in his own name, or in the name of any party entitled to give notice whether that party be his principal or not.

It has been held that a notice given by a party to a bill in the name of an indorser, but without his authority, is good;[84] so, too, a notice given by an agent which did not specify the principal's name.[85]

It has been stated that a tradesman's foreman or servant is not necessarily such an agent as can give a good notice,[86] but it is suggested that the same decision would not be reached today.

In whose favour notice enures

15–15   In preserving the liability of the drawer or indorsers what matters is whether they have been give notice, not whether the party, whom is maintaining the claim, gave the actual notice:

49.—(3) Where the notice is given by or on behalf of the holder, it enures for the benefit of all subsequent holders and all prior indorsers who have a right of recourse against the party to whom it is given.

(4) Where notice is given by or on behalf of an indorser entitled to give notice as hereinbefore provided, it enures for the benefit of the holder and all indorsers subsequent to the party to whom notice is given.

Hence a notice by the last indorsee to the drawer will operate as a notice for each indorser to the drawer; and if the payee or first indorsee has duly received notice, or has not been discharged by laches, a notice by him to the drawer will be equivalent to a notice from each indorser, and from the holder to the drawer. It has been held that a notice from an intermediate party may, in pleading, be described as a notice from the plaintiff.[87]

---

[82] *Jameson v. Swinton* (1809) 2 Camp. 373; *Wilson v. Swabey* (1815) 1 Stark. 34.

[83] *Jennings v. Roberts* (1855) 24 L.J.Q.B. 102, 4 E. & B. 615, see *per* Lord Campbell C.J., pp. 618, 619.

[84] *Rogerson v. Hare* (1837) 1 Jur. 71.

[85] *Woodthorpe v. Lawes* (1836) 2 M. & W. 109. As to effect of misdescription of principal, see *Harrison v. Ruscoe* (1846) 15 L.J.Ex. 100; and *ante*, para. 15–03.

[86] *East v. Smith* (1847) 16 L.J.Q.B. 292.

[87] *Newen v. Gill* (1838) 8 C. & P. 367.

Notice by a pledgee

A creditor who holds a bill as a collateral security is bound to present and give notice of dishonour, and is liable for the consequences if he omits to do so.[88]

15–16

Notice by acceptor

At common law a notice by the acceptor to the drawer was held good.[89] However the 1882 Act stipulates that for a notice to be valid it must be give by or on behalf of the holder or indorser, so that the acceptor cannot now give a valid notice unless acting as agent on behalf of the holder or an indorser.[90]

15–17

To whom notice should be given

As required by the 1882 Act, section 48, set out at the beginning of the chapter, notice of dishonour must be given to the drawer and each indorser.

15–18

Notice to all parties

It is the safest course for the holder to give notice himself to all the parties against whom he may wish to proceed within the time within which he is by law required to give it to his immediate indorser. If he merely gives notice to his immediate indorser, and it is not regularly transmitted to the antecedent parties, they are discharged. Even if it is so transmitted, the evidence required to trace the notice back to a remote party is more voluminous, and may be difficult to procure. The holder may thus be defeated by the delay of an intermediate indorser but, if he elects to give all the indorsers notice himself, he must do so within the time within which he is bound to give notice to his immediate indorser, and cannot claim a day for each indorser.[91]

15–19

If there is any delay in the circulation of the notice back through the several parties, even though the neglect of one is compensated by the extraordinary diligence of another, delay once committed discharges all the antecedent parties, and subsequent notices are invalid, for they are given by parties who are no longer liable on the bill.[92] It has been held that in a case where apparently all the parties lived in the same place, it is not enough that the drawer or indorser receives notice in as many days as there are subsequent

15–20

---

[88] *Peacock v. Pursell* (1863) 32 L.J.C.P. 266.

[89] *Shaw v. Croft* (1798) Chit. 11th ed., p. 230; *Rosher v. Kieran* (1814) 4 Camp. 87.

[90] See s.49(1), *ante*, para. 15–13, *cf.* Bayley, *Bills* (6th ed.), p. 250, approved in *Harrison v. Ruscoe* (1846) 15 L.J. Exch. 110, 112. Where a cheque is sent by post by bankers, who are the agents of the holder, to the drawee bank. It has been considered that the latter bank is constituted thereby the holder's agent, and ought therefore to give him notice of dishonour (*Bailey v. Bodenham* (1864) 33 L.J.C.P. 252, 255 (Erie C.J.)); and see *Lombard Banking Ltd v. Central Garage and Engineering Co. Ltd* [1963] 1 Q.B. 220. The Uniform Commercial Code, s.3–508, appears not to contemplate notice by an acceptor.

[91] *Rowe v. Tipper* (1853) 13 C.B. 249.

[92] *cf. Harrison v. Ruscoe* (1846) 15 L.J. Exch. 110, 111; and see *Yeoman Credit Ltd v. Gregory* [1963] 1 W.L.R. 343.

indorsers, unless it is shown that each indorsee gave notice within a day after receiving it; as, if any has been beyond the day, the drawer and prior indorsers are discharged.[93] Nor can a party in such a case, by waiving his own discharge, waive the discharge of antecedent parties. The defendant was the eighth, plaintiff the eleventh, indorser of a bill. The instrument passed through several subsequent hands, was dishonoured at maturity, and returned to the immediate indorsee of the plaintiff. It remained in his hands three days, and then the plaintiff paid it, and gave notice to the defendant, who received the notice in a shorter interval from the day of dishonour than would have elapsed had each party through whose hands the bill was returned taken the full time allowed by law for giving notice. Abbott C.J.: "In this case the plaintiff . . . was clearly discharged by the laches of the holder. Then can he, by paying the bill, place the prior indorsers in a worse situation than that in which they would otherwise have been? I think he cannot do so, and that in paying this bill he has paid it in his own wrong, and cannot be allowed to recover upon it against the defendant."[94]

No laches can be imputed to the Crown and, therefore, if a bill was seized under an extent before it was due, the neglect of the officer of the Crown to give notice of dishonour would not discharge the drawer or indorser.[95]

Special instances

15–21   Section 49(8) to (11) of the 1882 Act set out provisions where notice is given in special instances.

Agent

15–22   As notice may be given by leaving it at the counting-house or place of business,[96] so notice to an agent for the general conduct of business is sufficient notice to the principal, since the 1882 Act provides as follows:

49.—(8) Where notice of dishonour is required to be given to any person, it may be given either to the party himself, or to his agent in that behalf.

But notice to a man's attorney or solicitor is not sufficient,[97] nor can notice be given to a referee in case of need.[98] A verbal message left at the drawer's house with his wife has been held sufficient. "A person, not a merchant" says Bolland B. "who draws a bill of exchange, undertakes to have someone at his

---

[93] *Marsh v. Maxwell* (1809) 2 Camp. 210n.; see *Rowe v. Tipper, supra.*

[94] *Turner v. Leech* (1821) 4 B. & Ald. 451; *Smith v. Mullett* (1809) 2 Camp. 208, where equally the defendant appears to have received the notice, in spite of laches, earlier, reckoning by the number of indorsers than he otherwise would have done.

[95] Crown Proceedings Act 1947; *West on Extents* (1817 ed.), pp. 28, 29; *R. v. Renton* (1848), 2 Ex. 216; 17 L.J. Ex. 204. As to waiver of laches, see *post,* para. 15–33, s.50(2)(b).

[96] See *ante,* para. 15–06.

[97] *Crosse v. Smith* (1813) 1 M. & S. 545, where the message was a verbal one, but Lord Ellenborough seems to have held generally (at 554) that an attorney was not a proper person to give notice to.

[98] *Re Leeds Banking Co.* (1865) L.R. 1 Eq. 1.

house to answer any application that may be made respecting it when it becomes due."[99]

Personal representatives

In the case of the death of the drawer or indorser the 1882 Act provides: **15–23**

49.—(9) Where the drawer or indorser is dead, and the party giving notice knows it, the notice must be given to a personal representative if such there be, and with the exercise of reasonable diligence he can be found.

Under the 1882 Act the joint effect of this subsection and of section 50(2)(a)[1] appears to be to dispense with notice altogether where there is no personal representative or none who can, with reasonable diligence, be found.[2]

Bankruptcy

Prior to the passing of the 1882 Act it appeared that notice given to a **15–24** bankrupt drawer or indorser was invalid.[3] Now notice may be given to the bankrupt or his trustee:

49.—(10) Where the drawer or indorser is bankrupt, notice may be given either to the party himself or to the trustee.

Parties jointly liable

Where drawers or indorsers are jointly liable, though not partners, the 1882 **15–25** Act provides that:

49.—(11) Where there are two or more drawers or indorsers who are not partners, notice must be given to each of them, unless one of them has authority to receive such notice for the others.

It has been considered that, in the case of joint parties who are not partners, notice to one only will not bind even him,[4] and the 1882 Act seems to support this view. By section 16 of the Partnership Act 1890, notice to a partner who habitually acts in the partnership business is notice to the firm, except in the

---

[99] *Housego v. Cowne* (1837) 2 M. & W. 348. Where husband and wife were joint indorsers of a note and the wife left all business affairs in her husband's hands, it was held that notice to the husband was as good as against the wife (*Counsell v. Livingston* (1902) 4 O.L.R. 340).

[1] *Post,* para. 15–32.

[2] By s.3–508(7) of the Uniform Commercial Code, if any party is dead or incompetent, notice may be sent to his last known address or given to his personal representative.

[3] The cases cited in support of this view appear to have been *Ex p. Moline* (1812) 19 Ves. 216; *Ex p. Johnson* (1834) 3 Deac. & Ch. 433; *Ex p. Chappel* (1838) 3 Mont. & A. 490.

[4] Story, *Promissory Notes* (7th ed.), p. 410; Daniel, *op. cit.* (5th ed.), Vol. 2, para. 999a; *Beutel's Brannan* (7th ed., 1948), p. 1067; and see W.C.C. s.3–507.

case of fraud on the firm committed by or with the consent of that partner.[5] Notice to a continuing partner, after the dissolution of the partnership, binds a partner who has retired from the partnership in respect of the liability on a bill incurred previous to the dissolution of the partnership.[6]

Notice to acceptor not necessary

15–26   Neither the acceptor of a bill nor the maker of a note is, however, entitled to notice, since it is provided that

52.—(3) In order to render the acceptor of a bill liable it is not necessary to protest it, or that notice of dishonour should be given to him.

And by section 89(2),[7] this provision applies to the maker of a note.[8]

Even though an acceptance is qualified, that will not entitle the acceptor to notice. "Bills of exchange" says Abbott C.J. "of late years have been made payable by the acceptor, either at the houses of his friends or agents, they being expressly named in the acceptance, or at banking houses, or at houses merely described by their number in a certain street. It is most convenient that the same rule should be laid down as applicable to all these cases. The most plain and simple rule to lay down is this; that the effect of an acceptance in any of these forms is a substitution of the house, banker, or other person therein mentioned, for the house or residence of the acceptor, and, consequently, that the presentment at the house, or to the party named in the acceptance is equivalent to presentment at the house of the acceptor."[9] *A fortiori* it is unnecessary to have given the acceptor such a notice in any action against the drawer.[10]

Transferor not indorsing

15–27   If a man, not a party to a bill assigns without indorsement, he is not entitled to notice of dishonour.[11] And, as a general rule, a man transferring by delivery without indorsement a bill or note payable to bearer is not entitled to notice.

---

[5] Clearly, therefore, notice to a limited partner under the Limited Partnerships Act 1907 will not be sufficient. Since, in the case of limited companies, neither the individual shareholders nor the individual directors are its agents, notice to one of them is not notice to the company.

[6] *Goldfarb v. Bartlett and Kremer* [1920] 1 K.B. 639.

[7] *Post*, para. 24–01.

[8] *cf. Pearse v. Pemberthy* (1812) 3 Camp. 261; *Hough v. Kennedy* (1910) 13 W.L.R. 674; *Codville Co. v. Jordan* [1922] 1 W.W.R. (Can.) 1280, cases of accommodation maker of note to knowledge of plaintiff.

[9] *Treacher v. Hinton* (1821) 4 B. & Ald. 413, 415; *Smith v. Thatcher* (1821) 4 B. & Ald. 200.

[10] *Edwards v. Dick* (1821) 4 B. & Ald. 212.

[11] *Van Wart v. Woolley* (1824) 3 B. & C. 439; *Swinyard v. Bowes* (1816) 5 M. & S. 62. But a notice has been held to be in time, although an allowance be made for its transmission through a party not indorsing (*Clode v. Bayley* (1843) 12 M. & W. 51).

A transferor by mere delivery of a negotiable instrument, made or become payable to bearer, is not in general liable, either on the instrument or on the consideration.[12] He, therefore (unless in some excepted cases), requires no notice of dishonour. But also, if the bill or note payable to bearer were delivered on account of a pre-existing debt, that delivery is not, prima facie, a sale of the bill or note. On dishonour, therefore, of the bill or note, the liability of the transferor for the original debt revives. But in such a case the transferee will have made the bill or note his own, unless he has given due notice of dishonour.

Further, just as there may be an express contract that the instrument shall not amount to a payment if dishonoured, so there may be circumstances from which a court might infer that the intention and understood contract of the parties was that the instrument was not to be a payment, if dishonoured.[13]

It is conceived that in all cases where, in consequence of the dishonour of bills or notes made or become payable to bearer, a remedy arises on the consideration, the transferor is entitled to notice of dishonour.[14]

Guarantor

A man merely guaranteeing the payment of a bill, but not a party to it, is **15–28** not discharged by the neglect of the holder to give him notice of dishonour unless he has been actually prejudiced by such neglect.[15] (It is suggested that this is so even where he signs the back of a bill under such words as "Payment guaranteed", which would constitute a sufficient memorandum to satisfy s.4 of the Statute of Frauds.) And though a man indorses a bill, yet if he also gives a bond conditioned for its payment, absence of due notice of dishonour would not amount to a defence to an action on the bond.[16] As to backing a bill by the signature of the "backer" see *post*, paras 17–13 *et seq.*

FAILURE TO GIVE NOTICE

Effect of failure to give notice

The law presumes that, if the drawer has not had due notice, he is injured **15–29** because otherwise he might have immediately withdrawn his effects from the

---

[12] See *post*, para. 17–21, the 1882 Act, s.58(2).

[13] *Post*, para. 31–01, and see *Van Wart v. Woolley* (1824) 3 B. & C. 439.

[14] In *Smith v. Mercer* (1867) L.R. 3 Ex. 51, it is pointed out that an unindorsed bill is either taken in payment, in which case the transferor is discharged, dishonour notwithstanding, or it is taken with a right of recourse, in which case the transferor is not liable in the absence of notice; see also *Turner v. Stones* (1843) 1 Dowl. & L. 122, 131.

[15] *Hitchcock v. Humfrey* (1843) 5 M. & G. 559 and *Walton v. Mascall* (1844) 13 M. & W. 72 (agreements of guarantee in writing); *Carter v. White* (1883) 25 Ch.D. 666, 672 (surety by deposit of security): Cotton L.J. at 671: rule as to notice applies only to parties to bills not to persons interested without being parties (*Hitchcock v. Humfrey*), where the above passage is cited; *Mallough v. Dick* (1927) 1 W.W.R. 544. It is otherwise where the bill is not presented for payment when due (*Philips v. Astling* (1809) 2 Taunt. 206). The notorious insolvency of the acceptor before maturity excuses presentment and notice to the guarantor (*Holbrow v. Wilkins* (1822) 1 B. & C. 10; *Warrington v. Furbor* (1807) 8 East 242).

[16] *Murray v. King* (1821) 5 B. & Ald. 165.

hands of the drawee and that, if the indorser has not had timely notice, the remedy against the parties liable to him is rendered more precarious. The consequence, therefore, of neglect of notice is, that the party to whom it should have been given is discharged from all liability, whether on the bill or on the consideration for which the bill was paid.[17]

It has long been settled that the want of notice is a complete defence, and that evidence tending to show that the defendant was not prejudiced by the neglect is inadmissible, except in an action against the drawer who had no effects in the hands of the drawee.[18] If a man who is discharged for want of notice nevertheless pays the bill, he cannot recover against prior parties. But where an agent drew a bill on his principal for goods bought by the agent for the principal, and the bill was dishonoured, of which the agent had no notice, but the agent, being afterwards arrested on the bill, paid it, and sued his principal on the contract of indemnity, which the law implies in favour of the agent in such cases, it was held that the agent's not having insisted on the absence of notice as a defence to the action against himself did not preclude him from recovering the amount of the bill against his principal.[19]

Delay in giving notice

15–30   Whilst ss.(12), (13) and (14) impose a strict time-limit for the giving of notice, the rules are ameliorated where the delay in giving of notice is caused by circumstances beyond the control of the party responsible for the giving of such notice. As regards delay the 1882 Act provides as follows:

> **50.—(1) Delay in giving notice of dishonour is excused where the delay is caused by circumstances beyond the control of the party giving notice, and not imputable to his default, misconduct, or negligence. When the cause of delay ceases to operate the notice must be given with reasonable diligence.**

Delay in the post office, as we have seen, does not prejudice the sender.[20] But if the cause of delay is removed to the knowledge of the holder, notice must at once be given. Thus, where the holder was unable to find the drawer at the address given by the latter but, previous to the issue of the writ, in fact, obtained an effective address, it was held that notice ought to have been sent to that address.[21]

Ignorance of a party's residence will excuse neglect to give notice of dishonour, so long as that ignorance continues without neglecting to use the ordinary means for acquiring information. "When the holder of a bill does not know where the indorser is to be found, it would be very hard" says Lord Ellenborough, "if he lost his remedy by not communicating immediate notice

---

[17] *Bridges v. Berry* (1810) 3 Taunt. 130, where the consideration for the bill was time allowed for payment of an earlier bill; see also the 1882 Act, s.48, *ante*, para. 15–02.

[18] *Dennis v. Morrice* (1800) 3 Esp. 158; but notice in such a case is now excused (the 1882 Act, s.50(2)(c), (4), *post*, para. 15–34); *cf.* also *Hill v. Heap* (1823) Dow. & Ry. N.P. 57.

[19] *Huntley v. Sanderson* (1833) 1 Cr. & M. 467.

[20] The 1882 Act, s.49(15); *ante*, para. 15–05.

[21] *Studdy v. Beesty* (1889) 60 L.T. 647.

of the dishonour of the bill, and I think the law lays down no such rigid rule. The holder must not allow himself to remain in a state of passive and contented ignorance; but, if he uses reasonable diligence to discover the residence of the indorser, I conceive that notice given as soon as this is discovered is due notice of the dishonour of the bill, within the usage and custom of merchants."[22] Where the holder, in order to discover the residence of the indorser, had merely made inquiries at a certain house where the bill was made payable, Lord Ellenborough said: "Ignorance of the indorser's residence may excuse the want of due notice, but the party must show that he has used reasonable diligence to find it out. Has he done so here? How should it be expected that the requisite information should have been obtained where the bill was payable? Inquiries might have been made of the other persons whose names appeared on the bill, and application might have been made to persons of the same name with the defendant whose addresses are set down in the Directory."[23] Due diligence has, however been held to be a question of fact.[24] After the residence of the party is discovered, the holder has the same time to give notice as he would have had in the first instance.[25]

Nemo ad impossibile tenetur;[26] and, therefore it seems, on general principles, that the death or dangerous illness of the holder or his agent, or other accident not attributable to the holder's negligence, rendering notice impossible, may excuse it, or delay in giving it.[27] But where an indorser left home on account of the dangerous illness of his wife at a distance, and a letter containing notice of dishonour of a bill lay unopened at his shop during his absence, until after the proper time for giving his indorser notice, Lord Ellenborough held that the circumstances afforded no excuse for delay.[28] This decision appears to be based on the fact that the indorser had left no one behind in his shop who was authorised to open letters.

Dispensation of notice

The requirements as to the giving of notice are further relaxed by the **15–31**
provisions set out in s.50(2)of the 1882 Act. That subsection provides that notice of dishonour is dispensed with by reference to four categories. Subsections (2)(a) and (b) have general application, whilst subsections (c) and (d) set out when notice is dispensed with as regards the drawer and indorsers, respectively.

---

[22] *Bateman v. Joseph* (1810) 2 Camp. 461, 462; *Browning v. Kinnear* (1819) Gow. N.P.C. 81; *Baldwin v. Richardson* (1823) 1 B. & C. 245; *Chapcott v. Curlewis* (1843) 2 Moo. & R. 484; *Fleming v. McLeod* (1907) 39 S.C.R. 290; *Merchants Bank of Canada v. Cunningham* (1892) 1 Que. Q.B. 33.

[23] *Beveridge v. Burgis* (1812) 3 Camp. 262.

[24] *Bateman v. Joseph* (1810) as reported 12 East 433. It is a question for the jury whether the delay arose by reason of the indistinctiveness of the defendant's writing on the bill so that the notice could not be property addressed (*Hewitt v. Thomson* (1836) 1 Moo. & R. 543); see also *Siggers v. Brown* (1836) 1 Moo. & R. 520.

[25] *Firth v. Thrush* (1828) 8 B. & C. 387; *Dixon v. Johnson* (1855) 1 Jur. (N.S.) 70.

[26] Nobody can be required to do that which is impossible.

[27] Pothier, Contrat de Change, para. 144.

[28] *Turner v. Leech* (1818) Chitty (11th ed.), p. 226.

Notice cannot be given

15–32   Section 50(2) provides for notice to be dispensed with:

(a) when after the exercise of reasonable diligence, notice as required by this Act cannot be given to or does not reach the drawer or indorser sought to be charged; as already set out delay in the giving of notice may be excused where the matter is beyond the control of the party responsible for giving notice.[29] Once reasonable diligence to give notice has been attempted, but without success, notice is dispensed with.

Waiver

15–33   Additionally section 50(2) provides for notice to be dispensed:

(b) by waiver express or implied. Notice of dishonour may be waived before the time of giving notice has arrived, or after the omission to give due notice.

Thus where the drawer stated to the holder, a few days before the bill became due, that he would call and see if the bill had been paid by the acceptor, it was held that he had dispensed with notice.[30] A subsequent promise to pay or admission of liability is such a waiver. "A promise to pay may operate either as evidence of notice of dishonour, or as a prior dispensation, or as a subsequent waiver of notice."[31] A promise to pay, if made before the time for giving notice has expired is a dispensation; if made after that, it is a waiver independently of any question of actual notice.[32] And a payment of part, or an acknowledgement of liability,[33] though after action brought,[34] will be evidence of notice.[35]

It makes no difference that such promise, payment or acknowledgement was made under a misapprehension of the law, for every man must be taken to know the law[36] otherwise, a premium is held out to ignorance, and there is

---

[29] *Supra* para. 15–30.

[30] *Phipson v. Kneller* (1815) 4 Camp. 285; see also *Burgh v. Legge* (1839) 5 M. & W. 418; *Brett v. Levett* (1811) 13 East 213, 214; but see *Ex p. Bignold* (1836) 1 Deac. 712. Waiver of notice seems to enure for and against the same parties as notice itself (*Coulcher v. Toppin* (1866) 2 T.L.R. 657; *Bank of Toronto v. Bennett* (1925) 57 O.L.R. 326).

[31] *Cordery v. Colville* (1863) 32 L.J.C.P. 210, 211 (Byles J.).

[32] *Ibid.*; *Woods v. Dean* (1862) 32 L.J.Q.B. 1; *Kilby v. Rochussen* (1865) 18 C.B.(N.S.) 357. It was formerly considered that a promise to pay was only evidence from which a jury might presume that a notice had been received (*Hicks v. Beaufort* (1838) 4 Bing. N.C. 229).

[33] *Rogers v. Stephens* (1788) 2 T.R. 713; *Lundie v. Robertson* (1806) 7 East 231; *Horford v. Wilson* (1807) 1 Taunt. 12; *Wood v. Brown* (1816) 1 Stark. 217; *Margetson v. Aitken* (1828) 3 C. & P. 338; *Dixon v. Elliott* (1832) 5 C. & P. 437. For examples of insufficient acknowledgments, see *Dennis v. Morrice* (1800) 3 Esp. 158; *Borradaile v. Lowe* (1811) 4 Taunt. 93; *Lecaan v. Kirkman* (1859) 6 Jur. (N.S.) 17.

[34] *cf. Hopley v. Dufresne* (1812) 15 East 275.

[35] Many of the cases cited in this connection fail to draw the proper distinction between the effect of a promise as waiver of notice, and its effect as evidence of notice. In *Kilby v. Rochussen, supra*, the Court held a subsequent promise to be sufficient evidence of due notice, but would have amended if necessary by adding an averment of waiver.

[36] *Stevens v. Lynch* (1810) 12 East 38.

no telling to what extent this excuse might be carried.[37] On the other hand if the promise or acknowledgement is made under a misapprehension of fact, as, if the bill has been presented for acceptance and acceptance has been refused, a promise to pay, in ignorance of that circumstance, is no waiver of the consequence of laches.[38] But a promise to pay will entirely dispense with proof of presentment of notice, and will throw on the defendant the double burden of proving laches, and that he was ignorant of it.[39] Where it is only as to part of the sum, the plaintiff can only avail himself of it as a waiver *pro tanto*. A drawer of a bill for £200, who had not received due notice of dishonour, said: "I do not mean to insist on want of notice, but I am only bound to pay you £70." Abbott C.J.: "The defendant does not say that he will pay the bill, but that he is only bound to pay £70. I think the plaintiffs must be satisfied with the £70.[40] The acknowledgement or promise may be made by the attorney for the defendant, or by his clerk who has the management of the case.[41] It need not be made to the plaintiff, but may be made to another party to the bill, or to a stranger.[42] A promise to pay made by the drawer in expectation that a bill will be dishonoured, but before it is dishonoured, does not dispense with notice; for it is to be understood as a promise on condition that due notice is given.[43]

Though a party may waive the consequence of laches in respect of himself he cannot do so in respect of antecedent parties.[44]

It is fully established that notice means something more than knowledge.[45] Thus where one man was secretary of two companies, one of them being the drawer and indorser and the other the indorsee of a bill, and no notice of the dishonour was given, it was held that the knowledge of the secretary was not to be regarded as equivalent to notice, unless it was shown that it was his duty as regards the indorsee company to communicate his knowledge to the drawer company.[46]

In *Lombard Banking Ltd v. Central Garage and Engineering Co. Ltd*,[47] Scarman J. said that the courts have been ready to infer waiver of notice from very slight evidence:

"In the present case the evidence of waiver consists of conduct after action brought from which it is sought to infer waiver made before action brought. If there was a

---

[37] *Bilbie v. Lumley* (1802) 2 East 469.

[38] *Blesard v. Hirst* (1770) 5 Burr. 2670; *Goodall v. Dolley* (1787) 1 T.R. 712; *McFatridge v. Williston* (1892) 25 N.S. 11.

[39] *Taylor v. Jones* (1809) 2 Camp. 105; *cf. Stevens v. Lynch, supra; Swift Canadian Co. v. Duff* (1916) 38 O.L.R. 163.

[40] *Fletcher v. Froggatt* (1827) 2 C. & P. 569.

[41] *Standage v. Creighton* (1832) 5 C. & P. 406.

[42] *Potter v. Rayworth* (1811) 13 East 417; *Gunson v. Metz* (1823) 1 B. & C. 193. In *Rabey v. Gilbert* (1861) 30 L.J. Ex. 170, it was held that suffering judgment by default in an action at the suit of a second indorsee was evidence of notice or of a waiver of notice in an action by the first indorsee.

[43] *Pickin v. Graham* (1833) 1 Cr. & M. 725; and see *Prideaux v. Collier* (1817) 2 Stark. N.P.C. 57; *Baker v. Birch* (1811) 3 Camp. 107; *Wiggins v. Bellve* (1897) 15 N.Z.L.R. 540.

[44] *Roscow v. Hardy* (1810) 12 East 434; *Turner v. Leech* (1821) 4 B. & Ald. 451; *Marsh v. Maxwell* (1809) 2 Camp. 210, n.

[45] *Carter v. Flower* (1847) 16 M. & W. 743, 749; see also *Pickin v. Graham, supra*, at 727.

[46] *Re Fenwick, Stobart & Co.* [1902] 1 Ch. 507.

[47] [1963] 1 Q.B. 220, 233.

failure to give notice of dishonour in due time every fact pertinent to that failure was known to Rees Evans the director of the plaintiff company who had indorsed the bill by way of guarantee; he was also very well aware, even before the plaintiffs themselves knew, of the fact and of the reasons for dishonour. I find it inconceivable, that if he had not waived the requirements of due notice, upon the facts of this particular case the merest technicality, he would not have taken the point when he was seeking, under legal advice, leave to defend the action."

Dispensation as regards drawer

15–34   Notice of dishonour is dispensed with in five situations; in each case the need to give such notice is essentially made redundant since the drawer will be aware that the bill has not been accepted or met, whichever is applicable. Thus notice is dispensed with:

50.—(2)(c) As regards the drawer in the following cases, namely, (1) where drawer and drawee are the same person, (2) where the drawee is a fictitious person or a person not having capacity to contract, (3) where the drawer is the person to whom the bill is presented for payment, (4) where the drawee or acceptor is as between himself and the drawer under no obligation to accept or pay the bill, (5) where the drawer has counter-manded payment.[48]

Drawer/drawee same person

15–35   As set out in s.5(2) of the 1882 Act[49] where in a bill the drawee and the drawer are the same person the holder may treat the instrument either as a bill or as a note. If the holder elects to treat the instrument as a bill there is no reason why he should be given notice of dishonour, in his capacity as drawer, since, in his capacity as drawee, he is responsible for the non-acceptance or non-payment of the bill. Thus notice is expressly dispensed with. (Equally no notice need be given if the instrument is treated as a note, since the person is the maker of the note and thereby corresponds with the acceptor of a bill, to whom notice need not be given.)[50]

Fictitious drawee

15–36   The case of a drawee being a fictitious person or one incapable of contracting is provided for by section 5(2),[51] which enables the holder to treat the drawer as the maker of a note and as such not entitled to notice.

Presentment for payment at drawer

15–37   If the drawer of a bill makes it payable at his own house, this is evidence to go to the jury that it is a bill drawn for the accommodation of the drawer

[48] *Hill v. Heap* (1823) Dow. & Ry. N.P. 57.
[49] See *ante*, para. 3–09.
[50] See ss.89(2) and 52(3).
[51] *Ante*, para. 3–04, *post* para. 24–05.

himself, of the dishonour of which it is not necessary to apprise him. "I cannot understand", says Lord Tenterden, "why the drawer should with his own hands make the bill payable at his own house, unless he was to provide for the payment of it when at maturity."[52]

Insufficient funds in drawee's hands

The most common instance of this arises in relation to cheques, where the **15–38** bank, on whom the cheque is drawn, is under no obligation, as regards the drawer, to pay the cheque because there are insufficient funds in the drawer's account. If the drawer has insufficient funds at any time during the currency of the bills in the hands of the drawee, the latter will be under no obligation to accept or, if he has accepted, to pay (*vis-à-vis the drawer*), and the drawer will have no remedy against the acceptor or any other person if he is obliged to pay the bill; not being therefore prejudiced by want of notice, the drawer cannot set that up as a defence.[53]

But this case was distinguished in a later decision, where it was held that notice of dishonour for the accommodation of an indorsee must be given to the drawer, though he had no effects in the hands of the acceptor, as, on receipt of notice, the drawer would be entitled to call on the indorsee for the money, whereas in the former case there was no person from whom the drawer would have been entitled to recover.[54] Further, at common law, in order to be liable without notice, the drawer must have had no remedy against the acceptor or any other person.[55] Hence if a bill was drawn for the accommodation, not of the drawer, but of the acceptor, as the drawer might sue the acceptor, he was entitled to notice[56] and if the drawer in such a case chose to pay without notice, he could not sue the acceptor for *money paid* to his use, although he might sue on the bill.[57] So, it was no excuse for neglect to give notice to *an indorser*, that the drawer had no effects in the acceptor's hands.[58] Nor would the absence of effects in the hands of the maker of a *promissory note* be any excuse for want of notice to the indorser, at all events unless the indorser was the person who was to pay, and who had no remedy over against anyone; nor would it suffice to allege that he had not been damnified by the absence of

---

[52] *Sharp v. Bailey* (1829) 9 B. & C. 44.

[53] *Bickerdike v. Bollman* (1786) 1 T.R. 405. Absence of effects will excuse presentment for payment as against the drawer, or an accommodated indorser (1882 Act, s.46(2)(c) and (d)). Hence, where a cheque is dishonoured for want of funds, the drawer is chargeable without either presentment for payment or notice of dishonour, unless he had a reasonable expectation that it would be honoured (*Wirth v. Austin* (1875) L.R. 10 C.P. 689).

[54] *Cory v. Scott* (1820) 3 B. & Ald. 619; *Norton v. Pickering* (1828) 8 B. & C. 610. In such circumstances the drawer appears, as between himself and the acceptor, to have a remedy over against the acceptor, if, failing the indorser, the drawer himself has to pay, and therefore to be entitled to notice under s.50(2)(c), (4); *Cory v. Scott, supra*, p. 384.

[55] *Lafitte v. Slatter* (1830) 6 Bing. 623.

[56] *Ex p. Heath* (1813) 2 Ves. & B. 240; Bayley (6th ed.), p. 295. This seems to be consistent with s.50(2)(c), (4).

[57] *Sleigh v. Sleigh* (1850) 19 L.J. Ex. 345, distinguished in *Re Chetwynd's Estate* [1893] Ch. 13.

[58] *Wilkes v. Jacks* (1794) 1 Peake 267; *Brown v. Maffey* (1812) 15 East 216; *Foster v. Parker* (1876) 2 C.P.D. 18; see, further, *Corney v. Mendez da Costa* (1795) 1 Esp. 302; *Turner v. Samson* (1876) 2 Q.B.D. 23.

notice.[59] An intimation from the drawee that he could not meet the bill, but that the drawer must take it up, does not relieve the holder from the necessity of giving the drawer notice.[60] Where the acceptor remitted to the drawer a sum of money in part payment of his acceptance, it was held that such amount could be recovered by the holder as money paid to his use, but that he could not recover on the bill itself, since the drawer had received no notice.[61] The above cases do not appear to be affected by the 1882 Act, s.50(2)(c) and (d).

At common law, though the drawer had no effects in the hands of the drawee, yet if he had any reasonable expectation that the bill would be honoured, he was held to be entitled to notice of dishonour, as if he had consigned goods to the drawee, though, in fact, they never came to hand,[62] or had accepted bills for him,[63] or where there was a fluctuating balance as between drawer and drawee.[64]

The 1882 Act now, however, definitely provides that the question always is, whether the acceptor is *obliged* to pay and not whether the drawer *expects* that he will. An acceptor may indeed be under an obligation to pay, within the meaning of section 50(2)(c)(4), though he has not sufficient funds of the drawer's in hand to meet the bill. A course of dealing may prevail which would justify a drawer in drawing, although he has no value to the amount of the bill in the hands of the acceptor.[65]

Payment countermanded by drawer

15–39   The last instance in which notice is dispensed with as regards the drawer, is where the drawer himself countermands payment. This occurs, for example where the drawer of a cheque stops the cheque (*i.e.* instructs his bank not to make payment).

Notice where bill drawn by several on one of themselves

15–40   A further instance, not set out in s.50(2)(c), when notice may be dispensed with as regards the drawer, is where a bill is drawn by several persons upon one of themselves, since the acceptor is likewise a drawer, notice of dishonour is superfluous, as the dishonour must be known to one of them, and the knowledge of one is the knowledge of all.[66] But notice to someone in his capacity as secretary of one company is not notice to the same person as

---

[59] *Carter v. Flower* (1847) 16 M. & W. 743; *Reid v. Tustin* (1894) 13 N.Z.L.R. 745; *Brunelle v. Benard* (1919) 2 W.W.R. 288; *Jette v. Ducharme* (1928) 35 R.L.N.S. 20.
[60] *Staples v. Okines* (1795) 1 Esp. 332.
[61] *Baker v. Birch* (1811) 3 Camp. 107.
[62] *Robins v. Gibson* (1813) 3 Camp. 333; *Rucker v. Hiller* (1812) 16 East 43.
[63] *Spooner v. Gardiner* (1824) Ry. & M. 84; *Ex p. Heath* (1813) 2 Ves. & B. 240.
[64] *Orr v. Maginnis* (1806) 7 East 359; *Blackham v. Doren* (1810) 2 Camp. 503.
[65] See *Cumming v. Shand* (1860) 29 L.J. Ex. 129, 152 (Pollock C.B.).
[66] *Porthouse v. Parker* (1807) 1 Camp. 82; but in case of fraud a different rule would prevail (*Bignold v. Waterhouse* (1813) 1 M. & S. 255, 259).

secretary of another company, unless it is his duty to communicate the information to the other company.[67]

Dispensation as regards indorser

Notice of dishonour is dispensed with: **15–41**

50.—(2)(d) As regards the indorser in the following cases, namely, (1) where the drawee is a fictitious person or a person not having capacity to contract, and the indorser was aware of the fact at the time he indorsed the bill, (2) where the indorser is the person to whom the bill is presented for payment, (3) where the bill was accepted or made for his accommodation.

The first two instances of dispensation reflect similar provisions as regards the drawer; however where the drawee is fictitious, in the case of an indoser notice of dishonour is only dispensed with if the indorser was aware of the fact that the drawee was fictitious.

There is no comparable provision to s.50(2)(c); thus an indorser is entitled to notice of dishonour where payment is not met on a cheque because the bank has insufficient funds.

---

[67] *Per* Buckley J. in *Re Fenwick, Stobart & Co. Ltd Deep Sea Fishery Co.'s (Ltd) Claim* [1902] 1 Ch. 507, 511.

CHAPTER 16

DISHONOUR—NOTING AND PROTEST

16–01   NOTING and Protesting have been described as a procedure used to obtain formal proof that a bill or note has been presented and dishonoured.[1]

16–02   Noting is a minute made on the bill by the notary's clerk at the time of refusal of acceptance or payment. It consists of his initials, the month, the day, the year, the noting charges, and the reference to the notary's register. A ticket or label is also attached to the bill on which is written the answer given to the notary's clerk when he made the presentment.[2] A bill may be noted where no protest is either meant or contemplated, as in the case of many inland bills. The use of it seems to be that a notary, being a person conversant in such transactions, is qualified to direct the holder to pursue the proper conduct in presenting a bill, and may, upon a trial, be a convenient witness of the presentment and dishonour. In the meantime, the minute of the notary, accompanying the returned bill, is satisfactory assurance of non-payment or non-acceptance to the various parties by whom the amount of the bill may successively be paid.[3]

16–03   Protesting is a formal certification, signed by a notary, that a bill has been dishonoured. Under the 1882 Act it is only required on a foreign bill, since under certain foreign jurisdictions the fact of dishonour would not otherwise be recognised.

Necessity for and mode of protest

16–04   Immediately upon the dishonour of a bill at due presentment, whether by non-acceptance or non-payment, or of a note by non-payment, a right of recourse against the drawer or maker and the indorsers accrues to the holder; but in order to avail himself of this right he must (unless excused) give due notice of dishonour,[4] and in the case of a foreign bill (but not a note, s.89(4))[5] cause it to be protested, or at all events noted, on the day of dishonour or not later than the next succeeding business day.[6] If the bill is not duly protested, the drawer and indorsers are discharged from liability.[7]

---

[1] See para. 8.31 of the *Banking Services: Law and Practice Report* by the Review Committee (1989) CM.622.

[2] *Brooke's Notary*, 9th ed., 1939, pp. 253 *et seq.*

[3] The expenses of noting (as distinguished from those of protest) may be recovered from any party liable on an inland bill under s.57(1)(c); they may be included under the term "bank charges" on a specially indorsed writ (*Dando v. Boden* [1893] 1 Q.B. 318); see also *Lawrence & Sons v. Willcocks* [1982] 1 Q.B. 696.

[4] As to notice of dishonour, see Ch. 15.

[5] *Post*, paras 16–10 and 24–02.

[6] Bills of Exchange (Time of Noting) Act 1917 (7 & 8 Geo. 5, c. 48).

[7] See s.51(2).

By the law of some foreign countries[8] a protest is essential in the case of dishonour of any bill or note, whether inland or foreign, and it is for the sake of uniformity in international transactions that by English law as in that of the United States[9] foreign bills must be protested.[10] Besides, a protest affords satisfactory evidence of dishonour to the drawer, who, from his residence abroad, might experience a difficulty in making proper inquiries on the subject, and be compelled to rely on the representation of the holder. It also furnishes an indorsee with the best evidence to charge an antecedent party abroad; for foreign courts give credit to the acts of a public functionary such as a notary in the same manner as a protest under the seal of a foreign notary is evidence, in our courts, of the dishonour of a bill payable abroad. "A notary public by the law of nations has credit everywhere."[11]

The requirement that bills be protested is less common throughout the world than was formerly the case. The Banking Services: Law and Practice Report by the Review Committee recommended that the mandatory requirement that foreign bills be protested, in order to preserve the liability of the drawer and indorsers, be abolished; they recommended that protesting be retained on a voluntary basis.[12]

General provisions

The 1882 Act provides as follows: **16–05**

51.—(1) Where an inland bill has been dishonoured it may, if the holder think fit, be noted for non-acceptance or non-payment, as the case may be; but it shall not be necessary to note or protest any such bill in order to preserve the recourse against the drawer or indorser.

(2) Where a foreign bill, appearing on the face of it to be such, has been dishonoured by non-acceptance it must be duly protested for non-acceptance, and where such a bill, which has not been previously dishonoured by non-acceptance, is dishonoured by non-payment it must be duly protested for non-payment. If it be not so protested the drawer and indorsers are discharged.[13] Where a bill does not appear on the face of it to be a foreign bill, protest thereof in case of dishonour is unnecessary.

Inland bills

Inland bills are defined in s.4(2) of the 1882 Act.[14] As set out above there   **16–06**
is no requirement to protest an inland bill. However if there is any doubt about

---

[8] Uniform Law on Bills of Exchange and Promissory Notes, Geneva 1930, Art. 44.

[9] Uniform Commercial Code, s.3–509, official comment.

[10] See *Borough v. Perkins* (1703) 1 Salk. 131. The Act 9 Will. 3, c. 17, referred to in this case, was repealed by the 1882 Act. It required inland bills for £5 or upwards, payable a certain time after date, to be protested, the party neglecting to do so to be liable to all costs and damages. See also the argument in *Trimbey v. Vignier* (1834) 1 Bing.N.C. 151.

[11] *Hutcheon v. Mannington* (1802) 4 Ves. 823.

[12] See paras.8.31 and 8.32, and Recommendation 8(8) of the Report (1989) Cm.622.

[13] See *Bank of Nova Scotia v. Marcelino San Miguel* (1954) 214 F. (2d) 102. It is submitted that if a foreign bill is duly noted, the protest may be completed at any time (s.51(4) and s.93). A guarantor of a bill, whether or not his guarantee is written or evidenced on the bill itself or is contained in a separate document will not be discharged by failure to protest.

[14] *Ante* para. 5–01.

the nature of the bill it is advisable to protest it in order to preserve rights against a party, which may need to be enforced in a foreign jurisdiction where protesting is required. Whilst the 1882 Act provides for noting of an inland bill, the only advantage in doing so is evidential, in that it provides evidence of dishonour. Nonetheless the expenses of noting (as distinguished from that of protest) on inland bills are recoverable in summary proceedings in this country.

Foreign bills

16–07   The definition of a "foreign bill" is to be deduced from section 4 of the 1882 Act;[15] it is a bill, which is not an inland bill (which, in effect, includes one which on the face of it purports to be an inland bill).

Protest by notary

16–08   The protest should be made by a notary public.[16] A notary was anciently a scribe who only took notes or minutes and made short drafts of writings and other instruments, both public and private. He is at this day a public officer of the civil and canon law who, in England, derives his authority to practise from the Court of Faculties of the Archbishop of Canterbury, and the instrument of his appointment decrees "that full faith ought to be given, as well in judgment as thereout, to the instruments to be from this time made".[17] This appointment is also registered and subscribed by the Clerk of the Crown in Chancery. The Acts regulating the appointment of notaries are the Public Notaries Acts 1801 to 1943.

By the Commissioners for Oaths Act 1889 (as amended by the Commissioners for Oaths Act 1891), ambassadors, etc., consuls, pro-consuls, consular agents, and acting consul-generals, acting vice-consuls, etc., in any foreign place are empowered to do all notarial acts.

Householder's protest

16–09   The 1882 Act provides specially for the case where the services of a notary are not available at the place where the bill is dishonoured:

94. Where a dishonoured bill or note is authorised or required to be protested, and the services of a notary cannot be obtained at the place where the bill is dishonoured, any householder or substantial resident of the place may, in the presence of two witnesses, give a certificate, signed by them, attesting the dishonour of the bill, and the certificate shall in all respects operate as if it were a formal protest of the bill.

---

[15] *Ante* para. 5–01.

[16] As to how far a notary may make a notarial document in his own favour, see *Johnson v. Le Grange* (1908) 25 S.C. 823; *Ginnsberg v. Nepgen* (1910) 27 S.C. 62.

[17] *Burn's Ecclesiastical Law* (9th ed., 1842), Vol. 3, p. 2; *Brooke's Notary* (9th ed., 1939), p. 441. In Scotland, by the Law Agents (Scotland) Amendment Act 1896, s.2, no person but a law agent can, after 12 months from the passing of the Act, be admitted a notary public.

The form given in Schedule 1 to this Act may be used with necessary modifications, and if used shall be sufficient.

Protest of foreign note unnecessary

The provisions relating to protest do not apply to a foreign promissory note, **16–10** as far as proceedings in this country are concerned, for the 1882 Act contains the following exception:

89.—(4) Where a foreign note is dishonoured, protest thereof is unnecessary.

The reason for this exception has been stated to be that no action formerly lay upon a foreign promissory note except by virtue of the statute of Anne, and that that statute said nothing about protesting a note.[18] A foreign note should, however, always be protested if proceedings are intended in any foreign country.

Protest for non-acceptance and protest for non-payment

A bill protested for non-acceptance may, at the option of the holder, be **16–11** protested for non-payment, for the 1882 Act provides:

51.—(3) A bill which has been protested for non-acceptance may be subsequently protested for non-payment.

The rule is the same in the United States of America.[19] As in the case of protest of a foreign note, it may be advisable to effect this second protest if action is intended in a foreign country, for protest for non-acceptance does not always in foreign law (though it does in any country which has adopted the Geneva Convention)[20] excuse the subsequent protest for non-payment.

Time for protest

The time within which a bill must be noted or protested is settled by the **16–12** following provisions:

51.—(4) Subject to the provisions of this Act,[21] when a bill is noted or protested, [it may be noted on the day of its dishonour and must be noted not later than the next succeeding business day]. When a bill has been

---

[18] *Bonar v. Mitchell* (1850) 19 L.J. Exch. 302, 303.

[19] Uniform Commercial Code, s.3–509(2).

[20] Art. 44 of the Geneva Convention provides that: "Protest for non-acceptance dispenses with presentment for payment and protest for non-payment." Generally speaking, foreign law only entitled the holder to demand security, and not payment, after effecting protest for non-acceptance. There does not appear, therefore, to be much object in effecting this protest, unless it is desired to obtain such security, or, it seems, an acceptance for honour is offered.

[21] For other provisions, see s.51(9), *post*, para. 16–16, and s.93.

duly noted, the protest may be subsequently extended as of the date of the noting.

The words in brackets have, by section 1 of the Bills of Exchange (Time of Noting) Act 1917, been substituted for the words "it must be noted on the day of its dishonour".[22] The time for protesting is supplemented by the provisions of s.93, which extends the time for protesting provided that the bill has been noted for protest:

93. For the purposes of this Act, where a bill or note is required to be protested within a specified time or before some further proceeding is taken, it is sufficient that the bill has been noted for protest before the expiration of the specified time or the taking of the proceeding; and the formal protest may be extended at any time thereafter as of the date of the noting.

The actual protest, as distinguished from the noting, may be drawn up and completed at any time before the commencement of the suit,[23] or even before or during the trial, and antedated accordingly.[24]

Form of protest

16–13   A protest is a solemn declaration signed by the notary and must contain the following statements:

51.—(7) A protest must contain a copy of the bill, and must be signed by the notary making it, and must specify:

(a) The person at whose request the bill is protested:

(b) The place and date of protest, the cause or reason for protesting the bill, the demand made, and the answer given, if any, or the fact that the drawee or acceptor could not be found.

In practice protests are under the notary's official seal, though this is not required by law. When a protest is made for a qualified acceptance (which, by s.44(1),[25] may be treated as a dishonour of the bill), it must not state a general refusal to accept; otherwise the holder cannot avail himself of the qualified acceptance.[26]

Places of protest

16–14   As regards the place of protest the 1882 Act contains the following provisions:

---

[22] See the Act set out, Appendix 1.

[23] *Geralopulo v. Wieler* (1851) 20 L.J.C.P. 105, distinguishing *Vandewall v. Tyrrell* (1827) M. & M. 87.

[24] Buller, *Law of Trials at Nisi Prius* (7th ed., 1817), p. 272a, citing the unreported case of *Goostrey v. Mead* (1751), also referred to in *Orr v. Maginnis* (1806) 7 East 359, 361.

[25] *Ante*, para. 10–10.

[26] *Sproat v. Matthews* (1786) 1 T.R. 182; see also *Bentinck v. Dorrien* (1805) 6 East 199.

51.—(6) A bill must be protested at the place where it is dishonoured:

Provided that:

(a) **When a bill is presented through the post office, and returned by post dishonoured, it may be protested at the place to which it is returned and on the day of its return if received during business hours, and if not received during business hours, then not later than the next business day:**

(b) **when a bill drawn payable at the place of business or residence of some person other than the drawee has been dishonoured by non-acceptance, it must be protested for non-payment at the place where it is expressed to be payable, and no further presentment for payment to, or demand on, the drawee is necessary.**

Subsection (b) practically reproduces the provisions of the Act of 1832,[27] which dealt only with this question.

Lost bill

The loss, destruction[28] or wrongful detention of a bill is no excuse for the absence of protest.   **16–15**

51.—(8) Where a bill is lost or destroyed, or is wrongly detained from the person entitled to hold it, protest may be made on a copy or written particulars thereof.

Excuses for absence of protest

As to when protest is excused, or delay in noting or protesting is excused, it is provided that: **16–16**

51.—(9) Protest is dispensed with by any circumstance which would dispense with notice of dishonour. Delay in noting or protesting is excused when the delay is caused by circumstances beyond the control of the holder, and not imputable to his default, misconduct, or negligence. When the cause of delay ceases to operate the bill must be noted or protested with reasonable diligence.

Thus the circumstances excusing protest are those set forth in section 50(2)[29] relating to dispensing with notice of dishonour.

---

[27] 2 & 3 Will. 4, c. 98, repealed by the 1882 Act.

[28] As to action in a destroyed instrument, see *post*, para. 30–07.

[29] *Ante*, paras 15–31 *et seq*. The following authorities at common law may be consulted: *Legge v. Thorpe* (1810) 12 East 171 (drawer having no effects in hands of drawee and no reason to believe that the bill would be paid); *Gibbon v. Coggon* (1809) 2 Camp. 188; *Patterson v. Becher* (1821) 6 Moore C.P. 319; *Greenway v. Hindley* (1814) 4 Camp. 52 (waiver by drawer promising to pay on presentment of bill to him after due).

It seems clear that, by section 16(2) of the 1882 Act,[30] the drawer or any indorser may waive protest as against himself. This is usually done by writing the words "I waive protest", or some similar phrase.

Notice of protest

16–17   The fact that a bill has been protested does not excuse notice of dishonour being given. If the party to whom notice is sent is resident abroad it is sufficient to inform him of the protest without sending him a copy[31] it has even been held that it is unnecessary to include in the notice any reference to the bill having been protested.[32] Notice of the protest certainly is not necessary if the party resides within this country, though, at the time of non-acceptance, he may happen to be abroad[33] nor if, at the time of dishonour, he has returned home to this country. "If", says Lord Ellenborough, "the party is abroad he cannot know of the fact of the bill having been protested, except by having notice of the protest itself; but, if he be at home, it is easy for him, by making inquiry, to ascertain that fact."[34]

Additional provisions as to protesting

16–18   The main provisions as to protesting are set out in s.51 of the 1882 Act. However certain supplementary provions are contained elsewhere in the 1882 Act:

44.—(2) ... Where a foreign bill has been accepted as to part, it must be protested as to the balance.

67.—(1) Where a dishonoured bill has been accepted for honour supra protest, or contains a reference in case of need, it must be protested for non-payment before it is presented for payment to the acceptor for honour or referee in case of need.

In one case protest is equally necessary, whether the bill be inland or foreign, in accordance with the following provision:

(4) When a bill of exchange is dishonoured by the acceptor for honour it must be protested for non-payment by him.

A notarial certificate of the protest abroad of a foreign bill is evidence of that fact,[35] but a notarial protest under seal has been rejected as proof of the presentment of a foreign bill in this country.[36] Duplicate protests made out

---

[30] *Post*, para. 17–29.
[31] *Goodman v. Harvey* (1836) 4 A. & E. 870.
[32] *Ex p. Lowenthal* (1874) L.R. 9 Ch.App. 591.
[33] *Cromwell v. Hynson* (1796) 2 Esp. 511.
[34] *Robins v. Gibson* (1813) 1 M. & S. 288.
[35] *Geralopulo v. Wieler* (1851) 20 L.J.C.P. 105; *Anon.* (1699) 12 Mod. 345; Roscoe, N.P. (18th ed.), pp. 215, 387.
[36] *Chesmer v. Noyes* (1815) 4 Camp. 129.

from the notary's book, after action brought, have been held equivalent to originals drawn up at the time of the entry in the book.[37]

Where the drawee becomes bankrupt presentment for acceptance is not obligatory (1882 Act, s.41(2)(a)), yet in the case of a foreign bill protest is required.[38]

Protest for better security

Besides the protest for non-acceptance and for non-payment, the holder **16–19** may protest the bill for better security. Protest for better security is where the acceptor becomes bankrupt or insolvent or suspends payment before the bill falls due. In this case the holder may cause a notary to demand better security,[39] and, on its being refused, the bill may be protested, and notice of the protest may be sent to an antecedent party. The 1882 Act contains the following provision on the subject:

51.—(5) Where the acceptor of a bill becomes bankrupt or insolvent or suspends payment before it matures, the holder may cause the bill to be protested for better security against the drawer and indorsers.

It seems that the holder must wait till the bill falls due before he can sue any party, and the protest for better security will not excuse a subsequent protest for non-payment, if the bill be not met at maturity.[40] There does not appear any advantage from the protest more than from simple notice of the circumstances;[41] except that after such a protest there may be a second acceptance for honour,[42] whereas, without the intervention of a protest, there cannot be two acceptances on the same bill.[43]

On the other hand, many foreign Codes appear to allow the holder of a bankrupt's acceptances, after protest duly effected, to demand security from prior parties that the bill will be met at maturity. Should it be desired to obtain such security in the foreign country, a protest for better security drawn up in this country would presumably be sufficient, since, as already remarked, notarial acts are recognised by foreign courts.[44]

---

[37] *Geralopulo v. Wieler, supra.*

[38] For form of such protest, see *Brooke's Notary* (9th ed., 1939), p. 259, etc.; *cf.* also *La Banque Nationale v. Martel* (1899) Q.R. 17 S.C. 97. As to case of acceptor's bankruptcy before maturity, see the 1882 Act, s.51(5), *post*, para. 16–19.

[39] See *Brooke's Notary* (9th ed., 1939), p. 92; and form of protest, *ibid.* at p. 259.

[40] See Brooke, *op. cit.*, p. 92.

[41] Since protest for better security is not, unlike protest for non-payment, essential to maintain the holder's rights, it has been held not to be "necessary" within the meaning of s.57(1)(c), and the cost of such protest cannot therefore be recovered (*Ex p. Bank of Brazil* [1893] 2 Ch. 438).

[42] *Ex p. Wackerbath* (1800) 5 Ves. 574.

[43] *Jackson v. Hudson* (1810) 2 Camp. 447; see also 1882 Act, s.6(2).

[44] See *ante*, para. 16–04. As a general rule, after protest has been effected, application must be made, in the first instance, to any referee in case of need whose name appears on the bill; *cf.* Geneva Convention, Art. 55.

Scotland

16–20   Protest of an inland bill is optional and (as distinguished from mere noting) rarely resorted to.[45] But it is necessary in Scotland for the purposes of summary diligence. The 1882 Act specially excepts this matter in the following provision:

> **98. Nothing in this Act, or in any repeal affected thereby, shall extend or restrict, or in any way alter or affect, the law and practice in Scotland in regard to summary diligence.[46]**

Promise to pay evidence of protest

16–21   A promise to pay, made after dishonour by the drawee without denial of protest, is good prima facie evidence of protest[47] and is a waiver of notice thereof.[48]

---

[45] Unless an acceptance for honour is desired (1882 Act, s.65(1)). As to noting expenses, see *post*, para. 28–01.

[46] For summary diligence in Scotland, see Wallace and McNeil (8th ed., 1949), p. 182.

[47] *Campbell v. Webster* (1845) 15 L.J.C.P. 4; see also cases cited *ante*, para. 16–16, note 29 (excuses for absence of protest).

[48] *Ex p. Lowenthal* (1874) L.R. 9 Ch.App. 591.

CHAPTER 17

LIABILITIES OF PARTIES

Parties

A BILL of exchange does not represent a single contract but rather a series of contracts. The nature and extent of the liability of the parties to a bill depends upon the capacity in which that person became a party to the bill. In this chapter the liabilities of the following are considered: **17–01**

    (1) The drawee;

    (2) The acceptor;

    (3) The acceptor for honour;

    (4) The drawer;

    (5) The indorser;

    (6) A stranger;

    (7) A transferor;

    (8) An accommodation party.

In the main the liabilities of the parties is dealt with in sections 53 to 56 and 58 of the 1882 Act.

THE DRAWEE

The drawee is the person to whom the bill is addressed and who is required to pay.[1] In England, though not necessarily in Scotland,[2] the drawee of a bill is not liable to the holder until he accepts: **17–02**

53.—(1) . . . the drawee of a bill who does not accept as required by this Act is not liable on the instrument . . . [3]

Even though there may be an obligation, as between the drawer and drawee, to make payment the drawee incurs no liability on the bill until acceptance. The drawee may make payment. So in the case of a cheque (being a bill of exchange drawn on a bank), the bank, as drawee, owes a duty to its customer, the drawer, to pay the cheque provided it has sufficient funds, but incurs no liability on the instrument itself, since the bank does not sign it.

[1] Section 3(1).
[2] See the 1882 Act, s.53(2), *ante*, para. 1–15.
[3] The acceptance required by the Act is given in s.17, *ante*, para. 10–01.

Contractual obligation

17–03   The drawee may, however, place himself under obligation to accept. For instance, where the seller of goods draws on the buyer for the price and transmits to him the bill of exchange together with a bill of lading, to secure acceptance or payment of the bill, the buyer is bound to return the bill of lading if he does not honour the bill of exchange, and if he wrongfully retains the bill of lading, the property in the goods does not pass to him[4] and he is liable for conversion.[5] When shippers of goods discount a draft upon the consignee and authorise the discounters to hand to such consignee, upon his acceptance of the draft, a bill of lading indorsed by the shippers, the ownership of the goods is to be considered, by general mercantile usage, to pass to the consignee on his so accepting, but such inference may be modified or rebutted by particular arrangements between the shippers and the consignee.[6] But where, after payment at maturity of the bill of exchange it was found that the bill of lading was a forgery, it was held that the acceptor was not entitled to recover the amount of the bill of exchange from the person who had presented the bill for payment and to whom it had been paid, since in so presenting the bill such person did not warrant or represent the bill of lading to be genuine.[7] When a cheque is sent in respect of a promised renewal of an acceptance, the acceptor cannot take the cheque without renewing.[8]

If, upon the sale of goods, there is an agreement that the seller shall give credit, and also an agreement by the buyer to give an acceptance for the price, the period of credit stands though an acceptance is not given but, if damage can be proved, an action may lie against the buyer for breach of his contract to give such acceptance.[9] If, however, the agreed terms are cash on delivery with buyer's option of a bill and not, conversely, a bill with the option to pay cash, the seller can sue immediately upon the refusal to accept.[10]

No assignment

17–04   Even though the drawee may have funds available to make payment, a bill does not operate as a assignment of those funds.[11] The position differs in Scotland.

---

[4] Sale of Goods Act 1979, s.19(3): *Shepherd v. Harrison* (1871) L.R. 5 H.L. 116. A bill of exchange accompanied by a bill of lading is usually known as "a documentary bill"; for Dominion cases relating to this question, see *Bank of Australia v. Lohmann* [1919] Vict.L.R. 418; *Imperial Bank v. Hull* (1901) 5 Terr.L.R. 313; *Pantin v. Turner* (1899) 20 Natal L.R. 125.

[5] *Midland Bank Ltd v. Eastcheap Dried Fruit Co.* [1961] 2 Lloyd's Rep. 251; [1962] 1 Lloyd's Rep. 359.

[6] *The Prinz Adalbert* [1917] A.C. 586; *Brace & Co. v. Schmidt* (1920) Q.R. 31 Q.B. 1.

[7] *Guaranty Trust Co. of New York v. Hannay & Co.* [1918] 2 K.B. 623.

[8] *Torrance v. Bank of British North America* (1873) L.R. 5 P.C. 246.

[9] *Rabe v. Otto* (1903) 89 L.T. 562; *Mussen v. Price* (1803) 4 East 147.

[10] *Rugg v. Weir* (1864) 16 C.B.(N.S.) 471; *Anderson v. Carlisle Horse Clothing Co.* (1870) 21 L.T. 760.

[11] Section 53(1).

Liability complete

As we have already seen, every contract on a bill, including that of the **17–05**
drawee/acceptor, is incomplete and revocable till delivery.[12] The liability of
the acceptor, therefore, though irrevocable when complete, does not attach by
merely writing his name, but upon the subsequent delivery of the bill, or upon
communication to, or according to the directions of, the person entitled to the
bill that he has so accepted.[13] The acceptor is considered in all cases as the
party primarily liable on the bill. He is to be treated as the principal debtor to
the holder, and the other parties as sureties liable on his default.[14]

THE ACCEPTOR

Once the drawee of a bill accepts the bill, in accordance with the require-   **17–06**
ments of sections 17 to 19 of the 1882 Act,[15] he incurs a primary liability. The
liability assumed by the drawee on accepting the bill is thus stated by the 1882
Act:

54. The acceptor of a bill, by accepting it—
(1) Engages that he will pay it according to the tenor of his accep-
tance:
(2) Is precluded from denying to a holder in due course:

(a) **the existence of the drawer, the genuineness of his signature, and**
   his capacity and authority to draw the bill;

(b) **in the case of a bill payable to drawer's order, the then capacity of**
   the drawer to indorse, but not the genuineness or validity of his
   indorsement;

(c) **in the case of a bill payable to the order of a third person, the**
   existence of the payee and his then capacity to indorse, but not the
   genuineness or validity of his indorsement.

Liability of the acceptor

Once a bill is accepted the primary liability on the bill is that of the   **17–07**
acceptor; the liability of the drawer and indorsers is conditional, in that they
undertake to pay if the acceptor does not.[16] Thus a bill, accepted generally,

---

[12] 1882 Act, s.21(1).

[13] See s.21 and cases cited, *ante*, para. 9–02. See also *Smith v. Commercial Banking Co. of
Sydney* (1910) 11 C.L.R. 667, where on presentment of a draft on a bank for payment the proper
officer of the bank, in order to authorise payment, wrote his name on the face, and such signature
was held not to amount to an acceptance; though, *per* Griffith C.J., at 674, there might have been
due delivery if it could have been proved that the signature had been placed on the draft previous
to being handed over to the holder for actual presentment for payment.

[14] *Fentum v. Pocock* (1813) 5 Taunt. 192; see also s.54.

[15] *Ante*, Ch. 10.

[16] *Rowe v. Young* (1820) 2 Bligh H.L. 391.

need not be presented for payment to the acceptor,[17] nor is there any requirement to give notice of dishonour or protest the bill.[18] The phrase "according to the tenor of his acceptance" is included because an acceptor may make his acceptance conditional or partial,[19] in which event the extent of his liability will subject to the terms of acceptance.

Estoppels

17–08   As set out above s.54(2) provides that the acceptor is subject to a number of estoppels, but they operate only so far as a holder in due course is concerned. Hence the acceptor cannot maintain that the drawer's signature was forged[20] or to say that the payee being a bankrupt could not indorse,[21] or even to say that a second bankruptcy before the acceptance precluded him from indorsing, though the effect of such second bankruptcy was to vest, *ipso facto*, all the bankrupt's property in his assignees.[22] Nor can the acceptor plead that the drawer to whose order the bill was made payable was a corporation having no authority to indorse;[23] nor that the drawing (and first indorsing) was in the name of a deceased person.[24]

     In an action against an acceptor for refusal to pay his acceptance on the ground that it had been obtained by the fraud of a third party (with which, it was alleged, the plaintiff was tainted) and thus under mistake of fact, it was held that the mistake was not as to a fact affecting his liability.[25]

Indorsements

17–09   However, the estoppels to which the acceptor is subject do not extend to indorsements. The acceptor, therefore, is not precluded from showing that the indorsement of the payee is a forgery, and this is so, even though the instrument at the time of acceptance already bears what purports to be the indorsement of the payee.[26] It is immaterial that the payee whose name is indorsed on the bill is also the drawer, and that the signature of both appear to be in the same handwriting.[27] The only cases in which an acceptor is liable on his acceptance to a holder claiming through a forged indorsement are (i) where, at the time of the acceptance, the acceptor knew of the forgery and

---

[17] Section 52(1).

[18] Section 52(3).

[19] Section 19 *ante* paras 10–04 *et seq.*

[20] *Jenys v. Fawler* (1733) 2 Stra. 946; *Price v. Neal* (1762) 3 Burr. 1355; *Phillips v. im Thurn* (1866) L.R. 1 C.P. 463.

[21] *Drayton v. Dale* (1823) 2 B. & C. 293; *Braithwaite v. Gardiner* (1846) 8 Q.B. 473.

[22] *Pitt v. Chappelow* (1841) 8 M. & W. 616.

[23] *Halifax v. Lyle* (1849) 18 L.J.Ex. 197; see also s.22, *ante*, para. 16–09, as to minors.

[24] *Ashpitel v. Bryan* (1863) 32 L.J.Q.B. 91, affirmed 33 L.J.Q.B. 328.

[25] *Ayres v. Moore* [1940] 1 K.B. 278. The defendant succeeded because his acceptance had been obtained by fraudulent misrepresentation and the plaintiff was not a holder in due course.

[26] *Robarts v. Tucker* (1851) 16 Q.B. 560.

[27] *Smith v. Chester* (1787) 1 T.R. 654.

intended that the bill should be put into circulation by a forged instrument[28] and (ii) where the payee is a fictitious or non-existing person and, consequently, the holder does not need to make title through the indorsement, since, by section 7(3) of the 1882 Act, the instrument is payable to bearer.[29]

Similarly, where the bill is drawn and indorsed by procuration, the acceptance, though admitting the agent's authority to draw, does not admit his authority to indorse.[30]

The special duty to exercise care in framing a mandate to a bank does not exist in the same fashion in the instance of the acceptor of a bill of exchange.[31]

THE ACCEPTOR FOR HONOUR

The concept of acceptance for honour is described in Chapter 10.[32] The **17–10** liability of the acceptor for honour is thus defined:

66.—(1) The acceptor for honour of a bill by accepting it engages that he will, on due presentment, pay the bill according to the tenor of his acceptance, if it is not paid by the drawee, provided it has been duly presented for payment, and protested for non-payment, and that he receives notice of these facts.

(2) The acceptor for honour is liable to the holder and to all parties to the bill subsequent to the party for whose honour he has accepted.

The party accepting for honour is placed in the shoes of the party for whose honour he intervenes, both as regards his liability to subsequent parties and his rights against the antecedent parties, and in addition can recover against such party himself.[33] It has been stated that a person accepting for honour is entitled to recover against the person for whose honour he accepts, even though the acceptance be given without the orders or the knowledge of the person for whose honour it is given.[34]

The acceptor supra protest admits the genuineness of the signature of, and is bound by an estoppel binding on, the party for whose honour he accepts.

[28] *cf. Beeman v. Duck* (1843) 11 M. & W. 251; see *contra, Tucker v. Robarts* (1849) 18 L.J.Q.B. 169, 173; but the 1882 Act, s.54(2)(b), does not appear to countenance the latter view. Clearly the acceptor is not estopped from disputing the validity and genuineness of the indorsement, as distinguished from the drawer's then capacity to indorse (*Garland v. Jacomb* (1873) L.R. 8 Ex. 216).

[29] See *ante*, para. 3–04.

[30] *Robinson v. Yarrow* (1817) 7 Taunt. 455.

[31] *London Joint Stock Bank v. Macmillan and Arthur* [1918] A.C. 777, *per* Lord Haldane at 815; approved by Lord Scarman in *Tai Hing Cotton Mill Ltd v. Liu Chong Hing Bank Ltd* [1986] A.C. 80 and followed in *Commonwealth Trading Bank of Australia v. Sydney Wide Stores Pty* [1981] 14 S.C.L.R. 304 (High Court of Australia); and see *Scholfield v. Londesborough* [1896] A.C. 514.

[32] Para. 10–11.

[33] *cf.* Geneva Convention, Art. 58.

[34] Beawes (6th ed.), p. 569, para. 47; Pothier, *Contrat de Change*, para. 113. By Art. 127 of the French Code the acceptor for honour is, however, bound to notify without delay the fact of his acceptance to the person for whose honour he accepts.

Thus, where a bill was drawn in favour of a non-existing person or order, but the name of the drawer and the name of the payee and first indorser were both forged, and the defendant accepted for the honour of the drawer, it was held that the defendant was estopped from disputing the drawer's signature, and that the bill, though drawn in favour of a non-existing person, was negotiable, and payable to bearer.[35]

The undertaking of the acceptor supra protest is not an absolute engagement to pay at all events, but only a collateral conditional engagement to pay if the drawee, upon further presentment to him at maturity, persist in dishonouring the bill.[36] The bill at maturity must be presented to the drawee, and, if payment is refused, protested for non-payment before payment can be demanded of the acceptor supra protest.[37]

THE DRAWER

17–11   The liability of the drawer is thus defined by the 1882 Act:

55.—(1) The drawer of a bill by drawing it—

(a) engages that on due presentment it shall be accepted and paid according to its tenor, and that if it be dishonoured he will compensate the holder or any indorser who is compelled to pay it, provided that the requisite proceedings on dishonour be duly taken;

(b) is precluded from denying to a holder in due course the existence of the payee and his then capacity to indorse.

The liability of the drawer can be described as both secondary and conditional. By the terms of s.55(1)(a) the drawer does not himself undertake to pay the bill, but merely engages that the bill will be accepted and paid and undertakes, in the event of dishonour, to pay compensation to the holder or any indorser compelled to pay. The liability of the drawer has been likened to that of a surety, but it is not wholly accurate.[38] The liability of the drawer is conditional since it is dependent upon the holder taking the requisite steps upon dishonour.[39]

It may be pointed out that the drawer's undertaking applies only to what appears on the face of the bill under this section and that he is not precluded from asserting that the payee's indorsement was forged. On the other hand, the

---

[35] *Phillips v. im Thurn* (1866) L.R. 1 C.P. 463.

[36] *cf. Hoare v. Cazenove* (1812) 16 East 391, 394.

[37] See s.67, *ante*, paras 12–21 and 16–18.

[38] For example the Statute of Frauds has no application; see *McCall Brothers v. Hargreaves* [1932] 2 K.B. 423 at 429–430; cited with approval in *G. & H. Montage G.m.b.H v. Irvani* [1990] 1 W.L.R. 667 at 683.

[39] See Chs 15 and 16.

undertaking of the indorser extends to everything on the bill, whether on the face or the back, at the time when it leaves his hands.[40]

As regards cheques, the drawer is the person who signs the cheque, which is not intended to be accepted by the bank on whom it is drawn; by issuing the cheque the drawer engages that it will be met on presentation and is liable to the payee, if it is not paid.[41]

THE INDORSER

Every indorser of a bill is in the nature of a new drawer; and is liable to every succeeding holder in default of acceptance or payment by the drawee.[42] The liability of the indorser is stated thus in section 55 of the 1882 Act. **17–12**

(2) The indorser of a bill by indorsing it—

(a) **engages that on due presentment it shall be accepted and paid according to its tenor, and that if it be dishonoured he will compensate the holder or a subsequent indorser[43] who is compelled to pay it, provided that the requisite proceedings on dishonour be duly taken;**

(b) **is precluded from denying to a holder in due course the genuineness and regularity in all respects of the drawer's signature and all previous indorsements;[44]**

(c) **is precluded from denying to his immediate or a subsequent indorsee that the bill was at the time of his indorsement a valid and subsisting bill, and that he had then a good title thereto.**

An indorser, like the drawer, incurs a secondary and conditional liability. The indorser will not be liable to the drawer as such, whatever his liability to that person as named payee and holder may be.[45]

A STRANGER

No one can be liable on a bill whose name does not appear on it. In *Leadbitter v. Farrow* Holroyd J. observed "I apprehend that no action would **17–13**

---

[40] The limited extent of an estoppel can be seen from the case of *Aquaflite Ltd v. Jayman International Freight Consultancy Ltd* [1980] 1 Lloyd's Rep. 36 CA, in which a promise to send cheques where bills of exchange had been given for a repudiated contract was distinguished from the position that would have obtained had the cheques been delivered.

[41] See *post* para. 21–73.

[42] Cited with approval by Mustill L.J. in *G. & H. Montage G.m.b.H. v. Irvani* [1990] 1 W.L.R. 667 at 672C.

[43] By subsequent indorser is meant subsequent in time, see *McCall v. Hargreaves* [1932] 2 K.B. 423, applying *McDonald v. Nash* [1924] A.C. 625, and *National Sales Corporation v. Bernardi* [1931] 2 K.B. 188.

[44] See *Macgregor v. Rhodes* (1856) 25 L.J.Q.B. 318.

[45] See *G. & H. Montage G.m.b.H v. Irvani* [1990] 1 W.L.R. 667 at 672.

lie on the bill, except against those who are parties to it".[46] But if a person signs a bill other than as drawer or acceptor, he must do so either as an indorser or as a stranger; in either case he incurs the liabilities of an indorser:

56. Where a person signs a bill otherwise than as drawer or acceptor, he thereby incurs the liabilities of an indorser to a holder in due course.[47]

This section appears generally to have been construed as entailing that only a holder in due course might sue such a person but there seems to be no reason why it should be so restricted. It is, perhaps, more rational to read it as enacting that the liabilities incurred are those for which any indorser would normally be liable to a holder in due course, thus placing such a person in the same category as regards liabilities as any indorser in the strict sense; it can hardly mean that the liability is to no one but a holder in due course. It would seem to follow that he would be entitled to such privileges as are available to a strict indorser, for example the right to notice of dishonour,[48] though the Act is silent as to these.[49] In *G. & H. Montage G.m.b.H. v. Irvani*[50] Mustill L.J. considered the position of a stranger who simply "backs" the bill, by appending his signature without qualification or explanation. Such a "quasi-indorser" or "anomalous indorser" will be liable to subsequent parties in the event of dishonour; but he will not by his signature alone incur liability to the drawer/payee.[51]

Stranger not a guarantor

17–14   It is clear, however, that although one who backs a bill is in a sense a surety, he is not a guarantor as understood by the Statute of Frauds. There is a distinction between liability upon a bill and liability under an underlying contract of guarantee. In *McCall Brothers v. Hargreaves*[52] Goddard J. observed:

> "It would, I am sure, astonish most people to be told that the Statute of Frauds could ever be set up as an answer to a claim under a bill, and I am glad to find that there is nothing in the authorities which obliges me so to hold. It is true, no doubt, that the agreement which has been found to exist in all the cases cited, as well as in this case, is in one sense a contract of guarantee; but nonetheless an action will lie on the bill

---

[46] (1816) 5 M & S 345, 350; *Cardinal Financial Investments Corp. v. Central Bank of Yemen* [2001] Lloyd's Rep. Banking 1.

[47] Liability is excluded by adding the words sans recours to the signature; see *post*, para. 17–29.

[48] See Cour de Cassation (Ch.Com.), France November 4, 1970.

[49] However, earlier editions of Byles, commenting on this omission, remarked that the section "does not even style him an indorser so as to come in under s.57, but apparently leaves him, if compelled to pay, to his rights to be indemnified at common law".

[50] [1990] 1 W.L.R. 667.

[51] See *supra*, at p. 672.

[52] [1932] 2 K.B. 423, 429–430.

against a person who has indorsed it in these circumstances and with the intention I have found."[53]

A person may, of course, by a separate document undertake secondary liability for the payment of a bill, in which case he is a surety and the document must comply with the provisions of section 4 of the Statute of Frauds.

Steele v. M'Kinlay

In *Steele v. M'Kinlay*,[54] a case decided prior to the 1882 Act, the third **17–15** person had written his signature upon the bill after it had been drawn and accepted, but before its indorsement by the drawer. After the deaths of the drawer and the third person, the drawer's representatives sued the representatives of the third person upon the bill and it was held that the third person could not be regarded as an acceptor and that his liability could be established only by proof of a special contract to be answerable to the drawer for the acceptor, which contract, being different from that which the law merchant would infer from the mere signature as it appeared on the back of a bill, could be proved only by a memorandum in writing, which writing was absent. The distinction between a person who in the nature of things could be the indorser of a bill of exchange and a stranger who writes what, if he had the right to indorse, would be an indorsement on the bill, although he had no right to the property in it, was drawn by Lord Watson in *Steele v. M'Kinlay*.[55] He said:

> "I am of opinion that the character in which James M'Kinlay did become a party to the bill was, both in fact and law, that of an indorser; and that in determining his legal position the circumstances that M'Kinlay's indorsement was written before the bill was delivered to the drawer and the money advanced by him is quite immaterial. No doubt a proper indorsement can only be made by one who has a right to the bill, and who thereby transmits the right, and also incurs certain well known and well defined liabilities. But it is perfectly consistent with the principles of the law merchant that a person who writes an indorsement with intent to become a party to the bill shall be held—notwithstanding that he has not and therefore cannot give any right to its contents—to be subject, as in a question with subsequent holders, to all the liabilities of a proper indorser."

In the particular case James M'Kinlay had signed on the back of a bill drawn by Walker (for whom the plaintiff was trustee) on and accepted by the two sons of M'Kinlay. Both Walker and James M'Kinlay were dead and there was no evidence as to the purpose for which or the capacity in which M'Kinlay had signed.

All that Lord Watson appears to be saying here was that a drawer cannot normally sue an indorser on a bill, which was what the decision amounted to. So where it can be established that the signature was appended with the object of rendering the signatory liable in the event of dishonour, the principle of

---

[53] The passage was cited with approval in *G. & H. Montage* (*supra*) at 683.
[54] (1880) 5 App.Cas. 754.
[55] (1880) 5 App.Cas. 754, 782; and see Lord Sumner in *McDonald & Co. v. Nash & Co.* [1924] A.C. 625, 650, *infra*.

Steele v. M'Kinlay has no application, whether the holder is the drawer or not. Lord Blackburn, at 774, is in many respects to much the same effect as Lord Watson. The bill was drawn by Walker payable to "me or my order" and was indorsed by him. Apart, therefore, from the fact that no evidence regarding the purpose of M'Kinlay's indorsement was available, he would today probably be held liable not to the drawer as such, but to the payee and holder.

Gerald McDonald v. Nash

17–16   Subsequently Lord Sumner, in *Gerald McDonald & Co. v. Nash & Co.*,[56] sought to explain *Steele v. M'Kinlay*[57] and *Macdonald v. Whitfield*:[58]

> "What was held was that, though M'Kinlay was an indorser both in fact and in law and might in a question with subsequent holders be subject to all the liabilities of a proper indorser, he could not thus be interpolated as a party between drawer and acceptor. There is nothing here to touch the case of an indorser, who by arrangement and in order to make himself liable to the drawer, writes his name as indorser first, and for convenience leaves the drawer to write his name higher up, afterwards. On the other hand, *Macdonald v. Whitfield* is a case where the true liability of indorsers, who all indorse on the same occasion without any subsequent filling in of blanks, is held to depend on the actual agreement between them and not on the mere ritual observed in putting their hands to paper."

Liability to the drawer/payee

17–17   A third person signing a bill usually places his signature upon the back of it: hence he is said to "back" the bill and his signature is commonly called an indorsement.[59] The object of backing a bill is to increase its value by reason of the additional credit which it derives from the signature of the third person and it presupposes that the third person, by his signature, has made himself liable upon the bill. This is clearly the case where the bill has been discounted and the bill is in the hands of a holder in due course: the third person comes under an obligation to all subsequent holders precisely similar to that of the drawer. Under s.56 the indorsement, however, does not impose a similar obligation to prior parties,[60] in particular the drawer/payee. Ordinarily when, therefore, the drawer seeks to hold the stranger backing the bill liable, if the acceptor dishonours the bill, he is in effect treating the third person as a surety for the acceptor. A difficulty then arises under section 4 of the Statute of Frauds, because a contract of suretyship must be evidenced by some note or memorandum in writing. Different routes have been adopted to circumvent this difficulty. First, the difficulty does not arise where the bill is indorsed back

---

[56] [1924] A.C. 625.
[57] (1880) 5 App.Cas. 754, 769, *per* Lord Blackburn.
[58] (1883) 8 App.Cas. 733.
[59] See *Rolfe Lubell & Co. v. Keith and Greenwood* [1979] Lloyd's Rep. 35, in which the managing director and the secretary of a company which had accepted bills of exchange indorsed them "For and on behalf of" the company. It was held that the only construction to be placed on the indorsement was that they were personally liable; since none could pass a liability from himself to himself, the only way in which validity could be given to the indorsement was to construe it as binding some one other than the acceptor.
[60] *Montage v. Irvani* (*supra*) at 679.

to the drawer, who then enforces it as a holder in due course.[61] Secondly it is avoided where there is sufficient evidence in writing of an independent contract of suretyship,[62] so that there is a sufficient note or memorandum, such as to satisfy the requirements of the Statute of Frauds. Thirdly, the courts have found it possible to make a third party liable to the drawer /payee by what has been described as an "idiosyncratic . . . doctrine".[63] The device established in *Gerald McDonald & Co. v. Nash & Co.*[64] depends upon proof by evidence extrinsic to the bill, that such a third party intended to sign as surety for the acceptor, taking the case outside s.56, and enabling the third party to sue as indorser; the proof did not depend upon any written note or memorandum satisfying the requirements of the Statute of Frauds. This means could not be employed where what was relied upon was solely that written on the bills and no more.[65]

Indorsement before completion

A further complication is introduced where, as is frequently the case, the third person places his indorsement upon a blank form which is subsequently completed as a bill to drawer's order and indorsed by the drawer.   **17–18**

The leading case before the passing of the 1882 Act was *Steele v. M'Kinlay.*[66] After the passing of the 1882 Act, the principle of *Steele v. M'Kinlay* was applied in *Jenkins v. Coomber*[67] to a case where a bill was drawn to the drawer's order and the third person wrote his name upon the back of the bill before the drawer indorsed it. In an action by the drawer, it was held that the third person was not liable as an indorser under section 55 or as having incurred the liability of an indorser under section 56, since at the time when he put his name upon it the bill was not complete and regular on the face of it, as it required the drawer's indorsement; nor was he liable as a surety, since the provisions of the Statute of Frauds were not satisfied. This decision was distinguished in *McDonald v. Nash.*[68]

---

[61] *Wilkinson v. Unwin* (1881) 7 Q.B.D. 636; *Re Gooch* [1921] 2 K.B. 593; *Yeoman Credit Ltd v. Gregory* [1963] 1 W.L.R. 343, 348–354; [1962] 2 Lloyd's Rep. 302, 313–316.

[62] *Singer v. Elliott* (1888) 4 T.L.T. 524 in which the defendant had written to the plaintiff and spoken of his having guaranteed: held sufficient memorandum to satisfy the Statute of Frauds (but see Goddard J. in *McCall v. Hargreaves* [1932] 2 K.B. 423, 428); *Stagg, Mantle & Co. v. Brodrick* (1895) 12 T.L.R. 12. In *Yeoman Credit Ltd v. Gregory* [1963] 1 W.L.R. 343, it was held that there was no sufficient evidence of such an independent contract.

[63] See Mustill L.J. in *Montage v. Irvani (supra)* at 679H.

[64] See above.

[65] See *Montage v. Irvani (supra)* at 679H.

[66] (1880) 5 App.Cas. 754, doubting *Matthew v. Bloxsome* (1864) 33 L.J.Q.B. 209 in which the defendant placed his signature on the back of a bill which was accepted and completed by the plaintiffs, payable to their order; it was held that the defendant was liable to the plaintiffs as drawers of a bill payable either to bearer or to the plaintiffs' order.

[67] [1898] 2 Q.B. 168, approved in *Shaw & Co. v. Holland* [1913] 2 K.B. 15 but stated by Goddard J. in *McCall v. Hargreaves* [1932] 2 K.B. 423, 428 to be overruled by *McDonald (Gerald) & Co. v. Nash & Co.* [1924] A.C. 625 and *National Sales Corporation Ltd v. Bernardi* [1931] 2 K.B. 188.

[68] [1924] A.C. 625.

It is to be stressed, however, that in *Steele v. M'Kinlay*, owing to the death of the parties, there was no evidence as to the circumstances in which the third person came to write his name.

The report of *Mander v. Evans and Rose*[69] makes no reference to any earlier decision, but there it was held that a person who signed on the back of a bill which did not bear the signature of the drawer, and who had been requested to do so by the person who later accepted it, could not be liable to the drawer, for she had no intention of becoming liable to him and he was not a holder in due course as the bill was not complete and regular when he took it. But where there is clear evidence that the third person agreed to be liable on the bill to the drawer if the acceptor did not pay, the principle of *Steele v. M'Kinlay* has no application.[70] The bill is to be regarded as indorsed by the drawer to the third person and reindorsed by him back to the drawer.[71] The third person is therefore liable to the drawer upon the bill and not upon any independent contract of suretyship.[72] Further, the fact that the bill was incomplete when the third person put his name upon it is immaterial, since the drawer is entitled under section 20[73] to complete it.[74]

In completing the bill, the drawer may inadvertently place his own indorsement below that of the third person. In this case, the order in which the indorsements appear is disregarded and the drawer is entitled to enforce the bill in accordance with the intention of the parties.[75]

While the analogy of an indorsement back to the drawer may be permitted, it must be understood that there is no negotiation to the drawer and his signature as payee-indorser does not make him a holder in due course. His rights against the indorsers do not derive from such a status, but depend on the fiction indicated by Goddard J. in *McCall Brothers Ltd v. Hargreaves* that a bill payable to the drawer must be considered as indorsed to the defendant and indorsed back by the defendant to the payee.[76] It is submitted that the finding in *Lombard Banking Ltd v. Central Garage and Engineering Co.*[77] that the plaintiffs were holders in due course, was—in the light of the decision in *R. E. Jones Ltd v. Waring & Gillow*[78]—technically wrong, though it made, and could make, no difference to the result.

---

[69] (1888) 5 T.L.R. 75.

[70] *Wilkinson v. Unwin* (1881) 7 Q.B.D. 636; *McDonald (Gerald) & Co. v. Nash & Co.* [1924] A.C. 625; *McCall Bros. Ltd v. Hargreaves* [1932] 2 K.B. 423 and *ante*, para. 17–17.

[71] *Glenie v. Bruce Smith, per* A. T. Lawrence J. ([1907] 2 K.B. 507) approved in [1908] 1 K.B. 263 and followed in *National Sales Corporation Ltd v. Bernardi* [1931] 2 K.B. 188; *Re Gooch* [1921] 2 K.B. 593; 1882 Act, s.20.

[72] *McCall Bros. Ltd v. Hargreaves, supra.*

[73] See *ante*, para. 4–01.

[74] *McDonald (Gerald) & Co. v. Nash, supra,* followed in *National Sales Corporation v. Bernardi* [1931] 2 K.B. 188, and with dictum of Lord Watson in *Macdonald v. Whitfield (supra)*, applied in *Yeoman Credit Ltd v. Gregory* [1963] 1 W.L.R. 343. Hence, *Jenkins v. Coomber* [1898] 2 Q.B. 168 and *Shaw v. Holland* [1913] 2 K.B. 15, so far as they turn on this point, are no longer law; see *McCall Bros. Ltd v. Hargreaves, supra; Re Gooch* [1921] 2 K.B. 593.

[75] *National Sales Corporation v. Bernardi, supra* (applied in *Lombard Banking Ltd v. Central Garage & Engineering Co. Ltd* [1963] 1 Q.B. 220 and in *Durack and Others v. West Australian Trustee, Executor & Agency Co.* (1944) 72 C.L.R. 189); following *Glenie v. Bruce-Smith, supra,* and *Re Gooch, supra; McCall Bros. v. Hargreaves.*

[76] [1932] 2 K.B. 423, 430.

[77] [1963] 1 Q.B. 220.

[78] [1926] A.C. 670.

Dominion and American law

The parallel provision to section 56 in common law jurisdictions has been **17–19** provocative of much litigation, in Canada especially, the obvious result of attempts to devise a satisfactory method of guaranteeing payment of a bill or note by a third party somewhat akin to the aval of Continental law.

In Canada, the leading case on the subject is that of *Robinson v. Mann*,[79] a decision of the Supreme Court which a later decision described as a case which "has remained for many years unquestioned and been accepted throughout Canada as law".[80] It was there held that a third party indorsing a note not already indorsed by the payee may be liable as an indorser to such payee, and the Court was clearly of opinion that the effect of section 56 was to introduce the principle of the aval into English [*sic.*] law.[81] It is to be noted that to the words of the English 1882 Act the Canadian Bills of Exchange Act, by section 131, adds the words, "and is subject to all the provisions of this Act respecting indorsers", and it would appear that this addition was made with the intention of adopting the principle of the aval as already in force in the Province of Quebec.[82] There is nothing in the English cases above set out to justify the contention that the principle of the aval has been recognised by English, as distinguished from Canadian, law since the passing of the 1882 Act. In this respect, therefore, the English and Canadian cases are in sharp contrast.[83]

In Australia, section 61 is in the same terms as section 56 of the United Kingdom. It has been held by the High Court of Australia that where the defendant took a note, of which her husband was the maker, to the payee (such note being intended as a renewal of an earlier note) and the payee declined to renew it unless the defendant first indorsed it, which she accordingly did, the payee subsequently indorsing his name above that of the defendant and then again below it, the indorsements were in the order in which they were intended by the defendant to appear, and that the defendant was estopped from denying either that she was an indorser or that the payee was a holder in due course.[84] In New Zealand, the courts appear to take a very similar view to that contained in the Australian cases.[85]

In Ceylon, where a bank officer indorsed a cheque payable to a third party "Payment of cheque guaranteed, *per pro* Thomas Cook (Bankers) Ltd, D.", it

---

[79] (1901) 31 S.C.R. 484. In the headnote to this case, the word "indorsee" is a misprint for "indorser"; see addendum to volume. See also Falconbridge, *Banking and Bills of Exchange* (7th ed.), pp. 762, 763.

[80] *Grant v. Scott* (1919) 50 D.L.R. 250 (Davis C.J.), approving *Robinson v. Mann.*

[81] 31 S.C.R. 484, 486. The same view seems to have been taken in *Grant v. Scott* (1919) 59 S.C.R. 227, 230 (Brodeur J.).

[82] See *McDonough v. Cook* (1909) 19 O.L.R. 267, 273.

[83] See Falconbridge, *op. cit.*, pp. 762, 763, and as regards South Africa, Cowen (4th ed., 1966), pp. 220 *et seq.*

[84] *Ferrier v. Stewart* (1912) 15 C.L.R. 32, where the English cases of *Steele v. M'Kinlay* (1880) 5 App.Cas. 754; *Singer v. Elliott* (1888) 4 T.L.R. 524, and *Jenkins v. Coomber* [1898] 2 Q.B. 168, appear to have been distinguished on the ground that in all these cases the indorsement of the third party preceded that of the payee. This decision was shortly after followed in *Trimble v. Thorne* [1914] V.L.R. 41; see also *Freedman & Co. v. Dan Che Lin* (1905) 7 W.A.L.R. 179, where a person indorsing a note after the payee was held on the facts to be a joint maker.

[85] See *Erikssen v. Bunting* (1901) 20 N.Z.L.R. 388; *Cook v. Fenton* (1892) 11 N.Z.L.R. 505.

was held that he thereby turned the cheque into a bill of exchange, but that the defendant bankers were not liable as the signatory had no authority and anyone taking the cheque was put on inquiry by the procuration signature.[86]

In South Africa, Roman-Dutch law recognises the principle of the aval; it has been held that a person who indorses a note, which has not been indorsed by the payee, prima facie incurs the liability of an aval or surety for the maker to the lawful holder.[87] The payee in such case is not a holder in due course,[88] but the surety as such is not entitled either to presentment at due date or to notice of dishonour.[89]

The Uniform Commercial Code contains the following provisions in Part 4—Liability of Parties: Section 3–401. Signature.

(1) No person is liable on an instrument unless his signature appears thereon.

Section 3–402. Signature in Ambiguous Capacity.

Unless the instrument clearly indicates that a signature is made in some other capacity it is an indorsement.

The purpose of this last section is stated as:

> "The revised language is intended to say that any ambiguity as to the capacity in which a signature is made must be resolved by a rule of law that it is an indorsement. Parol evidence is not admissible to show any other capacity, except for the purpose of reformation of the instrument as it may be permitted under the rules of the particular jurisdiction. The question is to be determined from the face of the instrument alone, and unless the instrument itself makes it clear that he has signed in some other capacity the signer must be treated as an indorser.
>
> The indication that the signature is made in another capacity must be clear without reference to anything but the instrument."

The "aval"

17–20   As observed by Mustill L.J other systems of law have not needed to resort to the device adopted in *McDonald v. Nash*,[90] in order to render a stranger liable, since their laws recognised the concept of "aval".[91] Under the Geneva Convention, Chapter IV, Articles 30, 31 and 32, payment of a bill may be guaranteed by the signature of a third person appearing on the bill. This is

---

[86] *Addaicappa Chetty v. Thomas Cook (Bankers) Ltd* (1930) 31 Ceylon N.L.R. 385; and (1932) N.L.R. 443, PC.

[87] See Cowen, 4th ed. (1966), Ch. 13, p. 213, especially the comments on the law of England, p. 220; *Klopper v. Van Straaten* (1894) 11 S.C. 94; *Moti & Co. v. Cassim's Trustee* [1924] A.D. 720; *Cassimjee v. Maharaj* (1925) 46 N.L.R. 151.

[88] *Cook & Co. v. Estate Stephan* (1907) 11 Cape Times R. 660 (Villiers C.J.); *Ullman Bros. v. Davidson* [1903] T.S. 596.

[89] *Bethlehem v. Zietsman* [1908] E.C.C. 367.

[90] *Supra.*

[91] See *Montage v. Irvani* (*supra*) at 673.

called an aval.[92] A signature by way of aval is created by the placing of a signature on the bill together with the words "*bon pour aval*", "*bon pour aval pour les tires*" or some comparable wording. The person who thus signs the bill as surety assumes the same liability as the party for whom he intervenes. If, therefore, the aval is given on behalf of the acceptor, the person so giving it assumes the liability of an acceptor; if nothing is said, the aval is deemed to have been given for the drawer.

But:

> "An aval for the honour of the acceptor, even if on the bill, is not effectual in English law, as appears by *Jackson v. Hudson*.[93] That case cannot now be questioned after the lapse of so many years, even if it could have been successfully impugned at the time, which I do not think it could. But the indorsement by a stranger to the bill on it to one who is about to take it is efficacious in English law, and has effect as an aval. The effect, according to English law, of such an indorsement is recognised by Lord Holt in *Hill et al. v. Lewis*[94] and again in *Penny v. Innes*;[95] such an indorsement creates no obligation to those who were previously parties to the bill; it is solely for the benefit of those who take subsequently. It is not a collateral agreement, but one on the bill; and it is for that reason, and because the original bill by the custom of merchants has incident to it the capacity of an indorsement in the nature of an aval upon it, that such an indorsement requires no new stamp. The law of Scotland also gives effect to such an indorsement."[96]

THE TRANSFEROR BY DELIVERY

A bill which is payable to bearer can be negotiated merely by delivery.[97]   **17–21**
Thus there is no need for the holder of such a bill to indorse it. The 1882 Act provides that:

58.—(1) Where the holder of a bill payable to bearer negotiates it by delivery without indorsing it, he is called a "transferor by delivery".

(2) A transferor by delivery is not liable on the instrument.

(3) A transferor by delivery who negotiates a bill thereby warrants to his immediate transferee being a holder for value that the bill is what it purports to be, that he has a right to transfer it, and that at the time of transfer he is not aware of any fact which renders it valueless.

No liability on the instrument

It was long ago held that if the holder of a bill sends it to market without   **17–22**
indorsing his name upon it, neither morality nor the laws of this country will compel him to refund the money for which he sold it, if he did not know at the time that it was not a good bill.[98]

---

[92] For a statement of the aval in the law of England, Canada and the United States see Cowen, *Negotiable Instruments in South Africa* (4th ed., 1966), pp. 215–240.

[93] (1810) 2 Camp. 447, 448, approved in *Steele v. M'Kinlay* (1880) 5 App.Cas. 754, 772.

[94] 1 Salk. 132, 133.

[95] (1834) 1 C.M. & R. 439.

[96] Lord Blackburn in *Steele v. M'Kinlay* (1880) 5 App.Cas. 754, 772.

[97] Section 31(2).

[98] *Fenn v. Harrison* (1790) 3 T.R. 757, 759 (Lord Kenyon C.J.).

Liability for warranties[99]

17–23   But the transferor by delivery is to be held to warrant that the instrument is what it purports to be.[1] Thus a transferor by delivery of a bill purporting to be drawn abroad, not requiring therefore to be stamped with an inland stamp, was held to warrant that the bill was in fact so drawn and, therefore, liable to the purchaser, the bill not answering the description on it which was sold; the money was recoverable as paid in mistake of fact.[2] Where in the case of billbrokers a custom is proved of not indorsing bills discounted with their bankers, but of giving instead a general guarantee, the liability created by such guarantee has been held to be equivalent to that incurred by indorsement.[3]

No liability on the consideration

17–24   Subject to the exceptions referred to below, the general rule of the English law, as established by the authorities, is that the transferor is not liable to refund the consideration, if the bill or note so transferred by delivery without indorsement turns out to be of no value by reason of the failure of the other parties to it. For the taking to market of a bill or note payable to bearer without indorsing it, is prima facie a sale of the bill. And there is no implied guarantee of the solvency of the maker, or of any other party.[4]

When the bill is considered as sold

17–25   If a bill or note, made or become payable to bearer, is delivered without indorsement, not in payment of a pre-existing debt, but by way of exchange for goods, for other bills or notes, or for money transferred to the party delivering the bill at the same time, such a transaction has been repeatedly held to be a sale of the bill by the party transferring it, and a purchase of the instrument, with all risks, by the transferee.[5] So, where A gave a bankrupt, before his bankruptcy, cash for a bill, but refused to allow the bankrupt to indorse it, thinking it better without his name, and afterwards, on dishonour of the bill, proved the amount under the commission, the Lord Chancellor ordered the debt to be expunged, observing that this was a sale of the bill.[6] So,

---

[99] See also para. 17–27, below.

[1] As to American law see Uniform Commercial Code, s.3–417.

[2] *Gompertz v. Bartlett* (1853) 23 L.J.Q.B. 65 *per* Campbell C.J., citing *Jones v. Ryde* (5 Taunt. 488) and *Young v. Cole* (3 New Ca. 724). In the *Hamilton Finance* case ([1969] 1 Lloyd's Rep. 53), Mocatta J. declined to accept that drawers of an unstamped bill warranted that the bill was not void under the Stamp Acts.

[3] *Re Fox Walker & Co., ex p. Bishop* (1880) 15 Ch.D. 400.

[4] See *Camidge v. Allenby* (1827) 6 B. & C. 373, 385; *Rogers v. Langford* (1833) 1 Cr. & M. 637; *Lichfield Union (Guardians) v. Greene* (1857) 26 L.J.Exch. 140. Payment by "approved banker's bill" has been held to entitle the payer to the rights, *e.g.* to notice of dishonour, as well as to the liabilities of an indorser (*Smith v. Mercer* (1867) L.R. 3 Ex. 51). In America there seems to be considerable divergence of opinion in the case where the principal party on the instrument is insolvent; *cf.* Daniel (5th ed.), para. 737, where the correct view is said to be that the loss should fall upon the party holding the instrument at the time the insolvency was made known to him.

[5] *cf. Evans v. Whyle* (1829) 5 Bing. 485, 488 (Park J.); *McGlynn v. Hastie* (1918) 46 D.L.R. 20.

[6] *Ex p. Shuttleworth* (1797) 3 Ves. 368.

if a party discounts bills with a banker, and receives in part of the discount other bills, but not indorsed by the banker, which bills turn out to be bad, the banker is not liable. "Having taken them without indorsement", said Lord Kenyon, "he hath taken the risk on himself. They (*viz.*, the bankers) were the holders of the bill, and by not indorsing them, have refused to pledge their credit to their validity; and Richard Fydell (*viz.* the transferee) must be taken to have received them on their own credit only."[7] So, where, in the morning the plaintiff sold the defendant a quantity of corn, and, at three o'clock in the afternoon of the same day, the defendant delivered to the plaintiff in payment certain promissory notes of the bank of H, which had then stopped payment, but which circumstance was not at the time known to either party, Bayley J. said: "If the notes had been given to the plaintiff at the time when the corn was sold, he could have had no remedy upon them against the defendant. The plaintiff might have insisted on payment in money, but, if he consented to receive the notes as money, they would have been taken by him at his peril."[8]

Such seems the general rule governing the transfer by delivery, not only of ordinary bills of exchange and promissory notes, but also of bank notes. Nor is there any hardship in such a rule, for the remedy against the transferor may always be preserved by indorsement, or by special contract. The rule, however, is not without exceptions.

Exceptions

If a banker's note is given on account of a pre-existing debt, the note is not **17–26** to be considered as sold.[9] But if the banker fails and if the note is duly presented, and due notice is given of the dishonour, the remedy for the antecedent debt revives. "I agree", says Holt C.J., "the difference taken by my brother Darnell, that taking a note for goods sold is a payment, because it was a part of the original contract, but paper is no payment where there is a precedent debt. For when such a note is given in payment, it is always taken to be given under this condition, to be payment if the money be paid thereon in convenient time."[10]

Just as there may be an express contract which would make the transferor liable without indorsement, so there are other circumstances from which a court might infer that the intention, and implied contract of the parties, was that the notes were not to be payment if dishonoured.[11]

If, for example, a man asks another to change a bank note for him as a favour, and the banker fails, it is conceived that a jury would be justified in inferring an implied contract to refund the change, if the note was duly

---

[7] *Fydell v. Clark* (1796) 1 Esp. 447; *Bank of England v. Newman* (1700) 1 Ld.Raym. 442; *Emly v. Lye* (1812) 15 East 7; *Owenson v. Morse* (1796) 7 T.R. 64.

[8] *Camidge v. Allenby* (1827) 6 B. & C. 373.

[9] As pointed out by Lord Campbell C.J. in *Timmins v. Gibbins* (1852) 18 Q.B. 722, 726, it is difficult to say that there can be any case in which the debt is not antecedent to the payment.

[10] *Ward v. Evans* (1703) 2 Ld.Raym. 928; *Clerk v. Mundall* (1698) 12 Mod. 203; *Moore v. Warren* (1720) 1 Stra. 415; *Ex p. Blackburne* (1804) 10 Ves. 204; *Robson v. Oliver* (1847) 10 Q.B. 704.

[11] See *Van Wart v. Woolley* (1824) 3 B. & C. 439, 446.

presented and dishonoured, and due notice given.[12] It has been held that if a customer pays to his account with his banker notes of a bank which has failed, and the banker is guilty of no laches, the loss falls on the customer.[13] If a bank cashes at one branch a cheque payable at another branch of the same bank, and when such cheque reaches the branch on which it is drawn the drawer's balance there has been exhausted, and the cheque is consequently dishonoured, the amount paid to the holder may be recovered by the bank.[14] In all cases where the receiver of the notes seeks to return them he must do so within a reasonable time.[15]

Warranty of genuineness

17–27   The warranties contained in the 1882 Act, section 58(3),[16] do not impliedly involve a warranty of the solvency of the parties to the instrument.[17] On the other hand, a warranty of genuineness has long been required of the transferor by delivery.[18] And if the bill or note does not in this respect fully answer the warranty (though some signatures be genuine), yet the consideration entirely fails, and the money given for the bill may be recovered back, provided it be claimed within a reasonable time.[19]

In all cases, if notes or bills are transferred as valid when the transferor knows they are good for nothing, the suppression of the truth is a fraud, and he is liable. If, indeed, it can be shown that the transferor was aware of the insolvency of prior parties at the time of the transfer, then it is wholly immaterial whether the instrument was taken in payment of a pre-existing debt or not.[20]

Mocatta J. found it impossible, in an action to recover moneys paid by way of discounting unstamped bills, to imply a warranty by the drawers that the bills were not void under the Stamp Acts.[21]

---

[12] See *Rogers v. Langford* (1833) 1 Cr. & M. 637; *Turner v. Stones* (1843) 1 D. & L. 122.
[13] *Timmins v. Gibbins* (1852) 18 Q.B. 722.
[14] *Woodland v. Fear* (1857) 26 L.J.Q.B. 202; *Bell v. Cook* [1920] C.P.D. 125.
[15] cf. *Rogers v. Langford, supra*.
[16] *Ante*, para. 17–21.
[17] cf. *Gurney v. Womersley* (1854) 4 E. & B. 133, 134 (Lord Campbell C.J.). The Uniform Commercial Code, s.2–417(2), definitely requires a warranty of title. This is probably also the case under the English Code, since the words used in s.58(3) are "that he has a right to transfer it", and a right to transfer can hardly exist without a right to hold. Hence indirectly, he does perhaps warrant his title. A warranty of title is implied in the case of foreign bonds (*Raphael v. Burt* (1884) 1 Cab. & E. 325).
[18] *Jones v. Ryde* (1814) 5 Taunt. 488; *Bruce v. Bruce* (1814) 1 Marsh 165; *Fuller v. Smith* (1824) Ry. & M. 49; *Gurney v. Womersley, supra*.
[19] *Pooley v. Brown* (1862) 31 L.J.C.P. 134, where no claim was made on the bills for more than one year. A contemporaneous undertaking to be responsible for the payment of a note to the person to whom the note is transferred without indorsement, will not be available in the hands of a subsequent party, since it is not assignable with the note (*Re Barrington* (1804) 2 Sch. & Lef. 112).
[20] cf. *Camidge v. Allenby* (1827) 6 B. & C. 373, 382; *Loughman v. Barry* (1872) I.R. 6 C.L. 457.
[21] *Hamilton Finance Co. Ltd v. Coverley Westray Walbaum & Tosetti Ltd and Portland Finance Co. Ltd* [1969] 1 Lloyd's Rep. 53, 71.

ACCOMMODATION PARTY

An accommodation party is a person who has signed the bill, without **17–28** receiving value, for the accommodation of the drawer or some other part to the bill, *i.e.* so that the part accommodated can raise money on it.[22] The 1882 Act provides that:

28.—(2) An accommodation party is liable on the bill to a holder for value; and it is immaterial whether, when such holder took the bill, he knew such party to be an accommodation party or not.

But it is essential that the claimant shall be ignorant of any special purpose for which the bill has been given, if there has been a breach of duty to apply the instrument for that special purpose.[23]

EXCLUSION OF LIABILITY

Having set out the liabilities that are incurred by various parties it should be **17–29** noted that a person may draw or indorse a bill without incurring personal responsibility:

16. The drawer of a bill, and any indorser, may insert therein an express stipulation—
(1) Negativing or limiting his own liability to the holder.[24]
(2) Waiving as regards himself some or all of the holder's duties.

Thus the indorser may express in his indorsement that it is made with this qualification, that he shall not be liable on default of acceptance or payment by the drawee. Such qualified indorsement will be made by annexing the words *sans recours*, or "without recourse to me", or any equivalent expression. Where a cheque drawn by the first defendants in favour of the plaintiffs was indorsed by the second defendants *sans recours*,[25] Ridley J. held that the right given by section 16 of the 1882 Act so to indorse applied to any indorser, even a quasi-indorser under section 56, and was not confined to an indorser who could give a title to a bill. He thought it a strange but necessary deduction from the 1882 Act.[26] But any stipulation limiting the liability of the party making it must appear on the instrument itself, or it will only be effectual between the immediate parties, or against a transferee without value, and is powerless against a holder in due course. An agent buying bills for a principal is liable on his indorsement to his principal, however small his commission, unless he qualifies his indorsement.[27] But a written or even verbal agreement

---

[22] See s.28(1). See also paras 19–37 *et seq.*
[23] *Hornby v. McLaren* (1908) 24 T.L.R. 494.
[24] *cf. Beutel's Brannan* (7th ed., 1948), pp. 946 *et seq.*
[25] *Wakefield v. Alexander & Co. and Chaproniere & Co.* (1901) 17 T.L.R. 217.
[26] (1901) 17 T.L.R. 217. As regards the drawer he must not of course so limit his liability as to make the drawing conditional; unlike the indorser, who, by s.33, may conditionally indorse.
[27] *Groupy v. Harden* (1816) 7 Taunt. 159.

between an indorser and his immediate indorsee that the indorsee shall not sue the indorser, but the acceptor only, is a good defence on the part of the indorser against his immediate indorsee suing in breach of the agreement.[28]

Indeed, the contract between indorser and indorsee does not consist exclusively of the writing popularly called an indorsement, though that indorsement is a necessary part of it. The contract consists partly of the written indorsement, partly of the delivery of the bill to the indorsee, and may also consist partly of the mutual understanding and intention with which the delivery was made by the indorser and received by the indorsee. That intention may be collected from the words of the parties to the contract, either spoken or written, from the usage of the place, or of the trade, from the course of dealing between the parties, or from their relative situation.[29]

Representative capacity[30]

17–30   The case of a person indorsing in a representative capacity so as to negative personal liability is provided for by the 1882 Act as follows:

31.—(5) Where any person is under obligation to indorse a bill in a representative capacity, he may indorse the bill in such terms as to negative personal liability.

Whether the signature of the agent carries the liability of the principal or of the agent is a question of fact. Executors or administrators having to indorse may stipulate to pay out of the estate only or in any other manner may expressly negative their personal liability.[31]

TRANSFEREE SUBJECT TO EQUITIES

Indorsement before bill or note drawn or made

17–31   An indorsement may be made even before the bill or note itself is drawn or made, and such indorsement will, as already mentioned, render the indorser liable to subsequent parties.[32] Where A, in accordance with an agreement, indorsed blank bill forms, which B accepted and C subsequently drew to his own order and indorsed, it was held that A was estopped by section 20 from saying that his name was put upon the bills before C, the drawer, had indorsed his name thereon, and thereby made the bills complete and regular.[33]

---

[28] *Pike v. Street* (1828) M. & M. 226.
[29] *Castrique v. Buttigieg* (1855) 10 Moo.P.C. 94; *Kidson v. Dilworth* (1818) 5 Price 564. As to American law, see *Beutel's Brannan* (7th ed., 1948), p. 963.
[30] See s.26(1) for persons signing in a representative capacity.
[31] See s.31(5), *ante*, para. 9–13.
[32] 1882 Act, s.20 *ante*, para. 4–01; *Russel v. Langstaffe* (1780) 2 Doug. 514; *Schultz v. Astley* (1836) 2 Bing.N.C. 544.
[33] *Glenie v. Bruce Smith* [1918] 1 K.B. 263, approved in *McDonald (Gerald) & Co. v. Nash & Co.* [1924] A.C. 625; see further, *ante*, para. 17–18.

Indorsement after dishonour

An indorsement may be made either before or after acceptance. If a bill is **17–32** indorsed after refusal to accept, and notice thereof to the indorsee, or after it is due, these are circumstances which may reasonably excite suspicions as to the liability or solvency of the antecedent parties. An indorsee, therefore, of a bill dishonoured or after due, with notice thereof, has not all the equity of an indorsee for value in the ordinary course of negotiation. He is held to take the bill on the credit of his indorser, and has no superior title against the other parties.[34]

The 1882 Act assimilates the case of a bill, known to have been dishonoured, to one actually overdue, as follows:

36.—(5) Where a bill which is not overdue has been dishonoured any person who takes it with notice of the dishonour takes it subject to any defect of title attaching thereto at the time of dishonour, but nothing in this subsection shall affect the rights of a holder in due course.[35]

Overdue bill

Where a person takes a bill after it is overdue he takes it subject to all the **17–33** equities. Such a person cannot be a holder in due course.[36] "After a bill or note is due", said Lord Ellenborough, "it comes disgraced to the indorsee, and it is his duty to make inquiries concerning it. If he takes it, though he give a full consideration for it, he takes it on the credit of the indorser, and subject to all equities with which it may be encumbered; total absence or failure of consideration is a defence as between immediate parties."[37] The 1882 Act gives effect in the following provision to the common law rulings as to bills taken when overdue:

36.—(2) Where an overdue bill is negotiated, it can only be negotiated subject to any defect of title affecting it at its maturity, and thenceforward no person who takes it can acquire it or give a better title than that which the person from whom he took it had.

---

[34] *Crossley v. Ham* (1811) 13 East 498.

[35] This subsection appears to overrule such a case as *Goodman v. Harvey* (1836) 4 A. & E. 870, where it was held that the fact of the notarial marks of dishonour appearing on a bill was not sufficient of itself to impugn the holder's bona fides. It had long been established at common law that an indorsee without notice was not prejudiced by the fact that a bill had been dishonoured (*O'Keefe v. Dunn* (1815) 6 Taunt. 305; *Whitehead v. Walker* (1842) 10 M. & W. 696).

[36] Section 29(1)(a).

[37] *Tinson v. Francis* (1807) 1 Camp. 19. In *Sturtevant v. Ford* (1842) 4 M. & G. 101, 106, Cresswell J. says. "Perhaps a better expression would be that he takes the bill subject to all its equities." In equity it has been held that where an overdue bill of exchange was bought with stolen money, the claim of the person with whose money it had been bought was an equity attaching to the bill (*Re European Bank* (1870) L.R. 5 Ch.App. 358; *Young v. Macnider* (1895) 25 S.C.R. 272).

Formerly it was held that among the equities attaching to the instrument was that of the absence of consideration.[38] But an original absence of consideration is not apparently, at the present time, one of those equities which attach on the instrument and defeat the title of a holder for value of an overdue bill.[39] The original absence of consideration, therefore, in the case of "accommodation" acceptances, the object of which is to raise money, will not defeat the title of an indorsee for value of an overdue bill or note, even though the indorsee had notice of the fact when he took the bill, unless there was an agreement, express or implied, restraining the negotiation of the bill or note after it should have become due.[40]

A bill or note assigned in due time on the day of payment is to be considered as assigned before it is due.[41]

Defects in title

17–34   There is no exhaustive list as to what constitutes a defect in title, but it includes for example fraud, illegality, breach of an agreement between the acceptor and the payee that the bill was not to be negotiated.[42] The indorsee of an overdue bill is only prejudiced by defects of title affecting the bill at its maturity, and hence it is no defence to plead that the bill was accepted, etc., for an illegal consideration before maturity if, between that time and the maturing of the bill, it was negotiated for value in good faith.[43]

An indorsee of an overdue bill or note is liable to such defects of title only as attach on the bill or note itself, and not to claims arising out of collateral matters.[44] Therefore, the indorsee of an overdue note is not liable to a set-off

---

[38] *Tinson v. Francis, supra.*

[39] The point was first definitely decided in *Charles v. Marsden* (1808) 1 Taunt. 224, followed in *Sturtevant v. Ford, supra,* and approved apparently in *Lazarus v. Cowie* (1842) 3 Q.B. 459. The 1882 Act seems to uphold this view, since absence of consideration is not one of those defects of title specified in s.29(2) as attaching to the instrument. On the other hand, the defendant has always been allowed to set up that the instrument, indorsed overdue, has in fact been paid before indorsement (*Brown v. Davies* (1789) 3 T.R. 80; *Parr v. Jewell* (1855) 16 C.B. 684); see also *Lazarus v. Cowie, supra.*

[40] *Parr v. Jewell, supra,* at 712; see also *Stein v. Yglesias* (1834) 1 Cr.M. & R. 565; *MacArthur v. MacDowall* (1892) 23 S.C.R. 571. In *Carruthers v. West* (1847) 11 Q.B. 143, 146, the defendant's plea did not exclude a negotiation before maturity to a holder without notice, and thus the plea of an agreement restraining negotiations was bad. But failure of consideration has a different effect from its original absence in the case of an overdue bill, and inasmuch as a holder of an overdue bill is never a holder in due course (s.29(1)), a total failure of consideration would afford an acceptor a defence against a holder of an overdue bill, whether with notice or not.

[41] *cf.,* 1882 Act, s.36(4).

[42] See *Cardinal Investments Corp. v. Central Bank of Yemen* [2001] Lloyds Rep. Banking 1, where the Court of Appeal cited a passage from *Chalmers and Guest on Bills of Exchange* (15th ed., 1998) at p. 317 as to the meaning of "defect in title".

[43] *Chalmers v. Lanion* (1808) 1 Camp. 383; *Fairclough v. Pavia* (1854) 9 Ex. 690.

[44] *Holmes v. Kidd* (1858) 28 L.J.Ex. 112; *Merchants' Bank of Canada v. Thompson* (1911) 23 O.L.R. 502. Where interest is made payable at stated intervals, default in the payment of interest does not make the instrument overdue (*Union Investment Co. v. Wells* (1908) 39 S.C.R. 625); but see *Jennings v. Napanee Brush Co.* (1884) 8 C.L.T. 595, followed in *Moore v. Scott* (1907) 5 W.L.R. 8; 16 Man. 492, the latter being overruled on this point by *Union Investment Co. v. Wells* (1908) 39 S.C.R. 625. As to mere personal defences, see *post,* paras 18–32 to 18–34.

due from the payee to the maker,[45] even though the indorsee had notice, gave no consideration, and took the bill on purpose to defeat the set-off, for the holder is under no legal obligation to allow a debt to be set off against the claim on the bill, unless he has entered into a contract to that effect with the defendant, which contract would create an equity in favour of the defendant attaching to an overdue bill.[46] Yet where a negotiable instrument is deposited as a security for the balance of accounts, and is afterwards indorsed overdue, the state of the account, made by the person with whom the bill was deposited at the time of the indorsement to the plaintiff, may be gone into, in an action by the indorsee against the party originally liable.[47]

Where the bill is deposited as a security for the balance of a running account, but at the time when the bill becomes due the balance is in favour of the depositor, and the bill is not withdrawn by him, and afterwards the balance shifts in favour of the depositary, the depositary is not to be considered as the transferee of an overdue bill.[48]

As to when a bill payable on demand, such an instrument being in practice almost always a cheque, is to be deemed overdue, see section 36(3).[49]

Overdue note

A promissory note may have a maturity date and thus become overdue, so **17–35** that the provisions of s.36(2) are applicable in the same manner as they apply to a bill.[50] However it should be noted that, in relation to a note, the 1882 Act provides:

86.—(3) Where a note payable on demand is negotiated, it is not deemed to be overdue, for the purpose of affecting the holder with defects of title of which he had no notice, by reason that it appears that a reasonable time for presenting it for payment has elapsed since its issue.

A promissory note payable on demand is, it has been stated, quite unlike a cheque, since it is intended to be a continuing security, while a cheque is intended to be presented speedily.[51] So the fact that a note is made payable

---

[45] *Burrough v. Moss* (1830) 10 B. & C. 558; *Stein v. Yglesias* (1834) 1 Cr.M. & R. 565; *Whitehead v. Walker* (1842) 10 M. & W. 696; *Re Overend, Gurney & Co., ex p. Swan* (1868) L.R. 6 Eq. 344, *per* Sir R. Malins V.-C., at 360: " . . . the right of set-off . . . is not an equity attached to the bill itself". *Cardinal Finance Investment Corp.* (*supra*).

[46] *Oulds v. Harrison* (1854) 10 Ex. 572, 579, where it was held that the holder's right to circulate the bill is not restrained simply by the existence at the time of a debt of equal value; see also *Caldwell v. McDermott* (1895) 2 N.W.T.R. (Can.) 249.

[47] *Collenridge v. Farquharson* (1816) 1 Stark 259.

[48] *Atwood v. Crowdie* (1816) 1 Stark 483.

[49] *Post*, para. 21–93.

[50] See *Cardinal Finance Investments Corp. v. Central Bank of Yemen* [2001] Lloyd's Rep. Banking 1.

[51] *Brooks v. Mitchell* (1841) 9 M. & W. 15, 18 (Parke B.), where the note was about 15 years overdue; see also *Glasscock v. Balls* (1889) 24 Q.B.D. 13; *Venter v. Smit* [1913] T.P.D. 231; *Northern Crown Bank v. International Electric Co.* (1911) 24 O.L.R. 57.

with interest has been held to imply that it will be in negotiation for some time.[52]

Abandonment of bill by indorsee

17–36   Where an indorsee sends a bill back as useless, that is an abandonment of his rights as indorsee, and he cannot, by getting the bill again into his own hands, acquire a right to sue without a new indorsement.[53]

After action brought

17–37   The holder cannot transfer after action brought, so as to enable his transferee to sue also, if the latter was aware that the first action had been commenced.[54] But if the transferee had no notice, the transfer is good.[55]

After death of holder

17–38   After the death of the holder his personal representatives may transfer.[56] But where indorsement is necessary, and the testator has only written his name on the bill without delivery, the executor cannot complete the indorsement by mere delivery.[57]

After bankruptcy

17–39   After the holder's bankruptcy his trustee may transfer,[58] unless the bankrupt were merely agent or trustee, for, except in the case of bills in the debtor's reputed ownership, the bankruptcy laws have no operation on any property in the possession of the bankrupt, unless he has therein a beneficial interest.

By will

17–40   The words goods and chattels, or either of them, in a testamentary instrument will pass all the personal estate of the testator, including choses in action,

---

[52] *Barough v. White* (1825) 4 B. & C. 325, 327 (Bayley J.).

[53] *Cartwright v. Williams* (1818) 2 Stark. 340.

[54] *Marsh v. Newell* (1808) 1 Taunt. 109; *Jones v. Lane* (1838) 3 Y. & C. 281; but see *Deuters v. Townsend* (1864) 33 L.J.Q.B. 301, where this statement of the law is doubted; *Kennedy & Co. v. Vaughan* (1906) 37 N.B.R. 112. By s.3–112(d) of the Uniform Commercial Code an instrument is nonetheless negotiable because it authorises a confession of judgment if the instrument be not paid at maturity.

[55] *Columbies v. Slim* (1772) 2 Chit.Rep. 637; see also Chitty, *Bills* (11th ed.), p. 164; *Deuters v. Townsend, supra.*

[56] See *ante*, para. 7–24.

[57] *Bromage v. Lloyd* (1847) 1 Ex. 32. The bill or note belongs to the estate and not to the intended indorsee.

[58] *cf. Cohen v. Mitchell* (1890) 25 Q.B.D. 262, 267 as to bona fide transactions with bankrupt.

such as bills and notes. But where the bequest is of all goods and chattels in a particular place, bills and notes in general do not pass.[59] But it has been considered that such notes as are commonly treated as money will pass.[60]

Donatio mortis causa

A *donatio mortis causa* is a conditional gift by the donor in contemplation of death,[61] to take effect in the event of death.[62] There need, however, be no statement included to the effect that the gift is to be returned should the donor recover, since, if the gift is made in contemplation of death, such a condition is inferred.[63]

17–41

A bill of exchange or promissory note specially indorsed to the donee or made or become payable to bearer may, it appears, be the subject of a *donatio mortis causa* and even, it has been held, if the instrument be unindorsed,[64] though not in the case of the donor's own note.[65] Equally, too, a cheque which is payable to the donor's order but is unindorsed by him.[66] On the other hand, a cheque drawn by the donor upon his own banker cannot be the subject of a *donatio mortis causa*, because the death of the drawer is a revocation of the banker's authority to pay.[67] But where, in the donee's house, a cheque was handed to her bank manager shortly before the death of the donor, it was held that the gift was complete as the manager accepted the cheque in exercise of his authority.[68] The giving of the cheque is not an appropriation of the money in the hands of the banker: the cheque is a mere order to pay and unless

---

[59] *Joseph v. Phillips* [1934] A.C. 348.

[60] See *Stuart v. Bute* (1806) 11 Ves. 657, 661; *Brooke v. Turner* (1836) 7 Sim. 71; *Barry v. Harding* (1844) 1 Jo. & Lat. 475.

[61] *Duffield v. Elwes* (1827) 1 Bligh (N.S.) 497, 530; *Miller v. Miller* (1735) 3 P. Wms. 356, 357, where such a gift was said only to be good if made in the donor's last illness. As to this, see also *Blount v. Burrow* (1792) 1 Ves. 546, though the report in 4 Bro.C.C. 72 does not deal with the question. The gift must be conditional to take effect only on the death of the donor by his existing disorder, but there need not, it seems, be positive evidence that it was made in the donor's last illness; *cf.* Williams, Mortimer & Sunnucks, *Executors Administrators And Probate* (18th ed., 2000), p. 536, commenting on *Blount v. Burrow, supra.*

[62] Delivery to an agent of the donee will be good, but not a mere agent of the donor (*Farquharson v. Cave* (1846) 2 Coll. 356; *Powell v. Hellicar* (1858) 28 L.J.Ch. 355, distinguished in *Walker v. Foster* (1900) 30 S.C.R. 299). There must be an actual delivery (*Bunn v. Markham* (1816) 7 Taunt. 224; *Tate v. Hilbert* (1793) 2 Ves. 111; *Irons v. Smallpiece* (1819) 2 B. & Ald. 551), though such delivery, as is required for a gift inter vivos, is not necessary (*Re Wasserberg* [1915] 1 Ch. 195.)

[63] *Gardner v. Parker* (1818) 3 Madd. 184.

[64] *Veal v. Veal* (1859) 27 Beav. 303; *Ranking v. Weguelin* (1859) 27 Beav. 309; *Re Mead* (1880) 15 Ch.D. 651.

[65] *Re Leaper* [1916] 1 Ch. 579; *Holliday v. Atkinson* (1826) 5 B. & C. 501, 503.

[66] *Clement v. Cheesman* (1884) 27 Ch.D. 631.

[67] *Tate v. Hilbert* (1793) 2 Ves. 111; *Hewitt v. Kaye* (1868) L.R. 6 Eq. 198; *Beak v. Beak* (1872) L.R. 13 Eq. 489; *Re Mead* (1880) 15 Ch.D. 651; *Re Beaumont* [1902] 1 Ch. 889, dictum of Buckley J., 896, used in a different context, adopted by the Privy Council considering the effect of marking a post-dated cheque in *Bank of Baroda v. Punjab National Bank* [1944] A.C. 176; *Re Davis* (1902) 86 L.T. 889; *McLellan v. McLellan* (1911) 23 O.L.R. 654; (1912) 25 O.L.R. 214, distinguished in *Kendrick v. Dominion Bank* (1920) 48 O.L.R. 539.

[68] *Re While* [1928] W.N. 182.

cashed[69] or otherwise acted on[70] in the lifetime of the donor, it is worth nothing.[71]

A bank note,[72] and a banker's deposit note (accompanied by a cheque for the amount plus interest)[73] may also, it has been held, be handed over in contemplation of death as a *donatio mortis causa*.

---

[69] *Bouts v. Ellis* (1853) 17 Beav. 121. It is sufficient if the banker undertakes to hold the cheque for the donee (*Re Beaumont, supra*; see also *Re While* [1928] W.N. 182, where the gift of a second cheque failed because it was post-dated).

[70] As by payment into the donee's bank (*Rolls v. Pearce* (1877) 5 Ch.D. 730), or by registration (*Tate v. Hilbert, supra*).

[71] *Hewitt v. Kaye, supra*; *Re Swinburne* [1926] Ch. 38, disapproving *Bromley v. Brunton* (1868) L.R. 6 Eq. 275; *Re Owen (decd.), Owen v. Inland Revenue Commissioners* [1949] 1 All E.R. 901. It is submitted that the distinction between a bearer and an order cheque suggested by Malins V.-C. in *Rolls v. Pearce* (1877) 5 Ch.D. 730 cannot now be relied on: the death of the drawer is, by the 1882 Act, s.75, equally a revocation of authority to pay in either case.

[72] *Drury v. Smith* (1717) 1 P.Wms. 405; *Miller v. Miller* (1735) 3 P.Wms. 356.

[73] *Re Dillon* (1890) 44 Ch.D. 76, distinguishing *Re Mead* (1880) 15 Ch.D. 651; see also *Re Archer* (1914) 33 N.Z.L.R. 344; *McDonald v. McDonald* (1903) 33 S.C.R. 145; *Brown v. Toronto Trusts Corporation* (1900) 32 O.R. 319; *Re Gannon* (1898) 9 Queensland L.J. 52, and *cf. Delgoffe v. Fader* [1939] W.N. 303. As to deposit books of the Post Office Savings Bank, see *Re Ward, Ward v. Warwick* [1946] 2 All E.R. 206; of the *London Trustee Savings Bank, Birch v. Treasury Solicitor* [1950] 2 All E.R. 1198; and commercial banks, *Delgoffe v. Fader* [1939] 3 All E.R. 682 and *Birch v. Treasury Solicitor (supra)*; and as to National Savings certificates, see *Darlow v. Sparks* [1938] 2 All E.R. 235.

CHAPTER 18

RIGHTS OF PARTIES

Parties

THE essence of negotiability is that a transferee shall be capable of taking free **18–01** of equities, that transfer by mere delivery or by indorsement and delivery shall vest in him an absolute and indefeasible title; that he shall have the right to sue on the instrument in his own name. It is natural that certain conditions attach to the acquisition of such a title and these are set out in section 29 of the 1882 Act, which defines such a transferee, being a holder in due course.[1]

However not all holders are holders in due course, for a transferee may be a "holder for value" or a mere "holder", whose rights upon the bill are subject to equities which do not affect the holder in due course. When considering a lesser holding than that of a holder in due course and, any action which may be brought by such lesser holder, the relationship between him and the defendant must be taken into account. In this respect parties to a bill may be considered as immediate or remote, the former being parties in direct relation with each other and the latter being those who are not in such relationship.[2]

In this Chapter the following persons are considered: **18–02**

(1) The holder in due course;

(2) The holder obtaining title through a holder in due course;

(3) The holder for value;

(4) The payee-holder for value;

(5) The transferee by delivery;

(6) The indorsee;

(7) Payer for honour.

HOLDER IN DUE COURSE

Holder in due course

In considering the rights of the holder of a bill of exchange it may be **18–03** simplest first to address the holder in due course, since such a holder has superior rights as regards both immediate and remote parties.

---

[1] See *post* para. 18–04.
[2] See this paragraph discussed by Cumming-Bruce L.J. in *Jade International Steel Stahl und Eisen GmbH & Co. KG. v. Robert Nicholas (Steels) Ltd* [1978] 3 W.L.R. 39, 45.

Definition of a holder in due course

18–04   The 1882 Act gives the following definition:

29.—(1) A holder in due course is a holder who has taken a bill, complete and regular on the face of it, under the following conditions; namely,

(a) that he became the holder of it before it was overdue, and without notice that it had been previously dishonoured, if such was the fact;

(b) that he took the bill in good faith and for value, and that at the time the bill was negotiated[3] to him he had no notice of any defect in the title of the person who negotiated it.

A person who takes a negotiable instrument in contravention of section 123(1) or (3) of the Consumer Credit Act 1974 is not a holder in due course and is not entitled to enforce the instrument,[4] but nothing in the Act affects the rights of the holder in due course of any negotiable instrument.[5] A holder in due course is to be distinguished from a mere holder for value.[6] The payee may be a holder for value, but he cannot be a holder in due course, the instrument not having been "negotiated" to him, as understood by section 29(1)(b).[7]

18–05   The instrument must be a bill. If it is not issued, it is not a bill.[8] If the purported signature of the drawer is a forgery, the instrument is, again, not a bill. If the signature is that of the drawer but he has no capacity to contract, the instrument is not a bill; nor where the maker of a note signs in the reasonable belief that he is witnessing someone else's signature to another document.[9] A taker in due course in these cases has no rights against the drawer or the alleged drawer, though he may have rights against intermediate parties.[10] A valid signature on an instrument which is otherwise forged may render the instrument quasi negotiable by estoppel.[11]

---

[3] A bill is not negotiated to the payee (*Jones v. Waring & Gillow, supra*). The Appellate Division, in *Standard Bank of South Africa Ltd v. Sham Magazine Centre* (1977) (1) S.A. 484, contrasted "not negotiable" in s.29(1)(b)—or rather the South African equivalent— with "not transferable". Here it meant "transfer free of equities". See also *Bank of Montreal v. Tourangeau and Royal Bank of Canada* [1980] 118 D.L.R. (3d) 293 Can, where a bank holding an assignment of book debts of a company sued where the defendant had deposited cheques in payment with a second bank. In due course the cheques were indorsed over to the second bank and it was held that the assignee bank could not claim in conversion because it was not the payee or drawer or indorsee of the cheques and was not a holder in due course. The second bank, however, was held not to have taken the cheques in good faith; it was not a holder in due course and held the cheques for the plaintiff bank.

[4] Consumer Credit Act 1974, s.125(1).

[5] *ibid.* s.125(4); For the Consumer Credit Act 1974 in relation to negotiable instruments generally, see paras 8–10 *et seq.*

[6] 1882 Act, s.27(2).

[7] *Jones v. Waring & Gillow, supra.*, disapproving Fletcher Moulton L.J. in *Lloyds Bank Ltd v. Cooke* [1907] 1 K.B. 794, 807. See further para. 18–36 *post.*

[8] *Ingham v. Primrose* (1859) 7 C.B.(N.S.) 82.

[9] *Lewis v. Clay* (1897) 14 T.L.R. 149.

[10] See *Baxendale v. Bennett* (1878) 3 Q.B.D. 525 and *Smith v. Prosser* [1907] 2 K.B. 735, 741, 751–752.

[11] Paget, *Law of Banking* (9th ed., 1982), p. 316. The passage referred to has not been retained in subsequent editions.

Holder

In order for a transferee to become a holder in due course he must obviously **18–06**
qualify as a holder. A holder is defined as the payee or indorsee of a bill or
note who is in possession of it, or the bearer of the instrument;[12] the bearer
being defined as the person in possession of a bill or note payable to bearer.[13]
However as set out below the original payee of a bill, although falling within
the definition of a holder, does not become a holder in due course.[14]

Complete and regular

The phrase "complete and regular on the face of it" in s.29(1) means **18–07**
complete and regular on both the front and the back of the bill. The expression, therefore, includes the indorsements. In *Arab Bank Ltd v. Ross*[15] the
plaintiff bank sued as holders in due course of two promissory notes made by
the defendant in favour of "Fathi and Faysal Nabulsy Company", which were
indorsed "Fathi and Faysal Nabulsy". Contrary to what McNair J. had found,
the Court held on the facts that the indorsement was sufficient to pass a title
but that the bank were not holders in due course as the indorsement was
irregular. There appear to be no other decisions on the point, but it may safely
be said that if there is anything on the instrument, or any omission, which
should put a transferee on inquiry, there can be no compliance with the
condition of the section. If, for instance, an instrument is lacking in a material
particular, a transferee takes it at the risk of its not being what it may purport
to be; it is the same as was the case where a cheque was crossed "not
negotiable". If the instrument shows signs of having been altered, it cannot be
said to be regular.

Where a bill is payable to drawer's order and is indorsed not in blank, nor
specially to third party signatories, but restrictively, *i.e.* for collection, it is
nevertheless "complete and regular on the face of it".[16]

An alteration of the date on a cheque is a material alteration which prevents
the cheque from being regular on the face of it.[17]

Overdue or dishonoured

To be a holder in due course the transferee must become the holder before **18–08**
the bill becomes overdue and without notice that it has been dishonoured. As
regards when bills and notes on demand may be overdue, see section 36(3)[18]
and section 86(3);[19] as regards bills not payable on demand, see section 14.[20]
In addition the holder must take the without notice that it had been previously

---

[12] section 2.
[13] section 2.
[14] *Post*, para. 18–36.
[15] [1952] 2 Q.B.21, CA, *per* Denning L.J.
[16] *Per* Megaw J. in *Yeoman Credit Ltd v. Gregory* [1962] 2 Lloyd's Rep. 302, 316.
[17] *Estate Ismail v. Barclays* (D.C. & O.) [1957] 4 S.A. 17(T).
[18] *Post*, para. 21–93.
[19] *Ante*, para. 17–35.
[20] As amended by the Banking and Financial Dealings Act 1971, s.3(2), *post*, para. 12–06.

dishonoured. The dishonour may be for non-acceptance or for non-payment. Where the plaintiff knowingly took a cheque, drawn for the accommodation of a third party after it had been dishonoured, he was held not to be a holder in due course.[21]

The 1882 Act goes on to provide for the circumstances of a party taking a bill with notice of dishonour of a bill, which is not overdue:

36.—(5) Where a bill which is not overdue has been dishonoured any person who takes it with notice of the dishonour takes it subject to any defect of title attaching thereto at the time of dishonour, but nothing in this subsection shall affect the rights of a holder in due course.[22]

Good faith

18–09   Section 29(1)(b) requires a taking in good faith as a constituent in the status of holder in due course:

(b) That he took the bill in good faith and for value, and that at the time the bill was negotiated to him he had no notice of any defect in the title of the person who negotiated it.

The 1882 Act sets out what constitutes "good faith":

90. A thing is deemed to be done in good faith, within the meaning of this Act, where it is in fact done honestly, whether it is done negligently or not.

Mere negligence, however gross, not amounting to wilful or fraudulent blindness and abstinence from inquiry, will not of itself amount to notice of defect of title, though it may be evidence of it.[23] In *Lipkin Gorman v. Karpnale Ltd*[24] it was held that a gaming club, who had taken a draft payable to a firm of solicitors from a partner in the firm who was engaged in gambling, did not come within s.29(1)(b); it appears that, based on the evidence adduced, the judge concluded that the club had not taken the draft in good faith.[25]

---

[21] *Hornby v. McLaren* (1908) 24 T.L.R. 494.

[22] It would seem that *Goodman v. Harvey* (1836) 4 A. & E. 870 cannot now be considered to state the law. In view of the subsection it can hardly be asserted that notarial marks of dishonour on a bill do not put a transferee on inquiry.

[23] *Goodman v. Harvey* (1836) 4 A. & E. 870; *Jones v. Gordon, infra*, at 628 (Lord Blackburn); see also *Perth Discount Bank v. Stubbs* (1899) 1 W.A.L.R. 186. See also *Midland Bank Ltd v. Charles Simpson Motors Ltd* (1960) 7 *Legal Decisions Affecting Bankers* 251 and 1960 C.L.Y. 217.

[24] [1987] 1 W.L.R. 987.

[25] See pp. 994–995. The Court of Appeal affirmed the judge's finding that the section had not been satisfied, see [1989]1 W.L.R. 1340, at 1360

The equitable doctrine of constructive notice by which a man, who refrains through gross negligence from making inquiries, is held to have had notice, does not extend to negotiable instruments.[26]

Absence of notice of defect of title

Notice of illegality or fraud is either particular or general. Particular or express notice is where the holder had notice of the particular facts avoiding the bill.[27] But notice of the facts more or less in detail is not necessary in order to invalidate the title; it is sufficient if the holder had general notice.   **18–10**

General or implied notice is where the holder had notice that there was some illegality or some fraud vitiating the bill, though he may not have been apprised of its precise nature. Thus, if when he took the bill he was told in express terms that there was something wrong about it, without being told what the vice was, or if it can be collected from circumstances fairly warranting such an inference that he knew, or believed, or thought, that the bill was tainted with illegality or fraud, such a general or implied notice will equally destroy his title.[28]

"A wilful and fraudulent absence of inquiry into the circumstances, when they are known to be such as to invite inquiry, will (if the jury think that the abstinence from inquiry arose from a suspicion or belief that inquiry would disclose a vice in the bills) amount to general or implied notice."[29] There must, however, be something to put the holder on inquiry.[30]

For purposes of section 29, however, there is no question of constructive notice. Notice means actual notice—"a very different question from that which I shall have to consider when I come to section 82 of the Act, and the

---

[26] *London Joint Stock Bank v. Simmons* [1892] A.C. 201, 221 (Lord Herschell); and also *Manchester Trust Co. v. Furness* [1895] 2 Q.B. 539, *per* Lindley L.J. at 545: " . . . as regards the extension of the equitable doctrines of constructive notice to commercial transactions, the Courts have always set their faces resolutely against it". *Lloyds Bank v. Swiss Bankverein* (1913) 108 L.T. 143; *Union Investment Co. v. Wells* (1908) 39 S.C.R. 625; *Liquidators of Cape of Good Hope Building Soc. v. Bank of Africa* (1900) 17 S.C. 480. See also absence of good faith in *Bank of Cyprus London v. Jones* (1984) 3 New Law Journal 522.

[27] *Midland Bank v. Reckitt* [1933] A.C. 1, 19.

[28] *Oakley v. Ooddeen* (1861) 2 F. & F. 656; *May v. Chapman* (1847) 16 M. & W. 355; *Raphael v. Bank of England* (1855) 17 C.B. 161; and see *Keelan v. Norray Distributing Ltd* (1967) 62 D.L.R. (2d) 466; *Williams & Glyn's Bank Ltd v. Belkin Packaging Ltd* [1983] W.W.R. 481, Supreme Ct. Canada.

[29] *Jones v. Gordon* (1877) 2 App.Cas. 616, 625, citing with approval the above passage from *Byles on Bills* p. 119 and cases there cited; see also *Oakley v. Ooddeen, supra*; *Jones v. Smith* (1841) 1 Hare, 55; *Frey v. Ives* (1892) 8 T.L.R. 582; *Waterous Engine Co. v. Capreol* (1922) 52 O.L.R. 247; *Bank of Montreal v. Normadin* [1925] S.C.R. 587; *Royal Bank of Canada v. Grobe* (1928) 3 D.L.R. 93.

[30] *Guildford Trust v. Goss* (1927) 136 L.T. 725, in which moneylenders took post-dated cheques in repayment of loans, the fact of their being post-dated and that they were drawn by one partner, indorsed by another and were being dealt with by a third not being regarded by Branson J. as putting the transferees on inquiry. And see *Nelson v. Larholt* [1948] 1 K.B. 339, in which the defendant received cheques for value drawn by an executor in fraud of the testator; Denning J. held that the defendant could not escape liability because he knew or ought to have known of the executor's want of authority.

question whether the bank was negligent. It is not suggested that the bank had actual notice, but merely that it was put on inquiry."[31]

As to what amounts to defects in title, this is dealt with below.[32]

Payee not a holder in due course

18–11   A holder in due course, under section 29(1), is a person to whom a bill has been negotiated; and negotiation, under section 31, implies transfer by indorsement, where necessary, and delivery. Further, in section 21(2), which distinguishes immediate and remote parties, a holder in due course is included among remote parties. Hence, though the payee is included in the above definition of "holder", he is not a holder in due course.[33] Consequently, where the drawer is induced by the fraud of a third person to draw the instrument in favour of the payee, and, subsequently, the payee in his turn is induced by the fraud of the third person to give him value for it, nevertheless, though the payee in fact took it bona fide and for value, the instrument comes to his hands tainted with the fraud. The payee cannot enforce the instrument[34] and, if he has received payment before the fraud is discovered, must refund it, as being a payment under a mistake of fact.[35]

Rights of a holder in due course

18–12   The holder in due course has the rights of a holder, which are set out in section 38(1):

38. The rights of the holder of a bill are as follows:
(1) He may sue on the bill in his own name:

The rights and privileges conferred on the holder in due course are provided at s.38(2); the holder in due course:

38.—(2) holds the bill free from any defect of title of prior parties, as well as from mere personal defences available to prior parties among themselves, and may enforce payment against all parties liable on the bill.

Defects of title and personal defences are dealt with below.[36]

---

[31] *Per* Devlin J. in *Baker v. Barclays Bank Ltd* [1955] 1 W.L.R. 822, 834.

[32] See *post*, para. 18–26.

[33] This was formerly an open question. In *Lewis v. Clay* (1897) 67 L.J.Q.B. 224; *Herdman v. Wheeler* [1902] 1 K.B. 361, and *Talbot v. Von Boris* [1911] 1 K.B. 854, the opinion was expressed that the payee was not a holder in due course; but in *Lloyds Bank v. Cooke* [1907] 1 K.B. 794, 805, Moulton L.J. was of the contrary opinion (*post*, para. 18–40). The question has now been settled by *Jones v. Waring & Gillow* [1926] A.C. 670.

[34] *Herdman v. Wheeler* [1902] 1 K.B. 361. This was a case of an inchoate promissory note filled up in excess of authority, the drawer and payee being immediate parties. See also *Lloyds Bank v. Cooke* [1907] 1 K.B. 794.

[35] *Jones v. Waring & Gillow* [1926] A.C. 670. *Texas Gulf Trust Co. v. Notias* (Texas Civil App.) (1962) 352 S.W. (2d) 925, in which there was no negotiation to the payee and he was therefore not a holder in due course; but see Uniform Commercial Code, s.3–302(2).

[36] See paras 18–26 *et seq. post*.

TITLE THROUGH HOLDER IN DUE COURSE

Holder obtaining title through holder in due course

A holder, though not himself a holder in due course, can, if he make title **18–13** through such a holder, yet recover on a bill or note, since the 1882 Act provides:

29.—(3) A holder (whether for value or not) who derives his title to a bill through a holder in due course, and who is not himself a party to any fraud or illegality affecting it, has all the rights of that holder in due course as regards the acceptor and all parties to the bill prior to that holder.

A bill drawn in Germany on an English defendant and discounted by a German bank was dishonoured on presentation and returned by the English collecting agent to the discounting bank which debited the drawer and delivered the bill back to the drawer who sued on it in England. It was held by Donaldson J. and the Court of Appeal that, by virtue of section 29(3), the drawer derived his title from the German discounting bank which was a holder in due course and that he was not suing in his capacity as drawer.[37]

Under the subsection a holder making title through a holder in due course is precluded from enforcing a bill affected by fraud or illegality only if he was himself a party to it.[38] So long as he was not a party to it, it is immaterial that he had notice of it, since he stands in the shoes of the person from whom he received it.[39]

In the case of fraud, however, it is to be observed that if there is a mistake as to the nature of the transaction, induced by the fraud of a third person, so that the person sought to be made liable is in a position to say that he did not sign a bill at all, even a person who takes as a holder in due course cannot recover.[40]

In *Bank of Baroda v. Punjab National Bank* the point came up, but seems not to have been argued or decided, whether a holder of a post-dated cheque could be a holder in due course. The respondent bank had lent against such a cheque. Lord Wright said:[41] "If the certification on the cheque had been negotiable as an acceptance in the proper sense would have been, the respondent bank would prima facie have been entitled to claim as a holder in due course . . . " It is submitted that, by virtue of the fact that a postdated cheque is not invalid,[42] the postdating by itself would not be sufficient to deprive a holder of his absolute title.

---

[37] *Jade International Steel Stahl und Eisen GmbH & Co. G. v. Robert Nicholas (Steels) Ltd* [1978] 2 Lloyd's Rep. 13.

[38] *Robinson v. Reynolds* (1841) 2 Q.B. 196; *Thiedemann v. Goldschmidt* (1859) 1 De G.F. & J. 4.

[39] In *Baker v. Barclays Bank Ltd* [1955] 1 W.L.R. 822, Devlin J., at 833, said that he was not entirely clear how it benefits the bank to establish that the customer for whom they collected was a holder in due course. Presumably the learned judge was not referred to s.29(3).

[40] See *ante*, para. 7–01.

[41] [1944] A.C. 176, 191.

[42] 1882 Act, s.13(1).

HOLDER FOR VALUE

Holder for value

18–14   In ordinary language a holder for value would be taken to be a holder who
has given value; but the 1882 Act extends this by enacting in section 27
that:

**(2) Where value has at any time been given for a bill the holder is
deemed to be a holder for value as regards the acceptor and all parties to
the bill who became parties prior to such time.**

**(3) Where the holder of a bill has a lien on it arising either from
contract or by implication of law, he is deemed to be a holder for value to
the extent of the sum for which he has a lien.**

The reason for including these subsections—the first, at any rate, in the
absence of a definition of holder for value or of his right—is not altogether
obvious, nor what are the disabilities, if any, which such a holder suffers. It
would seem to be implied that the rights of any holder other than in due course
must be less than absolute and it would follow that he would be subject to
defects of title in or mere personal defences of prior parties,[43] but as to this the
1882 Act is silent and the cases do not offer a clear explanation.[44]

Value given at some stage

18–15   A holder for value includes a person who holds a bill for which value has
at some time been given, though not necessarily by the holder himself, but
does not exclude the possibility of his having notice of any fraud, illegality, or
other vice affecting the title, for a man may really give part or the whole value
for a bill or note, though he has full notice of the fraud or illegality of the
original consideration.

Immediate parties

18–16   Between immediate parties—that is, between the drawer and acceptor,
between the payee and drawer, between the payee and maker of a note,
between the indorsee and indorser—the only consideration is that which
moved from the claimant to the defendant, and the absence or failure of this
is a good defence to an action.
In *Churchill and Sim v. Goddard*,[45] Scott L.J., at 109 said:

" . . . if the consideration for a bill wholly fails then as between immediate parties
the contract created by the instrument is discharged and the acceptor released."

---

[43] section 38.
[44] See *per* Milmo J. in *Barclays Bank v. Astley Industrial Trust* [1970] 2 Q.B. 527, 538, and his
reference to *Midland Bank Ltd v. Reckitt* [1933] A.C. 1, Lord Atkin, at 18.
[45] [1937] 1 K.B. 92.

and at 110:

> " . . . as between immediate parties the defendant is entitled to prove absence of consideration moving from the plaintiff as a defence to an action on the bill . . . "

This case was referred to in argument in *Diamond v. Graham*;[46] none of the judgments refers to it, but Danckwerts L.J. said that there was nothing in the statute to require value to be given by the holder and that the notes in Byles (which, incidentally, go back to the 16th ed. (1899) at least) went beyond the terms of s.27(2). It would thus seem that the statement above that "Between immediate parties, the only consideration is that which moved from the plaintiff [claimant] to the defendant and the absence or failure of this is a good defence to an action" must be accepted with some reserve. Thus, where a bill was drawn in the regular course of trade and delivered to the payee's agent, before the consideration was given, and the payee's agent, who was to have paid the consideration, failed, the payee could not recover against the drawer.[47]

Remote parties

But, between remote parties—for example, between payee and acceptor, between indorsee and acceptor, between indorsee and remote indorser—two distinct considerations, at least, must come in question; first, that which the defendant received for his liability; and, secondly, that which the claimant gave for his title. An action between remote parties will not fail unless there is absence or failure of both these considerations:

18–17

> "The sole ground on which the defendant relies is that the acceptance was not binding on account of the total failure or insufficiency of the consideration for which it was given, the document on the delivery of which the acceptance was given having been forged and there never having been any other consideration whatsoever for the acceptance of the defendant. And this would have been a good answer to the action if the Bank had been the drawers of the bill. But the Bank are indorsees and indorsees for value and the failure or want of consideration between them and the acceptors constitutes no defence; nor would the want of consideration between the drawer and acceptors (which must be considered as included in the general averment that there was no consideration), unless they took the bill with notice . . . which is not averred . . . "[48]

---

[46] [1968] 1 W.L.R. 1061, CA. But see the comments of Robert Goff J. in *Hasan v. Willson* [1977] 1 Lloyd's Rep. 431, 441(2), para. 19–16, *post*.

[47] *Puget de Brasro v. Forbes* (1792) 1 Esp. 117, approved in *Astley v. Johnson* (1860) 5 H. & N. 137, where it was held that a promise to give consideration in money at a specified future time having been broken, parties liable on the bill have a right to treat the payment of money as the consideration, and not the promise to pay it; *Jackson v. Warwick* (1797) 7 T.R. 121. The agency must be specially pleaded (*Munroe v. Bordier*) (1849) 19 L.J.C.P. 133); see also *Poirier v. Morris* (1853) 2 E. & B. 89.

[48] *Robinson v. Reynolds* (1841) 2 Q.B. 196, *per* Tindal C.J., 211, followed in *Thiedemann Goldschmidt* (1859) 1 De G.F. & J. 4; *cf.* also *Agra and Masterman's Bank v. Leighton* (1866) L.R. 2 Exch. 56. A defence which fails to allege that none of the previous holders had given value is insufficient (*Hunter v. Wilson* (1849) 19 L.J. Ex. 8).

Thus it is no defence to an action by an indorsee for value against an acceptor that the acceptor received no value;[49] nor, on the other hand, that, though the acceptor received value, the indorsee gave none. On the same principle, if the acceptance was without consideration, and the plaintiff, the indorsee, knew it, he, as a general rule, can recover no more than he gave for the bill;[50] for suppose the bill to be for £100 and that the indorsee gave £60 for it, if he could recover £100 from an accommodation acceptor, the acceptor having recovered that sum of the drawer, the drawer might recover back £40 from the indorsee as money received to the drawer's use.[51] Equally, the fact that the indorsee holder of a cheque had received it from the payee in payment an antecedent debt smaller than the value of the cheque did not prevent him being a holder for value under section 27(2).[52]

Value given by a stranger

18–18   Although the matter is not conclusively settled, it is unlikely that section 27(2) was intended to allow the original validity of the instrument to be transformed where value has been provided by someone who never became party to the instrument.[53]

Lien of holder

18–19   A holder who has a lien on a bill is *pro tanto* a holder for value, since the 1882 Act provides that:

27.—(3) Where the holder of a bill has a lien on it arising either from contract or by implication of law, he is deemed to be a holder for value to the extent of the sum for which he has a lien.

Bankers have a general lien on all securities for money which are deposited with them as bankers, in the way of their business (*i.e.* not deposited with them in any other capacity, *e.g.* as bailees), and they have, therefore, a lien, even as against the true owner, on all bills and notes payable to bearer, although the customer who deposited them was not the real owner, and had no authority to give a lien.[54] Further, the banker's lien extends to cheques

---

[49] *Collins v. Martin* (1797) 1 B. & P. 648, 651. But as to failure of consideration, see below Chapter 19. The proposition in the text should perhaps be read as restricted in such cases, to a holder in due course, which in the language of the 1882 Act it would appear the bank in *Robinson v. Reynolds* were.

[50] *Wiffen v. Roberts* (1795) 1 Esp. 261. This case can no longer be relied on as an authority that an indorsee with notice can only recover the value given by him as against an accommodation acceptor.

[51] *Jones v. Hibbert* (1817) 2 Stark. 304.

[52] *MacKenzie Mills v. Buono, The Times,* July 31, 1986. See also *ex p. Newton* (1881) 16 Ch. D. 330.

[53] See *MK International Development Co. Ltd v. The Housing Bank, The Financial Times,* January 22, 1991, and see generally Ch. 19 below at paras 19–13 to 19–17.

[54] *Brandao v. Barnett* (1846) 3 B.B. 519; *London Chartered Bank of Australia v. White* (1879) 4 App.Cas. 413; *Freedman v. Dominion Bank* (1909) 37 Q.R.C.S. 535; *Kuhne v. African Banking Corporation* [1910] Eastern Districts Court L.R. (Cape) 443; see also *Johnson v. Robarts* (1875) L.R. 10 Ch.App. 505 *et seq*; Paget, *Law of Banking*, 11th ed. (1996), p. 523; *Cuthbert v. Roberts Lubbock & Co.* (1909) 25 T.L.R. 583, CA.

entrusted to him for collection and constitutes him a holder for value, if, for instance, the customer is in a position to draw against them before they are cleared.[55]

In the case of bills, notes and cheques pledged with a banker or other person, the lien which attaches, by the above section, until repayment of the loan constitutes the pledgee a holder for value to the extent of his lien, with a title independent of that of the pledgor and a right to sue in his own name. Nor is the position of the pledgee less advantageous in the case of other negotiable instruments.[56] The pledgee is not, however, in general entitled to sell or negotiate the instruments pledged,[57] the property in which remains in the pledgor, who can follow them into the hands of transferees with notice or into those of the pledgee's trustee in bankruptcy.[58] The position of the collecting banker as a holder for value is dealt with in the chapters covering cheques.[59]

The holder of a cheque who has a lien on it is by virtue of section 27(3) deemed to have taken that cheque for value within the meaning of section 29(1)(b) to the extent of the sum for which he has a lien.[60] The same view was taken by Ungoed-Thomas J.[61]

Party having a lien must be a holder

Section 27(3) refers to the holder of a bill having a lien. It follows that a party, with a lien, can only claim to be a holder for value if he is a holder. **18–20**

2. "Holder" means the payee or indorsee of a bill or note who is in possession of it, or the bearer thereof.

A person, not in possession of a bill and having no interest therein, is not a holder, and cannot sue in his own name.[62] But after action brought by a person having no interest in a bill and no authority to sue as agent, the

---

[55] *Sutters v. Briggs* [1922] 1 A.C. 1, 18, 20 (Lord Birkenhead C., Lord Sumner); *Midland Bank v. Reckitt* [1933] A.C. 1, 19 (Lord Atkin), *post*, para. 23–69 and see *Re Keever, A Bankrupt, ex p. Trustee of the property of the Bankrupt v. Midland Bank Ltd* [1967] Ch. 182; *sub nom. Re Keever, ex p. Cork v. Midland Bank Ltd* [1966] 2 Lloyd's Rep. 475; [1967] Ch. 182.

[56] *cf. London Joint Stock Bank v. Simmons* [1892] A.C. 201; *Fuller v. Glyn, Mills & Co.* [1914] 2 K.B. 168.

[57] See the American cases of *Brown v. Ward* (1856) 3 Duer 360; *Wheeler v. Newbould* (1857) 16 N.Y. 392; Daniel (5th ed.), para. 833; see also Paget, *op. cit.* p. 523. The pledgee's duty, if the amount of the advance be not repaid when due, is to hold the securities till maturity and then realise them.

[58] *cf. Thompson v. Giles* (1824) 2 B. & C. 422; *Ex p. Barkworth* (1858) 27 L.J.Bk. 5.

[59] See *post* paras 23–69 *et seq.*

[60] *Barclays Bank Ltd v. Astley Industrial Trust* [1970] 2 Q.B. 527, *per* Milmo J.; there was there an antecedent debt in the form of an overdraft.

[61] *Re Keever, A Bankrupt, ex p. Trustee of the Property of the Bankrupt v. Midland Bank Ltd* [1967] Ch. 182; [1966] 2 Lloyd's Rep. 475.

[62] *Emmett v. Tottenham* (1853) 8 Exch. 884, citing the unreported case of *Gill v. Chesterfield*; *Sainsbury v. Parkinson* (1851, 1852) 18 L.T.(o.s.) 198, 227. In a claim on the instrument, it must be definitely alleged that the plaintiff is the holder (*Marcuson v. Botha* [1913] T.P.D. 650; see also *Torney v. Mcneil* (1914) 28 W.L.R. (Can.) 565). If the plaintiff is neither payee nor indorsee in possession he cannot sue upon the bill in his own name (*Barney v. Lauzon* [1923] 2 W.W.R. 19).

constructive holder may ratify the proceeding.[63] A person in possession of an
unindorsed order bill is not a holder, though he gave value for the bill, and
cannot sue in his own name.[64] He has, however, by 1882 Act, section 31(4),[65]
the right to have the bill indorsed to him,[66] and will become a holder as from
the date of the indorsement subsequently made.[67]

A negotiation by means of a forged indorsement does not confer a good
title, but a negotiation by a thief of an instrument made or become payable to
bearer, will confer a good title on a holder for value in good faith, which will
not be divested by the conviction of the thief for the larceny.[68]

Indorsee "means a person who has the rights which are given by statute in
respect of a bill or cheque by virtue of an indorsement. Since the Cheques Act
1957, the term is not limited to one who has received a cheque with a
signature actually written on the back."[69]

RIGHTS OF HOLDER

Rights of holder

18–21   It is convenient to set out the rights accruing to the various types of holders
referred to above:

> **38. The rights and powers of the holder of a bill are as follows:**
> **(1) He may sue on the bill in his own name:**
> **(2) Where he is a holder in due course, he holds the bill free from any
> defect of title of prior parties, as well as from mere personal defences
> available to prior parties among themselves, and may enforce payment
> against all parties liable on the bill:**
> **(3) Where his title is defective (a) if he negotiates the bill to a holder in
> due course, that holder obtains a good and complete title to the bill, and
> (b) if he obtains payment of the bill the person who pays him in due
> course gets a valid discharge for the bill.**

Defects of title and personal defences

18–22   These concepts are central to the act, and their (non)-availability as
defences is the key feature of the negotiable character of bills.

---

[63] *Ancona v. Marks* (1862) 31 L.J.Ex. 163.

[64] *Good v. Walker* (1892) 61 L.J.Q.B. 736, but by reason of s.2 of the Cheques Act 1957, for
purposes of the definition of "holder" in s.2 of the Act of 1882 a collecting banker is the "bearer"
of a cheque which is unindorsed (*Midland Bank Ltd v. Harris* [1963] 1 W.L.R. 1021). A drawer
of an unindorsed bill to his own order is the holder thereof upon its being accepted (*Walters v.
Neary* (1904) 21 T.L.R. 146).

[65] *Post*, para. 18–49.

[66] *Cook v. Hoosain Mia* (1912) 33 N.L.R. 12. See also *Savory v. Gibbs* (1910) 20 C.T.R. 600;
Rorich v. Voortman [1920] O.P.D. 42.

[67] *Day v. Longhurst* (1893) 62 L.J.Ch.334.

[68] *Chichester v. Hill* (1882) 52 L.J.Q.B. 160; *Woodhead & Co. v. Gunn* (1894) 11 S.C. 4;
Ferguson v. Kemp [1919] 1 W.W.R. 537. *Aliter*, where there is no consideration and the proceeds
can be traced (*Banque Belge v. Hambrouck* [1921] 1 K.B. 321).

[69] *Per* Megaw J. in *Midland Bank Ltd v. Harris* [1963] 1 W.L.R. 1021, 1024; and see
Westminster Bank Ltd v. Zang [1965] 2 W.L.R. 824.

The expression "defects of title" appears in three provisions which give effect to that concept: first, as part of the definition of a holder in due course: by section 29(1)(b) a party can only be a holder in due course if at the time he takes the bill he has "no notice of any defect in the title of the person who negotiated it".

Second, by section 36 (2) an overdue bill "can only be negotiated subject to any defect of title affecting it at its maturity. And thenceforward no person who takes it can acquire or give a better title than that which a person from whom he took it had."[70]

Finally, by section 38((2) a holder in due course "holds the bill free from any defect of title of prior parties, as well as from mere personal defences available to prior parties among themselves ... ". The corresponding provision at section 38(3) simply confers on a person who complies with formal definition of a holder the power to convey a good title to the instrument.[71]

The operation of those sections is reasonably clear. A party who takes a bill **18–23** for value from a holder of it is[72] entitled to enforce it in accordance with its terms against all other parties unless one or more of the requirements of section 29 is not met.[73] Any subsequent holder "stands in his shoes" against anyone whom that holder in due course could have held liable.[74]

The only defences which may be raised against such a person go to the **18–24** validity of the instrument itself, that it is not a bill at all because, for example, the signature upon it is a forgery,[75] or was placed there in an entirely different capacity.[76]

It follows that anyone else[77] takes the bill subject either to defects of title **18–25** or to any personal defences which may be set up against him.

Defect of title

It seems that the phrase "defects of title" is intended to refer to matters **18–26** which before the Act would have been referred to as "equities attaching to the bill". The Act provides a (non-exhaustive) list of matters which amount to defects of title.

---

[70] Corresponding to the requirement at s.29(1)(a); in effect a negotiable instrument is only negotiable (in the sense of being capable of passing free from equities) while it is current. A person who takes an overdue bill can tell from its date that it ought to have been paid and is on inquiry that there may be some reason why it has not; he takes the bill "on the credit of the person from whom he receives it" (*Brown v. Davies* (1789) 3 Term Rep. 80).

[71] Not the *right*, as against other parties, to do so.

[72] And is prima facie presumed to be (s.30).

[73] *i.e.* the bill is incomplete, or irregular, or is overdue, or he has notice that it has been dishonoured, that it was not taken in good faith, or that he had notice of a defect of title in the person from whom he took it.

[74] section 29(3). In effect the intervention of a holder in due course "wipes the slate".

[75] section 24.

[76] Consider *non est factum*. See *Lewis v. Clay* (1898) 67 L.J.Q.B. 224, *Foster v. McKinnon* (1869) L.R. 4 C.P. 704, para. 7–01.

[77] Including a holder for value (as defined by s.27) but *ex hypothesi* someone to whom the bill has not been regularly indorsed, or who has not given value, or who has taken an irregular or overdue bill, or has taken it with notice of its dishonour or of some defect in the title of the person negotiating it.

29.—(2) In particular the title of a person who negotiates a bill is defective within the meaning of this Act when he obtained the bill, or the acceptance thereof, by fraud, duress, or force and fear, or other unlawful means, or for an illegal consideration, or when he negotiates it in breach of faith, or under such circumstances as amount to a fraud.

Fraud etc.

18–27   Fraud in the 1882 Act has been held to mean common law fraud,[78] but the remaining words are clearly wide enough to embrace undue influence as it is now understood and as distinct from duress. It is suggested that the section embraces any matters which would give the acceptor or drawer of the bill the right to rescind it against the payee as a matter of the general law, and equally may be met by matters (such as affirmation) which would be an answer.[79]

Illegal consideration

18–28   Instances of illegal consideration are dealt with in Chapter 19 below, in particular in connection with gaming contracts. Bills or notes have been held unenforceable where they have been taken as part of insolvent composition in fraud of other creditors.[80]

Failure of consideration

18–29   The mere absence of consideration was not an equity attaching to the bill[81] and does not it seems amount to any defect in title. As to the failure of consideration, see Chapter 19 below. It has been suggested that to negotiate a bill upon which the consideration has failed would itself be a breach of faith.[82]

Otherwise in breach of faith

18–30   By way of example, it would be a breach of such an obligation to negotiate a bill which had been delivered subject to an unfulfilled condition, or for a specified and limited purpose.[83]

[78] *Oesterreiche Landerbank v. S'Elite Ltd* [1981] 1 Q.B. 565, overruling the decision in *Banca Popolare di Novara v. John Livanos & Sons Ltd* to the effect that the term embraced a "fraudulent preference" *per se*, under the Bankruptcy Act 1914; the point does not arise under the language of the 1986 Insolvency Act. A transaction which infringes that Act may nonetheless, in fact, be fraudulent or it may be illegal on other grounds.

[79] See *Mills v. Oddy* (1835) 2 Cr. M. & R. 103; Compare *Archer v. Bamford* (1822) 3 Stark 175 (where the acceptor retained the benefit rather than repudiating the contract); *Dawes v. Harness* (1875) L.R. 10 C.P. 166. See also para. 26–31 below.

[80] *Cockshott v. Bennett* (1788) 2 T.R. 763; *Knight v. Hunt* (1829) 5 Bing. 432; *Bryant v. Christie* (1816) 1 Stark. 329; and see *Took v. Tuck* (1827) 4 Bing. 224; *Moidel v. Cohen* (1926) Q.R. 64 S.C. 441. *Wilson v. Ray* (1839) 10 A. & E. 82 *Smith v. Cuff* (1817) 6 M. & S. 160; *Horton v. Riley* (1843) 11 M. & W. 492; see also *Smith v. Bromley* (1781) 2 Doug. 695; *Atkinson v. Denby* (1862) 31 L.J.Ex. 362, *Banks v. Cheltenham Dairy Co.* (1910) 29 New Zealand L.R. 979; *Ex p. Milner* (1885) 15 Q.B.D. 605 *Wells v. Girling* (1819) 1 Brod. & B. 447 *Leicester v. Rose* (1803) 4 East 372.

[81] See above para. 17–33, nn. 39 and 40.

[82] See Chalmers & Guest, para. 707.

[83] And see further below "Where indorsee a trustee" at para. 18–50.

Consumer credit

Where a person negotiates a cheque in contravention of section 123(2) of   **18–31**
the Consumer Credit Act 1974, his doing so constitutes a defect in his title
within the meaning of the 1882 Act.[84]

Mere personal defences

The meaning of this phrase is uncertain; it is though clear that the Act   **18–32**
envisages a third category of defences to which a holder other than a holder
in due course may be subject, falling short of defects of title. The Act does not
define them, and there appears to be no express guidance in the case law.

Cowen[85] distinguishes between defences *in rem* and *in personam* and gives,   **18–33**
in illustration of the former, fraud, duress, minority, illegality, *inter alia*, and
of the latter, incapacity to sue the debtor, and counterclaim. He suggests that
"a remote party who is not a holder in due course may be met by defences *in
rem* but not by defences *in personam*", for which view he finds support in
English law. He sums up as follows:[86] "Whereas neither 'defects of title' nor
'mere personal defences' may be raised against a holder in due course, defects
of title may be raised against a remote party who is not a holder in due course,
but 'mere personal' or 'collateral' defences are not available against such a
holder." Falconbridge is to much the same effect: "a mere personal defence
is one which does not relate to the instrument or affect the holder's title, as for
example, a right of set-off arising out of another transaction between the
maker and the payee of a note. The defence may be good as between the two
parties between whom it arises, that is, between immediate parties, but it is not
available against a remote party."[87]

It is suggested that the term is apt to embrace a purely personal claim   **18–34**
arising out of a separate transaction in circumstances where it is not so related
to the transaction upon the bill as to amount to an equity upon it. That question
should depend upon the same matters as govern the general law as to whether
an assignee takes "subject to equities",[88] or to the availability of equitable set-
off.[89] A wholly separate cross-claim on the part of an earlier holder should not
be available against a remote holder of the bill any more than it would against
an ordinary assignee. It could be relied on between the relevant parties
"among themselves" in respect of liability on the bill. Note, however, that an
unliquidated cross-claim cannot be set-off against the liquidated claim on a
bill, even as between immediate parties.[90]

Title of original payee

The decision of the House of Lords in *R.E. Jones Ltd v. Waring & Gillow*   **18–35**
is discussed below, but it serves to note here that while the case decides that

[84] Consumer Credit Act 1974, s.125(2).
[85] See *Negotiable instruments in South Africa*, (4th ed., 1966), p. 272.
[86] *ibid.*, p. 274.
[87] Falconbridge, p. 667.
[88] See Chitty, 28th ed., Vol. 1 para. 20–68.
[89] See *Hanak v. Green* [1958] 2 Q.B. 9.
[90] See Ch. 26 below.

an original payee is not a holder in due course,[91] it does not follow that his title is defective merely because the instrument was procured wrongfully or by fraud. If, bona fide and for value, the payee receives a complete and regular instrument with no notice of (or participation in) any wrongdoing, there is no reason why he should not be treated as a bona fide purchaser for value and entitled to enforce it.

This appears to be the law.[92] Where, for example, the defendant was induced by the owner's fraud to purchase certain pictures at a sale by auction and gave a cheque for the price to the auctioneer, the auctioneer, who in the meantime had settled with the owner, was held entitled to enforce payment of the cheque, notwithstanding the principal's fraud.[93]

PAYEE-HOLDER FOR VALUE

Payee not a holder in due course

18–36   It would seem that no serious difficulty arose in regard to the status of a payee-holder for value before the decision of the House of Lords in *Jones v. Waring & Gillow*.[94] This was an action for the recovery of money paid under mistake of fact and the House, as judged by the speeches, took no account of the status of the respondents as holders of the cheque by which they obtained the money sought to be recovered. The respondents had pleaded that they were holders in due course of the cheque and that they had, therefore, an unimpeachable title and accordingly could not be called upon to repay. The House rejected the argument, held that the payee of a cheque could not be a holder in due course and, on this point, contented themselves with that.[95] The point seems to have had no effect on the (majority) judgment against the respondents, nor on the opinions of the minority. All the judges were of the same opinion in this respect (if the concurrence of Lord Atkinson extends to it) and they expressly denied the accuracy of the view of Fletcher Moulton

[91] The payee-holder is in effect the first person to whom the contractual promises embodied in a bill are made, and the first person entitled to sue on it. He either has a good title, or he does not, but that question does not depend on the instrument's negotiability; his title is not derived from a previous holder.

[92] *Hindle v. Brown* (1908) 98 L.T. 791, and see also *Watson v. Russell* (1862) 3 B.&S. 34 *per* Crompton J., *Talbot v. Von Boris* [1911] 1 K.B. 854, *Nelson v. Larholt* [1948] 1 K.B. 449, *Hasan v. Willson* [1977] 1 Lloyd's Rep. 431. Against that, see the other cases discussed below. It is however difficult to reconcile this proposition with the result in *Jones v. Waring & Gillow* (that the monies were repayable). *Quaere* whether that case can be explained by reference to the special requirements for valid past consideration (Ch. 19 and see Ch. 32, below on Payments under a mistake, paras 32–24 *et seq.*). On ordinary contractual principles a debtor would not (generally) have a defence arising out of his unilateral mistake of fact, or a misrepresentation for which the creditor was not in some way responsible.

[93] *Oesterreiche Landerbank v. S'Elite Ltd* [1981] 1 Q.B. 565.

[94] [1926] A.C. 670.

[95] Whilst the decision has been criticised (see Crawford and Falconbridge, *Banking and Bills of Exchange*, 8th ed., p. 1474), Professor Shea in his Report on Negotiable Instruments— Appendix A to the Banking Services: Law and Practice Report—ultimately recommended that the payee should not be a holder in due course; see paras 20.4–6 (1989) cm 1026.

L.J. in *Lloyds Bank v. Cooke*,[96] preferring that of Lord Russell of Killowen C.J. in *Lewis v. Clay*.[97]

In deciding that the payee could not be a holder in due course, the House did not deal with the implication of their decision and left in doubt what are the rights of a holder who, but for that decision could claim to be a holder in due course—a holder who complies with all the conditions of section 29 save that he took the instrument as payee instead of having it "negotiated" to him within the meaning of that section. The question falls to be considered from two points of view, from that of the instrument being a bill of exchange that is not a cheque and from that of its being a cheque; in the first case the payee-holder is, *vis-à-vis* the acceptor, a remote party, whereas in the second he is immediate in relation to the drawer, the party primarily liable.

It is, perhaps, important first to make clear that the decision went no further; it did not, specifically, at any rate, reduce the rights of a payee-holder for value below those of a holder in due course. And it is submitted that the decision did not affect the rights of a payee-holder for value whatever they may be.

Position prior to the 1882 Act

If it is accepted—and there seems little doubt—that prior to 1882 a payee could be a holder in due course or its then equivalent and that he had an indefeasible title, only from the wording of section 29 of the 1882 Act could it appear that the legislature intended to change the law. A review of the cases since that time shows no positive change in the position.   **18–37**

Lewis v. Clay

The first is that of *Lewis v. Clay* (to which the House referred in *R. E. Jones Ltd v. Waring & Gillow*). This was an action on a promissory note by the payee against one of the makers, the second of whom had been fraudulent in obtaining its value from the payee. Lord Russell of Killowen C.J. held that the plaintiff was not the holder in due course of the note, not being "a person to whom, after its completion by and as between the immediate parties, the bill or note had been negotiated. In the present case the plaintiff is named as payee on the face of the promissory note, and, therefore, is one of the immediate parties." Perhaps the significant part of this statement is that the parties were immediate to each other; is it implied that if the payee plaintiff was a remote party as regards the defendant the position would be different? The learned judge went on to say that even if the plaintiff had been a holder in due course it would have made no difference to the result; what, it is submitted, he meant was that even if the holder had taken in due course he would have had no title, since the drawer's signature to the note was obtained by fraud, he being under the reasonable impression that he was witnessing someone else's signature to another document altogether.   **18–38**

[96] [1907] 1 K.B. 794.
[97] (1897) 14 T.L.R. 149.

18–39   *Herdman v. Wheeler*[98] was the next case in which the question was raised,
again in an action by the payee of a promissory note. Channell J., speaking for
the whole Court, said[99] "On the whole, therefore, we are not prepared to hold
that the payee of a note can never be a holder in due course . . . [1] We have been
very reluctant to come to the conclusion that the judgment in favour of the
defendant is right, because it appears dangerous even to cast doubt upon a
payee's right to recover when he has taken a bill or note complete and regular
on the face of it honestly and for value . . . " But they concluded that
"negotiated" in section 20 (not section 29) meant transfer by one holder to
another, although by section 31(1) "A bill is negotiated when it is transferred
from one person to another in such a manner as to constitute the transferee the
holder of the bill."

Lloyds Bank v. Cooke

18–40   The decision next in time was the Appeal Court decision in *Lloyds Bank Ltd
v. Cooke*, which was based not on the terms of the 1882 Act, but on the ground
that the defendant was estopped as between himself and the plaintiffs from
denying the validity of the note. In the course of his judgment,[2] Fletcher
Moulton L.J. said (at 806) that the term "holder in due course" was intended
to be the equivalent of the term "bona fide holder for value" used prior to the
Act and could include the payee who had given full value in good faith (see
Lord Selborne in *France v. Clark*);[3] therefore, that he was led to the conclusion, by the language of the statute "that the Act did not intend to impair the
position of the payee as contrasted with that of an indorsee, and that a payee
who has given value in good faith is intended to come within its provisions as
a 'holder in due course' just as much as an indorsee. . . . Finding, therefore,
no indication in the Act of any intention to interfere with the position of a
payee of a negotiable instrument in this respect, I arrive with some confidence
at the conclusion that, in the circumstances of a case like the present, such a
payee since the Act still occupies the favourable position which he would
have had before the Act by virtue of the law of estoppel as applied to a case
where a promissory note has been signed in blank by the maker and entrusted
to another person to fill up." *A fortiori* the case of a valid and complete bill
delivered to the payee for value. But the learned Lord Justice was able to reach
the same conclusion from the definitions in the Act itself.[4]

Talbot v. Von Boris

18–41   A promissory note was again in question in *Talbot v. Von Boris*[5] and was
again decided on section 20, but Farwell L.J. approved the dictum of Fletcher

[98] [1902] 1 K.B. 361.
[99] *ibid.* at 372.
[1] *ibid.* at 375.
[2] [1907] 1 K.B. 794, 805, CA.
[3] (1884) 26 Ch.D. 257.
[4] *ibid.* at pp. 807–808.
[5] [1911] 1 K.B. 854.

Moulton L.J. referred to above. The case decided that duress (or fraud) must be shown to be that of the plaintiff if the defendant is to succeed.

Ayres v. Moore

30 years later came *Ayres v. Moore*,[6] which was an action, by the payee of **18–42** bills of exchange against the acceptor, which failed because the acceptance was obtained by fraud. In the course of his judgment, Hallett J. said of the argument that the plaintiff must be shown to be actually or notionally guilty of complicity in the fraud before that fraud can operate against him, " . . . if it were necessary for an immediate party to be personally tainted by the fraud that he might be deprived of his rights under the bill—then a great many provisions which the Legislature has thought fit to enact, and a great deal of discussion and argument in the cases, would be superfluous. In my view, it is precisely because a holder of a bill may be affected, although he is personally innocent of fraud, that there are those provisions for protecting a holder in due course. I do not think that an immediate party as such is likewise protected, and in my judgment, although no very clear authority has been cited to me, he is not." As to this, the payee of a bill is, *vis-à-vis* the acceptor, a remote party; and, further, the payee was not a holder in due course, not only because he was the payee, but because the bills were incomplete at the time he took them.

Arab Bank Ltd v. Ross

The last and most recent case is that of *Arab Bank Ltd v. Ross*,[7] in which the **18–43** bank sued as holders in due course of two promissory notes made by the defendant. The indorsement was irregular, which clearly defeated the plea. Nevertheless, the defendant failed to prove the fraud he alleged and it was held that the plaintiffs obtained a good title through the indorsements, which were valid. As Somervell L.J. put it: if the defendant "had succeeded in establishing that the notes had been obtained by fraud, but failed to establish the plaintiffs' knowledge, it may be that he could have succeeded once he had shown that by reason of the incompleteness of the note the plaintiff was not a holder in due course". It would seem to be implied in this that proof of fraud coupled with irregularity on the face of the instrument would defeat a person who took otherwise as a holder in due course.

Conclusion

Considering all these cases together the following points emerge: **18–44**

(1) that, apart from *R. E. Jones Ltd v. Waring & Gillow* and *Ayres v. Moore*, all were concerned with the payee of promissory notes, and were actions against the maker, an immediate party;

(2) that the decision in *R. E. Jones Ltd v. Waring & Gillow* did nothing, specifically, to derogate from the status of a payee of a cheque;

[6] [1940] 1 K.B. 278.
[7] [1952] 2 Q.B. 216.

(3) that the payee of a bill of exchange is, *vis-à-vis* the acceptor, a remote party.

It is thus submitted that where the payee of a bill takes in accordance with the conditions which must be fulfilled by a transferee before he can claim to be a holder in due course under section 29, he has the same rights *vis-à-vis* a remote party such as the acceptor and is not liable to be defeated either by defects of title or by any personal defence which the acceptor may set up against the drawer. It is only where, the instrument not being complete and regular on the face of it and, therefore, such as to put the taker on inquiry, or where other circumstances are such as to call for inquiry by him, that any defect of title within the meaning of section 27 will defeat him.

In *Lombard Banking Ltd v. Central Garage & Engineering Co. Ltd*[8] Scarman J. held that the plaintiffs were holders in due course of bills drawn by them to their own order and indorsed by them after the indorsements of the defendants. It is submitted that that could not be so, as the bills were not negotiated back to the drawers.

TRANSFEREE BY DELIVERY

Transferee by delivery

18–45 The 1882 Act does not define "transferee by delivery" but he is the transferee of a bill or note to bearer requiring nothing but delivery to complete the transfer. The person so transferring is a transferor by delivery, defined in section 58.[9] Bills and notes payable to bearer may circulate freely like money. The bona fide possessor is the true owner, for it is essential to the currency of bearer bills and notes that property and possession should be inseparable. Unless the indorser had a right to indorse[10] the indorsee of a bill payable to order, and not made payable to bearer by a blank indorsement, has no right to the bill, either so as to retain it against the real owner or to sue any party upon it. Whereas, if the cheque, bill or note be originally made or have since duly become payable to bearer, the title of the holder, both as against a former owner on the one hand and against the maker, acceptor, or indorser on the other, is not affected by any infirmity in the title of the transferor, provided the holder took it bona fide for value.

It was formerly considered that the transferee's title would be affected by want of due caution on his part, and that he would be liable in trover to the real owner, and unable to enforce payment against the parties to the instrument, if he were guilty of negligence in taking it. Thus, where a banker, in a small market town, changed a £500 Bank of England note for a stranger, without any further inquiry than merely asking his name, he was held liable, in trover, to a party from whom the note had been unlawfully obtained, Best C.J. observing: "The party's caution should increase with the amount of the note

[8] [1963] 1 Q.B. 220.
[9] *Ante*, para. 17–21.
[10] *Mead v. Young* (1790) 4 T.R. 28, unless there be an estoppel (1882 Act, s.24).

which he is called upon to change. A man may change a £20 note without asking a single question, but would that be right as to one of several thousands?"[11] But it is now settled that if a man takes honestly an instrument made or become payable to bearer, he has a good title to it, with whatever degree of negligence he may have acted, unless his gross negligence induces the jury to find fraud. "I believe", says Lord Denman, "we are all of opinion that gross negligence only would not be a sufficient answer where the party has given consideration for the bill. Gross negligence may be evidence of malafides, but is not the same thing. We have shaken off the last remnant of the contrary doctrine."[12]

Title of an agent

If the party presenting a bill or note payable to bearer is the mere agent of another, the agent's title is infected with the infirmity of his principal's title, although the principal is in the agent's debt; and the agent consequently may not be able to enforce payment of the maker.[13]   **18–46**

Title of pledgee

It makes no difference that the bill or note is only pledged, and not absolutely transferred; the pawnee acquires a property in it,[14] and is not liable in trover to the real owner, as in the case of goods improperly pledged.[15]   **18–47**

INDORSEE

Indorsee

The term indorsee is not defined in the 1882 Act, but as observed by Megaw J.:   **18–48**

> " . . . in the definition of 'holder' in section 2 of that Act [of 1882] 'indorsee' means a person who has the rights which are given by statute in respect of a bill or cheque by virtue of an indorsement. Since the Cheques Act 1957, it is not limited to one who has received a cheque with a signature actually written on the back."[16]

---

[11] *Snow v. Peacock* (1825) 2 C. & P. 215, 221; and see *Gill v. Cubitt* (1824) 3 B. & C. 466; *Crook v. Jadis* (1834) 5 B. & Ad. 909.

[12] *Goodman v. Harvey* (1836) 4 A. & E. 870, 876; *Willis v. Bank of England* (1835) 4 A. & E. 21; *Raphael v. Bank of England* (1855) 17 C.B. 161; *Carlon v. Ireland* (1856) L.J.Q.B. 113; see also *Uther v. Rich* (1839) 10 A. & E. 784, 790.

[13] *Solomons v. Bank of England* (1791) 13 East 135n. The fact that the agents are possessed of a lien cannot affect the legal consequence of their taking a bill when overdue (*Redfern v. Rosenthal* (1902) 86 L.T. 855). As to when the holder can recover in spite of the fraud of the other party's agent, *cf. Watson v. Russell* (1864) 34 L.J.Q.B. 93, distinguished in *Jones (R.E.) v. Waring & Gillow* [1926] A.C. 670; *Grant v. Harty* (1888) 6 N.Z.L.R. 444; *Ontario Bank v. Young* [1901] 2 O.L.R. 761; *Johnson v. Johnson* (1928) 2 D.L.R. 912.

[14] *Barber v. Richards* (1851) 6 Ex. 63; 1882 Act, s.27(3).

[15] *Collins v. Martin* (1797) 1 Bos. & P. 648. As to banker's lien, see *ante*, para. 18–19.

[16] *Midland Bank Ltd v. Harris* [1963] 1 W.L.R. 1021, *per* Megaw J. at 1024.

A valid transfer by indorsement vests in the indorsee a right of action against all the parties whose names are on the bill, in case of default of acceptance or payment; and against an innocent indorsee for value no prior party can set up the defence of fraud, duress, illegality or absence of consideration.[17]

Right to indorsement

18–49   The transferee for value of a bill may compel his transferor to indorse to him, since the 1882 Act provides that:

31.—(4) Where the holder of a bill payable to his order transfers it for value without indorsing it, the transfer gives the transferee such title as the transferor had in the bill, and the transferee in addition acquires the right to have the indorsement of the transferor.[18]

Further, by section 39 of the Supreme Court Act 1981, if the transferor refuses to comply with an order of the court directing him to indorse, the court may order the instrument to be executed by its nominee.[19] By section 31(4) the transferee must come within the definition of a "holder" in section 2 of the 1882 Act,[20] and there must be an intention on the part of the transferor to transfer the whole of the rights on the instrument.[21] Otherwise the transferee of an unindorsed bill has no right, apart from such direct order of the court, to sign his transferor's name as indorser.[22] Nor can he obtain a good title by an indorsement written after notice to him of a fraud.[23]

Where indorsee a trustee

18–50   Where a bill or note is merely indorsed to another, and deposited with him as a trustee, he can only use it in conformity with the stipulations on which he became the depositary of it.[24]

If the depositary of the bill indorses it over in breach of trust, the indorsee, with actual notice of the breach of trust, or constructive notice, as where he takes it overdue, can acquire no title to the bill as against the rightful owner,

---

[17] 1882 Act, s.29.

[18] It has been held in Canada that the transferor is not bound to give an unqualified indorsement unless some contract or equity requires him to assume responsibility on the bill (*Scott v. Ferguson* (1929) 3 D.L.R. 705).

[19] The court may direct the act to be done by the person obtaining the order.

[20] *Walters v. Neary* (1904) 21 T.L.R. 146, following *Watkins v. Maule* (1820) 2 Jac. & W. 237. Further as to "holder" of an unindorsed bill, see *Day v. Longhurst* (1893) 62 L.J. Ch. 334.

[21] *Good v. Walker* (1892) 61 L.J.Q.B. 736, where the instrument was transferred as pledge for a lesser sum, distinguishing *Hood v. Stewart* (1890) 17 R. 749, where the indorsement was omitted by mistake, and see *International Securities Ltd v. Gerard* (1916) 29 D.L.R. 77.

[22] *Harrop v. Fisher* (1861) 30 L.J.C.P. 283, distinguished in *Johnson v. L'Heureux* (1914) 27 W.L.R. 21; and see *Moxon v. Pulling* (1814) 4 Camp. 50.

[23] *Whistler v. Forster* (1863) 32 L.J.C.P. 161; *Imperial Bank of Canada v. Dennis* [1926] 3 D.L.R. 168.

[24] As to the consideration where the bill is deposited as security for the balance of a running account, see *ante*. As to when a banker suing as holder in due course is also a trustee, see *Barclays Bank Ltd v. Aschaffenburger Zellstoffwerke A.G.* [1967] 1 Lloyd's Rep. 387.

and can neither sue him on the bill, nor hold the bill against him.[25] If A is in possession of a bill accepted by B, and solely on B's behalf and without B's authority indorses the bill for value to C, who takes with notice of the want of authority, C has no right to retain the bill as against B notwithstanding his rights against A, for A could not retain the bill against B, and C has no better title than A has.[26]

So where the drawer of a bill of exchange deposited it with a creditor, and gave him authority to receive the proceeds and apply them in a specified way, and the drawer afterwards committed an act of bankruptcy, on which a commission issued, the creditor having, after the act of bankruptcy, delivered the original bill to the acceptor, and taken in lieu of it another bill it was held by Tindal C.J. that the creditor had been guilty of a conversion, and the assignees of the bankrupt might recover against him in trover.[27] But it would have been otherwise if the creditor had merely received the money, for that would not have amounted to a conversion unless the assignees proved a demand and a refusal (to deliver the bill) before due.[28]

Restrictive indorsements

A trust may be expressed on the bill itself by a restrictive indorsement, or **18–51** a restrictive direction appended to the payee's name, so that into whose hands soever the bill may travel it may carry a trust on the face of it.

In early cases it seems to have been thought that a man might indorse a bill with words bestowing a mere naked authority to receive it to his use, but transferring no interest in it.[29] Now, however, it is clear that by a restrictive indorsement a man may transfer such interest as he has in the bill to his immediate indorsee and, if he choose, may enable him to transfer such rights to others.

The 1882 Act deals with the subject of restrictive indorsements as follows:

35.—(1) An indorsement is restrictive which prohibits the further negotiation of the bill or which expresses that it is a mere authority to deal with the bill as thereby directed and not a transfer of the ownership thereof, as, for example, if a bill be indorsed "Pay D only", or "Pay D for the account of X", or "Pay D or order for collection".[30]

---

[25] *Goggerley v. Cuthbert* (1806) 2 N.R. (Bos. & P.) 170. If the acceptor is compelled to pay, he may sue the depositary: *Bleaden v. Charles* (1831) 7 Bing. 246 where the plaintiff abandoned his claim to reimbursement of the costs incurred in the action against him as acceptor; and see *Osborn v. Donald* (1864) 12 W.R. 9 and 831, Ex. Ch.

[26] *Evans v. Kymer* (1830) 1 B. & Ad. 528.

[27] *Robson v. Rolls* (1832) 1 Mood & R. 239.

[28] *Jones v. Fort* (1829) 9 B. & C. 764; but see this case criticised in *Exley v. Inglis* (1868) L.R. 3 Ex. 247, 252.

[29] See *Snee v. Prescot* (1743) 1 Atk. 245, 249; and that it could not be transferred without being also negotiated (*Edie v. East India Co.* (1971) 2 Burr. 1216, 1225, 1227). In *Evans v. Cramlington* (1687) Carthew 5, in error 2 Vent. 307, it was held that the effect of a drawing—"Pay B or order for the use of C"—constituted an equity only in C's favour, and that, if B indorsed to D, the legal right in the bill vested in D.

[30] *Williams, Deacon & Co. v. Shadbolt* (1885) 1 T.L.R. 417; *Lloyd v. Sigourney* (1829) 5 Bing. 525.

In addition to these examples of restrictive indorsements the following have also been held or said to be restrictive: "The within must be credited to D value in account";[31] "Pray pay the money to my servant for my use";[32] "Pay to the order of the D Bank to my credit";[33] "Deposit only to the account of (the payee)".[34] On the other hand, the following has been held not to constitute a restrictive indorsement: "Value in account with the O Bank".[35] Nor will the crossing of a cheque with the words "Account of J. F. Moriarty Esq., National Bank, Dublin" be sufficient to prevent further transfer.[36]

The question arose in *Yeoman Credit Ltd v. Gregory*[37] in which Megaw J. expressed the view:

"What one has to look to primarily here is all the facts and circumstances relating to these two signatures on the bill and the intention of the parties, which in this case is perfectly clear. The intention throughout of both parties was that, if Express Coachcraft Ltd, defaulted on the bill, the plaintiffs should be entitled to recover from the defendant.

I have come to the conclusion that it would be wrong to say that this form of indorsement is one which prevents the bill from being a bill which is complete and regular on its face, or which makes it something which is not complete and regular on its face. Just in the same way as the Courts have found it possible to say that the order of the indorsements is something which, if explained by extrinsic evidence, is not a fatal defect, so also I think the fact that the indorsement which is put on is a restrictive indorsement is not fatal when the facts and circumstances are explained by extrinsic evidence and when it appears that the intention at all times was that the defendant should be liable on Express Coachcraft Ltd's default. I think it is permissible under Sect. 20 of the Act, having regard to the intention of the parties, to treat this indorsement as though it had been made first as an indorsement in blank, which would validate the indorser's signature as an indorser, and, second, as a restrictive indorsement for collection just as though the indorsement had been written on in blank at one moment of time and at a subsequent moment of time there had been written above, as the holder was plainly entitled to do, a restriction."[38]

Effect of restrictive indorsement

18–52   The significance of this judgment lies in the holding that a bill bearing the particular restrictive indorsement (*i.e.* for collection) may be complete and regular on the face of it. Where a restrictive indorsement is intended to serve the double purpose indicated in Megaw J.'s judgment, construction of its effect is less easy. Further, the 1882 Act provides as regards the effect of a restrictive indorsement that:

---

[31] *Archer v. Bank of England* (1791) 2 Doug. 637.

[32] *cf. Edie v. East India Co., supra* at p. 1227.

[33] *Merchants Bank of Canada v. Brett* [1923] 2 D.L.R. 264.

[34] *Imperial Bank of Canada v. Hays and Earl Ltd* (1962) 35 D.L.R. (2d) 136, applying *Merchants Bank of Canada v. Brett* [1923] 2 D.L.R. 264; it was further held that the plaintiff, being a restrictive indorsee, was not a holder in due course.

[35] *Murrow v. Stuart* (1853) 8 Moo. P.C. 267. In the practically identical case of *Buckley v. Jackson* (1868) L.R. 3 Ex. 135, it was pointed out by Kelly C.B. that such an indorsement means only that value has been received, and been received in a certain manner, but that it in no way restricts the effect of the indorsement.

[36] *National Bank v. Silke* [1891] 1 Q.B. 435; see also *post*, para. 21–40.

[37] [1962] 2 Lloyd's Rep. 302.

[38] [1962] 2 Lloyd's Rep. 315.

35.—(2) A restrictive indorsement gives the indorsee the right to receive payment of the bill and to sue any party thereto that his indorser could have sued, but gives him no power to transfer his rights as indorsee unless it expressly authorise him to do so.

A, a merchant in New England, remitted a bill to B, his agent in London, indorsing it in this form: "Pay B, or his order, for my use". B discounted it with his bankers; he afterwards failed, and the bankers, to whom he was indebted in more than the amount of the bill, received payment of it at maturity from the acceptors. Held in an action for money had and received, that the bankers were liable to refund the money to A.[39]

In *Williams, Deacon & Co. v. Shadbolt*, bills were drawn by Darmer & Co. of Mobile, Alabama, and indorsed to the Bank of Mobile which indorsed them to the plaintiff bank "for collection for the account of the Bank of Mobile", which latter bank later went into liquidation indebted to the plaintiff bank. It is not clear from the report[40] that subsection (2) of section 35 was specifically mentioned. It was admitted for the defence that the Bank of Mobile were the real owners and holders of the bill but that their account with their customers had been settled. The case turned not on whether this was the fact, but whether the plaintiffs were holders with a right against the acceptors.

And as to the authorisation of further transfer:

35.—(3) Where a restrictive indorsement authorises further transfer, all subsequent indorsees take the bill with the same rights and subject to the same liabilities as the first indorsee under the restrictive indorsement.

A bill was indorsed by the payee in this form; "Pay A B, or order, for the account of C D", A B pledged it with the defendant, who advanced money upon it to A B personally. Held, that the defendant had sufficient notice, from the indorsement, that A B had no authority to raise money on the bill for his own benefit, and therefore could not defend an action of trover for the bill, brought by C D, his principal.[41]

PAYER FOR HONOUR

Payer for honour

Although instances are rare, the 1882 Act provides that anyone may **18–53** intervene and pay it for honour.[42]

---

[39] *Sigourney v. Lloyd* (1828) 8 B. & C. 622; affirmed on appeal, 5 Bing. 525.

[40] 1 T.L.R. 417; in *Paternott v. Mornimpex Hungarian Foreign Trading Co.* (1956) 58 Ceylon N.L.R. 44, it was held that an indorsement by the payees to a bank for collection was restrictive and an indorsement back by the restrictive indorsee gave the drawer no right to sue, unless it could be shown that the payees also were collecting agents for the drawer.

[41] *Treuttel v. Barandon* (1817) 8 Taunt. 100.

[42] section 68(1).

Effect of payment for honour

18–54   The effect of the payment for honour as regards the liabilities of the parties is as follows:

68.—(5) Where a bill has been paid for honour, all parties subsequent to the party for whose honour it is paid are discharged, but the payer for honour is subrogated to, and succeeds to both the rights and duties of, the holder as regards the party for whose honour he pays, and all parties liable to that party.

The payer for honour must therefore see that notice of dishonour is duly given to all prior parties.[43] Though the subsequent parties are discharged the payer for honour may rely on any title they may have.[44] The payer for honour, however, though he succeeds to the rights of the holder, does not thereby acquire a right to re-issue the bill.[45]

Further,

68.—(6) The payer for honour on paying to the holder the amount of the bill and the notarial expenses incidental to its dishonour is entitled to receive both the bill itself and the protest. If the holder do not on demand deliver them up he shall be liable to the payer for honour in damages.[46]

Lastly, the holder who refuses to take payment supra protest does so at his peril, since;

68.—(7) Where the holder of a bill refuses to receive payment supra protest he shall lose his right of recourse against any party who would have been discharged by such payment.

In this case also, as in the case of subsection (1) already noted, a distinction is to be observed between this provision and that contained in section 65(1), since in the latter case, *viz.*, of acceptance supra protest, the holder is not bound to allow such acceptance.

No payment for honour on notes

18–55   As no protest is necessary in case of dishonour of a note, whether inland or foreign, there is in general no payment supra protest.[47]

---

[43] *Goodall v. Polhill* (1845) 14 L.J.C.P. 146.
[44] *Ex p. Swan* (1868) L.R. 6 Eq. 344; Nouguier, pp. 584–591.
[45] *ibid.*
[46] For a form of receipt to be given by the holder, see Brookes (9th ed., 1939), p. 258.
[47] It has been said that the law merchant as to payment supra protest does not apply to promissory notes (Storey (7th ed.), s.453); but it is to be observed that s.89 of the 1882 Act does not exclude the application of s.68 to this class of instrument.

Chapter 19

CONSIDERATION

Introduction

AS a general principle in order for a promise to be binding, in English law, it **19–01** must either be made by deed or supported by "consideration".[1] As long ago as 1937 it was possible for the Law Revision Committee, in its sixth Interim Report (Cmd. 5449), to say that the doctrine of consideration was peculiar to the Anglo-American law, that the law of Scotland had always rejected the view that consideration was essential to the formation of a contract; and that the common law of England was alone in the view that a contract should not confer any rights on a stranger even although the sole object was to benefit him. The Committee's recommendations included that an agreement shall be enforceable if the promise or offer has been made in writing by the promisor or his agent, or if it is supported by valuable consideration past or present. The Committee's recommendations never received legislative approval.[2]

The Banking Services: Law and Practice Report by the Review Committee **19–02** recommended that the need for consideration as a test of negotiability should be abolished,[3] but again the recommendation has not been put into effect. The position remains, then, that the general law as to consideration applies to bills, except to the extent provided by the 1882 Act. The 1882 Act not only sets out what is meant by consideration, but provides that consideration (i) is presumed unless the contrary is proven, and (ii) may be constituted by an antecedent debt or liability.

The meaning of consideration

Under the 1882 Act consideration is the same thing as value; by section 2 **19–03** "value means valuable consideration", which, in section 27(1) is stated as constituted by:

(a) any consideration sufficient to support a simple contract;
(b) an antecedent debt or liability whether the bill is payable on demand or at a future time.[4]

---

[1] See *Chitty on Contracts*, Vol.1 (28th ed., 1999) p. 167.
[2] By section 1 of the Contracts (Rights of Third Parties) Act 1999 a contract made between A and B which complies with the requirements set out may confer enforceable rights on C, a non-party. Section 6(1) of that Act excludes its operation to bills of exchange, cheques and promissory notes. It may be, nonetheless, that rights conferred by that Act could amount to consideration sufficient to support a claim upon a bill where previously none could have been found.
[3] Cm.622 (1989), recommendation 8(4).
[4] See *ante* paras 2–15 and 2–16.

Presumption as to consideration

19–04   If a man seeks to enforce a simple contract the onus lies on him to establish that there was good consideration. But to this rule bills and notes are an exception. In the case of simple contracts, the law presumes that there was no consideration till a consideration appears; in the case of contracts on bills or notes, a consideration is presumed till the contrary appears, or at least appears probable,[5] for the 1882 Act provides:

30.—(1) Every party whose signature appears on a bill is prima facie deemed to have become a party thereto for value.

Strictly a claimant in pleading his statement of case, when suing on a bill, need not allege the consideration relied upon. It is suggested though that under the Civil Procedure Rules it is preferable to state the consideration given and essential where it is known that it is disputed.[6]

Presumption as to holder in due course

19–05   The 1882 Act goes further than providing that there is a presumption as to value, for it provides:

(2) Every holder of a bill is prima facie deemed to be a holder in due course; but if in an action on a bill it is admitted or proved that the acceptance, issue, or subsequent negotiation of the bill is affected with fraud, duress, or force and fear, or illegality, the burden of proof is shifted, unless and until the holder proves that, subsequent to the alleged fraud or illegality, value has in good faith been given for the bill.[7]

Subsection (2) settles and possibly alters the law. Before the 1882 Act it was not clear whether the onus was shifted both as to value and good faith on proof of fraud or illegality.[8] In *Tatam v. Haslar*[9] Denman J. said: "That was the old law as stated in *Hall v. Featherstone*[10] which has not, I think, been altered by this Act. The words 'if it is admitted or proved' mean no more than that some evidence of circumstances in the nature of fraud must be given

---

[5] In *Jones v. Thomas* (1837) 2 Y. & C. 498, the action was between attorney and client, and as between the parties themselves it was held that the attorney must prove the consideration for a note received by him from the client in circumstances of great suspicion.

[6] See Bullen & Leake & Jacob's *Precedents of Pleading*, Vol.1 (14th ed., 2001) p. 125.

[7] In *Thambirajah v. Mahesvari* (1961) Ceylon N.L.R. 519, the Supreme Court held that to claim the presumption, the plaintiff must first show that he is a holder, and, as the notes in question were not payable to bearer, he must show a valid indorsement to him.

[8] *Jones v. Gordon* (1877) 2 App.Cas. 616, 628 (Lord Blackburn), see also *Bailey v. Bidwell* (1844) 13 M. & W. 73, 76.

[9] (1889) 23 Q.B.D. 345.

[10] (1858) 3 H. & N. 284.

sufficient to be left to the jury"; but the 1882 Act has now clearly settled that the onus is so shifted.[11]

Good faith

"In good faith" means honestly, whether negligently or not (s.90).[12] Proof **19–06** of full value having been given is not absolutely inconsistent with want of good faith;[13] but where the person relied on as having given value in good faith is dead or cannot be called, proof of full value having been given by him would be strong evidence of good faith.[14] It is further clear that a holder with notice, being a transferee from a holder in due course, is not prejudiced by the fact of notice as he stands in the shoes of his transferor.[15]

Fraud, duress and illegality

The issues of fraud and other defects in title are dealt with in Chapter 18. **19–07** Though negligence is not constructive notice of fraud, etc., "wilfully shutting one's eyes to the means of knowledge" may be.[16] The defendant must still prove, not only the fraud or illegality, but also the claimant's knowledge of it. If the holder establishes that he is a holder in due course, having taken the bill in accordance with the conditions laid down in section 29,[17,18] then s.30(2) has no application.

---

[11] *Tatam v. Haslar* (1889) 23 Q.B.D. 345; Brown v. Israelstam (1909) 7 Transvaal H. 22. It is interesting that Brannan points out, p. 143, that the language of subs. (2) "is not quite correct; for the holder may be a holder in due course though the fraud or illegality was in the transfer to him". The same applies to a payee holder for value. The Uniform Commercial Code, s.5–408, under the heading "Purposes of Changes", makes a distinction between consideration and value: "'Consideration' refers to what the obligor has received for his obligation and is important only on the question of whether his obligation can be enforced against him." It does not say in what way value is distinguished. Cowen, p. 82, says: "It is now well settled that consideration in the sense of English law is foreign to the conception of a contract under Roman-Dutch law." In Ceylon, something less than is required by English law is normally adequate to support a simple contract, but in regard to bills of exchange s.27(1) of the Bills of Exchange Ordinance provides that valuable consideration may be constituted by "any consideration sufficient by the law of England". This is anomalous in view of the fact that the common law of Ceylon is Roman-Dutch.

[12] See para. 18–09.

[13] *Raphael v. Bank of England*, (1855) 17 C.B. 161 at 172 (Cresswell J.); *Harris v. Aldous* (1899) 18 N.Z.L.R. 499.

[14] Lord Esher M.R. favoured the editors of the 15th edition of this book with the following opinion on this subject: "If the plaintiff (or party giving the value relied on) can be called, no jury would, I think, be satisfied unless he is called to say that he had no knowledge of the fraud. But if he be dead, or cannot be called, proof of his having given full value would of itself by strong evidence of bona fides and ignorance of the fraud, there being no evidence of any suspicious circumstances." See also *Oakley v. Boulton, Maynard & Co.* (1888) 5 T.L.R. 60; *Noble v. Boothby* (1912) 22 W.L.R. (Can.) 232.

[15] s.29(3).

[16] *May v. Chapman* (1847) 16 M. & W. 355, 361 (Parke B.), approved in *Raphael v. Bank of England* (1855) 17 C.B. 161, 174 (Willes J.). In South Africa "constructive notice" is not the equivalent of bad faith, *per* Cowen in the Law of Negotiable Instruments in South Africa (4th eds. 1966), citing *John Bell & Co. v. Esselen* (1954) (1) S.A. 147, AD.

[17] *Barclays Bank v. Astley Industrial Trust* [1970] 2 Q.B. 527.

[18] Section 30 was also considered in *Mansavri v. Singh* [1986] 1 W.L.R. 1393, in relation to its possible conflict with the Bretton Woods Agreement Order 1946 (S.R. & O. No. 36).

The 1882 Act does not include within the instances where the burden of proof is shifted, the case of the defendant's proving that the bill has been lost, but it may be included under the general heading "illegality", since the finder of a lost bill or note acquires no property therein. There does not appear to be any direct authority on the subject.[19] Similarly the sub-section does not advert to bills being given under undue influence. But it is suggested that undue influence may be covered by "illegality" or "duress".[20]

Position of the payee

19–08 Subsection (2) does not apply to any case in which the holder, who is seeking to enforce a negotiable instrument, is the person to whom the instrument was originally delivered and in whose possession it remains.[21]

Accommodation bill

19–09 It was once held that the defendant, by showing the bill to be an accommodation bill, or that he received no value, could call on the plaintiff to prove consideration.[22] But it was subsequently settled that mere absence of consideration received by the defendant will not entitle him to call on the plaintiff to prove the consideration which the plaintiff gave. "There is, indeed", says Lord Abinger "a substantial distinction between them (*viz.* bills given for accommodation only, and cases of fraud), inasmuch as in the former case it is to be presumed that money has been obtained upon the bill. If a man comes into court without any suspicion of fraud, but only as the holder of an accommodation bill, it may fairly be presumed that he is a holder for value. The proof of its being an accommodation bill is no evidence of the want of consideration in the holder. If the defendant says, "I lent my name to the drawer for the purpose of his raising money upon the bill", the probability is that money was obtained upon the bill. Unless, therefore, the bill be connected with some fraud, and a suspicion of fraud be raised from its being shown that something has been done with it of an illegal nature, as that it has been clandestinely taken away, or has been lost or stolen, in which case the holder

---

[19] In *Paterson v. Hardacre* (1811) 4 Taunt. 114 it was treated as settled law that when a bill had been lost of fraudulently obtained, consideration must be proved; see also *Mills v. Barber* (1836) 1 M. & W. 425, 431. On the other hand, in *King v. Milsom* (1809) 2 Camp. 5, where the plaintiff sought to maintain trover for a lost note, it was held by Lord Ellenborough C.J. that the onus of proving consideration in good faith was not shifted to the defendant in the absence of "strong evidence of fraud". A distinction may perhaps be taken between the case of an instrument which has been lost in circumstances that may not constitute the keeping of it larceny by the finder, and that of one taken from the true owner by felony; the case of, *e.g.*, a bank-note which had been lost in a public place, it may be that the onus does not lie upon the holder to prove himself a holder in due course. But where it is proved that the note was stolen or improperly obtained the onus is clearly shifted to the holder (*De la Chaumette v. Bank of England* (1829) 9 B. & C. 208). As to larceny and felony, see today the Theft Act 1968, s.32(1)(a) by which the offence of larceny was abolished; and the Criminal Law Act 1967, s.1, by which all distinctions between felony and misdemeanour were abolished.

[20] *Ante* paras 6–12 and 18–27.

[21] *Talbot v. Von Boris* [1911] 1 K.B. 854, citing *Watson v. Russell* (1862) 3 B. & S. 34; (1864) 5 B. & S. 968.

[22] See *Heath v. Sansom* (1831) 2 B. & Ad. 291; *Thomas v. Newton* (1827) 2 C. & P. 606.

must show that he gave value in good faith for it, the *onus probandi* is cast upon the defendant.[23]

Adequacy of consideration

"The courts do not concern themselves with the adequacy of consideration, **19–10** but inadequacy of consideration may be evidence of bad faith or fraud[24]."

The cases cited do not take the matter very far, so much depending upon the circumstances. It seems clear beyond question, however, that if there is any question of fraud on the part of the claimant, he may not recover. Perhaps the best statement of the position is to be found in Lord Blackburn's judgment in *Jones v. Gordon*.[25]

" . . . I think it right to say that I consider it to be fully and thoroughly established that if value be given for a bill of exchange, it is not enough to show that there was carelessness, negligence, or foolishness in not suspecting that the bill was wrong, when there were circumstances which might have led a man to suspect that. All these are matters which tend to shew that there was dishonesty in not doing it, but they do not in themselves make a defence to an action on a bill of exchange. I take it that in order to make such a defence, whether in the case of a party who is solvent and *sui juris*, or when it is sought to be proved against the estate of a bankrupt, it is necessary to shew that the person who gave the bill, whether the value given be great or small, was affected with notice that there was something wrong about it when he took it. I do not think it is necessary that he should have notice of what the particular wrong was."

This is not a pure instance of inadequacy. A closer instance is to be found in the case of *Simons v. Cridland*[26] in which it was held that where a holder of a long overdue acceptance sues for payment, having given only a nominal sum for it, an injunction would be granted restraining the defendant from further proceeding, on the terms that the plaintiff gives judgment at law, to be dealt with as the court should direct. The defendant had taken a note subject to the equities and the plaintiff had a right to have an account taken. The American decision[27] referred to by Chalmers states the position in the words of Hunt J. to the effect that the argument of the plaintiff is that negotiable paper may be sold for such sum as the parties may agree upon and that whether such sum is large or small the title to the entire paper passes to the purchaser. This is true; and if the plaintiff had bought the notes of $500 before maturity and without notice of any defence and paid that sum the authorities show that the whole interest in the notes would have passed to him and he could have recovered the full amount due upon them.

---

[23] *Mills v. Barber, supra*, where it was stated that the judges who decided *Heath v. Sansom, supra*, had withdrawn the opinions, they had there expressed, views which had indeed already been dissented from: see *Whittaker v. Edmunds* (1834) 1 Moo. & R. 366; *Jacob v. Hungate* (1834) *ibid.* 445.

[24] See *Chalmers & Guest on Bills of Exchange* (15th ed., 1998) p. 229.

[25] (1877) 2 App.Cas. 616, 628; and, at 631, he said: "that since the repeal of the Usury laws we can never inquire into the question as to how much was given for a bill . . . ".

[26] (1862) 5 L.T. (N.S.) 523.

[27] *Dresser v. Missouri Co.* (1876) 3 Otto 92, U.S. Sup. Ct.; see also *Allen v. Davis* (1850) 20 L.J. Ch. 44, in which an inference of fraud was drawn.

NATURE OF CONSIDERATION

Consideration for a bill

19–11   The 1882 Act defines and extends what may amount to consideration by providing:

> **27.—(1) Valuable consideration for a bill may be constituted by—**
>
> **(a) Any consideration sufficient to support a simple contract;**
>
> **(b) An antecedent debt or liability. Such a debt or liability is deemed valuable consideration whether the bill is payable on demand or at a future time.**

Simple contract

19–12   It is submitted that subsection (1)(a) places bills and notes upon the same footing as other simple contracts in respect of what is an adequate consideration, other than an antecedent debt.[28] Certain specific instances are considered below.

Antecedent debt or liability

19–13   Section 27(1)(b) provides for an exception to the ordinary rules as to consideration, by providing that past consideration is acceptable as "valuable consideration". Such an antecedent debt or liability must be the liability of the promisor or drawer of the bill and not that of a stranger to the bill.[29]

Oliver v. Davis

19–14   This view is confirmed by the case of *Oliver v. Davis*[30] a Court of Appeal decision: the plaintiff had lent the Defendant £350 in whose favour Davis had drawn a post dated cheque for £400. Before the cheque was presented Davis persuaded Woodcock to draw in favour of the plaintiff. Woodcock learned of

---

[28] The view expressed above, approved in *Oliver v. Davis* [1949] 2 K.B. 727 by Denning L.J. (at 742), was adopted in *Crofts v. Beale* (1851) 11 C.B. 172 and *Crears v. Hunter* (1887) 19 Q.B.D. 341. Denning L.J. appeared not to be certain that the judgment of Hallett J. in *Ayres v. Moore* [1940] 1 K.B. 278 at 282 was in accord and he dissociated himself from it if it were not; "inadequacy of consideration affords no relevant answer to a demand made upon a promissory note" (*Adib el Hinnawi v. Yacoub Fahmi Abu el Huda el Faruqi* [1936] 1 All E.R. 638). The headnote which reproduces the above statement, is too wide in that the judgment of the Privy Council is to the effect that "having regard to the terms of the promissory note [which do not appear from the report], the alleged inadequacy of consideration affords no relevant answer to a demand upon it".

[29] In the review of the authorities which follow in Chalmers & Guest (15th ed.) paras 749–758 the view is likewise expressed that antecedent consideration must move to the promisee (para. 752). To similar effect is para. 34–064 of *Chitty on Contracts* (28th ed., vol. 2). On appropriate facts it might now be possible to find consideration in an antecedent right to enforce a contract to which the payee/promisee was not a party, by virtue of the Contracts (Rights of Third Parties Act) 1999 (see fn 2 above).

[30] [1949] 2 K.B. 727.

the true character of Davis and stopped payment. It was held that there was no valuable consideration within the meaning of section 27(1)(a) or (b), Evershed M.R. saying: "[T]he proper construction of the words antecedent debt or liability in paragraph (b) is that they refer to an antecedent debt or liability of the promisor or drawer of the bill and are intended to get over what would otherwise have been prima facie the result that at common law the giving of a cheque for an amount for which you are already indebited imports no consideration since the obligation is past and has already been incurred."[31]

Diamond v. Graham

Then came the case of *Diamond v. Graham*.[32] There Diamond agreed to lend one H £1,650 provided that H undertook to procure a cheque for £1,665 from Graham. Diamond gave H a cheque for £1,660, but H was unable to get in touch with Graham, so Diamond stopped the cheque. The next day H obtained a cheque from Graham in favour of Diamond for £1,665 and at the same time H gave Graham a cheque for £1,665. However, Graham's cheque was paid in before the parties had expected and was dishonoured, being returned with the answer "effects not cleared". The Court of Appeal unanimously upheld the decision of Megaw J., giving judgment for Diamond in an action on the dishonoured cheque. The decision can be justified on the ground that consideration had been given, by Diamond releasing his cheque to H, inferentially at the implied request of Graham. However Danckwerts L.J. observed that there was nothing in section 27(2) which required value to be given by the holder as long as value had been given for the cheque.[33]

19–15

Hasan v. Willson

However, it is difficult to regard the law at present as differing from the decision of Robert Goff J. (as he then was) in *Hasan v. Willson*.[34] The case concerned commission payments relating to a large stock of coins being sold by a foreign government. In relation to the proposed sale, which was to another government, one S had rendered himself liable to pay Hasan £50,000. Because S falsely represented to Willson that he had funds in P. Ltd, Willson agreed to give a cheque for £50,000 payable to Hasan in exchange for a cheque for £50,000 payable to him drawn on P. Ltd's account with the Midland Bank. It was quickly discovered that the cheque of P. Ltd would be dishonoured so Willson stopped his cheque. It was on this latter cheque that the action was brought. The question of consideration was the salient point and section 27 was considered as to whether the fact that the Plaintiff was a stranger meant that the consideration failed. In addition the point was taken that the cheque was obtained by fraud. It was indicated that, alone, such a defence would not have succeeded, but the drawer's right to countermand was good. The nub of the matter is that Robert Goff J. followed the views of Diplock and Sachs L.JJ. in *Diamond v. Graham* regarding Danckwerts L.J.'s

19–16

---

[31] *ibid.*, 735.
[32] [1968] 1 W.L.R. 1061.
[33] P.1064.
[34] [1977] 1 Lloyd's Rep. 431.

views, in that case as obiter, and applied Evershed M.R.'s dicta in *Oliver v. Davis*.[35]

MK International v. The Housing Bank

19–17   Finally it was observed by Mustill L.J., in *MK International Development Co. Ltd v. The Housing Bank*,[36] that the clear current of authority was in favour of the view that s.27(1)(b) applied only to the antecedent debt or liability of the promisor, and that the mere existence of debts owed by a third party was not sufficient.[37]

Forbearance

19–18   In the case of simple contracts in general the promise to pay the debt of another is not enforceable unless the promisee has suffered a detriment, as by forbearing to sue, or releasing the original debtor.[38] In the later cases in which a bill given for the debt of a third person has been recovered upon, such a consideration as indicated has been furnished by the promisee.[39]

A judgment debt is a good consideration for a note payable at a future day; for it imports an agreement on the part of the judgment creditor to suspend enforcement proceedings on the judgment till the maturity of the note.[40] So actual forbearance, at the request of a third party, to sue, though no promise binding at law have been made not to sue, may be a good consideration for a note by that third party.[41]

A subsisting debt due from a third person is a good consideration for a bill or note, if the instrument is payable at a future day, for then it amounts to an agreement to give time to the original debtor, and that indulgence to him is a consideration to the maker.[42] But if the instrument is payable immediately, it is conceived that the pre-existing debt of a stranger could not be a consideration, unless the instrument was taken in satisfaction, or unless credit had been given to the original debtor at the maker's request.[43] So, too, a debt due from the defendant and a third person is a good consideration.[44] It must be established that the person taking the stranger's instrument had authority to release the liability of the debtor in exchange for the instrument.[45]

---

[35] [1949] 2 K.B. 727.

[36] [1991] 1 Bank L.R. 74; *Financial Times*, January 27, 1991.

[37] See also *AEG (UK) Ltd v. Lewis*, *Times Law Reports*, December 29, 1992.

[38] *cf.* Addison, *Contracts* (11th ed., 1911), p. 3, and see the Statute of Frauds 1677, s.4.

[39] See, in addition to cases already cited, *Willers v. Stevens* (1846) 15 L.J. Ex. 108; *Walton v. Maskell* (1844) 14 L.J.Ex. 54; also *Sison v. Kidman* (1842) 11 L.J.C.P. 100, as explained in *Crofts v. Beale* (1851) 11 C.B. 172, 173 (Maule J.).

[40] *Baker v. Walker* (1845) 14 M. & W. 465.

[41] *Crears v. Hunter* (1887) 19 Q.B.D. 341, 346, distinguishing *Crofts v. Beale* (1851) 11 C.B. 172.

[42] *Balfour v. Sea Fire Life Assurance Co.* (1857) 3 C.B.(N.S.) 300. It is otherwise if the original debtor be dead and at the tie of the drawing or making of the instrument there can be no executors of his estate, nor administrators appointed (*Nelson v. Serle* (1839) 4 M. & W. 795).

[43] *cf. Crofts v. Beale* (1851) 11 C.B. 172, 173 (Jervis C.J.), applied in *Oliver v. Davis* [1949] 2 K.B. 727, in which the plaintiff sued on the cheque in his favour of the second defendant, given to meet the first defendant's debt to the plaintiff.

[44] *Heywood v. Watson* (1828) 4 Bing. 496.

[45] *AEG (UK) Ltd v. Lewis*, *Times Law Reports*, December 29, 1992.

Cross acceptances

If a man gives his acceptance to another, that will be a good consideration **19–19**
for a promise or for another bill or acceptance, though such first acceptance is,
after all, unpaid,[46] and, therefore, cross acceptances for mutual accommodation are respectively considerations for each other.[47]

Fluctuating balance

A fluctuating balance may form a consideration for a bill.[48] Where a **19–20**
banker's acceptances for his customer exceeded the cash balance in his hands,
and accommodation acceptances were deposited by the customer with the
banker as a collateral security, it was held that, whenever the banker's
acceptances exceeded the cash balance, the bankers held the collateral bills for
value.[49] In the case of bills deposited as a security for the balance of an
account current, the successive balances form a shifting consideration for the
bills. Thus, A & Co., bankers in the country, being pressed by the plaintiffs B
& Co., bankers in town, to whom they were indebted, to send up any bills that
they could procure, transmitted for account an accommodation bill accepted
by the defendant; when the bill became due the balance was in favour of A &
Co., but the bill was not withdrawn, and afterwards the balance between the
houses turned considerably in favour of B & Co., the plaintiffs, and was so
when A & Co. became bankrupt; B & Co. were held entitled to recover
against the defendant the accommodation acceptor.[50]

Compromise of a claim

The compromise of a disputed claim constitutes good consideration for an **19–21**
instrument, and it is immaterial that the claim is in fact unfounded, provided
that the person making it acts in good faith.[51] This principle was applied in
London and County Bank v. London and River Plate Bank,[52] where certain

---

[46] *Rose v. Sims* (1830) 1 B. & Ad. 521.
[47] *Cowley v. Dunlop* (1798) 7 T.R. 565; *Cuckler v. Buttivant* (1802) 3 East 72.
[48] *Pease v. Hirst* (1829) 10 B. & C. 122; *Collenridge v. Farquharson* (1816) 1 Stark. 259;
Richards v. Macey (1845) 14 M. & W. 484; and for a bond, *Henniker v. Wigg* (1843) 4 Q.B. 792.
An indorsement stating the consideration to be secure floating advances up to the sum of £100
within mentioned required an agreement stamp; *Cholmeley v. Darley* (1845) 14 M. & W. 344).
Prima facie the consideration for a note is the advance made or balance due at the time; and if the
payee asserts that it was given to secure a fluctuating balance, the burden of proof lies on him (*Re
Boys* (1870) L.R. 10 Eq. 467).
[49] *Bosenquet v. Dudman* (1814) 1 Stark. 1: and see *Bolland v. Bygrave* (1825) Ry. & M.
271.
[50] *Atwood v. Crowdie* (1816) 1 Stark. 483; see *Woodroffe v. Hayne* (1824) 1 C. & P. 600. As
to when a banker becomes a holder for value of his customer's cheques paid into the credit of the
account, see paras 23–69 *et seq*.
[51] *Cook v. Wright* (1861) 30 L.J.Q.B. 321; *Kingsford v. Oxenden* (1891) 7 T.L.R. 565; see also
Callisher v. Bischoffsheim (1870) L.R. 5 Q.B. 449; *Miles v. New Zealand, Alford Co.* (1886) 32
Ch.D. 266; *Smith v. Key* [1906] *Eastern Districts Court (Cape)* 46; *cf.* also *Van Dyk v. Udwin*
(1900) 17 Cape S.C. 56; *Tully v. Cresswell* (1913) 33 N.Z.L.R. 724; *Eastern Township Lumber
Co. v. Lynch* (1920) 48 N.B.R. 28.
[52] (1888) 21 Q.B.D. 535; see also *Bank of Australasia v. Curtis* [1927] N.Z.L.R. 247. For an
instance of partial failure of consideration when the Court refused a stay in respect of the amount
admitted see *Thoni GmbH v. R.T.P. Equipment* [1979] 2 Lloyd's Rep. 282, CA.

negotiable securities, which had been stolen from the defendants by their manager, came into the possession of the plaintiffs for value and without notice of any fraud. Subsequently the manager, by fraud, obtained the securities from the plaintiffs and restored them to the defendants, who did not know that the securities had been out of their possession. Some of the securities were not the securities actually stolen, but were of a like kind and value. When the plaintiffs claimed the return of the securities, the defendants were held to be entitled to retain them as bona fide holders for value, since they had a right of action against the manager for wrongful conversion of the securities, which was lost on the restoration, and consequently, in the absence of any evidence to the contrary, it was to be presumed that they accepted the securities in discharge of the manager's obligation to restore them.

Del credere agent

19–22   Where an agent, being a del credere agent,[53] assumes responsibility for the discharge by the buyer of his contractual obligations to the seller and, in exchange for the bills of lading, receives from the buyer a bill for the price made payable to himself and accepted by the buyer, the contract contained in the bill is a contract between the buyer and the agent and the consideration for it is the delivery of the bills of lading by which the buyer is enabled to get possession of the goods: and the fact that the buyer is subsequently entitled to reject the goods does not amount to a failure of consideration as between the parties to the bill.[54]

Moral obligation and natural affection

19–23   A moral obligation is in general insufficient but may, in some cases, be a consideration for a bill or note where there once existed a legal liability though it may have been barred by statute.[55] Thus, for example, where a bankrupt after his bankruptcy gave a promissory note to the plaintiff, one of his creditors, for part of his debt, it was held that it was given on good consideration.[56] Though a moral obligation is not sufficient, a court, in the exercise of its equitable jurisdiction, may decree the payment of a note given in circumstances creating a strong moral obligation to pay it.[57]

---

[53] A *del credere* agent is someone, who for a special commission, undertakes the liability of a surety for the due performabnce of contracts made by him on behalf of his principal; see *Bowstead & Reynolds on Agency* (17th ed., 1996) p.32.

[54] *Churchill and Sim v. Goddard* [1973] 1 K.B. 92.

[55] *cf. Eastwood v. Kenyon* (1840) 11 A. & E. 438, and cases there cited.

[56] *Trueman v. Fenton* (1777) Cowp. 544; *Brix v. Braham* (1823) 1 Bing. 281, where there was no fresh consideration for the bankrupt's promise. The consideration, in either case, seems to be an "antecedent debt or liability" within the 1882 Act, s.27(1)(b). A majority of the Court of Exchequer held that bill, given since the repeal of the usury laws, to repay a debt with usurious interest contracted before their repeal was binding (*Flight v. Reed* (1863) 32 L.J.Ex. 265, not followed in *Sharp v. Ellis* (1971) 20 F.L.R. 199 (Vict.S.C.)).

[57] *Re Whitaker* (1889) 42 Ch.D. 119. It is to be observed that the discretion in this case was not exercised except with the consent of all parties, the lunatics wife being made a consenting party, and his committee being joined as co-petitioner with the payee of the note.

Natural affection is not a good consideration in the case of a simple contract,[58] nor in the case of a bill,[59] nor can it be now held to be a good consideration for a bill or note given for the debt of a third party, unless there has been a forbearance given or a detriment suffered by the creditor.[60]

Some of the older authorities appear to assume that such a consideration as the debt of a third person, coupled or not with natural affection, might support an action on a bill or note in cases where no action might lie on a simple contract, and expressions are used to the effect that a bill "imports a consideration" and, although not a specialty, resembles a specialty. The law as laid down in subsection (1)(b) in respect of an antecedent debt was not so settled without some doubt in the case of instruments payable on demand.[61] The 1882 Act is now definitely conclusive of the matter;[62] the antecedent debt or liability of a third party is not within the subsection. In the Court of Appeal, Evershed M.R. said that: "An antecedent debt or liability of a third party *in vacuo* cannot form a valuable consideration. Some connection at the least must be shown between the receipt of the bill and the debt . . . "[63]

ILLEGAL CONSIDERATION

Illegal consideration

The consideration given for a bill or note must not be illegal. It is said that **19–24** the test whether a contract be contaminated with an illegal transaction is this: does the plaintiff require any aid from the illegal transaction to establish his case?[64] In *Thackwell v. Barclays Bank plc*[65] the authorities on this subject were reviewed by Hutchinson J., who refused to allow the plaintiff to recover under a forged indorsement, since the plaintiff was a party to the fraudulent transaction which caused the cheque to be drawn.[66]

It is, however, important to distinguish between illegality which avoids a negotiable security in the hands of any holder and illegality which merely shifts on to the holder of the instrument the onus of proving that he is a holder

---

[58] *Harford v. Gardiner* (1588) 2 Leon. 30.

[59] *Holliday v. Atkinson* (1826) 5 B. & C. 501.

[60] See *Poplewell v. Wilson* (1719) 1 Stra. 264 and, *per contra, Garnet v. Clarke* (1709) 11 Mod. 226.

[61] See *Currie v. Misa* (1875) L.R. 10 Ex. 153, and cases there cited; *Cousins v. Hanson* (1917) Q.R. 53 S.C. 185.

[62] *Mclean v. Clydesdale Bank* (1883) 9 App.Cas. 95, 115, (Lord Blackburn), followed in *Re City Sawmilling Co.* (1898) 17 N.Z.L.R. 14, and distinguished in *Bank of British North America v. McComb* (1911) 21 Man. 58; see also *Stott v. Fairlamb* (1883) 52 L.B.Q.B. 420; *Elkington v. Cooke Hill* (1914) 30 T.L.R. 670. United States Law is the same: see Uniform Commercial Code, s.3–303.

[63] *Oliver v. Davis* [1949] 2 K.B. 727 applied in *Hasan v. Willson* [1977] 1 Lloyd's Rep. 431, and see on the question of value, *ante*, para. 19–16. See also *Bonoir v. Siery Ltd* [1968] N.Z.L.R. 254.

[64] *Simpson v. Bloss* (1816) 7 Taunt. 246.

[65] [1986] 1 All E.R.676;

[66] The judge would have held against the plaintiff, even if he was innocent, on the basis of the public conscience test. This test was disapproved by the House of Lords in *Tinsley v. Milligan* [1994] 1 A.C. 340; see also *Universal Import Export GmbH v Bank of Scotland, Times Law Reports*, December 21, 1994.

in due course.[67] A holder in due course takes free of all past defects, including illegal consideration. Similarly a holder, who derives title to a bill through and who is not party to any illegality, has all the rights of a holder in due course.[68]

Considerations are illegal either at common law; or by statute.[69] Among considerations illegal at common law are those that violate the rules of religion or morality. Yet, while such considerations will avoid a simple contract or a bond,[70] in the case of a negotiable instrument they will not avoid it as against a transferee for value without notice, provided that he discharges the onus of proof under section 30(2) of the 1882 Act.[71] Otherwise they will only avoid the negotiable instrument as against a transferee who fails to discharge such onus or as between immediate parties.[72]

Further, contracts in contravention of public policy are illegal at common law. The doctrine by which contracts are held void as being against public policy must be applied with caution;[73] and if it is merely doubtful whether a contract is at variance with the public interest, it is not void.[74] In this case also it is submitted that there is no authority that at common law negotiable securities are void in all hands, if given in pursuance of such an agreement. Indeed, it seems that knowledge of the illegality must appear as against a holder for value to defeat his claim.[75]

If a bill originally given upon an illegal consideration is replaced by a fresh bill, the latter bill is also void,[76] unless the amount is reduced by excluding so much of the consideration for the original bill as was illegal.[77]

Enemy contracts

19–25   Contracts with a public enemy are illegal as contrary to public policy. A declaration of war imports a prohibition of commercial intercourse and correspondence with the inhabitants of the enemy country, and such intercourse,

---

[67] A negotiable instrument cannot be absolutely void except by statute; previously the only surviving example of such a statute was the Betting and Loans (Infants) Act 1892, s.5, but this provision has now been repealed, *ante*, para. 6–09.

[68] Section 29(3).

[69] See *Shaw v. Shaw* [1965] 1 W.L.R. 537 which concerned the Exchange Control Act 1947; and see also *Sharif v. Azad* [1967] 1 Q.B. 605.

[70] *cf. Collins v. Blanter*, 1 Smith's L.C. 13th eds., 406; (1767) 2 Wils. 341.

[71] See *ante*, para. 19–05.

[72] *Robinson v. Cox* (1741) 9 Mod. 263; *Wood v. Adams* (1905) 10 O.L.R. 631; *cf.* also *Fitch v. Jones* (1855) 24 L.J.Q.B. 293; *Flower v. Sadler* (1882) 10 Q.B.D. 572; *Jones v. Merionethshire Building Society* [1892] 1 Ch. 173; *Robinson v. Midland Bank* (1925) 41 T.L.R. 402.

[73] *Hyams v. Stuart-King* [1908] 2 K.B. 696, 710 (Barnes P.) citing *Mogal Steamship Co. v. McGregor* [1892] A.C. 25, 46 (Lord Bramwell); see also *Janson v. Driefontein Mines* [1902] A.C. 484; *Porter v. Freudenberg* [1915] 1 K.B. 857.

[74] *Richardson v. Mellish* (1824) 2 Bing. 229.

[75] *cf. Willison v. Patteson* (1817) 7 Taunt. 439, 448, where the Court considered that the plaintiff "was conusant of the purposes for which these bills were drawn": *Foster v. Driscoll* [1929] 1 K.B. 470 the observations of Hutchinson J. to the contrary in *Thackwell v. Barclays Bank plc* [1986] 1 All E.R. 676 at 689 must be doubted in the light of *Tinsley v. Milligan* (*supra*).

[76] *Chapman v. Black* (1819) 2 B. & Ald. 588; *Wynne v. Callander* (1826) 1 Russ. 293.

[77] *Preston v. Jackson* (1817) 2 Stark 237; and see *Hubner v. Richardson* (1819) Bayley, *Bills* (6th ed.), p. 527.

except with the licence of the Crown, is illegal.[78] It is not, however, the nationality of a person but his place of business during the war that is important.[79] Thus an Englishman carrying on business in an enemy's country has been held to be an alien enemy.[80] On the other hand, an alien enemy, living in this country under a licence, was long ago held entitled to sue.[81] The avoidance of contracts of this class is to be distinguished from the avoidance of negotiable securities given in connection with them, and is part of the general law of contract. Yet the remedy upon the bill may be suspended, as much as that on any other contract, during the duration of the war as regards an alien enemy who seeks to enforce it. It was held that unless a person is an alien enemy at common law the Trading with the Enemy Act does not make him one, and thus that a company incorporated in accordance with the laws of an allied country which came under enemy occupation is not precluded from suing in the English courts merely by reason of the fact that it continues to trade in its own country.[82] But this decision was reversed by the House of Lords, on the ground that occupation by an enemy rendered a country enemy territory and its residents disentitled to sue in the courts of this country.[83]

Agreements to conceal an arrestable offence

Considerations impeding the course of public justice, as dropping a crimi-   **19–26**
nal prosecution for a felony or a public misdemeanour, or suppressing evi-
dence, are illegal considerations.[84] Hence, where a holder for value of notes, on which a son had forged his father's name, induced the father to give security for meeting them as an alternative to prosecuting the son, the father receiving no consideration therefor, it was held that a security so given could not be enforced.[85] A threat to prosecute, however, does not necessarily vitiate

---

[78] *Esposito v. Bowden* (1857) 7 E. & B. 763, 779. A public declaration of war does not now appear to be essential, but war and war alone, and not merely that war is imminent, is sufficient (*Janson v. Driefontein Mines* [1902] A.C. 484, 494). See also *Zinc Corporation Ltd v. Hirsch* [1916] 1 K.B. 541; *Ertel Bieber & Co. v. Rio Tinto* [1918] A.C. 260; *Ottoman Bank v. Jebara* [1928] A.C. 269; *Schering v. Stockholms Enskilda Bank* [1946] A.C. 219; and *Arab Bank Ltd v. Barclays Bank* (D.C. & O.) [1954] A.C. 495.

[79] *Janson v. Driefontein Mines, supra*, at 505. Occupied territory was not necessarily enemy country within the trading with the enemy legislation of 1914 and 1915 (*Societe Anonyme Belges des Mines D'Aljustrel v. Anglo-Belgian Agency* [1915] 2 Ch. 409).

[80] *McConnell v. Hector* (1802) 3 B. & P. 113; *Willison v. Patteson, supra*. A bill drawn in an enemy country by an Englishman, detained there as a prisoner, may be sued on by the indorsee after the return of peace though indorsed to him while an alien enemy (*Antoine v. Morshead* (1815) 6 Taunt. 237).

[81] *Wells v. Williams* (1698) 1 Ld. Raym. 282.

[82] *Re An Arbitration between N.V. Gebr. van Udens Scheepvaart en Agentur Maatschappij and Sovfracht* [1942] 1 K.B. 222.

[83] *Sovfracht (V/O) v. van Udens Scheepvaart Agentuur Maatschappij (N.V. Gebr)* [1943] A.C. 203, in which, *inter alia, Societe Anaonyme Belge des Mines D'Aljustrel v. Anglo-Belgian Agency* [1915] 2 Ch. 409 was considered. As to the capacity of enemies to contract, see *ante*, para. 6–14.

[84] *Edgcombe v. Rodd* (1804) 5 East 294; *Societe des Hotels Reunis v. Hawker* (1913) 29 T.L.R. 578; *Becker v. Buchman* (1927) 2 W.W.R. 32. The distinction between felony and misdemeanour was abolished by s.5 of the Criminal Law Act 1967.

[85] *Williams v. Bayley* (1866) L.R. 1 H.L. 200; *Western Bank of Canada v. McGill* (1902) 32 Can.S.C.R. 581; *Pachal v. Schiller* (1914) 24 W.L.R. (Can.) 440; and Maclaren, *op. cit*, 206; see also *Lindley v. Ward* (1911) 2 C.P.R. 272, distinguishing *Williams v. Bayley, supra*; see now the Criminal Law Act 1967, s.5(1).

a subsequent agreement by the debtor to give security for a debt which he justly owes to his creditor[86] and if there is in fact no agreement to stifle a prosecution, the indorsement of a bill by the debtor to the creditor is valid.[87] A note given to the prosecutor for the expenses of the prosecution by the defendant after his conviction, the amount being suggested by the Court, who, in consideration of the note having been given, inflicted a lesser term of imprisonment on the defendant, has been held to be given for a good consideration.[88] So where the defendant was convicted for disobedience to a maintenance order, but sentence was deferred, and he then, on the suggestion of the overseers, gave a note in settlement of the matter, the note was held to be given for a good consideration, the defendant not having objected to the amount of the note when brought up for sentence.[89]

The Consumer Credit Act 1974

19–27   The extent to which the Consumer Credit Act 1974 affects the transfer and negotiability of bills, notes and cheques is dealt with in Chapter 8 (*ante*).

In addition to the restrictions on the taking, negotiation, and enforcement of bills, the Act also confers powers on the court to re-open "extortionate credit bargains"[90] which may have a considerable effect upon those who deal in bills whether or not under regulated agreements.

Section 137 of the Act enables the court, if it finds a credit bargain extortionate, to re-open the credit agreement so as to do justice between the parties. A credit agreement[91] means any agreement between an individual as defined by the Act[92] and any other person by which the creditor provides the debtor with credit of any amount; and credit bargain[93] means

   (i) Where no transaction other than the credit agreement is to be taken into account in computing the total charge for credit,[94] the credit agreement or

   (ii) where one or more transactions are to be so taken into account, the credit agreement and those other transactions taken together.

It will be seen that this section embraces credit agreements other than those regulated by the Act. Thus any credit agreement even those which are outside

---

[86] *Flower v. Sadler* (1882) 10 Q.B.D. 572, 576 (Cotton L.J.); see also *Groves v. Harris* (1941) 29 W.L.R. (Can.) 331; *Johnson v. Musselman* (1917) 37 D.L.R. 162, So, too, the substitution of a good bill for a forged one at the instance of the forger, if unaccompanied by any stipulation to stifle a prosecution for forgery, is not illegal (*Wallace v. Hardacre* (1807) 1 Camp. 45).

[87] *Flower v. Sadler, supra*, where the opinion was expressed by Brett and Cotton L.JJ. at 575, 576, that, even if the indorsement had been in pursuance of an agreement to stifle a prosecution, the acceptor could not, in an action on the bill by the creditor, raise the point.

[88] *Beeley v. Wingfield* (1809) 11 East 46.

[89] *Kirk v. Strickwood* (1833) 4 B. & Ad. 421; and see *Baker v. Townshend* (1817) 1 Moo.C.P. 120.

[90] CCA, s.137(1).

[91] CCA, s.137(2)(a).

[92] CCA, s.189.

[93] CCA, s.137(2)(b).

[94] CCA, ss.20(1), 189.

the financial limits set by the Act but made with an individual, as defined by the Act,[95] may be re-opened by the court.

By section 138 a credit bargain is extortionate if it requires the debtor or a relative of his to make payments (whether unconditionally, or on certain contingencies) which are grossly exorbitant or it otherwise grossly contravenes ordinary principles of fair dealing. This section further goes on to define a number of factors[96] to be taken into consideration of a general nature and others which are particular either to the debtor or to the creditor. As this section now replaces the earlier provisions in the Moneylenders Acts 1900 and 1927 some relationship may be thought to exist between what was previously "harsh and unconscionable" to that which is now "extortionate". However the present provisions apply to a much wider range of transactions than the earlier ones and it has been said that it is "idle" to look at the old Act,[97] and also "it is neither necessary nor permissible"[98] to look at earlier authorities.

It is outside the scope of this work to examine what may or may not be an extortionate bargain under the Act but simply to note that by virtue of section 139(2) the Court may, for the purpose of relieving the debtor or a surety from payment of any sum in excess of that fairly due and reasonable, by order:

(a) Direct accounts to be taken between any persons.

(b) Set aside the whole or part of any obligation imposed on the debtor or a surety by the credit bargain or any related agreement.

(c) Require the creditor to repay the whole or part of any sum paid under the credit bargain or any related agreement by the debtor or a surety, whether paid to the creditor or any other person.

(d) Direct return to the surety of any property provided for the purpose of the security, or

(e) Alter the terms of the credit agreement or any security instrument.

The result of these sections is that a credit agreement (within the meaning of the word credit as defined in the Act), whether the agreement is a regulated agreement or not, may be re-opened by the court with consequential results to those who take, negotiate, or enforce their apparent rights under a bill.

Wagering and Gaming[99]

A wagering contract has been defined as "one by which two persons   **19–28**
professing to hold opposite views touching the issue of a future uncertain
event, mutually agree that, dependent upon the determination of that event,

---

[95] CCA, s.189. For a more detailed discussion see Guest's *Encyclopaedia of Consumer Credit Law.*
[96] s.138(2) to (5).
[97] *A. Ketley Ltd v. Scott* [1981] I.C.R. 241.
[98] *Davies v. Limitloans Ltd* [1986] 1 W.L.R. 823.
[99] For a full discussion of the subject—see Volume II, *Chitty on Contracts* (28th ed., 1999) Ch. 40.

one shall win from the other, and that other shall pay or hand over to him, a sum of money or other stake".[1] Gaming has been defined to mean the playing of any game for money or money's worth, including horse-racing.[2]

Legislation affecting wagering and gaming

19–29　　　"The ground for treating gaming contracts in an exceptional way is to be sought in reasons of public policy and not in any respect in the essential qualities of the contracts themselves, and it is clear that the necessity for so doing was not felt in the ages during which our common law was formed, so that liabilities under which such contracts labour are entirely derived from statute law."[3] The statutes that govern the position are The Gaming Acts 1710, 1835,1845,1892 and 1968.

Historical development

19–30　　　The Act of 1710[4] were aimed at the avoidance of bills and other securities given for losses at certain specified games. A bill or note given for a gaming debt within the Act was void even in the hands of an innocent indorsee for value as against the party losing at play,[5] although it always has been valid as against any party other than the actual loser.[6] The 1710 Act was substantially modified by the Gaming Act 1835.[7] Section 1, the only section in force today, provides that securities, including bills and notes, which would under the 1710 Act have been absolutely void, shall be deemed and taken to have been drawn or made for an illegal consideration.[8] The effect of this amendment is to make such instruments enforceable at law in the hands of a third person who acquires them innocently,[9] but he must prove that the instrument was acquired for value and in good faith.[10]

The next Act, the Gaming Act 1845, repealed the 1710 Act, preserving, however, the effect of the Act as modified by the Act of 1835. Section 18 of the Gaming Act 1845, set out below, avoided contracts, by parol or in writing,

[1] *Carlill v. Carbolic Smoke Ball Co.* [1892] 2 Q.B. 484, at 490.

[2] See para: 40–013 of Vol.II, *Chitty on Contracts* (supra).

[3] *Per* Fletcher Moulton L.J. in *Moulis v. Owen* [1970] 1 K.B. 746, 758, where the history of the statutes is given.

[4] Gaming Act 1710 (Halsbury's Statutes (4th ed. Reissue), Vol. 5, p. 12).

[5] *Bowyer v. Bampton* (1741) 2 Stra. 1155; *Shillito v. Theed* (1831) 7 Bing. 405.

[6] *Bowyer v. Bampton, supra*; *Edwards v. Dick* (1821) 4 B. & Ald. 212.

[7] Gaming Act 1835, repealed except as to s.1, by the Gaming Act 1922 and the SLR Act 1874.

[8] This Act made a similar alteration in the case of bills given for a variety of considerations, which under a series of Acts had been declared void, as, for instance, bills void under the usury laws, bills given as ransom for prizes taken at sea, or to induce creditors to sign a bankrupt's certificate. In *Williams Hill (Park Lane) Ltd v. Hofman* [1950] 1 All E.R. 1013, Roxburgh J., at 1015, said that the section (s.1) meant what it said, that it referred to the whole instrument and not merely to part of it, and that "note" and "bill" meant instruments properly so described.

[9] *Sutters v. Briggs* [1922] A.C. 1, 10 (Lord Birkenhead C.), following *Dey v. Mayo* [1920] 2 K.B. 346, especially Atkin L.J. at 364. This section is not affected by the passing of the Gaming Act 1922.

[10] The Gaming Act 1710. See also *Woolf v. Hamilton* [1898] 2 Q.B. 337; *Robinson v. Benkel* (1913) 29 T.L.R. 475; *Hay v. Ayling* (1851) 16 Q.B. 423; *Jones v. Hilton* (1905) 25 N.Z.L.R. 494.

by way of gaming and wagering and prohibited the bringing of any suit for recovering any sum of money or valuable thing alleged to be won upon any wager, but without dealing further with negotiable securities given for wagering considerations.

In the meantime, the Gaming Act 1892 avoided promises to pay to any person money paid by him in respect of a gaming contract, void under section 18 of the Act of 1845, or any commission, etc., in respect of any such contract.[11] The last relevant Act in the chronology is the Gaming Act 1968 (which has been subject to various amendments) which is concerned with the regulation of gaming and wagers on games, and not with wagering and gaming contracts, save for section 16.[12]

Gaming and Wagering Contracts

By section 18 of the Gaming Act 1845 all contracts by way of gaming or wagering are void. The section is as follows: **19–31**

> "Contracts by way of gaming to be void, and wagers or sums deposited with stakeholders not to be recoverable at law-saving for subscriptions for prizes
> ... All contracts or agreements, whether by parole or in writing, by way of gaming or wagering, shall be null and void; and ... no suit shall be brought or maintained in any court of law and equity for recovering any sum of money or valuable thing alleged to be won upon any wager, or which shall have been deposited in the hands of any person to abide the event on which any wager shall have been made."[13]

The section is concerned with contracts, rather than merely "securities",[14] although clearly negotiable instruments fall within the ambit of the section. Thus a winner of a wager could not claim on a cheque provided to him by the loser as payment in settlement of the wager. A security given for a gaming consideration cannot be directly enforced nor can any action be brought on the original consideration.[15] The second limb of section 18 of the Gaming Act 1845, which provides that "no suit shall be brought or maintained ... for recovering any sum of money ... alleged to be won upon any wager", prevents the recovery of a lost bet even where there is a fresh promise for new consideration to pay it. Thus, if the loser of a bet gives a cheque for part thereof and promises to pay the balance of the sum owing by instalments in consideration of the winner forbearing to have him posted as a defaulter, that

---

[11] See *Saffery v. Mayer* [1901] 1 K.B. 11; *cf.* also *Brookman v. Mather* (1913) 29 T.L.R. 276. A note given to secure money advanced for the payment of racing debts was at one time thought not given for an illegal consideration within the Act of 1835, and could therefore be recovered upon as between immediate parties (*Ex p. Pyke* (1878) 8 Ch.D. 754); but, *per* Denning L.J. in *Macdonald v. Green* [1951] 1 K.B. 594, this is no longer good law; nor is such a case within the Act of 1892 (*Ex p. Lancaster* [1911] 2 K.B. 981, following *Ex p. Pyke, supra*, explained in *Macdonald v. Green* (*supra*)).

[12] Considered *post* para. 19–35.

[13] See *Luckett v. Wood* (1908) 24 T.L.R. 617; *Société des Hôtels Réunis (S.A.) v. Hawker* (1913) 29 T.L.R. 578.

[14] *cf.* the 1710 and 1835 Gaming Acts.

[15] *Carlton Hall Club v. Laurence* [1929] 2 K.B. 153; *Applegarth v. Colley* (1842) 10 M. & W. 723; *Moulis v. Owen* [1907] 1 K.B. 746.

amounts to a promise to pay the bet and unenforceable by reason of the statute.[16]

19–32   Contracts within the section, though, are void not illegal. Where an instrument is given in respect of a gaming or wagering transaction which falls within the Act of 1845 only, it is deemed to be given for no consideration.[17] Hence, the onus of proof lies on the defendant to show that the holder is not a holder for value or that he does not make title through a holder for value[18] and a holder for value is not disentitled to recover, though he has notice of the transaction, the consideration being void but not illegal.[19]

Securities

19–33   Securities provided for the payment of money lost under a gaming or wagering contract are governed by the 1710, 1835 and 1968 Act. Where the Act of 1835 applies, the instrument such as a bill, note or cheque, which under the earlier statute of 1710, would have been absolutely void is deemed to have been made, drawn, accepted, given or executed for an illegal consideration. Consequently the holder must prove that he, or some previous holder, gave value without notice. Section 1 of the 1835 Act reads:

> **"1. Securities given for considerations arising out of illegal transactions not to be void, but to be deemed to have been given for an illegal consideration**
> ... Every note, bill or mortgage which if this Act had not been passed would, by virtue of the said several lastly hereinbefore mentioned Acts or any of them, have been absolutely void, shall be deemed and taken to have been made, drawn, accepted, given or executed for an illegal consideration; and the said several Acts shall have the same force and effect which they would respectively have had, if, instead of enacting that any such note, bill, or mortgage should be absolutely void, such Acts had respectively provided that every such note, bill, or mortgage should be deemed and taken to have been made, drawn, accepted, given, or executed for an illegal consideration: Provided always, that nothing herein contained shall prejudice or affect any note, bill, or mortgage which would have been good and valid if this Act had not been passed."**

19–34   Although the regulation of gaming is governed by the Gaming Act 1968, the nineteenth-century Gaming Acts are left untouched. Nevertheless it is submitted that, where a gaming transaction is lawful, the common law position is resuscitated and so bills and notes given in respect of lawful gaming cannot today be impeached on the ground that they were given for an illegal consideration under the statutes which rendered them either void, or, for some purposes, unenforceable.

---

[16] *Hill v. William Hill (Park Lane) Ltd* [1949] A.C. 530, by a majority of four to three, overruling *Bubb v. Yelverton* (1870) L.R. 9 Eq. 471 and *Hyams v. Stuart-King* [1908] 2 K.B. 696.

[17] *Fitch v. Jones* (1855) 5 E. & B. 238, where it was considered that the presumption is not involved, as it would be if the consideration were an illegal one, that an indorsee is suing as a mere agent of the original holder.

[18] 1882 Act, s.29(3).

[19] *Lilley v. Rankin* (1886) 56 L.J.Q.B. 248, *Pollock v. Patterson & Co.* (1900) 19 N.Z.L.R. 94.

The Gaming Act 1968

This state of affairs appears not to have been affected by the Gaming Act **19–35** 1968; section 16, however, provides that neither the holder of a licence nor his agent may accept a cheque for cash or tokens for enabling a person to engage in gaming unless the cheque is not post-dated and is exchanged[20] for tokens to an equal amount. Furhtermore the cheque must be presented for collection not more than two banking days (within the meaning of s.92 of the 1882 Act) after receipt; it must follow that such a cheque is enforceable between the parties. For purposes of section 16 of this Act of 1968, an instrument in the form of a cheque but drawn on a bank which did not exist is a cheque.[21]

Sub-sections 4 and 5 of the Gaming Act 1968 provide that:

(4) Nothing in the Gaming Act 1710, the Gaming Act 1835, the Gaming Act 1845 or the Gaming Act 1892 shall affect the validity of, or any remedy in respect of any cheque which is accepted in exchange for cash or tokens to be used by a player in gaming to which this Part of this Act applies.[22]

(5) In this section "banking day" means a day which is a business day in accordance with section 92 of the Bills of Exchange Act 1882.

Gaming abroad

It is immaterial that the transaction in respect of which the security was **19–36** given took place in a foreign country and was lawful there. The Acts of 1710 and 1835 render a security given for a gaming debt or for money lent for the purpose of gaming illegal and void in the hands of the original holder, wherever the gaming may have taken place.[23] Thus, where the defendant in Algiers gave to the plaintiff a cheque drawn on an English bank, partly in payment of money lent by the plaintiff to the defendant for the purpose of playing at baccarat and, as to the balance, to be applied by the plaintiff in paying the defendant's losses at baccarat, it was held that, though the consideration for the cheque was lawful by French law, nevertheless no action could be maintained on the cheque here, since the transaction was governed by English law and, consequently, the cheque must be deemed to have been given for an illegal consideration.[24]

---

[20] See *Ladup v. Siu* (1984) 81 L.S.Gaz. 283, CA in which Dunn L.J. indicated that the signing of cheques after the chips were handed over contravened the Act.

[21] *Aziz v. Knightsbridge Gaming and Catering Services and Supplies Ltd, The Times*, July 6, 1982.

[22] See *Ladup v. Shaikh* [1983] Q.B. 225, in which it was held that s.16 did not override s.81 of the Act of 1882; *Crockford Club v. Mehta* [1992] 1 W.L.R. 355 at 365 explaining the purpose of s.16(4).

[23] *Moulis v. Owen* [1907] 1 K.B. 746; *Société des Hôtels Réunis v. Hawker* (1913) 20 T.L.R. 578; *cf.* also *Browne v. Bailey* (1908) 24 T.L.R. 644.

[24] *Moulis v. Owen* [1907] 1 K.B. 746, where, as the cheque was an English cheque, the *lex loci* solution is applied. *Quaere*, whether a security not in terms payable in England would be within the statute (*ibid.* at 755 (Cozens-Hardy L.J.)).

In the case of transactions taking place abroad, though no action can be brought upon the security, an action lies on the original consideration, if lawful by the foreign law.[25]

ACCOMMODATION BILLS

19–37   In common language, a bill, accepted or indorsed without any consideration moving to the party making himself liable on the bill, is called an accommodation bill; but, in strictness, an accommodation bill is not merely a bill accepted or indorsed without value received by the acceptor or indorser, as the case may be, but a bill accepted or indorsed without value by the acceptor or indorser to accommodate the drawer, or some other party; *i.e.* that the party accommodated may raise money upon it, or otherwise make use of it.

Meaning of accommodation party

19–38   An accommodation party is defined by the 1882 Act:

28.—(1) An accommodation party to a bill is a person who has signed a bill as drawer, acceptor, or indorser, without receiving value therefor and for the purpose of lending his name to some other person

Liability of an accommodation party

19–39   The liability is thus provided for:

(2) An accommodation party is liable on the bill to a holder for value; and it is immaterial whether, when such holder took the bill, he knew such party to be an accommodation party or not.[26]

But it is otherwise where the plaintiff takes the bill from a person who holds it for a particular purpose and is in fact guilty of a breach of duty in transferring it to the plaintiff, provided that the plaintiff, at the time of taking it, is cognisant of the circumstances.[27]

---

[25] *Quarrier v. Colston* (1842) 12 L.J.Ch. 57, followed in *Société Anonyme des Grands Etablissements du Touquet-Paris-Plage v. Baumgart* (1927) 136 L.T. 799; *Saxby v. Fulton* [1909] 2 K.B. 208; *cf. Moulis v. Owen, supra*, at 756.

[26] *Smith v. Knox* (1800) 3 Esp. 46; *Scott v. Lifford* (1808) 1 Camp 246; *Gatineau Co. v. Barnwell* (1924) 38 Que.K.B. 58, even though the instrument has been indorsed when overdue (*Charles v. Marsden* (1808) 1 Taunt. 224); for absence of consideration would not appear to be an equity attaching to the bill; see *Sturtevant v. Ford* (1842) 4 M. & G. 101. But if there be an agreement not to negotiate after due date it may be otherwise (*Parr v. Jewell* (1855) 16 C.B. 684, where the bill on maturity was cancelled and satisfied by a renewal, and was then reissued by the drawer). As to the transfer of an overdue accommodation bill, see *ante*, p. 197. Bills drawn specifically the one against the other, for the same amount, are not in this sense accommodation bills (*Burdon v. Benton* (1947) 9 Q.B. 843; see also *King v. Philips* (1844) 12 M. & W. 705).

[27] *cf. Hornby v. McLaren* (1908) 24 T.L.R. 494, where the plaintiff, who took a cheque drawn for the accommodation of a third party, after it had been dishonoured and with knowledge of that fact, was held not to be a holder in due course. The fact of notice must be clearly proved (*Middleton v. Barned* (1849) 4 Exch. 241).

A party who procures another to lend his acceptance thereby engages himself to take up the bill or else within a reasonable time before the bill becomes due to provide the accommodation acceptor with funds for so doing or, lastly, to indemnify the accommodation acceptor against the consequences of non-payment.[28] Where, therefore, the drawer of a bill, accepted for his accommodation, a week before the bill became due handed over bank notes to the accommodation acceptor, it was held that he could not himself have revoked this payment and consequently his bankruptcy before the bill became due did not amount to a revocation.[29]

Substitute bill

If a bill or note originally without any consideration is given up, another bill between the same parties being substituted for it, the giving up of the first bill is no consideration for the second, and both are alike incapable for want of consideration of being enforced between the immediate parties, though it is otherwise at the suit of the holder in due course.[30]   **19–40**

FAILURE OF CONSIDERATION[31]

Immediate Parties

Total failure

As between immediate parties[32] the entire failure of consideration has the same effect as its original and total absence and is a defence to an action brought on a bill or note. So, for example, in *Solly v. Hinde*[33] A appointed B his executor, and gave him a promissory note, payable on demand, for £100 in consideration of the trouble he would have in the office of executor after A's death. B, however, died first, and his executors brought an action on the note against A. It was held that, as the consideration for the note had totally failed, the action was not maintainable.   **19–41**

---

[28] *Reynolds v. Doyle* (1840) 1 M. & G. 753. Where the bill is proved to be an accommodation bill the party accommodated cannot sue the party granting the accommodation thereon even though the latter is admittedly in the former's debt, such debt being distinct from the subject-matter of the bill: *Raner v. Benjamin Bros* [1910] T.P.C. 1324.

[29] *Yates v. Hoppe* (1850) 9 C.B. 541. If the payment had been a fraudulent preference, it would, of course, have been otherwise.

[30] *Southall v. Rigg* (1851) 11 C.B. 481; *Edwards v. Chancellor* (1888) 52 J.P. 454. A substituted bill or note is in general held under the same title as the one it replaces (*Lee v. Zagury* (1817) 8 Taunt. 114, distinguished in *Mascarenhas v. Mercantile Bank of India* (1931) 47 T.L.R. 611; *Roblin in Vanalstine* (1917) 40 O.L.R. 99). Bills given after the repeal of the usury laws in renewal of bills void under those laws were valid between the parties, the antecedent pecuniary advance being a good consideration (*Flight v. Reed* (1863) 32 L.J.Ex. 265).

[31] See *Chitty on Contract* (28th ed., 1999) pp. 1489–1497.

[32] For meaning of immediate parties, see *ante*, para. 18–16.

[33] (1834) 2 Cr. & M. 516; *Wells v. Hopkins* (1839) 5 M. & W. 7. In *Churchill & Sim v. Goddard* [1937] 1 K.B. 92 Scott L.J. observed (p. 109) that "these authorities . . . call for no discussion, as there is no doubt as to the principle". See also *Mills v. Oddy* (1835) 2 Cr. M. & R. 103, *Abbott v. Hendrix* (1840) 1 M. & G. 791.

More recently the proposition has been applied *in Fielding & Platt Ltd v. Najjar,*[34] and stated in clear terms *in Nova (Jersey) Knit Ltd v. Kammgarn Spinnerei GmbH.*[35]

The discounter or purchaser of a bill which is forged may recover as for a total failure of consideration.[36]

Partial Failure

19–42   As between immediate parties the partial failure of consideration affords a *pro tanto* defence provided it is for a liquidated and ascertainable amount.[37]

Though partial failure or absence of consideration is a defence *pro tanto*, where part of the consideration is fraudulent or illegal, the instrument is vitiated altogether except as against a holder in due course or a transferee from one not being a party to the fraud or illegality.[38]

Remote Parties[39]

Holder in due course

19–43   The total failure of consideration is no defence against a holder in due course of the bill or someone claiming title under him,[40] and *a fortiori* nor is its partial failure.

Mere Holder

19–44   The total failure of the original consideration will defeat the claim of a subsequent holder who is not a holder for value.[41] By virtue of section 27(2)

---

[34] [1969] 1 W.L.R. 258, discussed below.

[35] [1977] 1 W.L.R. 713 at 722, 726, 732.

[36] *Hamilton Finance Co. Ltd v. Coverley, Westray Walbaum & Tosetti* [1969] 1 Lloyd's Rep. 53, *per* Mocatta J. citing *Jones v. Ryde* (1814) 5 Taunt. 488; *Gurney v. Womersley* (1854) 4 E. & B. 133.

[37] *Forman v. Wright* (1851) 11 C.B. 481; *Agra and Masterman's Bank v. Leighton* (1866) L.R. 2 Ex. 56 (Channell and Pigott BB.); *Goldie Co. v. Harper* (1899) 31 O.R. 284; *Nova (Jersey) Knit Ltd v. Kammgarn Spinnerei* [1977] 1 W.L.R. 713 at 720, 732; *Thoni GmbH KG v. R.T.P. Equipment Ltd* [1979] 2 Lloyd's Rep. 282, *MK International Development Co. Ltd v. Housing Bank* [1991] 1 Bank L.R. 74. See also *Barber v. Backhouse* (1791) 1 Peake 86; *Darnell v. Williams* (1817) 2 Stark. 166; *Day v. Nix* (1824) 9 Moore C.P. 159. Some earlier authorities apparently treated the claim on a bill as indivisible, so that partial failure or absence of consideration (even apparently if liquidated) could not be pleaded by way of defence (*Tye v. Gwynne* (1810) 2 Camp. 346; *Scott v. Gillmore* (1810) 3 Taunt 226; see also *Trickey v. Larne* (1840) 6 M. & W. 278; *Clark v. Lazarus* (1840) 2 M. & G. 167; *Warwick v. Nairn* (1855) 10 Exch. 762) but the modern law is clear.

[38] *Robinson v. Blank* (1706) 1 Burr. 1077, 1082; *Scott v. Gillmore, supra*; *Cruickshanks v. Rose* (1831) 1 Moo.& R. 100; *Moulis v. Owen* [1907] 1 K.B. 746, 753; *Browne v. Bailey* (1908) 24 T.L.R. 644; *Société des Hôtels Réunis v. Hawker* (1913) 29 T.L.R. 578. As to the position of a holder in due course see sections 29 and 38 of the 1882 Act, and above at paras 18–04 and 18–12. See now also *United City Merchants Ltd v. Royal Bank of Canada* [1982] Q.B. 208, and *Carney v. Herbert* [1985] A.C. 301 (Privy Council on appeal from New South Wales) dealing with severability of illegal consideration.

[39] For meaning of remote parties, see *ante*, para. 18–17.

[40] *Robinson v. Reynolds* (1841) 2 Q.B. 196; s.29(3).

[41] *Astley & Williams v. Johnson* (1860) 5 H. & N. 137. In such a case there will not be any effective consideration for the bill. See s.27(2) and above paras 18–14 *et seq*; where value has at any time been given a subsequent party is deemed a holder for value.

where value has at any time been given a subsequent holder will be deemed a holder for value, so the question can only arise where the original consideration has wholly failed and there has been no other, later, consideration given to support the bill.

For that reason it is difficult to see how a party could be a mere holder (as opposed to a holder for value) of a bill the consideration for which has *partially* failed. Upon any view, such a person's claim is subject to any liquidated, ascertained, failure of consideration.[42]

Holder for value

The position of a holder for value, who is not a holder in due course, is less **19–45** certain. The absence of consideration is not separately identified as a defect of title in section 29(2), and on the pre-Act authorities was not an "equity attaching to the bill".[43] Since value has *ex hypothesi* been given for the bill, it cannot be said that the bill is unenforceable for its absence.

However, there is in principle a distinction to be drawn between the original absence of consideration and its failure (whether total or partial).[44] In the former situation, the party becoming liable is generally an accommodation party for whom the Act makes specific provision,[45] and in any event has undertaken (gratuitously) an obligation on the bill which will be enforceable upon the provision of any subsequent consideration. It is not surprising that such a party should not have an "equity" attaching to the bill or enforceable against a subsequent purchaser of it.[46] In the latter case the party has not got what he bargained for. He would have a defence against his immediate party. In the case of total failure of consideration he might well be entitled to the return of the bill, and in the meantime could obtain an injunction to restrain its negotiation.[47]

Nonetheless opinions differ as to the availability of the defence of either total or partial failure of consideration and there is a dearth of modern authority. Chalmers & Guest suggest that total failure may be a defence against a remote holder for value with notice of it,[48] but that partial failure is

---

[42] But see Chalmers & Guest, para. 707, and 708 n. 44, Chitty (28th ed.) para. 34–097 where the possibility appears to be envisaged. Both cite *Agra and Masterman's Bank v. Leighton* (above) for the proposition. The Plaintiff bank in that case had discounted the bills which were indorsed in its favour, and would appear to have been at least holders for value.

[43] See above at para. 17–33 and notes 39 to 41.

[44] *ibid.*, esp. note 41.

[45] Section 28(2); reflecting the result of the earlier authorities appearing above at para. 17–33. The result is unsurprising—the party becomes a party to lend his credit to the bill.

[46] He would generally have no ground for complaining of, or restraining, its negotiation that being the purpose for which it is put into circulation. Consider the distinct situation of *Parr v. Jewel* (1855) 16 C.B. 684, or *Carruthers v. West* (1847) 11 Q.B. 143, concerning agreements restraining negotiation. If a bill is negotiated contrary to such an agreement, that is clearly a breach of faith included within the defects of title to which anyone other than a holder in due course takes subject.

[47] See Ch. 26 para. 26–09. If an injunction can properly be granted the Claimant's rights must amount to an equity attaching to the bill.

[48] Para. 707, citing *Lloyd v. Davis* (1824) 3 L.J. (OS) K.B. 38, *Traders Finance Corp. Ltd v. Casselman* (1960) 22 D.L.R. 2d 177.

not.[49] It is suggested in Chitty that partial failure is not a defence to a remote holder for value, and that total failure may not be.[50]

The defendant acceptor in *Archer v. Bamford* was liable because he had failed to wholly to rescind the contract; the consideration had not therefore failed, and the Court considered that had he done so then his defence, against the Plaintiff indorsee of the bill, would probably have succeeded. The knowledge of the Plaintiff in *Lloyd v. Davis* would now be dealt with as a reason why he was not entitled to the status of a holder in due course. Similarly, in *Watson v. Russell*, the party to whom the cheque had been paid (and from whom the proceeds were irrecoverable) was held to have purchased a negotiable security in good faith and for value; as far as the report shows there were no circumstances alleged by which he too would not now be found to be a holder in due course. The bank indorsee in *Robinson v. Reynolds* similarly recovered because they were holders who gave value and had no notice of the want of consideration, a holder in due course under the Act.

In short, the effect of these cases is met by the statutory distinction between a holder in due course (or someone claiming under him) and a holder (otherwise) for value. It is suggested that there is no reason in principle why a holder, albeit for value, but who is not a holder in due course should not be subject to the same defences of total or (liquidated) partial failure of consideration as might be raised against an immediate party.[51]

Bill to be treated as cash

19–46   The courts have repeatedly said that a bill of exchange or a promissory note is to be treated as cash and is to be honoured unless there is some good reason to the contrary. The fact that the Defendant has a counterclaim, even one arising out of the original consideration and which would otherwise give rise to an equitable set-off is no defence against any party.[52]

Identifying the consideration

19–47   Failure of consideration was the reason for the county court judgment in *Poliway Ltd v. Abdullah*,[53] in which the defendant repudiated a contract for the purchase of property which he had bought at an auction and for which he had given his cheque to the auctioneers for the deposit. In the Court of Appeal, Roskill L.J., in reversing the trial judge, held that

> "at the moment when the cheque was given and received by the auctioneers they warranted to the defendant their authority to sign the memorandum on the vendors'

---

[49] Para. 709. Citing *Archer v. Bamford* (1822) 3 Stark 175, *Ashley Colter Ltd v. Scott* [1942] 3 D.L.R. 538 at 541.

[50] Para. 24–101, citing *Archer v. Bamford* for the former proposition, and *Watson v. Russell* (1864) 5 B. & S. 968 for the latter, though noting *Lloyd v. Davis* to the effect that the holder could not sue if he knew when he acquired the bill that the consideration had failed.

[51] A holder who is not a holder in due course generally takes subject to defects of title and personal defences, see more generally "defects of title" in Ch. 18 above. There is no reason in principle why this should not include failure of consideration. Chitty (para. 34–101 n. 30) considers this view to be arguable.

[52] See below Ch. 26 under "Set-off Counterclaim and stay" at paras 26–27 *et seq.*

[53] [1974] 1 W.L.R. 493.

behalf and to receive the cheque payable to themselves as named payees in diminu-tion of the defendant's obligation to pay the full amount of the purchase price to the vendors."

He thought this the true consideration for the cheque and accordingly there was no question of failure.

In *Fielding & Platt Ltd v. Najjar*[54] the Defendant had executed a series of promissory notes in favour of the Plaintiff pursuant to an agreement for the manufacture and supply of machinery. After the first of the notes fell due, and was dishonoured, the Plaintiff suspended work on the contract. In proceedings for summary judgment upon the first two notes (which by then were due) the Defendant argued that there had been a failure of consideration. The Court of Appeal held that there was clearly consideration for the first note because at the time it fell due the Plaintiff was engaged in manufacture. However, by the time of the second note the Plaintiff had accepted the Defendants repudiation of the contract and were entitled only to damages under it. Lord Denning M.R. held that the consideration for the second and subsequent notes had failed, thought Widgery L.J. considered this only arguable, expressing the opinion that consideration was provided for all the notes by the Plaintiff entering into the original agreement.

GIFT INTER VIVOS

It seems, on general principles, that the payment of a bill of exchange, **19–48** promissory note or cheque, given by the acceptor, maker or drawer to the payee, as a gift *inter vivos*, cannot be enforced at the suit of the donee against the donor.[55] It follows, therefore, that a transferee for value from a donee can only recover the value given by him, and not the face value of the instrument. Thus, where a bill of exchange was accepted by the defendant as a present to the payee who indorsed it to the plaintiff for a small sum advanced to him, Lord Ellenborough held that the plaintiff was only entitled to recover so much as he had advanced on the bill.[56] The effect of a gift of a negotiable instrument, payable to bearer, or indorsed by the donor in blank, appears on principle to be that as between the donor and the donee, the donor cannot recover the bill back or receive the amount from prior parties, but the donee himself cannot sue the donor upon it. As between the donee and the other prior parties to the bill, they are liable to him.[57] If the bill is not transferable, or is payable to order and not indorsed, the effect of the gift of it is to vest both the legal property in the paper and the beneficial interest in the money in the donee,[58] who must, however, recover from prior parties in the donor's name.[59]

---

[54] [1969] 1 W.L.R. 357.

[55] *Easton v. Pratchett* (1835) 1 Cr. M. & R. 798, 808 (Lord Abinger C.B.); *Holliday v. Atkinson* (1826) 5 B. & C. 501, 503; *Milnes v. Dawson* (1850) 5 Exch. 948, 950.

[56] *Nash v. Brown* (1817) Chitty, 11th eds., p. 60. *Quaere*, whether this is consistent with s.30 of the 1882 Act.

[57] *Easton v. Pratchett* (1835) 1 Cr. M. & R. 798, 808.

[58] *Rummens v. Hare* (1876) 1 Ex.D. 169; see also *Barton v. Gainer* (1858) 27 L.J. Ex. 390.

[59] As to *donatio mortis causa*, see *ante*, para. 17–41.

CHAPTER 20

ALTERATION AND FORGERY

ALTERATION

Common law

20–01   AT common law it has been held that a deed, bill of exchange, promissory note, guarantee, or any other executory written contract, is avoided by an alteration in a material part, made while it is in the custody of the plaintiffs, although that alteration is by a stranger;[1] for a person who has the custody of an instrument is bound to preserve it in its integrity; and as it would be avoided by his fraud in altering it himself, so it shall be avoided by his laches in suffering another to alter it.

For a modern statement and application of the law as it applies to contractual documents, but not bills of exchange or banknotes, see *Raiffeisen Zentralbank Osterreich AG v. Crossseas Shipping Ltd.*[2]

Section 64 of the 1882 Act

20–02   The rules relating to alteration or rasure of deeds apply (at least for the most part) to other written contracts, and to bills and notes.[3] The common law rulings must now, however, be taken subject to the following express provisions of the 1882 Act:

64.—(1) Where a bill or acceptance is materially altered without the assent of all parties liable on the bill, the bill is avoided except as against a party who has himself made, authorised, or assented to the alteration, and subsequent indorsers.

Provided that

Where a bill has been materially altered, but the alteration is not apparent, and the bill is in the hands of a holder in due course, such holder may avail himself of the bill as if it had not been altered, and may enforce payment of it according to its original tenor.[4]

---

[1] *Davidson v. Cooper* (1844) 13 M. & W. 343; *Bank of Hindostan v. Smith* (1867) 36 L.J.C.P. 241; see, however, Taylor, *Evidence* (12th ed., 1931), paras 1820, 1827, doubting *Davidson v. Cooper, supra*; Phipson (15th ed., 2001) expresses no such doubt.

[2] [2000] 1 W.L.R. 1135. The guarantee sued on was not avoided by the unauthorised insertion of the address of an agent for service, since that was not (for various reasons) prejudicial to the debtor and it could not be inferred that the insertion was made fraudulently or with an improper motive.

[3] See *Master v. Miller* (1791) 4 T.R. 320, 321 (Ashhurst J.), but see above note and compare para. 20–20 below.

[4] For cheques held valid according to their original tenor see *Rapid Discount Corporation Ltd v. Thomas E. Hiscott Ltd* (1977) 76 D.L.R. (3d) 450.

Accident

The alteration contemplated by the subsection is an alteration to which all **20–03** parties might assent, and the subsection does not apply to the effects of a pure accident. Thus, where part of an instrument is effaced by the operations of a mouse, by the hot end of a cigarette, or by any of the other means by which an accidental disfigurement can be effected, the instrument is, nevertheless, enforceable.[5]

Alteration to a bill

Further, the alteration must be made in a bill; an alteration made in an **20–04** instrument which does not become a bill until after the alteration is not within the subsection.[6]

Operation of the proviso—holder in due course

The proviso introduces a principle in the case of bills and notes, which, it **20–05** has been stated, differs in the following respects from the rulings at common law: "Before the Act a material alteration was a complete defence, by whomsoever made, and avoided and discharged the bill, except as against a party who made or who assented to the alteration. Now under the proviso to section 64, a holder for value may, when a bill has been materially altered, but the alteration is not apparent, avail himself of the bill as if it had not been altered."[7]

Bank notes

The proviso does not cover the case of Bank of England notes, since such **20–06** instruments differ in many respects from ordinary promissory notes.[8]

Precautions against alteration

The acceptor of a bill is not bound to take precautions against fraudulent **20–07** alterations in the bill after acceptance. Thus, where an acceptor accepted a bill for £500 on a bill stamp sufficient for a much larger amount, and spaces were

---

[5] *Hong Kong and Shanghai Banking Corporation v. Lo Lee Shi* [1928] A.C. 181, where a bank note issued by the appellant bank was accidentally left in the pocket of a garment when it came to be washed and was reduced to a lump of paper; subsequently the note was restored to some extent and, with the exception of the number, the necessary particulars could be read and the holder of the note was held entitled to recover.

[6] *Foster v. Driscoll* [1929] 1 K.B. 470, 494 (Scrutton L.J.).

[7] *Scholfield v. Londesborough* [1895] 1 Q.B. 536, 552 (Lopes L.J.), where the phrase "holder for value" is used in place of the strictly accurate "holder in due course".

[8] *Leeds Bank v. Walker* (1883) 11 Q.B.D. 84.

left permitting subsequent alteration and insertion in the bill, the drawer subsequent to acceptance was thereby enabled to alter the amount of the bill to £3,500; but the acceptor was held not to have been guilty of negligence in accepting a bill so drawn, and to be only liable therefor to a holder in due course for £500, the amount for which his acceptance was originally given.[9]

20-08   On the other hand a customer in drawing a cheque upon his bank owes a duty not to complete it so as to facilitate its alteration.[10]

Apparent alteration

20-09   Whether an alteration is "apparent" or not within the meaning of the proviso to section 64(1) is a question not free from difficulty. In *Leeds Bank v. Walker*,[11] the view was expressed that if the party sought to be bound can at once discern some incongruity on the face of the instrument and point out to the holder that it has been materially and fraudulently altered, the alteration is to be regarded as an "apparent" one, even if the alteration is not obvious to all mankind.

20-10   This view appears, however, to be inconsistent with the decision in *Scholfield v. Londesborough*[12] and was not accepted in *Wollatt v. Stanley*,[13] where it was held that the test to be employed was whether the alteration was apparent to the holder without the intervention of the party bound; an intending holder would naturally examine the instrument before taking it, and if, on examining the instrument with reasonable care, the alteration would be observed and noticed, then the alteration would be apparent.

20-11   Since the proviso is inserted for the benefit of a holder in due course, it is difficult to see why an alteration which was not apparent to him, though exercising reasonable care, should be regarded as apparent because it might be apparent when pointed out by some person who, from his knowledge of the facts, might be in a position to detect it.

20-12   The onus of proving that an alteration is not apparent lies on the holder.[14]

---

[9] *Scholfield v. Londesborough* [1896] A.C. 514.

[10] *London Joint Stock Bank v. Macmillan* [1918] A.C. 777, and see Ch. 22 below at paras 22–09 *et seq.*

[11] 11 Q.B.D. 84, 90 (Denman J.); this concerned a materially altered Bank of England note, which the Judge held to be excluded from the operation of the section; but see note 13 below, reference to Denman J.

[12] [1895] 1 Q.B. 536, 552.

[13] (1928) 138 L.T. 620 (Salter J.); see also *Bank of Montreal v. Exhibit and Trading Co.* (1906) 11 Com.Cas. 250, where the addition of the word "Ltd" to the name of the payee was held, after inspection by the court, not to be "apparent"; *Gagnier v. Leblanc* (1921) 32 Que. K.B. 495; *Black v. Collin* (1917) 3 W.W.R. 225, where an addition of a rate of interest was equally so held, since such addition could only have been detected by very careful scrutiny: *Maxon v. Irwin* (1908) 15 O.L.R. 81; *Cunnington v. Peterson* (1898) 29 O.L.R. 346 (in these two cases the opinion of Denman J. in *Leeds Bank v. Walker* (*supra*) was expressly dissented from); *Brown v. Bennett* (1891) 9 N.Z.L.R. 487; and *Slingsby v. District Bank* [1932] 1 K.B. 544, 555 (Scrutton L.J.).

[14] *Woollatt v. Stanley* (1928) 138 L.T. 620.

Other jurisdictions

In South Africa all parties at the date of the alteration who did not assent **20–13** "must be regarded as if the alteration had not been made"; parties making or assenting to the alteration and subsequent indorsers are liable on the bill as altered.[15] Section 145 of the Canadian Act, section 69(1) of the Australian Act, and section 64(1) of the New Zealand Act follow the English Act. The Uniform Commercial Code, section 3–407 omits any reference to "apparent".

The High Court of Australia has held that to constitute a material alteration **20–14** within the meaning of section 69, it should be apparent upon inspection of the bill that its text has undergone a change, that the document shows some revision consistent with it having been made after issue. Starke J. said that it was not enough that a prudent businessman should be put upon inquiry or his suspicions aroused; the alteration must be visible as an alteration.[16] In that case, there was space beside the place for the maker's signature for the addition of the place of payment. Evatt J. dissented on the ground that the unauthorised insertion of a place of payment amounted to a material alteration, because one or more of the legal results mentioned in section 93 flows from the inclusion in the note of a place of payment.

Material alteration

The alteration, in addition to being "apparent", must, in order to avoid the **20–15** bill, be of a material character. The 1882 Act deals further with this question as follows:

64.—(2) In particular the following alterations are material, namely, any alteration of the date, the sum payable, the time of payment, the place of payment, and, where a bill has been accepted generally, the addition of a place of payment without the acceptor's assent.

Thus the unauthorised alteration of the date of a bill after acceptance, **20–16** whereby the payment would be accelerated, avoids the instrument, and no action can afterwards be brought upon it even by an innocent holder for a valuable consideration.[17] So where the drawer, without the consent of the acceptor, added to the acceptance the words "payable at Mr. Bidlake's 248, Chiswell Street", it was held that this was a material alteration, discharging

---

[15] See s.62(1).

[16] *Auto Finance Corpn of Australia v. Law* (1933) 49 C.L.R. 1. Section 93 requires presentment at a particular place in order to render the maker liable, where the note is in the body of it made payable at that place. *Quaere*, whether in this case the insertion was in the body of the note.

[17] *Master v. Miller* (1791) 2 H.Bl. 138; 1 Smith L.C., 13th ed., 807; *Vance v. Lowther* (1876) 1 Ex.D. 176; even though the alterations may in fact benefit the defendant (*Boulton v. Langmuir* (1897) 24 O.A.R. 618). So also an alteration made to obtain the indorsement of a further party (*Union Bank of Canada v. West Shore Land Co.* (1916) 23 B.C.R. 64); and see *Clement v. Renaud* [1956] 1 D.L.R. 695.

the acceptor.[18] A similar addition, made by or with the consent of the acceptor, was held not to invalidate the bill as against him, either at common law or under the then Stamp Act,[19] and would not invalidate under the provisions of section 64(1).[20]

20–17   The provisions of section 64(2) are not intended to be exhaustive. There may be material alterations other than those there dealt with;[21] and it has been stated that any alteration is material which would alter the business effect of the instrument if used for any business purpose for which such an instrument is used.[22]

Examples

20–18   The following alterations have been held to be material: The addition of the name of a new maker to a joint and several note without the consent of an original maker;[23] an alteration in the name of the payee of an order cheque by the addition of an initial,[24] or by an unauthorised addition to his description;[25] the alteration of the place where the bill purports to be drawn from a place inside to a place outside the British Isles, whereby the bill is changed from an inland bill to a foreign bill;[26] the alteration of a foreign bill by adding either on the face of the bill or to the indorsements the rate of exchange according to which the bill is to be paid;[27] the addition of the words "interest to be paid at six per cent. per annum" to a note providing in the body thereof for the payment of "lawful interest", even though written on the corner of the note

---

[18] *Cowie v. Halsall* (1821) 4 B. & Ald. 197; *Macintosh v. Haydon* (1826) Ry. & M. 362; *Burchfield v. Moore* (1854) 23 L.J.Q.B. 261; see also *Sims v. Anderson* [1908] V.L.R. 348; *Bellamy v. Williams* (1917) 41 O.L.R. 244. But where the place of payment is added in the margin of a note and not in the body it is otherwise (*Fulton v. McCardle* (1888) 6 N.Z.L.R. 365).

[19] *Stevens v. Lloyd* (1829) M. & M. 292; *Walter v. Cubley* (1833) 2 Cr. & M. 151.

[20] But in an action against the drawer, such an alteration seems to be material where made by the acceptor after issue without the drawer's consent, for such an alteration would vary the drawer's liability, even though to his benefit and not his prejudice; *cf. Stevens v. Lloyd*, *supra*, at p. 294.

[21] In *Suffell v. Bank of England* (1882) 9 Q.B.D. 555, decided shortly before the 1882 Act became law, it was held that the alteration of the number of a Bank of England note, though it did not vary the contract, was material in the sense of altering the note in an essential part; and hence a fraudulent alteration of the number avoided the note. This decision, which was followed in *Leeds Bank v. Walker* (1883) 11 Q.B. 84, but distinguished in *Hong Kong and Shanghai Banking Corporation v. Lo Lee Shi* [1928] A.C. 181, was based on the peculiar character of Bank of England notes as part of the currency, and the opinion was expressed by Jessel M.R. at 563, that in an ordinary case the alteration of the number on a bill of exchange or cheque might not be material.

[22] *Suffell v. Bank of England*, *supra*, at 562 (Brett L.J.).

[23] *Gardner v. Walsh* (1855) 5 E. & B. 82, approved on principle by Scrutton L.J. in *Koch v. Dicks* [1933] 1 K.B. 307; *Bolster v. Shaw* [1917] 1 W.W.R. 431; *Gill v. Doey* [1934] O.L.R. 406. Such an addition has, however, been held to operate as an indorsement (*Ex p. Yates* (1857) 27 L.J.Bk. 9).

[24] *Goldman v. Cox* (1924) 40 T.L.R. 744.

[25] *Slingsby v. District Bank* [1932] 1 K.B. 544.

[26] *Koch v. Dicks* [1933] 1 K.B. 307.

[27] *Hirschfield v. Smith* (1866) L.R. 1 C.P. 340, where the addition was, according to the learned Author, himself a member of the Court, made in red ink, the inference being, it is supposed, that it was intended as a memorandum only and not as part of the bill, but the report itself makes no mention of this fact.

and not in the body.[28] On the other hand, where a bill was addressed to A B & Co. and the acceptance was by A and B, and the address was afterwards altered to correspond with the acceptance, as the acceptors would be liable either way the alteration was held to be immaterial.[29] Similarly, the addition of the words "on demand" to a note specifying no time for payment is not a material alteration, as the legal effect of the note is not altered.[30] Again, the conversion of a blank indorsement into a special indorsement under section 34(4)[31] is an immaterial alteration.[32]

Ambiguous Instrument

In the case of an ambiguous instrument which at the option of the holder may be treated either as a bill or as a note,[33] an alteration in the name of the addressee, though it might affect its validity as a bill, is immaterial when the instrument is treated as a note.[34]   **20–19**

Prejudicial alteration

An alteration which is otherwise material does not cease to be material because it is prejudicial to the party making it.[35]   **20–20**

Inchoate bill

It is, perhaps, important to differentiate between material alterations made before the instrument is issued and those made thereafter. No one can obtain rights in a bill before it is issued and if the alteration is the drawer's or is made with his consent before issue it is not a material alteration within the section. Three persons joined, as drawer, acceptor and indorser, in the fabrication of an accommodation bill and the date was altered before it came into the hands of   **20–21**

---

[28] *Warrington v. Early* (1853) 23 L.J.Q.B. 47. An alteration of the rate of interest on a note avoids it (*Bellamy v. Porter* (1913) 28 O.L.R. 527); or striking out rate of interest, even though beneficial to maker (*Langley v. Lavers* (1913, N.S.) 13 E.L.R. 141), or filling in a rate after note signed by maker (*Allen v. Gray* (1917) 3 W.W.R. 1084; *Moreau v. Clouthier* (1925) 32 R.L.N.S. 233; *Wood v. Smart* (1914) 26 W.L.R. (Can.) 817). The following have also been held material alterations: striking out an agreement to renew an instrument (*Fulton v. McCardle* (1888) 6 N.Z.L.R. 365; *contra Maxon v. Irwin* (1907) 15 O.L.R. 81, *dissentiente* Falconbridge C.J.); the insertion in good faith, and though subsequently cancelled of the words "jointly and severally" before the words "promise to pay" in a note (*Banque Provinciale v. Arnoldi* (1901) 2 O.L.R. 624; *People's Bank v. Wharton* (1894) 27 N.S. 67); the alteration of the word "order" to "bearer" in the case of a cheque "certified" by a bank (*Re Commercial Bank of Manitoba* (1894) 10 Man.R. 171).

[29] *Farquhar v. Southey* (1826) M. & M. 14; *Rabinovitch v. Cohen* (1917) Q.R. 53 S.C. 174; *cf.* also *Bank of Montreal v. Exhibit and Trading Co.* (1906) 11 Com.Cas. 250.

[30] *Aldous v. Cornwell* (1868) L.R. 3 Q.B. 573; see 1882 Act, s.10(1)(b), also *Humphreys v. Bredell* [1913] T.P.D. 86, where the addition of the words "as surety and co-principal" before the name of a party, who was in fact such, held immaterial.

[31] *Ante*, para. 9–12.

[32] *Bird & Co. (London) Ltd v. Thomas Cook & Son Ltd* (1937) 156 L.T. 415.

[33] See *ante*, para. 3–09.

[34] *Haseldine v. Winstanley* [1936] 2 K.B. 101.

[35] *Koch v. Dicks* [1933] 1 K.B. 307, following *Gardner v. Walsh* (1855) 5 E. & B. 83. But compare, for documents other than bills of exchange, *Raiffeisen Zentralbank Osterreich AG v Crossseas Shipping Ltd* [2000] 1 W.L.R. 1135 (note 2 above).

a holder for value; it was held that, as the accommodation parties could not sue upon the bill *inter se*, it was not, till it came into the hands of a holder for value, an available instrument, and therefore that an alteration before that time did not avoid it.[36] But once the drawer becomes liable, an alteration, though before acceptance, avoids the bill.[37] A bill is not issued when, having been drawn, it is sent to the acceptor for acceptance; when, therefore the drawee asked that a longer time be allowed for payment and the bill was altered to give effect to that request with the consent of the drawer, it was held that the bill was not an available instrument when the alteration was made.[38]

Correction of a mistake

20–22   In previous editions it has been said that where an alteration is made with the object of correcting a mistake, the alteration is not material. There is no modern authority in terms for this proposition[39] and its general correctness is doubtful. It is difficult to see that the intention with which an alteration is made can bear on the question whether as a matter of law it is "material" within the meaning of the section. The correction of a mere typographical error, (unless for example, liable to confuse the identity of the payee) is unlikely to be material. It may be that a correction to reflect accurately the true common intention of the parties would not as between them be material, but it would seem better to regard this as depending upon implied assent.[40]

Stamp Acts

20–23   As bills of exchange and promissory notes do not today attract stamp duty,[41] the question of alteration which is material by the stamp laws no longer arises and material alterations are henceforth to be judged by reference to section 64 only. Hitherto, by virtue of the Stamp Act 1891, a material alteration rendered the instrument a new and different instrument requiring a new stamp.

Extinction of debt

20–24   An alteration by the drawer and payee of a bill payable to drawer's order, or the payee of a note, though it avoids the instrument, does not extinguish the

---

[36] *Downes v. Richardson* (1822) 5 B. & Ad. 674: "An accommodation bill is not issued until it is in the hands of some person who is entitled to treat it as a security available in law"; *Tarleton v. Shingler* (1849) 7 C.B. 812. An alteration of the date before issue without the consent of the acceptor avoids the acceptance (*Engel v. Stourton* (1889) 5 T.L.R. 444).

[37] *Walton v. Hastings* (1815) 4 Camp. 223.

[38] *Kennerley v. Nash* (1816) 1 Stzrk. 452.

[39] Compare *Brutt v. Picard* (1824) Ry & M 37; *Hamelin v. Bruck* (1846) 9 Q.B. 306; *London & Provincial Bank v. Roberts* (1874) 22·W.R. 402.

[40] But note *Raiffeisen Zentralbank Osterreich AG v. Crossseas Shipping Ltd* [2000] 1 W.L.R. 1135 (n.2 above) where it was said to be inappropriate to inquire whether the other party *would have assented* to the term inserted by amendment. This, it is submitted, is different from a finding that he impliedly assents to the correction of the bill to reflect his intention.

[41] Finance Act 1970 (c. 24), s.32 and Sched. 7, Pt. I, para. 1(2)(a).

debt,[42] but an alteration by an indorsee not only avoids the security as against all parties, but also extinguishes the debt due to the indorsee from the indorser.[43] For it would be unjust that the indorsee should compel the indorser to pay his debt when the indorsee has destroyed the instrument on which alone, in some cases, and on which preferably in all cases, the indorser should sue. To make the indorser liable on the consideration and give him a cross-action against the indorsee for the alteration would be to oblige him to rely on the indorsee instead of the antecedent parties, and to prove a fact of which he might have no evidence; it would besides introduce a needless circuity of action.

Failure of consideration

Looked at another way, the indorsee contracts to receive a valid bill. Where the indorser has destroyed the instrument and it is a nullity the consideration between him and the indorsee has failed just as if the bill were a forgery.[44]   **20–25**

Renewal of altered bill

If a bill is altered so that a man otherwise liable on it is discharged, he is not liable on a bill given in renewal of the altered bill, even though he had the means of discovering the alteration, unless he was actually apprised of it at the time when he gave the substituted bill.[45]   **20–26**

Decimalisation

The Decimal Currency Act 1969, s.3(2), made provision for an alteration of the sum payable by a bill consequent upon the introduction of a decimal currency: **20–27**

> "If a reference to an amount of money in the old currency contained in an instrument to which this section applies is altered so as to make it read as it would otherwise fall to be read in accordance with subsection (1) of this section, the alteration shall not affect the validity of the instrument and, in the case of a bill of exchange or promissory note, shall not be treated as a material alteration for the purposes of section 64 of the Bills of Exchange Act 1882."

The instruments to which the subsection applies are stated in subsection (3) as cheques and other instruments to which section 4 of the Cheques Act 1957 applies; bills of exchange other than cheques, promissory notes, money and postal orders; warrants issued by the Director of Savings for the payment of

---

[42] *Sutton v. Toomer* (1827) 7 B. & C. 416; *Atkinson v. Hawdon* (1835) 2 A. & E. 628; see *Sloman v. Cox* (1834) 1 Cr.M. & R. 471 unless the bill or note was taken in satisfaction of the debt (*McDowall v. Boyd* (1848) 17 L.J.Q.B. 295).

[43] *Alderson v. Langdale* (1832) 3 B. & Ad. 660, followed in *Wyton v. Hille* (1915) 25 Man.R. 772.

[44] Affording a defence as between those parties and entitling the indorsee to recover any consideration furnished by him. See *Hamilton Finance Co. Ltd v. Coverley, Westray Walbaum & Tosetti* [1969] 1 Lloyd's Rep. 53, *per* Mocatta J. citing *Jones v. Ryde* (1814) 5 Taunt. 488; *Gurney v. Womersley* (1854) 4 E. & B. 133.

[45] *Bell v. Gardiner* (1842) 11 L.J.C.P. 195.

money, documents issued by the Secretary of State for Social Services intended to enable a person to obtain payment of the sum mentioned in them, such document not being a bill of exchange, any other document which is intended to enable a person to obtain through a banker payment of any sum mentioned in the document, if drawn, made or issued before the appointed day, February 15, 1971.[46]

No substantial damages for conversion of altered instrument

20–28   In the combined appeals in *Smith and another v. Lloyds TSB Group plc*; *Harvey Jones Ltd v. Woolwich plc*[47] the Court of Appeal held that where an instrument is converted by a collecting bank following its material alteration, the instrument is worthless and no substantial damages for its face value can be recovered. The question had previously been the subject of controversy and conflicting decisions.[48]

FORGERY

General Definition in Criminal Law

20–29   Section 1 of the Forgery and Counterfeiting Act 1981 provides that: "A person is guilty of forgery if he makes a false instrument with the intention that he or another shall use it to induce somebody to accept it as genuine, and by reason of so accepting to do or not to do some act to his own or any other person's prejudice." Section 9(1) of the Act defines a false instrument.

20–30   Elsewhere, it has been said that forgery is the making or alteration of a writing to the prejudice of another man's right.[49] Forgery of an acceptance was a felony.[50] A crossing is a material part of a cheque; a material alteration of a bill, if made without authority, is a forgery. The splitting of a bank note into two amounts to the making of a false document within the section.[51]

Section 24 of the Act

20–31   Forged and unauthorised signatures are dealt with by section 24 of the Act which provides that:

---

[46] The likelihood of any such instruments remaining current or outstanding is of course extremely slim.

[47] [2000] 3 W.L.R. 1725.

[48] Including the two, opposite, first instance decisions under appeal. See also in particular (from among the cases cited) *Slingsby v. District Bank Ltd* [1931] 2 K.B. 588 and [1932] 1 K.B. 544, CA; *Slingsby v. Westminster Bank Ltd* [1931] 1 K.B. 173, and same at [1931] 2 K.B. 583; *Arrow Transfer Co Ltd v. Royal Bank of Canada* (1971) 19 D.L.R. 3d 420, (1972) 27 D.L.R. 3d 81; *Bank of Canada v. Nbank of Montreal* (1977) 76 D.L.R. (3d) 385, *Bank of Ceylon v. Kulatilleke* (1957) 59 N.L.R. 188.

[49] 4 Bla. Comm. 248.

[50] The distinction between felonies and misdemeanours was abolished by the Criminal Law Act 1967, s.1.

[51] *per* Lewis J. in *R v. Guy*, Chester Summer Assizes, *Law Journal*, November 1, 1945.

24. Subject to the provisions of this Act,[52] where a signature on a bill is forged or placed thereon without the authority of the person whose signature it purports to be, the forged or unauthorised signature is wholly inoperative and no right to retain the bill or to give a discharge therefor or to enforce payment thereof against any party thereto can be acquired through or under that signature, unless the party against whom it is sought to retain or enforce payment of the bill is precluded from setting up the forgery or want of authority.

Provided that nothing in this section shall affect the ratification of an unauthorised signature not amounting to a forgery.[53]

It is probable that from the language of the section (referring distinctly to forged or unauthorised signatures) and from the criminal law at the time the 1882 Act was passed[54] that "forged" within the section has a narrower meaning than "forgery" under the modern criminal law. The section appears to apply only where the signature is literally not that of the person whose signature it purports to be, or is made by someone purporting to sign in a representative capacity when he has in fact no such authority to do so.[55]   **20–32**

Effect

If a drawer's signature is forged then the (purported) instrument is not his bill at all. Likewise a forged acceptance is no acceptance at all.[56] Where an indorsement is forged, no party can derive title to the bill, or be a holder (still less holder in due course) through it as against parties prior to the forgery. The last lawful holder of the instrument remains its true owner, and if in possession, the holder of it.   **20–33**

It must be noted that (as the section expressly preserves) the acceptor of a bill or its indorser are precluded from denying to a subsequent holder in due course the geniuneness of prior signatures.[57] In effect a fresh bill is created, of which there may be a subsequent holder in due course.   **20–34**

A signature which is placed without authority may subsequently be ratified. Although a forgery cannot be ratified, circumstances may arise (see below) in which a party may be estopped from denying that a signature is not his.   **20–35**

---

[52] Namely, s.7(3), *ante*, para. 3–04; s.54(2), *ante*, para. 17–06; s.55(2), *ante*, para. 17–18; s.60, *post*, para. 22–47; s.80, and s.82.

[53] In the United States section 3–404 of the Uniform Commercial Code provides that an unauthorised signature becomes valid so far as its effect as a signature is concerned.

[54] The relevant statute was the Forgery Act 1861. Compare *Kreditbank Cassel GmbH v. Schenkers Ltd* [1927] 1 K.B. 826 where Scrutton L.J. approached the matter under the Forgery Act 1913.

[55] See *Morison v. London County and Westminster Bank Ltd* [1914] 1 K.B. 356 A forgery is generally regarded as a nullity (see *Motis v. Dampskibsselskabet* [1999] 1 All E.R. (Comm. Cas.) 571 at 579), and it appears that in such a case the rule that a stranger is not concerned with the internal management of a company does not apply (*Ruben v. Great Fingall Consolidated*) [1906] A.C. 439. The section does not, though, apply merely because an agent has exceeded his authority.

[56] See for a statement of the effect of forged acceptances: *Credit Lyonnais Bank Nederland NV v. ECGD* [1998] 1 Lloyd's Rep. 19, CA at 26 and 39 (The House of Lords decision on another point is at [2000] A.C. 486).

[57] Section 54(2)(a) and para. 17–08 and s.55(2)(b) and para. 17–12.

Bank mandate

20–36   A bank paying cheques on which the drawer's signature has been forged does not obtain a discharge as against its customer, for it pays without any mandate.[58]

No discharge

20–37   Where the title to a bill or note is made through a forgery, even a "bona fide holder for value" has in general no right to sue upon it,[59] or even retain it;[60] and, therefore, as a general rule, if the acceptor or maker pays one who derives his title through a forgery, he will not be discharged.

Estoppel in cases of forgery

20–38   A forgery is incapable of ratification,[61] but if the drawee has once admitted that the acceptance is in his own handwriting, and thereby given currency to the bill, he cannot afterwards exonerate himself by showing that it was forged.[62] To raise an estoppel by silence after knowledge of the forgery it must appear that there was a duty to disclose the fact of the forgery, that the silence was deliberate, amounting to a representation that the instrument was in order, and that, in consequence of such representation, the party seeking to set up the estoppel suffered detriment.[63]

20–39   Hence, if a disclosure made with the utmost diligence would yet have been too late to prevent the prejudicial step an estoppel does not arise.[64] Further, there is no duty to inform a person of a forged acceptance if his agent is already in possession of such information and chooses to withold it, unless the conduct of the agent would create in the mind of a person of ordinary

---

[58] See more generally Ch. 22, below, and for a discussion of the position when payment is made upon a joint account where one signature is forged or absent, para. 22–06.

[59] *Mead v. Young* (1790) 4 T.R. 28; *Kreditbank Cassel v. Schenkers* [1927] 1 K.B. 826.

[60] *Esdaile v. La Nauze* (1835) 1 Y. & Co.Ex. 394; *Johnson v. Windle* (1836) 3 Bing.N.C. 225; *Bobbett v. Pinkett* (1876) 1 Ex.D. 368. But if the bill or note held under a forged indorsement is surrendered by the holder for renewal and the new instrument is issued to him directly and is in his name, he is entitled to retain it (*Mascarenhas v. Mercantile Bank of India* (1931) 47 T.L.R. 611).

[61] *Brook v. Hook* (1871) L.R. 6 Ex. 89; *Wilkinson v. Stoney* (1839) 1 Jebb. & S. 509 (Ir.R).

[62] *Leach v. Buchanan* (1802) 4 Esp. 226. The passage in the text was approved in *Greenwood v. Martins Bank Ltd* [1932] 1 K.B. 371, 375.

[63] *Brown v. Westminster Bank Ltd* [1964] 2 Lloyd's Rep. 187; *Greenwood v. Martins Bank* [1933] A.C. 51; *Ewing v. Dominion Bank* [1904] A.C. 806, distinguished in *Connell v. Shaw* (1909) 39 N.B.R. 267, where no substantial loss was caused by the silence of the party whose signature was forged; see also *Bank of Ireland v. Evans' Charities Trustees* (1855) 5 H.L.C. 389; *Arnold v. Cheque Bank* (1876) 1 C.P.D. 578; *Patent Safety Gun Cotton Co. v. Wilson* (1880) 49 L.J.C.P. 713; and *cf. Lewes Steam Laundry Co. v. Barclay* (1906) 95 L.T. 444; *Kepitigalla Rubber Co. v. National Bank of India* [1909] 2 K.B. 1010; *Columbia Graphopone Co. v. Union Bank of Canada* (1916) 38 O.L.R. 326; *Ethier v. Labelle* (1907) Q.R. 33 S.C. 39. See also *Ontario Woodsworth Memorial Foundation v. Grozbord* (1966) 58 D.L.R. (2d) 21, Ontario CA. For an instance of a refusal to enforce a partial estoppel, see *Avon County Council v. Howlett* [1983] 1 W.L.R. 605.

[64] *McKenzie v. British Linen Co.* (1881) 6 App.Cas. 82.

intelligence a suspicion or belief that the agent meant to betray his principal's interest.[65]

By paying one forged acceptance a man is not estopped from setting up that defence in the case of another similar bill.[66]

20–40

Estoppel between bank and customer

In *Greenwood v. Martins Bank Ltd* it was held that where a customer's signature to a cheque is forged, it is the duty of the customer, on discovering the forgery, to inform the bank, and if he deliberately abstains from doing so, with the result that the bank loses its remedy against the forger, the customer is estopped from relying on the forgery; and it is immaterial that the bank was guilty of negligence in not detecting the forgery.[67]

20–41

That principle was acknowledged by the Privy Council judgment of Lord Scarman in *Tai Hing Cotton Mill Ltd v. Liu Chong Hing Bank Ltd*.[68] An employee of the Defendant Bank's customers issued forged cheques but the Court of Appeal in Hong Kong accepted that the customers owed a reciprocal duty of care to the bank in the conduct of the account to check their statements, and advise the bank of the forgeries thereby discovered. The customers appealed and Lord Scarman decided in their favour; his view being followed by other members of the Judicial Committee. The customers were not under a general duty to check their accounts and were not estopped from disputing the transactions; the only exceptions placing an onus on the customer were the principles enumerated in the cases of *Greenwood v. Martins Bank* and *London Joint Stock Bank v. Macmillan and Arthur*.[69] In the former case the customer had discovered a forgery and did not tell the bank and further forgeries followed; the latter case was an instance in which a customer had drawn a cheque leaving a space that permitted a non-apparent alteration upwards of both figures and words.

The banks sought to rely upon their contractual terms to impose a wider duty, but it was held that any such provision had to be in emphatic and unambiguous terms that would bring home to the customer beyond doubt that he was giving up his right to dispute the transactions on his account. Thus the particular written provisions contained in the mandate and correspondence with all three of the appellant bankers were of no avail.

20–42

The above case accords with the decision in *Wealdon Woodlands v. National Westminster Bank Plc*[70] where the Plaintiffs failed to observe forgeries reflected in a statement of account received from the bank but were not estopped from bringing an action against the bank.

20–43

---

[65] *Ogilvie v. West Australian Mortgage Co.* [1896] A.C. 257.

[66] *Morris v. Bethell* (1869) L.R. 5 C.P. 47; *Liquidators of Union Bank v. Beit* (1892) 9 Cape S.C. 109; *Simon v. Sinclair* (1907) 6 W.L.R. (Can.) 638.

[67] *Greenwood v. Martins Bank, supra* and see *Brown v. Westminster Bank Ltd* [1964] 2 Lloyd's Rep. 187. See also para. 22–15 below.

[68] [1986] A.C. 80. The judgment in terms states that it represents the law in England, not just Hong Kong. The decision was applied by the Court of Appeal of New South Wales in *National Australia Bank Ltd v. Hokit Pty Ltd* [1997] 6 Bank. L.R. 177. See also paras 22–09 *et seq.* below.

[69] [1917] A.C. 177.

[70] (1983) 133 New L.J. 719.

Knowledge or notice

20–44   It would seem that in order to give rise to an estoppel a party must have actual knowledge, or at least be "wilfully blind" to the forgery, and that constructive notice is not enough.[71]

Complete or partial nullity

20–45   In view of the meaning of forgery as defined by the Forgery Act 1981, it is clear from section 64(1) of the 1882 Act[72] that forgery does not necessarily corrupt absolutely. In *Kwei Tek Chao v. British Traders and Shippers Ltd*[73] Devlin J. said: " . . . if the forgery corrupts the whole of the instrument or its heart, then the instrument is destroyed; but if it corrupts merely a limb, the instrument remains alive, though no doubt defective". By way of example, the learned judge went on: " . . . if a man adds two noughts to a cheque, that is the end of it. It is no longer a cheque for, let us say, £10, because the original figure of £10 has been destroyed by the addition of two noughts. It is not a cheque for £1,000 because the figure of £1,000 is a forged figure. There is therefore nothing left of it and it must go. The same result would not necessarily follow, however, if a man were, for example, to forge the date on a cheque, because he thought that, it being overdue, there was a possibility that awkward questions might be asked."

The instruments in the case were bills of lading and not bills of exchange, and the example is, perhaps, not happily chosen, for in the hands of a "holder in due course" *vis-à-vis* the drawer the cheque, if the alteration was not apparent, would be a cheque for £10.

Conflict of laws[74]

20–46   It was held in *Embiricos v. Anglo-Austrian Bank*[75] that section 24 is declaratory of English law only, and does not control the general rule of international law. "I do not think that section 24 governs the case of an indorsement abroad"—*per* Vaughan Williams L.J. at 685. Romer L.J. at 686, said that the section "has not . . . the intention or effect of controlling the operation of private international law in a case such as the present".

20–47   In *Canada Life Assurance Co. v. Canadian Imperial Bank of Commerce*[76] a Canadian life assurance company drew cheques on its so-called "Agency" account with a New York bank. The cheques were cashed in New York by

---

[71] *Price Meats Ltd v. Barclays Bank plc* [2000] 2 All E.R. (Comm) 346, in which the authorities, including *Greenwood*; *Morison v. London County and Westminster Bank*, *McKenzie v. British Linen Co.* (1881) 6 App. Cas. 82; *Ogilvie v. West Australian Mortgage and Agency Corp. Ltd* [1896] A.C. 257; and the statement to the contrary in Paget (11th ed.), p. 348 (referring to *McKenzie*) are considered.

[72] *Ante*, para. 20–02.

[73] [1954] 2 Q.B. 459, 476 *sub nom. Chao v. British Traders and Shippers Ltd* [1954] 1 All E.R. 779, 787.

[74] See more generally Part IV, Ch. 25.

[75] [1905] 1 K.B. 677.

[76] (1980) 98 D.L.R. (3d) 670 (Can.).

forged indorsements and the life assurance company brought an action in Canada. The question for the Court was whether New York law or Canadian law applied. It was held that the former was applicable and the bank could rely on the endorsements as a good defence, despite the bill being an inland bill under the Canadian Bills of Exchange Act.

PART TWO

CHAPTER 21

THE CHEQUE—1

INTRODUCTION

CHEQUES, which are bills drawn on a banker and payable on demand, differ **21–01** from other bills of exchange in many respects. They are not intended as credit instruments, to be paid at a future date and in the meantime discounted or sold by the payee. Rather, the function of cheques is as a means of effecting immediate payment to the payee. Consequently cheques are not accepted by the drawee as a precursor to payment; and the drawee does not assume any liability on the cheque, but simply pays or not according to the sufficiency of the funds in its customer's account.[1]

Although historically cheques were negotiable, nowadays cheques are nor- **21–02** mally issued in a form that precludes their transfer by the payee to third parties. This change has been brought about by the Cheques Act 1992, which made provision for cheques crossed and marked "account payee" to be non-transferrable. As matters stand it seems that the 1992 Act effectively sounded the death-knell for cheques as negotiable instruments.

Reflecting their different nature and function, cheques are subject to certain **21–03** rules that set them apart from other bills. Part III of the 1882 Act, "Cheques on a Banker", contains most of the provisions that differentiate cheques. These provisions relate to presentment for payment,[2] revocation of the bank's authority to pay[3] and the form and effect of cheque crossings.[4] In addition, the Cheques Act 1957 contains important provisions for the protection of banks which collect payment of cheques and similar instruments or make payment upon them.

NATURE AND CHARACTERISTICS OF A CHEQUE

Definition

The definition of a cheque is provided by section 73 of the 1882 Act, as **21–04** follows:

73. A cheque is a bill of exchange drawn on a banker payable on demand.

Except as otherwise provided in this Part, the provisions of this Act applicable to a bill of exchange payable on demand apply to a cheque.

---

[1] *Bank of Baroda v. Punjab National Bank* [1944] A.C. 176, at 184.
[2] Sections 74 to 74C.
[3] Section 75.
[4] Sections 76 to 81A.

21-05   There are thus three requirements for a cheque: first, it conform to the definition of a bill of exchange; second, it must be drawn on a "banker"; and third, it must be payable on demand.

Cheque must be a bill of exchange

21-06   A cheque must be drawn unconditionally for a sum certain in money, to or to the order of a specified person or to bearer.[5] Any failure to comply with the definition of a bill of exchange[6] will disqualify the instrument as a cheque. So an instrument in cheque form but drawn payable to "cash" or "wages" or any other impersonal payee is not a cheque.[7] Likewise, a conditional order to a bank to pay a sum to the payee[8] and a document in the form of a receipt used for withdrawing money from a bank are not cheques.[9] Where the drawer's signature is a forgery, the instrument is not within the definition of a bill of exchange and is not a cheque.[10]

Certain other payment instruments are deemed cheques, or are made subject to the legislative provisions relevant to cheques.[11]

Drawn on a banker

21-07   As regards the requirement that a cheque must be drawn on a "banker", that expression is defined in the 1882 Act as including "a body of persons, whether incorporated or not, who carry on the business of banking".[12] Like most commercial activities the "business of banking" is one which evolves with the passage of time and it can be anticipated that the essential requirements of that business may also change. The nature of the business of banking is essentially one of fact and not law.[13]

---

[5] Section 3 of the 1882 Act.

[6] For the requirements of a bill of exchange, see para. 1–09 *ante.*

[7] *North and South Insurance Corporation Ltd v. National Provincial Bank Ltd* [1936] 1 K.B. 328; *Cole v. Milsome* [1951] 1 All E.R. 311; *Orbit Mining & Trading Co. Ltd v. Westminster Bank Ltd* [1963] 1 Q.B. 794.

[8] *Bavins Jnr & Sims v. London & South Western Bank Ltd* [1900] 1 Q.B. 270. Cf. *Nathan v. Ogdens Ltd* (1905) 94 L.T. 126.

[9] *Midland Bank v. Inland Revenue Commissioners* [1927] 2 K.B. 465, 473; *Brandon v. Bank of Montreal* (1926) 59 O.L.R. 268.

[10] *Arrow Transfer Co. Ltd v. Royal Bank of Canada* (1972) 27 D.L.R. (3d) 81, applied in *Koster's Premier Pottery Pty Ltd v. Bank of Adelaide* (1981) 28 S.A.S.R. 355. For a full discussion of the effect of forgery and alteration of bills of exchange see Chap. 20.

[11] Section 14(7), National Loans Act 1968 (deems certain Bank of England warrants to be cheques); Sections 4(2) and 5, Cheques Act 1957 (extends the protections given to collecting banks and the provisions of the 1882 relating to crossings to certain other instruments, see para. 23–14 *post*). See also Savings Bank Annuity Regulations 1969, S.I. 1969 No. 1342; the Premium Savings Bonds Regulations 1972, S.I. 1972 No. 765, as amended by S.I. 1976 No. 1543 and 1980 No. 767; the National Savings Stock Register Regulations 1976, S.I. 1976 No. 2012; the Savings Certificates (Yearly Plan) Regulations 1984, S.I. 1984 No. 779; the Savings Certificates Regulations 1991, S.I. 1991 No. 1031 and the Savings Certificates (Children's Bonus Bonds) Regulations 1991, S.I. 1991 No. 1407.

[12] Section 2. Note also that a building society carrying on the activity of providing banking services is entitled to be treated for all purposes as a bank and a banker: section 12(3) of the Building Societies Act 1997.

[13] See *Woods v. Martins Bank Ltd* [1959] 1 Q.B. 55 at 70.

The leading case as to the essential attributes of the business of banking **21–08** remains *United Dominion Trust v. Kirkwood*.[14] There, citing expert banking evidence which had been given at the trial, the Court of Appeal regarded the essential business of bankers as taking money from customers on running account, *i.e.* on an account from which withdrawals may be made by the customer from time to time upon demand. In the circumstances that prevailed in 1965, when *UDT v. Kirkwood* was tried, the payment and collection of cheques for customers were also essential conditions.[15] Given the increasing use of electronic funds transfers, it is possible that in future those services would no longer be regarded as essential.

Section 69(1) of the Banking Act 1987, until its repeal, prohibits any person **21–09** carrying on business in the United Kingdom from describing himself or holding himself out so as to indicate that he is a bank, a banker or is carrying on the business of banking unless he is an authorised institution or an exempted person. Authorisations under the Act are granted and may be revoked by the Financial Services Authority,[16] which publishes a list of authorised institutions. Alternatively, an institution based in another Member State of the E.C. may be treated as authorised in the United Kingdom if it is a credit institution[17] authorised in its home state and has complied with certain certification requirements.[18] If an institution is authorised, or treated as authorised, under the Banking Act 1987, then, provided it meets certain capital requirements, it is not prevented from carrying on business in the United Kingdom under a name which indicates that it is a bank, or a banker or is carrying on banking business.[19]

Thus the regime under the Banking Act 1987 is one whereby the privilege **21–10** of calling oneself a bank and of carrying on banking business is restricted to authorised institutions and to European credit institutions entitled to be treated as authorised. The fact that an institution may be authorised under that regime, so that it may accept deposits and carry on banking business, is an indication that its business might well include banking, but it is not necessarily determinative of that question, as the business actually carried on by the institution may be different from or less than that which its status would entitle it to carry on. Specifically, authorisation under the Banking Act 1987 may have been sought and obtained solely so that the institution can carry on a business which is no more than accepting deposits. Conversely, lack of authorisation and its consequential prohibition against carrying on the business of banking does not, of itself, preclude an argument that for the purposes of section 73 of the Bills of Exchange Act 1882 the unauthorised institution is a "banker"; for

---

[14] [1966] 2 Q.B. 431; see also *Re Roe's Legal Charge Park Street Securities v. Roe* [1982] 2 Lloyd's Rep. 370.

[15] *ibid.*, see pp. 446–447 (*per* Lord Denning M.R.), pp. 457–458 (*per* Harman L.J.), and pp. 465–566 (*per* Diplock L.J.).

[16] Sections 9 and 11 of the 1987 Act.

[17] A "credit institution" means an undertaking whose business is to receive deposits or other repayable funds from the public and to grant credits for its own account: Article 1 of the Directive of the European Parliament and the Council 2000/12/EC, a definition that follows the First Council Directive (1977/780/EEC) of December 12, 1977.

[18] Banking Coordination (Second Council Directive) Regulations 1992 (S.I. 1992 No. 3218), Regulations 3 and 47, paragraph 1 of Schedule 2 and paragraph 18 of Schedule 18.

[19] Section 67 of the Banking Act 1987.

the prohibition at section 69(1) of the Banking Act 1987 does not prevent any person from using the expression "bank" or "banker" in order to take advantage of, or comply with, other enactments, international agreements, rules of law or commercial usages or practices applicable to banks and bankers.[20]

21–11   Upon commencement of the Financial Services and Markets Act 2000, the regulatory regime relating to banks will change. The Treasury will specify by Order certain activities, which will include accepting deposits,[21] as "regulated activities".[22] It will be an offence for a person to carry on by way of business a regulated activity unless that person is an authorised person under the Act of 2000.[23] The prohibitions in sections 67 and 69 of the Banking Act 1987 against the use of banking names and descriptions and carrying on the business of banking will be replaced by the general prohibition against carrying on regulated activities unless authorised.

21–12   Under this new regime it will be very hard to argue that an institution which is not an authorised or exempt person under the Act of 2000 is nonetheless a banker, as without such authorisation or exemption that person could not lawfully accept deposits from the public. However the Act of 2000 moves away from the use of the terms "banker" and "business of banking" and is ultimately of no assistance in defining those terms. The Financial Services Authority, however, will employ "bank" as a defined term for the purposes of its prudential standards, restricting such definition to certain types of deposit-taking institutions and European credit institutions.[24]

Payable on demand

21–13   The third requirement of a cheque is that it must be payable "on demand". A bill is payable on demand if it is expressed to be so payable, or is expressed to be payable at sight or on presentation.[25] It is also payable on demand if no time for payment is expressed.[26] The latter is the normal form in which cheques are issued. As discussed below it has been contended that a post-dated cheque is not payable on demand, and hence not a cheque but a normal bill of exchange.

Dating and post-dating

21–14   Prima facie a cheque need not be dated,[27] but in practice no undated cheque would be paid by a bank without the drawer's consent and a bank's refusal to

---

[20] Section 69(4) of the 1987 Act.
[21] See paragraph 4 of Schedule 2 to the Act of 2000.
[22] Section 22 of the Act of 2000.
[23] Section 19 of the Act of 2000.
[24] Financial Services Authority: "Interim Prudential Sourcebook for Banks", section 3.5.1. This defines "bank", for the purposes of the FSA's sourcebook as "A firm with a Part IV permission to accept deposits other than (a) a building society; (b) a friendly society; (c) a credit union; and (d) a firm whose Part IV permission to accept deposits is subject to a limitation under s.40(7)(a) of the Act in relation to the accepting of deposits; and (2) an incoming EEA firm which is a credit institution". Further information can be obtained on the website: www.fsa.gov.uk.
[25] Section 10(1)(a) of the 1882 Act; see para. 2–15 *ante*.
[26] Section 10(1)(b) of the 1882 Act.
[27] Section 3(4)(a) of the 1882 Act; see para. 2–10 *ante*.

pay has been upheld.[28] The date on an undated cheque may be completed by the person in possession of it in accordance with section 20 of the 1882 Act.

A bill of exchange is not invalid by reason of its being ante-dated or post-dated.[29] And the date appearing on the cheque is deemed to be the true date of its drawing unless the contrary be proved.[30]   **21–15**

Post-dated cheques have long been held to be regular instruments.[31] A post-dated cheque does not become payable until the date shown upon it and a bank which pays it prematurely will not be entitled to debit the drawer's account.[32] If the drawer countermands payment before the date written upon the post-dated cheque, the drawee bank must not pay it.[33]   **21–16**

As a result of the deferral of the payee's ability to obtain payment, a post-dated cheque has been likened to a bill of exchange payable on a certain future date.[34] The view has also been expressed that a post-dated cheque is not truly payable "on demand", and hence not in fact a "cheque" within the definition at section 73 of the 1882 Act at all.[35] Such an argument has been rejected in Australia[36] but has yet to be the subject of decision in England. The nearest that the English courts have come to deciding the issue was probably the decision of the Court of Appeal in *Royal Bank of Scotland v. Tottenham*[37] in which it was held that a post-dated cheque was admissible in evidence when it was stamped with an amount of stamp duty that was appropriate for a cheque, but would have been insufficient for a bill of exchange. The Court of Appeal read section 13(2) of the 1882 Act,[38] as though it provides that "a cheque" (as opposed to "a bill") is not invalid by reason of its being post-dated.[39]   **21–17**

In *Bank of Baroda v. Punjab National Bank* the Privy Council considered the question of whether a post-dated cheque could be and had been accepted by virtue of a certificate added to it by the drawee bank. The analysis of the Privy Council proceeded upon the basis that a post-dated cheque is indeed a cheque, as opposed to a bill of exchange proper, and as such is not an instrument that is intended for acceptance. In the light of these authorities, the argument that a post-dated cheque is not to be regarded as payable on demand,   **21–18**

---

[28] *Griffiths v. Dalton* [1940] 2 K.B. 264.

[29] Section 13(2) of the 1882 Act.

[30] Section 13(1).

[31] *Gatty v. Fry* (1877) 2 Ex. D. 264; *Royal Bank of Scotland v. Tottenham* [1894] 2 Q.B. 715; *Hitchcock v. Edwards* (1889) 60 L.T. 636; *Carpenter v. Street* (1896) 6 T.L.R. 410; *Guildford Trust v. Goss* (1927) 43 TLR 167.

[32] *Pollock v. Bank of New Zealand* (1901) 20 N.Z.L.R. 174.

[33] *Keyes v. Royal Bank of Canada* [1947] 3 D.L.R. 161.

[34] *Forster v. Mackreth* (1867) 16 L.T. 23, 26.

[35] *Brien v. Dwyer* (1978) 141 C.L.R. 378, 407–408 *per* Aickin J. See also Hedley and Hedley, *Bills of Exchange and Bankers' Documentary Credits* (4th Ed.), p. 222 and Brindle and Cox, *The Law of Bank Payments* (2nd ed.), pp. 365–366.

[36] *Hodgson & Lee Pty Ltd v. Mardonius Pty Ltd* (1986) 78 A.L.R. 573, (1986) 5 N.S.W.L.R. 496, a decision of the Supreme Court of New South Wales, Court of Appeal.

[37] [1894] 2 Q.B. 715.

[38] Section 13(2): "A *bill* is not invalid by reason only that it is ante-dated or post-dated, or that it bears date on a Sunday." (*Emphasis added*)

[39] See Paget (11th ed.), pp. 242–243.

but as a bill of exchange payable at the date borne by it, is considered unlikely to prevail.

21–19   However, if (on the contrary view) a post-dated cheque is not truly payable on demand, not only would it not be a cheque, it would not be a bill at all. The date it bears is intended to mark the commencement of the indefinite period at which it may be paid on demand and is not intended to be a single fixed or determinable future time at which presentment for payment must be made,[40] failing which the drawer is prima facie discharged from liability.[41] On this view, therefore, a post-dated cheque could be described as an instrument which is payable on demand on or after a future date, being neither a true cheque nor a bill, but simply a written instruction to make payment. The implications of so treating post-dated cheques would be fairly limited, as sections 76 to 81A of the 1882 Act and the protection of section 4 of the Cheques Act 1957 are applicable to "any document issued by a customer of a banker which, though not a bill of exchange, is intended to enable a person to obtain payment from that banker of the sum mentioned in the document".[42]

21–20   Notwithstanding that it is considered that a post-dated cheque is a true "cheque" for the purposes of the 1882 Act, it may not be regarded as a cheque for all purposes. The normal function of cheques is to enable immediate payment, whereas a post-dated cheque is intended to enable deferred payment only. Thus, a partner of a solicitors' firm who had authority to issue cheques in the ordinary course of the firm's business lacked authority to issue a post-dated cheque for the purposes of obtaining credit;[43] an established practice amongst bankers of certifying cheques for payment did not extend to the certification of a post-dated cheque;[44] and a contractual provision permitting the payment of a deposit by cheque did not authorise the payment by post-dated cheque.[45]

Place of issue or payment

21–21   As in the case of a bill, a cheque is not invalid by reason that it does not specify the place where it is drawn or where it is payable.[46] As, however, banks usually have several branches, cheques indicate the branch on which they are drawn and the bank cannot be forced to pay elsewhere.[47]

Sum payable

21–22   The sum is usually expressed both by words and figures. Where there is a discrepancy between the two the sum denoted by words is the amount

---

[40] See ss. 3 and 11 of the 1882 Act. *Gaudet v. Comeau* [1936] 1 D.L.R. 754.
[41] Section 45(1) of the 1882 Act.
[42] Sections 4(2)(c) and 5 of the Cheques Act 1957.
[43] *Forster v. Mackreth* (1867) 16 L.T. 23
[44] *Bank of Baroda v. Punjab National Bank* [1944] A.C. 176.
[45] *Brien v. Dwyer* (1978) 141 C.L.R. 378.
[46] 1882 Act, s.3(4)(c).
[47] *Woodland v. Fear* (1857) 26 L.J.Q.B. 202, (1857) 7 E. & B. 519; *Prince v. Oriental Bank* (1878) 3 App. Cas. 325, 332–333; *Clare v. Dresdner Bank* [1915] 2 K.B. 576. Cf. *Arab Bank Ltd v. Barclays Bank* (D.C. & O.) [1954] A.C. 495.

payable;[48] the usual practice is to dishonour the cheque, though sometimes it would be paid if only the smaller amount was claimed. Where the amount of the cheque was expressed only in words, the cheque would usually be paid, but not if the amount was in figures only.[49]

CROSSED CHEQUES

History

The device of a "crossing" on the face of cheques is significant both to   **21–23** banks and their customers. First, the presence of a crossing prevents the cheque from being paid otherwise than to a banker. Second, by adding suitable words to a crossing, the drawer or holder of a cheque is able to render the cheque incapable of transfer. These are both important safeguards against theft. Third, a bank which pays a crossed cheque in good faith and without negligence is protected from liability provided that he pays the cheque in accordance with its crossing, a protection which relieves against the strict liability under the tort of conversion.[50] Finally, banks which collect payment of cheques for their customers (as banks invariably do) must be mindful of the crossings on those cheques, which may indicate that the cheque is incapable of transfer, and hence, that it should only be collected for the named payee.[51] A failure to heed the crossing can result in the collecting bank's incurring liability to the cheque's drawer or payee.

The custom of writing the name of a banker across the face of a cheque is   **21–24** said to have originated from the practice of the clearing house, where the clerks of the different bankers who did business there were accustomed to write across the cheques the names of their employers so as to enable the clearing house clerks to make up the accounts.[52] It first received legislative sanction by the Drafts on Bankers Act 1856, amended by the Drafts on Bankers Act 1858, which made the fraudulent obliteration of or alteration or addition to a crossing a forgery.[53] These Acts were repealed but substantially re-enacted by the Crossed Cheques Act 1876, which, in addition, by section 10, rendered a banker who paid a cheque in contravention of the crossing, general or special, liable to the "true owner" of the cheque for any loss he might have sustained owing to the cheque having been so paid, it having been held, under the Act of 1858, that the payee of a specially crossed cheque which had been stolen after he had indorsed it had no right of action against the drawee bank who had paid the cheque to a bank other than that named in the crossing.[54] The Act of 1876 also, by section 12, introduced the "not negotiable" crossing.

---

[48] 1882 Act, s.9(2), *ante*, para. 2–20.
[49] Question on Banking Practice (Institute of Bankers) (10th ed., 1965), No. 469.
[50] See Chap. 22 *post*.
[51] See Chap. 23 *post*.
[52] *Bellamy v. Marjoribanks* (1852) 7 Ex. 389, 402; see also *Carlon v. Ireland* (1856) 25 L.J. Q.B. 113.
[53] In *Simmonds v. Taylor* (1857) 27 L.J.C.P. 248, it had been held that, under the Act of 1856, the crossing was no part of the cheque, and its fraudulent alteration no forgery.
[54] *Smith v. Union Bank* (1875) 1 Q.B.D. 31.

21–25   The Bills of Exchange Act 1882 repealed the Act of 1876 but re-enacted its provisions with slight variations in sections 76–82. By the Cheques Act 1957 certain additional protections were afforded to bankers of cheques and other instruments. Then, by the Cheques Act 1992, new provisions were inserted at section 81A of the Bills of Exchange Act 1882 enabling cheques to be made non-transferrable by the addition of the words "account payee" or "a/c payee" to the crossing.

Crossings defined

21–26   A crossed cheque is defined in section 76 of the 1882 Act as follows:

76.—(1) Where a cheque bears across its face an addition of—

(a) The words "and company" or any abbreviation thereof between two parallel transverse lines, either with or without the words "not negotiable" or

(b) Two parallel transverse lines simply, either with or without the words "not negotiable";

that addition constitutes a crossing, and the cheque is crossed generally.

(2) Where a cheque bears across its face an addition of the name of a banker, either with or without the words "not negotiable", that addition constitutes a crossing, and the cheque is crossed specially and to that banker.

21–27   The words "and Co." are, in accordance with the terms of this section not an essential part of a general crossing; the two transverse lines drawn across the face of a cheque are by themselves sufficient to constitute such a crossing.[55] Where the crossing is a special one, the two transverse lines do not appear to be essential, the name of the bank written across the cheque being of itself sufficient to constitute such a crossing. It is however, usual in the case of a special crossing for the two lines to accompany it.

21–28   The crossing must be on the face of the cheque. A decision of the Cour de Cassation, given in Paris on December 18, 1961 was to the effect that a crossing on the back of the instrument giving a slight impression on the front was not enough; the crossing must be seen on the front otherwise than *en relief*.[56]

---

[55] In *Mather v. Bank of New Zealand* (1918) 18 S.R.N.S.W. 49, the Court held that where across the middle of a cheque just after the name of the payee two fine transverse lines roughly parallel were drawn an inch and an eighth long and one-sixteenth of an inch apart, the question whether the cheque was a crossed cheque was properly left to the jury.

[56] *Banque*, March 1962, 193. Article 37 of décret loi of October 30, 1935 requires a crossing to be *au recto* and thus a crossing by perforations is not permitted.

The effect of general and special crossings

The presence of a general or special crossing on a cheque circumscribes the **21–29** persons to whom payment may be validly made by the drawee. A cheque crossed generally may only be paid to a bank and a cheque crossed specially may only be paid to the bank to which it is crossed. The precise duties of the paying bank in this regard are set out in section 79 of the 1882 Act. By section 80 of the 1882 Act the paying bank is exonerated from liability if he makes payment in accordance with the crossing, in good faith and without negligence. These provisions are discussed in the next Chapter.[57]

Although a crossed cheque can be properly paid only to a banker, a payee **21–30** who is not a banker may nonetheless present the cheque himself to the branch on which it is drawn and if he is informed by the bank that the cheque will not be paid the cheque is treated as duly presented for payment and dishonoured.[58]

Not negotiable

Cheques may be marked "not negotiable", as provided by section 81 of the **21–31** 1882 Act:

81. Where a person takes a crossed cheque which bears on it the words "not negotiable," he shall not have and shall not be capable of giving a better title to the cheque than that which the person from whom he took it had.

Only crossed cheques can be marked "not negotiable", for this section does **21–32** not authorise the insertion or subsequent addition of those words, except where cheques are crossed. A distinction must be drawn for the purposes of this section between the concepts of "negotiation" and of "transfer". A negotiation is a specific type of transfer, capable of conferring on the transferee good title to the instrument transferred, even though the transferor himself did not possess good title.[59] Thus, a cheque marked "not negotiable" is freely transferable, but the holder of such an instrument is in an exceptional position since, though he is otherwise a holder in due course, he gets no new and independent title and no presumption as to the liability of antecedent parties is drawn in his favour.[60]

The section applies as much to a payee who takes a cheque crossed "not **21–33** negotiable" as it does to third party transferees, such as endorsees. Thus, where a signed, blank cheque form crossed "not negotiable" was fraudulently completed by an agent in favour of the respondent, as payee, to whom the

---

[57] See paras 22–35 *et seq.*

[58] *Ringham v. Hackett and Walmsley* (1980) 10 L.D.A.B. 206, (1980) 124 Sol. J. 221.

[59] See Chap. 8.

[60] See *Great Western Ry v. London and County Bank* [1901] A.C. 414; *Union Bank of Australia v. Shulte* [1914] V.L.R. 183; *Fisher v. Roberts* (1890) 6 T.L.R. 354; *Dungarvin Trust Pty Ltd v. Input Refrigeration Co. (Pty)* [1971] (4) S.A. 300 (T.); but it has been held otherwise where the cheque is an accommodation one: *Shapiro v. Ibrahim* [1918] Witwatersrand L.D. (S.A. 105).

agent was indebted, it was held that the payee was a person who took the cheque within the meaning of the section.[61]

21–34   The incidence in the United Kingdom of cheques marked "not negotiable" has dramatically declined as a result of the statutory recognition in the Cheques Act 1992 of the addition to the crossing of the words "account payee". Cheques issued in this form have now almost totally replaced those bearing a "not negotiable" crossing.

Cheques crossed and bearing the words "account payee"

21–35   The Cheques Act 1992 amended the 1882 Act by introducing entirely new provisions for the addition to crossed cheques of the words "account payee" or "a/c payee". Thus:

> **81A Non-transferable cheques**
> **Where a cheque is crossed and bears across its face the words "account payee" or "a/c payee", either with or without the word "only", the cheque shall not be transferable, but shall only be valid as between the parties thereto.**

21–36   It is often desirable for cheques to be issued in a form that allows payment to be made only to the named payee, as this reduces the opportunity for fraud in transmission of the payment. Transferable cheques falling into the wrong hands have proved to be quite easily used by fraudsters to obtain payment, usually through the mechanism of a forged indorsement.

21–37   It was possible before the passage of the Cheques Act 1992 to make a cheque non-transferable. This could be achieved either by describing the payee in the form "John Smith only" (and deleting the words "or order" from the pre-printed cheque form) or by adding the words "not transferable" to the cheque.[62] However, before the 1992 Act, the addition of "account payee" to the crossing on a cheque did not have any statutory recognition, nor did it make the cheque non-transferable. The words were seen as merely a direction or warning, addressed to the collecting bank, as to how the proceeds of the cheque should be applied[63] and insufficient, in the case of a cheque drawn to order or bearer, to make it non-transferable within the meaning of section 8(1) of the 1882 Act.[64] At the practical level, however, before 1992 the use of the words "account payee" may have somewhat hindered negotiation, as a collecting bank which disregarded them was vulnerable to being found negligent.[65] The subtleties of the legal position were largely lost on users of

---

[61] *Wilson & Meeson v. Pickering* [1946] 1 K.B. 422, at 429 and 430.

[62] See Section 8(1) of the 1882 Act, discussed in Chap. 8.

[63] *Akrokerri Mines Ltd v. Economic Bank* [1904] 2 K.B. 465, 472; approved by Atkin L.J. in *Importers Ltd v. Westminster Bank Ltd* [1927] 2 K.B. 297; *Morison v. London County and Westminster Bank Ltd* [1914] 3 K.B. 356; *Rhostar (PVT) Ltd v. Netherlands Bank of Rhodesia Ltd* (1972) 2 S.A.L.R. 703.

[64] *National Bank v. Silke, supra; Importers' Co. v. Westminster Bank* [1927] 2 K.B. 297, 309 (Atkin L.J.); and *Standard Bank of South Africa Ltd v. Sham Magazine Centre*, 1977 (1) S.A. 484 (A.D.) to the same effect.

[65] *Bellamy v. Majoribanks* (1852) 7 Exch. 389; *Bevan v. The National Bank Ltd* (1906) 23 T.L.R. 65.

cheques and there existed widespread misapprehension as to how a cheque might be made truly incapable of transfer.[66]

The introduction of section 81A changed the status of crossings accompanied by the words "account payee" so that cheques bearing such words are now not transferable and are only valid "between the parties thereto", meaning the original parties of drawer, drawee and payee. The vast majority of cheque books now issued in the United Kingdom bear a pre-printed crossing together with these words.

21–38

For the section to operate it appears that the exact words "account payee" or "a/c payee" must be used, either with or without the addition of the word "only". Moreover, there must be a crossing[67] and the words on the cheque must appear "across its face", which should be interpreted (in accordance with section 76, which uses the same expression) as meaning that the words are orientated transverse to the main text of the cheque. Whilst a departure from these requirements takes the cheque outside section 81A, if the intent of the drawer is clear it is likely that the cheque would still be regarded as non-transferable on the basis that it "contains words . . . indicating that it should not be transferable" within section 8(1) of the 1882 Act.

21–39

If a crossed cheque bearing the words "account payee" is mistakenly indorsed by the payee in favour of a third party the indorsee does not thereby become a party entitled to sue on the instrument as a cheque. However, as between payee and indorsee only there may well be a valid assignment. It is submitted that the situation is analogous to that in which an assignment is made of the benefit a contract in contravention of a term in the contract prohibiting assignment. In those circumstances, the purported assignment will often amount to a valid contract between the assignor and assignee.[68]

21–40

By whom cheque may be crossed

As to the person by whom a cheque may be crossed, either generally or specially, the 1882 Act provides as follows:

21–41

77.—(1) A cheque may be crossed generally or specially by the drawer.

(2) Where a cheque is uncrossed, the holder may cross it generally or specially.

(3) Where a cheque is crossed generally the holder may cross it specially.

(4) Where a cheque is crossed generally or specially, the holder may add the words "not negotiable".

(5) Where a cheque is crossed specially, the banker to whom it is crossed may again cross it specially to another banker for collection.

---

[66] See the Green Paper "Banking Services: Law and Practice" Report by the Review Committee (1989) Cm 622 and the White Paper "Banking Service Law and Practice" (1990) Cm 1026. Also, *Honourable Society of the Middle Temple v. Lloyds Bank* [1999] 1 All E.R. (Comm.) 193, 206–207 *per* Rix J.

[67] See section 76, discussed above, for the definition of a crossing.

[68] *Linden Gardens Trust Ltd v. Lenesta Sludge Disposals Ltd* [1994] 1 A.C. 85, 108, *per* Lord Browne-Wilkinson; *Chitty on Contracts*, 28th ed., para. 20–044.

(6) Where an uncrossed cheque, or a cheque crossed generally, is sent to a banker for collection, he may cross it specially to himself.

21–42   The term "holder" does not necessarily mean a holder who has taken a cheque for value; it includes every person who is in lawful possession[69] of the instrument, such as an agent for collection.[70] A bank, therefore, to whom a cheque is sent for collection, is not restricted to the right under subsection (6) of crossing the cheque specially to itself: like any other holder, it may cross it generally, or specially, to another bank, or make it not negotiable.[71]

21–43   It is notable that this section has not been amended to create a right for a holder to alter a crossing by adding the words "account payee". There could be no objection to such an action on the part of the payee or his agent, which would merely serve to ensure that payment is made for the payee's account. It may be that as the words "account payee" are not deemed to form any part of the "crossing", as defined by section 76, their addition to a crossing does not require the countenance of section 77, which is concerned only with the addition of crossings and words that form parts of crossings.

Crossing a material part of cheque

21–44   A crossing is a material part of a cheque, and its obliteration, alteration, etc., is unlawful, as provided by the 1882 Act:

78. A crossing authorised by this Act is a material part of the cheque; it shall not be lawful for any person to obliterate or, except as authorised by this Act, to add or to alter the crossing.

21–45   The practice has arisen of the drawer, at the request of the payee, striking out the crossing and writing on the cheque the words "pay cash" so that the cheque may be paid over the counter; there appears to be no objection to this practice, especially where there is a printed form of crossing already on the cheque, as the cheque is never effectively used as a crossed cheque.[72] The practice is called "opening" the crossing.

21–46   It is now standard practice for banks to provide cheque forms which contain a crossing to which are added the words "account payee". As already noted[73] it is doubtful whether those words are properly regarded as forming any part of the "crossing" for the purposes of the 1882 Act. In any event a drawer

---

[69] Presumably, a person who holds under a forged indorsement, however innocent he may be of the forgery, not being in lawful possession, is not a holder and cannot cross the cheque.

[70] *Akrokerri Mines Ltd v. Economic Bank* [1904] 2 K.B. 465, 472 (Bigham J.), approved in *Sutters v. Briggs* [1922] 1 A.C. 1, 16 (Lord Birkenhead C.).

[71] *Sutters v. Briggs* [1922] 1 A.C. 1.

[72] By a resolution of the Committee of London Clearing Bankers of November 7, 1912, it was decided that the full signature of the drawer must be appended to the alteration, and presentment must be made by the drawer or his known agent. In *Smith and Baldwin v. Barclays Bank* (1944) 5 *Legal Decisions Affecting Bankers*, 370 it was conceded that the opening of a crossing did not affect the status of the cheque as a crossed cheque. The concession is considered to have been wrongly made.

[73] See the discussion in relation to section 77 of the 1882 Act, above.

could legitimately delete those words from the cheque form if he wished to issue the cheque in transferable form, as the deletion would constitute an amendment of the form, not of a part of the issued cheque. Once a crossed cheque has been issued bearing the words "account payee", those words are undoubtedly a material part of the cheque. This follows either by necessary implication from the fact that the words "not negotiable", being a crossing but of less potency than the words "account payee", are deemed material. Or, if (which is considered doubtful) the words "account payee" are to be regarded as forming part of the crossing, they are expressly deemed a material part of the cheque under section 78. The payee, or another person, would not be entitled to delete or alter the words "account payee" without the authority of the drawer, as this would amount to material alteration of the cheque within the terms of section 64.

Other instruments that may bear crossings

The provisions of the 1882 Act as to crossed cheques are also applicable to **21–47** dividend warrants,[74] documents issued by customers of banks which, though not bills of exchange, are intended to enable a person to obtain payment from the banker of the sum mentioned in the document, documents issued by a public officer intended to enable a person to obtain payment from the Pay-master General or the Queen's and Lord Treasurer's Remembrancer, and drafts payable on demand drawn by a banker on himself (which are commonly referred to as "bankers' drafts").[75]

DRAWER'S RIGHT TO HAVE HIS CHEQUES PAID

Generally speaking, the drawee of a bill of exchange is not liable until he **21–48** adds his acceptance, and as cheques are not accepted,[76] the payee cannot enforce payment from the bank. However, the bank owes a duty to its customer, the drawer, to pay cheques drawn in proper form on it provided that the customer's account holds sufficient funds to meet the cheque,[77] or that the cheques are within an agreed overdraft.[78] If the bank breaches that duty by dishonouring a customer's cheques, for which it holds sufficient funds, the

---

[74] Section 95 of the 1882 Act.

[75] Sections 4(2) and 5 of the Cheques Act 1957.

[76] A cheque can be lawfully accepted: *Bellamy v. Marjoribanks* (1852) 7 Ex. 389, 404 (Parke B.); *Keene v. Beard* (1960) 8 C.B.(N.S.) 372. But it is only done in very unusual and special circumstances and would require strong and unmistakable words of acceptance: *Bank of Baroda v. Punjab National Bank* [1944] A.C. 176. Article 4 of the Geneva Convention prohibits the acceptance of a cheque, any *"mention d'acceptation portee sur le cheque est reputee non ecrite"*.

[77] *London Joint Stock Bank Ltd v. Macmillan and Arthur* [1918] A.C. 777, 789; *Joachimsom v. Swiss Bank Corporation* [1921] 3 K.B. 110, 127. *Bank of New South Wales v. Laing* [1954] A.C. 135, 154.

[78] *Rouse v. Bradford Banking Co. Ltd* [1894] AC 586, 596.

bank may be liable in damages for breach of contract and defamation.[79] If the funds in the account are insufficient to meet the cheque, the presentation of the cheque represents the customer's request that overdraft facilities be granted to permit payment of the cheque. The bank then has an option whether or not to comply with that request and incurs no liability if it chooses not to do so.[80]

21–49   The bank is entitled to reasonable time after the receipt of funds to the credit of a customer in which to pay.[81] What is reasonable time depends upon the circumstances of the case, which will vary according to whether the moneys paid in to credit are cash or cheques, etc., which have to be collected, and according to whether they are paid in at the branch at which the drawer's account is kept or at another branch. A drawee bank is not required to make inquiries before it considers whether it will pay or not, certainly not inquiries of other branches; but where it is guilty of delay in discovering that it has sufficient funds in hand to make payment, though they have not been credited to the customer's account, it may be liable for dishonour.

Drawer's claims for for wrongful dishonour of his cheques

21–50   Damages for wrongful dishonour of a customer's cheques are available in contract and may also be available in the tort of libel.

21–51   Contractual damages include both general damages for loss of credit and reputation[82] and special damages for losses that the customer may plead and prove that he has suffered. As regards general damages for loss of credit and reputation, the presumption that such damage has been suffered by the customer arises because of the exceptional nature of the contract between bank and customer, whereby the bank undertakes for consideration to sustain the credit of the customer.[83] It used to be the case that only customers who were "traders" benefited from a right to recover general damages.[84] However in *Kpohraror v Woolwich Building Society*[85] it was held by the Court of Appeal that even private individuals who are not traders are now entitled to claim general damages for injury done to their credit without proving any such specific damage. This reflects the changed conditions of society, where the

---

[79] "Other things being equal, in particular if the customer has sufficient funds or credit available with the bank, the bank is bound either to pay the cheque or dishonour it at once. There is no point in its saying in effect to the drawer or, indeed, to the holder if it has been transferred, 'I will pay if you present it again,' " *per* Lord Wright in Bank of *Baroda v. Punjab National Bank* [1944] A.C. 176, 184. If the bank decides to close the account, reasonable notice must be given: *Prosperity Ltd v. Lloyds Bank* (1923) 39 T.L.R. 372; *Joachimson v. Swiss Bank Corporation* [1921] 3 K.B. 110, 127.

[80] *Barclays Bank Ltd v. W. J. Simms Son & Cooke (Southern) Ltd* [1980] Q.B. 677, 699.

[81] *Marzetti v. Williams* (1830) 1 B. & Ad. 415.

[82] Damages for loss of reputation simpliciter are available only in the tort of defamation: *Joyce v. Sengupta* [1993] 1 W.L.R. 337, although it may be that damages are not so confined if the cause of action is not based upon words spoken or written: see *McGregor on Damages*, (16th Ed.) para. 229 discussing *Thurston v. Charles* (1905) 21 T.L.R. 659.

[83] *Wilson v. United Counties Bank Ltd* [1920] A.C. 102, 112.

[84] *Gibbons v. Westminster Bank Ltd* [1939] 2 K.B. 882.

[85] [1996] 4 All E.R. 119.

credit rating of individuals has become important for their personal transactions, including mortgages and hire-purchase as well as banking.[86] The availability of special damages for actual damage suffered by the customer depends upon whether, at the time that the bank-customer contract was made (which will often be the time that the customer's account was opened) it should have been reasonably in the contemplation of the parties that such damage might occur.[87]

When a cheque is dishonoured it is normally returned to the payee bearing   **21–52** a brief statement from the drawee bank of the reason for dishonour. This "answer" may be such as to provide the drawer with a claim in defamation against his bank, the test being whether the words used tend to lower the customer in the estimation of right thinking people generally.[88] The words "not sufficient" are capable of being defamatory and the defence of qualified privilege failed insofar as the insufficiency of funds which led to the dishonour of the cheque arose as a result of the bank's wrongly paying another cheque that had been countermanded.[89] The words "Refer to Drawer" are a common answer on cheques and are capable of being defamatory.[90]

The amount of damages to be awarded for loss of reputation and credit is   **21–53** "not nominal, nor excessive, but reasonable and temperate" and should reflect the natural and necessary consequences which must result from the bank's breach of contract.[91]

Ambiguous cheque or mandate

As a cheque is the drawer's mandate (*i.e.* his authority) to his bank, it is the   **21–54** customer's duty to ensure that his cheques are regular and unambiguous in form.[92] If there is ambiguity in the mandate, the bank which adopts a reasonable course cannot be made liable, but it may be incumbent on the bank in the case of a patent ambiguity for it to attempt to contact its customer first.[93] It follows also that the bank is entitled to make sure that the signature is that of his customer.

Bank suspects fraud or illegality

Exceptionally, cheques may be presented for payment in such circum-   **21–55** stances that the bank is, or should be, aware that the account signatory has

---

[86] *ibid.* at p. 124.

[87] *Hadley v. Baxendale* (1854) 9 Exch. 341. *Kpohraror v. Woolwich Building Society, supra.*

[88] *Sim v. Stretch* [1936] 2 All E.R. 1237. Whether the words are defamatory is not to be judged according to whether a particular class of person would attach special meaning to them, but according to what the words would suggest to an ordinary person of average intelligence: *Frost v. London Joint Stock Bank Ltd* (1906) 22 T.L.R. 760, CA.

[89] *Davidson v. Barclays Bank Ltd* [1940] 1 All E.R. 316.

[90] *Jayson v. Midland Bank Ltd* [1968] 1 Lloyd's Rep 409. Paget (11 Ed.), p. 338. See also *Pyke v. Hibernian Bank Ltd* [1950] I.R. 195 and *Svendssen v. State Bank* (58 American St.R. 522, 523). In earlier times, such an answer had been regarded as innocuous: *Plunkett v. Barclays Bank* [1936] 2 K.B. 107, following *Flach v. London and South Western Bank* (1915) 31 T.L.R. 334, 336.

[91] *Rolin v. Steward* (1854) 14 C.B. 595, at p. 605 *per* Lord Campbell C.J., and p. 607 *per* Williams J. Cited in *Kpohraror* [1996] 4 All E.R. 119, at 123.

[92] *London Joint Stock Bank Ltd v. Macmillan and Arthur* [1918] A.C. 777, 814 & 816.

[93] *European Asian Bank AG v. Punjab and Sind Bank* (No. 2) [1983] W.L.R. 642, 656. Paget (11th ed.), pp. 332–333.

abused his authority in signing the cheques and is attempting to defraud the customer. The bank acts as the customer's agent in paying the customer's cheques and, as such owes the customer a duty of care.[94] That duty is owed both as a matter of contract and tort.[95] In these circumstances the bank faces a dilemma: whether to comply with its mandate by promptly paying the cheques, or to give effect to its suspicions by delaying payment and making enquiries of the customer.

21–56 The standard of care expected of banks in such cases was considered by the Court of Appeal in *Lipkin Gorman v. Karpnale*.[96] According to May L.J., payment should only be delayed in circumstances such as would cause a reasonable cashier to refer payment of a cheque to his superior, and the superior would hesitate to authorise payment without enquiry.[97] According to Parker L.J., the test is whether if a reasonable and honest banker knew of the relevant facts he would have considered that there was a serious or real possibility albeit not amounting to a probability that his customer might be being defrauded.[98]

Tipping off

21–57 A distinct situation arises where the bank has reason to become suspicious as to the legality, or the customer's true ownership, of funds standing to the credit of the account. In these circumstances, the bank's dilemma is even more acute, as the avenue of making enquiries of the customer is fraught with difficulty.

21–58 If the bank is to avoid the possibility of incurring accessory liability to the owner of the moneys, it is incumbent on the bank to act honestly and not to be guilty of commercially unacceptable conduct in the context involved.[99] Yet, its basic duty is to comply with its customer's mandate. Moreover, if the bank suspects that the account holds the proceeds of criminal activity or is used for such purposes, it will be at risk of committing a crime unless it discloses its suspicions to the police and operates the account only so far as the police consent.[1]

---

[94] *Westminster Bank Ltd v. Hilton* (1926) 135 L.T. 358, 362, CA and (1926) 43 T.L.R. 124, 126, HL; *Royal Products Ltd v. Midland Bank Ltd* [1981] 2 Lloyd's Rep. 194, 198.

[95] *Barclays Bank plc v. Quinecare Ltd* [1988] 1 F.T.L.R. 507, 517.

[96] [1989] 1 W.L.R. 1340. See also *Barclays v. Quinecare (supra)*.

[97] *ibid.* at p. 1356.

[98] *ibid.* at p. 1378. *cf. Verjee v.CIBC Bank & Trust Co. (Channel Islands) Ltd*, Unreported, March 21, 2001: the bank is unlikely to be put on notice of the possibility of a fraud where the signatory to the account is the account-holder himself.

[99] *Royal Brunei Airlines Sdn Bhd. v. Philip Tan Kok Ming* [1995] 2 A.C. 378, 390. For discussions of the paying bank's position in relation to accessory liability see Warne & Elliott, *Banking Litigation* (1999) p. 13 *et seq.* and Paget (11th ed.), p. 398 *et seq.*

[1] Section 93A of the Criminal Justice Act 1988. If the bank knows or suspects that the moneys are the proceeds of drug trafficking, it is under a positive obligation to make such disclosure: section 52 of the Drug Trafficking Act 1994. Under ss.146 and 402(1)(b) of the Financial Services and Markets Act 2000 the Financial Services Authority will be empowered to prosecute for breaches of the Money Laundering Regulations 1993 (S.I. 1993 No. 1933) and to make rules in relation to the prevention and detection of money laundering. The FSA's draft Money Laundering Rules require the appointment by regulated firms of a Money Laundering Reporting Officer (rr. 2 and 8.1) who must promptly report suspicious transactions to the National Criminal Intelligence Service (rr. 5.2 and 6).

Once the bank has made that disclosure, or otherwise knows or suspects   **21–59**
that a police investigation is proposed or under way, the bank is obliged not
to disclose to any other person anything that may prejudice the investigation,
or it risks committing the criminal offence of "tipping off".[2]

In these circumstances, the bank may be prevented from airing its concerns   **21–60**
with the customer in order to probe whether its suspicions are well-founded.
At the same time, it may be obliged to follow directions from the police as to
whether and how payments out of the account should be made, which may
place the bank in breach of mandate.

A bank which finds itself embarrassed as to how it should proceed in order   **21–61**
on the one hand to avoid tipping off and on the other hand to avoid incurring
liability to its customer or to a third party to whom the funds belong may
apply to the court in proceedings to which the police (but not the customer or
the potential third-party claimant) are the defendant. In those proceedings the
court may make an interim advisory declaration.[3] The court will then determine what if any disclosure the bank may make to the customer or third party.[4]
Such a declaration may well be insufficient to stave off liability for breach of
mandate, if the bank has refused to pay the cheques of an innocent customer.[5]
But if there is evidence available to the bank that the customer is indeed
engaged in using the account for laundering the proceeds of crime, the
declaration is likely to permit the bank to deploy that evidence without
committing the defence of tipping off.

Revocation of the bank's authority to pay cheques

The 1882 Act provides as follows for the revocation of the banker's   **21–62**
authority to pay cheques drawn on him by his customer:

**75. The duty and authority of a banker to pay a cheque drawn on him
by his customer are determined by—**

(1) Countermand of payment:
(2) Notice of the customer's death.

Before a cheque is paid the customer may countermand its payment, or   **21–63**
"stop" the cheque, by instructing the bank not to pay it. The bank is entitled
to satisfy itself that the countermand is authorised[6] and may have agreed with

---

[2] Section 93D of the Criminal Justice Act 1988.

[3] Part 25(1)(b) of the Civil Procedure Rules.

[4] *Governor and Company of the Bank of Scotland v. A Ltd, B & C* [2001] EWCA Civ 52;
[2001] 1 W.L.R. 751.

[5] Query whether the bank might have a defence if in refusing payment of the customer's
cheques it was following the instructions of the police who suspected money laundering and the
bank had no information that refuted the suspicion. It would seem unjust that a bank, acting in
accordance with its duties under section 93A, were to incur liability to its customer in such
circumstances.

[6] A countermand by telegram may justify a bank in postponing the honouring of a cheque
pending inquiry as to the authenticity of the telegram; if, by reason of its negligence, the bank
overlooks the telegram and so has no actual notice of such countermand and honours the cheque,
it may be liable for negligence: *Curtice v. London City and Midland Bank* [1908] 1 K.B. 293. In
the words of Cozens-Hardy M.R., at 298, "Countermand is really a matter of fact. . . . There is
no such thing as a constructive countermand in a commercial transaction of this kind."

the customer in advance the proper form by which countermand should be made.[7] The countermand must not be expressed in ambiguous terms; it must unequivocally refer to the particular cheque which is stopped.[8] The countermand must be given to the particular branch upon which the cheque is drawn.[9] There is no breach of duty where the bank pays a cheque in the ordinary course of business before receiving notice of countermand.[10] If a bank overlooks the fact that payment of a cheque has been countermanded, it cannot debit the customer's account but it may have the right to recover some or all of the payment from the recipient.[11]

21–64   By subsection (2) the bank's authority to pay cheques ceases upon notice of the customer's death. There must be actual notice of the death to the bank, or knowledge of it.[12] The bank-customer relationship, by contrast, is automatically terminated upon death, the balance of the account being then an asset belonging to the customer's estate and vesting his personal representatives.[13] If the account is held in joint names, the death of one customer may not terminate the contract and the survivor may be entitled to operate the account.[14]

Bank's closure of the customer's account

21–65   If the customer's account is overdrawn, the overdraft will generally be subject to repayment on demand at any time. Consequently the bank can, by making demand, terminate the overdraft and with it the customer's entitlement to issue further cheques. However, the bank may be required by its contract with the customer to meet cheques issued by the customer within the agreed overdraft facility and before demand was made.[15]

If the customer's account is in credit, the bank is in normal circumstances[16] obliged to afford the customer some advance notice of the closure of the account, so that the customer has a reasonable period during which to make alternative banking arrangements.[17]

---

[7] Paragraph 3.2 of The Banking Code (January 2001) states that the bank will provide the customer with information about stopping a cheque.

[8] *Westminster Bank v. Hilton* (1927) 136 L.T. 315, (HL), where the cheque was post-dated to a date subsequent to the date of the countermand, and a wrong number was specified in the countermand. The decision was applied in *Shapera v. Toronto Dominion Bank* (1970) 17 D.L.R. (3d) 122 and *Giordano v. Royal Bank of Canada* (1972) 29 D.L.R. (3d) 38.

[9] *Burnett v. Westminster Bank Ltd* [1966] 1 Q.B. 742, 760.

[10] In *Bains v. National Provincial Bank* (1927) 137 L.T. 631, the cheque was presented and paid shortly after the advertised time of closing, but before the bank actually closed.

[11] *Barclays Bank Ltd v. Simms* [1980] Q.B. 677.

[12] *Kendrick v. Dominion Bank* (1920) 47 O.L.R. 372.

[13] *Tarn v. Commercial Banking Co. of Sydney* (1884) 12 Q.B.D. 294.

[14] Paget (11th ed.), p. 171. As to partnership accounts see Paget pp. 143–144 and section 33 of the Partnership Act 1890: in the absence of agreement to the contrary, the death of any one partner dissolves the partnership, but the surviving partners have authority to bind the firm and continue its business so far as necessary for winding up its affairs.

[15] *Williams & Glyn's Bank v. Barnes* [1981] Com. L.R. 205.

[16] The bank may be entitled to take the immediate action of freezing the customer's account when it becomes aware of a winding-up or bankruptcy petition: see *Hollicourt (Contractors) Ltd v. Bank of Ireland* [2001] Lloyds Rep. Bank. 1, paragraph 7, citing with approval Paget (11th ed.) p. 207.

[17] *Joachimson v. Swiss Bank Corp.* [1921] 3 K.B. 110, 125 & 127; *Prosperity v. Lloyds Bank Ltd* (1923) 39 T.L.R. 372. Paget (11th ed.) p. 116.

Customer's insolvency[18]

As regards the compulsory liquidation of companies section 127 of the   **21–66**
Insolvency Act 1986 provides:

In a winding up by the court, any dispositions of the company's property . . . made after the commencement of the winding up, is unless the court otherwise orders, void.

By section 129 of the Insolvency Act 1986 the winding up is deemed to   **21–67**
commence at the time of presentation of the winding-up petition, or if a
voluntary resolution had previously been passed, from the time of that resolution.

Neither the presentation of the winding-up petition[19] nor the making of the
winding-up order invalidates the bank's mandate to honour cheques.[20] Before
the winding-up order is made the directors still have control of the company's
assets, save that dispositions are avoided under section 127. In those circumstances, there is an obvious risk that directors who continue to make payments
after presentation of a winding-up petition without having obtained a valida-
tion order under section 127 may be doing so erroneously and in breach of
their fiduciary duties to the company. Consequently, banks normally freeze the
company's accounts when they receive notice of the petition, a practice that
has been judicially described as normal and prudent.[21] After a winding-up
order is made, the company's assets fall under the control of liquidator for the
purposes of being distributed to the creditors.[22] At this stage it is most unlikely
that the company's bank account will, or should properly, continue to be
operated according to the pre-liquidation mandate. If the customer is dissolved
the bank-customer relationship ceases and the mandate ends.[23]

If the bank makes payment upon cheques after presentation of the petition,   **21–68**
those payments are not avoided by section 127 as between the bank and the
customer, but only as between the customer and the payee.[24]

In the case of the bankruptcy of individuals analogous but more elaborate   **21–69**
provisions under section 284 of the Insolvency Act 1986 apply:

**284(1) Where a person is adjudged bankrupt, any disposition of prop-
erty made by that person in the period to which this section applies is void**

---

[18] See also Chap. 34.

[19] *Hollicourt (Contractors) Ltd v. Bank of Ireland* [2001] Lloyds Rep. Bank 1, 12, CA. *Coutts & Co v. Stock* [2000] 1 W.L.R. 906, 910.

[20] *Re Loteka Pty Ltd* (1989) 15 A.C.L.C. 620.

[21] *Hollicourt (supra)*, para. 7, *per* Mummery L.J.

[22] Section 143(1) of the Insolvency Act 1986.

[23] *Re Russian Commercial and Industrial Bank* [1955] Ch. 148. But, if the company is subsequently restored to the register, the company is deemed to have continued in existence as if its name had not been struck off the register: section 653(3) of the Companies Act 1985. This would retrospectively validate payments made by the bank on behalf of the company during the period in which it was struck off.

[24] *Hollicourt (supra)*, approving *Coutts & Co v. Stock* [2000] 1 W.L.R. 906. The same applies to payments made by the bank by means of bankers draft issued at the customer's request: *Tasmanian Primary Distributors Pty Ltd v. RC and MB Steinhardt Pty Ltd* (1994) 13 A.C.S.R. 92.

except to the extent that it is or was made with the consent of the court, or is or was subsequently ratified by the court.

(2) Subsection (1) applies to a payment (whether in cash or otherwise) as it applies to a disposition of property and, accordingly, where any payment is void by virtue of that subsection, the person paid shall hold the sum paid for the bankrupt as part of his estate.

(3) This section applies to the period beginning with the day of the presentation of the petition for the bankruptcy order and ending with the vesting . . . of the bankrupt's estate in a trustee.

. . .

(5) Where after the commencement of his bankruptcy the bankrupt has incurred a debt to a banker or other person by reason of the making of a payment which is void under this section, that debt is deemed for the purposes of any of this Group of Parts to have been incurred before the commencement of the bankruptcy unless—

(a) the banker or person had notice of the bankruptcy before the debt was incurred, or

(b) it is not reasonably practicable for the amount of the payment to be recovered from the person to whom it was made.

. . .

21–70   Where an individual customer become bankrupt, it seems by analogy with section 127 that the bank will be entitled to pay cheques which are presented to it after the time of presentation of the bankruptcy petition but before the bankruptcy order and to debit the customer's account accordingly. However, if the bank continues to pay the bankrupt's cheques after the date of the order its position is vulnerable. If the cheques diminish a credit balance, that balance is likely to represent property vested in the customer's trustee in bankruptcy,[25] who may bring a claim against the bank in negligence[26] or on the basis that the bank is constructive trustee of the moneys paid away.[27] If the payments result in an overdraft, that debt will have been incurred after bankruptcy and the bank will not be entitled to prove in the bankruptcy in respect of the debt unless it can bring itself within subsection 284(5), above. This requires that the bank had not received notice of the bankruptcy order and that it is "reasonably practicable" to recover the relevant payment from the payee.

Court order

21–71   The duty of a bank to honour its customer's cheques also ceases on service of a garnishee order[28] or on the bank receiving notice that a freezing order has been made against the customer. However, the bank should have regard to the

---

[25] Sections 306 and 307 of the Insolvency Act 1986. However it is possible that the credit balance may consist of or contain after acquired property of the bankrupt that is not within the bankrupt estate.

[26] cf. *Lipkin Gorman v. Karpnale* [1989] 1 W.L.R. 1340, discussed above at para. 21–56.

[27] *Royal Brunei Airlines v. Tan* [1995] 2 A.C. 378.

[28] See *post*, para. 26–17.

precise terms of such orders, as they may be limited to an amount less than the credit balance on the account or in other ways.

Mental incapacity

The bank's authority to pay cheques also ceases on the bank's receiving **21–72** notice that his customer is mentally incapable of giving a mandate.[29]

PRESENTMENT OF CHEQUES FOR PAYMENT

A holder's right of recourse against the drawer of a cheque arises if, and **21–73** only if, the cheque is dishonoured by non-payment.[30] Dishonour by non-payment occurs when the cheque is duly presented for payment and payment is refused or cannot be obtained, or when presentment of the cheque is excused[31] and the cheque is unpaid.[32]

Place and manner of presentment

On account of the huge numbers of cheques which are issued in the United **21–74** Kingdom daily special arrangements exist for handling their presentation. Most cheques are handed in to banks by their payees for collection. Unless the customer has requested special collection,[33] the collecting bank then, acting as the agent of the payee, submits the cheque to the drawee bank through the clearing system.[34]

At present, this system operates a three-day clearing cycle. On day one of **21–75** the cycle the cheque is processed by the collecting bank, or its agent, and its details are recorded electronically and sent to the paying bank. On day two the cheque is delivered to an Exchange Centre, or clearing house, where the members hand over the cheques drawn on other banks and receive the cheques drawn on themselves. On day three the drawee banks decide whether to pay the cheques or return them unpaid. Any dishonoured cheques are returned by first class post direct to the collecting bank branch or in some cases to a central returns unit within the collecting bank. The same day the banks settle the net balances due between them by means of adjustments of their respective accounts at the Bank of England. Banks which are not themselves members of

---

[29] *Drew v. Nunn* (1879) 4 Q.B.D. 661; *Daily Telegraph Newspaper Co. v. McLaughlin* [1904] A.C. 776; *Bradford Old Bank v. Sutcliffe* (1918) 34 T.L.R. 229; *The Imperial Loan Co. Ltd v. Stone* [1892] 1 Q.B. 599. *cf. Yonge v. Toynbee* [1910] 1 K.B. 215.

[30] Section 47(2) of the 1882 Act. See *ante*, para. 12–22.

[31] Section 46(2) of the 1882 Act. See *ante*, para. 12–16.

[32] Section 47(1) of the 1882 Act.

[33] A special collection is normally handled by the collecting branch itself, which will take or send the cheque direct to the branch of the paying bank for payment. Thus presentation for payment is expedited.

[34] For a general description of the clearing system see the web site of APACS (the Association for Payment Clearing Services): www.apacs.org.uk. For a more detailed description see *Brindle & Cox on the Law of Bank Payments* (2nd ed.), p. 374 *et seq*; also *Barclays Bank plc v. Bank of England* [1985] 1 All E.R. 385.

the clearing system[35] utilise the services of member banks on an agency basis.

21–76   The precise stages of the clearing cycle at which the payee's account with his bank is credited, the funds so credited attract interest and those funds may be withdrawn differ from bank to bank and are matters upon which banks should provide information to their customers.[36]

21–77   If the cheque is drawn by a customer of one branch of a bank and handed in for collection at another branch, the cheque is handled internally by that bank, normally through its clearing department which will send the cheque to the paying branch. If the cheque is handed in for collection at the very branch upon which it is drawn, then the branch will normally deal with its payment internally by adjusting the accounts of its two customers.

21–78   In order to comply with the requirement for presentment the payee of a cheque, or his bank, may adopt one of two courses now sanctioned by the 1882 Act, as amended: physical presentment of the cheque itself, or truncated presentment by notification of information contained on the cheque.

Physical presentment

21–79   The majority of cheques are physically presented for payment, in which case the presentation is subject to section 52(4) of the 1882 Act:

52(4) Where the holder of a bill presents it for payment, he shall exhibit the bill to the person from whom he demands payment, and when a bill is paid the holder shall forthwith deliver it up to the party paying it.

The proper time for physical presentment is at a reasonable hour on a business day.[37]

21–80   The proper place for physical presentment of cheques is now governed by alternative provisions at sections 45(4) and 74A of the 1882 Act, as follows:

45(4) A bill is presented at the proper place–

where a place of payment is specified in the bill and the bill is there presented.

. . .

74A Where the banker on whom a cheque is drawn—

(a) has by notice published in the London, Edinburgh and Belfast Gazettes specified an address at which cheques drawn on him may be presented, and

---

[35] There are currently 12 members of the Cheque and Clearing Credit Company Limited, the company that controls the clearing.
[36] Paragraph 3.2 of the Banking Code (January 2001).
[37] See section 45(3) and para. 12–08 *ante*.

(b) has not by notice so published cancelled the specification of that address,

the cheque is also presented at the proper place if it is presented there.

Cheques issued in the United Kingdom tend to have printed upon them the **21–81** address and sort code of the branch of the drawee bank at which the drawer's account is held. Unless section 74A applies or truncated presentment under section 74B is used, it is to that branch that the cheque must be physically presented in accordance with section 45(4). The contractual duty of the bank is to repay to its customer the moneys standing to the credit of his account if demand is made at the branch where the account is held.[38] So, if a cheque is presented for payment at a branch other than that upon which it is drawn, the bank is entitled to refuse payment.[39] The fact that cheques are customarily exchanged between banks at a clearing house does not involve any waiver of the drawer's right, or the holder's duty, to have presentment made at the customer's branch of the drawee bank.[40]

The alternative under section 74A of presentment at a designated place of **21–82** payment published by the drawee bank in the Gazette was introduced in 1996.[41] It is intended to permit banks to handle the physical presentment and payment of cheques centrally. However, if a bank has published such an alternative place for presentment, it is still open to payees to present cheques at the branches upon which they are drawn.

Truncated presentment

In 1989 the Jack Committee recommended that provision be made for the **21–83** "truncation" of cheque presentation, such that notifying the drawee of the information on the cheque, as opposed to the physical presentment of cheque itself, should qualify as due presentment for payment. Such a system was proposed as an aid to efficiency.[42]

The recommendation was implemented in 1996,[43] when sections 74B and **21–84** 74C were inserted into the 1882 Act, providing as follows:

74B(1) A banker may present a cheque for payment to the banker on whom it is drawn by notifying him of its essential features by electronic means or otherwise, instead of by presenting the cheque itself.

(2) If a cheque is presented for payment under this section, present-ment need not be made at the proper place or at a reasonable hour on a business day.

---

[38] *R. v. Lovitt* [1912] A.C. 212, 218, 219; *Clare v. Dresdner Bank* [1915] 2 K.B. 576; *Joachimson v. Swiss Bank Corporation* [1921] 3 K.B. 110, 127 *Arab Bank Ltd v. Barclays Bank* (D.C.O.) [1954] A.C. 495.

[39] *Woodland v. Fear* 26 L.J.Q.B. 202; *Prince v. Oriental Bank* (1878) 3 App. Cas. 325.

[40] *Barclays Bank plc v. Bank of England* [1985] 1 All E.R. 385.

[41] Section 74A was inserted by the Deregulation (Bills of Exchange) Order 1996, S.I. 1996 No. 2993, art. 3.

[42] Banking Services Law and Practice—Report by the Review Committee (1989) Cm 622, paras 7.38–7.45.

[43] The Deregulation (Bills of Exchange) Order 1996, S.I. 1996 No. 2993.

(3) **If, before the close of business on the next business day following presentment of a cheque under this section, the banker on whom the cheque is drawn requests the banker by whom the cheque was presented to present the cheque itself—**

(a) **the presentment under this section shall be disregarded, and**

(b) **this section shall not apply in relation to the subsequent present-ment of the cheque.**

(4) **A request under subsection (3) above for the presentment of a cheque shall not constitute dishonour of the cheque by non-payment.**

(5) **Where presentment of a cheque is made under this section, the banker who presented the cheque and the banker on whom it is drawn shall be subject to the same duties in relation to the collection and payment of the cheque as if the cheque itself had been presented for payment.**

(6) **For the purposes of this section, the essential features of a cheque are—**

(a) **the serial number of the cheque,**

(b) **the code which identifies the banker on whom the cheque is drawn,**

(c) **the account number of the drawer of the cheque, and**

(d) **the amount of the cheque is [sic][44] entered by the drawer of the cheque.**

74C. Section 52(4) above—

(a) **so far as relating to presenting a bill for payment, shall not apply to presenting a cheque for payment under section 74B above, and**

(b) **so far as relating to a bill which is paid, shall not apply to a cheque which is paid following presentment under that section.**

21–85   The features of the truncation system, therefore, are that only "bankers" may present cheques this way. The collecting bank may notify the drawee bank of the four "essential features" of the cheque by electronic means or otherwise. As there are no prescribed limits to the mode of notification a cheque could be presented for payment otherwise than by the exchange of computerised data; for instance, by means of a telephone conversation between the collecting and payee banks. Nor is there any prescribed place or time at which truncated presentment must be made, save that it must be made to the banker on whom the cheque is drawn. Presumably, however, the person and office to which the truncated presentment is made must have the actual or ostensible authority of the drawee bank to receive truncated presentments. The drawee is entitled the next business day following truncated presentment to require physical presentment of the cheque, in which case the truncated

---

[44] Subsection (6)(d) contains a misprint: "is" must be read as "as".

presentment is disregarded. Finally, presentment by the truncated method does not otherwise affect the duties of the collecting and paying banks as regards the collection and payment of cheques.[45]

The discretion of the drawee bank as to whether to require physical **21–86** presentment following upon and in place of truncated presentment means that, in practice, the adoption of truncation is consensual, as between banks. Full truncation, whereby cheques are not given to the drawee at all but stored by the collecting bank, is not yet employed.

A point which may have to be resolved is the consequence of an error in the information supplied by the collecting bank to the drawee. If one or more of the four "essential features" specified in subsection 74B(6) is inaccurately notified to the drawee, it is doubtful whether any presentment has occurred within subsection 74B(1). On this view, such a defective presentment would be a nullity and the payee would have to present the cheque again in order to render the drawer liable.

Time within which a cheque must be presented

Cheques differ from other bills payable on demand in respect of the time **21–87** within which they must be presented in order to render the drawer liable. Whereas unreasonable delay in presentment will in itself discharge the drawer of a demand bill, the drawer of a cheque is not discharged by mere delay except as provided by the 1882 Act in the following provision:

74. Subject to the provisions[46] of this Act—

(1) Where a cheque is not presented for payment within a reasonable time of its issue, and the drawer or the person on whose account it is drawn had the right at the time of such presentment as between him and the banker to have the cheque paid and suffers actual damage through the delay, he is discharged to the extent of such damage, that is to say, to the extent to which such drawer or person is a creditor of such banker to a larger amount than he would have been had such cheque been paid.[47]

(2) In determining what is a reasonable time regard shall be had to the nature of the instrument, the usage of trade and of bankers, and the facts of the particular case.

(3) The holder of such cheque as to which such drawer or person is discharged shall be a creditor, in lieu of such drawer or person, of such

---

[45] See Chaps 22 and 23 *post*.

[46] Section 46 as to excuse for non-presentment or delay in presentment.

[47] Practically the same rule prevails in America, for by the Uniform Commercial Code, s.3–502, a cheque must be presented for payment within a reasonable time after its issue or the drawer will be discharged from liability thereon to the extent of the loss caused by the delay. The doctrine of reasonable time in reference to the presentment of bills, notes, or cheques is otherwise unknown; it is strictly confined to the former British Dominions and the United States. In all other countries a specific time-limit is imposed by law. The Geneva Convention provides, in Art. 29, that "A cheque payable in the country in which it was issued must be presented for payment within eight days" from "the date stated on the cheque as the date of issue". "A cheque issued in a country other than in which it is payable must be presented within a period of 20 days or of 70 days according as to whether the place of issue and the place of payment are situated respectively in the same continent or in different continents."

banker to the extent of such discharge, and entitled to recover the amount from him.

21–88   At common law, if the drawer suffered actual damage by the delay in presentment of a cheque he was discharged altogether.[48]

The section appears to limit the extent to which a drawer is discharged by late presentment of the cheque to the rare circumstance where the drawee bank enters insolvency during the period between the issue and presentment of the cheque, leaving the drawer a larger (unsatisfied) creditor of the bank than he would have been if the cheque had been presented and paid within a reasonable time.

21–89   The section places the drawer of a cheque in a less advantageous position than the drawer of other bills payable on demand, who is discharged altogether by late presentment. However, the section does not include the case of an indorser of a cheque, who is therefore not to be distinguished from the indorser of a bill. Under the provision of section 45 of the 1882 Act due presentment of a bill for payment must, unless specially excused, be made in order to render the drawer and indorsers liable.[49]

21–90   The section is badly drafted for if, "at the time of such presentment", the drawer had lost the right to have the cheque paid through the liquidation of the bank, or through the staleness of the cheque (see below), on a literal reading of the phrase those circumstances would defeat his claim. This would deprive the section of its effect in the very circumstances in which it is intended to operate. It is submitted that the phrase must be read as "at the time at which presentment ought reasonably to have been made".

21–91   By delay the holder takes the risk of the bank's failure, the revocation of the bank's authority to pay owing to the drawer's death, countermand of payment by the drawer or the exhaustion of the balance by further drawings. Thus, from the point of view of maximising his chance of obtaining payment from the drawee, it is to his advantage to make presentment promptly. There is authority from before the 1882 Act, moreover, that if a creditor takes from a debtor the cheque of a third party, the creditor must present such cheque within a reasonable time, otherwise the debtor may be discharged from all liability.[50] The effect of delayed presentment of a cheque upon the liability of a party other than the drawer appears to be beyond the ambit of section 74, so it is possible that the old rule continues to apply.

Out-of-date cheques

21–92   Banks refuse to pay cheques which are presented well beyond the date that they bear. The practice of banks may differ from bank to bank[51] but individual banks should advise their customers of how they deal with out-of-date

[48] *Laws v. Rand* (1857) 27 L.J.C.P. 76 and cases there cited; also *King and Boyd v. Porter* [1925] N.I. 107, CA.

[49] See *ante*, para. 12–03.

[50] *Hopkins v. Ware* (1869) L.R. 4 Ex. 268; *Sawyer v. Thomas* (1890) 18 O.A.R. 129.

[51] The Jack Committee found that most, if not all, banks specified six months as the reasonable time within which a cheque must be presented: Banking Services Law and Practice—Report by the Review Committee (1989) Cmd 622, para. 7.51.

cheques.[52] The bank's practice in this regard may thus be made a matter of contract between the bank and its customer, operating by way of a limit upon the customer's mandate.[53] Unless discharged under section 74 (above), the cheque remains valid despite its late presentment and enforceable subject only to its becoming statute-barred under the Limitation Act 1980.[54]

The negotiation of overdue cheques

In the extremely rare cases in which cheques are nowadays negotiated, the **21–93** indorsee will be at risk if the cheque is "overdue". An overdue cheque, like an overdue bill, can only be negotiated subject to defects of title.[55] Bills on demand other than cheques are rarely met with in this country, except in relation to documentary credits, so that the following subsection of the 1882 Act may be considered to apply mainly in practice to the case of cheques. It defines an overdue instrument as follows:

36.—(3) A bill payable on demand is deemed to be overdue within the meaning and for the purposes of this section, when it appears on the face of it to have been in circulation for an unreasonable length of time. What is an unreasonable length of time for this purpose is a question of fact.

The authorities previous to 1882 cannot be relied on so far as they suggest **21–94** that a cheque, taken after more than a reasonable time has elapsed since its issue, is not taken subject to equities, unless taken in such circumstances as ought to have excited suspicion. In *Down v. Hailing*,[56] it was said that an overdue cheque was like an overdue bill, and Holroyd J. remarked that the cheque in question, five days old, had been in circulation for more than a reasonable length of time, but the court declined to lay down a definite rule of law as to that constituted reasonable time. In *London and County Bank v. Groome*,[57] where the earlier authorities are reviewed, Field J. was of the opinion that the real question for the jury was whether a stale cheque was taken in such circumstances as ought to have excited suspicion, the lapse of time (in this case, eight days) being, although not conclusive, a circumstance to be taken into consideration in coming to a conclusion on that question.

---

[52] The Banking Code (January 2001), para. 3.2.

[53] If there is no express contract permitting the bank to refuse payment of out-of-date cheques, there might be a contract implied by custom of bankers, but the point is without decision: see Paget (11 Ed.), p. 334.

[54] See Chap. 29.

[55] Section 36(2) of the 1882 Act; see *ante*, para. 17–33. A cheque, which has been dishonoured on countermand of payment, is within s.36(2) and (5), and accordingly a holder with notice thereof takes no better title than his transferor (*Hornby v. McLaren* (1908) 24 T.L.R. 494); and see s.29.

[56] (1825) 4 B. & C. 330.

[57] (1881) 8 Q.B.D. 288; see also *Serrell v. Derbyshire Ry* (1850) 9 C.B. 811, and *Rothschild v. Corney* (1829) 9 B. & Co. 388; *Ex p. Hughes* (1880) 43 L.T. 577. The question of a reasonable time for presentment has been left to the jury entirely as one of fact (*Wheeler v. Young* (1897) 13 T.L.R. 468).

PAYEE'S RECOURSE AGAINST THE DRAWER

The right of recourse

21–95   The drawer of a cheque engages that on due presentment the cheque will be paid and that if it is dishonoured he will compensate the holder (who, these days, will almost invariably be the payee),[58] or any indorser who has been compelled to pay upon it, provided that any requisite proceedings on dishonour have been taken.[59] The holder's right of recourse against the drawer and indorsers accrues immediately the cheque is dishonoured by non-payment.[60]

Notice of dishonour

21–96   The drawer of a cheque is, in his capacity as the drawer of a bill,[61] entitled to notice of dishonour unless such notice is excused or waived[62] but notice will not be necessary where the dishonour is due to the insufficiency of funds in or closure of the customer's account,[63] or when payment has been countermanded.[64] These are by far the most common circumstances in which a cheque will be dishonoured. However, circumstances might arise in which notice of the dishonour of a cheque is not dispensed with, such as where the bank is unable to pay as a result of its insolvency.[65] Normally, the dishonoured cheque, after receipt by the collecting bank, is returned to the customer, except in the case where the collecting bank is itself relying on it[66] or notice of dishonour is not excused or waived.

A cheque need not be protested even though drawn outside the United Kingdom, unless the fact that it was so drawn appears upon its face.[67]

Identifying the drawer—printed cheque forms

21–97   Cheque books issued to customers by banks ordinarily have the name of the bank's customer printed on the face of each cheque. If the customer is thus identified as a partnership, the signature on the cheque of one partner is interpreted as a signature on behalf of the firm, rendering the other partners parties to the cheque.[68] Conversely, if the customer is identified in print as a

---

[58] See: "Cheques crossed and bearing the words 'account payee' " *ante* para. 21–35.

[59] Section 55(1) of the 1882 Act.

[60] Section 47(2) of the 1882 Act.

[61] See *ante*, para. 21–06.

[62] Section 50(2)(b) of the 1882 Act. *May v. Chidley* [1894] 1 Q.B. 451; *cf. Bradley v. Chamberlyne* [1893] 1 Q.B. 439.

[63] Section 50(2)(c)(4) of the 1882 Act.

[64] Section 50(2)(c)(5) of the 1882 Act; *Fradlin v. Reichman* [1917] T.P.D. 573.

[65] If there were a failure to give notice of dishonour in these circumstances, discharging the drawer's liability on the cheque, the payee would in most circumstances still be entitled to bring proceedings against the drawer on the underlying debt for which the cheque was given in payment.

[66] In this connection see *Westminster Bank Ltd v. Zang* [1966] A.C. 182.

[67] Cheques are prima facie "inland bills" within s.4 of the 1882 Act, see also *Grant v. Vaughan* (1764) 3 Burr. 1516, decided on 9 Will. 3. c. 17 repealed by the 1882 Act.

[68] *Ringham v. Hackett and Walmsley* (1980) 10 L.D.A.B. 206; (1980) 124 Sol J 221.

company, signature by an individual is taken as made on behalf of the company, so the individual incurs no liability.[69] If the name of the company is incorrectly stated, an officer who signs the cheque may incur personal liability upon it.[70]

Drawer's defences

The defences available to a drawer of a cheque when sued by the payee are **21–98** those that may arise between the immediate parties to other bills of exchange. These include absence or total failure of consideration,[71] defences giving rise to an entitlement as against the drawer to rescind the cheque (such as fraud, undue influence or mistake)[72] and invalidity of the cheque itself (such as forgery of the drawer's signature or unauthorised alteration).[73]

Cheque guarantee cards

Banks often issue to their customers cheque guarantee cards, which are **21–99** intended as an assurance to traders who receive cheques in payment for goods or services that the cheque, if within a stated amount, will not be dishonoured for lack of funds. If a cheque is met for the drawer under the provisions of the card, the bank honours its own undertaking as principal, and not guarantor, to the trader and debits its customer's account.[74] Conditions governing cheque guarantee cards vary and may be set out on the card or incorporated by reference. It has been held, on one set of such conditions, that even a fraudster had the ostensible authority of the bank to contract on the bank's behalf with traders, making the bank liable to the payee under its guarantee.[75] However, the outcome might be otherwise where different conditions apply.[76]

Cheque not an assignment

A cheque, like a bill, does not operate as an assignment in favour of the **21–100** payee (except in Scotland, whose law in this respect is in agreement with French law): section 53.[77] The holder, therefore, of an unpaid cheque has no equitable claim on the bank on which the cheque is drawn.[78]

---

[69] *Bondina Ltd v. Rollaway Shower Blinds Ltd* [1986] 1 W.L.R. 517.

[70] Section 349(4) of the Companies Act 1985, see para. 6–04, *ante*.

[71] See para. 19–41, *ante*.

[72] See paras 18–26 *et seq.*

[73] See Chap. 20.

[74] *Re Charge Card Services Ltd* [1987] 1 Ch. 150, 166. *First Sport Ltd v. Barclays Bank plc* [1993] 1 W.L.R. 1229.

[75] *First Sport v. Barclays Bank (supra)*.

[76] See Brindle & Cox, *The Law of Bank Payments* (2nd Ed.), pp. 162–169.

[77] See *ante*, para. 1–15; *Rowlatt v. Garment Manufacturing Co.* (1921) 49 O.L.R. 166.

[78] *Hopkinson v. Forster* (1874) L.R. 19 Eq. 74; *Shand v. Du Buisson* (1874) L.R. 18 Eq. 283; *Bank of Louisiana v. Bank of New Orleans* (1873) L.R. 6 H.L. 352; *Schroeder v. Central Bank* (1876) 34 L.T. 735. A banker's deposit receipt, though not transferable, still less negotiable, may be equitably assigned (*Re Griffin* [1899] 1 Chap. 408). There may, however, be an equitable assignment of the proceeds of a cheque after the latter has been duly paid (*West v. Newing* (1900) 82 L.T. 260).

Travellers cheques

21–101   Travellers cheques are instruments issued by banks and other companies in the United Kingdom, as elsewhere in the world, to enable the purchaser to obtain cash, goods or services in other jurisdictions. Although a variety of forms of travellers cheques exist, the mechanism for their issue and payment is common. The purchaser signs each travellers cheque at the time of purchase. Then, at the point at which the travellers cheque is to be cashed or spent, he countersigns it and delivers it to a third party from whom he obtains value for it. Once countersigned, the instrument can be used by that third party to obtain payment from the issuer and it may also be regarded as a matter of commercial usage as freely negotiable.[79]

21–102   As no obligation to pay upon a travellers cheque arises unless or until it is validly countersigned, the payment obligation is one that is conditional. The instrument therefore does not qualify as a bill of exchange,[80] nor as a true cheque.[81]

21–103   The obligations as between the purchaser and the issuer are generally governed by a contract on the issuer's standard terms which is signed by the purchaser at the time of acquiring the travellers cheques. For this reason it is hard to draw general rules as to the legal incidents of travellers cheques. The case law is sparse in this country[82] and comprises cases in which the purchasers of travellers cheques have brought claims against the vendor for reimbursement of the value of travellers cheques which were lost or stolen before they were countersigned.

21–104   In *Fellus v. National Westminster Bank*[83] the terms of the contract stipulated that a refund would be made "providing the cheques were signed but not countersigned and there has been no undue negligence". It was held that "undue negligence" meant "excessive carelessness". Judged by that standard, a purchaser of £8,000 worth of travellers cheques was entitled to a refund of cheques which were apparently taken from the pocket of his overcoat, which he took off and carried over his arm as he shopped in Oxford Street in London. Equally another purchaser of £10,000 worth of cheques was entitled to a refund notwithstanding that his travellers cheques were in a jacket which he removed and left on a chair in a clothes shop whilst he briefly tried on a new jacket.

21–105   By contrast in *Braithwaite v. Thomas Cook Travellers Cheques*[84] the conduct of the purchaser of £50,000 of travellers cheques which were lost or stolen before countersignature was held to fall short of an express contractual requirement that he had "properly safeguarded each cheque against loss or theft". The purchaser spent the day carrying around the travellers cheques in

---

[79] See *Chitty on Contracts*, (28th ed.), para. 34–174.
[80] Section 3(1) of the 1882 Act.
[81] Section 73 of the 1882 Act.
[82] See Chitty (28th ed.), paras 34–173 *et seq.* which refers to the American case law on the subject.
[83] (1983) 133 N.L.J. 766.
[84] [1989] 1 Q.B. 553.

a plastic bag also containing, visibly, a carton of cigarettes. During the day he socialised and drank alcohol. Finally, still carrying the plastic bag, he took an Underground train home and promptly fell asleep, at which point the bag containing the cigarettes and travellers cheques was stolen. Judged by the particular contractual standard that applied, the purchaser's conduct deprived him of any contractual claim to a refund.

However, it is conceivable that a claim in the tort of conversion[85] might have succeeded in respect of the £34,000 worth of travellers cheques which the defendant paid in spite of forged countersignatures which had been added to them. It is hard to see that anyone other than the purchaser could have been the true owner[86] of those travellers cheques, as, not being countersigned by him, they had yet to attain a negotiable character. It is equally difficult to justify the issuer's payment of travellers cheques which did not bear any true countersignature. In these circumstances, a plea of conversion (which may indeed have been advanced after trial)[87] might well have had some prospects. **21–106**

A claim in conversion was raised against the issuer by the purchaser of travellers cheques in *El Awadi v. Bank of Credit and Commerce International*.[88] The purchaser's cheques were stolen from his car, where he had carelessly left them. Later the cheques, bearing forged countersignatures, were paid by the issuer. Hutchison J regarded the purchaser's claim in conversion as one of some substance, such that he described it as "distinctly arguable", without deciding the case on the basis of that claim. Rather, the case was determined again on the grounds of the contract between the purchaser and issuer of the travellers cheques. **21–107**

In this case the contract contained no express reference to a requirement that the travellers cheques be safeguarded to any particular level; but it provided for the refund of lost or stolen cheques "subject to approval by the issuer". It was argued on behalf of the issuer that there was no contractual right to a refund, merely a discretion granted to the issuer as to whether to award one. However this was rejected both as a matter of contractual interpretation and, more importantly, as a matter of law. It was held that it is a legal incident of contracts for the issue of travellers cheques that the issuer takes on an obligation of some kind to refund the value of lost or stolen cheques. This term, imposed by law, is not cut down by any implied term precluding recovery by the purchaser where the loss of the travellers cheques results from a lack of care or from recklessness. **21–108**

Consequently, a right of refund for travellers cheques that are lost or stolen before being countersigned arises as a matter of legal implication out of the sale and purchase of the travellers cheques. The extent to which that right is modified by any requirement for the safeguarding of the instruments is a **21–109**

---

[85] See paras 22–22 *et seq. post.*
[86] See paras 22–27 *et seq. post.*
[87] In the final paragraph of the judgment, the Judge records that a new claim might yet be advanced in respect of the £34,000 worth of paid travellers cheques (at 561).
[88] [1990] 1 Q.B. 606.

matter that is governed by the particular express terms agreed upon their purchase. Similarly, it is submitted, it is a matter of contract to what extent the issuer limits or excludes its prima facie liability to the purchaser in conversion where it pays travellers cheques that do not bear the true countersignature of the purchaser.

CHAPTER 22

THE CHEQUE—II

THE PAYING BANK'S LIABILITIES FOR BREACH OF MANDATE AND CONVERSION

A PAYING bank acts as its customer's agent. It is obvious that, the cheque **22–01** being the customer's authority or mandate to the bank to make payment on his behalf, the drawee bank is bound to act within the terms of that mandate and entitled to make sure that the signature to the cheque is that of its customer, the drawer. In addition, a cheque constitutes an item of personal property and the owner of the cheque is entitled to have the cheque dealt with by others, including the paying bank, in a manner that does not interfere with the owner's rights.

Accordingly, the drawee bank, in paying, runs two particular risks, that of **22–02** non-compliance with the mandate given to it by the drawer and, if the cheque has fallen into the wrong hands, the risk of conversion,[1] by which the bank may incur liability to the true owner of the cheque. Against these the bank has statutory protection which it may successfully plead only if it complies with certain conditions. The protection and the conditions are to be found in section 19 of the Stamp Act 1853, sections 60 and 80 of the 1882 Act and section 1 of the Cheques Act 1957.

The paying bank is exposed to liabilities other than for breach of mandate **22–03** and conversion. Other sources of civil and criminal liability on the part of paying banks are discussed in the preceding Chapter in the section "Drawer's Right to Have His Cheques Paid".[2]

Payment outside the mandate

There are many circumstances in which a bank may pay a cheque without **22–04** its customer's authority. It may be that the particular cheque has been counter-manded or that the bank's authority has been terminated by the customer's death or incapacity. These situations are discussed in the last Chapter. In these, as in other circumstances in which payment is made outside the mandate, the bank is not entitled to debit its customer's account with the amount of the cheque; and, if it does so, the customer may bring an action for the account to be re-credited.

A bank may, of course, also contravene the mandate by paying a cheque, or **22–05** purported cheque, that has not been signed by or on behalf of the customer, as where the customer's signature is a forgery.

---

[1] See paras 22–22 *et seq.*
[2] See paras 21–48 *et seq.*

22–06   In the case of joint accounts where the mandate requires cheques to be signed by both account-holders, if one signatory forges the signature of the other causing the bank to pay cheques in breach of the mandate, the innocent signatory has an independent cause of action for the damage he has suffered.[3]

Fraudulent alteration of the amount

22–07   A bank's mandate is to pay the true amount of a cheque and not some greater sum that may be entered without the customer's authority. If the sum for which the customer drew the cheque is fraudulently altered and increased, and the bank pays the larger sum, it will not generally be able to charge the customer with the raised amount but will have to bear the loss.[4] It is not clear whether in such circumstances the bank's authority to pay survives the alteration of the cheque to the extent that the bank remains entitled to debit the original amount of the cheque.[5] On the one hand, the unauthorised increase in the amount of the cheque constitutes a material alteration which, by section 64 of the 1882 Act, has the effect of avoiding the cheque. On the other hand, notwithstanding that the actual payment is without mandate, the bank should be able to rely upon the fact that the customer has in fact authorised part of the payment.[6] It is also possible that the payment will have discharged a debt in the original amount of the cheque owed by the customer to the payee, giving the bank an answer to that extent.[7]

Circumstances exonerating a bank that pays in breach of mandate

22–08   The law recognises certain situations in which the bank may be entitled to debit the customer's account, notwithstanding that the cheque has been materially altered, or has been paid contrary to the mandate. Thus the bank may be entitled to debit the customer's account if the customer has been negligent in the manner in which he has drawn the cheque, so as to facilitate its fraudulent alteration; or where the customer was aware of the forgery of his cheques, but failed to inform the bank; or where, although paid contrary to the terms of the mandate, a cheque was issued with the customer's actual authority; or where a cheque paid in breach of mandate discharges a debt owed by the customer to the payee of the cheque. These situations are discussed below.

---

[3] *Catlin v. Cyrus Finance Corporation* [1983] Q.B. 759. An earlier contrary decision in *Brewer v. Westminster Bank Ltd* [1952] 2 All E.R. 650, was not followed in *Catlin*'s case and is regarded as having been wrongly decided: see Paget, 11th ed., pp. 169–170.

[4] *Hall v. Fuller* (1826) 5 B. & C. 750; but see *London Joint Stock Bank v. Macmillan* [1918] A.C. 777, 825, 826 (Lord Shaw) where it is suggested that fraudulent alteration by the customer's employee or agent might, even in the absence of any negligence on the part of the customer, be the responsibility of the customer.

[5] The Privy Council in *Imperial Bank of Canada v. Bank of Hamilton* [1903] A.C. 49 treated the cheque in its original form as subsisting, the nullity applying only to the "cheque" in its raised amount. See Paget (11th ed.), pp. 377–378.

[6] See, by analogy, *London Intercontinental Trust Ltd v. Barclays Bank Ltd* [1980] 1 Lloyd's Rep. 241.

[7] *Liggett (Liverpool) Ltd v. Barclays Bank Ltd* [1928] 1 K.B. 48, discussed further below at paras 22–17 *et seq.*

Negligence by the customer in drawing the cheque

It is the duty of the customer in drawing a cheque to take usual and **22–09** reasonable precautions to prevent forgery, and if, owing to neglect of this duty, forgery takes place, the customer may be liable for the loss.[8] In *Young v. Grote*[9] the plaintiff was a customer of the defendant bankers, and on leaving home entrusted to his wife several blank forms of cheques signed by himself desiring her to have them filled up according to the exigencies of his business. Mrs Young subsequently, for the purpose of the business, required the sum of £50 2s. 3d., and she delivered one of the cheques so signed by her husband, the plaintiff, to a clerk of the plaintiff's, and asked him to fill it up with such sum. The clerk accordingly filled it up with that sum and showed the cheque so filled up to Mrs Young, who told him to get it cashed. As filled up by the clerk the word "fifty" in the body of the cheque began with a small letter in the middle of the line; at the bottom of the draft the figures £50 2s. 3d. were inserted but were placed at a considerable distance to the right of the printed "£". After showing the cheque so filled up to Mrs Young, and before presenting it for payment, the clerk inserted the words "three hundred and" before the words "fifty" and the figure "3" between the printed "£" and the figures "50 2s. 3d.", so that it then appeared to be a cheque for £350 2s. 3d. It was presented and the defendant bankers paid it. The Court held that gross negligence was to be imputed to the plaintiff or his agent, and that the bankers who had been misled by his lack of caution and thus induced to pay the money were not liable to be called upon to make good the loss.

The Court based its decision upon negligence[10] but difficulty was caused by **22–10** speculations in later cases as to what underlay or was supposed to underlie this decision.[11] As a result of these speculations *Young v. Grote* came to be regarded as of doubtful authority, and in the Privy Council decision of *Colonial Bank of Australia v. Marshall*[12] was treated as no longer law. However, the authority of the case was fully re-established by the unanimous decision of the House of Lords in the case of *London Joint Stock Bank v. Macmillan*,[13] where it was held, confirming the view expressed in the seventeenth edition of this book, that the decision in *Young v. Grote* was sound in principle.

In the case of *London Joint Stock Bank v. Macmillan* the respondents' firm, **22–11** which had an account at the appellant bank, entrusted to a clerk the duty of filling in the cheques for signature. The clerk presented to one of the partners of the firm for signature a cheque drawn in favour of the firm or bearer. There

---

[8] *London Joint Stock Bank v. Macmillan* [1918] A.C. 777 at 789, 793 (Lord Finlay C.). See also the reference to this case in the speech of Lord Scarman in *Tai Hing Cotton Mill Ltd v. Liu Chang Hing Bank Ltd* [1986] A.C. 80, 96.

[9] (1827) 4 Bing. 253; see also *ibid.* 12 Moo.P.C. 484.

[10] (1827) 4 Bing. 253, 259, 260, 261.

[11] *Schofield v. Londesborough* [1896] A.C. 514, 523 (Lord Haisbury C.); 536 (Lord Watson) 545 (Lord Macnaghten); *Robarts v. Tucker* (1851) 16 Q.B. 560, 580 (Parke B.); *Union Credit Bank v. Mersey Docks Board* [1899] 2 Q.B. 205, 211 (Bigham J.).

[12] [1906] A.C. 559.

[13] [1918] A.C. 777; see also *Trull v. Standard Bank of South Africa* (1892) 4 S.A.R. 203, 205. In *Standard Bank of South Africa v. Kaplan* (1922) C.P.D. 214, 223, Gardiner J.P. said: "The same [*Macmillan*] decision would doubtless have been come to under our law."

was no sum in words written in the space provided for the writing, and there were the figures "2.0.0" in the space intended for figures. The partner signed the cheque. The clerk subsequently added the words "one hundred and twenty pounds" in the space left for words and wrote the figures "1" and "0" respectively on each side of the figure "2", which was so placed as to leave room for the interpolation of the added figures. The clerk presented the cheque for payment and obtained £120 out of the firm's account. It was held by the House of Lords that the bank was entitled to debit the firm's account with the full amount of the cheque.

22–12   The facts differed somewhat from those in *Young v. Grote*, since in *Macmillan's* case the space for the amount in words was left entirely blank when the partner signed the cheque. As was pointed out,[14] this made the case a more favourable one from the bank's point of view than *Young v. Grote*. Lord Finlay stated that the question whether there was negligence as between banker and customer is a question of fact in each particular case, and can be decided only on a view of the cheque as issued by the drawer with the help of any evidence available as to the course of dealings between the parties or otherwise. If the existence in a cheque of blank spaces of an unusual nature and such as to facilitate interpolation is declared to be no evidence of a breach of a duty as between customer and banker, the duty would have little left to operate upon. Lord Shaw pointed out that not a word was said in *Young v. Grote* about estoppel, and that it would be safest indeed to put that decision on the ground on which the judges who tried the case themselves put it, namely, that of negligence.[15]

22–13   The contrary decision of the Privy Council in the case of *Colonial Bank of Australia* appears to have had no binding authority outside Australia[16] and in 1981 was repudiated even there when the High Court of Australia in *Commonwealth Trading Bank of Australia v. Sydney Wide Stores Pty Ltd*[17] preferred the *Macmillan* decision over the *Colonial Bank* decision.

22–14   The customer's duty to take precautions to prevent forgery does not extend to alterations in the cheque which are of an unusual nature and which cannot reasonably be anticipated, such as, for example, an addition to the description of the payee, whereby the form of indorsement is affected.[18]

Customer remains silent after learning of forgery

22–15   In *Greenwood v. Martin's Bank*,[19] the House of Lords held that where a customer was aware that his account was habitually operated by his wife's issuing cheques upon which the customer's signature was forged, the customer owed a duty promptly to bring that fact to the attention of the bank. As, on the facts, the customer's failure to do so had resulted in the bank losing its right to claim against the wife, the customer became estopped from asserting

[14] *ibid.* at 822 (Lord Haldane).
[15] *ibid.* at p. 827.
[16] *Varker v. Commercial Banking Company of Sydney Ltd* [1972] 2 N.S.W.L.R. 967
[17] [1981] 148 C.L.R. 304
[18] *Slingsby v. District Bank Ltd* [1932] 1 K.B. 544; approved in *Mercantile Bank of India v. Central Bank of India* [1938] A.C. 287, 301.
[19] [1933] A.C. 51.

that his signature had been forged. There is thus a duty on account-holders to draw to the attention of their bank instances of forgery of which they become aware, failing which the account-holder is at risk of becoming estopped from subsequently disowning forged cheques that are paid and debited to the account.[20] This duty does not, however, extend so far as to require a customer to check his account statements or to make such investigations as might with reasonable care have been undertaken and would have revealed to him the fact of the forgery.[21]

Cheque issued with customer's actual authority

In *London Intercontinental Trust Ltd v. Barclays Bank Ltd*[22] the mandate **22–16** required that the plaintiff's cheques be signed by two signatories. In breach of that mandate the bank paid a cheque bearing only one signature. However, it was held that the signatory had been authorised by the customer's board of directors to order the relevant transfer of funds. Thus, notwithstanding the breach of mandate, the payment was made with the customer's actual authority and the bank was entitled to debit the account.

Payments which discharge the customer's debts

It sometimes happens that a bank pays cheques drawn outside the mandate **22–17** to payees who are creditors of the bank's customer. In such situations a question arises as to whether the re-crediting of the customer's account with the amount of such payments would be inequitable, producing a windfall for the customer, whereby the customer has its debts paid at no cost to itself.

In *A.L. Underwood Ltd v. Bank of Liverpool and Martins*[23] the bank was **22–18** held liable for conversion of a company's cheques. However, in relation to the amount of damages payable by the bank to the company the Court of Appeal ordered an inquiry into whether the proceeds of the converted cheques were used to discharge liabilities of the company, and if so under what circumstances. The rationale of the inquiry was clearly that it was possible that such payments may have reduced the damage suffered by the company and Scrutton L.J. made reference to "the equitable doctrines under which a person who had in fact paid the debts of another without authority was allowed the advantage of his payment".[24]

It was held in *B. Liggett (Liverpool) Ltd v. Barclays Bank Ltd*[25] that the **22–19** same equity could relieve a paying bank against the consequences of its having paid cheques drawn outside the mandate to trade creditors of its customer. In that case Wright J. did not regard the absence of authority from the customer to make the payments as presenting an obstacle to operation of

---

[20] In relation to estoppel in cases of forgery see *ante* para. 20–38.
[21] *Tai Hing Cotton Mill Ltd v. Liu Chong Hing Bank Ltd* [1986] A.C. 80, PC; *Price Meats Ltd v. Barclays Bank plc* [2000] 2 All E.R. (Comm.) 346; *Patel v. Standard Chartered Bank* (unreported, April 6, 2001) Toulson J.
[22] [1980] 1 Lloyd's Rep. 241.
[23] [1924] 1 K.B. 775, CA.
[24] *ibid.* at 794.
[25] [1928] 1 K.B. 48.

the principle. The decision has been criticised on the basis that it is irreconcilable with prior and subsequent authority that a person who confers an
unsought benefit on another does not thereby entitle himself to an equitable
right of recoupment.[26]

22–20   The apparent flaw in the reasoning of Wright J. in *Liggett's* case is an
assumption that an unauthorised payment by the bank is capable of discharging its customer's debt to the payee. Only if the payment is authorised or
ratified by the customer is the customer's debt thereby discharged.[27] As
discussed above, it is sometimes possible to show that a payment made in
breach of mandate was nonetheless authorised by the customer. Similarly,
where a customer can be shown to have taken the benefit of an unauthorised
payment, for instance by treating the payment in its books as having discharged a trade debt, then the bank is likely to have a case of ratification.

22–21   It has also been observed that there will be circumstances in which a court
may intervene to prevent unjust enrichment either by the customer in having
his money from the bank as well as having the claim against the customer met,
or by the creditor who has double payment of the debt.[28] In the absence of any
of these circumstances, however, the fact that the payments made by a bank
in breach of mandate went to creditors of the account-holder affords the bank
no particular defence to a claim for the account to be re-credited with the
amount of the payments.

Conversion

22–22   Claims in conversion may be brought against paying banks and collecting
banks alike. So the principles discussed hereafter are relevant to the liability
of both. Their statutory protections against such claims, however, are different; those given to the paying bank being discussed in this Chapter, and those
given to the collecting bank in the next Chapter.

22–23   Conversion is a tort of strict liability. It occurs where one person assumes
and exercises dominion over a chattel inconsistent with the title of the true
owner.[29] Any voluntary act in relation to goods which is a usurpation of the
owner's proprietary or possessory rights is a conversion and it matters not that
the doer of the act of usurpation did not know and could not by the exercise
of reasonable care have known of the owner's interest in the chattel.[30]

22–24   A cheque, being a piece of paper, constitutes an item of personal property
that may be converted. So the "true owner" of the cheque is entitled to bring
a claim in conversion against parties who deal inconsistently with his rights of
ownership and possession. The usual measure of damages in any claim for

---

[26] Goff & Jones on the *Law of Restitution* (1998, 5th ed.), p. 156; see *Falcke v. Scottish Imperial Insurance Co.* (1886) 34 Ch.D. 234 and *Re Cleadon Trust Ltd* [1939] Ch. 286.

[27] *Crantrave v. Lloyds Bank* [2000] 3 W.L.R. 877, 882, CA citing Goff & Jones, *op. cit.* (5th ed.), p. 17. See also *Lloyds Bank plc v. Independent Insurance Co. Ltd* [2000] Q.B. 110, CA.

[28] *Crantrave* (*supra*), at 883.

[29] *Hollins v. Fowler* (1875) L.R. 7 H.L. 757, 782 *per* Brett J.

[30] *Marfani & Co. Ltd v. Midland Bank Ltd* [1968] 1 W.L.R. 956 at 970–971 *per* Diplock L.J.

conversion is the value of the property at the time of the conversion.[31] By a well-established legal fiction the value of a valid cheque, at any rate where the drawer has sufficient funds to his credit and the drawee bank is solvent, is taken to be the face value of the cheque.[32] It is no defence to a claim in conversion that the claimant would have suffered the same loss irrespective of the conversion;[33] nor that the claimant possesses valuable claims against others also guilty of conversion whom the claimant has chosen not to pursue.[34]

In cases where the cheque has been subject to an unauthorised material **22–25** alteration, however, the measure of damages is not the face value. In those circumstances, the cheque is void under section 64(1) of the 1882 Act and, although the matter has previously been in doubt, it is now established that the legal fiction has no application; such a "cheque", once altered becomes a worthless piece of paper, with no validity thereafter as an instrument, and no party can bring an action for damages in conversion for its face value because it no longer represents a chose in action for that amount.[35]

It is clear that a paying bank which pays a cheque to a person who is not **22–26** its true owner may incur liability in conversion. The cause of action has, for instance, received statutory recognition in section 79 of the 1882 Act, which provides for the liability of a bank to the true owner of a cheque, if the bank pays it inconsistently with the crossing.[36] Where a cheque which has been stolen is wrongfully presented for payment and paid, the source of the paying bank's liability in conversion is generally not the destruction of the value of the cheque: as has been pointed out, the cheque, if paid otherwise than to a holder is not discharged.[37] Rather, the paying bank commits acts of conversion by simply receiving, possessing and dealing with the cheque in circumstances which would not be countenanced by its true owner and hence are inconsistent with his rights of ownership and possession.

"True owner"

The person entitled to bring a claim for conversion of a cheque is the person **22–27** who is entitled to immediate possession of it.[38] That person is described both in the 1882 Act[39] and the Cheques Act 1957[40] as its "true owner". Neither Act

---

[31] *Lancashire and Yorkshire Rly Co. v. MacNicoll* (1918) 88 L.J.K.B. 601, 607; *Solloway v. McLaughlin* [1938] A.C. 247, 257–258; *Kuwait Airways v. Iraqi Airways (No. 3)* [2001] 1 All E.R. (Comm.) 557.

[32] *Morison v. London County and Westminster Bank Ltd* [1914] 3 K.B. 356, 379 *per* Phillimore L.J.; *Lloyds Bank Ltd v. Chartered Bank of India, Australia and China* [1929] 1 K.B. 40, 55–56 *per* Scrutton L.J.

[33] *Kuwait Airways v. Iraqi Airways (No. 3)* [2001] 1 All E.R. (Comm.) 557, CA.

[34] *International Factors v. Rodriguez* [1979] Q.B. 351, CA.

[35] *Smith v Lloyds TSB Group plc* [2000] 3 W.L.R. 1725, CA.

[36] See para. 22–39.

[37] Ellinger & Lomnicka on the *Modern Law of Banking* (1994, 2nd ed.), pp. 360–365; by section 59 of the 1882 Act a bill is discharged only upon payment in due course.

[38] *Marquess of Bute v. Barclays Bank Ltd* [1955] 1 Q.B. 202.

[39] Sections 79(2) and 80.

[40] Section 4.

defines that term, which is somewhat inapposite, as it does not fully reflect the importance of the immediate right to possession.[41]

22–28 A person who is not a party to a cheque can nonetheless be its true owner and entitled to sue for its conversion if, as against one of the parties, he has an immediate right to possession of it.[42] Where the instrument was made payable to a one-time agent by name only, but the description of the payee bore an indication as to the principal, it was held that the principal and not the agent was the true owner.[43]

22–29 The true owner of the cheque will ordinarily be the person who is entitled to the money represented by it or paid under it.[44]

In cases of misappropriation, the identity of the true owner depends upon whether the cheque has been delivered by the drawer to the payee. So if a cheque is stolen from a drawer, title remains in the drawer, who is its true owner.[45] And the payee of a cheque is the true owner once it is delivered to him either actually or constructively (as where the delivery is made to his agent).[46] But where a cheque is stolen in the course of transmission from drawer to payee a difficulty can arise. The authorities are unclear as to whether a cheque which is sent by post is delivered when it is posted or when it is received.[47] If it is uncertain whether a cheque was misappropriated whilst in the hands of the drawer or the payee, by section 21(3) of the 1882 Act the payee will unless the contrary be proved be presumed to have received a valid and unconditional delivery of the cheque, and hence be its true owner.[48]

22–30 If a cheque form has been obtained and filled in fraudulently by an agent of the account-holder, and there is no one with a better title, the account-holder is the true owner.[49] Different questions arise where the drawer intends that the cheque should be issued but has been induced by a fraud to issue it. In such cases the true owner may, depending upon the circumstances, be either the drawer or the payee.

22–31 The cases suggest that two principles come into play: first that if the drawer intends and authorises delivery of a cheque or draft to the payee, and this occurs, that may constitute a good delivery and confer title on the payee. Thus where drawers handed over bank drafts for the purpose of delivery to the payees of the drafts and the drafts were received and paid by the payee, a

---

[41] *Marquess of Bute v. Barclays Bank Ltd* [1955] 1 Q.B. 202, 211.

[42] *International Factors Ltd. v. Rodriguez* [1979] Q.B. 351.

[43] *Marquess of Bute v. Barclays Bank Ltd* [1955] 1 Q.B. 202.

[44] *Great Western Railway v. London & County Banking Co.* [1901] A.C. 414 at 418 *per* Lord Halsbury; *Morison v. London County and Westminster Bank Ltd* [1914] 3 K.B. 356 at 375 *per* Buckley L.J.

[45] *Akrokerri (Atlantic) Mines Ltd v. Economic Bank* [1904] 2 K.B. 465; *Lloyds Bank v. E.B. Savory & Co.* [1933] A.C. 201. *Marfani & Co. v. Midland Bank Ltd* [1968] 1 W.L.R. 956.

[46] *e.g.* see section 80 of the 1882 Act, which carries the implication that a drawer can no longer be the true owner of a crossed cheque once it has "come into the hands" of the payee.

[47] *Deveze, Re ex parte Cote* (1873) L.R. 9 Ch. App. 27, CA; *Kleinwort Sons & Co. v. Comptoir Escompté de Paris* [1894] 2 Q.B. 157. See also *Warwicke v. Noakes* (1791) Peake 68; *Norman v. Ricketts* (1886) 3 T.L.R. 182; *Thairlwall v Great Northern Railway* [1910] 2 K.B. 509; *Chitty on Contracts* (1999, 28th ed.) 22–056.

[48] *Surrey Asset Finance Ltd v. National Westminster Bank plc, The Times* November 30, 2000 (permission to appeal refused [2001] EWCA Civ 60, unreported January 24, 2001).

[49] *Morison v. London County and Westminster Bank Ltd* [1914] 3 K.B. 356; *Midland Bank v. Reckitt* [1933] A.C. 1.

presumption arose that the delivery to the payee was made with the authority of the drawers, notwithstanding that the drafts had been issued as a result of the fraudulent misrepresentations of third parties.[50] The second principle which applies is that a cheque which is given under a subsisting contract, even if voidable, gives a title to the cheque, at least until the contract is rescinded by the drawer. So, the drawer of a cheque which issued in settlement of a contract which he has been induced to enter by the fraud of a payee will not be its true owner if at the time that the cheque is collected and paid he remains unaware of the fraud and has not rescinded his contract with the fraudster.[51] However, if the fraud is such that the cheque is issued without even a voidable contract coming into existence, then the drawer remains its true owner.[52]

A person who obtains a bankers' draft assumes the risk of its misappropria- **22–32** tion as if he had obtained bank notes which were stolen from him.[53] But a principal whose agent dishonestly and without authority procures the issue of bankers' drafts payable to third parties has no title to the drafts.[54]

Paying bank's statutory protections

There are a number of statutory provisions affording protection to paying **22–33** banks which pay cheques and other instruments to persons other than their true owners. There is some overlap between these provisions, whose inter-relationship is not in every respect clear.[55] In summary, these fall into two categories, as follows:

(a) Protection afforded to banks paying crossed instruments

Section 80 of the 1882 Act[56]—this protects a bank and the drawer where the bank pays a crossed cheque in good faith and without negligence to another bank. Protection under this section is also extended, by virtue of section 5 of the Cheques Act 1957, to certain instruments other than cheques.

(b) Protection afforded to banks paying instruments in disregard of indorsements

(i) Section 19 of the Stamp Act 1853[57]—this section provides a protection **22–34** in the case of banks paying wrongfully indorsed drafts or orders, as opposed to bills or cheques, drawn upon a banker and payable to order on demand.

---

[50] *Midland Bank v. Brown Shipley* [1991] 1 Lloyd's Rep. 576; see also *Marquess of Bute v. Barclays Bank Ltd* [1955] 1 Q.B. 202, 212; *Lipkin Gorman v. Karpnale Ltd* [1991] 2 A.C. 240.

[51] *Tate v. Wilts and Dorset Bank Ltd* (1899) 1 L.D.A.B. 286.

[52] *Australian Guarantee Corporation Ltd v. Commissioners of the State Bank of Victoria* [1989] V.R. 617; see also *Great Western Railway Co. v. London & County Banking Co.* [1901] A.C. 414.

[53] *Smith v. Lloyds TSB Group plc* [2000] 3 W.L.R. 1725, 1737–1738 *per* Pill L.J.

[54] *Union Bank of Australia Ltd v. McClintock* [1922] 1 A.C. 240; *Commercial Banking Co. of Sydney v. Mann* [1961] A.C. 1.

[55] See Roy Goode, *Commercial Law* (1995, 2nd ed.), p. 611.

[56] *Post*, para. 22–35.

[57] *Post*, para. 22–45.

(ii) Section 60 of the 1882 Act[58]—this section provides protection in relation to the payment of wrongfully indorsed bills drawn on a bank payable to order on demand. Few cheques are nowadays issued to order, so the section has limited application.

(iii) Section 1 of the Cheques Act 1957[59]—this section permits a bank paying a cheque, bankers' draft or documentary payment instruction in good faith and in the ordinary course of business not to have regard to indorsements on it or to the absence of any such indorsements.

Section 80 of the 1882 Act—crossed cheques

22–35   Most cheques issued in the United Kingdom these days are crossed. The nature and effects of crossings are discussed in Chapter 21.[60] The crossing of a cheque has the effect of protecting the banker on whom the cheque is drawn, provided that payment is made strictly in accordance with the crossing, as provided by section 80 of the 1882 Act:

80. Where the banker, on whom a crossed cheque is drawn, in good faith and without negligence pays it, if crossed generally, to a banker, and if crossed specially, to the banker to whom it is crossed, or his agent for collection being a banker, the banker paying the cheque, and, if the cheque has come into the hands of the payee, the drawer, shall respectively be entitled to the same rights and be placed in the same position as if payment of the cheque had been made to the true owner thereof.

22–36   The payment must be made without negligence[61] and to a banker, or to the particular banker (or his agent, also being a banker) specified in in the crossing. If both the holder of a crossed cheque and its drawer are customers of the same bank and the holder hands in the cheque for collection into his account, the bank complies with the crossing by debiting the drawer's account and crediting the holder's account. In that situation the bank is regarded as having made payment to a banker, namely to itself.[62] The banker is not protected if the body of the cheque, as opposed to the crossing, has been materially altered. For in that situation the instrument is not a "cheque" at all, but a nullity and a mere worthless piece of paper and the bank cannot debit the drawer's account with its amount.[63] On the other hand, the bank does not by paying such a materially altered cheque convert anything of value such as to make it liable to a true owner other than the drawer.[64]

22–37   If the cheque has come into the hands of the payee and is paid in accordance with the crossing, section 80 also provides for the exoneration of the drawer,

---

[58] *Post*, para. 22–47.
[59] *Post*, para. 22–51.
[60] *Ante*, paras 21–26 *et seq.*
[61] *Slingsby v. District Bank* [1932] 1 K.B. 544.
[62] *Gordon v. London City and Midland Bank Ltd* [1902] 1 K.B. 242, CA, 274–275 (this point was not considered on appeal [1903] A.C. 240); *Carpenter's Co. v. British Mutual Banking Co.* [1938] 1 K.B. 511, 538 *per* MacKinnon L.J.
[63] *Slingsby v. District Bank* [1932] 1 K.B. 544.
[64] *Smith v. Lloyds TSB Group plc* [2000] 3 W.L.R. 1725.

who is placed in the same position as if payment had been made to the true owner, who will generally be the payee.

Where section 80 operates, the paying bank and drawer are "placed in the **22–38** same position as if payment of the cheque had been made to the true owner". Hence the paying bank is both relieved of any liability in conversion which would otherwise arise from its acts in paying the cheque, and it is also entitled to debit the drawer's account with the amount paid in the usual way.

Section 80 applies to crossed cheques, as to which section 79 provides as **22–39** follows:

79.—(1) Where a cheque is crossed specially to more than one banker, except when crossed to an agent for collection being a banker, the banker on whom it is drawn shall refuse payment thereof.

(2) Where the banker on whom the cheque is drawn which is so crossed nevertheless pays the same, or pays a cheque generally otherwise than to a banker, or if crossed specially otherwise than to the banker to whom it is crossed, or his agent for collection being a banker, he is liable to the true owner of the cheque for any loss he may sustain owing to the cheque having been so paid.

Provided that where a cheque is presented for payment which does not at the time of presentment appear to be crossed, or to have had a crossing which has been obliterated, or to have been added to or altered otherwise than as authorised by this Act, the banker paying the cheque in good faith and without negligence shall not be responsible or incur any liability, nor shall the payment be questioned by reason of the cheque having been crossed, or of the crossing having been obliterated or having been added to or altered otherwise than as authorised by this Act, and of payment having been made otherwise than to a banker or to the banker to whom the cheque is or was crossed, or to his agent for collection being a banker, as the case may be.

Although section 79(2) specifically provides for the liability of the paying **22–40** bank who pays in contravention of the crossing to the true owner of the cheque, it does not apparently enlarge the rights of the true owner or increase the liability of the paying bank. Rather, by the proviso contained in the section, it affords the bank an additional protection in cases where the bank pays without negligence and in good faith and the crossing had been the subject of undetectable additions or alterations. The additions and alterations referred to in the proviso are additions to and alterations in the original crossing, and not to or in the body of the cheque.[65]

A person may by his own conduct deprive himself of the right to complain **22–41** that the paying bank has failed to comply with the crossings on cheques. Where the payee of crossed cheques, being a trading firm and not bankers, gave its cashier ostensible authority to receive payment from the drawee bank, it was held that the payee was estopped from denying the authority of its

---

[65] *Slingsby v. District Bank* [1932] 1 K.B. 544.

cashier to receive payment and could not rely upon the bank's contravention of the crossing.[66]

Extension of section 80 to other instruments

22–42   Section 5 of the Cheques Act 1957 makes the protection arising under section 80 of the 1882 Act available where a bank pays certain instruments that are not cheques. Section 5 provides that:

> **5. The provisions of the Bills of Exchange Act 1882, relating to crossed cheques shall, so far as applicable, have effect in relation to instruments (other than cheques) to which the last foregoing section applies as they have effect in relation to cheques.**

This section extends to a variety of instruments, described in section 4 of the Cheques Act 1957,[67] the provisions of the 1882 Act in relation to crossed cheques. It would seem that in order for the bank which pays upon one of the instruments mentioned in section 4 of the 1957 Act to be entitled to rely upon the protection of section 80 of the 1882 Act, the instrument would have to be crossed and paid in accordance with the crossing.

Indorsed cheques and other indorsed instruments

22–43   Negotiable instruments are inherently vulnerable to theft and, where transfer requires indorsement, to the forgery of indorsements. Banks paying upon instruments with forged indorsements generally have no means of knowing that indorsement has been forged. Consequently, statutory protections have been enacted in their favour.

22–44   The importance of these protections has greatly diminished with the demise of the transferable cheque. As already noted, following upon the enactment of the Cheques Act 1992, in the United Kingdom nearly all cheques are now issued in non-transferrable form.[68] Consequently, the transfer by indorsement of cheques from one person to another is no longer a common practice in this country. Insofar as the practice has survived at all either in relation to cheques or certain other instruments drawn upon banks, the statutory protections are still available. These arise, in the sequence of their enactment, under section 19 of the Stamp Act 1853, section 60 of the Bills of Exchange Act 1882 and section 1 of the Cheques Act 1957.

22–45   The Stamp Act 1853 first authorised drafts on a banker drawn payable to order on demand to bear a penny stamp only, a rate of duty which had previously been confined to drafts payable to bearer. The consequent inevitable increase in the number of drafts payable to order necessitated further legal protection for the banker on whom such drafts should be drawn. It was for the paying banker to verify the genuineness of the indorsements on cheques drawn to order, and he would therefore, unless protected by statute,

---

[66] *Meyer & Co. v. Sze Hai Tong Banking Co.* [1913] A.C. 847, PC.
[67] See para 23–14, *post*.
[68] See para. 21–36 *ante*.

be exposed to the consequences of paying on forged indorsements.[69] Accordingly, section 19 of the Act of 1853 provides:

19. . . . any draft or order upon a banker for a sum of money payable to order on demand, which shall when presented for payment, purport to be indorsed by the person to whom the same shall be drawn payable, shall be a sufficient authority to such banker to pay the amount of such draft or order to the bearer thereof; and it shall not be incumbent on such banker to prove that such indorsement, or any subsequent indorsement, was made by or under the direction or authority of the person to whom the said draft or order was or is made payable either by the drawer or any indorser thereof.[70]

Though the rest of this act has long been repealed this section is still in force. It has no application to bills or cheques which are dealt with by the 1882 Act; but it appears to have been purposely left unrepealed by the Bills of Exchange Act 1882, in order that it might apply to drafts or orders which were not bills of exchange or cheques as defined by the 1882 Act with regard to which the Act is silent.[71] Thus, a draft payable to order on demand addressed by one branch of a bank to another branch of the same bank is not a cheque but it is within section 19 of the Act of 1853, and therefore a banker who bona fide pays such a draft to a holder claiming under a forged indorsement is protected.[72] It is also within section 1 of the Cheques Act 1957.[73] **22–46**

By section 60 of the Bills of Exchange Act 1882 section 19 of the 1853 Act was substantially re-enacted as follows: **22–47**

60. When a bill payable to order on demand is drawn on a banker, and the banker on whom it is drawn pays the bill in good faith and in the ordinary course of business, it is not incumbent on the banker to show that the indorsement of the payee or any subsequent indorsement was made by or under the authority of the person whose indorsement it purports to be, and the banker is deemed to have paid the bill in due course, although such indorsement has been forged or made without authority.

This provision protects only the banker on whom the bill or cheque is drawn: it does not protect a collecting banker.[74] Its object is to protect the paying bank against forged or unauthorised indorsements on order bills payable on demand. Hence, it applies to an indorsement by an agent in fraud **22–48**

---

[69] *Charles v. Blackwell* (1877) 2 C.P.D. 151, 156 (Cockburn C.J.).

[70] Extended by s.11 of the Court of Chancery (Funds) Act 1872 to any document authorising the payment of money issued by the Paymaster-General in pursuance of that Act.

[71] *Capital and Counties Bank v. Gordon* [1903] A.C. 240, 251, *per* Lord Lindley; *Carpenter's Co. v. British Mutual Banking Co.* [1938] 1 K.B. 511, CA.

[72] *Capital and Counties Bank v. Gordon, supra* (instruments in Class 3), repealed and re-enacted by the Cheques Act 1957.

[73] See section 1(2)(b) of the Cheques Act 1957.

[74] *Ogden v. Benas* (1874) L.R. 9 C.P. 513; see also *Arnold v. Cheque Bank* (1876) 1 C.P.D. 578.

of his principal.[75] Where, however, the paying bank fails to exact, where it should, a proper indorsement and pays upon an indorsement which is irregular, it is not protected by this section:[76] nor is it protected where the bill or cheque is materially altered, since the instrument has been avoided by the alteration[77] and the bank is under no duty to pay it.[78]

22–49   As the section is limited to order bills, it does not apply where the bill or cheque is non-transferrable and payable only to the payee (as in the case of cheques crossed and marked "account payee") or where a cheque is made payable to bearer. However, in those cases, the paying bank will usually have the protection of section 1 of the Cheques Act 1957, discussed below, which is not limited to instruments payable to order.

22–50   Section 60 requires that the paying bank acts in good faith and in the ordinary course of business. The fact that the banker is guilty of negligence does not necessarily deprive him of protection. Negligence is clearly not incompatible with good faith[79] and an act which is done negligently may yet be done in the ordinary course of business.[80] Where, however, the paying banker happens to be the collecting banker and commits an act of conversion as collecting banker, the fact that as paying banker he pays the cheques in good faith and in the ordinary course of business within section 60 does not exonerate him from liability for that conversion.[81]

22–51   Section 1 of the Cheques Act 1957 did not completely replace the then existing protective legislation for the paying bank. As seen, section 19 of the Stamp Act 1853 and sections 60 and 80 of the 1882 Act are still effective. Section 1 of the Cheques Act 1957 provides that:

1.—(1) Where a banker in good faith and in the ordinary course of business pays a cheque drawn on him which is not indorsed or is irregularly indorsed, he does not, in doing so, incur any liability by reason only of the absence of, or irregularity in, indorsement, and he is deemed to have paid it in due course.

(2) Where a banker in good faith and in the ordinary course of business pays any such instrument as the following, namely:

(a) a document issued by a customer of his which, though not a bill of exchange, is intended to enable a person to obtain payment from him of the sum mentioned in the instrument;

(b) a draft payable on demand drawn by him upon himself, whether payable at the head office or some other office of his bank;

---

[75] *Charles v. Blackwell* (1877) 2 C.P.D. 151. London bankers resolved in 1868 to pay cheques indorsed by procuration, without guarantee, except in special cases, and they have since followed the practice.

[76] *Slingsby v. District Bank* [1932] 1 K.B. 544, (CA).

[77] Section 64 of the 1882 Act.

[78] *Slingsby v. District Bank, supra.*

[79] See section 90 of the 1882 Act.

[80] So held in *Carpenters' Co. v. British Mutual Banking* [1938] 1 K.B. 511, CA by the majority of the Court (Slesser and Mackinnon L.JJ., Greer L.J. being of the contrary opinion).

[81] *ibid.*

he does not, in so doing, incur any liability by reason only of the absence of, or irregularity in, indorsement, and the payment discharges the instrument.

Section 1 is an extension of the protection afforded the paying bank to cover instruments, whether crossed or uncrossed in respect only of absence of, or irregularity in, indorsement. As regards cheques, section 1 extends protection to banks paying cheques which are payable to order or otherwise. It therefore goes beyond the scope of section 60 of the 1882 Act and, importantly, includes cheques which have been crossed and marked "account payee". As regards other categories of documents, section 1 extends the paying bank's protection to documents, not being bills of exchange, which are issued by customers to persons so that the recipient can obtain payment from a bank and to bankers drafts.   **22–52**

The section provides that where payment is made under subsection (1), the banker is deemed to have paid the instrument—a cheque—in due course; and where he pays one of the instruments mentioned in subsection (2), the payment discharges the instrument. Payment in due course is, by section 59(1) of the 1882 Act, "payment made at or after maturity of the bill to the holder thereof in good faith and without notice that his title to the bill is defective"; this can only apply to instruments covered by the 1882 Act, hence the provision that "payment discharges the instrument" in the case of those which are not cheques. The intention in either case is to relieve the bank of liability in conversion and to entitle it to debit its customer's account the amount of the cheque or instrument. As a matter of practice, following the enactment of the Cheques Act 1957 the Committee of London Clearing Banks advised its members still to require the indorsement of certain instruments, including those cashed across the counter.[82]   **22–53**

Forgery

The position of a bank in the case of forgery of a cheque that he pays depends on the nature of the forgery. Forgery of indorsement is mostly covered by the legislation just referred to, and the bank has a large measure of protection. Alterations to the crossing are covered by the proviso in section 79(2); protecting the bank in cases of undetectable alterations and additions. There is, however, no protection against forgery of the drawer's signature, for payment of such an instrument is payment without a mandate and the banker cannot debit his customer's account the amount paid away. He may seek to recover the money paid upon a forged cheque as money paid under a mistake of fact.[83] Such an action would lie in the first instance against the collecting bank to whom payment was made. Commonly, though, the collecting bank will have disbursed the funds before the forgery is discovered and will have a defence of change of position. If so, the action would have to be brought against the ultimate recipient of the cheque proceeds.   **22–54**

---

[82] See the memorandum of the Committee of London Clearing Bankers dated September 23, 1957, which is reproduced in Chalmers & Guest (15th ed.), pp. 706–709.

[83] See Chap. 32.

22–55   Other than his specific duties as regards his manner of drawing cheques[84] and reporting known frauds,[85] the customer does not owe the drawee bank any duty of care in relation to the general management of his affairs, or checking his account statements, so as to prevent frauds.[86] Nor does the payee of a cheque owe the drawee bank any duty of care to prevent the misappropriation of the cheque.[87]

Bank collects for one customer a cheque drawn by another customer

22–56   Where a bank, on which a cheque is drawn, is also the collecting bank it fulfils a dual role as both paying and collecting bank. If a cheque is paid in by a customer who is not the cheque's true owner and the bank pays the cheque by crediting that customer's account, it will avoid liability for conversion only if its actions meet both the requirements of section 60 of the 1882 Act and of section 4 of the Cheques Act 1957.[88] However, the bank's debiting and crediting of the respective accounts of its two customers counts as payment "to a banker" for the purposes of complying with the crossing.[89]

22–57   Where there are insufficient funds for payment of the cheque the bank comes under no liability if it returns the cheque unpaid.[90] But if the bank chooses to retain the cheque in order to see whether the cheque can eventually be paid that step will be taken in the capacity of agent for the payee. In those circumstances the bank comes under a duty to the payee to pay the cheque as and when sufficient funds are paid into the drawer's account and the bank is not entitled to prefer the interests of others by satisfying first its own claims as a creditor of the drawer, nor the interests of the payees of other cheques drawn on the same account and which are subsequently presented.[91]

Marking

22–58   Cheques are intended for immediate payment on presentment and consequently are not in the ordinary course accepted. Though, as bills of exchange, they are capable of being accepted if the banker so chooses.[92] But there was a usage amongst bankers of marking cheques for the purpose of clearance, the banker on whom the cheque is drawn becoming bound by marking it to the

---

[84] See *ante*, para. 22–09.

[85] See *ante*, para. 22–15.

[86] *Tai Hing Cotton Mill Ltd v. Lui Chong Hing Bank Ltd* [1986] A.C. 80, PC.

[87] *Yorkshire Bank plc v. Lloyds Bank plc*, *The Times* May 12, 1999.

[88] *Carpenters' Co. v. British Mutual Banking Co.* [1938] 1 K.B. 511—the case concerned s.82 of the 1882 Act, the antecedent to section 4 of the Cheques Act 1957.

[89] *ibid.* at 538. See section 79(2) of the 1882 Act.

[90] *Boyd v. Emmerson* (1834) 2 A. & E. 184.

[91] *Kilsby v. Williams* (1822) 5 B. & Ald. 815, followed in *Bank of British North America v. Standard Bank of Canada* (1917) 35 D.L.R. 761, 38 O.L.R. 570.

[92] *Bellamy v. Marjoribanks* (1852) 7 Ex. 389, 404; *Keene v. Board* (1860) 29 L.J.C.P. 287, 290 (Erie C.J.); "It would certainly require strong and unmistakable words to amount to an acceptance of a cheque"; *per* Lord Wright in *Bank of Baroda Ltd v. Punjab National Bank Ltd* [1944] A.C. 176, 188, on the certification of a post-dated cheque.

collecting banker, and this usage has been judicially recognised.[93] Marking does not satisfy the requirements of section 17 of the 1882 Act[94] and so it will not amount to an acceptance,[95] and it is difficult to see upon what grounds the banker can be held liable. No usage in favour of the holder of a marked cheque has ever been established in this country; and the marking, if intended to be a binding representation as to the drawer's credit, will not impose any liability upon the banker, unless signed by him,[96] and then, presumably, on the basis that the banker is estopped by reason of his representation.

As to certification of a post-dated cheque, see *Bank of Baroda Ltd v. Punjab National Bank Ltd*[97] and *Keyes v. Royal Bank of Canada.*[98]

---

[93] *Goodwin v. Robarts* (1875) L.R. 10 Ex. 337, 351; see also *Robson v. Bennett* (1810) 2 Taunt. 388, in which, at 396, Mansfield C.J. said that "the effect of that marking is similar to the accepting of a bill", which dictum the Privy Council in the Bank of Baroda case held not to be justified either to English or Indian law: "In the absence of relevant enactment or custom, the issue in England and India as to the effect of the certification of a cheque must be determined by the common law" [1944] A.C. 176, 187.

[94] See *ante*, para. 10–01.

[95] Nor is it within s.7 of the Indian Negotiable Instruments Act 1881. *Bank of Baroda Ltd v. Punjab National Bank Ltd* [1944] A.C. 176; Paget, *op. cit.* p. 318.

[96] By s.6 of Lord Tenterden's Act.

[97] [1944] A.C. 176.

[98] (1947) 3 D.L.R. 161.

CHAPTER 23

THE CHEQUE—III

THE COLLECTING BANK

The role of the collecting bank

23–01   THE payees of cheques almost generally rely upon a bank, normally being a bank at which the payee holds an account, to obtain payment from the drawee bank. Indeed so far as crossed cheques are concerned payment will only be made by the drawee to a bank.[1] A bank which receives cheques for the purposes of obtaining payment for its customer is known as a "collecting bank".

23–02   The function of the collecting bank is that of an agent for its customer. The agency commences when it receives the cheques for collection and ends when the customer becomes entitled to call upon the bank to pay him the proceeds of the cheque.[2] Most cheques are handled through the cheque clearing system,[3] and a collecting bank which is not itself a member of the system may use the services of another, which is a member, as its sub-agent. The presentment of the cheque for payment must (unless another location is specified in accordance with section 74A, or truncated presentment under section 74B is employed)[4] occur at the branch of the drawee bank at which the drawer's account is held.

23–03   Consequently, a collecting bank which hands over cheques at the clearing house to the drawee does not itself handle the final stage of presentment for payment, and for the purposes of the journey from clearing house to branch the cheque is entrusted to the drawee bank as the collecting bank's sub-agent.[5]

23–04   Not all cheques, however, are processed through the clearing. In particular, the customer may request "special collection" of a particular cheque, in which case the collecting bank arranges for the cheque to be delivered directly to the relevant branch of the drawee bank either by putting it in the post, or by using a messenger. Also the cheque may be drawn upon an account held with the collecting bank itself, in which case the presentment will be handled through the bank's internal procedures and it will not be necessary for the cheque to pass through the clearing.

---

[1] See paras 21–39 and 22–35, *ante.*

[2] See *Re Farrow's Bank Ltd* [1923] 1 Ch. 41, which was analysed and explained by Longmore J. in *Triffit Nurseries v. Salads Etcetera Ltd* [1999] 1 All E.R. (Comm.) 110. See also *Gaden v. Newfoundland Savings Bank* [1899] A.C. 281: the collecting bank, being an agent, becomes accountable to the customer for the amount of a cheque only when it has cleared.

[3] See para. 21–74, *ante.*

[4] See paras 21–80 and 21–84, *ante.*

[5] *Barclays Bank plc v. Bank of England* [1985] 1 All E.R. 385, 392.

Sources of liability for collecting banks

It is the duty of a collecting bank to present a cheque for payment and **23–05**
obtain an answer without delay.[6] If the collecting bank fails to present a
cheque with reasonable diligence after receiving it, or delays unreasonably in
advising the customer when the cheque has been dishonoured, the bank will
be liable to its customer for any loss arising from its delay.[7] If the fault lay not
in the collecting bank itself but in a sub-agent used by it, the collecting bank
will nonetheless be responsible[8] and, provided that the sub-agent is aware that
the cheque belongs to a customer and not to its immediate principal, the
collecting bank, it is possible that the sub-agent will owe a direct duty of skill
and care in tort to the customer.[9]

Where a bank collects cheques representing money to which the bank's **23–06**
customer is not entitled, for instance being the proceeds of a fraud, the
collecting bank may incur liability to the true beneficial owner of the monies
as a constructive trustee.[10] In order to incur such liability, the bank must either
be shown to have knowingly assisted in a dishonest or fraudulent design. This
requires that the bank should itself have behaved dishonestly.[11] Or, the bank
must have received money which was held in trust knowing that it was trust
property and either knowing that it was paid to the bank in breach of trust or
having itself dealt with the money in breach of trust. Again, a degree of
culpability is required in order for a bank to be liable in this way for "knowing
receipt". The Court of Appeal has held that the test is whether it is unconscionable for the bank to retain the benefit of the receipt.[12] If the collecting
bank has in all innocence paid over to its customer the proceeds of the
collection, or has otherwise innocently changed its position, it will have a
defence to such a claim.[13]

The most immediate risk confronted by a collecting bank is not in normal **23–07**
circumstances that occasioned by the possibility of impropriety in its own
actions, but rather that it may unwittingly handle a cheque for a customer that
has been stolen or otherwise misappropriated. If it does so, the bank runs the
risk of incurring liability to the true owner of the cheque.

Such liability might arise in any of three ways: first, the collecting bank **23–08**
may be liable to the true owner of the cheque in the tort of conversion; second,
having received the proceeds of a cheque that it has converted, the collecting
bank may incur liability for "money had and received"; third, prospectively,

---

[6] *Riedell v. Commercial Bank of Australia* [1931] V.L.R. 382, 389 *per* Mann J.; cited by
Bingham J., sitting as an arbitrator, in *Barclays Bank plc v. Bank of England* [1985] 1 All E.R.
385, 391. In fulfilling its duty of obtaining payment for the customer, the bank does not owe the
customer any duty to have regard to the tax implications for the customer of the bank's actions:
Schioler v. Westminster Bank [1970] 2 Q.B. 719.

[7] *Lubbock v. Tribe* (1838) 3 M & W 607; *Bank of Nova Scotia v. Sharp*, 57 D.L.R. (3d)
260.

[8] *Bowstead and Reynolds on Agency*, (16th ed.), p. 165.

[9] *cf. Henderson v. Merrett Syndicates Ltd* [1995] 2 A.C. 145.

[10] See *Penn & Shea on the Law Relating to Domestic Banking*, (2nd ed.) 9–007 *et seq.*

[11] *Royal Brunei Airlines Sdn Bhd v. Tan* [1995] 2 A.C. 378.

[12] *Bank of Credit and Commerce International (Overseas) Ltd v. Akindele* [2000] 3 W.L.R.
1423.

[13] See Paget, (11th ed.) pp. 429 *et seq.*

a cause of action is to be given by section 150 of the Financial Services and Markets Act 2000 to private persons insofar as they suffer loss as a result of the contravention by banks and others of certain rules made by the Financial Services Authority. It may be that a bank which collects a stolen cheque for a thief has contravened one of the Financial Service Authority's rules in relation to money laundering and that this has enabled the fraud to occur, exposing the bank to liability for breach of statutory duty.[14]

Conversion

23-09   A collecting bank that collects a cheque and receives payment of it on behalf of a person other than the cheque's true owner is vulnerable to an action for conversion by the true owner. The nature of this cause of action and the meaning of "true owner" are discussed in the preceding Chapter[15] in the context of the liabilities of the paying bank, as an action for conversion of a cheque can also be brought by the true owner against a paying bank.

23-10   The primary defence of a collecting bank to such an action is that it received payment of the cheque in good faith and without negligence: section 4 of the Cheques Act 1957 (discussed below).

Money had and received

23-11   The action for money had and received is a restitutionary claim that provides a personal remedy against the defendant by way of a debt which in certain circumstances is implied by law.[16] In the present context the claim for money had and received tends to arise when a claimant, being the true owner of a cheque, "waives" the tort of conversion on the part of the collecting bank, and elects to receive instead of damages for conversion judgment on the restitutionary basis.[17] That election need not be made at the time of issuing proceedings. Indeed, claims for the conversion of cheques very commonly contain an alternative plea for money had and received. The claimant's election can be left until he applies for judgment to be entered.[18]

23-12   A claim for money had and received is often less to a claimant's advantage than is the corresponding claim in conversion. The restitutionary remedy is subject to a defence that the recipient materially altered his position on the faith of having received the payment.[19] Typically this will occur if the collecting bank has paid over all or part of the proceeds of the cheque to its customer before it becomes aware of the circumstances.[20] However, in some circumstances the claim for money had and received can circumvent defences

---

[14] See paras 23–39 to 23–40, *post*.

[15] See paras 22–22 *et seq*.

[16] *Fibrosa Spolka Akcyjna v. Fairbairn Lawson Combe Barbour Ltd* [1943] A.C. 32, 62 *per* Lord Wright.

[17] *Marfani & Co. Ltd v. Midland Bank Ltd* [1968] 1 W.L.R. 956, 971; *Bavins Junior & Sims v. London & South Western Bank* [1900] 1 Q.B. 270.

[18] *United Australia Ltd v. Barclays Bank Ltd* [1941] A.C. 1, 19.

[19] *Morison v. London County & Westminster Bank Ltd* [1914] 3 K.B. 356, 386.

[20] Merely crediting the money to the customer's account does not amount to a change of position, as the account can be re-debited: *Bavins Junior & Sims v London & South Western Bank* [1900] 1 Q.B. 270.

that are available to a claim in conversion. In particular, it may be that the purported "cheque" which is converted in fact lacks validity as such and is not in itself a valuable instrument, for whose conversion damages are measured by the face value of the instrument. If such a purported cheque is collected and payment received, the collecting bank's liability in conversion will be for nominal damages only,[21] but, having received payment, the collecting bank's liability in the restitutionary claim will prima facie be for the amount of the proceeds of payment received by it.[22]

Section 4 of the Cheques Act 1957

The vulnerability of the collecting bank to the claims of true owners of **23–13** cheques and other instruments, whether brought in conversion or for money had and received, has long been mitigated by statutory protection.[23] The effect of this protection has been to relieve a collecting bank from liability insofar as it acts in good faith and without negligence.

The present such protection is found at section 4 of the Cheques Act 1957, **23–14** which provides:

4.—(1) Where a banker, in good faith and without negligence—

(a) receives payment for a customer of an instrument to which this section applies; or

(b) having credited a customer's account with the amount of such an instrument, receives payment thereof for himself;

and the customer has no title, or a defective title, to the instrument, the banker does not incur any liability to the true owner of the instrument by reason only of having received payment thereof.

(2) This section applies to the following instruments, namely:

(a) cheques (including cheques which under section 81A(1) of the Bills of Exchange Act 1882 or otherwise are not transferable);[24]

(b) any document issued by a customer of a banker which, though not a bill of exchange, is intended to enable a person to obtain payment from that banker of the sum mentioned in the document;[25]

---

[21] *Smith v. Lloyds TSB Group* and *Harvey Jones Ltd v. Woolwich plc* [2000] 3 W.L.R. 1725, CA.

[22] *Bavins Junior & Sims v. London & South Western Bank* [1900] 1 Q.B. 270

[23] Prior to the passing of the Cheques Act 1957, the protection afforded to a collecting banker was to be found in section 82 of the Bills of Exchange Act 1882, the Bills of Exchange (Crossed Cheques) Act 1906 and, in regard to certain other instruments, in section 17 of the Revenue Act 1883, and the Bills of Exchange Act (1882) Amendment Act 1932. The Cheques Act 1957 repealed all of these and largely re-enacted them in section 4.

[24] The words in brackets were inserted by s.3 of the Cheques Act 1992.

[25] An example of such an instrument is one in cheque form but drawn payable to "cash"; see *North and South Insurance Corporation Ltd v. National Provincial Bank Ltd* [1936] 1 K.B. 328; *Cole v. Milsome* [1951] 1 All E.R. 311; *Orbit Mining & Trading Co. Ltd v. Westminster Bank Ltd* [1963] 1 Q.B. 794.

(c) any document issued by a public officer which is intended to enable any person to obtain payment from the Paymaster General or the Queen's and Lord Treasurer's Remembrancer of the sum mentioned in the document but is not a bill of exchange;

(d) any draft payable on demand drawn by a banker upon himself, whether payable at the head office or some other office of his bank.

(3) A banker is not to be treated for the purposes of this section as having been negligent by reason only of his failure to concern himself with absence of, or irregularity in, indorsement of an instrument.

23–15   By section 6 of the Cheques Act 1957 that Act is to be construed as one with the Bills of Exchange Act 1882.

The meanings of certain of the terms used in the earlier Act and also in section 4 of the 1957 Act ("banker",[26] "cheque"[27] and "true owner")[28] are discussed in the previous two Chapters. Certain other expressions appearing in section 4 require separate consideration.

"Customer"

23–16   The payment must be received on behalf of a "customer" of the collecting bank, otherwise the bank is not protected. To constitute a person a customer there must be some sort of an account, either a deposit or current account, or some similar relation.[29] In *Great Western Railway v. London and County Bank* it was suggested that if a person without an account lodged cheques for collection, as opposed to exchanging them for cash across the counter, that might constitute the person a "customer" of the bank.[30] But, if the proceeds of the cheque, once collected are not to be held on an account in the name of that person, it is doubtful whether the true relationship of bank and customer is established and hence whether this requirement of the section is met.[31]

23–17   Once the relation is established, the length of time during which it has subsisted is immaterial: a person may be a customer, though the account is opened by means of the actual cheque which becomes the subject-matter of the action. A person is treated as a customer of the bank even if he uses a

---

[26] See paras 21–07 et seq., *supra*.

[27] See para. 21–04, *supra*.

[28] See paras 22–27 et seq., *supra*.

[29] See *Great Western Ry v. London and County Bank* [1901] A.C. 414; *Lacave v. Credit Lyonnais* [1897] 1 Q.B. 148; *Matthews v. Brown & Co.* (1894) 63 L.J.Q.B. 494; *Importers' Co. v. Westminster Bank* [1927] 2 K.B. 297, 305, where it is said by Bankes L.J. that banks do various kinds of business, in all of which the persons with whom the banks do the business may properly be called customers.

[30] [1901] A.C. 414, at 422 *per* Lord Brampton.

[31] See *Commissioners of Taxation v. English Scottish and Australian Bank* [1920] A.C. 683, 687; *cf. Tate v. Wilts and Dorset Bank Ltd* (1899) 1 L.D.A.B. 286, in which it was conceded that a person who intended to open an account with the proceeds of a cheque which he paid in for collection was not a "customer" for these purposes at the time of the collection, a view with which Darling J. agreed (pp. 288–289). An agreement to open an account may suffice: *Ladbroke v. Todd* (1914) 30 T.L.R. 433.

branch other than his own branch for the purposes of receiving cheques for collection.[32]

A fraudster may become a customer of a bank by opening an account under **23–18** a false name.[33] But where the alias used by the fraudster corresponds to the name of a real person or company, that person or company does not come into contractual relations with the bank so as to be owed the duties that a bank owes to its customer.[34]

One bank may be the customer of another bank. If a bank that is not a **23–19** member of the clearing house employs a clearing bank to clear cheques entrusted to it for collection, it is a customer of the clearing bank, which is thus protected by section 4.[35]

"Receives payment"

Section 4 of the Cheques Act 1957 like its predecessor, section 82 of the **23–20** Bills of Exchange Act 1882, requires that the bank shall have received payment of the instrument, and protects the bank from "any liability to the true owner of the instrument by reason only of having received payment thereof".

A collecting bank will necessarily receive payment of a cheque which is **23–21** paid. However, the receipt of payment is not the only act which would be capable of amounting to a conversion if the cheque is collected for a person other than the true owner. Each material step taken to collect payment would be such a conversion. However, it is implicit that the protection afforded by the section extends to all such steps and not merely to the receipt of payment.[36]

As is made plain by subsections 4(1)(a) and 4(1)(b) it makes no difference **23–22** to the protection whether at the time that the collecting bank receives payment of the cheque or other instrument the bank receives payment for the customer, or having already credited the customer's account with the amount of the cheque, for itself. It became necessary for the legislation to spell this out following the decision of the House of Lords in *Gordon v. Capital & Counties Bank*.[37] In that case it was held that the section 82 of the 1882 Act only protected a bank which received payment of a cheque in the capacity of agent for its customer and that, having credited the account before receiving payment, the defendant bank received payment for itself and was not entitled to protection.

---

[32] This is implicit in the reasoning of the majority and minority opinions of the House of Lords in *Lloyds Bank v. E.B. Savory & Co.* [1933] A.C. 201, having been doubted by Lawrence L.J. below: [1932] 2 K.B. 122, 140.

[33] *e.g. Ladbroke v. Todd* (1914) 30 T.L.R. 433; *Marfani & Co. Ltd v. Midland Bank Ltd* [1968] 1 W.L.R. 956; *Lumsden & Co. v. London Trustee Savings Bank* [1971] 1 Lloyd's Rep. 114.

[34] *Robinson v. Midland Bank Ltd* (1925) 41 T.L.R. 402; *Stoney Stanton Supplies v. Midland Bank Ltd* [1966] 2 Lloyd's Rep. 373, CA.

[35] *Importers' Co. v. Westminster Bank* [1927] 2 K.B. 297; *Honourable Society of the Middle Temple v. Lloyds Bank plc* [1999] 1 All E.R. (Comm.) 193.

[36] *Gordon v. Capital & Counties Bank* [1903] A.C. 240, HL, at 244; *Marfani & Co. Ltd v. Midland Bank Ltd* [1968] 1 W.L.R. 956, CA, at 971.

[37] [1903] A.C. 240, HL.

23–23   That decision led to the enactment of the Bills of Exchange (Crossed Cheques) Act 1906, which provided that a banker receives payment of a crossed cheque for a customer within the meaning of section 82, notwithstanding that he credits his customer's account with the amount of the cheque before receiving payment thereof.[38] Both section 82 of the 1882 Act and the Act of 1906 were repealed and replaced by the Cheques Act 1957. Although the wording of section 4 of the 1957 Act does not precisely follow that of the 1906 Act and there is a significant extension of the categories of instrument to which the protection applies, there is no reason to suppose that Parliament intended to change the circumstances in which a collecting bank may claim protection in respect of an instrument that is covered.[39]

23–24   If a clearing bank receives payment of a cheque as agent for another bank and remits the payment to its principal, the clearing bank's receipt of the payment is sufficient to satisfy the requirement in section 4.[40]

"Good faith"

23–25   The bank must act in good faith, which is distinct from the requirement that it must act without negligence. A thing is done in good faith where it is in fact done honestly, whether it is done negligently or not.[41]

"Without negligence"

23–26   The onus of proof that the collecting bank acted without negligence rests upon the bank.[42] In deciding the question of whether in relation to any given cheque the bank has been guilty of negligence, it is necessary to have regard to the particular meaning of negligence in this context and to the standard of care by which its presence is judged.

The meaning of "negligence"

23–27   The collecting bank does not owe to the true owners of cheques that he collects any general duty of skill and care. Rather it owes a strict liability duty not to convert the property of the true owner and not to receive money representing the proceeds of such a conversion. Against those liabilities the bank is relieved, under section 4, subject to the proviso that he must have acted without negligence (and in good faith). Therefore, "negligence" in this context does not bear its usual sense of breach of a legal duty of skill and care.

---

[38] Section 1 of the Bills of Exchange (Crossed Cheques) Act 1906.

[39] In previous editions of this work it was questioned whether the introduction of the phrase "for himself" in subsection 4(1)(b) might have represented a material change in the law. However, it is considered doubtful whether this could be so. Insofar as any payment received after the crediting of the customer's account is not received for the banker "himself" so as to come within subsection 4(1)(b), it will be received "for a customer" within subsection 4(1)(a). So, it is submitted, the introduction of the phrase, "for himself", does nothing to limit the ambit of the protection.

[40] *Importers Co. Ltd v. Westminster Bank Ltd* [1927] 2 K.B. 297, 306.

[41] s.90 of the 1882 Act, see *ante*, para. 18–09.

[42] *Lloyds Bank v. Savory* [1933] A.C. 201, 229 *per* Lord Wright; *Marfani & Co. Ltd v. Midland Bank Ltd* [1968] 1 W.L.R. 956, 965 *per* Nield J.

This point was made in *Orbit Mining and Trading Co. Ltd v. Westminster Bank Ltd*[43] by Harman L.J., at 824, who said:

> "It is difficult to see what the standard of negligence is in a case where, as here, outside the statute there can be no duty by the defendant to the plaintiff: they are in no contractual relationship and in the absence of duty there is no negligence. Negligence, I think, is equivalent to carelessness. It is the price which the bank pays for the protection afforded by the Act in cases where the common law doctrine of conversion would leave the bank without defence."

The "carelessness" of which Harman L.J. speaks is, of course, not care-   **23–28** lessness with regard to the interests of the collecting bank's customer, who hands in the cheque, but with regard to the true owner of cheque whose property is thereby being converted.[44]

The net effect of the collecting bank's strict liability duty not to convert   **23–29** cheques and its qualified protection against that liability was described by Diplock L.J. in *Marfani & Co. Ltd v. Midland Bank Ltd*,[45] as follows:

> "It is . . . in my view, clear that the intention of the subsection and its statutory predecessors is to substitute for the absolute duty owed at common law by a banker to the true owner of a cheque not to take any steps in the ordinary course of business leading up to and including the receipt of payment of the cheque, and the crediting of the amount of the cheque to the account of his customer, in usurpation of the true owner's title thereto a qualified duty to take reasonable care to refrain from taking any such step which he foresees is, or ought reasonably to have foreseen was, likely to cause loss or damage to the true owner.
>
> "The only respect in which this substituted statutory duty differs from a common law cause of action in negligence is that, since it takes the form of a qualified immunity from a strict liability at common law, the onus of showing that he did take such reasonable care lies upon the defendant banker. Granted good faith in the banker (the other condition of the immunity), the usual matter with respect to which the banker must take reasonable care is to satisfy himself that his own customer's title to the cheque delivered to him for collection is not defective, *i.e.*, that no other person is the true owner of it."

The question of whether negligence is present is to be judged leaving aside   **23–30** the benefit of hindsight. The question should in strictness be determined separately with regard to each cheque that is collected; and the test of negligence is whether the transaction of paying in any given cheque coupled with the circumstances antecedent and present was so out of the ordinary course that it ought to have aroused doubts in the bankers' mind and caused them to make inquiry.[46]

---

[43] *Orbit Mining and Trading Co. Ltd v. Westminster Bank Ltd* [1963] 1 Q.B. 794.

[44] *Bissell & Co. v. Fox Brothers & Co.* (1885) 51 L.T. 633, 666, approved on appeal (1886) 53 L.T. 193, 194 *per* Baggallay L.J.

[45] [1968] 1 W.L.R. 956, at 972.

[46] *Commissioners of Taxation v. English, Scottish And Australian Bank Ltd* [1920] A.C. 683, 688 *per* Lord Dunedin; applied in *Lloyds Bank Ltd v. The Chartered Bank of India, Australia and China* [1929] 1 K.B. 40, 59 and in *Lloyds Bank Ltd v. E.B. Savory & Co.* [1933] A.C. 201, 230.

23–31   The particular antecedent circumstances that might be relevant to whether the bank's customer is in possession of cheques to which he is not entitled are discussed in the next section, "Standard of Care". It is a difficult question whether a bank can be convicted of negligence in relation to its collection of a cheque or cheques on the grounds that if it had not been negligent in relation to an earlier collection for the same customer the fraudulent character of the customer's behaviour would have been detected and the later cheque or cheques would not have been paid in, or if paid in would not without negligence have been collected.[47] Such a line of argument, if accepted, would amount to placing banks under a positive duty of care to the owners of cheques in general to detect and prevent ongoing frauds; whereas their true duty is not to convert such cheques as are given to them for collection. It is, moreover, a well-established principle that the question of negligence should be determined separately with regard to each cheque that is collected.[48] It is submitted that it is only at a stage at which the whole operation of the customer's account of itself is such as should give rise to a reasonable suspicion of fraud that antecedent conversions overlooked by the bank comprise evidence of negligence in relation to the collection of later cheques.

23–32   The relevant point in time at which the question of negligence is determined in relation to the collection of any one cheque is the time when the bank pays out the proceeds of the cheque to its customer, so depriving the true owner of his right to follow the money into the bank's hands.[49]

The standard of care

23–33   The standard of care to be applied is to be judged by the practice of careful bankers. Whilst the court is entitled to find that a given practice of bankers does not comply with the standard of care that a prudent bank should apply, it will be hesitant before condemning as negligent a practice generally adopted by those engaged in banking.[50] However, if a practice is one that omits to protect against an obvious risk, the mere fact that it is long established and that the risk seems not previously to have materialised is insufficient justification for the practice.[51]

23–34   As society and commerce change so the practice of banking is also subject to changes over time. So cases decided decades previously may be a poor guide to present banking practice.[52]

---

[47] This would appear to have been at least part of the reasoning in *Midland Bank Ltd v. Reckitt* [1933] A.C. 1, 16–17; see also *Nu-Stilo Footwear Ltd v. Lloyds Bank Ltd* (1956) 7 L.D.A.B. 121.

[48] *Commissioners of Taxation v. English, Scottish And Australian Bank Ltd* [1920] A.C. 683 at 688 *per* Lord Dunedin. *Lloyds Bank Ltd v. The Chartered Bank of India, Australia and China* [1929] 1 K.B. 40 at 59; *Lloyds Bank Ltd v. E.B. Savory & Co.* [1933] A.C. 201 at 230.

[49] *Marfani & Co. Ltd v. Midland Bank Ltd* [1968] 1 W.L.R. 956 at 975.

[50] *Marfani & Co. Ltd v. Midland Bank Ltd* [1968] 1 W.L.R. 956 at 975; see also *Commissioners of Taxation v. English, Scottish And Australian Bank Ltd* [1920] A.C. 683 at 689; *Importers Company Ltd v. Westminster Bank Ltd* [1927] 2 K.B. 297 at 302–303.

[51] *Lloyds Bank Ltd v. E.B. Savory & Co.* [1933] A.C. 201 at 235.

[52] *Marfani & Co. Ltd v. Midland Bank Ltd* [1968] 1 W.L.R. 956 at 972 and 976.

The internal regulations and procedures of a collecting bank may help to **23–35**
elucidate the standard of care in a given case. The court will have regard to
such evidence.[53] But the standards adopted internally by a particular institution are not in themselves decisive, as they may be set either higher or lower
than the law requires.[54] It is obvious that a bank's duties cannot be set higher
than is consistent with its ability to carry on banking business efficiently.[55] A
bank is not required to go about the business of collecting cheques with the
microscopic attention to detail of an amateur detective, nor to be abnormally
suspicious.[56]

Specific aspects of the standard of care are identified and discussed in the
following sections.

Opening the account

The thieves of cheques have historically operated in two principal ways so **23–36**
as to obtain payment of stolen cheques: (1) opening an account in the name
of the payee, or (2) forging an indorsement on the stolen cheque so that it
appears to have been transferred to the thief. As a result of the introduction of
the Cheques Act 1992 nearly all cheques are now issued bearing the words
"account payee" added to the crossing and such cheques are incapable of
transfer. Banks within the United Kingdom can be expected to understand the
effect of the "account payee" crossing, and not without very good reason to
accept such a cheque otherwise than for an account of the named payee
(although overseas banks cannot necessarily be relied upon in the same
way).[57] Therefore, the second type of fraud is now more difficult for the thief.
It can be anticipated that fraudulent account opening may now be seen as the
softer option for those seeking to misappropriate cheques. However, that
avenue also is less readily exploited than in the past, as a consequence of the
passage of legislation aimed at preventing money laundering.

Since long before the advent of such legislation the courts have recognised **23–37**
that good banking practice requires a bank to take some steps to verify the
identity of a new customer who opened an account. The object of such steps
is largely to prevent fraud, so any failure to comply with good practice in this
regard that results in the bank's not being in a position to detect fraudulent use

---

[53] *e.g. Lloyds Bank v. E.B. Savory & Co.* [1933] A.C. 201, 221; *Thackwell v. Barclays Bank plc*
[1986] 1 All E.R. 676.

[54] *Motor Traders Guarantee Corp. Ltd v. Midland Bank Ltd* [1937] 4 All E.R. 90, 96;
Penmount Estates Ltd v. National Provincial Bank Ltd (1945) 5 L.D.A.B. 418, (1945) 173 L.T.
344; *Orbit Mining & Trading Co. Ltd v. Westminster Bank Ltd* [1963] 1 Q.B. 794, at 818 & 826;
Lumsden & Co. v. London Trsutee Savings Bank [1971] 1 Lloyd's Rep. 114, 121;

[55] *Commissioners of Taxation v. English, Scottish And Australian Bank Ltd* [1920] A.C. 683,
690; *Honourable Society of the Middle Temple v. Lloyds Bank plc* [1999] 1 All E.R. (Comm.) 193,
215.

[56] *Lloyds Bank Ltd v. The Chartered Bank of India, Australia and China* [1929] 1 K.B. 40, 73;
Marfani & Co. Ltd v. Midland Bank Ltd [1968] 1 W.L.R. 956 at 963 and 966, *per* Nield J. at first
instance, and at 981 on appeal, *per* Cairns J.

[57] *The Honourable Society of the Middle Temple v. Lloyds Bank plc* [1999] 1 All E.R. (Comm.)
193.

of the account for the collection of cheques qualifies as an antecedent circumstance relevant to the question of negligence.[58]

23–38   Nowadays banks are under specific legal duties to identify new customers imposed upon them by anti-money laundering legislation.[59] The Money Laundering Regulations 1993[60] establish duties upon banks and others to maintain procedures for the identification of customers, the keeping of records and the reporting of instances of money-laundering.[61] These are bolstered by further duties to make employees aware of the bank's procedures and of the requirements of the law in relation to the prevention of money laundering[62] and to provide appropriate staff training.[63] Contravention of these duties is a criminal offence.[64] Guidance Notes[65] as to the standards to be obeyed in order to comply with these requirements have been provided by the Joint Money Laundering Steering Group (JMLSG), a collective body of several trade associations.

23–39   Upon the coming into force of the Financial Services and Markets Act 2000, responsibility for establishing rules in relation to money laundering falls upon the Financial Services Authority.[66] The first set of such rules is contained in the FSA's "Money Laundering Sourcebook".[67] These rules, which provide a civil regulatory framework, co-exist with the 1993 Regulations, which establish the requirements imposed by criminal law. Their prime requirement is that banks and others must take reasonable steps to find out who their clients are by obtaining evidence of the identity of any client who comes into contact with them to be able to show that the client is who he claims to be.[68] In assessing compliance with that duty the FSA has regard to the Guidance Notes of the JMLSG.[69] The Sourcebook also requires that banks take reasonable steps to ensure that their staff are aware of their responsibilities and of the law in relation to money laundering[70] and train their staff accordingly.[71]

23–40   In the light of these provisions, banking practice in relation to identifying new customers is now well-defined and stringent. A bank which facilitates a cheque-collection fraud by breaching the requirements of the Money Laundering Regulations or the Money Laundering Sourcebook can expect to be found

[58] *Ladbroke & Co. v. Todd* (1914) 30 T.L.R. 433; *Hampstead Guardians v. Barclays Bank Ltd* (1923) 39 T.L.R. 229; *Lloyds Bank v. E.B. Savory & Co.* [1933] A.C. 201; *Orbit Mining & Trading Co. Ltd v. Westminster Bank Ltd* [1963] 1 Q.B. 794, 813–814; *Marfani & Co. Ltd v. Midland Bank Ltd* [1968] 1 W.L.R. 956; *Lumsden & Co. v. London Trustee Savings Bank* [1971] 1 Lloyds Rep. 114.

[59] There are likely to be legislative developments. At the time of going to press a "Proceeds of Crime" Bill intended to strengthen the money laundering regime is before Parliament.

[60] S.I. 1993 No. 1933. The Regulations were passed in implementation of the E.C. Money Laundering Directive of June 1991 (91/308/EEC) and came into force on April 1, 1994.

[61] Regulation 5(1)(a).

[62] Regulation 5(1)(b).

[63] Regulation 5(1)(c).

[64] Regulation 5(2).

[65] "Guidance Notes for Mainstream Bankers, Lending and Deposit Taking Activities" published by the Joint Money Laundering Steering Group, 10 Lombard Street, London EC3 9EL.

[66] Section 146 of the Financial Services and Markets Act 2000.

[67] Introduced by the Money Laundering Sourcebook Instrument of June 21, 2001.

[68] Rule ML 3.1.3.

[69] Guidance ML 3.1.4.

[70] Rule ML 6.2.1.

[71] Rule ML 6.3.1.

guilty of negligence in relation to the relevant collection. If the victim of the fraud is a private person, that person is also given a cause of action by section 150 of the Financial Services and Markets Act 2000 in respect of losses he has suffered as a result of the contravention of certain designated provisions of the Money Laundering Sourcebook.[72] That cause of action may have the additional advantage to the victim of permitting the recovery of damages, above and beyond the amount of the cheque in question, insofar as the fraud has occasioned the victim other foreseeable losses.

Examining the cheque

The collecting bank should be alert to the possibility that the cheque may bear on its face a warning that the customer may have misappropriated it.[73]   **23–41**

The most obvious indication of a possible misappropriation would be that a cheque to whose crossing have been added the words "account payee", or similar, is paid into the account of a customer other than the payee. Following the Cheques Act 1992[74] such cheques are non-transferable. So, although section 4 protection can still apply to such cheques,[75] a bank which collects an "account payee" cheque for a customer other than the named payee should be aware of the likelihood that the customer has a defective title to the cheque, and possibly no title at all. In anything other than very special circumstances, the bank is likely to be held negligent if it collects an "account payee" cheque for a person who is recognisably not the payee.   **23–42**

Given the number of cheques that are handled every day, it is probably not practicable for cashiers to examine the signatures of drawers, of whom, in any event, they are likely to have no knowledge.[76]   **23–43**

The practicalities of the bank's business are, of course, of considerable relevance. A cashier is not expected to have the same degree of insight as a manager, nor the opportunity to make the kind of deductions that might put a manager on his guard. So if there is insufficient reason for a cheque to be referred by a cashier to higher authority, and for whatever reason no such referral in fact occurs, the bank is unlikely to be found negligent.[77]   **23–44**

Employees, agents and fiduciaries

The collecting bank's duty of inquiry is of particular importance where it knows or ought to know that the customer is in a fiduciary position and the form of the cheque indicates that the money which it represents may be the property of the customer's principal. Where, therefore, an employee pays into   **23–45**

---

[72] See the Table at Schedule 5 to the Sourcebook.

[73] *Lloyds Bank Ltd v. E.B. Savory & Co.* [1933] A.C. 201, 229.

[74] See para. 21–35, *ante*.

[75] Section 4(2)(a) of the Cheques Act 1957 was amended by the Cheques Act 1992 to include specific reference to "account payee" cheques.

[76] *Orbit Mining and Trading Co. Ltd v. Westminster Bank Ltd* [1963] 1 Q.B. 794, 824.

[77] *Ross v. London County Westminster and Parr's Bank Ltd* [1919] 1 K.B. 678, 685; *Bevan v. The National Bank Ltd* (1906) 23 T.L.R. 65, 69; *Motor Traders Guarantee Corp. Ltd v. Midland Bank Ltd* [1937] 4 All E.R. 90, 95; *Honourable Society of the Middle Temple v. Lloyds Bank plc* [1999] 1 All E.R. (Comm.) 193, 227–228.

his private account cheques drawn by third persons in favour of his employer, or drawn by his employer in favour of third persons, there may be a duty of the banker to inquire.[78] However, it is no part of a bank's duty continually to keep itself abreast of the identity of the customer's employer.[79]

23–46 It is immaterial whether the customer is employed by an individual, by a firm, or by a limited company. In *A. L. Underwood Ltd v. Bank of Liverpool and Martins*,[80] the duty was held to extend to a "one-man company". There a Mr Underwood had converted his business into a private company, in which he held all the shares but one and of which he was sole director. Cheques payable to the company were indorsed by him as director and paid into his private account for collection. The collecting bank was held to be guilty of negligence as it treated the director as identical with the company and overlooked the materiality of the cheques' being drawn in the company's favour.

23–47 A customer who is a solicitor is in a somewhat unusual position. On the one hand such a customer is very likely to be handling money belonging to others. On the other hand, by reason of his standing and honourable profession, it is reasonable for a bank to expect a solicitor to be competent and honest.[81] In relation to the operation of solicitors' client accounts, banks and building societies are afforded specific statutory protection by section 85 of the Solicitors Act 1974, which provides:

> **Where a solicitor keeps an account with a bank or a building society in pursuance of rules under section 32—**
>
> (a) **the bank or society shall not incur any liability, or be under any obligation to make any inquiry, or be deemed to have any knowledge of any right or any person to any money paid or credited to the account, which it would not incur or be under or be deemed to have in the case of an account kept by a person entitled absolutely to all the money paid or credited to it;**

23–48 The purpose of this section appears to be to entitle a bank or building society to assume that moneys coming into a solicitor's client account are being dealt with properly. In *Lipkin Gorman v. Karpnale Ltd*, at first instance, Alliott J. took the view that the intention of the Legislature was not to give the

---

[78] *Lloyds Bank v. Savory* [1933] A.C. 201, 229–230 *per* Lord Wright. The duty is clearer where the cheques are indorsed by the servant *per pro: Bissell v. Fox* (1885) 53 L.T. 193; *Lloyds Bank v. Chartered Bank of India, Australia & China* [1929] 1 K.B. 40. See also *Carpenters' Co. v. British Mutual Banking Co.* [1938] 1 K.B. 511.

[79] *Orbit Mining & Trading Co. Ltd v. Westminster Bank Ltd* [1963] 1 Q.B. 794, 825 *per* Harman L.J.

[80] [1924] 1 K.B. 775; see also *Hannan's Lake View v. Armstrong* (1900) 5 Comm. Cas. 188; distinguished in *Liquidator of Cape of Good Hope Building Society v. Bank of Africa* (1900) 17 Cape S.C. 480.

[81] *e.g. Paramount Estates Ltd v. National Provincial Bank Ltd* (1945) 5 L.D.A.B. 418, 423. *Bank of Baroda v. Rayarel* [1995] 2 F.L.R. 376, [1995] Fam Law 610.

bank a special advantage in maintaining and operating a solicitor's client account but only to ensure that there was no special disadvantage.[82]

However, where a solicitor paid money into his overdrawn account by means of cheques drawn on the account of a third party and signed by the solicitor himself under a power of attorney, the bank should have made inquiries.[83]

The fact that a cheque has been signed on behalf of a drawer by a person **23–49** in a representative capacity is by no means unusual or suspicious or a circumstance that of itself requires investigation. A cashier may see hundreds of such cheques every day.[84] But a signature "by procuration" operates as notice that the agent has but a limited authority to sign[85] and the fact that such a signature appears on a cheque is a circumstance of which a collecting bank may have to take account.[86]

Previous conduct of the account

Where the past conduct of an account shows that the customer has been in **23–50** the habit of issuing cheques for which the account contains insufficient funds, this circumstance may demand that the bank employ particular circumspection when collecting cheques for the customer.[87] In today's business environment such matters would seem very hard for a cashier to keep in mind for each and every customer of his branch, but a manager might perhaps be expected to access such account information and take account of it, in the event that reference is made to him.[88]

Large cheques

The larger the amount of the cheque, the greater the opportunity of profit to **23–51** fraudsters and the greater the risk run by the bank in collecting it. A cheque

---

[82] [1987] 1 W.L.R. 987, 997. The point did not arise on appeal [1989] 1 W.L.R. 1340. *Paget on Banking*, (11th ed.), at pp. 154–155, expresses a contrary view based upon the legislative history of the section.

[83] *Midland Bank Ltd v. Reckitt* [1933] A.C. 1, HL.

[84] *Orbit Mining & Trading Co. Ltd v. Westminster Bank Ltd* [1963] 1 Q.B. 794, 824 *per* Harman L.J.

[85] Section 25 of the 1882 Act. See para. 7–08, *ante*.

[86] See *Midland Bank Ltd v. Reckitt* [1933] A.C. 1, HL where Lord Atkin, at 16, disapproves the view expressed by Lord Reading C.J. in *Morison v. London County & Westminster Bank Ltd* [1914] 3 K.B. 356, 368 that s.25 of the 1882 cannot confer a right to recover the proceeds of a cheque once it has been paid. However, it would appear from the reasoning expressed in Lord Atkin's opinion, taken as a whole, that he did not consider that s.25 is sufficient without more to put a bank on inquiry whenever it collects a cheque drawn "*per pro*". Thus, in practical terms there seems little to fault Lord Reading C.J's view that the fact that a cheque is signed "*per pro*" "is not to be entirely disregarded. . . . when considering whether the bank has acted without negligence it is to be borne in mind with other facts and circumstances": *Morison's* case at 368.

[87] *Motor Traders Guarantee Corp. Ltd v. Midland Bank Ltd* [1937] 4 All E.R. 90.

[88] See, for example, *The Honourable Society of the Middle Temple v. Lloyds Bank* [1999] 1 All E.R. (Comm.) 193, where, at 228, Rix J. comments that it ought not to be difficult for a clearer's computer system to disclose the fact that the customer had never used the clearer's services before, or not for a long time previously, and comments "Automation brings its advantages as well as its limitations."

in an uncharacteristically large amount for a given customer may constitute an aspect of suspicious circumstances demanding inquiry.[89]

Making inquiries

23–52   A bank whose suspicion is aroused should not refrain from making inquiries for fear of offending its customer,[90] unless the inquiry would, in any event, be futile as well as offensive.[91]

If the bank does inquire into circumstances that have aroused its suspicion, it is not expected to have in mind and ask its customer every question that a lawyer might raise in cross examination.[92] And if the bank makes reasonable inquiries to which it receives plausible responses, it is exonerated from negligence.[93] A rather more difficult question that can arise is whether a bank which has failed to make a particular inquiry, or take some other precaution, can be heard to argue that its failure did not influence events, as the fraud would still have proceeded undetected even if the inquiry had been made or the precaution taken.[94]

23–53   In a number of cases, the court has expressed the view that a bank simply cannot be heard to say that its negligence made no difference to events.[95] That view can be justified with regard to the fact that the bank's liability arises in conversion, a tort of strict liability, and there is nothing in section 4 to suggest that negligence must be causative of loss in order to deprive the bank of protection.

23–54   On other occasions, however, courts have attached relevance to the question of whether the bank's negligence was causative of the true owner's loss.[96] And if the circumstances are such that it can be affirmatively shown that a particular negligent oversight by the bank was entirely inconsequential, it would seem illogical for the negligence to count against the bank. This is illustrated by an example given in Marfani's case by Cairns J.:[97]

> "If, for example, it were found that, on opening an account, the bank official had failed to ask the prospective customer for his address, that would plainly be the

---

[89] *Lloyds Bank Ltd v. Chartered Bank of India, Australia and China* [1920] 1 K.B. 40; *Commissioners of Taxation v. English Scottish and Australian Bank* [1920] A.C. 683, 690; *Orbit Mining & Trading Co. Ltd v. Westminster Bank Ltd* [1963] 1 Q.B. 794, 815 *per* Sellers L.J.; *The Honourable Society of the Middle Temple v. Lloyds Bank* [1999] 1 All E.R. (Comm.) 193, 228 *per* Rix J.

[90] *A. L. Underwood Ltd v Bank of Liverpool and Martins* [1924] 1 K.B. 775, 793 *per* Scrutton L.J.

[91] *Marfani & Co. Ltd v. Midland Bank Ltd* [1968] 1 W.L.R. 956, 977 *per* Diplock L.J.

[92] *Penmount Estates Ltd v. National Provincial Bank Ltd* (1945) 5 L.D.A.B. 418, 425.

[93] *e.g. Smith & Baldwin v. Barclays Bank Ltd* (1944) 5 L.D.A.B. 370.

[94] See Paget, (11th ed.) pp. 461–462; Chalmers & Guest, (14th ed.), pp. 744–745.

[95] *A. L. Underwood Ltd v. Bank of Liverpool and Martins* [1923] 1 K.B. 775, at 789 *per* Bankes L.J. and 798 *per* Atkin L.J.; *Lloyds Bank Ltd v. E.B. Savory & Co. Ltd* [1932] 2 K.B. 122, CA, at 148 *per* Greer L.J. and [1933] A.C. 201, HL at 233, *per* Lord Wright; *Thackwell v. Barclays Bank plc* [1986] 1 All E.R. 676, 684 *per* Hutchison J.; *Lumsden & Co. v. London Trustee Savings Bank* [1971] 1 Lloyd's Rep. 114, 121 *per* Donaldson J.

[96] *Marfani & Co. Ltd v. Midland Bank Ltd* [1968] 1 W.L.R. 956, at 976–977 *per* Diplock L.J. and at 979–980 *per* Cairns J; *Ladbroke & Co. v. Todd* (1914) 30 T.L.R. 433, 434 *per* Bailhache J.; *Baker v. Barclays Bank Ltd* [1955] 1 W.L.R. 822 at 838 *per* Devlin J.; *Honourable Society of the Middle Temple v. Lloyds Bank plc* [1999] 1 All E.R. (Comm.) 193, 226 *per* Rix J.

[97] *Marfani & Co. Ltd v. Midland Bank Ltd* [1968] 1 W.L.R. 956, at 980.

omission of a proper precaution. If, however, it were shown that, on the following day, the customer had voluntarily disclosed a perfectly genuine and respectable address to the bank, it seems to me that it would be impossible to hold that the bank had forfeited the protection of the section by the initial piece of carelessness. In my opinion, if the bank can show that in all probability a particular precaution would have been unavailing, the failure to take that precaution is not such negligence as deprives them of the protection. The burden of proof on the bank is no doubt heavy, but I do not think that it can be so heavy as to require them to prove with certainty that the precaution would have been useless."

It is submitted that the true owner of a cheque is entitled to be protected against *the risk* that negligence in the collection of the cheque may have prejudiced his position, and not merely the fact of this occurring. The threshold at which negligence on the part of the bank becomes so demonstrably innocuous as to be regarded as irrelevant remains unclear on the authorities, but on any view is set at a high level and will rarely be attained. **23–55**

Collection through branches

For the convenience of their customers it has for many years been the practice of banks to allow a customer of any of their branches to pay into any other branch cheques for collection. The branch which receives the cheques sends them for collection. This practice, when applied to cheques payable to third persons, led to difficulties if the cheques had been misappropriated, for the receiving branch had no knowledge of the customer's circumstances and, therefore, though it saw his cheques, had no reason to make inquiries; while the customer's branch never saw the cheques and did not therefore know that they were payable to third persons and might have been misappropriated by the customer. In *Lloyds Bank v. Savory*,[98] the effect of this practice was considered. It was held that there could be no splitting of knowledge between the branches and that the banker could be in no better position than if the cheques had been paid into the customer's branch. The practice was on its very face inconsistent with provident precautions against a known risk and therefore amounted to negligence; the mere fact that the practice was usual and long established and that in the past no losses seemed to have ensued was not a justification. Therefore, if misappropriated cheques are collected without having been seen by the customer's own branch, this is likely to constitute a negligent procedure. **23–56**

Clearing bank acting on behalf of the collecting bank

Only a minority of banks have direct access to the cheque clearing system operated in the United Kingdom. Those that do not have direct access commonly utilise the services of one of the members of the clearing system to collect payment of cheques on their behalf. In *Importers Co. Ltd v. Westminster Bank Ltd*[99] the Court of Appeal held that the protection of section **23–57**

---

[98] [1933] A.C. 201.
[99] [1927] 2 K.B. 297.

4 is available to clearing banks acting for other, non-clearing banks in this way. On the particular facts of the case, the clearing bank discharged its burden of establishing that it had received payment of the plaintiff's cheques, which were crossed cheques marked "account payee only", without negligence. The Court of Appeal rejected a contention by the plaintiff that such cheques may not be handled unless the clearing bank can be sure it is acting on behalf of the payee. Otherwise, however, the extent to which the clearing bank owed any duty to the true owner to scrutinise cheques was not decided. On the facts of the case, there was nothing that any such scrutiny could have revealed so as to put the clearing bank upon inquiry.

23–58   The duties of the clearing bank were considered again by Rix J. in the *Commercial Court in Honourable Society of the Middle Temple v. Lloyds Bank*.[1] In that case *Lloyds Bank* acted as clearing agent for a Turkish bank, which sent it an English cheque drawn by the Middle Temple in favour of its insurers, Sun Alliance Insurance Ltd. The cheque was crossed "a/c payee" and was in a sum of about £183,000. It had been intercepted and fraudulently passed to the Turkish bank for collection at one of its branches in Istanbul. The cheque was cleared and collected and the proceeds remitted to the Turkish bank, whence they were rapidly dissipated.

23–59   Rix J. regarded a clearing bank undertaking the role of sub-agent for collection as having some duty to the true owner beyond merely obeying the collecting bank's instructions in order to bring itself within section 4 of the Cheques Act 1957. He held that the test was whether there was anything in the circumstances which was noticed or was such that it ought to have been noticed by the clearing bank. This test was to be applied against the background that a clearing bank handles huge numbers of instruments each day and no test should be applied that would render its business impossible. In considering what was practicable or negligent, regard must be had to the way in which business is done to the practice of bankers.[2] Rix J. accepted that the position of the clearing bank was distinct from that of the its immediate principal, the collecting bank. For the clearing bank never has the opportunity to vet the customer, nor to compare the customer's name on the paying in slip with the name of the payee on the cheque.[3]

23–60   Where a clearing bank acts on behalf of another bank based in the United Kingdom, it is entitled to assume that such bank has performed the usual scrutiny required of cheques such that, in particular, any "account payee" cheques are being collected only for customers of the same name as the payee. However, the same does not necessarily apply where a clearing bank receives cheques from a foreign bank. In that case there is a duty on the clearing bank to establish at least that the foreign bank is aware of the significance in English law of the words "account payee" when appearing on an English cheque and the clearing bank, unless it has taken steps to do so, cannot assume that that the foreign bank has discharged its responsibilities under English

---

[1] [1999] 1 All E.R. (Comm.) 193.
[2] *ibid.* 215.
[3] *ibid.* 218.

law.[4] As Lloyds Bank had not taken any such steps, it was unable to bring itself within the protection of section 4.[5]

However, the particular facts of the case rendered Lloyds Bank negligent on a quite independent score. As a result of an inquiry as to whether the cheque was going to be paid the stolen cheque was specifically drawn to the attention of the manager, who looked at the cheque in order to answer the inquiry. The cheque then became the subject of individual attention, and it was reasonable to expect the manager to notice that a very substantial cheque drawn in favour of a well-known English insurance company had been received from a Turkish bank with no obvious reason to be handling such an item and no history of remitting substantial commercial cheques for clearance. Moreover, the inquiry after fate stated that the Turkish bank's customer was "indeed in a difficult position", indicating that the cheque was not being collected for the payee, a very large and reputable insurance company. In those somewhat unusual circumstances, a duty of inquiry arose, which was not satisfied by Lloyds Bank.[6]

23–61

Whilst Lloyds Bank was therefore liable to the true owner, Middle Temple, in conversion its status as agent for the Turkish bank entitled it to be indemnified against the damages it had to pay. The agent's right to an indemnity in respect of actions performed at its principal's behest is a principle of general application.[7] The circumstances equally gave rise to an implied warranty by the Turkish bank to Lloyds Bank that its customer was entitled to the proceeds of the cheque.[8]

23–62

Conduct of the true owner

In *Lumsden & Co. v. London Trustee Savings Bank*[9] it was held that a defence of contributory negligence was available to an action for conversion of a cheque brought by the true owner against a collecting bank. That defence was removed in respect of any proceedings founded upon conversion by the Torts (Interference With Goods) Act 1977 and then reinstated by section 47 of the Banking Act 1979, which provides:

23–63

In any circumstances in which proof of absence of negligence on the part of a banker would be a defence to proceedings by reason of section 4 of the Cheques Act 1957, a defence of contributory negligence shall also be available to the banker notwithstanding the provisions of section 11(1) of the Torts (Interference With Goods) Act 1977.

Accordingly, whether he is sued in conversion or for money had and received the collecting bank is entitled to raise a plea of contributory negligence on the part of the true owner. The court will in those circumstances

23–64

---

[4] *ibid.* 224–225.
[5] *ibid.* 227.
[6] *ibid.* 227–229.
[7] *ibid.* 232; see *Bowstead & Reynolds on Agency* (16th ed.) p. 325; *Sheffield Corp. v Barclay* [1905] A.C. 392; *Yeung v. Hong Kong and Shanghai Banking Corp.* [1981] A.C. 787.
[8] *ibid.* 235.
[9] [1971] 1 Lloyd's Rep. 114.

apply the principle in section 1 of the Law Reform (Contributory Negligence) Act 1945, as follows:

Where any person suffers damage as the result partly of his own fault and partly of the fault of any other person or persons, a claim in respect of that damage shall not be defeated by reason of the fault of the person suffering the damage, but the damages recoverable in respect thereof shall be reduced to such extent as the court thinks just and equitable having regard to the claimant's share in the responsibility for the damage . . .

23–65   Before the defence of contributory negligence became available, it was suggested that where the transactions complained of were incidents in a series of similar transactions, the failure of the true owner to discover the misappropriation and to challenge the validity of the payments at an earlier date entitled the collecting bank to assume that there is no cause for suspicion or inquiry: in other words, the bank was "lulled to sleep" by the conduct of the true owner.[10] Subsequently it was pointed out that mere repeated inadvertence by the true owner could not, as the law then stood, affect his rights.[11] Nowadays, under section 47 of the Banking Act 1979 such inadvertence would probably be regarded as "fault" sufficient to count as contributory negligence and reduce damages.

23–66   Where the true owner of cheques expressly or impliedly authorises another person to have them collected in a manner that would, but for that authority, be irregular, he is deprived of any claim in conversion.[12]

OTHER INSTRUMENTS COVERED BY SECTION 4

23–67   The categories of instrument, apart from cheques, to which the protection of section 4 of the Cheques Act 1957 applies are given in subsection 4(2), as follows:

(b) any document issued by a customer of a banker which, though not a bill of exchange, is intended to enable a person to obtain payment from that banker of the sum mentioned in the document;

(c) any document issued by a public officer which is intended to enable any person to obtain payment from the Paymaster General or the Queen's and Lord Treasurer's Remembrancer of the sum mentioned in the document but is not a bill of exchange;

---

[10] *Morison v. London County and Westminster Bank* [1914] 1 K.B. 256.

[11] *Bank of Montreal v. Dominion Gresham Guarantee and Casualty Co.* [1930] A.C. 659; *Lloyds Bank v. Chartered Bank of India, Australia and China* [1929] 1 K.B. 40 at 60 *per* Scrutton L.J. and 79 *per* Tomlin J.; *Lloyds Bank v. Savory* [1933] A.C. 201; *Carpenters' Co. v. British Mutual Banking Co.* [1938] 1 K.B. 511, 535 (Slesser L.J.).

[12] *Lumsden & Co. v. London Trustee Savings Bank* [1971] 1 Lloyd's Rep. 114; *Souhada v. Bank of New South Wales* [1976] 2 Lloyd's Rep. 444; see also *Lloyds Bank v. Chartered Bank of India, Australia and China* [1929] 1 K.B. 40 at 56 *per* Scrutton L.J.

(d) any draft payable on demand drawn by a banker upon himself, whether payable at the head office or some other office of his bank.

The definition of "bank" and "banker" for the purposes of the Bills of Exchange Act 1882 and the Cheques Act 1957 is discussed elsewhere.[13]   **23–68**

The terms of subsection (2)(b) are wide enough to include a document issued by a customer of a bank in the form of a cheque but made out to an impersonal payee, such as to "cash or order".[14]

The instruments described in subsection (2)(d) are commonly referred to as "bankers drafts" or "bank drafts". These do not qualify as cheques[15] because, not being "addressed by one person to another",[16] they are not bills of exchange.

By statutory instrument section 4 is also made applicable to certain warrants issued by the Director of Savings.[17]

THE BANK AS HOLDER OF ORDER CHEQUES

Before the Cheques Act 1992 cheques were commonly issued in a negotiable form, typically being payable to a named payee "or order".[18] The   **23–69**
collecting bank, like any other third party, was capable of acquiring a title to an order cheque as holder,[19] holder for value,[20] or holder in due course.[21] If the collecting bank acquired the status of holder in due course, it took the order cheque free from any defect of title of prior parties.[22] As such it had a good defence to any claim by a prior party, such as by the drawer or payee, in conversion or for money had and received. Consequently, over the years a body of case law developed as to the circumstances in which a collecting bank was, or was not, entitled to the status of holder in due course of a negotiable cheque. This was supplemented by the statutory intervention of section 2 of the Cheques Act 1957, which facilitates the negotiation of order cheques to banks.

---

[13] See paras 21–07 et seq., ante.

[14] An example of such an instrument is one in cheque form but drawn payable to "cash"; see North and South Insurance Corporation Ltd v. National Provincial Bank Ltd [1936] 1 K.B. 328; Cole v. Milsome [1951] 1 All E.R. 311; Orbit Mining & Trading Co. Ltd v. Westminster Bank Ltd [1963] 1 Q.B. 794.

[15] Defined in section 73 of the 1882 Act.

[16] Section 3 of the 1882 Act.

[17] Regulation 8(2) of The Premium Savings Bonds Regulations 1972 (S.I. 1972 No. 765) as amended (S.I. 1980 No. 767); reg. 22(2) of The National Savings Stock Register Regulations 1976 (S.I. 1976 No. 2012); reg. 7(2) of The Savings Certificates (Yearly Plan) Regulations 1984 (S.I. 1984 No. 779); reg. 7(2) of The Savings Certificates Regulations 1991 (S.I. 1991 No. 1031); reg. 7(2) of The Savings Certificates (Children's Bonus Bonds) Regulations 1991 (S.I. 1991 No. 1407).

[18] For the various other categories of negotiable bills see section 8 of the 1882 Act and para. 8–03, ante.

[19] Section 2 of the 1882 Act. See para. 18–06, ante.

[20] Section 27 of the 1882 Act. See para. 18–14, ante.

[21] Section 29 of the 1882 Act. See para. 18–04, ante.

[22] Section 38 of the 1882 Act.

23–70   Since the Cheques Act 1992 nearly all cheques in the United Kingdom have been issued in non-transferrable "account payee" form.[23] It is impossible for a collecting bank to become a holder in due course of such a cheque. For this reason the law concerning the negotiation of cheques to banks has little continuing relevance. However, as it remains legally possible to issue cheques in a negotiable form some discussion of the principles applicable to their collection is merited.

23–71   A bank may give value for an order cheque by encashing it for the holder or by crediting him with it in account with the intention that he may at once draw against it. Where, for instance, a bank accepted for collection a cheque which it was asked to collect for a new account and gave its customer part of its value in cash, the bank was held to be a holder in due course.[24]

23–72   Whether or not the bank is a holder in due course depends on the circumstances in which it took the order cheque. In short the bank must take a negotiable cheque which is complete and regular on its face, not being overdue and without notice of its previous dishonour, in good faith and for value without notice of any defect in its customer's title: section 29(1) of the 1882 Act.

23–73   Clearly the bank takes an order cheque for value if it gives the customer cash in exchange.[25] The actual exchange of cash is however not necessary if the cheque is treated as cash as soon as it is paid into the customer's account and the customer is entitled, either expressly or by a course of business, to draw against it. Thus the cheque may have been paid in upon the express condition that the amount of it shall be at once placed to the customer's credit,[26] or for the express purpose of reducing an overdraft;[27] or there may be nothing more than an understanding or course of practice under which the customer is at once credited with the amount of the cheque and allowed to draw against it before clearance.[28]

23–74   A bank may also become a holder for value by virtue of having a lien on the order cheque, as where the bank collects for an overdrawn account or for an account which becomes overdrawn during the process of collection. Section 27(3) of the 1882 Act provides that:

27.—(3) Where the holder of a bill has a lien on it arising either from contract or by implication of law, he is deemed to be a holder for value to the extent of the sum for which he has a lien.

---

[23] See para. 21–35, *ante.*

[24] *Midland Bank v. Charles Simpson Motors Ltd* [1960] C.L.Y. 217.

[25] *Great Western Ry v. London and County Bank* [1901] A.C. 414.

[26] *Ex p. Richdale* (1882) 19 Ch.D. 409; *National Bank v. Silke* [1891] 1 Q.B. 435; *Royal Bank of Scotland v. Tottenham* [1894] 2 Q.B. 715.

[27] *M'Lean v. Clydesdale Bank* (1883) 9 App.Cas. 95.

[28] *Capital and Counties Bank v. Gordon* [1903] A.C. 240. A banker who has allowed his customer habitually to draw against uncleared cheques cannot withdraw the privilege without notice (*Armfield v. London and Westminster Bank* (1883) 1 Cab. & E. 170; *Freeman v. Standard Bank* [1905] Transvaal H. 26); see in this connection *Westminster Bank Ltd v. Zang* [1966] A.C. 182.

A bank has a lien on all securities and valuables of its customer which come **23–75** into its hands in its capacity as banker in the ordinary course of his business.[29] Where, therefore, the customer is indebted to the bank on an overdraft, the lien arises immediately a cheque is paid in for collection—presumably by implication of law.[30]

Section 2 of the Cheques Act 1957 provides that: **23–76**

2. A banker who gives value for, or has a lien on, a cheque payable to order which the holder delivers to him for collection without indorsing it, has such (if any) rights as he would have had if, upon delivery, the holder had indorsed it in blank.

Thus the collecting bank is able to become the holder of an order cheque[31] **23–77** without having to obtain the previous holder's indorsement of it. The section was introduced in order to speed up the process of cheque collection by removing the necessity for customers to indorse cheques when handing them in for collection. However, as a matter of practice following the enactment of the Cheques Act 1957 the Committee of London Clearing Bankers advised its members still to examine and obtain indorsements on a variety of instruments.[32]

The facts of *Westminster Bank Ltd v. Zang*[33] provided the Court of Appeal **23–78** and House of Lords with the opportunity of interpreting section 2. The defendant drew an order cheque in favour of the managing director of a company—personally, not as such—which cheque the payee paid in to the company's overdrawn account with the plaintiff bank. The cheque was dishonoured and the bank handed it to the payee's solicitors in order that he might sue the drawer. The payee's action was dismissed for want of prosecution and the bank thereupon recovered the cheque and itself sued the drawer. As the cheque was never indorsed by the payee, the bank relied upon section 2 in seeking to establish itself as holder of the cheque.

The defendant argued that: **23–79**

(a) the cheque was not delivered to the bank by the holder, but by the payee as the company's agent;

(b) that section 2 required that the cheque be delivered for collection for the account of the holder, and that as the cheque was collected for the account of the company, which was not the payee, the section did not apply;

[29] *Currie v. Misa* (1867) 1 App.Cas. 554, HL and *Brandao v. Barnett* (1846) 3 C.B. 519, HL.

[30] *Re Keever, a bankrupt, ex p. Trustee of the Property of the Bankrupt v. Midland Bank Ltd* [1967] Ch. 182; Ungoed-Thomas J. (at 191) further held that handing a cheque in for collection in circumstances which create a lien is a "contract, dealing or transaction" within the meaning of s.45 of the Bankruptcy Act 1914; and see *Barclays Bank Ltd v. Astley Industrial Trust Ltd* [1970] 2 Q.B. 527. Now see the Insolvency Act 1986 s.284.

[31] See para. 8–03, *ante* for the categories of negotiable bill.

[32] See Chalmers & Guest (15th ed.), pp. 706–709.

[33] [1966] A.C. 182, CA and HL.

(c) the bank lost its lien when it delivered the cheque to the payee's solicitors.

The first argument was rejected by the Court of Appeal. The second argument was rejected by the House of Lords. But the third argument prevailed. Thus the bank, having neither given value nor having preserved its lien, was unable to bring itself within section 2 and was not entitled to sue upon the cheque.

23–80   The collecting bank's role of agent for collection of an order cheque on behalf of its customer is not necessarily incompatible with the bank's at the same time being a holder of the cheque.[34]

---

[34] *Barclays Bank v. Astley Industrial Trust* [1970] 2 Q.B. 527, 538.

PART THREE

CHAPTER 24

THE PROMISSORY NOTE

Promissory note defined

THE 1882 Act thus defines a promissory note: **24–01**

83.—(1) A promissory note is an unconditional promise in writing made by one person to another signed by the maker, engaging to pay, on demand or at a fixed or determinable future time, a sum certain in money, to, or to the order of, a specified person or to bearer.

Application of the 1882 Act

In construing promissory notes, Part II of the 1882 Act, relating to bills of **24–02**
exchange, must be taken into account for, by section 89(1), certain of its
provisions must, *mutatis mutandis*, be applied.[1]

The extent of the application to promissory notes of the provisions relating
to bills is thus stated:

89.—(1) Subject to the provisions in this part,[2] and except as by this section provided, the provisions of this Act relating to bills of exchange apply, with the necessary modifications, to promissory notes.

(2) In applying those provisions the maker of a note shall be deemed to correspond with the acceptor of a bill, and the first indorser of a note shall be deemed to correspond with the drawer of an accepted bill payable to drawer's order.

(3) The following provisions as to bills do not apply to notes; namely provisions relating to—

(a) Presentment for acceptance;

(b) Acceptance;

(c) Acceptance supra protest;

---

[1] For a recent example of the Court applying the provisions of the section—see *Cardinal Finance Investments Corporation v. Central Bank of Yemen* [2001] Lloyds Rep. Banking 1.

[2] As to other provisions in this part see especially s.86(3) (overdue note): and *ante*, para. 17–35.

(d) Bills in a set.

(4) Where a foreign note is dishonoured, protest thereof is unnecessary.[3]

In addition to the above differences between a bill and a note, the rule as to overdue instruments is not so strict in the case of a note payable on demand as in the case of bills and cheques.[4]

Contracting words

24-03   A note made payable at a particular place in the body thereof must be presented there in order to render the maker liable,[5] even though the note does not state that payment shall be made at such place "only and not elsewhere", as is required in the case of a bill.[6] Again, a note may be made not only joint, but joint and several, while the acceptance on a bill must be either joint or several.

No precise words of contract are essential in a promissory note,[7] providing that the legal effect is an unconditional promise to pay and also that there is evidence of the intention of the parties to make a promissory note.[8] Thus a document, which is no more than a receipt for money containing the terms on which the money is to be repaid and not intended to be negotiable, does not constitute a promissory note.[9]

It having been held by Lord Holt that a promissory note was not negotiable at common law,[10] the statute of 1704[11] was passed to get over the difficulty.[12] This statute (now repealed by the 1882 Act, Sched. II) did not, however, attempt to define a note as such. An instrument running "I promise to account with A B or order for £50, value received by me" has been held a good note within the Statute of Anne.[13] So, "I do acknowledge myself to be indebted to A in £100, to be paid on demand for value received" was held to be a good note within the same statute, the words "to be paid" amounting to a promise

---

[3] See *ante*, para. 16–10.
[4] See *post*, para. 24–10.
[5] See *post*, para. 24–11.
[6] 1882 Act, s.19(2)(c); *ante*, para. 10–07.
[7] *Brooks v. Elkins* (1836) 2 M. & W. 74.
[8] *Sibree v. Tripp* (1846) 15 M. & W. 23; *cf. Jackson v. Slipper* (1869) 19 L.T. 640; and see *Akbar Khan v. Attar Singh* [1936] 2 All E.R. 545; *Wirth v. Weigal Leygonie & Co. Ltd* [1939] 3 All E.R. 712. In *Syndic in Bankruptcy of Nasrallah Khoury v. Khayat* [1943] 2 All E.R. 406, PC, it was held that instruments drawn "I shall pay to the order of . . . two thousand gold Turkish pounds . . . " were promissory notes and not undertakings to deliver gold. See also *Dickie v. Singh*, 1974 S.L.T. 129. See also *Clayton v. Bradley* [1987] 1 W.L.R. 521.
[9] *Clayton v. Bradley* [1987] 1 W.L.R.521.
[10] *Buller v. Crips* (1703) 6 Mod. 29; *Clerke v. Martin* (1701) 2 Ld.Raym. 757.
[11] 3 & 4 Anne, c. 8.
[12] The correctness of Lord Holt's view seems to have been by no means accepted at the time. The statute of Anne bears the significant preamble: "It has been held that". See *Goodwin v. Robarts* (1875) L.R. 10 Ex. 337, 349 (Cockburn C.J.); *Grant v. Vaughan* (1764) 3 Burr. 1516, 1528 (Lord Mansfield C.J.).
[13] *Morice v. Lee* (1725) 8 Mod. 362; *Chadwick v. Allen* (1725) 2 Stra. 706.

to pay, the Court observing that the same words in a lease would amount to a covenant to pay rent.[14]

The sum payable on a promissory note will be "certain", as in the case of a bill, though it is payable with interest, or by stated instalments, with or without a proviso making the whole due on default of any instalment, or according to an indicated rate of exchange, or one to be ascertained as directed by the note itself.[15] If interest appears as a reference to a rate which is clearly determinable, the note would seem not to be invalidated as a negotiable instrument; *quaere* floating rates in general.

Instalments

As regards a note payable by instalments, the particular time of payment for each instalment must be stated, otherwise it will not be a note.[16] Presentment and notice of dishonour will probably be required when each instalment falls due, in order to charge indorsers, but laches as to one instalment will in ordinary cases only discharge indorsers as to that one. A note payable by instalments cannot be indorsed for less than the entire sum due upon it.[17]   **24–04**

Instruments treated as notes

Where an instrument in the form of a bill is not addressed to any drawee, a written acceptance by any one may be construed as a promise to pay, and the instrument may be a valid promissory note.[18] And where, for an executed consideration, a note was given, expressed to be "for £20 borrowed and   **24–05**

---

[14] *Casborne v. Dutton* (1727) Sel.N.P., 13th ed., vol. I, 329. In the following cases the words used have been held to constitute good promissory notes: *Wheatley v. Williams* (1836) 1 M. & W. 533 ("Gentlemen, I have received the imperfect books which, together with the costs overpaid on the settlement of your account, amounts to £80 7s., which sum I will pay you within two years from this date. I am, Gentlemen, your obedient servant, THOS. WILLIAMS"). *Ellis v. Mason* (1839) 7 Dowl. P.C. 598 ("John Mason, 14th February, 1836, borrowed of Mary Anne Mason, his sister, the sum of £14 in cash, a loan, in promise of payment of which I am truly thankful for"); *Hutley v. Marshall* (1882) 46 L.T. 186 ("Three months' notice I promise to pay S.H. interest 5 per cent. per annum for £500 value received"). In the following cases the words used were held not to be sufficient: *Jarvis v. Wilkins* (1841) 7 M. & W. 410 ("I undertake to pay to Mr. Robert Jarvis the sum of £6 4s. for a suit of clothes ordered by Daniel Page"; a guarantee). *Sibree v. Tripp* (1846) 15 M. & W. 23 ("Memo. Mr. Sibree has this day deposited with me £500 on the sale of £10,300 £3 p.c. Spanish, to be returned on demand"). *Hyne v. Dewdney* (1852) 21 L.J.Q.B. 278 ("Borrowed, this day, of Mr. John Hyne, Stonehouse, the sum of £100 for one or two months; cheque £100 on the Naval Bank", a simple acknowledgement). A banker's deposit note worded thus: "Received £150 to account for on demand", is not a "security for money" (Hopkins v. Abbott (1875) L.R. 19 Eq. 222). The following instruments were held not to be notes within the Stamp Act 1815: "I have received the £20 which I borrowed of you, and I have to be accountable for the same sum with interest" (*Horne v. Redfearn* (1838) 4 Bing. N.C. 433). "Borrowed of Mr. J. White the sum of £200 to account for on behalf of the Alliance Club at two month's notice if required" (*White v. North* (1849) 3 Ex. 689).

[15] 1882 Act, s.9, *ante*, para. 2–20. A note payable by instalments was held to be within the Statute of Anne (*Oridge v. Sherborne* (1843) 11 M. & W. 374).

[16] *Moffat v. Edwards* (1841) Car. & M. 16. Unless the note specially so provides, the failure to pay an instalment does not authorise the holder to sue for the whole of the balance (*Van der Westhuizen v. Lochner* (1908) 18 C.T.R. 446).

[17] The 1882 Act, s.32(2), *ante*, para. 9–06, forbids a partial indorsement.

[18] *Peto v. Reynolds* (1854) 9 Ex. 410, 415, 416 (Parke, Alderson and Martin BB.), approved in *Mason v. Lack* (1929) 140 L.T. 696; *Haseldine v. Winstanley* [1936] 2 K.B. 101.

received", but at the end were the words "which I promise never to pay", Lord Macclesfield rejected the word never[19] for a contract ought to be expounded in the sense in which the party making it apprehended that the other party understood it.[20] The Court may, but will not necessarily, hold that an instrument, which fails to qualify as a bill of exchange, can be enforced as a promissory note.[21] In *Credit Agricole Indosuez v. Ecumet (U.K.) Ltd*,[22] an instrument, which was subject to the law of the United Arab Emirates, arguably failed to meet the requirements of UAE law so as to constitute a bill of exchange. The Court declined to give summary judgment on an alternative claim that by accepting the instrument in return for the release of documents, the defendants had made a promissory note. Tomlinson J. observed:

"I should hesitate long before concluding . . . that what is on this hypothesis an acceptance of an instrument intended by the presenter and by the acceptor to be a bill of exchange can nonetheless take effect as the making of a promissory note on the discovery of defects which prevent it from being a bill of exchange."

Under the 1882 Act, an instrument may, for certain purposes, be treated as a promissory note, though it is not in note form:

5.—(2) Where in a bill drawer and drawee are the same person, or where the drawee is a fictitious person or a person not having capacity to contract, the holder may treat the instrument, at his option, either as a bill of exchange or as a promissory note.

Such an instrument is not strictly a bill, for it is not drawn by one person on another.[23]

It was held, upon the Statute of Anne, that an instrument payable to the maker's order was not a note, until indorsed, when it became payable to order or to bearer, according as the indorsement was blank or special,[24] and this is now recognised in the following provision of the 1882 Act:

83.—(2) An instrument in the form of a note payable to maker's order is not a note within the meaning of this section unless and until it is indorsed by the maker.

A note made by the maker to himself and another or a joint note by the maker and others to himself is not a valid instrument until indorsement and delivery, for without indorsement such an instrument is open to the objection

---

[19] See *Simpson v. Vaughan* (1739) 2 Atk. 32 (Lord Hardwicke).

[20] *Allan v. Mawson* (1814) 4 Camp. 115.

[21] *Novaknit Hellas S.A. v. Kumar Bros International Limited* [1998] Lloyds Rep. Banking 287.

[22] Unreported, Tomlinson J., March 29, 2001.

[23] See *ante*, para. 3–09, and *Re British Trade Corporation* [1932] 2 Ch. 1.

[24] *Brown v. De Winton* (1848) 17 L.J.C.P. 281; *Gay v. Lander* (1848) 17 L.J.C.P. 286, and cases there cited. In *Absolon v. Marks* (1847) 11 Q.B. 19, the defendant was held liable on a note made by himself and others, promising to pay "to our and each of our order" and proved to have been indorsed by him.

that the same party is both promisor and promisee thereon.[25] A note, however, by the maker and others to himself, if several as well as joint, may be valid at the suit of the payee as to the several contracts of his co-makers.[26]

Fixed or determinable future time

An instrument expressed to be payable on a contingency is not a promissory **24–06** note, see 1882 Act, section 11. A promissory note payable "on or before" a given date was held by a majority of the Court of Appeal in *Williamson v. Rider*[27] to be uncertain, as the words introduced a contingency. Ormerod L.J., dissenting, preferred to adopt the meaning of the words in the notice to quit in *Dagger v. Shepherd*[28] to the effect that "there is a fixed date for payment . . ., that the promisor binds himself to pay on that date, and if he fails can be sued under his promissory note, but if he chooses to pay—and it is purely a matter for him—at an earlier date . . . then the holder of the bill is under an obligation to accept that payment".[29]

In *Claydon v. Bradley*[30] the Court of Appeal held that they were bound by the majority decision in *Williamson v. Rider* and decided that a note expressed "to be paid back in full by 1 July 1983" was not a promissory note. However, Dillon L.J.[31] seemed to indicate that he preferred the reasoning of Ormerod L.J.'s dissenting judgment:

> "In the present case the time for payment was bound to arrive; the money was payable on 1 July 1983 if it had not been repaid, at the option of the payer, before."

It is submitted that this practical approach is to be preferred, but the Court of Appeal is now clearly bound by the majority view in *Williamson v. Rider* and it seems that only a decision of the House of Lords will alter the position.

Joint and several notes[32]

A note may be made by two or more makers. As to this the 1882 Act **24–07** provides as follows:

---

[25] *Moffat v. Van Millengen* (1787) 2 B. & P. 124; *Mainwaring v. Newman* (1800) *ibid.* 120; *Teague v. Hubbard* (1828) 8 B. & C. 345; *cf. Foster v. Ward* (1883) Cab. & E. 168. These cases, however, relate to actions between a partner and his firm, or between firms having partners in common, and in this respect they are no longer authorities.

[26] *Beecham v. Smith* (1858) 27 L.J.Q.B. 257.

[27] [1963] 1 Q.B. 89.

[28] [1946] 1 K.B. 215.

[29] *Williamson v. Rider* [1963] 1 Q.B. 89; Ormerod L.J.'s dissenting view was followed in the Canadian Supreme Court in *John Burrows Ltd v. Subsurface Surveys Ltd* (1968) 68 D.L.R. (2d) 354 in which a note provided that the maker may pay "on account of principal from time to time the whole or any portion thereof upon giving thirty (30) days' notice", and in *Creative Press v. Harman and Harman* (1973) I.R. 313, in which a note was "drawn" payable "on or before the 1st November, 1970", the Court approving *John Burrows v. Subsurface Surveys (supra)* and not *Williamson v. Rider*.

[30] [1987] 1 W.L.R. 521.

[31] At 525.

[32] See the Civil Liability (Contributions) Act 1978.

85.—(1) A promissory note may be made by two or more makers, and they may be liable thereon jointly, or jointly and severally according to its tenor.

A note signed by more than one person and beginning "we promise", etc., is a joint note only. Joint and several notes usually express that the makers jointly and severally promise. To cover the case of an instrument somewhat ambiguously worded, the 1882 Act provides as follows:

85.—(2) Where a note runs "I promise to pay" and is signed by two or more persons it is deemed to be their joint and several note.[33]

So a note beginning in the singular "I promise" and signed by one partner for himself and his co-partners is the joint note of all, and the party signing is not severally liable.[34] Where a note ran "I, J.C., promise to pay", and it was signed "J.C. or else H.B.", it was held not to be a note within the Statute of Anne as regards H.B., since it was a conditional promise on his part.[35]

A joint and several note, though on one piece of paper, comprises, in reality and in legal effect, several notes. Thus, if A, B and C join in making a joint and several promissory note there are, in effect, four notes. There is the joint note, of the three makers, and there are also the several notes of each of the three.[36]

The joint note may be valid though the several notes are void.[37] Yet for some purposes it is still one contract. Thus, an alteration which effects the liability of one maker vitiates the entire instrument—for instance, where a new maker is added to a joint and several note.[38]

Contract of maker

24–08   The maker of a note is the party primary liable on it, and is in the position of the acceptor of a bill:

88. The maker of a promissory note by making it—
(1) Engages that he will pay it according to its tenor;
(2) Is precluded from denying to a holder in due course the existence of the payee and his then capacity to indorse.

---

[33] *March v. Ward* (1792) 1 Peake 177, followed in *Clerk v. Blackstock* (1816) Holt N.P.C. 474.

[34] Ex p. *Buckley* (1845) 14 M. & W. 469, 475, overruling *Hall v. Smith* (1823) 1 B. & C. 407, where it was held that such a note was the several note also of the party signing; see also *Maclae v. Sutherland* (1845) 3 E. & B. 1.

[35] *Ferris v. Bond* (1821) 4 B. & Ald. 679.

[36] *Beecham v. Smith* (1858) 27 L.J.Q.B. 257; see *King v. Hoare* (1844) 13 M. & W. 494, 505 (Parke B.). In such a case the payee might sue the three, or each singly; he could not do both: *Streatfield v. Halliday* (1790) 3 T.R. 779); but under the CPR, r. 19.1 any number of defendants may be joined as parties to a claim.

[37] *Maclae v. Sutherland* (1854) 3. E. & B. 1; or the joint note may be discharged in bankruptcy, leaving the separate notes intact (*Simpson v. Henning* (1875) L.R. 10 Q.B. 406).

[38] *Gardner v. Walsh* (1855) 5 E. & B. 83; see, further, *Flanagan v. The National Bank Ltd* [1939] I.R. 352.

Delivery

As in the case of a bill, delivery is necessary in order to render the maker's   **24–09**
engagement operative.

**84. A promissory note is inchoate and incomplete until delivery thereof
to the payee or bearer.**[39]

Presentment

The maker of a note is not discharged if a note is not presented for payment,   **24–10**
for the liability of the maker to pay according to the tenor of the note is
absolute, except as provided by s.87(1).[40] The position of an indorser of a note
is as follows:

**86.—(1) Where a note payable on demand has been indorsed, it must
be presented for payment within a reasonable time of the indorsement. If
it be not so presented the indorser is discharged.**
**(2) In determining what is a reasonable time, regard shall be had to the
nature of the instrument, usage of trade, and the facts of the particular
case.**[41]

The question of what is a reasonable time under sections 45(2), 74(2)
(cheques), and 86(2), is a question of fact.[42]
A promissory note payable on demand differs from a bill payable on
demand or a cheque, in this respect: the bill and the cheque are probably
intended to be presented and paid immediately, and the drawer may have good
reasons for desiring to withdraw his funds from the control of the drawee
without delay; but a promissory note payable on demand is very often
originally intended as a continuing security, and afterwards indorsed as such.[43]
Indeed it is not uncommon for the payee, and afterwards for the indorsee, to
receive from the maker interest periodically for many years on such a note.
Sometimes the note is expressly made payable with interest, which clearly
indicates the intention of the parties to be, that though the holder may demand
payment immediately, yet he is not bound to do so.[44]
If transferred by indorsement, there appears nothing to exclude bank notes
(other than those of the Bank of England) from the operation of section 86(1)

---

[39] *Chapman v. Cottrell* (1865) 34 L.J. Ex. 186.
[40] *Post* para. 24–11.
[41] *Shute v. Robins* (1828) M. & M. 133.
[42] *Wheeler v. Young* (1897) 13 T.L.R. 468 (decided on s. 74(2)); see also *Serle v. Norton* (1841)
2 Moo. & R, 401, 403 (Lord Abinger C.B.); *Firth v. Brooks* (1861) 4 L.T. 467; *Harris Abattoir
Co. v. Maybee* (1914) 31 O.L.R. 453; *Campbell v. Riendeau* (1892) Q.R. 2 Q.B. 604. In *Chartered
Bank of India v. Dickson* (1871) L.R. 3 P.C. 574, 584n., and *Bank of British North America v.
Haslip* (1914) 31 O.L.R. 442, the question was regarded as one of mixed law and fact.
[43] *Brooks v. Mitchell* (1841) 9 M. & W. 15; see also s.86(3), *ante*, para. 17–35.
[44] *cf. Barrough v. White* (1825) 4 B. & C. 325, 327.

and (2).[45] If transferred by delivery, the question arose whether they were taken in complete satisfaction or not,[46] and whether in respect of an antecedent debt or not.[47] If not taken as satisfaction, the transferee must circulate or present them the day after he receives them, in order to enable him, in the event of the bank failing, to sue the person from whom they were received on the consideration that was given for them.[48]

The same rules which govern the presentment and circulation of bank notes also applied to such bankers' paper as might be fairly considered part of the circulating medium of the country. Such were the bills of a country banker on his London correspondent.[49]

Place of presentment

24–11   A note must be presented where a note is made payable at a particular place:

87.—(1) Where a promissory note is in the body of it made payable at a particular place, it must be presented for payment at that place in order to render the maker liable. In any other case, presentment for payment is not necessary in order to render the maker liable.

(2) Presentment for payment is necessary in order to render the indorser of a note liable.

(3) Where a note is in the body of it made payable at a particular place, presentment at that place is necessary in order to render an indorser liable; but when a place of payment is indicated by way of memorandum only, presentment at that place is sufficient to render the indorser liable, but a presentment to the maker elsewhere, if sufficient in other respects, shall also suffice.

To entitle the maker to presentment for payment at a particular place, it is not necessary, as in the case of a bill (see s.19(2)),[50] that the note should be expressly payable at that place "only and not elsewhere". It is sufficient to state the place of payment in the body of the note.[51] The mere mention of the place of payment, however, in the margin or at the foot of the note, as distinguished from the body thereof, is to be treated as a memorandum only

[45] Bank of England notes, being legal tender, are equivalent to cash; see *post*, para. 24–14; the Bank of England today has a monopoly of note issue in the United Kingdom.

[46] See *ante*, para. 17–25.

[47] *Ante*, para. 19–13; but *cf. Lichfield Union (Guardians) v. Greene* (1875) 26 L.J.Ex. 140, 142.

[48] *Camidge v. Allenby* (1827) 6 B. & C. 373.

[49] *ibid.*; *Shute v. Robins* (1828) N. & M. 133; today there are no notes issued by banks in England and inter-bank settlements are made by means of drafts on the Bank of England.

[50] *Ante*, para. 10–07.

[51] *Sanderson v. Bowes* (1811) East 500; *Corporation Securities Ltd v. Royal Bank* [1935] 2 D.L.R. 173; but see *Schonemier v. King and Jardine* (1929) 50 B.C.R. 174. It is immaterial that the place of payment was inserted merely for the purpose of giving jurisdiction to a particular court (*Josolyne v. Roberts* [1908] 2 K.B. 349).

and not as part of the contract.[52] Where a note written in the French language bore at the foot the words "payable à la fin d'octobre 1843. Chez M. Legrelle", the Court thought that, by English law, it would be necessary to aver and prove a presentment at Legrelle's, and that the expression "Chez", etc., although separated by a full point from the words fixing the date of payment, were not, on that account merely, to be regarded only as a memorandum.[53] Where the whole of the body of the note was in print, including the mention of the place of payment, which appeared at the bottom of the note, this latter was held to be part of the note, and not a mere memorandum.[54] Since the passing of the 1882 Act, a statement of a place of payment written by the maker across the face of the note has been held to be a mere memorandum.[55]

Where a bill is drawn by one branch of a bank upon another and the holder exercises his option under section 5(2)[56] to treat it as a promissory note, the address of the drawee, though properly part of the instrument when treated as a bill, forms no part of the contract contained in it when treated as a promissory note, but is a memorandum only; hence, the instrument, though a promissory note by virtue of section 5(2) is not in the body of it made payable at a particular place.[57]

Where a promissory note is payable at either of two places, presentment at either of them will suffice. Thus where a country bank note was made payable both at Tonbridge and in London, presentment in London was held sufficient, though it was proved that, had it been presented at Tonbridge, the nearest place, it would have been paid.[58] But it is conceived that presentment of a cheque to the London agents of the drawer's bankers, though described on the cheque as agents, is insufficient, for the obligation to pay a cheque must in general depend on the state of the drawer's account, which the London agents may not know.[59]

The presentment for payment need not be on the day that the note matures, unless there is an express stipulation to that effect (section 52(2)[60]; applied to notes by section 89). The mere statement of a place of payment in the body of the note is not such a stipulation; and, though it renders presentment for payment necessary,[61] the maker is not discharged by a failure to present at that place on the day of maturity.[62]

---

[52] *Williams v. Waring* (1829) 10 B. & C. 2; *Exon v. Russell* (1816) 4 M. & S. 505; *Price v. Mitchell* (1815) 4 Camp. 200; and even if the statement in the memorandum commence with the words "payable at" (*Masters v. Baretto* (1849 8 C.B. 433; *Harvey & Co. v. Daugherty* [1914] T.P.D. 655).

[53] *Vanderdonckt v. Thellusson* (1849) 19 L.J.C.P. 12.

[54] *Trecothick v. Edwin* (1816) 1 Skarkt. 468; see *contra, Curtis v. Rattray* [1913] W.L.D. 181.

[55] *Stevenson v. Brown* (1902) 18 T.L.R. 268.

[56] *Ante*, paras 3–09 and 24–05.

[57] *Re British Trade Corporation* [1932] 2 Ch. 1.

[58] *Beeching v. Gower* (1816) Holt.N.P.C. 313; see *contra Naidoo v. Naidoo* (1910) 10 H.C.G. 352. As to a cheque payable in either of two places but customarily as a London cheque, see *Forman v. Bank of England* (1902) 18 T.L.R. 339.

[59] *Bailey v. Bodenham* (1864) 33 L.J.C.P. 252, 254 (Byles J.).

[60] *Ante*, para. 12–02.

[61] *Britannia Electric Lamp Works Ltd v. Mandler (D.) & Co.* [1939] 2 K.B. 129.

[62] *Gordon v. Kerrs* (1898) 35 S.L.R. 469.

Dominion and American Law

24–12   The corresponding provisions of the Canadian Bills of Exchange Act (ss.183, 184) have given rise to much difficulty.[63] They differ to some extent in their wording from section 87 of the 1882 Act; in particular, it is provided by section 183(2) that the maker is not discharged by the omission to present at the place named in the body of the note on the day it matures, but that if action is brought before such presentment the costs are to be in the discretion of the Court.[64] Two conflicting views have been expressed. According to one view, there must be a presentment for payment before action; and, unless presentment is proved, the action will fail. Since, however, it is the duty of the maker to be in a position to pay the note when presented, he will be deprived of costs if he failed to keep sufficient funds to meet the note at the place named, from maturity till action brought.[65] According to the other view, presentment for payment before action is not essential; but if the maker has performed his duty by keeping sufficient funds at the place named to meet the note, the plaintiff will be disentitled to costs.[66]

The South African law, with the exception of that of Natal, provides (Cape, s.86(1); Transvaal, s.86(1); Orange Free State, s.86(1)), that presentment is unnecessary where the particular place mentioned is the place of business of the payee and the note remains in his hands. Summary judgment (provisional sentence) cannot, however, be obtained without an allegation that the note, if made payable in the body thereof at a particular place, has been presented for payment.[67] A presentment after maturity is a valid presentment.[68]

The Australian Act reproduces section 87 in its section 93, as does the New Zealand Act in section 88. Section 68 of the Indian Negotiable Instruments Act 1881 covers both bills and promissory notes in similar terms.

In the United States of America there is no equivalent to section 87(1); presentment for payment is governed by section 3–501 of the Uniform Commercial Code and is applicable to both bills and notes.

---

[63] See generally Falconbridge, Banking and Bills of Exchange (7th ed., 1969), pp. 897 *et seq.*

[64] Falconbridge, *op. cit.* p. 898, says that the subsection "enjoys the distinction of being perhaps the most obscure provision of the Canadian Bills of Exchange Act, with the possible exception of the similar provision in s.93" (relating to bills).

[65] *Warner v. Symon-Kaye Syndicate* (1894) 27 N.S.R. 340; *Jones v. England* (1906) 7 Terr.L.R. 440; *Albert v. Marshall* (1913) 48 N.S.L.R. 34; *Morgan v. Shaw* [1926] 1 D.L.R. 828.

[66] *Merchants' Bank of Canada v. Henderson* (1897) 28 O.R. 360, followed in *Freeman v. Canadian Guardian Life Insurance Co.* (1908) 17 O.L.R. 296; *Robertson v. North Western Register Co.* (1910) 19 Man.R. 402; *Bank of Commerce v. Bellamy* (1915) 25 D.L.R. 133 (where the divergent views on the question are discussed by the Court); *Hayden Clinton National Bank v. Dixon* (1916) 26 D.L.R. 694; *Anderson v. Hiestead* (1916) 10 W.W.R. 636; 34 W.L.R. 474; *Flexlume Sign Co. v. Ettenberg* (1916) O.R. 50 S.C. 308; *Sinclair v. Deacon* (1919) 7 E.L.R. 222; *Sparks v. Conmee* (1919) 45 O.L.R. 202; *Schonemier v. King and Jardine* (1929) 50 B.C.R. 174.

[67] *Van Niekerk v. Wolmarans* [1906] T.S. 19; see also *Kuper v. Zwiegelaar* (1906) 23 S.C. 748. Presentment after the issue of the summons but before trial is not sufficient (*Rippon v. Ohlssohn's Cape Breweries* [1907] T.S. 113). In *Pillemer v. Israelstam* [1911] W.L.D. 39, an amendment was not allowed.

[68] *cf. Michaelson v. Lowenstein* [1905] T.S. 324.

Bank notes

A bank note is a promissory note, made by a banker, payable to bearer on **24–13** demand and intended to circulate as money.[69] According to Lord Mansfield:

> "Bank notes are not goods, not securities nor documents for debts, nor are they so esteemed; but are treated as money, as cash, in the ordinary course and transactions of business, by the general consent of mankind, which gives them the credit and currency of money, to all intents and purposes. They are as much money as guineas themselves are, or any other current coin that is used in common payments as money or cash. They pass by a will which bequeaths all the testator's money or cash, and are never considered as securities for money, but as money itself. On payment of them, whenever a receipt is required, the receipts are always given as for money, not as for securities or notes. So, on bankruptcies they cannot be followed as identical [*sic*], and distinguishable from money, but are always considered as money or cash."[70]

Like money, bank notes could not, at common law, be taken in execution,[71] but may be taken by virtue of the Judgments Act 1838.

Legal tender

Gold coin was formerly the only legal tender above 40s.[72] Today, by the **24–14** Coinage Act 1971, gold coins made by the Mint, in accordance with the Act and of a minimum weight, are legal tender for any amount; other coins for stated amounts. Bank notes were, nevertheless, a good tender, unless objected to on that account.[73] The Currency and Bank Notes Act 1954 enacted that all notes issued by the Bank of England in England and Wales and those of denomination of less than £5 in Scotland and Northern Ireland are legal tender. By the Gold Standard Act 1925, the Bank of England, until otherwise directed by proclamation, is not bound to pay its notes in gold coin.[74]

Negotiable sterling certificate of deposit[75]

In general, Certificates of Deposit issued by banks are not promissory notes **24–15** since they are not intended to be negotiable. However new instruments, such

---

[69] As to the power of the Bank of England to issue promissory notes, see para. 24–14. Notes of the Bank of Canada are promissory notes within the meaning of s.176(1) of the Bills of Exchange Act R.S.C. 1952, c. 15 (*Bank of Canada and Bank of Montreal v. Bay Bus Terminal (North Bay) Ltd*, Sup.Ct. June, 1977).

[70] *Miller v. Race* (1758) 1 Burr. 452; 1 Sm.L.C., 13th ed., 524; *Miller v. Miller* (1735) 3 P.Wms. 356.

[71] *Knight v. Criddle* (1807) 9 East 48.

[72] 56 Geo. 3, c. 68, s.11.

[73] *Grigby v. Oakes* (1801) 2 B. & P. 526.

[74] s.1(2), suspended by the Gold Standard (Amendment) Act 1931.

[75] By s.55 of the Finance Act 1968, a " 'certificate of deposit' means a document relating to money, in any currency, which has been deposited with the issuer or some other person, being a document which recognises an obligation to pay a stated amount to bearer or to order, with or without interest, and being a document by the delivery of which, with or without endorsement, the right to receive that stated amount, with or without interest, is transferable".

Such certificates are included in the definitions of "securities" and "security" in s.42(1) of the Exchange Control Act 1947.

as negotiable certificates of deposit, have come into usage. Such certificates
are probably not promissory notes for they contain no promise to pay, nor are
they obviously unconditional; the deposit is, however, allegedly payable to
bearer if the certificate is presented for payment through an authorised bank.
The nature of the certificates has not been judicially considered; they are
alleged to be negotiable, which is probably true only in the sense that the
issuing bank is estopped from denying the right of the bearer to payment.
They are treated as negotiable by the City of London[76] and today are probably
negotiable by custom.[77]

Pledge of collateral security

24-16   **83.—(3) A note is not invalid by reason only that it contains also a
pledge of collateral security with authority to sell or dispose thereof.**[78]

Thus a promissory note is not the less a note because it contains a recital
that the maker has deposited title deeds with the payee as a collateral security,
or a pledge of collateral security with power to sell,[79] or because it refers to
an agreement, where it does not appear that the agreement qualifies the
notes,[80] or because it contains such words as: "No time given to, or security
taken from, or composition or arrangement entered into with, either party
hereto shall prejudice the rights of the holder to proceed against any other
party."[81]

Promissory notes often accompany other securities, such as mortgages, bills
of sale, etc., as affording a more speedy remedy in case of default: they may
be valid though the instruments which they accompany are invalid.[82] If
indorsed away, the fact that the indorsement is in breach of faith affords no
defence against a holder in due course.[83]

"IOU"

24-17   A mere acknowledgment of a debt does not amount to a promissory note;
if there are no words amounting to a promise, the instrument is merely
evidence of a debt and may be received as such between the original parties.

[76] *Customs & Excise Commissioners v. Guy Butler (International) Ltd* [1977] Q.B. 377,382.

[77] See Negotiability by Estoppel, *post* para. 8–04.

[78] And see *Sockalingham Chettiar v. Ramanayake* [1937] A.C. 230.

[79] *Wise v. Charlton* (1836) 4 A. & E. 786; *Fancourt v. Thorne* (1846) 9 Q.B. 312.

[80] *Jury v. Barker* (1858) 27 L.J.Q.B. 255; applied in *National Bank of Iowa City v. Rooney*
(1913) 24 Western L.R.(Can.) 163. See also *Lecomte v. O'Grady* (1918) 57 Can.S.C. 563.

[81] *Kirkwood v. Carroll* [1903], 1 K.B. 531 overruling *Kirkwood v. Smith* [1896] 1 Q.B. 582, and
approving *Yates v. Evans* (1892) 61 L.J.Q.B. 446.

[82] *Monetary Advance Co. v. Cater* (1888) 20 Q.B.D. 785.

[83] *Glasscock v. Balls* (1889) 24 Q.B.D. 13. As to the position of the parties in case of
bankruptcy, see *Baines v. Wright* (1885(16 Q.B.D. 330.

An acknowledgment is frequently made in an abbreviated form, thus:

LONDON, January 1, 1965.

Mr A B

IOU £100

C D.

An acknowledgment of a debt in this form is called an IOU. An IOU is not a negotiable instrument.[84] It is evidence of an account stated, but not of money lent.[85] An IOU jointly signed by a debtor and surety has been held to be evidence to go to a jury of an account stated by the debtor and surety jointly.[86] An IOU ought to be regularly addressed to the creditor by name; but though not addressed to anyone it will be evidence for the plaintiff if produced by him.[87] This rule was convenient and safe for if, before the alteration of the law making parties to the action competent witnesses, the IOU were given (as it often is) when no one but the plaintiff and defendant was present, it would have been impossible for the plaintiff to prove how he became possessed of it; but if the IOU were given to a third party, the defendant had ordinarily the means of proving it.

An IOU requires no stamp.

Gaming considerations

An action will not lie upon an IOU given in respect of a gaming debt, and **24–18** prior to the fusion of law and equity a bill would have lain in equity to discover whether an IOU were given for a gaming debt.[88] An action is, however, maintainable on an IOU given in respect of money lent to pay a gaming debt incurred abroad in a country where such gaming in lawful.[89]

POST OFFICE MONEY AND POSTAL ORDERS

The Post Office has authority by statute to issue money and postal orders for **24–19** the remittance of small sums of money and to make regulations with respect

---

[84] See *Wilkinson v. L'Eaugier*, 2 Y. & C. Ex. 363, 369 (Lord Abinger C.B.). An IOU will not pass under a testamentary clause bequeathing "securities for money" (*Barry v. Harding* (1844) 1 Jo. & Lat. 475; *cf. Hopkins v. Abbott* (1875) L.R. 19 Eq. 222, 228).

[85] *Fesenmayer v. Adcock* (1847) 16 M. & W. 449.

[86] *Buck v. Hurst* (1866) L.R. 1 C.P. 297. An IOU by a surety would seem to have been void under the Statute of Frauds and, though the point was not taken in *Buck v. Hurst, supra,* it might be questioned whether an IOU was a sufficient promise in writing to satisfy the Mercantile Law Amendment Act 1856, s.3; *cf. Holmes v. Mitchell* (1859) 7 C.B. (N.S.) 361; *Gould v. Coombs, infra.*

[87] *Curtis v. Rickards* (1840) 1 M. & G. 46, followed in *Fesenmayer v. Adcock, supra; Douglas v. Holme* (1840) 12 A. & E. 641. For a case where a debt was equitably assigned, the IOU to the assignor being replaced by an IOU to the assignee, see *German v. Yates* (1915) 32 T.L.R. 52.

[88] *Wilkinson v. L'Eaugier* (1836) 2 Y. & C.Ex. 363.

[89] *Quarrier v. Colston* (1842) 12 L.J.Ch. 57, followed in *Sazby v. Fulton* [1909] 2 K.B. 208; but as to the case of a cheque, as distinguished from an IOU, given in such circumstances, see *ante,* paras 19–28 *et seq.*

thereto. Postal orders are money orders in a special form.[90] Neither is a negotiable instrument.

Thus postal orders for an amount not exceeding two pounds are issued payable on demand at any time within three months of the last day of the month of issue (or later on payment of a commission) at any post office, except at a few specified small offices.[91] A poundage duty is paid, together with the principal sum, at the time of issue. The sender should fill in the payee's name, and if possible name of the office where the order is to be payable. Postal orders may, in accordance with the postal regulations, be crossed either generally or specially.[92] Forgery or fraudulent alteration of a money order or the crossing thereon was felony; and if the order be cut, defaced, or mutilated, or any erasure or alteration be made, payment may be refused.[93] A banker, receiving payment for a principal on a postal order or document purporting to be such order, is not thereby rendered liable to anyone except his principal, but this protection does not extend to the latter.[94]

The maximum amount for which post office money orders (other than postal orders) may be issued is £50, and they are not legally payable after the expiration of six months (in the case of all inland and of most foreign money orders) from the end of the month of issue, except on special terms. If payable in the United Kingdom they may, in accordance with the Post Office regulations, be crossed by any holder.[95]

A banker collecting forged pension warrants of the Colonial Customs Service does not warrant that they are genuine, that the pensioner is still alive.[96]

---

[90] Post Office Act 1969, s.7(1)(b) as substituted by British Telecommunications Act 1981 s.58.

[91] Outside the United Kingdom they are also payable at offices within the British Commonwealth and protectorates and in the Republic of Ireland.

[92] The Post Office (Postal Order) Scheme 1971, para. 8, made under the Post Office Act, 1969, s.28.

[93] Postal orders were introduced by the Post Office (Money Orders) Act 1880, amended and extended to British foreign dominions, (*viz.*, those other than the United Kingdom, the Channel Islands, and the Isle of Man) by the Post Office (Money Orders) Act 1883. For the present law see the Post Office Act 1953, s.21 and the Post Office Act 1969, s.70. Postal Orders are not negotiable; the regulations of the Post Office definitely forbid them to be regarded as such, and every postal order has the words "not negotiable" printed on its face.

[94] Post Office (Money Orders) Act 1880, s.3 re-enacted by s.21(3) of the Act of 1953. This provision is an extraordinarily wide one, since it does not require the postal order to be crossed by the holder to the banker for collection, nor does it require good faith or absence of negligence on the banker's part. No reported case appears to deal with this proviso, for in the case of *Fine Art Society v. Union Bank* (1886) 17 Q.B.D. 705, the instruments under discussion were apparently money orders, not postal orders, and therefore did not come within the purview of the Act.

[95] Post Office Act 1953, s.23; Money Order Warrant, 1947 (S.R. & O. 1947 No. 656), reg. 5. Money orders appear to have been in use as long ago as 1840; see 3 & 4 Vict. c. 96, s.38. In *Fine Art Society v. Union Bank, supra*, it was held that a banker placing instruments described as Post Office orders to the credit of one customer instead of to another, who was in fact the true owner, was liable to the latter for the conversion of the instruments, since they were not negotiable.

[96] *Gowers v. Lloyds and National Provincial Foreign Bank Ltd* [1938] 1 All E.R. 766.

PART FOUR

CHAPTER 25

CONFLICT OF LAWS

Application

WHERE any contract on a bill or note has been made in a foreign country, or   **25–01**
where a bill is a foreign bill within the 1882 Act, section 4, the rights and
liabilities thereto may have to be ascertained by a reference to foreign law.
The use of bills of exchange in international trade makes it commonplace for
such questions to arise.

Sources

The principles to be applied in the United Kingdom are partly those   **25–02**
generally obtaining in cases of contract where there is a conflict of laws,[1] and
partly are settled by express provisions of the 1882 Act, in particular under
section 72.[2] Broadly, as discussed below, that section provides by subsection
(1) for issues relating to the form and formal validity, by subsection (2) for
matters of "interpretation" (probably including legal consequences), by subsection (3) for the duties of the holder and by subsection (5) for determination
of the date of maturity.[3] Where section 72 is not strictly applicable the
common law rules (preserved by section 97) are to be applied, though it seems
that the principles of section 72 may be applied by analogy.[4]

The Rome Convention

The Convention, which was implemented in England by the Contracts   **25–03**
(Applicable Law) Act 1990, specifically excludes "obligations arising under
bills of exchange, cheques and promissory notes and other negotiable instruments to the extent that the obligations arising under such other negotiable
instruments arise out of their negotiable character".[5] The Convention may
nonetheless govern other contracts pursuant to which bills are issued.

---

[1] A consideration of the general principles is beyond the scope of this work. Reference should
be made to Dicey & Morris on the *Conflict of Laws*, 13th Edition (2000). This Chapter is
concerned only with the particular issues which arise upon bills, notes and cheques, on which see
also Dicey & Morris, *op. cit.* para. 33R–326 *et seq.*, and Chalmers & Guest, para. 1751 *et
seq.*

[2] In Australia, section 77; in Canada, sections 160 to 164; in New Zealand section 72, and in
South Africa, section 70.

[3] Subsection (4) was repealed by the Administration of Justice Act 1977.

[4] See *G. & H. Montage GmbH v. Irvani* [1990] 1 W.L.R. 667, CA; *Banco Atlantico v. British
Bank of the Middle East* [1990] 2 Lloyds Rep. 504. As Dicey & Morris point out, the Act was
intended to and does largely reproduce the effect of earlier cases.

[5] Art. 1(2)(c). For the position of negotiable instruments other than bills, notes or cheques see
Dicey & Morris at paras 33R–314 to 33–324.

Geneva Conventions

25–04   The basic law in those countries which have adopted the Geneva Convention of 1930 "for the settlement of certain conflict of laws in connection with bills of exchange and promissory notes" is contained in League of Nations, Treaty Series, Vol. CXLIII, 1933–1934, 319, Articles 2 to 9 inclusive. The Continental rules relating to cheques are to be found in Geneva Convention No. 3317 of March 19, 1931.[6]

Several contracts/Several law

25–05   As the Act explicitly recognises by the opening words of section 72, a bill of exchange may embody a chain of several distinct contracts (drawing, acceptance, indorsement and so on) each of which may be subject to different laws. The "several laws" approach is adopted on the continent[7] and in America.[8]

Overview

25–06   The first question in many cases is whether an issue is to be resolved in accordance with the "*lex loci contractus*" or the "*lex loci solutionis*". By the *lex loci contractus* (or *celebrationis*), every contract is in general to be regulated by the laws of the country in which it is made, which alone are binding proprio vigore on aliens as well as on natural-born citizens or subjects, and the parties to the contract may generally be taken to have contemplated the legal consequences which those laws deduce from such a contract. According to the *lex loci solutionis* where a contract is made in one country to be performed in another, the law to be applied is that of the country where the contract is to be performed.

25–07   With limited exceptions (discussed below) the Act applies the *lex loci contractus*. This result has been criticised,[9] as being in conflict with general principles. On the other hand, there is much to be said for applying a certain (if sometimes arbitrary) rule to negotiable instruments in preference to a more sophisticated, but inevitably less certain, inquiry into the "proper law".[10]

25–08   Furthermore, the departure from general principles is not so serious if it is remembered that the *lex loci solutionis* could only be applied where the contract was to be performed in a country other than where it was made. As a bill of exchange is regarded as a series of contracts, the fact that the acceptance is in one country and the indorsement in another does not necessarily involve, under the ordinary rules of conflict of laws, the application of the *lex loci solutionis*. It is within the contract of acceptance or indorsement

---

[6] See also the United Nations Convention on International Bills of Exchange and International Promissory Notes (UNCITRAL).

[7] Under the conventions mentioned above.

[8] Restatement, Ch. 8: Introductory Note to Topic 4 Negotiable Instruments, noted by Dicey & Morris who observe that this "may perhaps be regarded as one of the few aspects of the conflict of laws on which there exists a widespread consensus of opinion throughout the world".

[9] See particularly below (paras 25–27 to 25–33) in connection with the wide view of section 72(2).

[10] See the view expressed in Chalmers & Guest at para. 1759.

itself that there must be a difference between the place of making and the place of performance. Consequently, in many of the cases, the distinction does not arise, since the place of making and place of performance are the same.

FORM AND FORMAL VALIDITY

Section 72(1)

This section embodies the general law applicable to contracts, and the **25–09** provisos are in the nature of exceptions. It is limited to the validity in point of form only, as distinct from validity depending on contractual capacity, lawful consideration, etc., which lies outside the provisions of the 1882 Act[11]:

72. Where a bill drawn in one country is negotiated,[12] accepted, or payable in another, the rights, duties, and liabilities of the parties thereto are determined as follows:

(1) The validity of a bill as regards requisites in form is determined by the law of the place of issue, and the validity as regards requisites in form of the supervening contracts, such as acceptance, or indorsement, or acceptance supra protest, is determined by the law of the place where such contract was made.

Provided that—

(a) **Where a bill is issued out of the United Kingdom it is not invalid by reason only that it is not stamped in accordance with the law of the place of issue:**

(b) **Where a bill, issued out of the United Kingdom, conforms, as regards requisites in form, to the law of the United Kingdom, it may, for the purpose of enforcing payment thereof, be treated as valid as between all persons who negotiate, hold, or become parties to it in the United Kingdom.**

General Effect

It would seem that the principle which underlies the section is that of the *lex* **25–10** *loci contractus* and that, apart from proviso (b), there is no room for the application of the *lex loci solutionis* except where the two coincide. The effect of subsection (1), taken without the provisos, would appear to be that if the form of a bill, of its drawing, acceptance or indorsement, renders the instrument invalid in the place in which it is issued or the intervening act is done, it will be invalid in the United Kingdom.

---

[11] See *post*, paras 25–39 *et seq.* (Illegality) and paras 25–53 *et seq.* (Capacity).
[12] As to "negotiated", see s.31, *ante*, paras 8–02, 9–03.

Proviso (b)

25–11   So, generally, the law to be applied in deciding the formal validity of any contract on a bill is the *lex loci contractus* but the proviso contained in section 72(1)(b) qualifies this general rule by entitling the holder, who becomes a party to the bill in the United Kingdom, to recover payment thereof, provided that it conforms as regards the requisites of form to the law of the United Kingdom, but solely against a party who has held, negotiated or become a party to it in the United Kingdom.[13] It seems, further, that such a holder might recover where the bill was invalidated abroad by some supervening defect in form, though valid at its issue.

25–12   In a case before the 1882 Act, where a promissory note, made in France by A in favour of B, both being domiciled Frenchmen, was indorsed in blank by B to the plaintiff in France, it was held that, as the indorsement was bad by French law, the plaintiff could not recover upon the note in England.[14] In this case the *lex loci contractus* and the *lex loci solutionis* were the same.

25–13   In *Bradlaugh v. De Rin*,[15] where bills drawn in Belgium were accepted in England and indorsed by several persons abroad, the last indorsement being by G in Paris in blank, and the bills indorsed and remitted to the plaintiff as G's agent in London, it was considered by the majority of the Court of Common Pleas that if the plaintiff could not sue by the law of France, neither could he by English law. On appeal in the Exchequer Chamber the French law was held to entitle the plaintiff to recover but the principle of the decision in the court below remained unshaken.[16] Assuming that the plaintiff became a party to the bills in England by receiving them after indorsement in Paris he would now be entitled to recover under the proviso. Otherwise the indorsement in blank would be interpreted according to the law of the place where it was made. Proviso (b) is an exception as regards United Kingdom parties *inter se*.

25–14   In *Koechlin et Cie v. Kestenbaum Brothers*[17] a bill drawn in France to the order of a French principal was accepted in England payable at a London bank and subsequently returned to France, where it was indorsed by the duly authorised agent of the principal in his own name. When presented for payment, payment was refused on the ground that it did not bear the principal's indorsement, but merely the indorsement of the agent in his own name. At the trial evidence was given that by French law an indorsement could be validly made by a duly authorised agent in his own name, and the Court held that the validity of the indorsement was a question of form, which, under section 72(1), fell to be determined by French law, and the principal was accordingly held entitled to recover.

25–15   The question whether a bill is conditional or not has been held to be a question relating to the "requisites in form" within the meaning of section

---

[13] See *Wynne v. Jackson* (1826) 2 Russ. 351, on which a bill void under German law was indorsed to an English firm; held, that an indorsee could sue the English indorser but not the German drawer. And see *Trimbey v. Vignier* (1834) 1 Bing.N.C. 151 (foreign maker).

[14] *Trimbey v. Vignier* (1834) 1 Bing.N.C. 151.

[15] (1870) L.R. 5 C.P. 473; in C.P. (1868) L.R. 3 C.P. 538.

[16] *ibid.*

[17] [1927] 1 K.B. 889.

72(1), which must therefore be determined by the law of the place of issue.[18]

In *Re Marseilles Extension Railway and Land Co.*[19] bills drawn in the   **25–16**
English form in France on an English drawee to the drawer's order were indorsed in blank by the drawer in France to an Englishman domiciled in England. This form of indorsement was irregular under the then French law, so that the bills were irregular at their first issue. The bills were subsequently indorsed in England to the applicants, who were held entitled to enforce payment against the acceptor on the ground that the bills were English bills and that the French indorsement in blank was immaterial. The bills in question pre-dated the Act. Since the Act, the ground of the decision is untenable, as the bills, by virtue of section 4, were foreign bills and not inland bills, but proviso (b) appears to apply to such a case. The proviso probably applies, in favour of a holder in this country, to the case also where it is a subsequent indorsement which is invalid by the law of the country where it is made.

"For the purpose of enforcing payment"

The expression in section 72(1)(b), "for the purpose of enforcing payment   **25–17**
thereof", has been held not to include the obtaining of a declaration that the holder who has been paid is entitled to retain the money, and that the proviso did not apply where an action was brought for the purpose, not of obtaining payment, but for that of preventing the defendants, the acceptors, recovering the money they had paid as such acceptors.[20]

Proviso (a)—Foreign stamp laws[21]

As to proviso (a), it was long ago held that bills or notes drawn or made in   **25–18**
a foreign state do not require, in order to be valid in this country, a stamp of the country where they are made or drawn.[22] On the other hand, if the instrument were, by the revenue law of the foreign country, owing to the want of a stamp, not merely inadmissible in evidence but absolutely void, with the result that there was no contract at all in the place where it was made, it was formerly held that the instrument could not be enforced here.[23] But it seems clear that in view of the wording of section 72(1)(a), such a bill would be enforceable here.[24]

---

[18] *Guaranty Trust Co. of New York v. Hannay* [1918] 1 K.B. 43, where Bailhache J. held that the bill in question, though unconditional by English law, was conditional by the law of America, the place of issue, and therefore not a negotiable instrument. The Court of Appeal ([1918] 2 K.B. 623) held that the bill was unconditional, both by English and by American law, and expressed no decided opinion as to the application of the section.

[19] (1885) 30 Ch.D. 598.

[20] *Guaranty Trust Co. of New York v. Hannay* [1918] 1 K.B. 43. In the Court of Appeal ([1918] 2 K.B. 623) this point was not dealt with.

[21] In England the requirement for stamp duty to be paid on bills was abolished by the Finance Act 1970.

[22] *James v. Catherwood* (1823) 3 D. & R. 190, 191; but see also Story, *Conflict of Laws* (8th ed.), p. 346, note (4).

[23] *Bristow v. Secqueville* (1850) 19 L.J.Ex. 289, discussing *Alves v. Hodgson* (1797) 7 T.R. 241.

[24] See Chalmers & Guest, para. 1770, Dicey & Morris, para. 33–336.

Place of issue

25–19   The place of issue is where the first delivery took place, not necessarily where the signature was affixed.[25]

25–20   In contrast, Article 3 of the Geneva Convention for the settlement of certain conflicts of Laws "in connection with cheques, March 19, 1931" reads:

> "The form of any contract arising out of a bill of exchange or promissory note is regulated by the laws of the territory in which the contract has been signed. Nevertheless it shall be sufficient if the forms prescribed by the law of the place of payment are observed.
>
> If, however, the obligations entered into by means of a bill of exchange or promissory note are not valid according to the provisions of the preceding paragraph, but are in conformity with the laws of the territory in which a subsequent contract has been entered into, the circumstances that the previous contracts are irregular in form does not invalidate the subsequent contract.
>
> Each of the High Contracting Parties may prescribe that contracts by means of a bill of exchange and promissory note entered into abroad by one of its nationals shall be valid in respect of another of its nationals in its territory, provided that they are in the form laid down by the national law."

INTERPRETATION

Section 72(2)

25–21   The 1882 Act further provides that:

72. Where a bill drawn in one country is negotiated, accepted, or payable in another, the rights, duties, and liabilities of the parties thereto are determined as follows:

. . .

(2) Subject to the provisions of this Act, the interpretation of the drawing, indorsement, acceptance, or acceptance supra protest of a bill, is determined by the law of the place where such contract is made.

Provided that where an inland bill is indorsed in a foreign country the indorsement shall as regards the payer be interpreted according to the law of the United Kingdom.

The other provisions referred to seem to be the remaining provisions of this section and section 53, as to funds in the hands of the drawer:[26]

Meaning of "interpretation"

25–22   While subsection (1) clearly relates only to formal validity, what "interpretation" means is more doubtful and contentious. Subjection (2) cannot be

---

[25] *Chapman v. Cottrell* (1865) 34 L.J. Ex. 186; 1882 Act, s.2.

[26] See para. 21–100. On that issue Article 6 of the Geneva Convention for the settlement of certain conflicts of laws in connection with bills of exchange and promissory notes, June 7, 1930 provides that "The question whether there has been an assignment to the holder of the debt which has given rise to the issue of the instrument is determined by the law of the place where the instrument was issued."

construed as an extension of subsection (1) and it would seem reasonable to think that form has no place in it and that it decides the rights and liabilities of the parties *inter se*. This view is supported by the opening words of section 72 subject to which it must be read.

Construction

No great difficulty is concerned where the question can be characterised as one of construction, or the literal effect of the form in which the contract is made. The word clearly covers matters of construction, that is to say, the legal interpretation of the words used in the instrument. Thus, the question whether an acceptance is general or qualified is determined under the subsection by the law of the place of acceptance, *i.e.* the *lex loci contractus*.[27] **25–23**

In *Haarbleicher and Schumann v. Baerselman*[28] a bill drawn on the defendants in favour of a Hamburg banker was indorsed *für mich*. After acceptance, the bill was deposited by the plaintiffs as security and later sold to the Bank of England. It was dishonoured at maturity and returned to the plaintiffs who sued as indorsers and holders for value. The defence was that *für mich* was a restrictive indorsement within section 35 of the 1882 Act, but the plaintiffs contended that by section 72(2) the effect of the indorsement was to be judged by the law of the place where the contract was made. It was held that the question was one of foreign law and, therefore, of fact; and that the indorsement was an open not restrictive one. **25–24**

In *Bank Polski v. Mulder*,[29] bills were drawn in Poland in Dutch currency payable in Amsterdam. The Court of Appeal, affirming the opinion of Tucker J.,[30] held that the acceptance, being a London acceptance, fell to be determined according to the law of England, and by its terms was general, not qualified. **25–25**

Similarly in *G. & H. Montage GmbH v. Irvani*[31] a discrepancy between the words and figures appearing in a contract of aval was to be resolved in accordance with the law of Germany, where that contract was made. **25–26**

Legal Effect

The more difficult question is whether "interpretation" extends more generally to the legal consequences of an act. If the subsection is confined to the narrower sense just described, there being no other provision of the 1882 Act in point, it follows that the legal effect of the different acts specified is left to be determined by the ordinary rules governing the conflict of laws. **25–27**

Chalmers took the view that "the term 'interpretation' . . . clearly included the obligations of the parties as deduced from such interpretation."[32] **25–28**

[27] *Sanders v. St. Helens Smelting Co.* (1906) 39 N.S.L.R. 370.
[28] (1914) 137 L.T.J. 564.
[29] [1942] 1 K.B. 497; *Sanders v. St. Helens Smelting Co. Ltd* (1906) 39 N.S. 370.
[30] [1941] 2 K.B. 166.
[31] [1990] 1 W.L.R. 667.
[32] Bills of Exchange (9th ed., 1927), See now Chalmers & Guest (15th ed.) at para. 1782–1784.

25–29   On the other hand Falconbridge has argued that this view "is chiefly responsible for the difficulty of reconciling the statute with principle ... ", and continues: "The effect or obligation of each contract, including, apparently, the measure of damages on dishonour, as well as questions of intrinsic validity, would all be left to be governed, independently of the statute, by the proper law of each contract, that is, usually by the law of the place of performance of each contract", and he suggests that the "result would be substantially, though not exactly, in accord with the solution proposed by the Geneva Convention of 1930, that is, that the obligations of the acceptor of a bill or the maker of a note are governed by the law of the place in which the instrument is payable, and that the effect of the signature of any other party is governed by the law of the place in which the signature is affixed".[33]

25–30   Dicey and Morris observe that there is "great force in the argument in favour of a narrow construction of subsection (2) and in favour of the application of the *lex loci solutionis* to the validity and effect as distinguished from the interpretation of bills and notes and of the contracts contained in them."[34]

25–31   There is, however, a series of judicial opinions expressing the view that the word "interpretation" extends to and includes the legal effect of the different acts[35] and, though it is tempting, having regard to the ambiguity of the word, to construe "interpretation" in the strict sense and to leave the extent of the obligations arising out of the acts to be determined by the ordinary rules, this solution of the difficulty appears to be incorrect.[36]

25–32   The weight of recent dicta is clear. In *Nova (Jersey) Knit v. Kammgarn Spinnerei*[37] Lord Wilberforce observed that "the word 'interpretation' appears to bear a wide meaning but even if it does not extend to matters of substance, these would be governed by the proper law, which in the present case would be the same". In *G. & H. Montage GmbH v. Irvani*[38] Mustill L.J. noted that "It has been common ground throughout, and rightly so in my opinion, that the word 'interpretation' in subsection (2) embraces the respective obligations created by the acts of drawing, indorsing and accepting the bill."

---

[33] Falconbridge, at p. 835.

[34] *Conflict of Laws*, 13th ed. 2000 para. 33–344; but they also note (para. 33–330) that "in the law of negotiable instruments there is a strong case for applying one system of law to the form of each contract, the formation of the contract, and the capacity of the parties to make it, and it is therefore submitted that the formation of the contract, including the need for, and the meaning of, consideration, and the capacity of the parties should be governed by the law of the place where the contract was made".

[35] *Alcock v. Smith* [1892] 1 Ch. 238, 256 (Romer J.); *Embiricos v. Anglo-Austrian Bank* [1904] 2 K.B. 870, 875 (Walton J.); *Koechlin et Cie v. Kestenbaum Brothers* [1927] 1 K.B. 889; see also *London and Brazilian Bank v. Maguire* (1895) Q.R. 8 S.C. 358 and *Republica de Guatemala v. Nunez* [1927] 1 K.B. 669, CA. See also p. 258 *supra*.

[36] *Koechlin et Cie v. Kestenbaum Brothers, supra*; but see *Guaranty Trust Co. of New York v. Hannay* [1918] 2 K.B. 623, 670 (Scrutton L.J.); *Embiricos v. Anglo-Austrian Bank* [1905] 1 K.B. 677. 685 (Vaughan Williams L.J.); Falconbridge, *Banking and Bills of Exchange* (7th ed.), pp. 834 *et seq*.

[37] [1977] 1 W.L.R. 713 at 718.

[38] [1990] 1 W.L.R. 667, at 675. The views, and criticism, expressed in both Chalmers & Guest and the previous edition were noted, and the authorities referred to in the preceding paragraph were considered. The same view (in reliance on that case) was stated in *Banco Atlantico v. BBME* [1990] 2 Lloyd's Rep. 504 at 507 col. 1 (Bingham L.J.).

If this is so the result is that the 1882 Act (except in the proviso), appears **25–33** to depart from the ordinary rules and to accept the *lex loci contractus* even where, apart from the 1882 Act, the *lex loci solutionis* would be applied. There is though a dearth of clear modern authority where the issue was directly in point. There remain uncertainties as to the extent to which the subsection applies in connection with particular issues discussed below.

Inland Bills

The proviso to section 72(2) of the 1882 Act applies the *lex loci solutionis* **25–34** to inland bills in accordance with the decisions before the 1882 Act.[39] It is to be observed that the proviso only applies "as regards the payer", and hence not to the question which of two parties is entitled to claim as holder of an inland bill indorsed abroad.[40]

Transfer

Several of the cases concern the validity and effect (in particular whether **25–35** free or subject to equities) of a transfer of the instrument abroad. Cases turning on the formal requirements for[41] or proper construction of[42] a foreign indorsement present no difficulties within the scheme of the 1882 Act, as explained above.

In *Alcock v. Smith*[43] the transfer in Norway of an overdue inland bill sold **25–36** at auction pursuant to a Norwegian court order was held to have been free of equities, in accordance with Norwegian law, so that the title of a subsequent purchaser prevailed.

In the case of *Embiricos v. Anglo-Austrian Bank*,[44] a foreign cheque **25–37** payable in London, was transferred in Austria by a forged indorsement, which was effective by Austrian law to convey a title to a bona fide holder for value, and it was held that the transfer must be governed by Austrian law. In that case, the Court of Appeal accepted the rule of international law that the validity of the transfer of movable chattels must be governed by the law of the country in which the transfer takes place, as applying to the transfer of bills or cheques by indorsement.[45]

Neither case is decided explicitly on the ground that section 72 governed **25–38** the law applicable to the transaction. Instead, the result is based on the proposition, which must be taken to be well established, that the effect as to

---

[39] *Robinson v. Bland* (1960) 2 Burr. 1077; *De la Chaumette v. Bank of England* (1829) 9 B. & C. 208; *Cooper v. Waldegrave* (1840) 3 Beav. 282; *Lebel v. Tucker* (1867) L.R. 3 Q.B 77; *cf. Re Marseilles Extension Railway and Land Co.* (1885) 30 Ch.D. 598, 601–604.

[40] *Alcock v. Smith* [1892] 1 Ch. 238.

[41] For example *Koechlin et Cie v. Kestenbaum Brothers*, above.

[42] For example *Haarbleicher and Schumann v. Baerselman*, above.

[43] [1892] 1 Ch. 238. The cases of *Lacave v. Credit Lyonnais* [1897] 1 Q.B. 148 and *Kleinwort & Co. v. Comptoir d'Escompte de Paris* [1894] 2 Q.B. 157 are to be distinguished on the ground that the defendant banks in both cases were collecting banks only, and were not indorsees or assignees. See also *Canada Life Assurance Co. v. Canadian Imperial Bank of Commerce* (1980)98 D.L.R. (3d) 670 (CAN).

[44] [1905] 1 K.B. 677.

[45] The Court of Appeal on this point followed *Alcock v. Smith, supra*.

title of the transfer of a negotiable instrument is governed by the law of the place where the transaction takes place.[46]

Illegality

25–39   There have been a number of cases dealing with the enforcement of bills where a question of illegality has been raised, particularly in connection with exchange control.[47]

25–40   In *De Beeche v. South American Stores Ltd*,[48] a lease provided for payment of rent in Chile by first class bills on London. Subsequent legislation in Chile made it impossible for the lessees to perform their contract in this respect without committing breaches of Chilean law and they were accordingly held to be discharged from their obligation to pay rent in the manner provided. The place of performance was Chile and the rights and duties of the parties were governed by Chilean law.

25–41   On the other hand, in *Kleinwort, Sons & Co. v. Ungarische Baumvolle Industrie Aktiengesellschaft and Hungarian General Creditbank*,[49] the first defendants, who were a Hungarian company, drew certain bills upon the plaintiffs, bankers in London. The bills were accepted and discounted by the plaintiffs for the benefit of the first defendants, upon their undertaking, guaranteed by the second defendants, a Hungarian bank, to pay the amount of the bills in sterling at maturity. This was not done, and the defendants contended that they were excused because the Hungarian exchange regulations made it illegal for Hungarian subjects to pay sums sterling in London except with the consent which had not been given, of the Hungarian National Bank. The Court of Appeal, however, rejected this contention on the ground that payment had to be made, not in Hungary, where it would have been unlawful, but in London. The rights and duties of the parties were accordingly governed by English law and the Hungarian regulations had no application.

25–42   Conversely, in *Re Banque des Marchands de Moscou (Koupetschesky) (No. 2)*, Roxburgh J. held that drafts drawn on an English bank by a Russian bank, which had been dissolved, in favour of a customer of the latter were illegal because they violated Russian law.[50]

---

[46] See Chalmers & Guest at para. 1806 *et seq.* and Dicey and Morris at para. 33–349 *et seq.* Both distinguish to a greater or lesser extent between the contractual issue and the question of title. The extent of the indorser's/transferor's liability on the bill would, on the "wide" view of section 72(2) be governed by the law of the place of transfer (completed by delivery). The effect of treating the question of title as governed by section 72 is, as pointed out by Dicey & Morris (para. 33–353) to introduce an anomaly because of the distinction drawn by the proviso in the case of inland bills.

[47] In England the Exchange Control Act 1947 was repealed by the Finance Act 1987. The discussion of its provisions which appeared in the previous edition has not been retained, the cases decided under it turning on questions of construction of the Act, see *Contract and Trading Co. (Southern) Ltd v. Barbey & others* [1960] A.C. 244, *Cummings v. London Bullion Co. Ltd* [1952] 1 K.B. 327 and *Credit Lyonnais v. P.T. Barnard & Associates Ltd* [1976] 1 Lloyd's Rep. 557.

[48] [1935] A.C. 148.

[49] [1939] 2 K.B. 678.

[50] [1954] 1 W.L.R. 1108.

In general it seems that a bill may be unenforceable because of illegality[51] **25–43**
where the consideration for it is illegal in England, if that is the place of
payment, and even if the acceptance is not subject to English law.[52] Equally
a bill may be unenforceable if the consideration, though lawful in England, is
contrary to foreign law,[53] but not, apparently, merely because payment would
involve the payer in a breach of foreign law if that is not the law of the
contract, or of the place of performance.[54]

Bretton Woods

A number of more recent cases have involved the Bretton Woods Agree- **25–44**
ments Order 1946, made under the Bretton Woods Agreements Act 1945.
Article 8, section 2, of the Schedule to the Order provides that:

> "Exchange contracts which involve the currency of any member [of the Inter-
> national Monetary Fund] and which are contrary to the exchange control regulations
> of any member maintained or imposed consistently with this Agreement shall be
> unenforceable in the territories of any member."

The statutory prohibition does not depend upon any questions of conflicts **25–45**
of, or the applicable, law. Its effect was considered in *United City Merchants
(Investments) Ltd and others v. Royal Bank of Canada and others*[55] in which
an attempt was made to avoid Peruvian Exchange control. The transaction was
the sale of a glass fibre forming plant to Peruvian buyers to be paid for by
irrevocable credit. By arrangement between the parties, the sale price was
doubled with the object of achieving a deposit of half the amount in the United
States. It was held by the Court of Appeal that the transaction offended against
Peruvian currency and was accordingly an infringement of the Bretton Woods
Agreement. It was further held, however, that there was nothing to prevent
payment under the credit for the value of the goods supplied: in the words of
Lord Diplock: " . . . the sellers are entitled to judgment for that part of the
second instalment which was not a monetary transaction in disguise".

It is unclear whether a bill of exchange could be similarly enforced *pro* **25–46**
tanto. It is, though, clear that the suggestion in *Sharif v. Azad* that, even if the
transaction infringes the Bretton Woods Agreement, a cheque drawn in connection with it is nonetheless to be regarded as autonomous and therefore
enforceable, is untenable, following the *United City Merchants* case as applied
in *Mansouri v. Singh*.[56]

---

[51] Subject to the status of a holder in due course or someone deriving title under him (Ch. 18);
that status may depend in a case with a foreign element on the effect of the transfer as described
above. Compare Dicey & Morris para. 33–345 where it is suggested that "all contracts contained
in the bill are effected".

[52] *Moulis v. Owen* [1907] 1 K.B. 746, applying *Robinson v. Bland* (1760) 2 Burr. 1077.

[53] *Re Banque des Marchands de Moscou (Koupetschesky) (No. 2)*, above.

[54] *Kleinwort, Sons & Co. v. Ungarische Baumvolle Industrie Aktiengesellschaft*, above.

[55] [1983] A.C. 168. See also *Sharif v. Azad* [1967] 1 Q.B. 605, CA; *Wilson Smithett & Cope
Ltd v. Terruzzi* [1976] Q.B. 683; *Batra v. Ebrahim* [1982] 2 Lloyd's Rep. 11 and *Mansouri v.
Singh* [1986] 1 W.L.R. 1393.

[56] [1986] 1 W.L.R. 1393 at 1403.

Consideration

25–47   The need for consideration, or what may constitute it, is not specifically addressed by section 72. The view of Dicey & Morris[57] is that all such matters as formation, capacity and consideration ought all to be subject to one system of law, in practice the *lex loci contractus*. Chalmers & Guest[58] suggest that the question is probably, by analogy, governed by the law of the place where the contract was made. Whether or not section 72(2) ought to be read so widely as to cover the question, this would be consistent with the common law approach to the validity of the contract.

25–48   It was long before the 1882 Act held that an acceptance void or avoided by the law of the country where it is given, is not binding here. By the law of Leghorn, if a bill was accepted and the drawer then failed, and the acceptor had not sufficient funds of the drawer in his hands at the time of acceptance, the acceptance became void. An acceptor at Leghorn, in these circumstances, instituted a suit at Leghorn, and his acceptance was thereupon vacated. Afterwards he was sued in England as acceptor, and then filed his bill for an injunction and relief. Lord Chancellor King granted a perpetual injunction, enjoining the plaintiff from suing on the bills.[59]

Measure of damages

25–49   It is clear that the damages recoverable upon dishonour of a bill are a matter of substantive law, not the *lex fori*.[60] Under English law the measure is generally prescribed by section 57 of the 1882 Act.[61]

25–50   It is less clear how the relevant law is ascertained.[62] It has been said that, as distinct from the formal validity or interpretation of the contract, it may well be that the law to be applied as to any defaulting party is the law of the place at which such party undertakes that he himself will pay, which would in general be the place where he made the contract, except in the case of an acceptor.[63]

25–51   On the other hand, there is much to be said for the view that the extent of a party's liability ought to be determined in accordance with the *lex loci contractus*, in accordance with the general rule under section 72 as it seems now to be applied.[64] Neither approach seems consistent with Article 4 of the Geneva Convention, by which the obligation of the acceptor is to be judged

---

[57] Para. 33–330 (not extending to issues of legality, discussed above).

[58] Para. 1774.

[59] *Burrows v. Jemino* (1726) 2 Stra. 733; see also *Wynne v. Callander* (1826) 1 Russ. 293.

[60] *Re Gillespie, Ex parte Robarts* (1886) 18 Q.B.D. 286, 292; *Re Commercial Bank of South Australia* (1887) 36 Ch. D. 522.

[61] As to damages in general, see *post*, Ch. 28.

[62] That this question has not been decided suggests it is of more academic interest than practical significance.

[63] *Allen v. Kemble* (1848) 6 Moo.P.C. 314, 321–322. Chalmers, *Bills of Exchange* (13th ed., 1964), p. 243 (but see now Chalmers & Guest, para. 1463–1465, where a different view is taken by the present editors); McGregor, *Damages* (15th ed., 1988) para. 1067 *et seq.*, paras 850 *et seq.* This proposition was apparently advanced in previous editions.

[64] Now proposed by Chalmers & Guest (para. 1465). Dicey & Morris, note only that the pre-Act cases are not consistent, though tending towards the *lex loci solutionis*, and that a common law rule to this effect could survive under section 97 of the Act.

by the law of the place in which the instrument is payable; and those of other parties according to the law of the place where their signatures are affixed.

On any view, the contracts upon the bill are to be regarded severally and **25–52** may be subject to different laws. Consequently an indorser might be liable for a higher rate of interest than he could recover from the drawer in a different place,[65] or the drawer for a higher rate than he could recover from the acceptor. Thus, where a bill was drawn in California on a drawee in Washington, and the rate of interest varied in the two places, in an English action against the drawer it was held that the Californian rate of interest was recoverable; but in an action against the acceptor, the Washington rate of interest would alone be recoverable.[66]

Capacity

The subsection makes no provision for determining which law shall apply **25–53** in relation to contractual capacity. Section 22(1) of the 1882 Act provides that as a matter of English law capacity is co-extensive with that governing contracts generally, and subject to the relevant laws governing corporations.[67]

In *Cooper v. Cooper*,[68] Lord Macnaghten said that "it has been doubted **25–54** whether the personal competency or incompetency of an individual to contract depends on the law of the place where the contract is made or on the law of the place where the contracting party is domiciled. Perhaps in this country the question is not finally settled, though the preponderance of opinion here as well as abroad seems to be in favour of the law of domicile. It may be that all cases are not to be governed by one and the same rule." However, Lord Greene M.R. in *Baindail v. Baindail*,[69] held that the *lex loci* and not the *lex domicilii* determined the matter. Dicey & Morris note that the preponderance of opinion now favours the latter view.[70]

In *Bondholder Securities Corporation v. Manville*,[71] a Canadian court held **25–55** that the capacity of a married woman domiciled in Canada to make a promissory note in Florida was governed by the law of Florida. As Chalmers & Guest note[72] this is consistent with the general principle to be found in section 72, and is the view preferred by Dicey & Morris.[73]

This approach conflicts with the general approach taken on the continent.[74] **25–56** Article 2 of the Geneva Convention applies what it calls the "national" law:

[65] Story, *op. cit.* para. 314.

[66] *Gibbs v. Fremont* (1853) 9 Ex. 25; following *Allen v. Kemble, supra; Cougan v. Banks* (1817) Chitty, 11th ed., 437; but see *Cooper v. Waldegrave* (1840) 2 Beav. 282.

[67] See Ch. 6 above.

[68] (1888) 13 App.Cas. 88, 108.

[69] [1946] P. 122 at 128.

[70] See Rule 179 and paragraphs 32–214 and following for a much fuller discussion of the question than is appropriate here.

[71] [1933] 4 D.L.R. 699; Dicey & Morris, para. 33–330 suggest that *Re Soltykoff* [1891] 1 Q.B. 413 adopts the same principle.

[72] Para. 1775.

[73] Para. 33–330.

[74] See Dicey & Morris at 32–217, though they note the position has been varied in both France and Germany.

"The capacity of a person to bind himself by a bill of exchange or promissory note shall be determined by the national law. If this national law provides that the law of another country is competent in the matter, this latter law shall be applied.

A person who lacks capacity, according to the law specified in the preceding paragraph, is nevertheless bound, if his signature has been given in any territory in which according to the law in force there, he would have the requisite capacity.

Each of the High Contracting Parties may refuse to recognise the validity of a contract by means of a bill of exchange or promissory note entered into by one of its nationals which would not be deemed valid in the territory of the other High Contracting Parties otherwise than by means of the application of the preceding paragraph of the present article."

DUTIES OF HOLDER

Subsection 72(3)

25–57   Where laws conflict, the duties of the holder are to be regulated as follows:

72.—(3) The duties of the holder with respect to presentment for acceptance or payment and the necessity for or sufficiency of a protest or notice of dishonour, or otherwise, are determined by the law of the place where the act is done or the bill is dishonoured.

25–58   The protest and notice of dishonour are part of the contract, and not incidents of the remedy for the breach of it. This subsection determines which rules must be applied.

25–59   Before the Act it was held that where a bill was drawn in England on an acceptor in France, notice of dishonour by the indorsee in England to his indorser in England was good if it conformed with the law of France, though too late according to English law.[75] In a similar case it was held that notice, good according to the law of France, was due notice according to English law.[76] So where a bill drawn in England payable in Spain—a country where no notice of dishonour for want of acceptance is required—was dishonoured there for want of acceptance, and, after the lapse of several days, intimation of that fact was given to the indorsee in England, who immediately gave notice to his indorser, it was held by the Court of Appeal that the indorser was liable.[77]

25–60   And where a cheque drawn in Yugoslavia payable in Holland could not be presented owing to the German occupation of Holland, Stable J. felt fortified by *Re Francke & Rasch*[78] in holding that the law of England applied.[79]

25–61   These cases seem to be consistent with the above subsection enabling the holder to recover, if he has given a notice of dishonour sufficient by the law of the place where the bill is dishonoured, whether or not sufficient by the law

[75] *Rothschild v. Currie* (1841) 1 Q.B. 43.
[76] *Hirschfeld v. Smith* (1866) L.R. 1 C.P. 340.
[77] *Home v. Rouquette* (1878) 3 Q.B.D. 514.
[78] [1918] 1 Ch. 470.
[79] *Cornelius v. Banque Franco-Serbe* [1942] 1 K.B. 29.

of the place where notice is given or received. But this right depends on his having duly presented. A draft in favour of A drawn on a German drawee must be presented for payment within three weeks of its being drawn and if it is not, neither the payee nor a transferee from him may recover from the drawer in England.[80]

More recently, in *G. & H. Montage v. Irvani*[81] the plaintiff (a German   **25–62** company) sued on bills which had been accepted in Germany and to which a director of the drawee had added his signature by way of aval. The contract of aval was governed by, and fell to be construed in accordance with, German law.[82] The bills were payable in London but were dishonoured. No notice of dishonour was given to the defendant, and though the bills were protested that was done late in respect of some of them. It was held that the necessity for, and requirements of, notice of dishonour and protest were governed by English law, but that the requirements in the 1882 Act[83] did not as a matter of that law apply to a party liable upon an aval.

RATE OF EXCHANGE

Section 72(4) (repealed)

As to the calculation of the rate of exchange where a bill is drawn abroad   **25–63** in foreign currency on this country,[84] it was formerly provided that:

72.—(4) Where a bill is drawn out of but payable in the United Kingdom, and the sum payable is not expressed in the currency of the United Kingdom, the amount shall, in the absence of some express stipulation, be calculated according the rate of exchange for sight drafts at the place of payment on the day the bill is payable.

This subsection was repealed by the Administration of Justice Act 1977,   **25–64** following the House of Lords' decision in *Miliangos v. George Frank (Textiles) Ltd*.[85] The following discussion is retained because though a party is entitled to claim judgment in foreign currency he is not obliged to do so. Circumstances may still arise which were outside the terms of the statute, or in which the same principles may now fall to be applied.[86]

---

[80] *Franklin v. Westminster Bank Ltd, The Times*, May 14 and July 17, 1931; Mann, *The Legal Aspect of Money* (3rd ed., 1971), pp. 321, 456.

[81] [1990] 1 W.L.R. 667, CA.

[82] See above para. 25–32.

[83] Sections 48 and 51(2).

[84] A similar principle applies in the case of a bill payable abroad in currency of the United Kingdom (*Ottoman Bank v. Jebara* [1928] A.C. 269). The 1882 Act makes no provision for a bill drawn in the United Kingdom in foreign currency, but in *Cohn v. Boulken* (1920) 36 T.L.R. 767, where a cheque was drawn in England on an English bank for an amount in foreign currency, it was held that the rate of exchange should be that ruling at the date of trial. This decision was not followed in *Uellendahl v. Pankhurst, Wright & Co.* [1923] W.N. 224 or in *Peyrae v. Wilkinson* [1924] 2 K.B. 166, in which cases the rate of exchange prevailing when payment became due was adopted: see generally *S.S. Celia v. S.S. Volturno* [1921] 2 A.C. 544.

[85] *Miliangos v. George Frank (Textiles) Ltd* [1976] 1 Lloyd's Rep. 201, HL; [1976] A.C. 443.

[86] See also Ch. 28 below at paras 28–22 *et seq.*

25–65   This subsection received important interpretation by Mocatta J. in *Barclays Bank International Ltd v. Levin Bros. (Bradford) Ltd.*[87] After referring to the House of Lords' judgment in *Miliangos v. George Frank (Textiles) Ltd*[88] which allowed judgment to be given in a foreign currency, he said:

> "the very restrictive wording of the subsection merely provided a formula to ascertain the amount of sterling which an acceptor should pay on the date of maturity in order to discharge his obligation under a bill of exchange, if he chose to pay that bill of exchange in sterling and not in the currency in which it was drawn. Accordingly, the function of the subsection ended with the day of payment and it had no statutory effect upon the sum recoverable by the indorsee when no payment had been made on the date of maturity and the indorsee subsequently sued the acceptor."

Once judgment is given in currency, the judgment debtor, if he wishes to pay in sterling, must take the risk of an alteration in the exchange, and the conversion will be at the date of payment however that may come about.

25–66   In the case of a promissory note payable in "gold Turkish pounds", the rule of section 72(4) was applied (the Palestine Ordinance being in the same terms and expressly stating that the 1882 Act declares the law in Palestine); this, although the note was made in Palestine, Lord Wright saying that "the essence of the rule applies in a case where the sum is not expressed in the United Kingdom or Palestine currency and is payable in the United Kingdom or Palestine".[89]

25–67   *Woodhouse A. C. Israel Cocoa Ltd S.A. v. Nigerian Produce Marketing Co. Ltd* concerned a contract for the sale of cocoa which provided for payment in £ sterling in London or in £ Nigerian in Lagos. The sellers were later asked whether temporarily they would accept payment against documents in sterling in Lagos, to which they replied in the affirmative. Devaluation, which had been foreseen, followed, and the buyers asserted a right to pay in sterling in Lagos on the basis of parity. The sellers maintained that the agreement reached earlier related only to the currency and that sterling to the full contract price in Nigerian pounds must be provided. Roskill J. held that the contractual letters did not have the effect of substituting the £ sterling for the £ Nigerian as the currency of the contract. He was reversed on appeal on the ground that the letter by which the sellers agreed that payment might be made in sterling altered the money of payment, not the money of account.[90]

DATE OF MATURITY

Subsection 72(5)

25–68   The due date of a bill due in one country and payable in another is determined as follows:

---

[87] [1977] Q.B. 2.70, 275, [1977] 1 Lloyd's Rep. 51.
[88] *Miliangos v. George Frank (Textiles) Ltd* [1976] 1 Lloyd's Rep. 201, HL; [1976] A.C. 443.
[89] *Syndic in Bankruptcy of Salim Nasrallah Khoury v. Khayat* [1943] A.C. 507, PC at 514.
[90] [1971] 1 Lloyd's Rep. 25. See also *W. J. Alan & Co. Ltd v. El Nasr Export and Import Co.* [1971] 1 Lloyd's Rep. 401.

72.—(5) Where a bill is drawn in one country and is payable in another, the due date thereof is determined according to the law of the place where it is payable.

Where, owing to a state of war prevailing in the country where a bill is payable, the time of payment is postponed by law, the contract of the indorser is correspondingly enlarged.[91] The due date being dependent on foreign law, if maturity is postponed by emergency legislation in the foreign country an action on the bill cannot be maintained in this country while such legislation is in force.[92] **25–69**

OTHER MATTERS

Foreign discharge

Where the defendant gave the plaintiff, in a foreign country where both were resident, a bill of exchange drawn by the defendant on a person in England, which bill was afterwards protested here for non-acceptance, and the defendant afterwards, while still resident abroad, became bankrupt there, and obtained a certificate of discharge by the law of that state, it was held that such certificate was a bar to an action here, founded upon an implied assumpsit to pay the amount of the bill, because the implied contract was made abroad.[93] So payment of part in discharge of the whole of a debt, though ineffectual by the law of England, will nevertheless bar the whole debt even here, if the payment was made in a foreign country by the law of which it would have that effect.[94] **25–70**

Payment in due course of a bill in accordance with the *lex loci solutionis* will clearly discharge it. But a discharge by the law of a place where the contract was neither made nor to be performed is not a discharge in any other country.[95] Therefore, to an action against the acceptor of an English bill, the discharge of the acceptor under a bankruptcy in Australia is no defence.[96] It was held otherwise in the case of a Scots bankruptcy for that operated under a direct enactment of the Imperial legislature.[97] **25–71**

Foreign Limitation Acts

Statutes of limitation in general affect the remedy only, and not the substance of the contract. Formerly this was treated as a matter for the *lex fori* so **25–72**

[91] *Rouquette v. Overmann* (1875) L.R. 10 Q.B. 525.
[92] *Re Francke and Rasch* [1918] 1 Ch. 470, applying *Rouquette v. Overmann* (1875) L.R. 10 Q.B. 525; and see *Cornelius v. Banque Franco-Serbe* [1941] 2 All E.R. 728.
[93] *Potter v. Brown* (1804) 5 East 124.
[94] *Ralli v. Dennistoun* (1851) 6 Exch. 483. Art. 7 of the Geneva Convention provides that: "The question whether acceptance may be restricted to part of the sum or whether the holder is bound to accept partial payment is governed by the law of the country in which the bill of exchange is payable. The same rule governs the payment of promissory notes."
[95] Story, *op. cit.* para. 342; *Smith v. Buchanan* (1800) 1 East 6.
[96] *Bartley v. Hodges* (1861) 30 L.J.Q.B. 352.
[97] *Phillips v. Allan* (1828) 8 B. & C. 477.

that where by the law of the country where the contract was made the plaintiff would have had 40 years to bring his action, yet, as he sued in England, it was held that he must bring his action within six years.[98] On the other hand, though the payee of a French promissory note must, if he had sued in France, have brought his action there within five years, it was held that he might here bring his action at any time within six years.[99] A different result was said to follow where the foreign law extinguished the debt, when the *lex fori* would likewise then regard the debt as extinguished, subject to the qualification that both the parties have resided within the jurisdiction of the *lex loci contractus* during the whole prescribed period, so that it has actually operated upon the case.[1]

The Foreign Limitation Periods Act 1984

25–73   This Act now governs the position. By section 1 of that Act the English Court is not to apply the English limitation rules[2] unless English law is the (or a) *lex causae*. That is subject to section 2, by which the foreign limitation law may be disapplied (in favour of the English *lex fori*) if their application imposes undue hardship upon any party or person who may become a party. Undue hardship does not arise merely because the foreign limitation period is shorter, but does include a situation where it conflicts with public policy.[3]

25–74   For relevant purposes it would seem that the governing law of each party's obligation is that determined in accordance with section 72.[4]

Set-off

25–75   The availability of set-off may depend on its characterisation. If the set-off claimed is "judicial" and in the nature of a procedural remedy then it would appear to depend on the *lex fori*.[5] The availability of set-off arising in other contexts, particularly insolvency, will depend on the law of the country where the set-off arises.[6]

---

[98] *British Linen Co. v. Drummond* (1830) 10 B. & C. 903.

[99] *Huber v. Steiner* (1835) 2 Bing.N.C. 202; *Harris v. Quine* (1869) L.R. 4 Q.B. 653; *Casanova v. Meier* (1885) 1 T.L.R. 245; see also *Don v. Lippmann* (1837) 5 C. & F. 1.

[1] *Huber v. Steiner* (1835) 2 Bing.N.C. 202, 211 (Tindal C.J.) citing Story, *Conflict of Laws* (1st ed.), para. 582 (9th ed., *ibid.*); but see 1 Smith L.C., 13th ed., 683, 684, where the qualification is disputed.

[2] As to which see Ch. 29 below.

[3] For a discussion of these issues and the principles to be derived from the cases see Dicey & Morris at para. 7–043 to 7–044.

[4] See Chalmers & Guest, para. 1831.

[5] A full discussion is beyond the scope of this work. See Derham, *Set-Off*, 2nd ed. 1996, Wood, *English and International Set-Off*, (1989).

[6] *cf. Macfarlane v. Norris* (1862) 2 B. & S. 783. In *Allen v. Kemble* (1848) 6 Moo.P.C. 314, the drawer and indorser in Demerara of a bill payable in the United Kingdom were allowed to set off a debt due from a bankrupt indorsee, which was a valid set-off by the law of Demerara, but not by the law of the United Kingdom. But this proceeded on the ground that Demerara was the *locus contractus* of the drawer and indorser. The remedy being sought in the Demerara court, the *lex fori* was the same as the *lex loci contractus*. The decision in *Allen v. Kemble* was approved in *Rouquette v. Overmann* (1875) L.R. 10 Q.B. 525. And see now the discussion in *In re Bank of Credit and Commerce International S.A. (No. 10)* [1997] A.C. 213.

Condition precedent to action

Where by the law of the foreign country a criminal prosecution must be a   **25–76**
preliminary to a civil action, the absence of such a previous prosecution is no
defence to an action here.[7]

Pleading and evidence

Foreign law should be specifically pleaded. It will in general be assumed   **25–77**
that the law of a foreign country is the same as the law of this country in
respect of negotiable instruments until the contrary is proved, the burden of
proof lying on the party alleging any difference.[8]

---

[7] *Scott v. Seymour* (1862) 31 L.J.Ex. 457.
[8] *Brown v. Gracey* (1821) Dow. & Ry.N.P. 41 n.; *Nouvelle Banque de l'Union v. Ayton* (1891) 7 T.L.R. 377; *Guaranty Trust Co. of New York v. Hannay* [1918] 2 K.B. 623, 655 (Warrington L.J.); *Standard Bank of Canada v. Wildey* (1919) 19 N.S.W.S.R. 384. The Acts for ascertaining colonial and foreign law are the British Law Ascertainment Act 1859 and the Foreign Law Ascertainment Act 1861.

PART FIVE

CHAPTER 26

PROCEDURE—I: FORM OF ACTION, PARTIES AND SUMMARY JUDGMENT[1]

Action on the bill or the consideration

WHEN a bill is dishonoured the holder may at his option sue on the bill, or **26–01** (as between immediate parties) upon the consideration for it. A claim on the bill has several advantages. First, the sum payable is certain in amount.[2] Second, less evidence is necessary, and the claimant will have the benefit of a number of statutory presumptions.[3] Third, in an action on the bill the burden is upon the defendant to show that the bill has been paid (or generally to raise any other defence) whereas in an action on the consideration if the defendant shows that a bill, cheque or note has been given the burden will be upon the claimant to show that it has not been honoured. Fourthly, and most importantly, the defences available to the claim on the bill are fewer, and in particular it is not generally open to the defendant to raise any cross claim for unliquidated damages (even where that would be available as an equitable set-off to a claim on the consideration) to defeat or delay payment of the bill.[4]

In any case where the status or validity of the bill is disputed, it is prudent **26–02** and common practice to include an alternative claim upon the consideration or underlying transaction.

Where a bill is avoided because of an innocent material alteration, this does **26–03** not prevent an action being brought upon the underlying consideration.[5]

Title to sue

Generally,[6] the holder of the bill in possession of it is the only person who **26–04** can then sue on it.[7] But he is not the holder if he has not possession at the time the writ is issued.[8] It is a good defence that at the time of action brought the

---

[1] "Action" includes a counterclaim or set-off—1882 Act, s.2.
[2] See Ch. 28 "Damages Interest and Costs".
[3] See Ch. 27 "Pleading and Evidence".
[4] See *post*, paras 26–27 *et seq.*
[5] *Payana v. Pana Lana* [1914] A.C. 618.
[6] See though below, para. 26–07 (Order bill transferred without indorsement).
[7] *Emmett v. Tottenham* (1853) 8 Ex. 884. As to the rights of a holder in due course under the 1882 Act, s.38, see *ante*, pp. 219, 229. A subsequent party, who has been compelled to pay a part of the bill at the suit of the holder, may sue a prior party in an action for money paid to his use (*Pownal v. Ferrand* (1827) 6 B. & C. 439). A payee who has, on dishonour by the maker, paid part of a note to the indorsee, should, on getting it back from him, sue the maker for the balance due to him, in his own name, unless he has the indorsee's authority to sue in his name: see *Coleman v. Biedman* (1849) 7 C.B. 871.
[8] *Lloyds Bank Ltd v. Dolphin, The Times*, December 2, 1920, 3 *Legal Decisions Affecting Bankers*, p. 230; and see *Westminster Bank Ltd v. Zang* [1966] A.C. 182.

bill was outstanding in the hands of an indorsee[9] but if the indorsee held the bill as an agent or trustee for the plaintiff, the plaintiff, though not in actual possession of the bill, may sue,[10] even though the agent's authority depends on a ratification after action brought.[11]

Holder a trustee

26–05   Where the holder holds the bill wholly or in part as trustee for someone else, the defendant may raise against the trustee any defence or set-off which he could raise against the other person behind the trustee to the extent of that person's interest.[12]

Transferee by delivery

26–06   Where a bill which is payable to bearer is negotiated by delivery without indorsement, the transferor (a transferor by delivery) gives only the limited warranties identified in section 58 of the Act. Such a transferor may be sued by his transferee if a holder for value upon those warranties (if false), or upon the underlying consideration if any for which the bill was given.

Order bill transferred without indorsement

26–07   The person to whom an order bill has been delivered for value without the indorsement of the previous holder is entitled to call for the bill to be indorsed.[13] If the previous holder is unable or unwilling to complete the indorsement the court may order that its own officer or appointee be authorised to do so.[14] In an appropriate case such relief may be sought at the same time as an action upon the bill.[15] The transferee of such a bill acquires no greater rights or title to the bill than the transferor and will be bound by any fraud or other matters of which he has notice prior to the indorsement.[16]

Action for delivery up or injunction

26–08   The person entitled to immediate possession of a bill may bring proceedings for its delivery up as though it were any other property. In an appropriate case such an order may be made summarily.

---

[9] cf. *Davis v. Reilly* [1898] 1 Q.B. 1; *Price v. Price* (1847) 16 M. & W. 232; *Jaganathan v. Dorasami* [1906] T.S. 483; *Fidelity Trust Co. v. Terminal Land and Investment Co.* (1927) 4 D.L.R. 532.

[10] *Stones v. Butt* (1834) 2 Cr. & M. 416; *National Savings Bank v. Tranah* (1867) L.R. 2. C.P. 556.

[11] *Ancona v. Marks* (1862) 31 L.J.Ex. 163.

[12] *Thornton v. Maynard* (1875) L.R. 10 C.F. 695; *Barclays Bank Ltd v. Aschaffen-burger Zellstoffwerke A.G.* [1967] 1 Lloyd's Rep. 387.

[13] Section 31(4) of the Act

[14] Supreme Court Act 1981, s.39, *Savage v. Norton* [1908] 1 Ch. 290.

[15] *Walters v. Neary* (1904) 21 T.L.R. 146.

[16] See generally Ch. 18 above and, in particular, para. 18–45.

An injunction may be granted to restrain the transfer or indorsement of a **26–09** bill where it has been fraudulently or improperly obtained,[17] or where its negotiation would otherwise (as against the person applying) be wrongful,[18] or where the consideration for it has wholly failed.[19] Such relief may be valuable where there is a risk that the bill will otherwise be negotiated to a holder in due course whose claim would prevail over any personal defences available.

Rectification

Cases may arise in which the instrument needs rectification, as where the **26–10** plaintiff's name is by accident inserted as that of the drawer, in which case a court can rectify the error by striking out the plaintiff's name.[20]

Action for conversion

A bill, note or cheque is treated as any other piece of moveable property, **26–11** and the true owner may bring an action in conversion against any person dealing wrongfully with it. In practice such claims most commonly arise in the case of stolen cheques or drafts against the collecting (or more rarely) paying banks. The liabilities of banks in such cases, and the statutory defences available to them, are considered in Chapters 22 and 23 above.

Multiple parties liable

The claimant is entitled to join, at his option, all or any or the parties liable **26–12** to him on a bill or note as defendants in one action.[21] Should he not do so, a named defendant may wish to claim a contribution, or an indemnity against a third party not a party to the action (as in the case of a holder of a bill suing a subsequent, in preference to a prior, indorser). Such a party may be joined under the procedure governing "Part 20 claims",[22] and in an appropriate case may also be joined as an additional defendant.[23]

This may also be done in cases where the liability arises, whether on an **26–13** express or implied contract, collaterally to the bill on which action is

---

[17] See *Lloyd v. Gurdon* (1818) 2 Swan 180; *Hood v. Aston* (1826) 1 Russ. 412; *Green v. Pledger* (1844) 3 Hare 165; *Thiedemann v. Goldschmidt* (1859) 1 De G.F.& J. 4; *Day v. Longhurst* (1893) 62 L.J. Ch. 334. The shift of the onus of proof provided for by s.30(2) does not apply to such proceedings and the burden remains on the party seeking to establish fraud (*Hawkins v. Troop* (1890) 7 T.L.R. 104).

[18] For example where delivery of the bill remains subject to an unfulfilled condition, or was for a particular purpose.

[19] *Patrick v. Harrison* (1792) 3 Bro. C.C. 476; *Bainbrigge v. Hemmingway* (1865) 12 L.T. 74.

[20] *Druiff v. Parker* (1868) L.R. 5 Eq. 131. As to whether the court should give effect to the real intention of the parties to a bill, whereon is an erroneously placed signature, without a previous rectification, *cf. Steel v. M'Kinlay* (1880) 5 App. Cas. 754, 773, 774 (Lord Blackburn), criticising *Matthews v. Bloxsome* (1864) 33 L.J.Q.B. 209.

[21] See CPR Part 19 and rule 19.1.

[22] See generally CPR Part 20.

[23] CPR Part 19.

brought,[24] as, for instance, where an accommodation drawer sued by the holder seeks to join an accommodation indorser on his verbal promise that the drawer should not have to pay.[25]

26–14   By section 3 of the Civil Liability (Joint Contribution) Act 1978 a judgment against one of two or more persons jointly liable to the claimant no longer operates as a bar to an action, or the continuance of an action, against the other or others.[26] The claimant cannot be compelled to join other persons jointly liable with the defendant.

Proceedings for contribution

26–15   Joint debtors equally liable as between themselves (not being general partners)[27] were at common law severally entitled to contribution,[28] even against the executor of a contributory.[29] Therefore, one of several joint or joint and several makers of a note who paid more than his share might maintain an action against another for contribution, and by the Mercantile Law Amendment Act 1856, section 5, it was provided that a surety or joint debtor, who had paid a debt, should be entitled to the assignment of all securities held by the creditor, and also, on giving a proper indemnity, to sue his principal or co-surety or co-debtor in the creditor's name, and that his own payment should not be pleadable in bar.[30]

Party liable in different capacities

26–16   At one time, if a party was liable on a bill in two or more capacities, he might be the object of several actions on the same bill at the suit of the same plaintiff.[31] It is clear that he could now be, and should be, sued in a single action.

Garnishee proceedings

26–17   The moneys represented by a bill of exchange are attachable by garnishee order, which suspends execution until the bill matures and restrains the judgment debtor in the interim from dealing with the bill.[32]

---

[24] As in *Macdonald v. Whitfield* (1883) 8 App. Cas. 733, where a collateral contract was implied, approving *Reynolds v. Wheeler* (1861) 30 L.J.C.P. 350. The claim of the defendant against the third party must be on an express or implied contract (*Wynne v. Tempest* [1897] 1 Ch. 110).

[25] *Batson v. King* (1859) 28 L.J.Ex. 327; *Wildes v. Dudlow* (1874) L.R. 19 Eq. 198.

[26] Because of this section the former RSC Ord. 15, r. 4(3) was revoked and no comparable provision appears in the CPR. A defendant is no longer entitled to apply for a stay until the claimant joins all other persons jointly liable.

[27] *Sadler v. Nixon* (1834) 5 B. & Ad. 936.

[28] *Edger v. Knapp* (1843) 6 Sc.N.R. 707.

[29] cf. *Priory v. Hembrow* (1841) 8 M. & W. 873.

[30] *Batchellor v. Lawrence* (1861) 9 C.B.(N.S.) 543.

[31] *Wise v. Prowse* (1821) 9 Price 393.

[32] *Hyam v. Freeman* (1890) 35 S.J. 87; *Jones v. Thompson* (1858) 27 L.J. Q.B. 235.

SUMMARY JUDGMENT

The power of the Court to give judgment speedily and without trial is **26–18**
particularly important in connection with bills of exchange, cheques and
promissory notes. The procedure is now governed by Part 24 of the CPR,
which by rule 24.2 provides that:

"The court may give summary judgment against a claimant or defendant on the
whole of a claim or on a particular issue if—

(a) it considers that—

(i) that claimant has no real prospect of succeeding on the claim or issue;
or

(ii) that defendant has no real prospect of successfully defending the claim
or issue; and

(b) there is no other compelling reason why the case or issue should be disposed
of at a trial."

Under that power the Court may resolve any question of law or construction
which arises, and it may impose conditions,[33] including the payment into court
of the sum claimed.[34]

Real prospect of success

The burden for a party wishing to resist such a judgment is to establish a   **26–19**
real prospect of success; this does not require a probability of success. It is not
appropriate for the court under such an application to attempt to try disputed
questions of fact,[35] but the court is equally not bound to accept an assertion at
its face value.[36]

Dicta can be found suggesting that the defendant in an action on a bill faces   **26–20**
a higher test than one in an ordinary action. For example[37] in *Credito Italiano
v. Birnhak*[38] in which fraud was pleaded in defence, it was held that the

---

[33] CPR r.24.6 and CPR r.3.1(3). Under 24PD para. 4 the court may make a conditional order
where "it appears to the court possible that a claim or defence may succeed but improbable that
it will do so". Compare the previous practice of making leave to defend conditional if the defence
was "shadowy", *Paclantic Financing Co. Inc. v. Moscow Narodny Bank Ltd* [1984] 1 W.L.R.
930. It was formerly common where leave was given to defend in whole or in part a claim on a
bill or cheque to require the payment into court of the disputed sum, see for example *Thoni GmbH
v. R.T.P. Equipment Ltd* [1979] 2 Lloyd's Rep. 282, and *All Trades Distributors v. Agencies
Kaufman* (1969) 113 S.J. 995, CA. Given the numerous powerful dicta about the importance of
enforcing payment of bills this approach may well be followed.

[34] See in particular CPR 24PD para. 5. Generally where there is a genuine claim or defence a
condition should not be imposed which it is impossible for a party to fulfill (*MV Yorke Motors (a
firm) v. Edwards* [1982] 1 W.L.R. 444 and now *Chapple v. Williams* (1999) L.T.L. December 8,
1999, C.A. A condition of payment may be imposed where despite the apparent absence of assets
there is evidence that a company with no assets is nonetheless able to raise funds (*Foot & Bowden
v. Anglo Europe Corp. Ltd*, February 17, 2000, CA, unreported.

[35] *Swain v. Hillman, The Times*, November 4, 1999.

[36] See more generally Civil Procedure at 24.2.3; *Glaxo Group Ltd v. Dowelhurst Ltd* [1999] All
E.R. (D) 1288); *Britannia Building Society v. Prangley* (2000) L.T.L. June 12, 2000, Ch. D. For
the high point under the (previous) provisions of RSC Ord. 14 see *National Westminster Bank v.
Daniel* [1993] 1 W.L.R. 1453; [1994] 1 All E.R. 156.

[37] *cf.* the previous edition of this work, at p. 376.

[38] [1967] 1 Lloyd's Rep. 314.

defendants had failed to raise the triable issue of fraud; Sachs L.J. there said:

" . . . the plaintiffs are suing upon a document of a type upon which the commerce of Europe largely depends and the courts are careful not to give leave to defend unless they find that there have been stated upon oath facts which afford to the defendants a prima facie defence raising an issue fit to be tried. The time-honoured phrase in relation to such an issue is 'a triable issue,' the words used in many authorities including the judgment of Lord Justice Greer in the case of *Powszechny Bank v. Paros* [1932] 2 K.B. 353, at p. 359."

26–21   While the claimant on a bill has a number of advantages[39] it is reasonably clear that there is no additional special burden upon the defendant as to the standard of proof in respect of those matters which can properly be raised as a defence.[40]

Holder in due coures and onus of proof

26–22   Where the defendant shows that there was fraud in the negotiation of the bill the burden shifts to the holder to show that he is a holder in due course.[41] The mere statement in the plaintiff's evidence that he took the bill in good faith and for value is not necessarily sufficient to decide the issue in his favour.[42] The holder is, in that case, required to prove that he gave value in good faith without notice of the fraud.[43] If his claim to have done so is established by clear, unchallenged evidence, the allegation of fraud does not constitute a defence and the holder is entitled to judgment.[44] An allegation falling short of fraud will not be sufficient to shift the onus of proof, as where the defendant gave the bill to a person against whom he claimed a set-off and sought to put the indorsee from that party to proof that he was a holder in due course.[45]

Other compelling reason

26–23   Exceptionally there may be circumstances not amounting to a defence on the merits but in the light of which summary judgment ought not to be given.[46]

---

[39] In particular the presumptions in his favour, and unavailability of defences against him if he is a holder in due course, and the non-availability of unliquidated set-offs (as to which see below).

[40] Certainly this appears to be the case in the light of the more robust test established under Part 24 of the CPR (and foreshadowed by the later decisions under RSC Ord. 14 noted above). See the discussion in *Solo Industries UK Ltd v. Canara Bank* [2001] E.W.C.A. CTV 1041 distinguishing (in a documentary credit case) the high evidential burden on a party seeking to restrain payment under a credit from the burden on a bank seeking to establish grounds for defending a claim.

[41] Section 30(2) of the 1882 Act.

[42] *Tatam v. Haslar* (1889) 23 Q.B.D. 345; *Bank für Gemeinwirtschaft Aktiengesellschaft v. City of London Garages Ltd* [1971] 1 W.L.R. 149, CA.

[43] *Powszechny Bank v. Paros* [1932] 2 K.B. 353, approving *Fuller v. Alexander* (1882) 52 L.J.Q.B. 103; 47 L.T. 443; *cf. Engel v. Stourton*, 5 T.L.R. 444 and *Millard v. Baddeley* [1884] W.N. 96; *Bank of Ottawa v. Alder* (1912) 17 B.C.L.R. 378; *Farmer v. Ellis* (1901) 2 O.L.R. 544; and see *Jade International Steel Stahl und Eisen G.m.b.H. & Co. KG v. Robert Nicholas (Steels) Ltd* [1978] 1 Q.B. 917.

[44] *Bank für Gemeinwirtschaft v. City of London Garages* (*supra*).

[45] *Edwards v. Davis* (1888) 4 T.L.R. 385; and see *Engel v. Stourton* (1889) 5 T.L.R. 444 (a case of material alteration).

[46] Under the former provisions (RSC Ord. 14) leave to defend would be given where there was "some other reason" for trial.

Once Bramwell B. considered that the power to sign judgment was not **26–24** intended "to apply to cases in which the defendant might reasonably say, 'I do not know if your case is well founded or not, but I require you to prove it,' " and added, "The case is like that of a defendant under Keating's Act[47] applying for leave to defend in an action on a bill of exchange on which he is sued as guarantor", in which case he would have been admitted to defend, where there had been no acknowledgment by him of the debt or anything else to show that his object in defending was merely delay.[48] That approach would not now be followed where, in the absence of a properly triable defence, the claim could be proved under Part 24. A defendant would need to demonstrate exceptional circumstances requiring investigation.[49]

In proceedings in the Queen's Bench Division of the High Court, or in the **26–25** County Court, a party charged with fraud (among other matters) is entitled to require the action to be tried by a jury, unless the court is satisfied that because of the subject matter that is inappropriate.[50] Such an application should be made within 28 days of service of the defence.[51] This is a substantive right which cannot be excluded by the CPR or procedural directions, and by itself may afford a compelling reason why the matter should go to trial.[52]

Trial of issue

Where a particular issue or issues can be identified which, though inap- **26–26** propriate for summary determination under Part 24, can be separately identi- fied and decided, the court's general powers of case management[53] may well now be invoked to order a split trial of those questions.

SET-OFF, COUNTERCLAIM OR STAY

Autonomy of the Bill

The courts have repeatedly emphasised the commercial importance of the **26–27** independence of the contract upon a bill from its underlying subject matter. In the words of Lord Denning M.R. in *Fielding & Platt v. Najjar*:[54] " . . . a bill of exchange or promissory note is to be treated as cash. It is to be honoured unless there is some good reason to the contrary."[55] In particular, as will be seen, although the court has jurisdiction to entertain a counterclaim in an

---

[47] Bills of Exchange Act 1855.
[48] *Lloyds Bankings Co. v. Ogle* (1876) 1 Ex.D. 262, 264.
[49] *In Solo Industries UK Ltd v. Canara Bank* [2001] E.W.C.A. CTV 1041 Mance L.J. (holding that there was a defence with a real prospect of success) considered that the factual uncertainty resulting from the claimant's failure to provide disclosure ordered of it would at least have justified finding that there was another "compelling reason" (para. 71).
[50] Section 69 of the Supreme Court Act 1981, s.66 of the County Courts Act 1984.
[51] CPR r.26.11
[52] Though cases in which such a charge could be established summarily are by their nature extremely rare.
[53] See generally under CPR Part 3.
[54] [1969] 1 W.L.R. 357, 361, CA.
[55] See also *Montechhi v. Shimco (U.K.) Ltd* [1979] 1 W.L.R. 1180 at 1183.

action upon a bill,[56] the existence of such a claim will not generally operate as a defence to, a bar to summary judgment for, or a ground for staying execution of, moneys due under a bill.

26–28   In *Nova (Jersey) Knit Ltd v. Kammgarn Spinnerei GmbH*[57] the plaintiffs sued on bills of exchange drawn by them and accepted by the defendants. The House of Lords held that English law applied, as the bills, although accepted in Germany, were delivered in London (see s.2 of the Bills of Exchange Act 1882, definition of "Acceptance"). An agreement between the parties provided for disputes to be referred to arbitration, and the defendants sought to stay the proceedings on that ground, they having claims to damages. The House of Lords held[58] that there was, as to the claim on the bills, no dispute.

26–29   Lord Wilberforce said:[59] "[A seller] may demand payment in cash; but if the buyer cannot provide this at once, he may agree to take bills of exchange payable at future dates. These are taken as equivalent to deferred instalments of cash. Unless they are to be treated as unconditionally payable instruments, . . . , which the seller can negotiate for cash, the seller might just as well give credit . . . ." Lord Russell expressed it this way:[60] "It is in my opinion well established that a claim for unliquidated damages under a contract for sale is no defence to a claim under a bill of exchange accepted by the purchaser; nor is it available as set-off or counterclaim. This is a deep rooted concept of English commercial law. A vendor and purchaser who agree upon payment by acceptance of bills of exchange do so not simply upon the basis that credit is given to the purchaser so that the vendor must in due course sue for the price under the contract of sale. The bill is itself a contract separate from the contract of sale. Its purpose is not merely to serve as a negotiable instrument, it is also to avoid postponement of the purchaser's liability to the vendor himself, a postponement grounded upon some allegation of failure in some respect by the vendor under the underlying contract, unless it be total or quantified partial failure of consideration."

Unliquidated cross-claims

26–30   The result is that it is well established[61] that even between immediate parties, cross claims for unliquidated damages, may not be set up in answer to

---

[56] See now s.49(2) of the Supreme Court Act 1981.

[57] [1977] 1 W.L.R. 713 The decision was distinguished in *Williams & Glyn's Bank v. Belkin Packing* (1983) 6 W.W.R. 481 (Supreme Court of Canada). The propositions derived from the case have recently been reaffirmed by the Court of Appeal in *Safa Limited v. Banque du Caire* [2000] 2 Lloyd's Rep. 600 (a documentary credit case, though on exceptional facts, where the paying bank had grounds for defending the claim on the basis, *inter alia*, that it might have been the victim of misrepresentation).

[58] Lord Salmon dissenting on this point.

[59] p. 721.

[60] pp. 732–733.

[61] See *Glennie v. Imri* (1839) 3 Y. & C. Ex. 442; *Trickey v. Larne* (1840) 6 M. & W. 278; *Warwick v. Nairn* (1855) 10 Ex. 762; *James Lamont & Co. Ltd v. Hyland Ltd* [1950] 1 K.B. 585; *Brown Shipley & Co. Ltd v. Alicia Hosiery Ltd* [1966] 1 Lloyd's Rep. 668; *Cebora SNC v. SIP Industrial Products Ltd* [1976] 1 Lloyd's Rep. 271; *Montecchi v. Shimco UK Ltd* [1979] 1 W.L.R. 1180; *Montebianco Industrie Tessilli SpA v. Carlyle Mills (London) Ltd* [1981] 1 Lloyds Rep. 509.

a claim upon a bill.[62] This is the case even if such cross-claims would otherwise entitle the party liable to rely upon the defence of equitable set-off.[63] It follows that a cross claim which is for a liquidated sum may be relied on. The principles appear to be unaffected by the procedural changes implemented by the Civil Procedure Rules.[64]

Other defences

The principle described above only precludes reliance by way of the **26–31** defence of set-off upon an unliquidated cross-claim. The (arguable) existence of a defence to liability is an answer to an application for summary judgment.[65] As between immediate parties at least there is no reason why an innocent misrepresentation inducing the bill, or entitling the party liable to rescind the contract in consideration of which it was drawn, should not amount to a defence.[66]

Failure of consideration

A total failure of consideration may be relied on as a defence against an immediate party, or against a subsequent holder provided he is not a holder for value. Similarly, a partial failure of consideration, provided it is for an ascertainable liquidated sum, may be relied on *pro tanto* at least between immediate parties.[67]

Possible discretion

Occasionally the courts have indicated that there may be room for the use **26–32** of a discretion of the court in situations when there is a partial failure of consideration. In *Montebianco Industrie Tessili S.p.A. v. Carlyle Mills (London)*[68] Stephenson L.J. stated:

[62] This is an important characteristic of claims upon bills, but it is not the only context in which such a principle can be found. Similar principles apply to documentary credits, recently discussed in *Solo Industries UK Ltd v. Canara Bank* [2001] E.W.C.A. CTV 1041. An unliquidated cross-claim may not, for example, be set-up in answer to, or set-off against, the liability of a mortgagor—see *National Westminster Bank plc v. Skelton* [1993] 1 W.L.R. 72 (note), applying the principle in *Mobil Oil Co. Ltd v. Rawlinson* (1981) 43 P.& C.R. 221; In *Esso Petroleum Co. Ltd v. Milton* [1997] 1 W.L.R. 938 (CA) the same principle was applied to a direct debit mandate. In other contexts it is not uncommon for contracts to provide expressly that payment should be due without set-off.

[63] As to which see *Hanak v. Green* [1958] 2 Q.B. 9. It is helpful in understanding the cases to bear in mind that ordinarily, where a right to set-off in equity is established in accordance with the principles set out in that case, this operates as a substantive defence, and not merely a cross-claim upon which a cross-judgment may be entered or pending which execution may be stayed. Neither applies in the case of bills of exchange (see below).

[64] *Safa Limited v. Banque du Caire* [2000] 2 Lloyd's Rep. 600, at p. 605 *per* Waller L.J.

[65] The availability of defences depends upon the status of the holder claiming to enforce the bill, see above Ch. 18, particularly at paras 18–22 to 18–35.

[66] Consider *Safa Limited v. Banque du Caire* [2000] 2 Lloyd's Rep. 600 and *Solo Industries UK Ltd v. Canara Bank* [2001] E.W.C.A. CTV 1041. See also the discussion by Hickman in New Law Journal October 5, 2001 p. 1445 considering these cases together with the (now doubted) decision in *Clovertogs Ltd v. Jean Scenes Ltd* [1982] Com.L.R. 88, and para. 18–27, above.

[67] See above "Failure of Consideration" at paras 19–41 to 19–45.

[68] [1981] 1 Lloyd's Rep. 509.

" . . . we cannot consider this case as a case of total failure of consideration when . . . it would be beyond argument that the Defendants should have leave to defend, so we are in the position of partial failure of consideration where we have a discretion . . . what this Court has to do is to exercise its discretion anew . . . to decide whether we ought to apply the well-known ordinary principle relating to the enforcement of bills of exchange or whether we should, without eroding the principle, meet the justice of the case by making an exception to it."

26–33   Similarly it was suggested by Stephen J. that there might be exceptional circumstances in which such matters could be raised by defence but that" . . . without such strong grounds a counterclaim ought not to be allowed in an action on a bill, cheque or note which was not disputed."[69] In another case Thesiger L.J. suggested that a good counterclaim sufficiently connected might be pleaded as a defence.[70]

26–34   In the *Montebianco* case the assumed discretion was not exercised and the principle set out in *Nova (Jersey) Knit*[71] was applied. With respect to the learned Lord Justice it would seem that any departure from that principle would have the result of eroding the general rule behind it. The principle is well established, and earlier dicta must be regarded as doubtful.

No stay of execution or restraint by injunction

26–35   The same cases establish that the existence of the unliquidated counterclaim affords no ground for a stay of execution in respect of the judgment on the bill. Various attempts have been made to get round this rule. They have almost invariably failed.

26–36   In *Montecchi v. Shimco (U.K.) Ltd*[72] two plaintiffs brought separate actions against the defendant in respect of two dishonoured bills. In each case the defendant counterclaimed for damages on the ground that goods supplied by the plaintiffs were defective. Both plaintiffs obtained summary judgment, but in the first action the Master granted the defendant a stay of execution until the hearing of the counterclaim whilst in the second the Master refused a stay. On

---

[69] *Newman v. Lever* (1887) 4 T.L.R. 91; and see *James Lamont & Co. Ltd v. Hyland Ltd* [1950] 1 K.B. 585; *Brown, Shipley & Co. Ltd v. Alicia Hosiery Ltd* [1966] 1 Lloyd's Rep. 668, applied in *Cebora S.N.C. v. S.I.P. (Industrial Products) Ltd* [1976] 1 Lloyd's Rep. 271 distinguishing *Saga of Bond Street Ltd v. Avalon Promotions Ltd* [1972] 2 Q.B. 325 and *Barclays Bank Ltd v. Aschaffenburger Zellstoffwerke, A.G.* [1967] 1 Lloyd's Rep. 387. In *Saga of Bond Street Ltd v. Avalon Promotions Ltd* the plaintiffs obtained a default judgment which the master and judge in chambers refused to set aside on the ground that they had no discretion. The judgment was obtained before the defendant had any knowledge of the writ, which was returned through the dead letter office. Referring to *Brown, Shipley & Co. Ltd v. Alicia Hosiery Ltd (supra)* Salmon L.J. said that he did not view that case or any other as laying down the proposition that the court had no discretion and is bound in every case where the claim rests on a dishonoured bill of exchange to give judgment for the plaintiff unconditionally. This view was said by Waller L.J. in *Safa v. Banque du Caire* to have been "negatived" by the *Nova (Jersey)* decision. See also *A/S Catherineholm v. Norequipment Trading Ltd* [1972] 2 Q.B. 314, following *Saga of Bond Street Ltd v. Avalon Promotions*, applying Denning L.J. in *R. v. London County Quarter Sessions Appeals Committee, ex p. Rossi* [1956] 1 Q.B. 682, 684 and disapproving *Thomas Bishop Ltd v. Helmville Ltd* [1972] 1 Q.B. 464 (CA).

[70] *Anglo-Italian Bank v. Wells* (1878) 38 L.T. 197, 201. In *Oscar Harris v. Vallarman* [1940] 1 All E.R. 185 Slesser L.J. held it to be arguable that a cross-claim might be, since the Judicature Acts, available as a defence. This view cannot stand in the light of the *Nova (Jersey)* case.

[71] *Supra* at p. 377.

[72] [1979] 1 W.L.R. 1181.

appeal Pain J. removed the stay in the first action but in the second Jupp J. granted a stay and a Mareva-style injunction[73] restraining the plaintiff from dealing with the proceeds of execution or removing the moneys from the jurisdiction.

The Court of Appeal stated the law in unequivocal terms: **26–37**

" . . . it is elementary that as between the immediate parties to a bill of exchange, which is treated in international commerce as the equivalent of cash, the fact that the Defendant may have a counterclaim for unliquidated damages arising out of the same transaction forms no sort of defence to an action on a bill of exchange and no ground upon which he should be granted a stay of execution of the judgment in the action for the proceeds of the bill of exchange."[74]

As to the Mareva point Bridge L.J. continued:[75]   **26–38**

"I am far from saying that in no circumstances whatever could such an injunction as was granted by Jupp J. in (this) case be granted to restrain a Plaintiff from dealing with the fruits of a judgment in this type of situation . . . [It] seems to me that the basis of the Mareva injunction is that there has to be a real reason to apprehend that if the injunction is not made, the intending Plaintiff in this country may be deprived of a remedy against the foreign Defendant whom he seeks to sue. . . . Certainly no case has been cited to us in which such an injunction was granted when there was not every reason to apprehend that without such injunction the Plaintiff creditor would be defeated."

In other words a freezing injunction will not be granted merely to prevent   **26–39** a claimant from enjoying the fruits of judgment pending the hearing of a counterclaim. Equally, a stay will not be granted on the sole basis that a claimant has no assets in the jurisdiction with which to satisfy a potential counterclaim.[76]

Insolvency

An unliquidated claim for damages may nonetheless be raised as a cross-   **26–40** claim in answer to a statutory demand.[77]

---

[73] These are now termed "freezing injunctions" under CPR Part 25.

[74] *per* Bridge L.J. at 1183.

[75] At pp. 1183–1184.

[76] *Cebora S.N.C. v. S.I.P. (Industrial Products) Ltd* [1976] 1 Lloyd's Rep. 271 at 280 *per* Sir Eric Sachs.

[77] *Hofer v. Strawson* [1999] 2 B.C.L.C. 336; *The Times* April 17, 1999.

CHAPTER 27

PROCEDURE—II: PLEADING AND EVIDENCE

Forum

27–01 ACTIONS may be brought in the High Court or County Court.[1] Claims relating to bills or cheques may fall within the subject matter of the specialist lists established under CPR Part 49.

Commencement

27–02 Proceedings are commenced by the issue of the Claim Form.[2] Generally proceedings may not be commenced until there is a cause of action upon the bill, which will not be until its maturity even if the acceptor has refused payment.[3] Under CPR 16 PD para. 3.1 parties are encouraged to serve particulars of claim together with the claim form; service of them is generally[4] necessary for any judgment to be obtained. There is no necessity for a prior demand on the maker of a note unless it is specified to be payable at a particular place (in which case a conforming presentment for payment is required), the commencement of proceedings being sufficient,[5] but a party issuing a claim form without demand could expect, if the note was then paid, to be penalised in costs.[6]

Statements of Case—General

27–03 There are under the Civil Procedure Rules no prescribed forms for statements of case, which are required to be a "concise statement of the facts". The substantial volume of old case law dealing with technical requirements of

---

[1] The Civil Procedure Rules apply to both. An action may not be commenced in the High Court unless it is for a sum exceeding £15,000. A description of the rules is beyond the scope of this work and reference should be made to Civil Procedure. See also Bullen Leake & Jacob's *Precedents of Pleading*.

[2] In accordance generally with CPR Part 7, or CPR Part 8 where that procedure is appropriate.

[3] *Wells v. Giles* (1836) 2 Gale 209, *Kennedy v. Thomas* [1894] 2 Q.B. 759; *Gelmini v. Morriggia* [1913] 2 K.B. 549, 552; (cf. *Westaway v. Stewart* (1908) 8 W.L.R. 907, *Thibeault v. Gauthier* (1928) 34 R. du Jur. 190) though notice of dishonour might be given. A claim might perhaps be allowed to include a claim for payment a bill which has not yet matured where it is one of a series claims on which are brought together, or where injunctive or other relief is sought prior to maturity.

[4] Practice in the Commercial Court is different.

[5] *Rumball v. Ball* (1711) 10 Mod. 38; *Norton v. Ellam* (1837) 2 M. & W. 461.

[6] *Macintosh v. Haydon* (1826) Ry. & M. 362, but particularly under modern practice.

pleading, and the matters which might be proved under various averments, is now obsolete.[7]

The formal requirements for the contents of statements of case are set out **27–04** in CPR Part 16 and the practice direction supplementing that Part. Where a claim is brought in specialist proceedings under CPR Part 49 reference should also be made to the relevant practice guide. In general terms, if the statement of case sets out properly the facts relied on, the claim will not be defeated by a technical objection to the form. Where under the approach favoured by the CPR the parties have clearly identified their positions, and the matters in dispute, it is sensible for the claimant to set out his case upon those issues in detail. It is suggested that this course is appropriate even in respect of those matters which, by virtue of a presumption arising under the Act, are presumed in his favour or in respect of which the burden is upon the defendant. If a matter is denied, reasons must be given.

Statements of case must be verified by a statement of truth in accordance **27–05** with CPR Part 38. Provided they are so verified they may stand as evidence in interlocutory proceedings.

Presumptions—General

The Act contains a number of statutory presumptions, some of which will **27–06** be referred to below. Prima facie presumptions may be displaced by evidence; their effect is to shift the onus of proof. In some cases matters are conclusively presumed in favour of a holder in due course; and a defence which purports to deny them without also denying (giving proper reasons) the claimant's status as such a holder would be liable to be struck out.[8] In other cases a party is absolutely precluded from denying a matter, and consequently any attempt to do so could be struck out as a matter of law.

Particulars of Bill

The particulars of claim should state the date, amount and parties to the **27–07** bill.[9] Where a bill is payable at usance, this should be specifically stated.[10]

CPR PD 16 para. 8.3 requires a party relying on a written contract to attach **27–08** or serve with his particulars of claim a copy of the contract. Doing so avoids

---

[7] Indeed much of it has for some time not reflected practice. References to that case law are not maintained in this edition save where relevant to a matter which remains good practice. Similarly previous editions have considered many decisions relating to rules of evidence which are no longer relevant and these too are omitted. It should be noted that while, generally, the previous rules were more technical and restrictive, they include cases in which parties were allowed under a general averment or denial to establish by evidence facts which now (and for some time) ought to be specifically pleaded, and which they would not be allowed to raise without amendment or proper notice to the other side.

[8] Under CPR Part 3, or in practical terms judgment could be entered upon the claim, or issue, pursuant to CPR Part 24.

[9] *Walker v. Hicks* (1877) 3 Q.B.D. 8, *Manchester Advance Co. Ltd v. Walton* (1892) 62 L.J.Q.B. 158.

[10] *Meggadow v. Holt* (1691) 12 Mod. 15; *Buckley v. Campbell* (1708) 1 Salk. 131. A usance must be proved and will not be judicially noticed

the need to transcribe the terms of the instrument (which may be highly material if the proper construction or effect is in dispute), as well as providing all the material for an application for summary judgment should one follow.

27–09   It has been said that a claim on a foreign bill should state it to be so, because of the presumption that a bill is an inland bill until the contrary is shown, and that the claimant might otherwise be obliged to amend if the defendant denies the acceptance of it as an inland bill,[11] but if the circumstances of the bill appeared from the face of the pleading (or its face) and/or the question is not material, then this may no longer be considered important.

Amount and Interest

27–10   The amount claimed, which may be in foreign currency,[12] should be stated. Particulars of the interest claimed should be set out in accordance with CPR 16.4(2).[13]

Status of claimant

27–11   The claimant should state the capacity in which he sues. It was held in *Arab Bank v. Ross*[14] that a pleading in which the Plaintiff claimed as a holder in due course was sufficient to enable him to succeed as a holder for value.[15]

27–12   By section 30(2) of the Act every holder is presumed to be a holder in due course, unless one of the factors mentioned there is shown, in which case the burden shifts to the claimant to show that value has subsequently been given in good faith for the bill.[16]

Capacity of Parties to the bill

27–13   Evidence may be given to explain the capacity or circumstances in which persons have become parties to a bill, even where this is contrary to the

---

[11] *Armani v. Castrique* (1844) 13 M. & W. 443; *cf.* Bullen and Leake.

[12] *Barclays Bank International v. Levin Bros (Bradford)* [1977] Q.B. 270, and see Ch. 28 below. The information required by CPR PD 16 para. 10 must be provided.

[13] See also s.44A of the Adminstration of Justice Act 1979, inserted by s1 of the Private International Law (Miscellaneous Provisions) Act 1995: the court has power to direct that interest should run on a judgment expressed in foreign currency at a rate other than that prescribed under the Judgments Act 1838. The Court will generally be prepared to enter a judgment in default for where interest is claimed at a rate equal to or lower than the Judgment Act rate.

[14] [1952] 2 Q.B. 216.

[15] Romer L.J. expressed the view that a party intending to rely in the alternative on his status as a holder for value should specifically say so. It is respectfully suggested that this is redundant.

[16] *Siffman v. Grydy* [1909] T.S. 568 is to the effect that fraud must be proved "up to the hilt". This seems to reflect no more than the generally high civil burden for such an allegation, which must be specifically alleged and proved. A properly formulated allegation of fraud is sufficient to displace the onus, see the cases cited at para. 26–22 above.

appearance of the instrument. "[I]t is a well established rule of law that the whole facts and circumstances attendant upon the making, issuing and trans-ference of a bill may legitimately be referred to for the purpose of ascertaining the true relation to each other of the parties who put their signature upon it, either as makers or indorsers, and that reasonable inferences derived from these facts and circumstances are admitted to the effect of qualifying, altering or even converting the relative liabilities which the law merchant would otherwise assign to them."[17]

Principal and surety

In the case of a note on its face joint or joint and several, the introduction **27–14** of equitable principles since the Judicature Acts now enables a surety in all cases[18] to give evidence to show that the creditor was affected with knowledge that he was but a surety and in consequence to set up any defence arising out of the law of principal and surety.[19] Where the question arises between the principal debtor and sureties, or between the sureties *inter se* in an action for indemnity or contribution, such evidence has always been admissible.[20]

Delivery

No contract upon a bill is complete until it has been delivered,[21] nonetheless **27–15** delivery by all prior parties is conclusively presumed in favour of a holder in due course.[22] Against a party other than a holder in due course, there is a prima facie presumption of delivery, but this may be rebutted by evidence. If delivery is denied, then proper reasons should now be given. Evidence may be adduced to dispute valid delivery or to show that delivery was without authority, subject to a condition, or for a special and limited purpose other than the transfer of property in the instrument.[23]

Consideration

By section 30(1) there is a rebuttable presumption that any party signing a **27–16** bill became a party to it for value, and it is not therefore strictly necessary to plead consideration. It is nonetheless sensible to state the consideration where this is practicable, and especially when it is known to be in dispute.

---

[17] *Per* Lord Watson in *Macdonald v. Whitfield* (1883) 8 App.Cas. 733.
[18] Formerly it was otherwise: *Price v. Edmunds* (1830) 10 B. & C. 578; *Strong v. Foster* (1855) 17 C.B. 201.
[19] See Ch. 33. Early examples include *Hollier v. Eyre* (1842) 9 Cl. & F. 1, 45; *Davies v. Stainbank* (1855) 6 De G.M. & G. 679; *Greenough v. M'Clelland* (1860) 30 L.J.Q.B. 15; *Overend, Gurney & Co. v. Oriental Finance Co.* (1874) L.R. 7 H.L. 348.
[20] *Reynolds v. Wheeler* (1861) 30 L.J.C.P. 350; *Godsell v. Lloyd* (1911) 27 T.L.R. 383.
[21] Section 21(1).
[22] Section 21(3).
[23] Section 21(2).

27–17   Conversely, if the defendant wishes to deny that consideration was given for the bill[24] then he should properly set out the reasons.

Indorsements

27–18   It is not strictly necessary to set out each indorsement appearing on a bill, but it is sensible to set them out, certainly if the manner in which the claimant acquired title is in issue.

27–19   Indorsements are deemed to have been placed on the bill in the order in which they appear,[25] and to have been made before the bill was overdue,[26] but in each case subject to proof to the contrary.

27–20   A defendant has a right at the trial to call on the plaintiff to read any indorsements that may be on the bill.[27]

Presentment

27–21   In a claim for dishonour by non-acceptance, the fact circumstances of presentment for acceptance (or alternatively the matters dispensing with it) should be set out. In a claim following dishonour by non-payment against the drawer or an indorser, and (whether or not strictly necessary) against the acceptor, the presentment and subsequent dishonour (or the circumstances dispensing with presentment) should likewise, as material facts, be set out.

Proceedings on dishonour

27–22   Notice of dishonour, (and where required noting and protest), is a constituent of the cause of action against a drawer or indorser, so in an action against such a party the particulars of claim should set out the giving of such notice, or alternatively plead the facts by which notice was dispensed with.[28]

27–23   Notice of dishonour may be proved by inference from other matters. After the bill is due a promise to pay, or a part payment,[29] or the offer of it,[30] or any admission of liability,[31] whether before or after the period of giving notice has

---

[24] Note that the action can be maintained if value has at any time between the parties been given for the bill (s.27(2)), and it is no defence for an accommodation party to allege its absence (s.28(2)).

[25] Section 32(5).

[26] Section 32(6).

[27] *Richards v. Frankum* (1840) 9 C. & P. 221. As to agreements by clerks in fraud of their employers, see *Bosanquet v. Foster* (1841) 9 C. & P. 659; *Bosanquet v. Corser* (1841) 9 C. & P. 664. A holder may strike out indorsements which are not necessary to his title, and a series of indorsements in blank may be so irrelevant. However it has been held that at trial indorsements not pleaded or relied on should be struck out (*Mayer v. Jadis* (1836) 1 M. & Rob. 247) in which case the remedy against the indorsers is lost. Whether or not that remains good, it is preferable to plead the indorsements thereby preserving rights against all parties.

[28] *Fruhauf v. Grosvenor* (1892) 61 L.J.Q.B. 717; *May v. Chidley* [1894] 1 Q.B. 451; *Roberts v. Plant* [1895] 1 Q.B. 597.

[29] *Horford v. Wilson* (1807) 1 Taunt. 12.

[30] *Dixon v. Elliott* (1832) 5 C. & P. 437.

[31] *Mills v. Gibson* (1847) 16 L.J.C.P. 249; *Jackson v. Collins* (1848) 17 L.J.Q.B. 142. Even though the admission had been made to a person other than the subsequent plaintiff (*Rabey v. Gilbert* (1861) 30 L.J.Ex. 170).

expired, is prima facie (but not conclusive evidence)[32] of notice.[33] If such matters are relied on as waiver of the requirement of notice of dishonour, this should be specifically pleaded.

Payment

Payment must in all cases be pleaded. Under the former practice it was **27–24** held, in a case where the only issue for the jury was whether any interest was due on the bill, that the defendant could not tender evidence of payment of principal without a plea of payment.[34] A plea of payment must be supported by proof of actual payment in money[35] but where a bill has been given in satisfaction of another bill and ultimately paid, in an action on the first bill it will be sufficient to plead such payment.[36] Where the defendant pays part only of the plaintiff's claim into court, he must in his pleading distinctly indicate the nature of his defence as to the residue, and not merely deny that the plaintiff sustained more damage than the sum paid in.[37]

Material Alteration

Where an alteration appears on the face of a bill or note, it lies on the **27–25** claimant to show that it was made under such circumstances as not to avoid the instrument.[38] The rule is reasonable. If it lay on the defendant, (an acceptor for example), sued by an indorsee, to show that the alteration was improperly made, it might be a great hardship, for he may have no means of proving that the bill went unaltered from his hands, or of showing the circumstances of a subsequent alteration. The burden of explaining an alteration imposes no hardship on the claimant: if the bill was altered while in his hands, he may and

---

[32] *Bell v. Frankis* (1842) 11 L.J.C.P. 300.

[33] Other early cases cited in previous editions as illustrations include *Booth v. Jacobs* (1834) 3 Nev. & M. 351 (a letter from the defendant containing no promise of payment, but merely an ambiguous allusion to the bill being dishonoured, was held sufficient to warrant the jury finding that the defendant had received due notice of dishonour); *Wilkins v. Jadis* (1831) 1 Moo. & R. 41 (the sending a person by the defendant, the drawer, to the plaintiffs two days after the bill had become due, to inform him that he, the drawer, had been defrauded of the bill, and that he should defend any action upon it, was left by Lord Tenterden to the jury as evidence to prove notice of dishonour); *Brownell v. Bonney* (1841) 1 Q.B. 39 (a statement by the defendant to a third party that he should pay the bill. and not avail himself of the informality of the notice, held to be evidence of due notice); *Campbell v. Webster* (1845) 15 L.J.C.P. 4 (a conditional promise to pay, although the condition be not complied with); but see *Pickin v. Graham* (1833) 1 Cr. & M. 725. and see *Curlewis v. Corfield* (1841) 1 Q.B. 814; *Britton v. Milsom* (1892) 19 O.A.R. 96, distinguished in *Swift Canadian Co. v. Duff* (1916) 38 O.L.R. 163.

[34] *Adams v. Palk* (1842) 3 Q.B. 2.

[35] *Morley v. Culverwell* (1840) 7 M. & W. 174.

[36] *Thorne v. Smith* (1851) 10 C.B. 659.

[37] *cf. Tattersall v. Parkinson* (1847) 16 L.J.Ex. 196. As to payment into court, see generally, Ord. 22.

[38] *Johnson v. Duke of Marlborough* (1818) 2 Stark. 313; *Henman v. Dickinson* (1828) 5 Bing. 183; *Knight v. Clements* (1838) 3 Nev. & P. 375. It has been held that the giving of an authority to draw, accept, etc., bills did not ratify an alteration, made prior to such authority, of a bill accepted by the person giving the authority, and altered by the person to whom the authority was given *Sutton v. Blakey* (1897) 13 T.L.R. 441); but in this case the alteration was but to correct a mistake, which at common law never avoided the instrument; see *ante*, para. 20–22. It is said that the presumption against the legality of an alteration is confined to the cases of a bill or note, and of a will; *cf.* notes to *Master v. Miller*, 1 Smith L.C., 13th ed., 807.

ought to account for it; if before, then he took it with a mark of suspicion on its face, which ought to have induced him either to refuse it, or to require evidence of the circumstances under which the alteration was made.

Lost Bills[39]

27–26   It is not strictly necessary to produce the bill at trial since it may be proved by secondary evidence,[40] and a defence that the bill has been lost or destroyed must be positively pleaded.[41]

27–27   It has been held, on section 87 of the Common Law Procedure Act 1854, that a judge has no power on defendant's application to order a stay of proceedings until the plaintiff furnishes an indemnity to the court's satisfaction.[42] In the light of that it has previously been said that the proper course to adopt is for the defendant to plead the loss of the bill and not to ask for an indemnity, it then being for the claimant to tender an indemnity and move to strike out the defence so far as founded on the loss of the bill.[43] This is hardly appropriate under modern practice, and it is suggested that an indemnity should be sought (or offered) at the earliest stage, with the defendant then applying to dismiss the action unless it is provided.[44] A claimant who commences an action without offering an indemnity will incur liability for the defendant's costs up to the time of his having such indemnity.[45]

BILLS AND NOTES AS EVIDENCE

General

27–28   There are a number of early cases, referred to below, in which decisions have turned on, or the courts have expressed views upon, the inference to be drawn from the existence or form of bills or cheques or receipts upon them. It is extremely rare now for a case to be decided in the absence of positive evidence in some form as to the circumstances, and these cases can be regarded as no more than indications of what inferences may be drawn. Even for that purpose, they must be considered in the light of modern commercial and banking practice.

---

[39] See generally Ch. 31 below.

[40] *Shearn v. Burnard* (1839) 10 A & E 593.

[41] *Blackie v. Pidding* (1848) 6 CB 196, *Charnley v. Grundy* (1854) 14 C.B. 608.

[42] *Aranguren v. Scholfield* (1856) 1 H. & N. 494. The bond of the plaintiff has been held insufficient where the amount involved was large, a surety or sureties being required in addition, the Court inclining to the view that such was the practice at the time of the decision in *Walmsley v. Child* (1749) 1 Ves.Sen. 341 (*Orton v. Brett* (1899) 12 Man. 448).

[43] See section 70 of the Act, discussed in Ch. 31.

[44] The defendant could apply under Part 24 on the grounds that the claim has no prospect of succeeding unless an indemnity is given so that the court might make an order under section 70.

[45] *King v. Zimmerman* (1871) L.R. 6 C.P. 446; see also *Tessier v. Caille* (1902) Q.R. 25 S.C. 207. In South Africa the courts appear to hold the view that execution should be stayed till an indemnity be given; *cf. Bodania Co. v. Mahomed* [1906] T.S. 520. The holder is not bound to apply under s.69, but on offering an indemnity has a good cause of action under s.70 against the defendant (*Phillips v. Wobbe* (1916) 7 C.P.D. 359).

Bills and Notes

A bill or note as between immediate parties is evidence of money lent,[46] but   **27–29**
as between immediate parties only.[47] It may also be evidence of an account
stated when due,[48] and is admissible as a paper or writing to prove the
defendant's receipt of so much money, and even though it has been invalidated as a bill or note by alteration.[49] Similarly, it has been held that an
indorsement is prima facie evidence of money lent by the indorsee to the
indorser,[50] and of an account stated.[51]

Prima facie all negotiable instruments, and indeed, all payments, are to   **27–30**
extinguish an existing debt, not to create a new one,[52] *i.e.* prima facie they are
repayments.

Cheques

A cheque presented and paid is not in itself evidence of money lent or   **27–31**
advanced by the banker to the customer, but prima facie evidence of repayment by the bank.[53] A cheque, not presented, is not evidence of money
previously lent to the drawer by the payee.[54] In other words, the mere
circumstance of one man drawing a cheque in favour of another is no evidence
of a debt due from the drawer.

It was at one time held that the mere production of a cheque drawn by the   **27–32**
debtor in favour of the creditor and paid by the banker was not evidence of

---

[46] *Clerke v. Martin* (1701) 2 Ld.Raym. 757; and the form of action was, prior to the statute of
Anne, in the case of notes, for money lent, and not upon the note itself (*Grant v. Vaugham* (1764)
3 Burr. 1516, 1525 (Lord Mansfield C.J.)); Bayley, *Bills* (6th ed.), p. 362; *Morgan v. Jones* (1830)
1 C. & J. 162, 167, distinguished, as regards a cheque, in *Baxter v. Foster* [1955] C.L.Y.B.
183.

[47] *cf. Bayley, op. cit.*, *Waynam v. Bend* (1808) 1 Camp. 175; *Bentley v. Northouse* (1827) M. &
M. 66; *Eales v. Dicker* (1829) M. & M. 324. Formerly the principle appears not to have been
confined to immediate parties; *cf. Bayley*, p. 362.

[48] *Wheatley v. Williams* (1836) 1 M. & W. 533; *Irving v. Veitch* (1837) 3 M. & W. 90; *Fryer v.
Roe* (1852) 12 C.B. 437 and see *Rhodes v. Gent* (1821) 5 B. & Ald. 244.· An IOU is evidence of
an account stated, but not of money lent: see *ante*, para. 24–17.

[49] *Sutton v. Toomer* (1827) 7 B. & C. 416. As to when a party can sue on the consideration for
an altered bill or note, see *ante*, para. 26–03. An unstamped or insufficiently stamped bill could
not, until stamp duty was abolished by the Finance Act 1970, be evidence of a contract or any part
of it: *Jardine v. Payne* (1831) 1 B. & Ad. 663; and see *Hamilton Finance Co. Ltd v. Coverley
Westray Walbaum Tosetti Ltd* and *Portland Finance Co. Ltd* [1969] 1 Lloyd's Rep. 53. An
unstamped note has, however, been admitted to show that it was given in respect of a void and
illegal agreement (*Nash v. Duncomb* (1831) 1 M. & R. 104).

[50] *Kessebower v. Tims* (1782) Bayley, *op. cit.*, p. 363.

[51] *Burmester v. Hogarth* (1843) 11 M. & W. 97, 101.

[52] *Welch v. Seaborn* (1816) 1 Stark. 474; *Pearce v. Davis* (1834) 1 Mood. & R. 365.

[53] In default of sufficient evidence that the customer was overdrawn at the time he drew such
cheque (*Fletcher v. Manning* (1844) 12 M. & W. 571; see also *Allaire v. King* [1908] Q.R. 33 S.C.
343; *Harty v. Grattan* (1916) 35 O.L.R. 348; *Trudeau v. Hemsley* (1935) Q.R. 74 S.C. 40). *Kilsby
v. Williams* (1822) 5 B. & Ald. 815; *Pott v. Clegg* (1847) 16 M. & W. 321.

[54] *Pearce v. Davis* (1834) 1 Moo. & R. 365; nor if presented and paid is it evidence of a loan
by the drawer to the payee, but rather of a repayment (*Cary v. Gerrish* (1810) 4 Esp. 9; *Graham
v. Cox* (1848) 2 C. & K. 702; *cf Aubert v. Walsh* (1812) 4 Taunt. 293).

payment of a particular debt.[55] It was said[56] that the payee should be required to write his name across it or indorse it to show that it had passed through his hands.

27–33   Since 1957 it has not been common practice for collecting banks to require their customer's indorsements, or for cheques to be indorsed. Accordingly, s3 of the Cheques Act 1957[57] provides that : "3. An unindorsed cheque which appears to have been paid by the banker on whom it is drawn is evidence of the receipt by the payee of the sum payable by the cheque."[58]

Receipt

27–34   A general receipt on the back of a bill is not of itself evidence of the payment by the drawer, though he produces the bill, for "prima facie the receipt on the back imports that it was paid by the acceptor".[59] Evidence is admissible to explain the receipt,[60] and the circumstances may show the contrary.[61]

Protest

27–35   It has been held that a protest is not evidence to support due presentment. In *Chesmer v. Noyes*[62] it was material to show that a bill drawn abroad on Bristol had been duly presented, and a protest by a notary under seal was offered which contended that by the usage of merchants this was evidence of dishonour of a foreign bill. Lord Ellenborough held that a protest might be sufficient to prove a presentment in a foreign country, but presentment of a foreign bill in England must be proved in the same manner as if it were an inland bill or a promissory note.

---

[55] *Egg v. Barnett* (1800) 3 Esp. 196. It was held not necessary to go on and show that the debtor paid the cheque to his creditor: *Mountford v. Harper* (1847) 16 M. & W. 825, distinguishing *Lloyd v. Sandilands* (1818) Gow 15; *Boswell v. Smith* (1833) 6 C. & P. 60.

[56] This statement is to be found in previous editions.

[57] Which contains other provisions dispensing with the need for indorsement, see above para. 23–76.

[58] 5 & 6 Eliz. 2, c. 36. In *Westminster Bank Ltd v. Zang* [1966] A.C. 182 Lord Reid commented (at 221) that the section could not be construed so as to exclude cheques which the payee had directed should be paid to the account of a third person, and observed that it "makes it clear—if there were any doubt—that an unindorsed cheque which appears to have been paid by the payee's banker is, without evidence as to who actually received the money, in itself prima facie evidence of the receipt of the money by the payee".

[59] *Scholey v. Walsby* (1791) 1 Peake N.P.C. 34 *per* Lord Kenyon.

[60] *Graves v. Key* (1832)3 B. & Ad. 313.

[61] *Phillips v. Warren* (1845) 14 M. & W. 379.

[62] (1815) 4 Camp. 129.

CHAPTER 28

DAMAGES, INTEREST AND COSTS

Basis under the Act

WHERE a bill is dishonoured by non-acceptance or by non-payment or a note **28–01**
is dishonoured by non-payment,[1] or a cheque is dishonoured on presentment
for payment,[2] the measure of damages for which the holder is entitled to sue
is provided by section 57 of the Act:

**57. Where a bill[3] is dishonoured,[4] the measure of damages, which shall
be deemed to be liquidated damages, shall be as follows:**

**(1) The holder may recover from any party liable on the bill, and the
drawer who has been compelled to pay the bill may recover from the
acceptor, and an indorser who has been compelled to pay the bill may
recover from the acceptor or from the drawer, or from a prior
indorser—**

(a) The amount of the bill:

**(b) Interest thereon from the time of presentment for payment if the
bill is payable on demand, and from the maturity of the bill in any
other case:**

**(c) The expenses of noting, or, when protest is necessary and the
protest has been extended, the expenses of protest.**

By section 97(2) the rules of common law including the law merchant shall **28–02**
also apply, except where they are inconsistent with the express provisions of
the 1882 Act.[5]

Amount

The amount of the bill is the sum for which it is drawn and, presumably, if **28–03**
the bill provides on the face of it for interest, interest for the currency of the

---

[1] By the 1882 Act, s.89(2), s.89(2), the maker of a note is deemed to correspond with the
acceptor of a bill, and the first indorser with the drawer of an accepted bill payable to the drawer's
order.

[2] By s.73, a cheque is a bill of exchange drawn on a banker, payable on demand, with the
difference that the drawer is the person primarily liable, the banker not being an acceptor. By an
anomaly the drawer appears to be discharged by want of notice of dishonour, unless waived or
excused. Section 73 appears to extend s.57 to cheques, English and foreign, so far as it is
applicable to bills on demand, and save that no person is in the position of an acceptor.

[3] By virtue of s.89(1), s.57(1) applies also to promissory notes.

[4] In view of subs. (2) it would seem reasonable to think that subs. (1) applies only to bills
dishonoured in the British Isles as defined by s.4(1).

[5] See *Re Gillespie, ex p. Robarts* (1886) 18 Q.B.D. 286, CA.

bill would be added. Such interest is recoverable not as damages, but as debt.[6]

Amounts in foreign currency

28-04 Until 1975, if the bill were drawn in a foreign currency, the sterling equivalent was to be calculated as at the date of dishonour,[7] but today the point does not generally arise, since the recognition of the power of the English Courts to give judgment in foreign currency.[8]

INTEREST

Contractual provision

Interest may be payable by the express terms of the instrument. In that event, the interest due up to maturity[9-10] will be part of the amount within the terms of section 57(1)(a).[11]

Date from which interest payable

It was long held at common law that bills and notes, specified to be payable with lawful interest, carried interest from their date, whether payable after date,[12] or on demand,[13] or after the happening of an event certain to happen, though the time of happening was uncertain.[14] This is declared by the Act:—

9.—(3) Where a bill is expressed to be payable with interest, unless the instrument otherwise provides, interest runs from the date of the bill, and if the bill is undated from the issue thereof.

[6] *Watkins v. Morgan* (1834) 6 C. & P. 661; *Hudson v. Fossett* (1844) 13 L.J.C.P. 141. Where there was a collateral agreement to pay interest at a fixed amount per month, if a bill was not paid at maturity, it was held that the creditor could not sue for the interest, having indorsed the bill over (*Florence v. Drayson* (1857) 1 C.B.(N.S.) 584). Where there was a like agreement, and the plaintiff recovered on the bill in one action, he was allowed to recover the agreed interest in a second action up till the date of judgment on the bill (*Florence v. Jenings* (1857) 26 L.J.C.P. 274).

[7] *Syndic in Bankruptcy of Salim Nasrallah Khoury v. Khayat* [1943] A.C. 507, PC, overruling *Cohn v. Boulken* (1926) 36 T.L.R. 767, according to which the date was the day of the trial; the former would have been followed by Mocatta J. in *Barclays Bank International Ltd v. Levin Brothers (Bradford) Ltd* [1977] Q.B. 270 if it were not for the decision of the House of Lords in *Miliangos v. George Frank (Textiles) Ltd* [1976] A.C. 443, HL(E). See also below: "Re-exchange".

[8] *Miliangos v. George Frank (Textiles) Ltd, supra,* Administration of Justice Act 1977, s.4 repealing the 1882 Act, s.57(2).

[9-10] Referred to as "interest proper" in s.57(3).

[11] See 28–03 above. For illustrations of cases in which there was a further agreement to pay interest following maturity, see above note 6. In such a case there is no reason why the interest should not simply be claimed as interest due under a contract, though it is not part of the bill.

[12] *Kennerley v. Nash* (1816) 1 Stark. 452; *Dorman v. Dibden* (1826) Ry. & M. 381.

[13] *Hopper v. Richmond* (1816) 1 Stark. 507, 508; *Weston v. Tomlinson* (1826) Chitty, 11th ed., p. 434.

[14] *Roffey v. Greenwell* (1839) 10 A. & E. 222. So also where a note, payable with interest, was not enforceable till the death of one of the makers, interest ran from the date of the note *Richards v. Richards* (1831) 2 B. & Ad. 447.

Interest following maturity

The Act distinguishes between "interest proper" described above, and   **28–05**
forming part of the sum due upon the bill, and "interest as damages", being
discretionary interest not forming part of the amount of the bill. Additionally,
there is overlap with the modern statutory provisions entitling the court to
award interest.[15]

Historical basis

The explanation for the language is historical. Where interest was not made   **28–06**
payable by the terms of the bill, it could nonetheless be recovered in the nature
of damages for the non-payment of the principal debt.[16] The right to interest
was long ago recognised.[17] Bills and notes, by the usage of trade, carry
interest from the time of maturity; but the court was not bound to give more
than nominal interest, or, indeed, any interest at all.[18]

Interest in discretion of court

Section 57 recognises this principle, and makes interest part of the measure   **28–07**
of damages on dishonour of a bill, and further, by subsection (3), recognises
the qualification that interest may be withheld, wholly or in part, if justice
requires it:

> "**Where by this Act interest may be recovered as damages, such interest may,
> if justice require it, be withheld wholly or in part, and where a bill is expressed
> to be payable with interest at a given rate, interest as damages may or may not
> be given at the same rate as interest proper.**"

The discretion to give or to withhold interest, or to give it at a rate less than
that expressed on the bill (in the latter case as regards interest subsequent to
maturity only) is in the court.[19]

---

[15] Supreme Court Act 1981, s.35A, County Courts Act 1984, s.69. It is commonplace for both
s.57 of the Act, and the relevant general provision to be pleaded. There seems to be no distinction
in practice in the manner in which they are applied.

[16] *Ex p. Marlar* (1746) 1 Atk. 151 (Lord Hardwicke C.); *Cameron v. Smith* (1819) 2 B. & Ald.
305, 307 (Abbott C.J.); *Re Burgess* (1818) 2 Moo. 745; *Du Belloix v. Waterpark* (1822) 1 Dow
& Ry. 16; *Ex p. Charman* [1887] W.N. 184 (Lord Esher M.R.). There is a difference between the
two; see *N.V. Ledeboter and van der Held's Textielhandel v. Hibbert* [1947] 1 K.B. 964; 63 T.L.R.
334.

[17] *Lithgow v. Lyon* (1805) Coop.Ch.Ca. 29; *Lowndes v. Collens* (1810) 17 Ves. 27; *Laing v.
Stone* (1828) 2 Man. & R. 561; *cf.* also *Blaney v. Hendricks* (1771) 2 W.Bl. 761.

[18] *Cameron v. Smith, supra*, approved in *Webster v. British Empire Co.* (1880) 15 Ch.D. 169,
175, 176; *Ex p. Charman, supra*; *Spaethe v. Anderson* (1889) 18 N.Z.L.R. 149.

[19] *Ex p. Charman* [1887] W.N. 184; *London and Universal Bank v. Clancarty* [1892] 1 Q.B.
689. In *Riches v. Westminster Bank Ltd* [1943] 2 All E.R. 725, the Court of Appeal held that the
judge in the court below had rightly exercised his discretion, in awarding interest at four per cent
under the Law Reform (Miscellaneous Provisions) Act 1934, s.3, against the contention of
defendants that the claim for interest was not pleaded. See also Morris J. at pp. 967–968 in *N.V.
Ledeboter and Van der Held' Textielhandel v. Hibbert* [1947] 1 K.B. 964; 63 T.L.R. 334. In *Keene
v. Keene* (1857) 27 L.J.C.P. 88 the Court declined to interfere with the decision of the Master to
award ten per cent, that being the amount due on the bill, and the discretion may be applied on
an application for summary judgment (*London and Universal Bank v. Clancarty, supra*).

Time for which payable

28–08   Where interest is not expressly made payable in the instrument, the date from which it is to be calculated is the time for presentment for payment if the bill is payable on demand,[20] or the maturity of the bill in any other case, as provided by section 57(1)(b).[21]

28–09   In general (but subject to the court's discretion) interest is to be computed down to final judgment. "Carrying down (*viz.* to judgment) the interest", says Lord Mansfield, "does a plaintiff complete justice. It is agreeable to the principles of the common law, and interferes with no statute. It takes from defendants the temptations to make use of all the unjust dilatories of chicane. For, if interest is to stop at the commencement of the suit, where the sum is large, the defendant may gain by protracting the cause in the most expensive and vexatious manner, and the more the plaintiff is injured, the less he will be relieved."[22] On the other hand the court may well decline to award interest where the Claimant has delayed in bringing or pursuing his claim.

Rate of interest

28–10   There is no prescribed rate of interest.[23] It is common for interest to be claimed and awarded at a rate equivalent to that under the Judgment Act 1838,[24] but in a commercial case it may be more appropriate to seek a reasonable rate at or just above base rate. If a high rate is asked there may be difficulty in entering a default judgment.[25]

---

[20] Where there has been no demand before action, interest may be given from the date of service of the writ (*Pierce v. Fothergill* (1835) 2 Bing.N.C. 167); a demand may be dispensed with where it is patently useless, as where a bank has closed its doors (*Re East of England Banking Co.* (1868) L.R. 6 Eq. 368).

[21] In this connection, see *Bank Polski v. Mulder* [1942] 1 K.B. 497, 500, *per* Lord Greene M.R.; and see *Blake v. Lawrence* (1802) 4 Esp. 147 as to a promissory note payable by instalments. It would seem that because a cause of action cannot arise until there is a party capable of suing, money due to an estate carried interest only from the date of demand by an administrator when appointed: *Murray v. East India Co.* (1821) 5 B. & Ald. 204.

[22] *Robinson v. Bland* (1760) 2 Burr. 1077, 1088; but a valid tender by the defendant will prevent interest from running, *Dent v. Dent* (1813) 3 Camp. 296. Where the holder was an alien, resident in an enemy country, interest was held to run not from maturity but from the date of the declaration of peace (*Biedermann v. Allhausen & Co.* (1921) 37 T.L.R. 662), on the ground that by reason of the war it would have been illegal for the defendants to pay and thus there was no breach of duty. The same reasoning was applied in *N.V. Ledeboter and Van der Helds' Textielhandel v. Hibbert* [1947] 1 K.B. 964; 63 T.L.R. 334. See these cases and *Wolff v. Oxholm* (1817) 6 M. & S. 92, discussed in *The Berwickshire* [1950] P. 204; also *Stevenson v. Aktiengesellschaft für Cartonnagen Industrie* [1918] A.C. 239 (not a claim on a bill).

[23] See Practice Note (Claims for Interest) (No. 2) (1983) [1983] 1 W.L.R. 377, where the short term investment account rate is said to be a "safe guide". The formal requirements for pleading interest are set out at CPR 16.4 and see para. 27–10 above.

[24] Presently eight per cent. As to interest on judgments generally see CPR Part 40.

[25] See now CPR Part 12 (rule 12.6) and CPR Part 14 (rule 14.14). Both provisions in fact refer to interest claimed under the Supreme Court Act and County Courts Act, but the same principles would appear to apply where interest is claimed as liquidated damages under the Act, see *Elliott v. Roberts* (1891) 36 S.J. 92, as explained in *Lawrence & Sons v. Willcocks* [1892] 1 Q.B. 696.

As against drawer and indorser

It was once held that the drawer or indorser was liable to pay interest only **28–11** from the time that he himself received notice of dishonour,[26] but this view seems clearly incompatible with the provisions of section 57(1), since interest from presentment or maturity is recoverable thereunder from "any party" without distinction.

Interest on accommodation bills

The right to claim interest as liquidated damages under section 57(1)(b) is **28–12** confined to actions upon dishonoured bills, cheques or notes,),[27] but interest can instead be claimed under section 35A of the Supreme Court Act 1981 (or s.69 of the County Courts Act 1984).

Payment into court

Where money is paid into court on a security carrying interest, interest must **28–13** be paid, not merely to the commencement of the action, but to the time of payment into court, or the Claimant may proceed in the action for the difference.[28]

Interest after principal paid

Though the principal has been paid, the Claimant may proceed for interest, **28–14** unless it has been incurred by his negligence.[29] So where for the amount of the principal on an overdue bill another bill was given, and afterwards paid, it was held that an action lay on the original bill for the interest.[30]

Interest on failure to pay by bill

An engagement to give a bill will create a liability to interest on a contract, **28–15** which would not otherwise carry it. Thus where goods are sold to be paid for by a bill which is not given, interest is recoverable as part of the price of goods and may be recovered in an action for goods sold and delivered[31] such interest is to be calculated as from the date when the bill would have been due, if accepted.[32] This principle is of less importance now that the court has power

---

[26] *Walker v. Barnes* (1813) 5 Taunt. 240.

[27] And therefore the procedure by specially indorsed writ was formerly not available on a claim for interest by an accommodation acceptor, who had been compelled to pay the bill, against the party accommodated: *Ryley v. Master* [1892] 1 Q.B. 674.

[28] *Kidd v. Walker* (1831) 2 B. & Ad. 705.

[29] *Laing v. Stone* (1828) 2 Man. & R. 561.

[30] *Lumley v. Musgrave* (1837) 4 Bing.N.C. 9.

[31] *Marshall v. Poole* (1810) 13 East 98; *Farr v. Ward* (1837) 3 M. & W. 25; see *Benjamin's Sale of Goods* (1st ed., 1974), p. 724.

[32] *Slack v. Lowell* (1810) 3 Taunt. 157; *Boyce v. Warburton* (1810) 2 Camp. 480. As to evidence from which a jury may infer an agreement to pay by bill or note, see *Davis v. Smyth* (1841) 8 M. & W. 399.

to award interest generally,[33] and that interest on business debts may be payable by statute.[34]

Guarantor

28–16   A party who guarantees due payment of a bill is liable for interest.[35]

Noting and protest

28–17   The holder is, further, entitled to recover:

57.—(1)(c) The expenses of noting, or when protest is necessary, and the protest has been extended, the expenses of protest.

28–18   A claim for the expenses of protest must be confined to the case of a claim on the dishonour of a foreign bill only, since only in that case is protest "necessary" within the meaning of this subsection. Thus a claim for the expenses of a protest for better security has been considered not to come within this subsection.[36]

28–19   Noting, though otherwise but an incipient protest, appears to be distinguishable from the actual protest, as far as this subsection is concerned. Thus at one time it was the common practice of London bankers to cause all inland bills, if dishonoured by non-payment, to be noted after six o'clock of the day of maturity,[37] and it has been held that the expenses of such noting may be inserted in a specially indorsed writ under the heading "bank charges",[38] but if such noting is subsequently extended to protest, the costs of the latter are not recoverable, the bills being inland bills, and protest thereof not being "necessary".

Banker's commission

28–20   Where a foreign bill was dishonoured in London, the Court refused to allow the holder to recover banker's commission, brokerage and stamps for postage from the acceptor, since these charges were not specified as recoverable under section 57(1).[39]

28–21   But where a foreign drawer was liable, by the law of the place of drawing, to reimburse such expenses to the holder, he was held entitled to include these

---

[33] Supreme Court Act 1981 s.35A; County Courts Act 1984 s.69.

[34] Late Payment of Commercial Debts (Interest) Act 1998.

[35] *Ackermann v. Ehrensperger* (1846) 16 M. & W. 99. So a surety on a note, who has paid the same at maturity, may claim for interest in the bankruptcy of the principal debtor (*Ex p. Davies* (1897) 66 L.J.Q.B. 499). As to the damages recoverable by a surety who has paid a bill to the holder, see *post*, para. 33–12.

[36] *Re English Bank of River Plate* [1893] 2 Ch. 438. As to when special expenses may be recovered, see *post*, para. 28–18.

[37] *Wharton's Law Lexicon, sub tit.* Noting.

[38] *Dando v. Boden* [1893] 1 Q.B. 318. It is otherwise in *Natal (National Bank of South Africa v. Collins & Kersler* (1905) 26 Natal L.R. 333).

[39] *Banque Populaire de Bienne v. Cave* (1895) 1 Com.Cas. 67, distinguishing *Prehn v. Royal Bank of Liverpool* (1870) L.R. 5 Ex. 92; and see also *Re English Bank of River Plate, supra*. See *ante*, para. 28–18.

expenses in the damages recoverable by way of re-exchange from the English acceptor, the common law being applied under section 97(2), the Court considering that section 57(1) was not addressed to this point, and that in consequence there was nothing inconsistent with the application of section 97.[40]

RE-EXCHANGE[41]

The holder of a bill dishonoured abroad had, until the passing of the Administration of Justice Act 1977, instead of the damages set out in section 57(1), the right to claim damages as follows: **28–22**

57—(2) In the case of a bill which has been dishonoured abroad, in lieu of the above damages,[42] the holder may recover from the drawer or an indorser, and the drawer or indorser who has been compelled to pay the bill may recover from any party liable to him, the amount of the re-exchange with interest thereon until the time of payment.

It has been held that the damages allowed by this subsection are the only damages allowed to the holder of an instrument dishonoured abroad, and that the holder cannot claim the damages allowed by subsection (1), though the latter subsection is not in terms limited to bills dishonoured in this country.[43] However, the subsection was repealed by section 4(2) of the 1977 statute, and, subject to questions of conflicts of laws[44] it would appear that the starting point in such a case would be the English measure prescribed by section 51(1)(a).[45]   **28–23**

Theory of Re-exchange

Re-exchange was the amount for which a plaintiff might draw on the defendants, so as to reimburse himself in respect of the dishonour of a bill; in other words, the cost of buying the currency necessary to meet the sterling requirement at the time and place of dishonour plus the incidental expense of obtaining it in a foreign country. The existence and amount of it depended on the rate of exchange between two countries. The theory of the transaction was this: a merchant in London indorses a bill for a certain number of Austrian   **28–24**

---

[40] *Re Gillespie, ex p. Robarts* (1886) 18 Q.B.D. 286, as to re-exchange recoverable under s.97(2) and to the common law rules; see also *ante* p. 149.

[41] Since it is now possible to enforce a currency judgment in the English courts, the rights provided by re-exchange are of less importance. It is though possible that a situtation may arise where an understanding of the common law (and law merchant) principles are relevant.

[42] *Viz.* the damages set out in s.57(1), that is to say, the amount of the bill, interest noting, and protest where necessary.

[43] *Re Commercial Bank of South Australia* (1887) 36 Ch.D. 522; and *cf. Re Gillespie, supra.*

[44] Chapter 25 above.

[45] It should be noted that the two subsections did not provide an exhaustive scheme, see *Re Gillespie* (above), where the liability of the London acceptor on the dishonoured bill to indemnify the foreign drawer extended to the re-exchange for which the drawer had been liable, applying the common law by s.97(2). Section 57(2) did not apply to a bill dishonoured in England (whatever its currency).

schillings, payable at a future date in Vienna. The holder is entitled to receive in Vienna, on the day of the maturity of the bill, a certain number of Austrian schillings. Suppose the bill to be dishonoured. The holder is now, by the custom of merchants, entitled to immediate and specific redress, by his own act, in this way. He is entitled, being in Vienna, then and there to raise the exact number of Austrian schillings by drawing and negotiating a cross bill, payable at sight, on his indorser in London, for as much English money as will purchase in Vienna the exact number of Austrian schillings, at the rate of exchange on the day of dishonour; and to include in the amount of that bill the interest and necessary expenses of the transaction. This cross bill was called in English a redraft, in French *retraite*, in German *Ruckwechsel*, and in Italian *rivalsa*. The amount for which it is drawn is called in English re-exchange, in French *rechange*, and in Italian *ricambio*. If the indorser pays the redraft or cross bill, he has fulfilled the engagement of indemnity. If not, the holder of the original bill may sue him on it, and will be entitled to recover in that action the amount of the redraft or cross bill, with the interest and expenses thereon. The amount of the verdict will thus be an exact indemnity for the non-payment of the Austrian schillings in Vienna on the day of the maturity of the original bill.

28–25   According to English practice, the redraft or cross bill was seldom drawn, but the right of the holder to draw it was settled by the law merchant of all nations, and it is only by a reference to this supposed bill that the re-exchange—in other words, the true damages in an action on the original bill—can be scientifically understood and computed.

Special customs

28–26   A custom among London merchants that the holder may at his election sue his indorser, either for the sum which the indorser received of him for the bill, or for the re-exchange, is inconsistent with the obligation appearing on the bill when interpreted by the law merchant, and, therefore, evidence of such a custom is inadmissible.[46] A custom, however, of having a fixed instead of a fluctuating rate of exchange between two countries is not of necessity, it seems, bad in law, as inconsistent with the nature of re-exchange; but the existence of the custom must be strictly proved.[47] In one case, at least, such a custom appears to have been recognised.[48]

Other special expenses

28–27   Expenses to which the holder of a bill is put other than those allowed under section 57(1), or section 97(2), cannot, it would seem, be claimed, even where

---

[46] *ibid.*

[47] *Willans v. Ayers* (1877) 3 App. Cas. 133. The custom as to allowing a fixed percentage by way of liquidated damages does not apply in the absence of an agreement, express or implied, to allow re-exchange. The Court relied on the fact that the bills were sent abroad, *viz.* to Australia, not to employ the proceeds there, but to have them remitted to London where the bills were drawn by the drawers on themselves in Australia. In the Supreme Court of South Australia the view was taken that the bills, being in fact promissory notes, gave no right to re-exchange; but *cf. Forbes v. Marshall* (1855) 11 Ex. 166.

[48] *Auriol v. Thomas* (1787) 2 T.R. 52, cited in *Willans v. Ayres, supra* at p. 145.

the writ is not specially indorsed, unless there is a special contract alleged to pay the same.[49] Thus, where action was brought for breach of contract for refusing to honour acceptances of the plaintiff's drafts, banker's commission and telegraphic expenses were allowed the plaintiffs as damages naturally flowing from the defendant's breach, but it would have been otherwise had action been taken on the acceptances themselves[50] such expenses would, however, presumably have been recoverable had the defendants been liable for re-exchange.[51] In an action by payee against acceptor the costs of postage were allowed on a count for money paid, a letter of the defendants having directed the plaintiff to charge the postage to his account.[52]

Damages for conversion

In trover the rule formerly was that the plaintiff was entitled to damages **28–28** equal the value of the article converted "at the time of the conversion", and therefore, in trover for bills and notes, interest was only calculated down to the time of conversion.[53] But by the Civil Procedure Act 1833, s.29, the jury might give damages over and above the value of the goods at the time of the conversion.

In the case of a cheque or other order drawn on a banker the Court of **28–29** Appeal, in a series of decisions "culminating in *Morison*'s case[54] and *Underwood*'s case[55] have surmounted the difficulty by treating the conversion as of the chattel, the piece of paper, the cheque under which the money was collected, and the value of the chattel converted as the money received under it . . . "[56] It has been said that this applies even where the instrument is not negotiable.[57]

Mitigation

On the question of mitigation of damage by a wrongdoer, Scrutton L.J. in **28–30** *Lloyds Bank Ltd v. Chartered Bank of India, Australia and China*,[58] said that it could not be settled by mere proof of receipt without more; but in *Underwood v. Bank of Liverpool*[59] both Scrutton and Atkin L.JJ. seemed to think

---

[49] *Banque Populaire de Bienne v. Cave*, (1895) 1 Com.Cas. 67, at 69.

[50] *Prehn v. Royal Bank of Liverpool* (1870) L.R. Ex. 92, 97, where the action was commenced when the bills were still current.

[51] As to expenses involved in re-exchange, see *supra*.

[52] *Dickinson v. Hatfield* (1831) 1 Moo. & R. 141. In *Kendrick v. Lomax* (1832) 2 C. & J. 405, 409, the Court declined to decide whether the cost of posting and noting were in general recoverable, but as regards noting the question is now settled by s.57(1)(c).

[53] *Mercer v. Jones* (1813) 3 Camp. 477; *Henderson v. Williams* [1895] 1 Q.B. 521; *Solloway v. McLaughlin* [1938] A.C. 247. But see *Greening v. Wilkinson* (1825) 1 C. & P. 625; as to the choice of the day of judgment for assessing damages, see *Sachs v. Miklos* [1948] 2 K.B. 23, CA; *Munro v. Willmott* [1949] 1 K.B. 295; and Denning J., in *Beaman v. A.R.T.S.* [1948] 2 All E.R. 89, 93.

[54] [1914] 3 K.B. 356.

[55] [1924] 1 K.B. 775.

[56] *Per* Scrutton L.J. in *Lloyds Bank v. Chartered Bank of India, Australia and China* [1929] 1 K.B. 40, 55.

[57] *Bavins v. London and South Western Bank* [1900] 1 Q.B. 270.

[58] *Supra*.

[59] *Supra*.

that payments by the sole director in charge of liabilities of the plaintiff company might reduce damages. In *Edmondson v. Nuttall*[60] Byles J. expressed the view that "you could not mitigate damages for conversion of a bag of money by showing that the defendant had, out of the bag of money converted, paid the debt of the plaintiff". This was mentioned by Scrutton L.J. in *Underwood*'s case, to the effect that the learned judge could not have had in mind "the equity doctrines under which a person who had in fact paid the debts of another without authority was allowed the advantage of his payments".[61]

Materially altered instrument

28–31   While the face value measure of damages for conversion is now well established, it will not apply where the instrument has, prior to the conversion, been avoided by a material alteration.[62]

COSTS

General Principles

28–32   The statutory power to award costs is now contained in section 51 of the Supreme Court Act 1981, and the rules governing costs are set out in parts 43–48 of the Civil Procedure Rules. The same general principles will apply to cases involving bills, notes or cheques. The paragraphs which follow set out illustrations from the previous case law which may provide guidance as to how in particular situations the court's discretion should be exercised.

Proceeding for costs only

28–33   Though, after the principal sum due on a bill has been once paid, or levied upon the goods of the party ultimately liable, the holder cannot recover it again from any other of the parties, yet if other actions were pending at the time of payment, he may proceed in them for costs, without recovering any part of the principal sum.[63]

28–34   A payment after action brought will not prevent the holder from proceeding for his costs.[64] Where an acceptor or maker pays on action brought without

---

[60] (1864) 17 C.B.(N.S.) 280, 297.

[61] See also the discussion in Ch. 32 paras 32–31 to 32–33.

[62] *Smith and another v. Lloyds TSB Group plc, Harvey Jones Ltd v. Woolwich plc* [2000] 3 W.L.R. 1725. See above para. 20–28.

[63] *Toms v. Powell* (1806) 7 East 536; *Godard v. Benjamin* (1813) 3 Camp. 331; *Holland v. Jourdine* (1815) Hold N.P.C. 6; *Goodwin v. Cremer* (1852) 18 Q.B. 757.

[64] *Toms v. Powell* (1806) 7 East 536; and see now CPR Part 45, and CPR rule 12.9 (default judgment for costs).

previous demand the court will take the question of costs into considera-tion.[65]

Multiple parties

An indorser, who had to pay the costs of an action against himself, could **28–35** not, at common law, sustain an action for those costs against the acceptor[66] nor does section 57 of the Act entitle him to claim such costs against any prior party. However, in the event that the indorser were to join in the prior parties to any action against him, provided his conduct in defending the claim was not unreasonable, it is likely that the court would order the party ultimately liable to bear the costs.

Accommodation party

The distinction between a bill without consideration and an accommodation **28–36** bill, strictly so called,[67] is of importance on the question of costs. A party accepting a bill merely without consideration (as if, for example, he does not know the state of accounts between himself and the drawer), if he is after-wards sued on the bill, cannot charge the drawer with the costs of defending the action,[68] whereas the acceptor of an accommodation bill, properly so called, who is compelled by an action to pay it, may have a claim upon the drawer for all the expenses of such action.[69] But an accommodation acceptor has no right to charge the party accommodated with the costs of an action to which the accommodation acceptor had evidently no defence.[70]

Security for costs

Security for costs may in the case of a bill of exchange be ordered against **28–37** a foreign plaintiff.[71]

---

[65] *Macintosh v. Haydon* (1826) Ry. & M. 362.

[66] *Dawson v. Morgan* (1829) 9 B. & C. 618.

[67] As to accommodation bills, see the 1882 Act, s.28(1); *ante*, para. 19–37.

[68] *Bagnall v. Andrews* (1830) 7 Bing. 217, 222.

[69] *Jones v. Brooke* (1812) 4 Taunt. 464; *Stratton v. Matthews* (1848) 18 L.J.Ex. 5. The acceptor may recover, as for money paid to the drawer's use, whether or not the action is defended at the drawer's express or implied request (*Howes v. Martin* (1794) 1 Esp. 161; *Garrard v. Cottrell* (1847) 10 Q.B. 679).

[70] *Roach v. Thompson* (1830) M. & M. 487; *Beech v. Jones* (1848) 5 C.B. 696. The outcome would now depend on the terms of the indemnity to be implied.

[71] *Banque du Rhone v. Fuerst Day Lawson, Promat S.A. (Third Parties)* [1968] 2 Lloyd's Rep. 153, CA. See CPR Part 25 for the modern law as to security for costs. It does not follow that because a claimant is foreign security will be awarded.

CHAPTER 29

LIMITATION OF ACTIONS

Statutes of limitation

29–01   A claim against a party liable upon a bill of exchange, cheque or promissory note is a claim in simple contract, now governed by the Limitation Act 1980, s.5. That section provides that an action founded on a simple contract shall not be brought after the expiration of six years from the date on which the cause of action accrued.

Persons under a disability

29–02   By section 28(1) of the Limitation Act 1980, it is provided that if any person entitled to the action shall at the time of the action accrued, be under a disability, then such person may bring action at any time before the expiration of six years from the date when the person ceased to be under a disability or died, whichever event first occurred, notwithstanding that the period of limitation has expired.[1-2]

When time begins to run

29–03   The period of limitation begins to run for the benefit of a party liable upon a bill or note (as well as on any other contract) from the time that the right of action[3] by the then holder first accrued against him, rather than the date when the present holder acquired that right.[4] If, for example, a promissory note is transferred three years after it became due, the transferee's claim against the drawer will be statute barred at the expiry of a further three years, only, in his hands.

Once time begins to run it never stops, even though circumstances arise in which it is impossible to sue, as if, for example, the debtor dies before action and no executor is appointed.[5]

And so in an action on a bill by an administrator, who has not taken out administration till after the bill became due, it was decided that the statute ran, not from the time the bill fell due, but from the time of granting letters of

---

[1-2] See *Scarpellini v. Atcheson* (1845) 7 Q.B. 864. In the case of infancy or unsoundness of mind the section shall not apply unless the plaintiff proves that the person under disability was not, at the time the right of action accrued, in the custody of a parent. The disability formerly attaching to a feme covert was removed by the Married Women's Property Act 1882 (*Lowe v. Fox* (1885) 15 Q.B.D. 667).

[3] Though at that time an action and judgment would have been fruitless (*Emery v. Day* (1834) 1 Cr.M. & R. 245).

[4] *Whitehead v. Walker* (1842) 9 M. & W. 506.

[5] *Rhodes v. Smethhurst* (1840) 6 M. & W. 351; *Smith v. Hill* (1746) 1 Wils. 134. An order for administration by the Court will however operate to suspend the running of time (though not to revive claims already barred): *Re Greaves* (1881) 18 Ch. D. 551.

administration, for there can be no action till there is a party capable of suing.[6]

For the purposes of computing time the day on which the event giving rise **29-04** to the cause of action occurred is generally not counted.[7] The maker of a note or the acceptor of a bill has the whole of the day on which the instrument is due to make payment; the cause of action against him is not complete until the commencement of the following day, which is to be counted for the purposes of limitation.[8] In the event that the period so calculated expires on a day when the Court offices are closed the Limitation Act will be construed so as to permit the commencement of proceedings upon the first subsequent day when they are open.[9]

The date on which the cause of action accrues will depend on the terms of **29-05** the instrument, and the nature of the liability of the party against whom it has arisen.

Therefore, on a bill payable at a certain period after the date, the statute runs, not from the time the bill was drawn, but from the time when it fell due.[10] And this is also as to the account stated of which the bill may be evidence.[11] As, upon a bill drawn payable after sight, there is no right of action till presentment, so without such presentment the statute does not begin to run.[12] If a note is payable at a certain period after sight, the statute runs from the expiration of that period after the exhibition of the note to the maker.[13]

A note payable at a certain period after demand is like a note payable after sight; the demand and the lapse of the specified time after the demand are conditions precedent, and the statute runs from the time when the note falls due.[14]

If a bill or note is payable on demand, no demand other than action brought is necessary, apart from the question of costs, to enforce payment.[15] And, though at common law bills payable at sight may have been subject to a

---

[6] *Murray v. East India Company* (1821) 5 B. & Ald. 204. The statute runs against an executor from the time the bill falls due, for he can commence an action before probate.

[7] *Marren v. Dawson Bentley & Co. Ltd* [1961] 2 Q.B. 135; *Kirby v. Leather* [1965] 2 Q.B. 367, *Pritam Kaur v. S. Russell & Sons Ltd* [1973] Q.B. 336.

[8] *Gelmini v. Morriggia* [1913] 2 K.B. 549, *per* Channell J. In *Marren v. Dawson Bentley*, Havers J. (following *Radcliffe v. Bartholemew* [1892] 1 Q.B. 161) considered that he was differing from the view of Channell J. There is in fact no inconsistency: in either case the first day to be counted is the first full day on which there is a complete cause of action.

[9] *Pritam Kaur (supra)* overruling *Gelmini* on this point. See also *The Clifford Maersk* [1982] 1 W.L.R. 1292. In *Swainston v. Hetton Victory Club* [1983] 1 All E.R. 1179 it was held that since the relevant complaint could (as the context required) have been presented to the tribunal by delivery through its letter box on a Sunday it was inappropriate to construe the time permitted as extending to the next business day.

[10] *Wittersheim v. Carlisle* (1791) 1 H.Bl. 631.

[11] *Fryer v. Roe* (1852) 12 C.B. 437.

[12] *cf. Holmes v. Kerrison* (1810) 2 Taunt. 323.

[13] *ibid.* As to notes payable three months after sight with interest, see *Way v. Bassett* (1845) 15 L.J.Ch. 1.

[14] *Thorpe v. Booth* (1826) Ry. & M. 388; *Thorpe v. Coombe* (1826) 8 Dow & Ry.K.B. 347; and see *Moore v. Petchell* (1856) 22 Beav. 172; and *Re Rutherford, Brown v. Rutherford* (1880) 14 Ch.D. 687. Any payment on account will rank as a demand (*Sparham v. Carley* (1892) 8 Man. L.R. 246).

[15] *Capp v. Lancaster* (1597) Cro.Eliz. 548; *Rumball v. Ball* (1711) 10 Mod. 38. As to costs *cf. Mackintosh v. Haydon* (1826) Ry. & M. 362, 363; para. 28-34 above.

different rule,[16] section 10(1)(a) of the 1882 Act now appears to place them on the same footing. Therefore on a bill or note payable on demand or at sight, unless the instrument is accompanied by some writing restraining or postponing the right of action, the statute runs as against the acceptor or maker, from the date of the instrument, or date of delivery, if that is delayed, and not from the time of the demand.[17]

29–06   By section 21(1) of the 1882 Act "Every contract on a bill, whether it be the drawer's, the acceptor's, or an indorser's, is incomplete and revocable, until delivery of the instrument in order to give effect thereto". No cause of action can therefore accrue until there has been effective delivery of the instrument. Delivery may in certain circumstances be shown to have been conditional or for a special purpose only.[18] In that event, the cause of action will not accrue and time will not begin to run until the condition has been satisfied or the purpose met.[19]

So where the maker of a note gave it to a third person, to be delivered to the payee after certain events should happen, the statute was held to run, not from the date of the note, but from the time of its delivery to the payee.[20]

Where a note payable on demand was given to a bank, accompanied by an agreement that the note should be held as a security for advances, the Court of Exchequer decided that the statute did not begin to run against the note till after advances made, and a claim made as for debt. The learned judge (Martin B.), however, who tried the case appears to have thought otherwise, or at least to have doubted.[21]

A promissory note payable at sight which in the body of it is made payable at a particular place must be presented at that place in order to render the maker liable (s.87(1)),[22] and the statute does not begin to run until it is presented there. It is otherwise, however, where the place of payment is specified in a memorandum only and not in the body of the note. The statute then runs from the date of the note.[23]

29–07   As against parties secondarily liable no right of action arises until there has been a presentment for payment to the party primarily liable, and hence as against the drawer or indorser of a bill or the indorser of a note payable on demand time will run only from the time when the cause of action against him is complete.[24]

---

[16] cf. Norton v. Ellam (1837) 2 M. & W. 461, 464 (Parke B.).

[17] ibid; Christie v. Fonsick (1812) Sel.N.P., 13th ed., p. 301; Bachand v. Lalumiere (1902) Q.R. 21 S.C. 449; Campbell v. Imperial Bank of Canada (1924) 35 O.L.R. 318; see also Re George Francis v. Bruce (1890) 44 Ch.D. 627. In Megginson v. Harper (1834) 2 Cr. & M. 322, it was assumed that the statute ran from the date of the note, which was payable on demand. In all cases of qualified acceptance, where, in accordance with s.52(2), presentment for payment is required in order to render the acceptor liable, the time probably runs from the date of presentment both as regards the acceptor and as regards subsequent parties, whose liability by s.45 is contingent on a due presentment. So, too, where presentment is required to the maker of a note made payable in the body thereof at a particular place by s.87(1).

[18] See generally above paras 9–01 to 9–02.

[19] See for example In re Bethell (1887) 34 Ch.D. 561, discussed below.

[20] Savage v. Aldren (1817) 2 Stark. 232.

[21] Hartland v. Jukes (1863) 32 L.J.Exch. 162.

[22] Ante, paras 12–14, 24–11.

[23] Re British Trade Corporation [1932] 2 Ch. 1, CA.

[24] Re Boyse (1886) 33 Ch.D. 612; cf. Re Bethell, supra.

If a bill is dishonoured by non-acceptance, and afterwards by non-payment, the statute runs against the holder from the refusal to accept.[25] As regards a drawer or indorser time runs from the date of receipt of notice of dishonour but if notice is excused, from the date of dishonour itself.[26]

If a note is payable by instalments, and contains a provision that, if default is made in payment of one instalment, the whole shall be due, the statute runs from the first default against the whole amount of the note.[27]

A bill accepted in blank and not completed for more than six years thereafter is valid in the hands of a holder in due course and, as against him, time does not begin to run until the completed bill falls due.[28] But a payee who retains an incomplete acceptance for more than six years may not thereafter complete it and sue the acceptor on it.[29]

Cheques

The drawer of a cheque "engages that on due presentment it shall be ... paid **29–08** according to its tenor ... ".[30] Though the drawer is the party primarily liable upon a cheque[31] presentment for payment, and notice of dishonour (unless dispensed with) are necessary to render him liable upon it. In principle no cause of action can accrue against the drawer until those events have happened, or been dispensed with.[32]

In previous editions of this work it has been said that "In the case of a cheque the statute runs against the drawer from the time when the cheque was given to the payee". That proposition is based on the judgment of Stirling J in the case of *In re Bethell*,[33] citing the earlier decisions of *Norton v. Ellam*[34] and *Robinson v. Hawksford*.[35] The former case concerned a note payable on demand, not a cheque, and under such an instrument the cause of action accrues immediately without a demand. The issue in the latter case was whether the drawer's liability on a cheque had been discharged by the holder's failure to present it in a reasonable time, a point now covered by section 74 of the 1882 Act. On this, Patteson J. (in the passage particularly relied on by Stirling J.) observed that "if [no inconvenience] has resulted, I see nothing unreasonable in a presentment, I should even say, at any time within six years". This decision was followed in *Laws v. Rand*.[36]

---

[25] *Whitehead v. Walker* (1842) 9 M. & W. 506; *Wilkinson v. Verity* (1871) L.R. 6 C.P. 206, 209 (Willes J.).

[26] See *Kennedy v. Thomas* [1894] 2 Q.B. 759.

[27] *cf. Hemp v. Garland* (1843) 4 Q.B. 519; *Reeves v. Butcher* [1891] 2 Q.B. 509.

[28] *Montague v. Perkins* (1853) 22 L.J.C.P. 187.

[29] *cf. Re Bethell* (1887) 34 Ch.D. 561.

[30] Section 55(1)(a) of the 1882 Act, and see generally above para. 17–11.

[31] And indeed, save in the now rare case of a cheque which is capable of indorsement and indorsed, the only party liable.

[32] See *In re Boyse* (1886) 33 Ch. D. 612.

[33] (1887) 34 Ch. D. 561 "such a cheque ought to have been presented within six years from the time when it was given, and that the time under the Statute of Limitations began to run when the cheque was sent to the Claimant ... ".

[34] 2 M. & W. 461.

[35] 9 Q.B. 52.

[36] (1857) 3 C.B.N.S. 442. See also *Alexander v Burchfield* 7 M. & G. 1067, 8 Scott N.R. 563.

Neither case is in fact any authority that limitation runs from the date of issue (or delivery) of the cheque,[37] and in principle it should not, but only from the date when following dishonour notice of dishonour is given or dispensed with.[38]

It is suggested that this does not leave the drawer of a cheque exposed indefinitely to a claim upon late presented cheques. The practice of banks in returning cheques regarded as stale is well established and their entitlement as against their customer to decline to pay a cheque in such circumstances is, even absent express agreement, probably a matter of implication.[39] Presentment for payment is dispensed with in that situation[40] and a cause of action against the drawer immediately accrues to the holder, who will have up to six years from that date[41] to bring his action.

29–09   Post-dated cheques present their own problems of analysis.[42] It is suggested that no cause of action can accrue against the drawer until after the date borne by the cheque, and that the date of its accrual will then depend upon the same considerations.

Non-acceptance

29–10   The drawee of a bill is not liable upon it merely by being so named. Whether the drawer has an action against the drawee for non-acceptance will depend upon the relations between them. In one action by the drawer of a bill against the drawee for non-acceptance, it was held that time ran not from the date of refusal to accept but from that when the drawer sustained damage.[43] It is suggested that the question depends upon the nature of the drawee's obligation to accept, and if contractual time would run from the point of breach. In the case of cheques, banks are generally obliged to honour the mandate of their customer,[44] and a claim in breach of contract for wrongful dishonour will accrue at the time of presentment, or re-presentment, for payment.

CLAIMS TO INDEMNITY AND CONTRIBUTION

Indemnity

29–11   Upon the contract which the law implies to indemnify an accommodation acceptor, it has been held that the statute begins to run from the time at which

---

[37] Indeed, if anything they suggest otherwise; if the holder can present the cheque six years less one day after delivery, how long after that date might he bring proceedings?

[38] See Chalmers & Guest at para. 1475 where this is said to be arguable in principle.

[39] See above para. 21–92.

[40] Section 46(2)(c) of the 1882 Act.

[41] The date from which the drawee bank becomes entitled to treat the cheque as stale cannot be stated with certainty and (absent contractual agreement with its customer) will be a matter of evidence as to practice.

[42] See above, paras 21–14 *et seq.*

[43] *Huntley v. Sanderson* (1883) 2 L.J.E. 204.

[44] See above para. 21–48.

the plaintiff is damnified by actual payment.[45] This accords with the general law in such cases.[46] The relevant limitation period will be six years, as the claim to an indemnity is treated as being upon a simple contract.

Contribution

The right to claim contribution against a party jointly liable arises upon payment of more than the due proportion and time generally runs from that point; the limitation period is again six years.[47] The paying party may additionally be entitled to claim a contribution by virtue of the Civil Liability (Contribution) Act 1978. Such a claim is subject to a limitation period of two years from the date of any judgment or award or the earliest date at which the amount to be paid is agreed with the creditor[48] but it is suggested that this does not operate to bar an action on the separate cause of action arising by law.

29–12

In either case, where the claim to contribution or indemnity has been the subject of express agreement, those terms will determine the relevant date for accrual of the cause of action.

29–13

ACKNOWLEDGMENT AND PART PAYMENT

Statutory basis

The law as to acknowledgment and part payment is now contained in sections 29–31 of the Limitation Act 1980.[49] Section 29(5) provides that:

29–14

"where any right of action has accrued to recover . . . (a) any debt or liquidated pecuniary claim . . . and the person liable or accountable for the claim acknowledges the claim or makes any payment in respect of it the right shall be treated as having accrued on and not before the date of the acknowledgment or payment".

What constitutes acknowledgment

An acknowledgment must be in writing and signed by the person making it,[50] though it may be made by an agent of the debtor.[51] Beyond that the statute deliberately[52] attempts no definition of what form of words may constitute an acknowledgment, and it is a question of fact in each case. In *Spencer v. Hemmerde*[53] Lord Sumner recognised that "The decisions on the exact meaning and effect of the words employed by generations of shifty debtors are

29–15

---

[45] *Reynolds v. Doyle* (1840) 1 M. & G. 753; *Brown v. Gillon* (1915) 10 Magistrates' Cases (N.Z.) 96. It is otherwise if the action is brought on the bill itself in the case of accommodation indorsers (*Webster v. Kirk* (1852) 17 Q.B. 944).

[46] See more generally Halsbury's Laws vol. 20 "Guarantee and Indemnity" para. 276.

[47] *ibid.* paras 277–278.

[48] Limitation Act 1980, s.10.

[49] Previously (though with some differences) sections 23–25 of the Limitation Act 1939.

[50] Limitation Act 1980, s.30(1). The requirement has existed since the Statute of Frauds Amendment Act 1928 (Lord Tenterden's Act) as amended by the Mercantile Law Amendment Act 1856.

[51] Section 30(2)(a), and see below.

[52] Law Reform Committee 21st Report para. 2.64.

[53] [1922] 2 A.C. 507 at 534.

irreconcilable". Decisions on the facts of an earlier age may provide some guidance, but must be approached with caution.

29–16   A promise to pay, or a simple acknowledgment of the fact that a debt is due and outstanding (which will generally imply such a promise)[54] present little difficulty. Where, however, the acknowledgment is coupled with other expressions, the question arises whether they nullify or qualify the implied promise to pay, or leave it absolute. This is a question for the Court. If the added words amount to a refusal to pay, there is no promise, express or implied; if they import a condition, the acknowledgment is qualified by the condition and no liability arises unless the condition is shown to have been performed.[55] Thus where the maker of a note after previously promising to pay by a certain date unless war broke out, wrote subsequently to say that, owing to the outbreak of war, he was quite unable to fix a date, the Court held that there was no unqualified promise and that therefore the plea of the statute succeeded.[56]

29–17   If, on the other hand, the added words do not impose any conditions and neither deny the debt nor negative the acknowledgment, the acknowledgment prevails and the debtor is liable. In particular, mere words of hope or fear, or mere statements of present inability to pay, do not qualify the acknowledgment. Thus, where in an action by the payee against one of the makers of a note the defendant had written to the plaintiff as follows: "The old account between us, which has been standing over so long, has not escaped our memory, and as soon as we can get our affairs arranged we will see you are paid", this was held to be a sufficient acknowledgment.[57] So too, where the acceptor of a bill had written to the solicitor of the plaintiff, the drawer, as follows: "I admit I owe your client the sum of £210 5s., but I cannot meet this liability at the moment, although I hope to call upon you within fourteen days to make a definite proposal for repayment of that amount." It was held to be sufficient acknowledgment.[58]

29–18   An effective acknowledgment need not quantify the debt outstanding but need only recognise that a debt is due.[59] Where in an action by the payee against the maker of a note for £100 it was proved that the defendant had used expressions in letters to the plaintiff's wife importing that he was willing that an account should be taken between himself and the plaintiff, and, though denying indebtedness beyond the amount of £40, that he would pay what was found to be due, this was held to be sufficient evidence of a new promise to

---

[54] *ibid*; where the previous cases are reviewed.

[55] *Tanner v. Smart* (1827) 6 B. & C. 603, distinguished in *Cooper v. Kendall* [1909] 1 K.B. 405; see also *Wood v. Tromenhauser* (1914) 32 O.L.R. 370.

[56] *Fettes v. Robertson* (1921) 37 T.L.R. 581.

[57] *Chasemore v. Turner* (1875) L.R. 10 Q.B. 500.

[58] *Cooper v. Kendall* [1909] 1 K.B. 405; *Parson v. Nesbitt* (1915) 60 S.J. 89; see also *Brown v. Mackenzie* (1913) 29 T.L.R. 310.

[59] *Dungate v. Dungate* [1965] 1 W.L.R. 1477 (CA), see also *Good v. Parry* [1963] 2 Q.B. 418, *Kamouh v. Associated Electrical Industries International Limited* [1980] Q.B. 199. It is generally not, though, sufficient to acknowledge only that a debt might be due. A mere promise to pay "the balance" without more has been held to entitle the plaintiff to nominal damages only (*Dickinson v. Hatfield* (1831) 1 Mood. & R. 141; *Kennett v. Milbank* (1831) 8 Bing. 38., but a different result might now be reached.

take the case out of the statute, and the plaintiff was entitled to recover the entire sum found to be due.[60]

Part payment

To bring the statue into operation any payment made must be "in respect **29–19** of" the claim or debt, but "A payment of a part of the . . . interest due at any time shall not extend the period for claiming the remainder then due, but any payment of interest shall be treated as payment in respect of the principal debt".[61] That a payment of interest suspends limitation of the principal sum accords with the earlier law.[62] It appears that any sum paid, whether expressed to be in respect of principal or interest, in respect of the entire sum due under a bill is effective to preserve the right to claim the whole sum due.[63]

Indorsements of the payment of interest may be recorded on the bill itself, **29–20** and are presumed to have been written at the time they bear date.[64] Such an indorsement would seem capable of amounting to an acknowledgment under section 30 provided the requirements are met, and be clear evidence of part payment.[65]

It is not necessary to prove an express declaration by the debtor to appro- **29–21** priate any payment made to the particular debt if his intention can be inferred.[66] A payment made generally on account is paid in respect of the whole sum due at any time.[67] In the absence of appropriation by the debtor the creditor has the right to appropriate the payment as he sees fit.[68] Where there is a running account between the debtor and creditor, and in the absence of any express or implied appropriation a payment is applied first to the oldest debt, in accordance with the rule in *Clayton's case*.[69] A payment may be appropriated to a statute-barred debt[70] but this will no longer operate to revive the balance of the debt.[71]

Payment can be made other than in cash and no money need change hands **29–22** if value or credit is in fact given.[72]

---

[60] *Langrish v. Watts* [1903] 1 K.B. 636. Compare *Surrendra Overseas Limited v. Government of Sri Lanka* [1977] 1 W.L.R. 565, discussed below.

[61] Limitation Act 1980, s.29(6).

[62] *Bealy v. Greenslade* (1831) 2 C. & J. 61; *Evans v. Davies* (1836) 4 A. & E. 840; *Purdon v. Purdon* (1842) 10 M. & W. 562; *Maber v. Maber* (1867) L.R. 2 Ex. 153.

[63] This was the view of the original author, and that expressed in previous editions, notwithstanding dicta in *Collyer v. Willock* (1827) 4 Bing. 313, where, however, the payment was not on behalf of the entire debt, the defendant expressly repudiating the interest. The result may be different where interest is payable in periodic instalments.

[64] *Smith v. Battens* (1834) 1 Mood. & R. 341.

[65] In the case of *In re Rutherford, Brown v. Rutherford* (1880) 14 Ch. D. 687 they were held to be evidence of a demand having been made rendering the note payable and so by the time of action statute barred. Compare the view of Hall VC in that case that interest could properly, and would ordinarily, have been paid without any such demand, which may be the better view.

[66] *Waters v. Tompkins* (1835) 2 C.M. & R. 723; *Walker v. Butler* (1856) 6 E. & B. 506; *cf. Worthington v. Grimsditch* (1845) 7 Q.B. 479.

[67] *Re Footman Bower & Co. Ltd* [1961] Ch 443.

[68] See generally Chitty, para. 22–061.

[69] *Clayton's Case* (1816) 1 Mer. 572, and see generally Chitty, paras 22–059 *et seq.*

[70] *Mills v. Fowkes* (1839) 5 Bing NC 455, *Stepney Corporation v. Osofsky* [1937] 3 All E.R. 289. Chitty, para. 22–063.

[71] Limitation Act 1980, s.29(7), see below.

[72] *Re Wilson* [1937] Ch. 675; *Maber v. Maber* (1867) L.R. 2 Ex. 153.

29–23   However, where a payment is made of part of a debt (or acknowledgment of it given) coupled with a denial that any further sum is due, that does not operate to postpone limitation as to the balance.[73]

By and to whom acknowledgment or payment to be made

29–24   An acknowledgment may be made by the agent of the debtor.[74] This presumably includes a person acting within his ostensible authority.[75] Solicitors can be agents for this purpose.[76] Auditors of a company certifying its accounts for a statutory purpose are not.[77] The acknowledgment must be given to the creditor or his agent.[78] A man cannot give an acknowledgment to himself.[79]

29–25   The same requirements apply to payments. A payment by the maker of a promissory note to the payee, who had negotiated the note to his bankers who had in turn transferred it to the Plaintiff bank, was held not to be a sufficient acknowledgment, as it was not payment to the person then entitled to receive it.[80] There may be occasions when a person who is not, or is no longer, the holder of an instrument nonetheless has apparent authority to receive payment.[81]

Effect of Acknowledgment or Part Payment

29–26   The statutory effect is in either case that the relevant cause of action is treated as having accrued on the date of the acknowledgment or payment. It follows that as long as the acknowledgment or payment was made to the holder of a bill at the time, a subsequent holder will be able to rely upon it against the debtor.[82] A debt may be acknowledged on successive occasions, however, no acknowledgment or part payment can revive a cause of action once it has become statute-barred.[83]

---

[73] *Surrendra Overseas Limited v. Government of Sri Lanka* [1977] 1 W.L.R. 565. This can explain cases such as *Collyer v. Willcock* (1827) 4 Bing. 313 (payment of principal, denying interest due), *Morgan v. Rowlands* (1872) L.R. 7 Q.B. 493. Similarly payment of part into court will not take a note out of the statute: *Reid v. Dickons* (1833) 5 B & Ad. 49; *Long v. Greville* (1824) 3 B. & C. 10.

[74] Limitation Act 1980, s.30(2)(a).

[75] Compare *Linsell v. Bonsor* (1835) 2 Bing. N.C. 241 (payment by agent in excess of authority).

[76] *Wright v. Pepin* [1954] 1 W.L.R. 635.

[77] *Re Transplanters (Holding Co.) Ltd* [1958] 1 W.L.R. 822. See also *Re Gee & Co. (Woolwich) Ltd* [1975] Ch. 52.

[78] Limitation Act 1980, s.30(2)(b).

[79] *Ledingham v. Bermejo Estancia Co. Ltd* [1947] 1 All E.R. 749.

[80] *Stamford, Spalding & Boston Banking Co. v. Smith* [1892] 1 Q.B. 765.

[81] Consider *Clark v. Hooper* (1834) 10 Bing. 480, where payment to an administrator under void letters of administration was held to take a note out of the statute in an action by an administrator under valid letters, distinguished in *Stamford v. Smith* (above) on the ground that there might be an exception in the case of a person filling a representative capacity, or who was believed to fill that capacity.

[82] This was suggested to be the position in *Gale v. Capern* (1834) 1 A. & E. 102 and *Cripps v. Davis* (1843) 12 M. & W. 159, relied on in earlier editions of the work for this proposition. The result follows now from the statutory mechanism applying in all cases, not just to bills.

[83] Limitation Act 1980, s.29(7). This marked a change in the law, and earlier cases speaking of "reviving" the rights under a bill (as did previous editions of this work) are not now good law, at least in this respect.

The acknowledgment of a debt binds the person making it (and his successors) but does not bind any other party.[84] On the other hand a payment made in respect of a debt or claim binds all persons liable in respect of it.[85] This would appear to apply to parties jointly liable in the same capacity on a bill, but does not apply to a person liable in a different capacity. Under the earlier law payment of interest by the indorser of a promissory note did not take the note out of the statute as against the maker.[86] It was, after some conflicting authorities, held that payment of a dividend by the assignees of an insolvent maker of a joint and several note would not take the note out of the statute as against his co-makers, for there was no acknowledgment of more being due,[87] but it is not clear that the same result would now be reached.

29–27

Bills, Notes and Cheques as acknowledgments or payments

The giving or a bill or cheque can amount to payment or acknowledgment of the whole or part of a debt due.[88] In *Marreco v. Richardson*[89] it was held that the giving of the instrument was an act from which a promise to pay the balance might be inferred. In that case, although the parties had agreed that the cheque (taken in part payment) should not be presented for some time, the period of limitation ran from the date of its delivery, and not from the date when it was subsequently presented and paid. The reasoning was that a promise to pay the balance could be inferred on the occasion of delivery of the cheque, but not from the later fact of its payment. On the law as it then stood, payment by itself was not sufficient to restart the period of limitation, but only evidence of conduct from which a promise to pay could be inferred.[90] That is no longer the law.

29–28

Time when payment made

Although the ratio of *Marreco v. Richardson* depended upon the time at which a promise to pay could be inferred, Farwell L.J. went on, following earlier dicta of Byrne J,[91] to hold that the giving of a cheque or other instrument operated as a conditional payment, subject to the condition subsequent that the instrument be honoured, and that provided the instrument is honoured, payment is effective as at the date of delivery. Different results have

29–29

---

[84] Limitation Act 1980, s.31(6).

[85] *ibid*, s.31(7).

[86] *Harding v. Edgecumbe* (1859) 28 L.J.Ex. 313.

[87] *Davies v. Edwards* (1851) 21 L.J.Ex. 4.

[88] *Turney v. Dodwell* (1854) 3 E. & B. 136; *Irving v. Veitch* (1837) 3 M. & W. 90.

[89] [1908] 2 K.B. 584, expressly following the reasoning of *Gowan v. Forster* (1832) 3 B & Ad 507 and *Turney v. Dodwell* (above).

[90] *ibid*, p. 588.

[91] In *Felix Hadley & Co. v. Hadley* [1898] 2 Ch. 680, in which the question was whether bills and cheques which had been given in respect of trade debts, but which had not yet been paid, were included in the trade debts sold at the relevant date. Byrne J. held that the debts for which bills or cheques had been taken had been paid, albeit conditionally, and so were not included in the sale.

been reached in other contexts.[92] Nonetheless Farwell L.J.'s dictum has recently been applied by the Court of Appeal in *Homes v. Smith*,[93] though not in the context of limitation. Apart from the breadth of the dicta in those cases, which concern different aspects of the relationship between the parties,[94] there would seem to be no reason in principle why the later payment of a cheque should not operate separately as a part payment made by the debtor's bank (as his agent) causing time to run again from that later date.[95]

Note twenty years old

29–30   Independently of the statute, if a note is 20 years old,[96] it will be presumed to have been paid, in the absence of circumstances tending to repel the presumption.[97]

[92] See *Re Hone* [1951] Ch. 85, in which Harman J. doubted the general application of Farwell L.J.'s dictum, and held that payment of a cheque after the making of a receiving order was contrary to the Bankruptcy Act 1914. In *Re Owen* [1949] 1 All E.R. 901 Romer J. held that gifts made by cheques drawn before, but paid after, a date three years before death were dispositions within that time for the purposes of estate duty, following *Re Swinburne* [1926] Ch. 238 in which the giving of a cheque which remained unpaid at the date of death was held not to be an effective *inter vivos* gift. In *Parkside Leasing v. Smith* [1985] 1 W.L.R. 310 at 316, Scott J. held (in the context of income tax) that interest was received when the cheque representing it was paid, and not when it was delivered, noting the narrowness of the ratio in Marreco (316). See also para. 31–02 below.

[93] [2000] Lloyds Rep. Banking 139. By contract between the vendors and purchasers of a property the vendors had agreed to accept a lesser sum than the whole balance outstanding provided payment was made by 2 p.m. on the 25th. A matter of hours before the deadline, the purchasers tendered a cheque for the lesser sum. The vendors were not bound to accept this, but it was held that they did so by receiving and presenting it for payment. The cheque was honoured, but after the deadline. Lord Wolf M.R. held, expressly following *Marreco* and doubting *Re Hone*, that payment was effectively made in time, by the delivery and acceptance of the cheque. Reliance was also placed on passages from the House of Lords decision in *DPP v. Turner* [1974] A.C. 357 concerning the suspensory effect on the underlying debt of payment by cheque.

[94] It is sufficient to support the results that the underlying obligation was (conditionally) discharged when it was replaced by the obligation on the cheque, and not necessary to go on to hold that this amounted at that date to actual payment either of the amount of the cheque or any part of a greater balance due.

[95] Especially so where, as in *Marreco v. Richardson*, the date for presentation had been expressly deferred. The cheque would remain subject to any countermand of the debtor in the meantime. In the event of dishonour, the fact of delivery could still be construed as an effective acknowledgment.

[96] Such, for 200 years, has been the common law as to a bond. The defence was introduced by the Civil Procedure Act 1833, s.3.

[97] *Duffield v. Creed* (1803) 5 Esp. 52; *Re Rutherford, Brown v. Rutherford* (1880) 14 Ch.D. 687; See *Douglass v. Lloyds Bank Ltd* [1929] 34 Com. Cas. 263 (circumstances in which repayment of bank deposit may be inferred).

PART SIX

CHAPTER 30

LOST BILLS AND NOTES

Title of finder

THE finder of a lost bill or note acquires no property in it, so as to enable him to **30–01** defend an action of conversion brought by the rightful owner. Equally such a finder has no title to sue the acceptor of a bill or the maker of a note. If the finder transfers a lost bill or note which is payable to bearer, his transferee, provided that he took it honestly, is entitled both to retain the instrument against the loser, and to compel payment from the parties liable thereon.[1] In the case of a crossed cheque marked "not negotiable",[2] a transferee only takes his transferor's title, and hence this danger is averted. Where a bill is transferable only by indorsement a forgery can convey no title, and a payment by an acceptor or other party to a man claiming under a forged instrument will not exonerate him.[3] A bank, which received a cheque on the basis that it would either apply the sum to the purchase of shares or return it to the drawer, does not owe a duty of care to the bank, on whom the cheque is drawn, not to lose it.[4]

Loss in the post

It is settled that if bills or notes are lost or stolen out of letters put into the **30–02** post office, then no action lies against the Post Office.[5] "The case of the Postmaster", says Lord Mansfield, "is in no circumstances whatever similar to that of a common carrier; but he is like all other public officers, such as the Lords Commissioners of the Treasury, the Commissioners of the Customs and Excise, the Auditors of the Exchequer, etc., who were never thought liable for any negligence or misconduct of the inferior officers in their several departments."[6]

Notice of loss

It is advisable that the loser should immediately give notice of the loss to **30–03** the parties liable on the bill; for they will thereby be prevented from taking it

---

[1] *cf. ante*, para. 18–45.
[2] It is suggested that in practice a cheque would not be made payable to bearer.
[3] See *ante*, para. 20–37.
[4] See *Yorkshire Bank plc v. Lloyds Bank plc* (1999) T.L.R. 362.
[5] See today The Post Office Act, s.29. In *Ose Gesellschaft v. Jewish Colonial Trust* (1937) 43 T.L.R. 398, a customer of the defendants, who were bankers, had instructed them to transmit a sum of money abroad, and the defendants sent the money by cheque in a registered letter. The cheque was stolen in transmission and paid under a forged indorsement. The customer, who was debited with the amount of the cheque, unsuccessfully sued the defendants for negligence, the negligence alleged being the omission to insure the letter. See *American Express Co. & Another v. British Airways Board, The Times*, November 25, 1982.
[6] *Whitfield v. Despencer* (1778) 2 Cowp. 754; *Lane v. Cotton* (1700) 1 Salk. 17; see also *Bainbridge v. Postmaster-General* [1906] 1 K.B. 178.

up without due inquiry. Public advertisement of the loss should also be given; for if any person whosoever discounts it with notice of the loss, that will be such strong evidence of fraud that he can acquire no property in it.[7] But public notice is of itself neither sufficient nor indispensable. To operate at all, it must be brought home to the party to be affected by it.[8]

Presentment and notice of dishonour

30–04   The party who has lost or destroyed a bill must, nevertheless, make application to the drawee for payment at the time it is due, and give notice of dishonour; for the bill might still have been paid, with or without an indemnity, and the prior parties, by not having been advised of the dishonour, may have been prevented from pressing their respective remedies against parties liable to them.[9]

Remedy of a holder

30–05   The 1882 Act affords the loser of a bill not overdue the following remedy to the holder:

> **69. Where a bill has been lost before it is overdue, the person who was the holder of it may apply to the drawer to give him another bill of the same tenor, giving security to the drawer if required to indemnify him against all persons whatever in case the bill alleged to have been lost shall be found again.**
>
> **If the drawer on request as aforesaid refuses to give such duplicate bill he may be compelled to do so.**

It should be noticed that this section applies to the case of the drawer only. There appears to be no means of compelling the acceptor or indorser to renew their signatures on the instrument obtained under this section. Nor does the section appear to apply to the maker of a note, since he is not in the position of the drawer of a bill under the 1882 Act, section 89(2). The former holder of a lost bill is not under any compulsion to apply for a replacement; he may instead bring an action on the lost bill under s.70.[10] If he does apply to the drawer for a replacement, the drawer is entitled to require an indemnity against claims by other persons in the event that the bill should be found.

If the loser obtains a judgment or order under this section he may, on failure of compliance by the drawer, have the document executed by a nominee of the Court.[11]

---

[7] It was formerly considered that advertisement was in some cases essential to the plaintiff's right to recover on a stolen instrument (*Snow v. Peacock* (1826) 3 Bing. 406, 411); but now it is clearly immaterial, since even gross negligence on the part of the person who has taken the instrument is not *ipso facto* equivalent to mala fides on his part; see *ante*, para. 18–09.

[8] See, *e.g. Raphael v. Bank of England* (1855) 17 C.B. 161.

[9] *Thackray v. Blackett* (1811) 3 Camp. 164.

[10] *Post* para. 30–06.

[11] Supreme Court Act 1981, s.39.

Action on lost bill

Where action is taken on a lost instrument, the 1882 Act invests the Court or a judge with the following power:

70. In any action or proceeding upon a bill, the court or a judge may order that the loss of the instrument shall not be set up, provided an indemnity be given to the satisfaction of the court or judge against the claims of any other person upon the instrument in question.

This section, which is a reproduction of the still unrepealed section 87 of the Common Law Procedure Act 1854,[12] alters the common law rule whereby action could not be brought on a lost bill or note, if negotiable, even though an indemnity had been tendered to the defendant[13] and it was lost when overdue,[14] and when unindorsed by the holder.[15] Nor could action be brought on the consideration.[16] But it was otherwise where the instrument was not negotiable.[17] The only effective remedy afforded the holder of a lost instrument was by resorting to a court of equity.[18]

For the provisions of this section to be applied the instrument must comply strictly with the definitions of a bill, note or cheque contained in the 1882 Act. Section 87 of the Common Law Procedure Act 1854 appears to have been retained because it applies to all negotiable instruments, not merely to instruments covered by the definitions in the 1882 Act.[19] A remedy similar to that contained in the 1882 Act can therefore presumably only be obtained in the case of other negotiable instruments if action is taken in the Supreme Court, the superior courts of common law at Westminster specified in the Act of 1854 being now merged therein, whereas the remedy afforded by the 1882 Act may be obtained in any court.

---

[12] That Act applied only to proceedings in the Superior Courts or common law at Westminster and to those in the county palatine courts of Lancaster and Durham; there is no such limitation in the 1882 Act. The Statute Law Revision Act 1892, repeals the words "bill of exchange or other" in s.87, so as to leave it applicable only to other negotiable instruments.

[13] *Pierson v. Hutchinson* (1809) 2 Camp. 211.

[14] *Hansard v. Robinson* (1827) 7 B. & C. 90.

[15] *Ramuz v. Crowe* (1847) 1 Ex. 167; but see also *Rolt v. Watson* (1827) 4 Bing. 273, and *Long v. Bailie* (1805) 2 Camp. 214n., where loss of a bill specially indorsed to the plaintiff was not allowed to be set up.

[16] *Crowe v. Clay* (1854) 9 Ex. 604; *Champion v. Terry* (1822) 3 Brod. & B. 295.

[17] *Wain v. Bailey* (1839) 10 A. & E. 616.

[18] *Rolt v. Watson, supra*, at p. 274; Chitty, *Bills*, 11th ed., p. 189, and note (o) the Stat. 9 Will. 3, c. 17, s.3. remained a dead letter at common law, since the common law courts could not compel the plaintiff to furnish, or the defendant to accept, an indemnity; see *Ex p. Greenway* (1802) 6 Ves. 812; *Davies v. Dodd* (1817) 4 Price 176, where the plaintiff had previously failed at common law ((1812) 4 Taunt. 602), the Court indicating that his remedy was on the statute; *King v. Zimmerman* (1871) L.R. 6 C.P. 466; Bayley J. (*Bills*, 6th ed., Ch. V, note (38)), inferred from the judgment of Lord Hardwicke C. in *Walmsley v. Child* (1749) 1 Ves. Sen. 341, that the equity of the statute would comprehend indorsements.

[19] Circular notes appear to be within s.87 of the Act of 1854 (*Conflans Quarry Co. v. Parker* (1867) L.R.3 C.P.1). The removal of the term "bill of exchange" as already noted, *supra*, note 12, from s.87 by the SLR Act 1892, appears to affect only the case of an instrument within the 1882 Act.

Destroyed instrument

30–07   As to the case of an instrument destroyed, not lost, there is common law
authority that an action lies, and secondary evidence is admissible of the
contents of the bill, on its destruction being proved,[20] and accordingly a bill
in equity was dismissed in such a case on the ground that the plaintiff had a
remedy at law.[21] On the other hand, the suggested distinction between the case
of a destroyed and that of a lost negotiable bill was apparently not recognised
in a case on a lost bill, and it seems to have been thought that no action would
lie in either case, the remedy being by bill in equity.[22] The distinction is now
of slight importance. If sound, it would perhaps enable a plaintiff to sue on a
destroyed bill without giving an indemnity, as, if a right of action existed at
common law on a destroyed bill, that right was necessarily independent of any
indemnity.[23] Neither section 69 of the 1882 Act nor section 70 in express
terms applies to destroyed bills.[24]

Loss of half of instrument

30–08   It remains to consider the case of a half note, the other half of which has
been lost.[25] Thus, where the holders sued on the half of a £5 note, the other
half having been stolen from the Leeds mail, Lord Ellenborough said:

> "Payment can be enforced at law only by the production of an entire note, or by
> proof that the instrument, or the part of it which is wanting, has been actually
> destroyed. The half of this note taken from the Leeds mail may have immediately
> got into the hands of a bona fide holder for value; and he would have had as good
> a right of suit upon that as the plaintiffs upon the other half which afterwards
> reached them. But the maker of a promissory note cannot be liable, in respect of it,
> to two parties at the same time."[26]

It is, however, doubtful how far the argument from the liability of the maker
on the second half would be held valid at the present day. The holder of the
first half has a good title and no notice; the holder of the second half has a bad

---

[20] *Pierson v. Hutchinson, supra,* at p. 212 (Lord Ellenborough C.J.); *Woodford v. Whitely*
(1830) Mood. & M. 517 (Parke J.); *Blackie v. Pidding* (1848) 6 C.B. 196; *cf. Clarke v. Quince*
1834 3 Dowl.P.C. 26. As to the destruction of a note of the Bank of Canada, see *The Bank of
Canada and the Bank of Montreal v. Bay Bus Terminal (North Bay) Ltd and Another,* Canadian
Supreme Court, June 1977.

[21] *Wright v. Maidstone* (1855) 24 L.J.Ch. 623.

[22] *Hansard v. Robinson* (1827) 7 B. & C. 90, 95; 9 D. & R. 860, 863; *cf.* Chitty, *op. cit.,*
p. 190.

[23] *cf.* Daniel, 5th ed., paras 1481, 1482.

[24] The parallel provisions of the Canadian Act have been held to apply to a note presumably
destroyed (*Pillow Co. v. L'Esperance* (1902) Q.R. 22 S.C. 213); Maclaren, *op. cit.,* p. 416.
Intentional destruction may be cancellation under the 1882 Act, s.63(1) but not destruction by
mistake or accident.

[25] The position is different where, after sending his first half, the sender changes his mind and
refuses to send the second half. In this case, the property in the first half does not pass to the
recipient who must return it to the sender (*Smith v. Mundy* (1860) 3 E. & E. 22).

[26] *Mayor v. Johnson* (1813) 3 Camp. 324.

title and notice. But it may be a question whether a half note is for all purposes a negotiable instrument.[27]

Conversion of lost bill or note

If a lost bill or note is in the hands of a party who has no right to retain it,   **30–09** as for example, it is still in the possession of the finder, or of a transferee who has taken it from him under circumstances amounting to fraud, the true owner may sue for conversion. If it has been wrongfully paid by the acceptor or maker to such holder the true owner may sue the person receiving payment for money had and received.[28] The true owner may, also, sue the banker or any other person who has wrongfully dealt with the instrument for conversion without a previous demand of the bill.[29] The damages in conversion, or for money had and received, is the face value of the instrument.

---

[27] In *Redmayne v. Burton* (1860) 2 L.T. 324, Willes J. was indeed of opinion that a bank was bound to pay on a half note without indemnity, as any person taking a half note would take it with notice.

[28] *Downs v. Halling* (1825) 4 B. & C. 330; *Bobbett v. Pinkett* (1876) 1 Ex.D. 368.

[29] *Lovell v. Martin* (1813) 4 Taunt. 799. As to the loss of an instrument when sent by post in payment, see *ante*, para. 30–02.

CHAPTER 31

BILL OR NOTE AS PAYMENT

Bill as conditional payment

31–01   IT was once considered that a simple contract could not be satisfied by any similar executory contract, unless it was founded on a new consideration, or was such as to give an immediate right of action upon breach thereof,[1] for that was merely substituting one cause of action for another. The delivery of a valid bill or note though, even for a less sum than that claimed,[2] if accepted in satisfaction, suspended the creditor's remedy for a debt, and if he either received the money on the instrument, or was guilty of laches, it operated as a complete satisfaction.[3] Since 1933 satisfaction may be executory.[4]

In this chapter the word "payment" is not always used in its strict legal sense. A plea of payment by bill means in law that the bill has been taken in satisfaction; but in the popular sense payment by bill may merely mean that a bill has been given for and on account of the debt.[5]

Whether a bill is taken in complete satisfaction, or merely as conditional payment, is a question depending on the facts of each case. The onus lies on the party alleging that the bill operated as a complete satisfaction of the original debt. The presumption of fact being the other way,[6] since, as already stated, if a bill or note is taken on account of a debt and nothing is said at the time, the legal effect of the transaction is that the original debt remains, but the remedy for it is suspended till maturity of the instrument in the hands of the creditor.[7]

Where the bill is given as conditional payment only, notwithstanding that it is pursued to judgment, an action will lie, if the judgment is unsatisfied, on the original contract whether it is a specialty or not.[8]

If a bill is given in respect of arrears of rent it will not, in the absence of special agreement, extinguish the claim for such rent or suspend the right of distress pending the maturity of the bill, unless it is given in satisfaction and

[1] Good v. Cheeseman (1831) 2 B. & Ad. 328, 335 (Parke B.); cf. Chitty, Contracts (28th ed., 1999), para. 23–015.

[2] Sibree v. Tripp, 15 M. & W. 23.

[3] Cf. Peacock v. Purssell (1863) 32 L.J.C.P. 266; 3 & 4 Anne, c. 8, s.7.

[4] British Russian Gazette and Trade Outlook Ltd. v. Associated Newspapers Ltd [1933] 2 K.B. 616.

[5] Maillard v. Argyle (1843) 6 M. & G. 40, 45, 46; Currie v. Misa (1875) L.R. 10 Ex. 153, Lush J., at 163.

[6] Goldshede v. Cottrell (1836) 2 M. & W. 20; Sibree v. Tripp, supra; Bottomley v. Nuttall (1858) 28 L.J.C.P. 110; Bidder v. Bridges (1887) 37 Ch.D. 406; Re Romer and Haslam [1893] 2 Q.B. 286.

[7] Allen v. Royal Bank of Canada (1926) 134 L.T. 194, 196; this passage was cited in Crockfords Club Ltd v. Mehta [1992] 1 W.L.R. 355 at 360 by Henry J. (upheld by the Court of Appeal).

[8] Wegg-Prosser v. Evans [1895] 1 Q.B. 108, following and explaining Drake v. Mitchell (1803) 3 East 251, and overruling Cambefort v. Chapman (1887) 19 Q.B.D. 229; cf. also Curtis v. Rush (1814) 2 Ves. & B. 416; Roycroft v. Uglum [1922] 1 W.W.R. 78.

not merely for and on account of the rent due.[9] But the giving of a bill for rent due is some evidence, though not conclusive, of an agreement by the landlord to suspend his right of distress pending the maturity of the bill.[10]

Cheque as payment

Where a cheque is offered in payment, it amounts to a conditional payment **31–02** of the amount of the cheque which, if accepted operates as a conditional payment from the time when the cheque was delivered; if the cheque is not met on presentation, the payment is subject to a condition subsequent which means that the sum which was due becomes due once more.[11]

However, as between a bankrupt and his trustee, it has been held that in order for there to be payment the cheque in question had to be cleared.[12]

Cheques until cleared cannot be considered as payment in cash under the allotment provisions of the Companies Act.[13] But upon a question whether a debt has been paid, the mere production of a cheque drawn by the debtor in favour of the creditor and paid by the banker is not conclusive evidence of payment. It must be further shown that the cheque passed through the creditor's hands. In previous editions it was said that for this purpose it was prudent to cause the payee to write his name across the cheque or to indorse it. Since the Cheques Act 1957, the need for indorsement has largely disappeared, which would have meant that the drawer of a cheque would have no evidence that the amount had been received by the payee. However, section 3 of the Cheques Act provides that:

> **"3. An unindorsed cheque which appears to have been paid by the banker on whom it is drawn is evidence of the receipt by the payee of the sum payable by the cheque."**

This section appears not yet to have been considered by the courts.[14] It is not necessary to go on and show that the debtor paid the cheque to his creditor.[15]

When the acceptor or other party liable on a bill proposes to pay by a cheque, the holder should not give up the bill till the cheque is paid.[16] It has

---

[9] *Palfrey v. Baker* (1817) 3 Price 572; *Davis v. Gyde* (1835) 2 A. & E. 623.

[10] *Palmer v. Bramley* [1895] 2 Q.B. 405. As to the admissibility of parol evidence of an agreement to take a bill in payment of rent, see *Henderson v. Arthur* [1907] 1 K.B. 10.

[11] *Homes v Smith* [2000] Lloyds Rep. Banking 139 at 143.

[12] *Re Hone (a bankrupt), ex p. The Trustee v. Kensington Borough Council* [1951] Ch. 85; in *Homes v Smith* (*supra*) the Court observed that this did not represent the general position. See also *The Brimnes* [1974] 2 Lloyd's Rep. 241; [1975] Q.B. 929, in which charterers' agents instructed the bank to transfer payment from their account to that of the owners; it was held that time of payment was when the order was implemented. See also *The Laconia* [1976] Q.B. 835; *The Zographia M.* [1976] 2 Lloyd's Rep. 382 and *Delbrueck & Co. v. Barclays Bank International Ltd* [1976] 2 Lloyd's Rep. 341.

[13] *Mears v. Western Canada Pulp and Paper Co.* [1905] 2 Ch. 353; *Re National Motor Mail Coach Co.* [1908] 2 Ch. 228.

[14] *Egg v. Barnett* (1800) 3 Esp. 196.

[15] *Mountford v. Harper* (1847) 16 M. & W. 825, distinguishing *Lloyd v. Sandilands* (1818) Gow 15; *Boswell v. Smith* (1833) 6 C. & P. 60.

[16] *Ward v. Evans* (1703) 2 Ld.Raym. 928; *Vernon v. Boverie* (1684) 2 Show. 296; see also *Nash v. De Freville* [1900] 2 Q.B. 72.

been held that the holder is not guilty of neglect in giving up the bill before the cheque is paid;[17] but it is not usual with London bankers to exchange bills for cheques, and it is doubtful whether they would be protected in so doing. If a creditor, however, in payment of any other debt than a bill or note, takes a cheque, and the banker fails, or the cheque is dishonoured, the creditor's remedies remain entire[18] but if he takes a stranger's cheque or acceptance, though offered payment in cash by his debtor, that may discharge the debtor, as the creditor abides the hazard of the security he takes.[19] If he takes the cheque of the debtor's agent, that is the same as if he takes the debtor's own cheque, and the latter will not be discharged, unless the creditor by taking such security has led the debtor to believe the debt will be discharged, and so to have been prejudiced by dealing with his agent as if he had discharged the debt.[20] Although a creditor has a legal right to demand notes or cash, he waives that right if he expressly asks for payment by cheque.[21] If payment of a cheque is stopped, the debt instantly revives as though it had never been given.[22]

A cheque is normally conditional payment; " . . . the giving of a cheque for a debt is payment conditional on the cheque being met, that is, subject to a condition subsequent, and if the cheque is an actual payment *ab initio* and not a conditional one".[23]

Where a cheque is sent in settlement of a debt for a larger amount, the creditor need not accept it but he may collect it, maintaining his rights, and sue for the difference.[24]

In *D. & C. Builders Ltd v. Rees*,[25] the plaintiffs, being in financial straits, had accepted a cheque for less than the sum due in full settlement. The Court of Appeal held that they could nevertheless sue for the balance.

In *Homes v. Smith* an agreement between the parties provided that a lesser sum would be accepted instead of the larger amount due if received by the payment time. It was held that where a cheque was tendered pursuant to the agreement, but not by the time stipulated, it was open to the payee to reject the mode of payment; but if the cheque was accepted no claim lay for the larger amount.[26]

---

[17] *Russell v. Hankey* (1794) 6 T.R. 12, followed in *Ridley v. Blackett* (1796) 2 Peake 62.

[18] *Everett v. Collins* (1810) 2 Camp. 515; *Marsh v. Pedder* (1815) 4 Camp. 257; *Tapley v. Martens* (1800) 8 T.R. 451. Where, under a foreclosure, a mortgagee assented to the auctioneer taking a cheque for the deposit and it was dishonoured, the acceptance of the cheque was held reasonable and the mortgagee was held entitled to the costs of the abortive sale (Farrer v. Lacy (1885) 31 Ch.D. 42; see also *Stembridge v. Morrison* (1913) 33 N.Z.L.R. 621).

[19] *Everett v. Collins, supra*;

[20] *Wyatt v. Hertford* (1802) 3 East 147.

[21] *Cubitt v. Gamble* (1919) 35 T.L.R. 223.

[22] *Cohen v. Hale* (1878) 3 Q.B.D. 371; *cf. Elliott v. Crutchley* [1904] 1 K.B. 365; *Russell v. Hellaby* [1922] N.Z.L.R. 186.

[23] *Per* Farwell L.J. in *Marreco v. Richardson* [1908] 2 K.B. 584, 592–593; see also *Homes v. Smith (supra). Cf.Private Motorists Provident Society v. Moore* [1988] F.L.R. 372, for an example of an exception to the general rule.

[24] *Day v. McLea* (1889) 22 Q.B.D. 610; and see *D. & C. Builders Ltd. v. Rees* [1966] 2 Q.B. 617, CA.

[25] [1966] 2 Q.B. 617, applying *Pinnel's Case* (1602) 5 Co.Rep. 1179.

[26] [2000] Lloyds Rep. Banking 139.

Acceptance of cheque "in full and final settlement"[27]

It is not uncommon for cheque to be sent "in full and final settlement". The **31–03** question arises as to whether the presentment of such a cheque constitutes an acceptance of the amount proffered, debarring any further claim. For the issue to arise it must be plain that the cheque is proffered on such a basis;[28] furthermore there must be an actual dispute, which is capable of being settled. Where the cheque bore a form of receipt "in full and final settlement", the creditor, in accepting the cheque, was not deprived of the right to sue for the balance if the receipt is not consistent with the purpose of the underlying transaction.[29] Whether the presentment of a cheque offered in full and final settlement will amount to an acceptance of the amount of the cheque is a question of fact. If the cheque is accepted and cashed without qualification or a passage of time elapses, then there is strong evidence from which inference is likely to be drawn that the cheque was accepted in full settlement.[30]

Bill as collateral security

A creditor may agree to take a bill as collateral security for a debt already **31–04** due without affecting his present right to sue for that debt. A creditor who takes from his debtor, as a collateral security only, a bill indorsed by his debtor, as he is trustee of the rights, so he is bound by the duties, of a holder. If he neglects to present or give notice of dishonour to his debtor, the debtor is discharged; for no one but the actual holder can perform these duties.[31]

Bill or note in payment of a solicitor's bill

Where a promissory note payable at a future date is given for a solicitor's **31–05** bill, the 12 months run from the time the note was paid, and not from the time it was given, unless it was agreed to treat it as payment at that time.[32] A solicitor cannot evade his obligation to deliver a bill of costs by taking a bill of exchange from his client for an agreed amount.[33] For costs due to him he has a lien on any bill of exchange[34] or cheque[35] belonging to his client but in his (the solicitor's) possession.

---

[27] For a full discussion of the topic see Foskett, *The Law and Practice of Compromise* (4th ed,1996) pp.26–35.

[28] *Rustenburg Platinum Mines Ltd. v. SAA* [1979] 1 Lloyds Rep. 19.

[29] *Neuchatel Asphalte Co. v. Barnett* [1957] 1 W.L.R. 356.

[30] See the cases cited in *Foskett* (*supra*).

[31] *Peacock v. Pursell* (1863) 32 L.J.C.P. 266.

[32] *Sayer v. Wagstaff* (1844) 5 Beav. 415; *Re Harries* (1844) 13 M. & W. 3; *Re Romer and Haslam* [1893] 2 Q.B. 286. As to what will amount to the instrument being taken as payment, see *Re Currie* (1846) 9 Beav. 602; *Re Harper and Jones* (1847) 10 Beav. 284.

[33] *Ray v. Newton* [1913] 1 K.B. 249; see also *Moore v. Sprague* (1917) 34 T.L.R. 113; *Kruger v. Coles* [1909] T.S. 172.

[34] *Gibson v. May* (1853) 4 De G. & M. 512.

[35] *Hanson v. Reeve* (1857) 27 L.J. Ch. 118.

Bills of a third person

31–06   If the debtor, instead of paying the creditor, directs him to take a bill of a third person, which the creditor does, and the bill is dishonoured, the liability of the original debtor revives;[36] and it is not necessary to give the original debtor, who is not himself a party to the bill, a notice of the dishonour.[37] The bill or note must be presented within a reasonable time.[38]

So if the creditor, not having the option of taking cash, takes of his own accord a bill of his debtor's agent, the debtor is not discharged.[39] But if the debtor refers his creditor to a third person for payment generally, and the creditor, having the option of taking cash, elects to take a bill which is dishonoured, the original debtor is discharged.[40]

Bill given to agent

31–07   The consequence of giving a bill to an agent—an auctioneer, for example—who has no authority to receive anything but cash, is, that the party giving the bill is not discharged from the demand of the principal, although the bill falls due at the period when the debt ought to have been discharged, and is regularly paid to the holder.[41] In *Meyer v. Sze Hai Tong Banking Co.* the plaintiff's cashier received, in exchange for cheques payable to the plaintiff, the defendant's cheques on other banks; it was held that the giving of such cheques was payment.[42]

What a creditor must prove

31–08   Where a debtor indorses a bill to his creditor, the creditor cannot sue for his debt without proving presentment of the bill and notice of dishonour.[43] But where the debtor does not indorse it, it has been held that it is sufficient for the creditor, when suing for the original debt, to show that the bill still remains in

---

[36] *Marsh v. Pedder* (1815) 4 Camp. 257; *Taylor v. Briggs* (1827) M. & M. 28; *March v. Thorburn* (1888) Newfoundland S.C. 357; and see *Bolton v. Richard* (1795) 6 T.R. 139.

[37] *Swinyard v. Bowes* (1816) 5 M. & S. 62, approved in *Holbrow v. Wilkins* (1822) 1 B. & C. 10, 12. The case of *Smith v. Mercer* (1867) L.R. 3 Ex. 51, appears to be distinguishable since in that case payment by "approved banker's bill" was a term of the contract.

[38] *cf. Chamberlyn v. Delarive* (1767) 2 Wilson 353.

[39] *Robinson v. Read* (1829) 9 B. & C. 449; *Marsh v. Pedder* (1815) 4 Camp. 257, 262; but it seems notice of dishonour must be given (*Smith v. Mercer, supra*).

[40] *Strong v. Hart* (1827) 6 B. & C. 160; *Smith v. Ferrand* (1827) 7 B. & C. 19; *Rogers v. Calgary Brewing Co.* (1917) 56 Can.S.C.R. 165; and see *Baillie v. Moore* (1846) 15 L.J.Q.B. 169.

[41] *Sykes v. Giles* (1839) 5 M. & W. 645; *Williams v. Evans* (1866) L.R. 1 Q.B. 352; *Blumberg v. Life Interests Corporation* [1896] 1 Ch. 171; affirmed 1 Ch. 27; *Johnston v. Boyes* [1899] 2 Ch. 73; *Collings v. City of Calgary* (1917) 55 Can.S.C.R. 406; *International Sponge Co. v. Andrew Watt & Sons* [1911] A.C. 279; *Bradford v. Price* (1923) 92 L.J.K.B. 871. A cheque taken by an agent only authorised to take cash amounts to a payment in cash when honoured; if dishonoured the agent is liable for the damage occasioned by his breach of authority (*Pape v. Westacott* [1894] 1 Q.B. 272, distinguishing Bridges v. Garrett (1870) L.R. 5 C.P. 451); see also *Delory v. Guyett* (1920) 47 O.L.R. 137; *AEG (UK) Ltd. v. Lewis* [1992] T.L.R. 656; and *ante*, para. 7–13.

[42] [1913] A.C. 847.

[43] *Kearslake v. Morgan* (1794) 5 T.R. 513; *Bridges v. Berry* (1810) 3 Taunt. 130.

his hands, without proving presentment,[44] or notice of dishonour[45] for that is presumptive evidence of dishonour, sufficient to throw it on the defendant to show that the bill has been paid.[46]

Effect on lien

The taking of a bill or note in payment will, in general, determine a lien. **31–09** Thus, where the owner of a ship having a lien on the goods, until the delivery of good and approved bills, took a bill of exchange in payment, and though he objected to it at the time, afterwards negotiated it, it was held that such negotiation amounted to an approval of the bill by him, and to a relinquishment of his lien on the goods.[47] Where, however, the vendor takes a bill in payment and negotiates it he will not thereby necessarily lose his lien if the bill is unpaid; but he may do so if, in the circumstances, the negotiation is equivalent to payment. Thus, where the vendor of hay took the vendee's note and discounted it through his agent with the plaintiff bank, the agent failing to hand over the money, and on the dishonour of the note, the bank purchased the hay from the vendee, returning his note, it was held that discount of the note amounted to payment and determined the lien.[48] But where the vendors of iron rails drew on the vendees for the price and negotiated the bills, it was held that they had not lost their lien on the acceptor's insolvency, their sole security being the value of the acceptances, while they remained liable as drawers to subsequent holders.[49]

Under section 38(1) of the Sale of Goods Act 1979, a seller of goods is to be deemed an "unpaid seller" if he has taken a bill or other negotiable instrument as conditional payment (and, as already stated,[50] every such payment is prima facie conditional), and the instrument is dishonoured, and, further, under section 39(1), an "unpaid seller" has a lien on the goods for their price while he is in possession of them. On the sale of real property the taking and negotiating of a note or bill by the vendor does not amount to a relinquishment of his lien on the land for the unpaid purchase money.[51]

Covenant to pay note when due

A covenant to pay in promissory notes implies and includes a covenant to **31–10** pay the notes when due.[52]

---

[44] *Goodwin v. Coates* (1832) 1 Mood. & R. 221.

[45] *Bishop v. Rowe* (1815) 3 M. & S. 362; but see *Smith v. Mercer, supra.*

[46] Where a debt is secured by a promissory note no equitable assignment of the debt can be complete or perfect until the note is delivered to the assignee in bearer form and no further act on the part of the assignor is necessary to give the assignee title *(Ramcharan v. Arima Bus Service Co.* (1966) 10 W.I.R. 375, Trinidad & Tobago CA).

[47] *Horncastle v. Farran* (1820) 3 B. & Ald. 497.

[48] *Bunney v. Poyntz* (1833) 4 B. & Ad. 568; but this case is said to be inconsistent with *Gunn v. Bolchow, Vaughan & Co.* (1875) L.R. 10 Ch. 491 *(Re Defries & Sons Ltd* [1909] 2 Ch. 423).

[49] *Gunn v. Bolckow, Vaughan & Co., supra; Re Rankin and Shilliday* [1927] N.I. 162.

[50] *Ante* para. 31–01.

[51] *Ex p. Loaring* (1814) 2 Rose 79; *Grant v. Mills* (1813) 2 V. & B. 306; see *Macreth v. Symons* (1808) 15 Ves. 329. As to the effect of taking a void cheque, see *Bond v. Warden* (1845) 14 L.J.Ch. 154.

[52] *Dixon v. Holdroyd* (1857) 27 L.J.Q.B. 43.

CHAPTER 32

PAYMENTS MADE UNDER A MISTAKE

General

32–01   IN recent years there have been many developments in the law governing the recovery of payments made under a mistake, with the recognition of a general concept of unjust enrichment and corresponding general defence of change of position. A full review of the relevant law is well beyond the scope of this work.[1] The principles will be summarised below, with illustrations of their application in the case of negotiable instruments and cheques, and the special considerations which apply to them. The reasoning, and the results, of earlier cases must be read in the light of the new, and more liberal, principles.

Historical Basis

32–02   The entitlement to recover monies paid under a mistake as monies had and received is long established, albeit with considerable debate and uncertainty as to its proper analysis. A useful modern starting point is Goff J.'s classic statement in the case of *Barclays Bank Ltd v. W.J. Simms Ltd*:[2]

> "*From this formidable line of authority certain simple principles can be deduced: (1) If a person pays money to another under a mistake of fact which causes him to make the payment, he is prima facie entitled to recover it as money paid under a mistake of fact. (2) His claim may however fail if (a) the payer intends that the payee shall have the money at all events, whether the fact be true or false, or is deemed in law so to intend; or (b) the payment is made for good consideration, in particular if the money is paid to discharge, and does discharge, a debt owed to the payee (or a principal on whose behalf he is authorised to receive the payment) by the payer or by a third party by whom he is authorised to discharge the debt; or (c) the payee has changed his position in good faith, or is deemed in law to have done so.*"

Unjust Enrichment

32–03   In the landmark decision of *Lipkin Gorman v. Karpnale*[3] the House of Lords recognised that claims for recovery in such cases should be guided by a general principle of unjust enrichment, and subject to a general defence of change of position. The language of that case has very quickly been assumed in a number of subsequent decisions. In *Banque Financière v. Parc (Battersea) Ltd*[4] Lord Steyn framed the test for the grant of remedy in wide terms:

---

[1] Reference should be made, in particular, to Goff and Jones, *The Law of Restitution* (5th ed.).
[2] [1980] Q.B. 677 at 695. See also the decision of Kerr J. in *National Westminster Bank Ltd v. Barclays Bank International Ltd* [1975] Q.B. 654.
[3] [1991] 2 A.C. 548.
[4] [1999] A.C. 221 at 227.

(a) has A been enriched, (b) was that at the expense of B, (c) was the enrichment unjust, and (d) are there any defences? Despite the breadth of those propositions, and the range of their possible applications, for present purposes (payment under a mistake) it appears that (subject to the development of the defence of change of position) the principles to be applied are consistent with the traditional analysis.

Mistake of Fact or Law

In *Kleinwort Benson Ltd v. Lincoln City Council*[5] the House of Lords held   **32–04**
that a mistake of law could found an action for the recovery of money, on the same basis as a mistake of fact.

Mistake "as between payer and payee"

In *Barclays v. Simms*[6] Goff J. rejected the proposition that in order to be   **32–05**
effective to ground a right of recovery the relevant mistake had to be one "between the payer and the payee", observing that this requirement would be inconsistent with the decision in *Jones v. Waring & Gillow*.[7] In general terms, it is clear that the mistake need only be that of the payer (as in *Barclays v. Simms* itself).[8] In the same passage he recorded that it was implicit that the mistake need not be the mistaken belief of the payer that he was liable to pay the money to the recipient.

Nonetheless, there is at least one respect in which the party seeking to   **32–06**
recover may need to demonstrate that the mistake was common to the parties or that the recipient knew of or was responsible for it. It is clearly a defence that the money has been received for good consideration, in particular including the discharge of an existing obligation.[9] To recover money paid pursuant to a contract, including a bill, it is necessary to establish that the contract itself should be set aside or was not enforceable. A unilateral mistake will not generally suffice if the contract is otherwise binding.[10] If the payer did believe that he was discharging an obligation, he will need to show that belief to have been mistaken.

---

[5] [1999] 2 A.C. 349. The decision reversed the effect of some two centuries of authority, though this development was prefigured by a number of observations (see for example *Woolwich Building Society v. IRC* [1993] A.C. 70) in the light of the unsatisfactory and frequently artificial distinctions drawn between fact and law in the cases. The decision went by 3:2 majority, with Lord Browne Wilkinson and Lord Lloyd dissenting on the basis that a payment made under a settled view of the law subsequently changed by judicial decision ought not to have a right of recovery.

[6] At 694.

[7] Discussed at length below, paras 32–24 *et seq.*

[8] The cases said to support the proposition are considered in the judgment of Goff J. and are reviewed in Paget (11th ed.) at p. 360.

[9] See in particular p. 695 in the judgment of Goff J., "note c". Also, *Lipkin Gorman v. Karpnale* (above).

[10] See there. This proposition, particularly in the context of bills, is discussed further below under "discharge of an obligation".

Negligence not a defence

32–07   Dicta can be found in the earlier cases suggesting that moneys paid on a bill are not recoverable if there has been any negligence on the part of the person making payment.[11] *Kelly v. Solari*[12] as explained in *Imperial Bank of Canada v. Bank of Hamilton*[13] established that mere negligence on the part of the payer is not a defence to such an action. Indeed, in *Barclays v. Simms* itself, the fact that the bank had overlooked its own customer's countermand did not preclude recovery. Similarly, despite suggestions to the contrary, it is clear that recovery is not precluded because a bank has failed to recognise a signature as a forgery, and that the bank making payment does not impliedly represent that the signature is genuine, only that it so believes.[14]

Money paid to an agent

32–08   Money, which is paid to an agent as such, is recoverable in his hands, but the agent will have a defence if he has in good faith accounted to his principal for the sum received. This includes a bank which, having received payment for its customer, has in good faith allowed the customer to withdraw the monies.[15] The defence can now be seen as consistent with the general defence of change of position, but has been long and distinctly recognised.

Estoppel

32–09   It is well established that a party claiming to recover moneys paid under a mistake might be estopped from recovery if by his actions or conduct he represented that the recipient was entitled to the moneys and the recipient had, to his detriment, relied on that representation.[16] A full discussion of the cases in which sums have been mistakenly paid (or overpaid) is beyond the scope of this work.[17]

32–10   It is clear that merely making payment does not by itself amount to a representation on the part of the paying bank that the payee is entitled to the

---

[11] See for example *Price v. Neal* (1762) 3 Burr. 1354, *Smith v. Mercer* (1815) 6 Taunt. 76, cited in earlier editions of this work.

[12] (1841) 11 L.J. Ex. 10.

[13] [1903] A.C. 49, PC.

[14] See *National Westminster Bank Ltd v. Barclays Bank International Ltd* [1975] Q.B. 654.

[15] See generally Paget, (11th Ed.) p. 365; *Buller v. Harrison* (1777) 2 Cowp. 565; *Deutsche Bank v. Beriro & Co.* (1895) 1 Com. Cas. 123 and 255; *Continental Caoutchouc and Gutta Percha Co. v. Kleinwort Sons & Co.* (1904) 90 L.T. 474, 9 Com. Cas. 240; *Kleinwort Sons & Co. v. Dunlop Rubber Co.* (1907) 97 L.T. 263; *Gowers v. Lloyds and National Provincial Foreign Bank Ltd* [1938] 1 All E.R. 766; *Thomas v. Houston Corbett & Co.* [1969] N.Z.L.R. 151; *National Westminster Bank Ltd v. Barclays Bank International Ltd* [1975] Q.B. 654; *Australia and New Zealand Banking Group v. Westpac Corp* (1988) 62 A.L.J.R. 292. Compare *Admiralty Commissioners v. National Provincial and Union Bank of England Ltd* (1922) 127 L.T. 452.

[16] See, for applications of the principles, *Skyring v. Greenwood*, 4 B. & C. 281; *Standish v. Ross* (1849) 3 Exch. 27; *Durrant v. Ecclesiastical Commissioners* (1880) 6 Q.B.D. 234; *Baylis v. Bishop of London* [1913] 1 Ch. 127; *Holt v. Markham* [1923] 1 K.B. 504; *Larner v. LCC* [1949] 2 K.B. 683; *Lloyds Bank Ltd v. Brooks* (1950) Legal Decisions Affecting Bankers 161; *Lloyds Bank Ltd v. Jiwani* [1976] 1 W.L.R. 964; *Avon County Council v. Howlett* [1983] 1 W.L.R. 605.

[17] For a fuller discussion see Paget, p. 367 *et seq.* and Goff & Jones.

funds, or that the drawer's signature is genuine.[18] A representation may of course be made expressly or impliedly in response to a specific request.[19] As between a bank and its own customer, on the other hand, it is usually relatively easy to identify a representation arising from account statements or a confirmation of balances.

The mere fact that money has been spent is not a detriment so as to preclude **32–11** its recovery, but it will be inequitable to require repayment if the defendant has changed his mode of living in reliance on the availability of funds.[20] More usually the defendant will seek to point to a specific item of expenditure or transaction entered into on the faith of receipt of the moneys, and in each case it is a question of fact whether the elements of an estoppel are shown.

In *Avon County Council v. Howlett*[21] it was held that if the defendant can **32–12** establish an estoppel this generally operates as a complete defence and not *pro tanto*, but this must now be read subject to the authorities considered in the next section.

Estoppel and Change of Position

In *Lipkin Gorman v. Karpnale* the House of Lords did not attempt to define **32–13** or limit the scope of the general defence that the defendant has changed his position in good faith. The relationship between that principle and the general restitutionary defence was addressed in *National Westminster Bank plc v. Somer International (UK) Ltd*.[22] The bank had, by mistake, credited the company's account with US$ 76,708 intended for another beneficiary. They advised the company that a dollar payment it was expecting had been received, and the company despatched goods to an aggregate value of about £13,000 in the belief that the payment represented a reduction on the trading account with its customer. When the bank discovered the mistake and claimed to be entitled to debit the account, the company argued that as it had relied to its detriment (by despatching the goods)[23] the bank was estopped from disputing the payment, and furthermore that such an estoppel operated as a rule of evidence, and could not be applied *pro tanto*.[24]

The Court of Appeal, following the decision in *Scottish Equitable v.* **32–14** *Derby*,[25] held that, though the defences of estoppel and change of position remain distinct, it was open to the Judge to have concluded that it would be unconscionable for the company to retain the moneys over and above the extent of its detriment where there was such a disproportion between the amounts. Robert Walker L.J. in the Scottish Equitable case expressed approval in principle of the argument that since the claim to recovery was subject to the

[18] See *National Westminster Bank Ltd v. Barclays Bank International Ltd* [1975] Q.B. 654.
[19] Consider *Midland Bank plc v. Brown Shipley & Co. Ltd* [1991] 1 Lloyds Rep. 576.
[20] See *Skyring v. Greenwood* and *Holt v. Markham*. See also the discussion in the *Somer* case (below); it would appear that reflecting the difficulty in such cases of identifying specific expenditure or detriment the courts take a more general attitude to proof of detriment.
[21] [1983] 1 W.L.R. 605.
[22] [2001] E.W.C.A. Civ. 970.
[23] A further alleged detriment was not established on the evidence.
[24] *Avon County Council v. Howlett* [1983] 1 W.L.R. 605.
[25] [2000] 3 All E.R. 793 (Harrison J.) and [2001] 3 All E.R. 818 (Court of Appeal).

general defence of bona fide change of position, it would not be inequitable to require restoration of the balance, and hence no estoppel should arise. Nonetheless, on the present authorities, the decisions in both cases rested on the narrower ground that the case fell within the dicta in *Avon County Council v. Howlett* that even under the established principles of estoppel there might be cases where it was unconscionable for the defendant to seek to rely upon it to the full extent of the sum paid.[26]

The Rule in *Cocks v. Masterman*[27]

32–15   There is a line of authority apparently advancing a further, or at least more generous, defence on the part of the recipient of moneys paid upon a negotiable instrument.

32–16   In *Cocks v. Masterman* the Plaintiff bankers had paid a bill against the forged acceptance of their customer, in ignorance of the forgery which they did not discover until the following day. They reclaimed the amount of the bill from the holder's bankers, but failed. The judgment of the Court was given by Bayley J., who said:

> " . . . we are all of opinion that the holder of a bill is entitled to know, on the day when it becomes due, whether it is an honoured or dishonoured bill, and that, if he receive the money and is suffered to retain it during the whole of that day, the parties who paid it cannot recover it back. The holder, indeed, is not bound by law (if the bill be dishonoured by the acceptor) to take any steps against the other parities to the bill till the day after it is dishonoured. But he is entitled so to do, if he thinks fit, and the parties who pay the bill ought not by their negligence to deprive the holder of any right or privilege. If we were to hold that the Plaintiffs were entitled to recover, it would be in effect saying that the plaintiffs might deprive the holder of a bill of his right to take steps against the parties to the bill on the day when it becomes due."

32–17   The principle was re-stated in wider terms by Mathew J. in *London and River Plate Bank v. Bank of Liverpool*[28] " . . . that when a bill becomes due and is presented for payment the holder ought to know at once whether the bill is going to be paid or not. If the mistake is discovered at once, it may be the money can be recovered back; but if it be not, and the money is paid in good faith, and is received in good faith, and there is an interval of time in which the position of the holder may be altered, the principle seems to apply that money once paid cannot be recovered back." The judgment continues with two strands of reasoning: first, the commercial importance that the holder of a bill should know promptly its fate, and second that "in such a case it is manifest that the position of a man of business may be most seriously compromised even by the delay of a day".

---

[26] As the Court noted, until re-considered by the House of Lords the defences will remain distinctly available in principle (see in contrast dicta of Jonathan Parker J. in *Philip Collins v. Davis* [2000] 3 All E.R. 808). In practice, the decision appears to put the matter very much on the same basis, and the comments in the cases give a very clear indication of the likely development of the law.

[27] 9 B. & C. 902.

[28] [1896] 1 Q.B. 7.

It is suggested that there are two different principles embodied in these **32–18** passages. The first is that a decision on payment must be taken promptly, and that once taken is irrevocable: the holder of a valid bill is entitled to know its fate.[29] That proposition is uncontroversial, but it is not the point at issue where what is claimed is the recovery of a payment on the grounds that the decision to pay was mistaken. The second proposition is no more than the application of the conventional estoppel rules, where in the context of negotiable instruments detrimental reliance can be immediately identified[30] from the loss of the opportunity to take the ordinary steps consequent on dishonour.[31]

On that basis, the supposed rule has been more often distinguished than **32–19** applied. It has been held not to apply in the case of a forged bank note.[32] It was held not to apply to a cheque the amount of which had been fraudulently increased where there were no indorsers to whom notice should be given,[33] and similarly of no application to a simple forged cheque.[34] In *Barclays Bank v. Simms* it was held not to apply since, payment having been countermanded, notice of dishonour was dispensed with.

In the same case Goff J. observed of this rule that "It is not merely **32–20** stringent, but very technical. It is possible that if, in due course, full recognition is accorded to the defence of change of position, there will be no further need for any such stringent rule and the law can be reformulated on a more rational and less technical basis." If the rule remains of any vestigial relevance, it appears to amount to no more than this: where there are one or more indorsers who may (notwithstanding the grounds for alleged avoidance of the payment) be liable on the bill, prima facie there will be a detriment capable of supporting an estoppel arising from the inability to give prompt notice of dishonour.[35]

Payments discharging an obligation

It is well settled that a payment is not recoverable if it has been received in **32–21** good faith and in discharge of a debt. In addition to "proposition 2(b)" as stated by Goff J. and set out above, the proposition has recently been confirmed by the Court of Appeal in terms in *Lloyds Bank plc v. Independent Insurance Co. Ltd.*[36]

Two different sorts of issue may arise. First, whether there was in fact an **32–22** obligation to be discharged. Second, whether, assuming there was a debt, the

---

[29] The commercial effect of this is embodied in the rules and practice governing presentation and payment of cheques, see above, paras 21–74 to 21–75.

[30] And perhaps, more favourably to the holder in such a case presumed without evidence.

[31] This was the view expressed by Robert Goff J. in *Barclays v. Simms* (above) at 701.

[32] *Leeds and County Bank Ltd v. Walker* (1883) 11 Q.B.D. 84.

[33] *Imperial Bank of Canada v. Bank of Hamilton* [1903] A.C. 49, PC.

[34] *National Westminster Bank Ltd v. Barclays Bank International Ltd* [1975] Q.B. 677.

[35] Chalmers & Guest point out (para. 1561) that even in such a case, the circumstances would appear to amount to a good excuse for delay in giving notice of dishonour (s.50(1)), in which case it would remain for the recipient to demonstrate that he had in fact been prejudiced. In *Barclays v. Simms* Goff J. rejected (at 702) a different argument, that no dishonour took place until the money was reclaimed.

[36] [2000] 1 Q.B. 110, discussed further below. See also *Kerrison v. Glyn Mills Currie & Co.* 81 L.J.K.B. 465, *Kleinwort Benson v. Lincoln C.C.* [1999] 2 A.C. 349 at 407 and the discussion in Goff & Jones at p. 204ff.

payment sought to be recovered was for some other reason ineffective to discharge it. The latter question is discussed below, under "Payments by banks".

32–23   In the former case, it is clear that it is open to the party seeking to recover the moneys paid to show that the transaction pursuant to which they were ostensibly due was unenforceable or liable to be set aside.[37]

R. E. Jones Ltd v. Waring & Gillow Ltd[38]

32–24   This was an action by the drawer of a cheque to recover its proceeds from the payee. A man named Bodenham was indebted to Waring & Gillow. By a series of wholly fraudulent representations he induced R.E Jones Limited to draw two cheques totalling £5,000 in favour of Waring & Gillow which he delivered to them purportedly in settlement of his liability. The cheques were subsequently replaced by a single cheque for that sum, sent directly by post between them. Though two members of the House considered that there was a defence on the basis of estoppel, all were agreed that subject to any available defences, the moneys were repayable. It was argued on behalf of Waring & Gillow that they were holders in due course, that consequently their title as holders of the cheque was indefeasible, and therefore that the moneys could not be reclaimed. This argument failed because under the Act the original payee of an instrument is not a "holder in due course".[39]

32–25   In that case, Lord Sumner observed that "It is not necessary to decide whether Waring & Gillow Ltd could have sued on the cheque as holders in due course, since the cheque was paid . . . It seems to me further that even if Waring & Gillow Ltd could have sued Jones Ltd to judgment on the cheque for 500l, this would not conclude the matter, unless it were also held that no cross-action for money had and received would also lie, which I am not prepared now to say."[40]

32–26   It is a startling, and unsatisfactory, proposition that a party may on the one hand be fully entitled to enforce payment of an unpaid instrument, and yet on the other obliged immediately to restore the proceeds as money paid under a mistake.[41] This result, if it is right, is particularly at odds with the considerations of commercial certainty and finality, which can be found in dicta throughout the cases. More fundamentally, it offends against common sense. It is suggested that despite the dictum above, this does not represent the law.

32–27   When a cheque or bill is given in satisfaction of an underlying obligation, that generally operates as a discharge of the obligation, subject to the condition subsequent that the bill be paid.[42] Unless the bill is dishonoured, the

---

[37] See *Barclays v. Simms* at 695 "footnote c".

[38] [1926] A.C. 670. The case is widely cited for determining that under the 1882 Act the original payee of an instrument is not a holder in due course (see Ch. 18 below).

[39] It is unfortunate that emphasis upon the statutory definition seems to have obscured the real issue posed by the defence, which is whether (irrespective of their statutory designation) Waring & Gillow were entitled to say that they received the moneys in discharge of a debt.

[40] At 695.

[41] Albeit this is the view expressed in Chalmers & Guest at para. 1049.

[42] See the cases cited at paras 29–29 and 31–02 above.

obligation is replaced by the undertaking embodied in the bill. That undertaking is in turn discharged by payment of the bill (or in the other circumstances described in this chapter). If the bill was binding on and enforceable against the payer, then the moneys will have been paid over in discharge of a real obligation[43] and will not be recoverable.

It is suggested that despite the dicta, this accords with the reasoning and the result in *Jones v. Waring & Gillow*. All members of the house started from the premise that the payment was prima facie recoverable. Though less clearly stated than it might be, this was on the basis that Waring & Gillow had given no consideration.[44] They were treated, as far as the payment was concerned, as volunteers as against Jones, which indeed they were. The antecedent debt of *Bodenham* could not, without more, amount to good consideration for Jones Ltd's promise to Waring & Gillow,[45] and they would accordingly have been able to defend any claim brought on it. **32–28**

Payments made by banks

In practice, almost all payments are made by or through the agency of banks on behalf of their customers. If the payment instruction is genuine and within the mandate the bank is entitled to debit its customer's account; it is for all practical purposes the customer's money which is paid and any claim for its recovery (on the ground of mistake or otherwise) must be brought by the customer. **32–29**

Different considerations arise where the relevant mistake is not that of the customer, but the bank itself, or when an issue arises between the bank and its customer as to its entitlement to debit the latter's account. Those issues are inextricably linked with the question whether the payment is effective to discharge an underlying debt on the part of the customer.[46] **32–30**

The "*Liggett* Defence"

In *B. Liggett (Liverpool) Ltd v. Barclays Bank Ltd*[47] an action was brought by the company against the bank reclaiming the amount of various cheques that had been paid and debited to its account. The circumstances in which the cheques were drawn varied, but materially though they were all drawn at the instigation of a director of the company, all failed to comply with the terms of the company's mandate. Wright J. held that the bank was (in principle) entitled to set up the fact that the proceeds of the cheques had been paid to **32–31**

---

[43] This pre-supposes that the bill is genuine, and not a forgery or one which has been destroyed by material alteration (Ch. 20 above), but no difficulty arises for present purposes in the latter case since there is no question of liability on such a (non) bill.

[44] Lord Sumner (at 691) noted that the earlier cheques were not consideration for their replacement, and that "*they issued [*the cheque*] to discharge their obligation, and there being no obligation in fact*", Lord Carson (at 700) distinguished *Watson v. Russell*, 3 B. & S. 34; 5 B. & S. 968 on the basis that "*there was an existing contract upon which a sum was due*".

[45] See above, Ch. 19 "Consideration" at paras 19–13 to 19–17.

[46] See, for an illustration, the approach of Goff J. in *Barclays v. Simms* at 699, but note also the discussion below of the circumstances in which a bank might be entitled to debit its customer's account.

[47] [1928] 1 K.B. 48.

trade creditors of the company, in discharge of indebtedness, and for the purpose of purchasing stock which the company had received. He regarded this as an application of an equitable doctrine "under which a person who has in fact paid the debts of another without authority is allowed to take advantage of his payment". He derived that statement of principle from the decision in *A.L. Underwood v. Bank of Liverpool and Martins.*[48]

32–32   The decision has been the subject of much subsequent comment, and though it has been applied,[49] it was explained in *In re Cleadon Trust Ltd*[50] as being consistent only with there having been actual authority for the discharge of the customer's debts.

32–33   The principle of the *Liggett* decision is sound in cases where the payment does discharge, or comes to have the effect of, discharging the debt.[51] It does not, at least as it is now understood, assist in identifying whether the payment in fact has that effect.

Absence of authority

32–34   The clearest illustration is the case of a cheque upon which the customer's signature is simply forged, in which case there is no authority or mandate at all to make payment.[52] Any money paid over is the bank's, which (subject to any defence on the part of the payee) it is entitled to recover, it having been mistaken as to the genuineness of the cheque.[53] Since the customer did not sign the cheque there is no question of the payment discharging a liability upon it as such.[54]

32–35   Furthermore, as a general proposition, subject to any adoption or ratification of it, a payment by a stranger without authority does not discharge a debt. So in such a case, even if the practical result of the forgery is that the money ends up in the hands of a creditor, the bank is not entitled to the benefit of the payment against its customer.

32–36   In *Crantrave Ltd v. Lloyds Bank plc*[55] the Defendant bank paid the sum of £13,497.50 standing to the customer's account with it to solicitors acting for

---

[48] [1924] 1 K.B. 775. That was a claim in conversion by which the company claimed damages in the amount of various cheques indorsed and then paid into the account of its sole director. The Court of Appeal ordered an inquiry to ascertain which of various payments made with the proceeds were used to discharge the company's liabilities, with Scrutton L.J. making reference to *Bannatyne v. MacCiver* [1906] 1 K.B. 103 and *Reid v. Rigby* [1894] 2 Q.B. 40.

[49] See for example *Lloyds Bank Ltd v. Chartered Bank of India Australia and China* [1929] 1 K.B. 40, as noted in Paget p. 341.

[50] [1939] Ch. 286.

[51] See *Crantrave Ltd v. Lloyds Bank plc* [2000] Q.B. 917, discussed further below.

[52] The same result arises if payment is made on a cheque or instrument which is avoided by material alteration. See *Imperial Bank of Canada v. Bank of Hamilton* [1903] A.C. 49, PC; also *Hall v. Fuller* (1826) 5 B. & C. 750; *Colonial Bank of Australia Ltd v. Marshall* [1906] A.C. 559. This is though subject to any estoppel arising against the customer out of the "Macmillan" duty (*London Joint Stock Bank Ltd v. Macmillan* [1918] A.C. 777—see Ch. 20 above).

[53] For an illustration see *National Westminster Bank Ltd v. Barclays Bank International Ltd* (above).

[54] Unless the customer has adopted the forgery or ratified the payment, which (as explained below) is one explanation of principles referred to in the *Liggett* case.

[55] [2000] 1 Q.B. 917.

a judgment creditor who had obtained a garnishee order nisi, but not absolute, since the garnishee proceedings were stayed and the company subsequently went into liquidation. The liquidator obtained summary judgment against the Bank, who had sought to argue that since the payment, though without authority, partially satisfied a judgment debt they should be entitled to the benefit of the equity described in *Liggett*. The Court of Appeal rejected that argument, since the Bank had no authority of any sort on behalf of their customer.

Absence of funds

At the other extreme is the situation where a bank pays a cheque in the **32–37** erroneous belief that its customer has sufficient funds to meet it, or over-looking the fact that its customer does not. It is clear that in such a case the cheque operates as a request by its customer for facilities, as well as an instruction to make the payment, and that the bank, though not under any obligation to its customer to do so, makes the payment with its customer's authority and is entitled to debit the account. Similarly, it is clear in such a case that the mistake by the bank is a matter between it and its customer, and that the money is not recoverable from the payee, whose debt is discharged.[56]

The point is well illustrated by the recent case of *Lloyds Bank plc v.* **32–38** *Independent Insurance Co. Ltd.*[57] This was an attempt by the Bank to recover from Independent the proceeds of an electronic payment. The bank had been instructed to make the payment by its customer, but had done so in the erroneous belief that funds had arrived for its customer's account in an amount sufficient to cover the payment. The claim failed. It was held that notwithstanding a stipulation for its own benefit that it would honour its customer's instruction when able to do so, the bank in fact had authority to make the payment on behalf of the customer. On that basis the payment was effective to discharge the customer's debt to Independent, and could not be recovered by the bank.

Payment with authority despite mandate

The terms of the customer's mandate determine the extent of the bank's **32–39** *obligation* to honour payment instructions, but a payment which is contrary to the mandate may nonetheless in fact be authorised by the customer.[58] A payment on a bill or cheque in such circumstances would be effective to discharge it, and the customer's obligation, would be irrecoverable from the payee, but could properly be debited to the customer's account.

---

[56] See *Barclays Bank v. Simms* (above) at 700.
[57] [2000] 1 Q.B. 110.
[58] See *London Intercontinental Trust Ltd v. Barclays Bank Ltd* [1980] 1 Lloyds Rep. 241.

Adoption or ratification

32–40   Though originally made without authority, the payment may be adopted or ratified by the person on whose behalf it is purportedly made, and so be effective to discharge the debt.[59]

Apparent authority

32–41   It is difficult to think of a clearer representation of the authority of an agent to pay a debt than drawing a cheque upon a bank and delivering it to the creditor.[60] Nonetheless, such apparent authority was insufficient in *Barclays Bank v. Simms* for the payment to operate as a discharge of liability.[61] In *Lloyds Bank v. Independent Insurance*[62] Waller L.J. expressed the view, *obiter*, that apparent authority would not have been sufficient for the payment to have discharged the debt. Accordingly, on the present state of the authorities it would seem that a payment which is made by the bank apparently within its authority from its customer, but in fact contrary to a countermand or in excess of its actual authority, is not effective to discharge the customer's liability on the cheque, and may be recovered from the payee.[63]

32–42   If that is the position, it is a result which can be criticised, particularly in the case of payment of a cheque or bill in the hands of the payee or, *a fortiori*, a holder in due course.[64] The analogy drawn by Goff J. in *Barclays v. Simms* between the absence of authority in the case of forgery and its absence following countermand is not complete; in the former case no question of apparent authority arises,[65] nor is there any underlying obligation. capable of discharge. In the latter there is a debt upon the bill, to which there is (*ex*

---

[59] See Crantrave, above. This is in part at least a possible explanation for the result in *Liggett*. If the customer conducts himself towards the creditor so as to take advantage of the payments, he could not complain against the bank about them. Though a forgery may not be ratified, it can be adopted, and the payment by the bank (even if made on a forged cheque) would be capable of ratification.

[60] For an apparently contrary view see Goff & Jones, p. 210, and also the observations of Waller L.J. in *Lloyds Bank v. Independent Insurance* at 122. The drawer of a cheque warrants that the bank will pay it. He must represent that the bank is authorised by him to do so, and that is a continuing representation. It is submitted that normally the recipient of a cheque (*a fortiori* its proceeds) assumes that, if and when paid, the payment is made in accordance with the cheque and on behalf of the drawer (and not on behalf of the bank or someone else entitled to ask for it back). He may not consciously advert to the question in terms of authority, but that is implicit in the assumption which he does make: that the payment discharges the debt and the money becomes his to keep.

[61] Though the point was not, apparently, argued in terms before the Judge.

[62] [2000] 1 Q.B. 110 at 121–123. The reasoning was based on the origin of ostensible authority in the law of estoppel. While the customer might have been estopped from disputing the bank's authority against Independent, it did not follow that the bank were, or that Independent would have been precluded from asserting against the customer that it had not been paid; if on the facts Independent were not entitled to claim from their original debtor, then a defence of change of position would be available.

[63] The point does not seem to have been clearly decided. In *Crantrave* (above) May L.J. distinuished the *Liggett* case on the grounds that there was no actual or "purported authority".

[64] See Goff & Jones at pp. 210–211 for a discussion of the various arguments and a defence of the decision.

[65] See above Ch. 20 at para. 20–32 and n. 5.

hypothesi) no defence on the part of the drawer.[66] If the holder presents a valid cheque for payment, and is paid what he is owed by the person on whom it is drawn, it might be thought that he should be entitled to keep the money.[67] If that were the result,[68] it would be left to the bank to seek reimbursement from its customer on the grounds of *Liggett*, and the customer to dispute that, or claim damages for any loss which he could show he had in fact suffered.

[66] If it could be shown that the cheque or bill was itself unenforceable, then payment could be recovered in any event, see above. Conversely, Goff & Jones' comment (p. 211, n. 48) that if the bank were (as other systems provide) subrogated to the payee's rights, that would "render the drawer liable as if he had not stopped the cheque", but the whole point is that the drawer *is liable*: it is his countermand which (as against the payee) is wrongful. Procedurally the resolution of those questions in proceedings to which, if necessary all three parties (drawer, payee, bank) are parties is no more cumbersome than in the separate actions envisaged by Goff J. in *Simms* (at 703), indeed it would be better that all issues be determined together.

[67] Suppose, conversely, the money is recoverable but the payee can make out a defence of change of position as to part. Is the debt of the drawer discharged *pro tanto*? Can the bank rely on that partial discharge to debit its customer's account? Can the payee sue the customer for part of the balance of the cheque?

[68] Which would be consistent with the importance placed elsewhere upon commercial certainty. There is moreover one additional argument arising from the operation of the Act. The drawer "engages" that a cheque will be paid on presentment (s.55). If it is presented and paid, that promise is in fact met, and the bill is discharged (s.59, which requires that the payment should be by or on behalf of the drawee, not the drawer). Whether as between the drawer and his bank the payment is authorised is on the face of it irrelevant.

CHAPTER 33

THE LAW OF PRINCIPAL AND SURETY IN ITS APPLI-
CATION TO BILLS AND NOTES[1]

Introduction

33–01   A party liable on a bill is said sometimes to bear to the holder the relation of principal debtor, sometimes of surety only. But in *Re Conley*[2] Lord Greene M.R. refuted this:

> " . . . in the case of a bill accepted for value the relationship between drawer and indorsers on the one hand and the acceptor on the other is referred to as one of suretyship by Cockburn C.J. and Lush and Quain JJ. in *Rouquette v. Overmann*.[3] We have the authority of the House of Lords for saying that the relationship is not one of suretyship though it is analogous thereto; *Duncan Fox v. North and South Wales Bank*."[4]

In this chapter, therefore, the term "surety" is used in the text in the sense in which Lord Greene used it, *i.e.* that it does not of necessity entail the assumption of personal liability by the "surety".

It is a general rule of law that a discharge of the principal is a discharge to the surety, for the engagement of the surety, being but an accessory to the principal's agreement, terminates with it. The effect of a discharge or indulgence by the holder to parties liable on a negotiable instrument may be considered as follows: what parties to a bill or note are principals, and what parties are sureties; what conduct of the holder will discharge the surety; how the discharge of the surety may be prevented; how it may be waived; what conduct of the creditor to the surety will discharge the principal debtor; what are the rights of sureties?

Principal or surety

33–02   "Suppose the bill to have been accepted and indorsed for value. The acceptor is the principal debtor, and all the other parties are sureties for him, liable only on his default. But though all the other parties are, in respect of the acceptor, sureties only, they are not, as between themselves, merely co-sureties, but each prior party is a principal in respect of each subsequent party. For example, suppose a bill to have been accepted by the drawee, and

---

[1] See, in general, *Rowlatt on Principal and Surety* (5th ed., 1999).
[2] [1938] 2 All E.R. 127, 131.
[3] (1875) L.R. 10 Q.B. 525.
[4] (1880) 6 App.Cas. 1, *per* Lord Selborne at 11, 13, 14 (quoting Lord Eldon L.C. in *Ex parte Younge*, 3 V. & B. 40) and Lord Blackburn at 19.

afterwards indorsed by the drawer and by two subsequent indorsers to the holder. As between the holder and the acceptor, the acceptor is the principal debtor and drawer and indorsers are his sureties. But as between the holder and the drawer, the drawer is a principal debtor, and the subsequent indorsers are his sureties. As between the holder and the second indorser, the second indorser is the principal, and the subsequent, or third, indorser is his surety."[5] A discharge, therefore, to the prior parties, the principals, is a discharge to the subsequent parties, the sureties; but a discharge to the subsequent parties, the sureties, is not a discharge to the prior parties, the principals.

Where a bill is payable to the order of a third person, the payee is a subsequent party, and so a surety for the drawer. He stands in the same situation as the first indorsee and the second indorser of a bill drawn payable to the indorser's order.[6]

It follows, therefore, that a discharge to the acceptor is a discharge to all the parties to the bill for, if it were not so, either they could sue the acceptor or they could not. If they could, the discharge to the acceptor would be frustrated; if not, the parties must pay the bill without a remedy over, which would extend their liability beyond their contract. Similarly a discharge to an indorser is no discharge of the prior indorsers, for they have no remedy against the discharged indorser; but it is a discharge of the subsequent indorsers, for if the holder could notwithstanding recover against them, and they could recover against the prior discharged indorser, his discharge would be frustrated; if they could not, they must pay the bill without a remedy over. A security given by the drawer cannot discharge the acceptor whose liability is prior to that of the drawer.[7]

Accommodation bills

It was formerly held that where a bill was accepted without consideration for the accommodation of the drawer, the drawer was to be considered the principal debtor, and the acceptor as his surety; and, therefore, that time given to the drawer by a holder with knowledge of the accommodation acceptance would discharge the acceptor,[8] but time given to the acceptor would not discharge the drawer.[9] But this distinction was afterwards overruled at law, the acceptor, in all cases of accommodation bills as well as others, being considered as the principal debtor. though the holder, at the time of making the agreement, or even of taking the bill, knew the acceptance to have been

33–03

---

[5] This passage from Byles, 11th ed., was cited with approval by Brett L.J. in *Horne v. Rouquette* (1878) 3 Q.B.D. 514, 518. An indorser who has paid a bill is entitled to the indemnity of the acceptor (*Duncan Fox & Co. v. North & South Wales Bank* (1880) 6 App.Cas. 1).

[6] *Claridge v. Dalton* (1815) 4 M. & S. 226, which decided that time given to an indorsee by the payee does not discharge the drawer who, having no effect in the hands of the drawee is not discharged by want of notice of dishonour. Le Blanc J. regretted that the rule in *Bickerdike v. Bollman*, 1 T.R. 405 for dispensing with notice was ever introduced.

[7] *Smith v. Knox* (1800) 3 Esp. 46, 47; *Claridge v. Dalton, supra; Hall v. Cole* (1836) 6 Nev. & M. 124 in which the plaintiff had given time to a party prior to the defendant who was accordingly discharged.

[8] *Laxton v. Peat* (1809) 2 Camp. 185.

[9] *Collott v. Haigh* (1812) 3 Camp. 281.

without value.[10] It was otherwise in equity where the holder had notice[11] and the equitable doctrine was available under an equitable plea.[12] and it is now beyond dispute that a holder, whether he has knowledge or not of the accommodation acceptance or making at the time he takes the instrument, discharges the accommodation party, if, after knowledge of his true character as a party to the instrument and of the real principal, he gives indulgence to the latter.[13]

The maker of an accommodation note, similarly, is a surety.[14]

Joint and several note

33–04   Although the rule was otherwise at common law, it is now indisputable that if of two parties to a joint and several note one is in fact a surety,[15] any indulgency given by the creditor after knowledge of the position to the real principal will discharge the surety in accordance with the established principles of equity.[16] It has further been laid down that if persons contract originally as principals, but afterwards by arrangement *inter se* one becomes a surety as between himself and the other, the creditor, after notice thereof, will discharge the surety by giving time to or releasing the other.[17] Where a note is indorsed by two persons as co-sureties for the maker, their rights *inter se* are to be regulated by reference to the rights of co-sureties.[18]

Discharge of surety by conduct of creditor

33–05   Whilst a contract of suretyship is not a contract *uberrimae fidei*, a creditor is under a duty to disclose to the surety arrangements made between the principal debtor and the creditor which make the terms of the principal

---

[10] *Fentum v. Pocock* (1813) 5 Taunt. 192; see also *Harrison v. Courtauld* (1832) 3 B. & Ad. 36; *Price v. Edmunds* (1830) 10 B. & C. 578; it is otherwise where the holder on taking the instrument agreed to treat the accommodation party as surety (*Manley v. Boycot* (1853) 2 E. & B. 46 and *Bellingham v. Hurley The Times*, April 4, 1908, CA).

[11] *Davies v. Stainbank* (1855) 6 De G.M. & G. 679.

[12] *Pooley v. Harradine* (1857) 7 E. & B. 431; *Greenough v. M'Celland* (1860) 30 L.J.Q.B. 15.

[13] *Overend, Gurney & Co. v. Oriental Finance Co.* (1874) L.R. 7 H.L. 348.

[14] *Bechervaise v. Lewis* (1872) L.R. 7 C.P. 372.

[15] Whether two parties to an instrument are principals or principal and surety depends on the facts (*Mutual Loan Association v. Sudlow* (1858) 5 C.B. (N.S.) 449, 453 (Byles J.), applied in *Wauthier v. Wilson* (1912) 28 T.L.R. 239, CA).

[16] *Pooley v. Harradine* (1857) 7 E. & B. 431; *Greenough v. M'Celland* (1860) 30 L.J.Q.B. 15. From the decision in *Overend, Gurney & Co. v. Oriental Finance Co.* (1874) L.R. 7 H.L. 348 it is clear that the doubt expressed in *Pooley v. Harradine, supra*, is set at rest, and the equity arises in favour of the surety from the moment the creditor has notice of the relation, whether he had it when he became holder of the instrument or not (see *Overend, Gurney & Co. v. Oriental Finance Co., supra*, at 354, 360 (Lord Cairns C.)). As to the nature of the equity not depending on any contract with the creditor varying the written instrument, but on his knowledge of the true relation of the joint debtors rendering it inequitable for him to prejudice the rights of the surety, see generally, *Pooley v. Harradine, supra; cf.* also *Leicestershire Banking Co. v. Hawkins* (1900) 16 T.L.R. 317.

[17] *Rouse v. Bradford Banking Co.* [1894] A.C. 586, 591; *Goldfarb v. Bartlett* [1920] 1 K.B. 639; *Schwartz v. Bielschowsky* (1911) 21 Man. 310; but dealings prior to such notice will not discharge the surety: *Royal Bank of Canada v. Wagstaffe* (1919) 46 O.L.R. 372.

[18] *Macdonald v. Whitfield* (1883) 8 App.Cas. 733 (P.C.).

contract something materially different, in a potentially disadvantageous respect, from those which the surety might expect.[19] Concealment from the surety of any material stipulation in the original contract releases the surety.[20] Similarly the surety is discharged if the actual original contract between the creditor and the principal debtor varies in the slightest degree from that for which the surety had stipulated.[21] So, in all transactions subsequent to the original contract, the surety's remedies, both at law and in equity, against the principal debtor, whether in his own name or in the name of the creditor, must be preserved intact by the creditor.[22]

The holder of a bill of exchange is not obliged to use active diligence in **33–06** order to recover against the acceptor,[23] in the absence of any agreement to do so.[24] He may defer suing him subject to any time limitation, he may even promise not to press him, or not to sue him, if the promise is not binding in law. Thus, where the executrix of an acceptor verbally promised to pay the holder out of her own estate, provided that he would forbear to sue, and he forbore accordingly, it was held that, the agreement being invalid under the Statute of Frauds,[25] the drawer was not discharged.[26] But if the holder once destroys or suspends, or, by a binding agreement with the acceptor,[27] contracts to destroy or suspend his right of action against the acceptor, the drawer and indorsers are at once discharged, unless the agreement giving time contains a stipulation that the holder shall, in case of default, have judgment at a period as early as he could have obtained judgment if hostile proceedings had continued.[28] But if the agreement contained a stipulation that a judgment should be given, it was not necessary to aver in a plea disclosing such an agreement that the time within which the plaintiff might have obtained judgment was postponed.[29]

If the creditor engages with the surety that he will enforce payment from the principal debtor within a certain time, his neglect to do so is a good defence in equity.[30]

---

[19] *Levett v. Barclays Bank plc* [1995] 1 W.L.R. 1260.

[20] *Pidcock v. Bishop* (1825) 3 B. & C. 605; *Stone v. Compton* (1838) 5 Bing. N.C. 142; *Brown v. Wilkinson* (1844) 13 M. & W. 14.

[21] See *Bonser v. Cox* (1843) 6 Beav. 110; *Polak v. Everett* (1876) 1 Q.B.D. 669; *Croydon Gas Co. v. Dickinson* (1876) 2 C.P.D. 46; *cf.* also *Holme v. Brunskill* (1877) 3 Q.B.D. 495 and *National Bank of Nigeria Ltd v. Awolesi* [1964] 1 W.L.R. 1311.

[22] As to the duty of the creditor, see *Watts v. Shuttleworth* (1860) 5 H. & N. 235, affirmed on appeal (1861) 7 H. & N. 353; *Wulff v. Jay* (1872) L.R. 7 Q.B. 756; *Rainbow v. Juggins* (1880) 5 Q.B.D. 422, CA.

[23] *cf. Orme v. Young* (1815) Holt N.P. 84; *Eyre v. Everett* (1826) 2 Russ. 381; *Trent Navigation v. Harley* (1808) 10 East. 34.

[24] *Bank of Ireland v. Beresford* (1818) 6 Dow H.L. 233, 239.

[25] 29 Car. 2, c. 3.

[26] *Philpot v. Briant* (1828) 4 Bing. 717.

[27] *Moss v. Hall* (1850) 5 Ex. 46. But an agreement with a stranger will not have this effect (*Fraser v. Jordan* (1857) 26 L.J.Q.B. 288; *Lyon v. Holt* (1839) 5 M. & W. 250); see also *Royal Bank of Canada v. Wagstaffe* (1919) 46 O.L.R. 372.

[28] *Kennard v. Knott* (1842) 4 M. & G. 474; *Michael v. Myers* (1843) 6 M. & G. 702. Receipt of interest in advance is not necessarily a giving of time (*Rayner v. Fussey* (1859) 28 L.J. Exch. 132).

[29] *Kennard v. Knott, supra; Issac v. Daniel* (1846) 15 L.J.Q.B. 149; *Moss v. Hall, supra.*

[30] *Lawrence v. Walmsley* (1862) 31 L.J.C.P. 143; *Watson v. Alcock* (1853) 22 L.J.Ch. 858.

33–07   Payment by the principal discharges the surety; but payment of money, which has to be refunded as being a fraudulent preference, is no payment so as to discharge a surety.[31]

The acceptor of a bill, or maker of a note, is bound to pay on the day the bill or note falls due, and therefore he cannot plead in his own discharge a subsequent tender.[32] But a drawer or indorser is not bound to pay till notice and request; though he is not entitled to a reasonable time thereafter within which to pay, yet a plea of tender after the bill be due, but before action commenced, may be good if pleaded by a drawer or indorser.[33] Therefore payment with interest, or tender thereof, by the acceptor or maker, though after the bill or note has been dishonoured, but before action brought against the drawer or indorser, will, it seems, discharge the latter parties, though it will not discharge the acceptor or maker.

A release to the acceptor or maker discharges the indorsers; and a release of one of several acceptors jointly liable, or of one of several makers jointly and severally liable, is a release of all.[34] If, however, it appears on the face of the deed that it was the paramount intention of the parties that the others should be held liable, this intention will be carried into effect by disregarding the form of the deed and construing the release as a covenant not to sue.[35]

The sureties are discharged by a general covenant not to sue, for that will enure as a release,[36] unless it is qualified by a reserve of remedies against the surety[37] or by a covenant not to sue within a particular time,[38] though it does not in law amount to a release,[39] or suspend the action.[40]

A written or verbal agreement, on good consideration, not to sue the acceptor at all, or not to sue him within a specified time, discharges the drawer and indorsers[41] but if such agreement is without consideration, or not made with the principal or otherwise void, the indorsers are not discharged.[42] Giving time to an apparent surety, who is really the principal, will discharge the acceptor, who, though apparently the principal, is only the surety to the

---

[31] *Pritchard v. Hitchcock* (1843) 6 M. & G. 151; *Petty v. Cooke* (1871) L.R. 6 Q.B. 790.

[32] *Hume v. Peplow* (1870) 8 East 168.

[33] *Siggers v. Lewis* (1834) 1 Cr. M. & R. 370, explaining *Walker v. Barnes* (1813) 5 Taunt. 240; *Soward v. Palmer* (1818) 8 Taunt. 277.

[34] See *Jenkins v. Jenkins* [1928] 2 K.B. 501 and *ante*, para. 14–07.

[35] *Henderson v. Stobart* (1850) 5 Exch. 99; *Prince v. Barker* (1855) 4 E. & B. 760.

[36] *Ayliff v. Scrimsheire* (1688) 1 Show. 46.

[37] *Price v. Barker, supra.* Where a release contains a proviso reserving the rights of the creditor against the surety, the instrument, by the very force of the proviso, is prevented from being a release and is cut down to a convenant not to sue (Rowlatt, *Principal and Surety* (4th ed., 1982), p. 170).

[38] Formerly at law a parol agreement by the creditor not to sue was no discharge to the surety of a liability contracted by deed (*Davey v. Prendergrass* (1821) 5 B. & Ald. 187); but it was otherwise in equity (*Rees v. Berrington* (1795) 2 Ves. 540), and the equitable principle would now prevail.

[39] *Ayliff v. Scrimsheire, supra.*

[40] There must, however, be an actual legal discharge of the principal debtor, not a mere intention or contemplation of releasing him (Rowlatt, *op. cit.*, p. 178).

[41] *Moss v. Hall* (1850) 5 Ex. 46; the court will not estimate the value of the consideration (*ibid.* at 49).

[42] *Arundel Bank v. Goble*, K.B. 1817; Chitty, 11th ed., p. 300, approved in *Philpot v. Briant* (1828) 4 Bing. 717; *Clarke v. Birley* (1888) 41 Ch.D. 422. Where the written agreement expressly reserves rights against the surety, or the surety assents to the indulgence, see *post*, para. 33–09.

knowledge of the creditor.[43] So also an acceptor, who is only a surety to the knowledge of the holder, may be discharged by the release of the drawer of a bill of earlier date to procure a renewal of which, or similar indulgence, the later acceptance has been given.[44]

The taking of a new bill from the acceptor, payable at a future day, discharges the indorsers.[45]

Misappropriation or misusing, or losing any security for the debt held by the creditor, discharges the surety.[46]

Where the creditor was unable to recover against the principal debtor on account of a set-off existing between them, the surety could plead the set-off by way of equitable defence on the ground that as soon as the surety's obligation is absolute he has the right in equity to be exonerated by his principal.[47]

Giving indulgence to a principal does not discharge a surety after judgment obtained against the latter.[48]

Part payment by the principal or by the surety will only discharge the surety[49] *pro tanto*.

A mere offer to give time to the acceptor not acted upon will not discharge the drawer.[50]

The taking of a judgment by consent or judge's order from the acceptor, though payable by instalments, will not discharge the indorsers, provided that the last instalment is not postponed beyond the period when, in the ordinary course of the action, judgment and execution might have been had.[51] But the instrument must be executed with the statutory formalities.[52]

The obtaining of a judgment against any one party, without satisfaction, is no discharge for any other party.[53]

If the acceptor becomes bankrupt, the holder may prove and receive a dividend without prejudice to his remedies against other parties, for the acceptor is, in case of bankruptcy, discharged, not by the act of the holder, but by act of law.[54]

---

[43] *Overend, Gurney v. Oriental Finance Co.* (1874) L.R. 7 H.L. 348. s.28, though making the accommodation party liable to a holder for value with notice, does not appear to conflict with the principle established by this decision.

[44] See *Ex.p. Webster* (1847) De G. 414; 11 Jur. 175.

[45] *Gould v. Robson* (1807) 8 East 576; *English v. Darley* (1800) 2 B. & P. 61; *Goldfarb v. Barlett* [1920] 1 K.B. 639.

[46] *Pearl v. Deacon* (1857) 26 L.J.Ch. 761; *Wulff v. Jay* (1872) L.R. 7 Q.B. 756.

[47] *Bechervaise v. Lewis* (1872) L.R. 7 C.P. 372.

[48] *Pole v. Ford* (1816) 2 Chit. 125; *Bray v. Manson* (1841) 8 M. & W. 668; *Jenkins v. Robertson* (1854) 23 L.J.Ch. 816; *Butcher & Sons v. Woods* (1891) 12 Natal L.R. 358.

[49] *Walwyn v. St. Quintin* (1797) 1 B. & P. 652.

[50] *Hewet v. Goodrick* (1826) 2 C. & P. 468; *Badnall v. Samuel* (1817) 3 Price 521.

[51] *Jay v. Warren* (1824) 1 C. & P. 532; and see *Lee v. Levy* (1825) B. & C. 390; *Hulme v. Coles* (1872) 2 Sim. 12; *Price v. Edmunds* (1830) 10 B. & C. 578; *Whitfield v. Hodges* (1836) 1 M. & W. 679; *Kennard v. Knott* (1842) 4 M. & G. 474.

[52] *Watson v. Alcock* (1853) 22 L.J.Ch. 858.

[53] *Claxton v. Swift* (1685) 2 Show. 481; Ord. 16, r. 8/6.

[54] *cf. Ex p. Jacobs* (1875) L.R. 10 Ch. 211, 213. A surety for a bankrupt was held not to be discharged by the creditor's signing the bankrupt's certificate even after notice from the surety not to do so (*Browne v. Carr* (1831) 7 Bing. 508); see also *Langdale v. Parry* (1823) 2 D. & R. 337.

Second bill as collateral security

33–08   Though the taking of a fresh bill from the acceptor in lieu of the dishonoured bill discharges the other parties, it will not have that effect if the
second bill or second security, whatever it be, was given as a collateral
security.[55] Where, a bill having been dishonoured, the acceptor transmitted a
new bill for a larger amount to the payee, but had not any communication with
him respecting the first, and the payee discounted the second bill and indorsed
the first to the plaintiff, it was held that the second bill was merely a collateral
security and that the receipt of it by the payee did not amount to giving time
to the acceptor of the first bill, so as to exonerate the drawer. "In cases of this
description", said Abbott C.J., "the rule laid down is that, if time be given to
the acceptor, the other parties to the bill are discharged; but in no case has it
been said, that taking a collateral security from the acceptor shall have that
effect. Here the second bill was nothing more than collateral security."[56] B,
being indebted to A, procured C to join with him in giving a joint and several
promissory note for the amount, and afterwards having become further
indebted and, being pressed by A for further security, by deed reciting the
debt, and that for a part a note had been given by him and C, and that A having
demanded payment for the debt, B had requested him to accept a further
security, assigned to A all his household goods, etc. as a further security, it was
held that his did not affect the remedy on the note against C.[57] So, where one
of the three partners, after a dissolution of partnership, undertook by deed
made between the partners to pay a particular partnership debt on two bills of
exchange, and that was communicated to the holder, who consented to take
the separate notes of the one partner for the amount, strictly reserving his right
against all three, and retained possession of the original bills, the separate
notes having proved unproductive, it was held that he might still resort to his
remedy against the other partners, and that the taking, under these circumstances, the separate notes, and even afterwards renewing them several times,
did not amount to satisfaction of the joint debt.[58]

Though the drawee may not have accepted the bill, yet it is conceived that
the holder, by giving up the bill to him and taking from him a substituted bill
at a longer date, would discharge the prior parties, though he has given due
notice of dishonour. If, however, the holder, being unable to obtain payment
at maturity of the original bill, takes a further bill from the acceptor as
collateral security and gives due notice of dishonour of the original bill, his
remedies on the original bill would not be affected, and as between himself
and the drawee there would be a good consideration for the new bill.

Prevention of discharge of surety

33–09   It has been repeatedly held, and is now well established, that a giving of
time by the creditor to the principal debtor will not discharge the surety, if

---

[55] *Gordon v. Calvert* (1828) 4 Russ. 581; *Calvert v. Gordon* (1828) 7 B. & C. 809.
[56] *Pring v. Clarkson* (1822) 1 B. & C. 14, see the observations on this case, Bayley, *Bills* (6th
ed.), p. 347.
[57] *Twopenny v. Young* (1824) 3 B. & C. 208.
[58] *Bedford v. Deakin* (1818) 2 B. & Ald. 210.

there is an agreement between the creditor and the principal that the surety shall not be thereby discharged,[59] although the surety himself is no party to the stipulation, or even has no notice of it,[60] for the surety's rights are not thereby affected, since, if he in fact pays the debt, he can at once proceed against the principal.[61] The stipulation, reserving rights against the surety, must in general appear on the face of the instrument giving time, and cannot, if the indulgence is in writing, be proved by parol.[62] But where the surety is an assenting party to the reservation of rights against himself, his assent may be proved by parol.[63]

No indulgence to an acceptor or other prior party will discharge an indorser if the indorser previously consents to it. Thus, where the acceptor, having been arrested by the holder, offered him a warrant of attorney for the amount of the bill payable by instalments, and, the holder mentioning the offer to the drawer, the drawer said, "You may do as you like, for I have had no notice of the non-payment," it was held that this amounted to an assent, and that the drawer (who, in fact, had had notice) was not discharged by the indulgence.[64]

Waiver of effect of indulgence

Wherever the surety, with knowledge of the facts, assents either by words **33–10** or acts to what has already been done, such subsequent assent will be a waiver of his discharge without any new consideration.[65] Therefore, where time had been given, and the drawer, aware of the fact, but ignorant of the law, and conceiving himself still liable, said: "I know I am liable, and if Jones (*viz.*, the acceptor) does not pay it I will", the drawer was held to have waived his discharge.[66] But where a bill was renewed, and an indorser said, "It was the best thing that could be done", it was held that this was no recognition of his liability.[67]

Discharge by conduct of holder

If the principal and sureties are jointly or jointly and severally liable, *e.g.* if **33–11** they are joint and several makers of a note, then a discharge to a surety by the

---

[59] *Burke's Case* (undated), referred to in *Ex p. Gifford* (1802) 6 Ves. 805, 809; *Boultbee v. Stubbs*. (1811) 18 Ves. 20; *Ex p. Glendinning* (1819) Buck 517; *Ex p. Carstairs* (1820) ibid. 560; *Nichols v. Norris* (1831) 3 B. & Ad. 41n; *Cowper v. Smith* (1838) 4 M. & W. 519; *North v. Wakefield* (1848) 13 Q.B. 536; *Owen v. Homan* (1853) 4 H.L.Cas. 997. A clause appearing on the face of a note to the effect that time given to or security, etc., taken from one party shall not prejudice the holder's rights against any other party does not invalidate the note as such (*Kirkwood v. Carroll* [1903] 1 K.B. 531).

[60] *Webb v. Hewitt* (1857) 3 Kay & J. 438.

[61] *Oriental Finance Co. v. Overend, Gurney & Co.* (1871) L.R. 7 Ch. 142, 150 (Lord Hatherley C.). Where, however, the instrument amounts to a release, rights cannot be reserved against the surety, for then the debt is gone at law (*Webb v. Hewitt, supra.*).

[62] *Ex p. Glendinning, supra; Lewis v. Jones* (1825) 4 B. & C. 506.

[63] *Ex p. Harvey* (1854) 23 L.J.Bk. 26; *Wuke v. Rogers* (1852) 21 L.J.Ch. 611; *Gorman v. Dixon* (1896) 26 Can.S.C.R. 87.

[64] *Clark v. Devlin* (1803) 3 B. & P. 363.

[65] *Mayhew v. Crickett* (1818) 2 Swanst. 185; *Smith v. Winter* (1838) 4 M. & W. 454, 467.

[66] *Stevens v. Lynch* (1810) 12 East 38.

[67] *Whithall v. Masterman* (1809) 2 Camp. 179; but *cf. Clark v. Devlin* (1803) 3 B. & P. 363.

creditor releasing him, or entering into a compromise with him, and erasing his name from the note, will be a discharge of the co-surety, and also of the principal debtor[68] but the discharge, in this case, does not proceed on the law of principal and surety.

Rights of sureties

33–12   The measure of damages which a surety, himself a party to the bill or note, such as a drawer or an indorser, who has been compelled to pay the amount thereof to the holder, may recover from his principal, such as the acceptor, maker or prior indorser, is regulated by section 57,[69] He may also avail himself of the Part 20 procedure by bringing a claim against his principal or principals .[70]

If one who is surety on a joint and several note, signed by the principal, pays the amount, though without any request or compulsion by the creditor, he may recover it of the principal.[71] A surety on payment of the debt is entitled to existing securities,[72] and the right extends to securities of which the surety did not know when he made himself liable,[73] even to securities which came into existence after that time.[74] A contract to indemnify a surety entitles the surety to interest.[75]

If a surety pays money to the creditor under a mistake as to the fact supposed to constitute his liability, he may recover it back.[76]

A surety who has paid for his principal is a creditor who may be barred by a composition deed, though he has not consented to it.[77]

Contribution

33–13   Where the sureties are not, as between themselves, principal and surety, as in the case of a prior and subsequent indorser of a bill or note, but merely co-sureties, as in the case of two or more joint or joint and several makers of a note, if one is called on to pay the whole debt, the others shall severally contribute in equal proportions. And though the same debt is secured by different instruments, executed by different sureties, and though one portion

---

[68] *Nicholson v. Revill* (1836) 4 A. & E. 675; *cf. Stevens v. Hughes* (1885) 1 T.L.R. 415; *Cardwell v. Smith* (1886) 2 T.L.R. 779; and see *Bogart v. Robertson* (1905) 11 O.L.R. 295.

[69] See *ante*, para. 28–01. A drawer, or indorsee, who, though not compelled to pay, being discharged as by want of notice, chooses to do so, is not entitled to any indemnity from a prior party; *cf. Horne v. Rouquette* (1878) 3 Q.B.D. 514, 519.

[70] CPR Part 20.

[71] Or the co-surety's proportion of the co-surety (*Pitt v. Purssord* (1841) 7 M. & W. 538).

[72] *Goddard v. Whyte* (1860) 2 Giff. 449; and to what has been realised on them (*Gray v. Seckham* (1872) L.R. 7 Ch. 680).

[73] *Duncan, Fox & Co. v. N. and S. Wales Bank* (1880) 6 App.Cas. 1, followed in *Aga Ahmed Ispahany v. Crisp* (1891) 8 T.L.R. 132.

[74] *Scott v. Knox* (1838) 2 Jones 778 (Ir.Rep.). On giving a proper indemnity the surety may sue in the creditor's name (Mercantile Law Amendment Act 1856, s.5); *Batchellor v. Lawrence* (1861) 9 C.B. (N.S.) 543).

[75] *Petre v. Duncombe* (1851) 20 L.J.Q.B. 242; *Ex p. Davies* (1897) 66 L.J.Q.B. 499.

[76] *Mills v. Alderbury Union* (1849) 3 Exch. 590: as to the recovery of money paid in mistake of fact generally, see Paget (11th ed., 1996),353–371.

[77] *Hooper v. Marshall* (1869) L.R. 5 C.P. 4.

of the debt is secured by one instrument, and one by another, and different sureties execute each, still there is mutual contribution; even though the surety seeking contribution did not at the time of the contract know that he had any co-sureties,[78] for the right of a co-surety to enforce contribution does not depend upon contract, but upon the equity of the case.[79] The relation in which co-sureties on a bill stand to the holder of the bill has no bearing on the relation in which they stand to each other. Thus where one co-surety A was in fact the drawer, and the other co-surety B the indorser of a bill, it was held that A could nevertheless recover from B contribution as co-surety, though he could not sue him on the bill itself.[80]

A surety has a right of action against his principal for every sum that he pays,[81] and a right of action against his co-surety as soon as he has paid more than his own due proportion of the debt.[82] He has a fresh right of action against the co-surety for every sum that he pays beyond that amount.

Where one co-surety to a bond receives a security, such as a promissory note, from the principal debtor, he is nevertheless entitled to contribution from another co-surety, unless it is found as a fact that the security was given with the intention of discharging him, and not merely as a collateral security.[83]

Determination of liability by notice

It has been held that a surety on a continuing guarantee has a right to determine his liability for future advances by notice.[84] Thus a guarantee of payment of all bills discounted by A for B for 12 months may be revoked within that period as to all bills not discounted at the date of the revocation.[85]   **33–14**

Backing a bill

Sometimes a person not liable on a bill indorses it with a view to guaranteeing payment by the acceptor to the drawer, oral evidence being admissible to show the intention behind the indorsement.[86] The Bills of Exchange Act 1882, s.56 provides that such person incurs the liabilities of an indorser. If no such evidence is available or the bill was incomplete at the time, there must be a   **33–15**

---

[78] *Deering v. Winchelsea* (1800) 2 B. & P. 270; *Mayhew v. Crickett* (1818) 2 Swanst. 185.

[79] See *Craythorne v. Swinburne* (1807) 14 Ves. 160, 169.

[80] *Reynolds v. Wheeler* (1861) 30 L.J.C.P. 350, approved in *Macdonald v. Whitfield* (1883) 8 App.Cas. 733; *Godsell v. Lloyd* (1911) 27 T.L.R. 383; *Lacombe v. Labonte* (1920) Q.R. 59 S.C. 17.

[81] The fact that the bill is unenforceable is not necessarily a bar to his right of action, if he has in fact paid it (*Re Chetwynd's Estate* [1938] Ch. 13).

[82] *Davies v. Humprhreys* (1840) 6 M. & W. 153; *Browne v. Lee* (1827) 6 B. & C. 689; *Cowell v. Edwards* (1800) 2 B. & P. 268; *cf. Fox v. Toronto General Trusts Corporation* [1934] 4 D.L.R. 759.

[83] *Done v. Whalley* (1848) 17 L.J.Ex. 225.

[84] *Brocklebank v. Moore* (1823), *Lloyds v. Harper* (1880) 16 Ch. 290.

[85] *Offord v. Davies* (1862) 31 L.J.C.P. 319.

[86] *Mcdonald v. Nash* [1924] A.C. 625; and see *ante.* paras 17–14 *et seq.*

memorandum in writing to satisfy the Statute of Frauds.[87] In *G. & H. Montage GmbH v. Irvani*, it was held that the Statute of Frauds did not apply where liability was sought to be established against a party signing bills, but that in any event, if the Statute did apply there was a sufficient note or memorandum in the bills and correspondence for the purposes of s.4.[88]

[87] *McCall v. Hargreaves* [1932] 2 K.B. 423.
[88] [1990] 1 W.L.R. 667.

INSOLVENCY OF PARTIES

The insolvency regime

The insolvency of companies and individuals is dealt with by the Insolvency **34–01** Act 1986 and the Insolvency Rules 1986.

Although the insolvency regimes are contained in one Act, there are important differences between them. The 1986 Act repealed and replaced provisions contained in the Bankruptcy Act 1914 and the Companies Act 1985.

The 1882 Act expressly reserves the rules in bankruptcy in the following **34–02** provision:

97–1 The rules in bankruptcy relating to bills of exchange, promissory notes and cheques, shall continue to apply thereto notwithstanding anything in this Act contained.[1]

By contrast with the old law[2] the Insolvency Act 1986 and the Insolvency Rules 1986[3] make separate and distinct provisions for the insolvency of individuals and the insolvency of companies. The provision in the Companies Act 1985 which applied the law in bankruptcy to the winding up of companies has been repealed.[4] There is apparently a lacuna, in that, although the law relating to bankruptcy no longer applies to company liquidations, section 97 of the 1882 Act has not been amended. It is likely that the court will construe the reference in section 97 to "bankruptcy" as a reference to the rules relating to insolvency, both of individuals and of companies.[5] The respective provisions of the Insolvency Rules which apply to bankruptcy and to companies are similar. In this chapter, reference is made to "the insolvent", which unless the context otherwise requires is a reference to insolvent individuals and to insolvent companies. Similarly, references to "the insolvency" are references to bankruptcy and to liquidation.

---

[1] See *Re Keever, ex p. Cork v. Midland Bank Ltd* [1967] Ch. 182; [1966] 2 Lloyd's Rep. 475 *per* Ungoed-Thomas J. at 482.

[2] Section 317 of the Companies Act 1948 and s.612 of the Companies Act 1985 provided that certain rules in force for the time being under the law of bankruptcy should apply in the winding up of companies.

[3] As amended by the Insolvency (Amendment) Rules 1987.

[4] Section 612 of the Companies Act 1985 was repealed by the Insolvency Act 1985.

[5] It is beyond the scope of this book to review fully the new insolvency provisions. For a full treatment see Peter Totty and Michael Jordan, *Insolvency.*

Petitioning creditor's debt

34–03   A bill, note, or cheque of the amount of £750 or more may be a good petitioning creditor's debt.[6]

It has been held that interest due on a bill cannot be added to the amount of the debt in order to make a sufficient petitioning creditor's debt[7] unless specially made payable on the face of the instrument.[8] However, interest is provable in an insolvency at the judgment debt rate on any debt arising by virtue of a written instrument from the date of the instrument to the commencement of the insolvency,[9] and the decisions under the old law should be read in the light of these new rules.

Bill not yet due

34–04   The fact that the bill is not yet due does not preclude the creditor from relying upon it. In bankruptcy, section 267(2)(b) of the Insolvency Act provides that a petition may be presented if the debt is for a liquidated sum payable to the petitioning creditor either immediately or at some certain future time and is unsecured.[10] Section 124 of the Insolvency Act enables a contingent or prospective creditor to petition for the winding up of a company. Under the old law, where the debtor had accepted a bill and at maturity it was agreed with the creditor that the bill would be indefinitely renewed so long as interest was paid, and a renewal bill was given, it was held that the creditor could present a petition based upon the original debt because it was a liquidated sum payable at some future time, though the renewal bill was not yet due.[11] The same result would occur under the present law.

Bills outstanding

34–05   Where the arrangements for taking a bill from the debtor operated as an agreement not to sue not merely during the currency of the bill but afterwards, notwithstanding dishonour, so long as the bill was outstanding in the hands of a third party,[12] it followed that the bill had to be in the possession of the creditor at the time the bankruptcy notice was issued. It follows that the bill must be in the possession of the creditor at the date when a statutory demand is served upon the debtor if one is served,[13] but, if no statutory demand is

---

[6] Insolvency Act 1986, s.123 and s.267.

[7] *Re Burgess* (1818) 8 Taunt. 660; at the time of this decision the debt had to amount to £100.

[8] *Cameron v. Smith* (1819) 2 B. & Ald. 305.

[9] See Insolvency Rules 4.93, 4.94, 6.113 and 6.114. Section 322(2) of the Insolvency Act 1986 provides that where a bankruptcy debt bears interest, that interest is provable as part of the debt except in so far as it is payable in respect of any period after the commencement of the bankruptcy. There is no equivalent of s.322 in relation to company liquidation.

[10] These words are taken from s.4(1)(b) of the Bankruptcy Act 1914, as to which *cf. Re: Barr ex p. Wolfe* [1896] 1 Q.B. 616, 618 (Vaughan Williams J.). The law is the same as the law in Australia (*David v. Malouf* (1908) 5 C.L.R. 749).

[11] *Re Barr ex p. Wolfe, supra.*

[12] *Belshaw v. Bush* (1851) 11 C.B. 191; *Davis v. Riley* [1898] 1 Q.B. 1; *ante* para. 14–06.

[13] A statutory demand which is not complied with shows the debtor's inability to pay his debts as they fall due. In relation to companies see s.123 of the Insolvency Act 1986. In relation to individuals see s.268 of the Insolvency Act 1986.

made, the bill need only be in the possession of the creditor at the date when the petition is issued,[14] Thus, under the old law, a debtor in part satisfaction of a compromise judgment accepted a bill drawn by a creditor, who indorsed it in blank and handed it to his bankers, the latter, however, declined to discount it, and on presentment by the bank at maturity it was dishonoured. The bank subsequently threatened the debtor with proceedings but none were in fact taken. A bankruptcy notice was then issued by the creditor founded on the original debt for which the bill was given, and the bill was subsequently thereto handed back to the creditor by the bank. It was held that the bankruptcy notice and the receiving order made thereon must be set aside, since the debt was not one on which a bankruptcy notice could be served, for at the time of the issue of the bankruptcy notice, the bill was outstanding in the hands of a third party, *viz*, the bank.[15]

Bill due

A bill at maturity must be presented and due notice of dishonour given to the drawer (or to the indorser), or it will not constitute a good petitioning creditor's debt against him.[16]   **34–06**

Debt must exist

The debt must have existed at the date of the commencement of the insolvency.[17] Thus under the old law, where a petitioning creditor had accepted a bill for the accommodation of the bankrupt previous to the act of bankruptcy, but subsequently to such act had paid the same, it was held that this payment, being after an act of bankruptcy, did not support the commission, for not till actual payment of the bill did the accommodation acceptor become a creditor of the bankrupt.[18] A bill or note which could not be sued on at law[19] is not a good petitioning creditor's debt.[20]   **34–07**

Date of bill not conclusive

Under the old law it was held that the presumption laid down in section 13(1) of the 1882 Act[21] (that a date on a bill is a true date) does not apply in an insolvency. The petitioning creditor had to show by extrinsic evidence that the debt existed before the petition was issued, and, where the debt was the   **34–08**

---

[14] A statutory demand is less likely to be required in every case in relation to a company whereas, in relation to an individual, there must be either a statutory demand or an unsatisfied execution: see s.286 of the Insolvency Act 1986.

[15] *Re a Debtor ex p. the Debtor* [1908] 1 K.B. 344, followed in *Nathan v. Green* [1921] V.L.R. 121, and distinguished in *Re Duncan and Abbott* [1919] N.Z.L.R. 97.

[16] *Cooper v. Machin* (1842) 1 Bing. 426, 428. The liability of the drawer during the currency of the bill is only a contingent one and as such would be provable in an insolvency. And see ss.45 and 48 of the 1882 Act.

[17] That is subject to the effect of s.284(5) discussed below.

[18] *Ex p. Holding* (1821) 1 G. & J. 97.

[19] *Richmond v. Heapy* (1816) 1 Stark at 204.

[20] *Ex p. Page* (1821) 1 G. & J. 100.

[21] *Ante* para. 2–13.

subject of a statutory demand, before that demand was served.[22] Similarly, the date of acceptance or indorsement could not be inferred from the drawing or making;[23] but the date had to be proved.[24] It is suggested that there is no reason why under the present insolvency regime the presumption in section 13(1) of the 1882 Act should not apply.

Bills honoured after presentation of the petition

34-09   The general practice of banks is to freeze a company's bank account upon receiving notice of a winding-up petition.[25] This is because of section 127 of the Insolvency Act 1986, which contains provisions dealing with the disposition of property after the commencement of winding up a company. It provides:

> **In a winding up by the court, any disposition of the company's property . . . made after the commencement of the winding up is, unless the court otherwise orders, void.**

In the case of compulsory liquidation, the winding up of a company is deemed to commence at the time of the presentation of the petition.

In *Hollicourt (Contracts) Ltd v. Bank of Ireland*[26] it was held that where cheques were drawn on a company's account and paid by the bank, after the presentation of a winding-up petition, section 127 of the 1986 Insolvency Act did not enable the company to recover the amounts so paid from the bank. The court held that the section only invalidated dispositions by a company of its property to the payees of the cheques, and enabled the company to recover the amounts disposed of to those payees.

The position of bankers who pay against bills drawn on insolvent individuals is governed by section 284 of the Insolvency Act 1986. Section 284(1) provides:

> **(1) Where a person is adjudged bankrupt any disposition of property made by that person in the period to which this section applies is void except to the extent that it is or was made with the consent of the court or is or was subsequently ratified by the court.**

This provision applies during the period beginning with the day of the presentation of the petition, and ending with the vesting of the bankrupt's

---

[22] See in relation to the old law *Sinclair v. Baggaley* (1838) 4 M. & W. 312, 318; *Anderson v. Wesion* (1840) 6 Bing. N.C. 296 at 301; *cf. Wright v. Lainson* (1837) 2 M. & W. 739; *Fletcher v. Manning* (1844) 12 M. & W. 571.

[23] *Cowie v. Harris* (1827) M. & M. 141.

[24] *Rose v. Rowcroft* (1815) 4 Camp 245.

[25] See *Paget's Law of Banking* (11th ed., 1996) p. 207.

[26] [2001] 1 A.E.R. 289; following *Coutts & Co. v. Stock* [2000] 1 W.L.R. 906 and disapproving dicta in *Re Gray's Inn Construction Co. Ltd* [1980] 1 W.L.R. 711.

estate in the trustee.[27] By analogy with section 127 a bank will be entitled to meet cheques presented to it during the relevant period.

In the case of individuals, additional provisions apply. The debts arising out of payments made by banks which are void pursuant to section 284 of the Insolvency Act 1986, but which may have arisen after the commencement of the bankruptcy are protected by section 284(5), which provides:

Where after the commencement of this bankruptcy the bankrupt has incurred a debt to a banker or other person by reason of the making of a payment which is void under this section, that debt is deemed for the purposes of any of this group of parts to have been incurred before the commencement of the bankruptcy unless

(a) **that banker or person had notice of the bankruptcy before the debt was incurred,[28] or**

(b) **it is not reasonably practicable for the amount of the payment to be recovered from the person to whom it was made.[29]**

There is no equivalent saving provision in relation to companies, but, petitions to wind up companies are advertised, and therefore banks have a reasonable opportunity to take notice of them. Bankruptcy petitions are not advertised, and bankruptcy orders may take some time to be advertised.

Garnishee order[30]

Where a judgment debtor is owed money by a third party, a judgment **34–10** creditor can obtain an attachment order from the court (a garnishee order) requiring that third party to discharge the debt by paying the amount due to the judgment creditor.[31] Although not a matter of insolvency it is convenient to deal with the subject in this Chapter.

Except where the order is for the attachment of a limited sum, a banker on whom a garnishee order is served in respect of a debt due from him to his customer, the judgment debtor, is entitled to dishonour cheques drawn on any credit balance over and above the amount of the judgment debt[32] and it is immaterial, where the customer is a solicitor, that the cheques are drawn upon a client account which has been opened by the solicitor for the purpose of

---

[27] Section 284(3).

[28] It is not clear what might constitute notice of the bankruptcy. Since the bankruptcy does not commence until the bankruptcy order is made it is arguable that notice of the bankruptcy petition is not sufficient.

[29] This provision derives from s.4 of the Bankruptcy Act 1926. That provision did not work satisfactorily, and a question remains over whether it will work satisfactorily in this limited sphere.

[30] For a fuller treatment of this subject see Paget, *op. cit.* pp. 467 *et seq.*

[31] RSC Ord. 49 under the CPR.

[32] *Rogers v. Whiteley* [1892] A.C. 118; as to current practice see *Paget's Law of Banking* (11th ed.), pp. 468–469.

keeping clients' moneys separate from his own.[33] But where a garnishee order
is served on the drawer of a cheque between its delivery for value and its
payment, there is no obligation on him to stop payment.[34] It will be otherwise,
however, if a cheque is given in respect of a debt accruing due after service
of a garnishee order nisi.[35] Moneys due under a bill of exchange on maturity
are attachable when the bill matures.[36]

Unless appropriately drawn, a garnishee order does not attach the balance
of a joint account, inasmuch as there is no debt due to the judgment debtor;
the debt is a joint debt.[37] Where the account is in the name of a wife whose
husband supplied all the funds, it was held that there was a resulting trust in
favour of the husband and that the balance could not be attached by the wife's
creditors.[38] Nor does it apply to an account in the name of a liquidator, if it is
the company which is cited as the judgment debtor.[39] Further, it does not apply
to sums paid to the banker for the credit of the customer after the service of
a garnishee summons.[40] It will, however, attach a balance which the customer
has instructed the banker to transfer elsewhere or to someone else, providing
that there has been no communication to the transferee before service of the
order.[41]

To defeat the office holder[42] the attachment must be completed before the
commencement of the insolvency.[43] A garnishee order nisi will not be made
absolute if insolvency intervenes between the date of the order nisi and the
application for the order absolute. That is because the court in its discretion is
required to do justice between all of the creditors.[44] Nothing short of the
receipt of money is sufficient to allow the garnishor to keep the fruits of his
judgment.[45] In *Re Caribbean Products (Yam Importers) Ltd*[46] it was held that
the reference to the "benefit of the execution or attachment" in what was
section 325 of the Companies Act 1948 included the right to take the
necessary steps to complete the execution or attachment. The Insolvency Act
1986 retains that wording.[47] However, if the order absolute has not been
obtained prior to insolvency any effective remedy has been lost.

---

[33] *Plunkett v. Barclays Bank* [1936] 2 K.B. 107.
[34] *Elwell v. Jackson* (1884) Cav. & E. 362 there being no *debitum in praesenti* or a *debitum infuturo*.
[35] *Edmunds v. Edmunds* [1904] P. 362.
[36] *Hyam v. Freeman* (1890) 35 S.J. 87.
[37] *Hirschorn v. Evans* [1938] 2 K.B. 801.
[38] *Harrods v. Tester* [1937] 2 All E.R. 236, CA; following *Marshall v. Crutwell* (1875) L.R. 20 Eq. 328.
[39] *Lancaster Motor Co. (London) Ltd v. Bremith Ltd* [1941] 1 K.B. 675.
[40] *Heppenstall v. Jackson* [1939] 1 K.B. 585.
[41] *Rekstin v. Severo Sibirsko Gosudarstvennoe Akcionernoe Obschestvo Konseverputj and the Bank for Russian Trade Ltd* [1933] 1 K.B. 47; but see *Delbrueck v. Barclays Bank International Ltd* [1976] 2 Lloyd's Rep. 341.
[42] Who may be either an administrator, a liquidator or a trustee in bankruptcy.
[43] See ss.10(1), 11(3), 183(1) and 346(1) of the Insolvency Act 1986.
[44] *Roberts Petroleum Ltd v. Kenny Ltd* [1983] A.C. 192.
[45] *George v. Thompson's Trustee* [1949] Ch. 322, in which the money had been paid into court but, owing to a breakdown in the court administration, had not been paid out on the creditor's application.
[46] [1966] 1 Ch. 331.
[47] See s.183 in relation to companies and s.346 in relation to individuals.

PROOF OF DEBTS

Production of the bill

Unless the office holder allows, a proof in respect of money owed on a bill **34–11** of exchange, promissory note, cheque or other negotiable instrument or security cannot be admitted unless there is produced the instrument or security itself or a copy of it, certified by the creditor or his authorised representative to be a true copy.[48] Further, subject to section 70 of the 1882 Act as to lost instruments,[49] and to the general dispensing power of the court,[50] where a dividend is paid on a bill of exchange or other negotiable instrument, the amount of the dividend shall be endorsed on the instrument, or on a certified copy of it, if required to be produced by the holder for that purpose.[51]

Under the similar provisions of the old law it was held that bills held by a bank "pending discount", *i.e.* during inquiries into the solvency of the acceptors, the banker meanwhile making some advances to the customer on the credit of the bills, were not securities which the banker was bound to value in proving under the bankruptcy of the customer.[52] This decision was explained in *Dawson v. Isle*[53] where Warrington J. said: "When that case is really examined I think it will be found that the question whether the bill became the property of the banker or not was never in question at all. The bill became the property of the banker but the question was whether he held it as security only or as his own property so that he could prove against the bankrupt's estate for the value on the bill." And, later, "It seems to me that the whole point was that the bill was not indorsed to the bank merely for the purpose of collection; it was indorsed to the bank for the purpose of being credited against money which the customer owed to the bank."

Voting

A creditor cannot vote in respect of a debt on, or secured by, a current bill **34–12** of exchange or promissory note unless he is willing to treat the liability to him on the bill or note of every person who is liable on it antecedently to the company, and against whom an insolvency order has not been made,[54] as a security in his hands, and to estimate the value of the security and for the purposes of entitlement to vote but not for dividend to deduct it from his proof.[55]

---

[48] Insolvency Rules 1986, Rules 4.87 and 6.108. Bills which are held by the creditor as security must be specified in the proof.

[49] As to ordering an indemnity see *ante* para. 30–06.

[50] *Ex p. Greenway* (1802) 6 Ves. 812.

[51] Insolvency Rule 11.6(5).

[52] *Ex p. Schofield, re Firth* (1879) 12 Ch.D. 337. This case was in fact decided upon the provisions of the Bankruptcy Act 1869 and the Rules of 1870.

[53] [1906] 1 Ch.D. 633 at 638.

[54] In the case of companyies the company should not have gone into liquidation, in the case of individuals a bankruptcy order should not have been made.

[55] Insolvency Rules 4.67(5) and 6.93(5). There is a similar provision in relation to administration orders in Rule 2.25.

When the holder may prove

34–13   Debts are defined as any debt or liability to which the insolvent is subject at the commencement of the insolvency, and any debt or liability to which the insolvent may become subject after the commencement of the insolvency by reason of any obligation incurred before the commencement of the insolvency, and any interest provable thereon.[56]

It is immaterial whether the debt or liability is present or future, whether it is certain or contingent or whether its amount is fixed or liquidated, or is capable of being ascertained by fixed rules or as a matter of opinion.[57] Liability means a liability to pay money or money's worth, including any liability under an enactment, any liability for breach of trust, any liability in contract, tort or bailment and any liability arising out of an obligation to make restitution.[58] Provable debts must be proved in accordance with the procedure laid down in the Insolvency Act 1986 and the Insolvency Rules 1986.[59]

In almost all cases where an insolvent would be liable to an action by the holder of a bill or note, the holder may prove on the insolvent's estate for the amount, and if more than one party to the bill is insolvent he may prove against all, although he may not receive more than 100p in the pound. Where a creditor has been paid part of his debt or a dividend in an insolvency has been declared[60] he may thereafter prove only for the balance. But if he has properly proved for the whole debt and he receives part from a party liable the proof stands.[61] Whatever would be a defence to an action will be an answer to such proof.[62]

The good part of a bill may in some cases in the event of insolvency be separated from the bad. Thus in one case, where a stock-jobber having a large sum of money in his hands to be employed in stock-jobbing transactions diverted part to his own use (contrary to the law applying to stock-jobbers at that time), and gave promissory notes to his employer, they were allowed to be proved only to the extent of the money diverted from the illegal purpose of the stock-jobber's own use.[63] It has been held that the equity is that where the consideration consists of two parts, one bad and the other good, the bill shall stand as to what is good.[64]

---

[56] In relation to individuals this definition appears in s.382 of the Insolvency Act 1986. In relation to companies this appears from Rule 13.12 of the Insolvency Rules. The effect of the fact that the provisions relating to proof of debts in a liquidation were apparently overlooked in the Insolvency Act 1986 and only appear in the Rules is unclear. It is thought unlikely that the court would refuse to apply the rules on an argument that they may be *ultra vires* the Insolvency Act 1986. Interest is provable in a bankruptcy by s.322(2) of the Insolvency Act 1986, and in liquidation by Rule 4.93(1).

[57] Insolvency Act 1986 s.382(3), and Rule 13.12(3).

[58] Insolvency Act 1986 s.382(4), Rule 13.12(4).

[59] In bankruptcy see s.322 and Rules 6.96 to 6.107. In liquidation see Rules 4.73 to 4.94 and Rule 12.3.

[60] *Cooper v. Pepys* (1741) 1 Atk. 107; *Ex p. Wildman* (1750) 1 Atk. 110; *Ex p. Taylor* (1857) 26 L.J. Bank. 58. These cases should apply under the new law.

[61] *Ex p. Taylor* (1857) 26 L.J. Bank 58; *Ex p. Cama* (1874) L.R. 9 Ch. 686.

[62] *Ex p. Smith* (1789) 3 Bro.C.C. 1; *Ex p. Barclay* (1802) 7 Ves. 596; *Ex p. Gifford* (1802) 6 Ves. 805; *Ex p. Wilson* (1805) 11 Ves. 410; *Ex p. Dewdney* (1808) 15 Ves. 479; *Ex p. Heath* (1813) 2 V. & B. 240.

[63] *Ex p. Bulmer* (1807) 13 Ves. 313.

[64] *Ex p. Mather* (1797) 3 Ves. 373.

Where bill discounted for small amount

If an insolvent discounts a bill for a small fraction of its nominal value the **34–14** transaction may be set aside as a transaction at an undervalue[65] and an order made restoring the position to what it would have been had the transaction not been entered into. Under the old law the question was whether the transaction was a fraud on creditors.[66] It is unlikely that many transactions will be attacked on that basis because it is far simpler to prove that the transaction was entered into at an undervalue.

Though the purchase or discounting of a bill for a small fraction of its nominal amount should not be regarded as necessarily implying or suggesting that there was fraud in the inception or preparation of the bill,[67] yet it is an important element in considering whether the man who gave the undervalue was acting bona fide. Thus if bills are issued for a discount in contemplation of insolvency, it is of extreme importance that the discounter knew that fact. So where a man purchased for £200 bills, accepted in fraud of the acceptor's creditors, of the face value of the bill of £1,700, manifestly knowing that both the drawer and the acceptors were hopelessly insolvent, and that the drawer could pay nothing at all, but that the acceptors, if made bankrupt, had assets sufficient to pay a dividend, and where it was obvious that the drawer had no good claim against the acceptors on these bills, it was held that the purchaser of the bills must be considered to have had notice that the bills were a fraud on the acceptors' creditors, and that he therefore could only prove for the sum actually paid by him.[68]

Bills not due

When a creditor has proved for a debt of which payment is not due at the **34–15** date of the declaration of dividend, he is entitled to a dividend equally with other creditors, but subject to the creditor's admitted proof being reduced by a percentage calculated as 5 per cent, multiplied by the number of months between the declaration of dividend and the date when payment of the creditors debt would otherwise be due, divided by 12.[69] Other creditors are not

---

[65] *Ante* pp. 459–460.

[66] Transactions which are a fraud on creditors may be set aside pursuant to s.423 of the Insolvency Act 1986. An application under this section need not be made in insolvency proceedings (*e.g.*, a bankruptcy or liquidation), replacing as it does s.172 of the Law of Property Act 1925.

[67] *Re Gommersall* (1875) 1 Ch.D. 137 at 146.

[68] *Jones v. Gordon, supra*, affirming *Re Gommersall* (1875) 1 Ch.D. 137. In this case Lord O'Hagan (2 App. Cas. at 626) and Bagally L.J. (1 Ch.D. at 147), both appear to have inclined to the view that the purchaser being privy to the fraudulent transaction, no proof should be allowed at all. However, that would result in a windfall to the creditors. *Re Gommersall* was distinguished in *Re Aylmer, ex p. Crane* (1893) 1 Mans. 391, where a creditor was allowed to prove for £1,056 the amount of three notes given in revival of a debt to the payee, extinguished by a former bankruptcy of the maker, who received no consideration for such agreement to revive beyond the discounting of his further £100 note for £54 cash.

[69] Insolvency Rules 1986, Rule 11.13.

entitled to interest out of surplus funds[70] until all creditors who have debts payable at a future time have been paid the full amount of their debts.[71] Interest accruing after the commencement of the insolvency calculated at the judgment debts rate is payable out of any surplus remaining after payment of all debts.[72]

Proof of bill or note on demand or after notice

34–16   The holder of a note payable on demand may prove though no demand has been made before notice of the petition.[73] A note payable at 12 months' notice with interest, is provable against the estate of the maker, though he has become insolvent before any notice is given.[74]

Irregular bill or note

34–17   A bill or note defective in its necessary form, or void for want of a stamp,[75] or payable on a contingency,[76] or expressed to be payable otherwise than in money,[77] is not, as a bill or note, provable. But a lender may prove in respect of the notes given for money lent to meet a lost bet, if not falling within section 1 of the Gaming Act 1835.[78]

Person not a party

34–18   A bill, as such, cannot be proved against a person who is not a party to the instrument,[79] though he gives a written engagement, not on the bill, to guarantee the payment of it[80] but the holder may prove on such an engagement made before the insolvency.[81] In other cases the estate may be liable to proof for the consideration, though not for the bill itself.[82]

---

[70] Under s. 189(2) or s.328(4) of the Insolvency Act 1986.

[71] Rule 11.13(3).

[72] Section 189 in relation to companies, s.328(4) in relation to individuals. As to the proof of interest see Rules 4.93 and 6.113.

[73] Applying by analogy with the old law *Ex p. Beaufoy* (1787) Cookes B.L. (8th ed.), 180.

[74] *Clayton v. Gosling* (1812) 5 B. & C. 360; *Ex p. Elgar* (1826) 2 G. & J. 1; *Ex p. Dowman* (1827) 2 G. & J. 241; s.382 of the Insolvency Act 1986 and Rule 13.12 of the Insolvency Rules 1986.

[75] *Ex p. Manners* (1811) 1 Rose 68; stamp duty on bills and notes was abolished by the Finance Act 1970 s.32.

[76] *Ex p. Tootell* (1798) 4 Ves. 372.

[77] *Ex p. Imeson* (1815) 2 Rose 225; *Ex p. Davison* (1817) Buck 31; at the time of these decisions, notes issued by the Bank of England were not legal tender.

[78] See Denning L.J. in *Macdonald v. Green* [1951] 1 K.B. 594.

[79] *Ex p. Roberts* (1789) 2 Cox Eq. 171; *Ex p. Bird* (1851) 4 De. G. & S. 273.

[80] *Ex p. Harrison* (1789) 2 Cox Eq. 172; *Re Barrington* (1804) 2 Scho. & Lef. 112; *Ex p. Hustler* (1821) 1 G. & J. 9.

[81] *Ex p. Bell* (1810) 1 Mont. and Gregg B.L. 194; and see *Ex p. Blackburne* (1804) 10 Ves. 204; *Ex p. Rathbone* (1818) Buck 215.

[82] *ibid.*; *Ex p. Robinson* (1817) Buck 113.

Bill passed without indorsement

It has been held that a person who passes a bill without indorsement, and   **34–19**
takes it up after the acceptor has gone into insolvency, will not be allowed to
prove it against the acceptor's estate.[83]

Drawer and Drawee the same

Where the drawer and drawee are the same person only one proof is   **34–20**
allowed.[84]

Mutual accommodation bills

Difficulties arise where there has been mutual accommodation between the   **34–21**
insolvent and other parties, with or without a specific exchange of securities.

Mutual accommodation with specific exchange is where the acceptance of
A is exchanged for the acceptance of B to the same amount. In this case each
party is bound to pay his own acceptance, and in paying it, is not considered
as surety for the other.[85] It is not essential, in order to constitute a specific
exchange of securities, that the acceptances given in exchange should be the
acceptances of the party giving them, or that the amounts or dates should be
exactly the same.[86]

Under the old law, a party to a specific exchange of paper was allowed to
prove the bankrupt's paper payable on demand, having only taken up his own
similar note the day after the commission against the bankrupt.[87] Where there
were five cross acceptances on each side, and those of A were discounted by
K, but not those of K in A's hands, and A's acceptances were proved by the
holders in his bankruptcy, and a dividend paid on those proofs, A's assignee
was not entitled to prove against K's estate on the five unnegotiated acceptances of K in A's favour.[88] Under the Insolvency Act 1986 a creditor is
probably able to prove on a bill not yet due as a contingent debt, his own
counter-bill being as yet undue, since a surety is entitled to prove though he
has not paid or been called on to pay.[89]

Mutual accommodation without specific exchange will not create a debt
from the acceptor to the drawer. But the acceptor is to be considered as a
surety, and may recover what he pays as money paid to the drawer's use.

---

[83] Applying the decision in bankruptcy in *Ex p. Isbester* (1810) 1 Rose 30.

[84] *Banco de Portugal v. Waddell* (1880) 5 App.Cas. 161.

[85] *Rolfe v. Caslon* (1795) 2 H.Bl. 570; *Cowley v. Dunlop* (1798) T.R. 565; *Buckler v. Buttivant* (1802) 3 East 72.

[86] *Buckler v. Buttivant* (1802) 3 East 72.

[87] *Ex p. Beaufroy* (1787) Cooke B.L. (8th ed.), 180; *Ex p. Clanricade* (1787) *ibid.* 182. The proof will not be admitted until the counter-bill is taken up or the insolvent's estate is exonerated from the original debt: see Cooke at p. 183. Otherwise the proof would offend the rule against double proof.

[88] *Ex p. Solarte* (1832) 2 D. & C. 261.

[89] Insolvency Act 1986 s.382(3), Rule 13.12(3). *Re Paine ex p. Read* [1897] 1 Q.B. 122; *Re Blackpool Motor Car Co.* [1901] 1 Ch. 77.

Where there is mutual paper, but not a specific exchange, both parties becoming insolvent, the cash balance only is to be proved for, the bills on both sides being excluded, though there is an excess of bad paper on one side, the true principle being that proof should only be admitted for that sum for which an action would have been maintained by the one party against the other, if the bills had remained in the situation in which they were actually found and there had been no insolvency.[90] This principle is limited to cross-accommodation acceptances. Where there is no cross-accommodation and the acceptances on one side are given independently for valuable consideration, such acceptances cannot be excluded, but must be taken into account in fixing the amount of the proof.[91] Further, even in the case of cross-accommodation bills, the principle has no application where the bills are in the hands of third parties.[92] In this case the third party may prove for the whole of each bill against the estate of each of the parties to it, and receive dividends as far as the amount really due to him.[93]

If the holder of a bill has proved against the estate of the person for whose accommodation the bill was accepted, there can be no further proof by anyone to whom the bill is returned, or by the accommodation acceptor when he pays it.[94]

Proof for expenses, re-exchange, etc.

34–22   Expenses of protest, re-exchange, etc., are provable provided that they had arisen prior to the commencement of the insolvency.[95]

Several insolvencies

34–23   Where there are several insolvencies of different parties to a bill or note, the holder may prove for the whole amount of the money due to him upon the bill or note. However, he may not receive more than the whole amount due. If before the insolvency of one party, or before proof is submitted, he receives payment of part of the debt from another party, he can only prove for the residue.[96]

---

[90] *Ex p. Waljer* (1898) 4 Ves. 373; *Ex p. Earle* (1801) 5 Ves. 833. If the holders of the bills have been paid and one estate yields a surplus, the other may then prove against it for the balance due on the mutual paper (*Ex p. Rawson* (18210 Jac. 274; *Ex p. Laforest* (1833) 2 D.& C. 199).

[91] *Re Charles ex p. Macredie* (1873) L.R. 6 Ch.App. 535, 537, *per* Lord Selbourne; *Ex p. Cama* (1874) L.R. 9 Ch.App. 686 at 689.

[92] *Ex p. Cama, supra.*

[93] *Ex p. Lee* (1721) 1 P.Wms. 782; *Ex p. King* (1786) Cooke B.L. (8th ed.), p. 177; *Ex p. Crossley* (1791) 3 Bro.C.C. 237; *Ex p. Bloxham* (1803) 8 Bes. 531; *Fentum v. Pocock* (1813) 5 Taunt 192; *Jones v. Hibbert* (1817) 2 Stark 304; *Ex p. Cama, supra*; *Ex p. Newton* (1880) 16 Ch.D. 330.

[94] *Re Lynn, ex p. Read* (1822) 1 G. & J. 224; *Re Oriental Bank* (1871) L.R. 7 Ch. 99.

[95] By virtue of s.382(3) of the Insolvency Act 1986 in relation to individuals, and Rule 13.12(3) in relation to companies.

[96] *Ex p. Wyldman* (1750) 2 Ves.Sen. 113. The holder may prove against the acceptor without deducting the value of a security from the drawer (*Ex p. Parr* (1811) 18 Ves. 65).

English and foreign insolvencies

Where an estate is insolvent both in England and in a foreign country, and **34–24** the holder of a bill receives a dividend in the foreign insolvency, he is not allowed to prove again in England until all the creditors have received a dividend equivalent to the dividend received by the holder in the foreign insolvency.[97]

Joint and separate estate

The law relating to insolvent partnerships has been changed by the Insol- **34–25** vency Act 1986 as applied by the Insolvent Partnerships Order 1994.[98] Insolvent partnerships are now wound up by the court as unregistered companies.[99]

Where a creditor holds the joint and several security of partners for the same debt, he cannot, as a general rule prove in both the joint and several estates.[1] Where the names of two firms appear on the bills and there are common partners in the two firms, double proof is generally allowed.[2] Similarly, where the same person is the sole general partner of two limited partnerships, the holders of the bills drawn upon one of the firms and accepted by the sole general partner may prove in the insolvency of the other firm.[3]

If a partner accepts a bill in the firm's name for a private debt, it cannot be proved against the firm's estate,[4] except if in the hands of a holder in due course[5] or it can be shown to have been accepted with the consent of the partners[6] in a trading partnership.[7]

Bills acquired after the acceptor's insolvency

A holder who has bought up the notes of acceptors of the insolvent after the **34–26** insolvency will be admitted to prove,[8] provided that, at the time of the insolvency, they were in the hands of a person entitled to prove.[9]

---

[97] Applying *Ex p. Wilson* (1872) L.R. 7 Ch.App. 490; *Banco de Portugal v. Waddell* (1880) 5 App.Cas. 161. There is presently no realistic prospect of an EEC Convention being introduced which may affect this.

[98] The Insolvent Partnerships Order 1986 was revoked and replaced by the 1994 Order as from December 1, 1994.

[99] The Insolvent Partnerships Order 1994, paras 7 and 8.

[1] Applying *Ex p. Hinton* (1847) De.G. 550.

[2] *Ex p. Honey* (1871) L.R. 7 Ch. 178.

[3] *Re Barnard* [1932] Ch. 269.

[4] *Ex p. Holdsworth* (1841) 1 Mont.D. & G. 475.

[5] *Ex p. Bushell* (1844) 3 Mont.D. & G. 615.

[6] *Ex p. Thorpe* (1836) 3 M. & A. 716.

[7] *Dickinson v. Valpy* (1829) 10 B. & C. 128.

[8] *Ex p. Lee* (1721) 1 P.Wms. 782; *Ex p. Thomas* (1747) 1 Atk. 73; *Ex p. Brymer* (1788) Cooke B.L. (8th ed.), p. 187; *Ex p. Deey* (1796) 2 Cox Eq. 423; *Cowley v. Dunlop* (1798) 7 T.R. 565; *Houle v. Baxter* (1802) 3 East 177; *Joseph v. Orme* (1806) 2 N.R.(B. & P.) 180; *Mead v. Braham* (1814) 3 M. & S. 91.

[9] *Ex p. Rogers* (1820) Buck 490. There must have been a provable debt at the commencement of the insolvency.

Set-off

34–27   The rules relating to set-off and mutual credit are in all material respects the
same as the old rules.[10] Where before the insolvent enters into insolvency
there have been mutual credits, mutual debts or other mutual dealings between
the insolvent and the creditor, an account is taken of what is due from each
party to the other in respect of the mutual dealings, and the sums due from one
party are set off against the sums due from the other. Only the balance of the
account is provable in the insolvency, or alternatively, is payable to the
liquidator or trustee.[11]

The term "mutual credit" is a wider term than "mutual debt".[12] The mutual
credit must be such as was intended to result in a debt.[13] Where, in consideration of the insolvent's acceptance, the defendant promised to indorse a bill to
the bankrupt, such promise was not the subject of mutual credit[14] but a
promise to accept has been held to be a subject of set-off as, unlike an
indorsement which is but a guarantee, an acceptance necessarily terminates in
a debt.[15] There must be mutuality of debts between the parties, so that a joint
debt cannot be set off against a several debt.[16]

There may be mutual credit in an insolvency, though one of the debts
constituting it is not due, as when a bond, bill or note is payable at a future
date.[17] It would appear that unmatured and contingent debts can be set off
under the rules.[18]

An acceptance of an insolvent has been the subject of a set-off notwithstanding that it was not due at the time of the insolvency and was in the hands
of an indorsee.[19] An acceptor may set off a sum due to him from the insolvent
as against his acceptance, though the latter was not due at the commencement
of the insolvency and was then in the hands of a third party.[20] It has also been
held that an indorser to a bill who became a party to it before the commencement of the insolvency could set it off on subsequently becoming a holder.[21]

---

[10] The old law was contained in s.31 of the Bankruptcy Act 1914. In relation to companies the
new law is contained in Rule 4.90, and in relation to individuals it is contained in s.323 of the
Insolvency Act 1986.

[11] Rule 4.90, s.323 of the Insolvency Act 1986. A right to set-off under these provisions
provides a good defence to an action on the bill see: *Willmot Brothers Ltd v. North West Thames
Regional Health Authority* (1984) 26 B.L.R. 51.

[12] *National Westminster Bank Ltd v. Halesowen Presswork and Assemblies Ltd* [1972] A.C.
785; *Rolls Razor Ltd v. Cox* [1967] 1 Q.B. 522.

[13] *Eberle's Hotels and Restaurants Co. v. Jonas* (1887) 18 Q.B.D. 459; *Rolls Razor v. Cox,
supra*.

[14] *Rose v. Simms* (1830) 1 B. & Ad. 521.

[15] *Gibson v. Bell* (1835) 1 Bing.N.C. 743.

[16] *Re Pennington & Owen* [1925] 1 Ch. 825.

[17] *Ex p. Prescot* (1753) 1 Atk. 230; *Atkinson v. Elliott* (1797) 1 T.R. 378.

[18] *Re BCCI (No. 8)* [1998] A.C. 214; In *Re Carreras Rothmans Ltd v. Freeman Matthews
Treasure Ltd* [1985] Ch. 207 it was held that a contingent obligation could not be set off. *In Re
Charge Card Services Ltd* [1987] Ch. 510 Millett J. analysed the authorities and held that it
could.

[19] *Collins v. Jones* (1830) 10 B. & C. 777.

[20] *Bolland v. Nash* (1828) 8 B. & C. 105.

[21] *McKinnon v. Armstrong* (1877) 2 App.Cas. 531.

There are several old decisions which indicate that set-off may be available in specific instances.[22]

PROPERTY DIVISIBLE AMONG CREDITORS

Trust property

The property[23] of the insolvent divisible among creditors does not include **34–28** property held on trust for any other person.[24]

The law has been stated that where the debtor is to collect and remit there is a trust, but that where the debtor is to use and repay on demand then there is no trust.[25] Accordingly, where A, who had no account at the bank, was in the habit of having cheques collected for him by the bank, he was held entitled to claim out of the estate of the bank sums not yet remitted to him at the date of the bankruptcy.[26] In the case of a banker and customer, the ordinary relation is that of debtor and creditor and not of trustee and *cestui que trust*.[27]

Appropriated securities

Where goods are specifically appropriated prior to the insolvency for the **34–29** purpose of meeting bills of exchange, or a second set of bills has been specifically appropriated to meet a first set, the holder of the bills has been held entitled thereto as against the creditors.[28]

When and to what extent securities or remittances in the hands of an acceptor, who afterwards becomes insolvent are available in favour of the holder of the bill, is a question involving many difficulties and it has accordingly given occasion to much discussion. This question can seldom arise, except when both drawer and acceptor are insolvent, for it is a matter of indifference to the bill-holder from what parties or funds he receives payment.

[22] See generally *Alsager v. Currie, supra; Baker v. Lloyds Bank Ltd* [1920] 2 K.B. 322; *Smith v. Hodson* (1791) 4 T.R. 211; *Ex p. Wagstaff* (1806) 13 Ves. 65; *Russell v. Bell* L.J.C.P. 117; *Key v. Flint* (1817) 8 Taunt 21; *Ex p. Flint* (1818) 1 Swanst. 30; *Buchannon v. Findlay* (1829) 9 B. & C. 739; *Groom v. West* (1838) 8 A. & E. 758 at 772; *Re. Gross* (1871) L.R. 6 Ch. 632; *Clarke v. Fell* (1833) 4 B. & Ad. 404, distinguished in *Ex p. Barnett, re Deveze* (1874) L.R. 9 Ch. 293; *Smith v. Hodson* (1791) 4 T.R. 211.
[23] Property is defined in s.436 of the Insolvency Act 1986. In relation to bankruptcy, the definition is extended by s.283(4).
[24] Section 283(3) of the Insolvency Act 1986. There is no equivalent provision in relation to companies, however, there can be no doubt that property held on trust cannot be distributed to the creditors, see for example: *Quistclose Investments Ltd v. Rolls Razor Ltd* [1970] A.C. 567; *Carreras Rothmans Ltd v. Freeman Matthews Treasure Ltd, supra.*
[25] *Re Brown, ex p. Plitt* (1889) 6 Morr. 81 at 82.
[26] *ibid.*
[27] *Foley v. Hill* (1848) 2 H.L.C. 28; *Re Agra and Masterman's Bank, ex p. Waring* (1866) 36 L.J.Ch. 151.
[28] *Ex p. Imbert* (1851) 26 L.J.Bk. 65; *Ex p. Flower* (1835) 4 Dea. & C. 449. As to what is a sufficient appropriation, see *Bailey v. Culverwell* (1828) 8 B. & C. 448; *Frith v. Forbes* (1862) 4 De. G.F. & J. 409; *Re Broad* (1884) 13 Q.B.D. 740; *Ex p. Dever* (1884) 13 Q.B.D. 766; *Phelps v. Comber* (1885) Ch.D. 813, approved on *Robey & Co.'s Perseverance Ironworks v. Ollier* (1872) L.R. 7 Ch.App. 695; *Brown, Shipley v. Kough* (1885) 29 Ch.D. 848; *Konig v. Brandt* (1901) 84 L.T. 748.

The general rule seems to be that when both the drawer and the acceptor of a bill have become insolvent, and bills, securities, or funds have been remitted by the drawer to the acceptor, and specifically appropriated to cover the acceptor's liability on his acceptance, the holder of the bill may avail himself of them; they do not belong to the acceptor's general creditors and do not pass to his trustee in bankruptcy or liquidation.[29]

Rule in *ex parte Waring*

34-30   Although this principle applies most frequently in the case of actual insolvency, yet it is not essential to its application that the insolvency should have been ascertained by a bankruptcy order, winding-up order, or resolution to wind up the company. It is enough if the parties are practically insolvent.[30] The securities need not be deposited by a party to the bill; it will suffice if the depositor is liable in respect of the transaction for which the bill was drawn.[31] To fall within this rule the holder must be entitled to prove against both the insolvent estates; where, therefore, the bill had been dishonoured for non-acceptance it was held not to come within it.[32]

Deposited and appropriated funds

34-31   Where the customer of a banker had lodged a sum of money with a bank to meet an acceptance of his made payable at a correspondent of the banker's, and the acceptor failed before its maturity, it was held that the drawer could not recover against the banker, there having been no privity of contract between him and the banker.[33] An acceptor who has deposited money with a bank to meet a bill, has on the bank's failure only the rights of an ordinary

---

[29] The original and leading case on the subject is *Ex p. Waring* (1815) 19 Ves. 345, which has been frequently followed and distinguished; *Re New Zealand Banking Co.* (1867) L.R. 4 Eq. 226, 229 (Lord Romilly M.R.); *Ex p. Dever, re Suse (No. 2)* (1885) 14 Q.B.D. 611, 623, where it was pointed out that there need not be an appropriation of a security to meet a particular bill.

[30] *Powles v. Hargreaves* (1853) 3 De G.M. & G. 430; *Bank of Ireland v. Perry* (1871) L.R. 7 Ex. 14; *City Bank v. Luckie* (1870) L.R. 5 Ch. 773; *Re Barned's Bank, ex p. Joint Stock Discount Co.* (1875) L.R. 10 Ch. 198. But the estate of the remitter must still be within the jurisdiction of the court (*Re Yglesias* (1875) L.R. 10 Ch. 635). As to the doctrine laid down in *Powles v. Hargreaves, supra,* see now *Royal Bank of Scotland v. Commercial Bank of Scotland* (1882) 7 A.C. 366.

[31] *Ex p. Smart* (1872) L.R. 8 Ch. 220.

[32] *Vaughan v. Halliday* (1874) L.R. 9 Ch. 561. The funds or moneys claimed for the benefit of the bill-holders must not be absolutely and entirely the property of, and in the possession of, one of the parties only, as when an agent consigns goods to his principal, and both fail, the agent having no right to have the goods specifically appropriated to take up the bills (*Ex p. Banner* (1876) 2 Ch.D. 278); see also *Ex p. Lambton* (1875) L.R. 10 Ch. 405.

[33] *Moore v. Bushell* (1857) 27 L.J.Ex. 3; *Hill v. Royds* (1869) L.R. 8 Eq. 290, followed in *Auchteroni v. Midland Bank* [1928] 2 K.B. 294. As to what will amount to specific appropriation under such circumstances, see *Farley v. Turner* (1857) 26 L.J. Ch. 710. Absent insolvency, the position may be otherwise where the Contracts (Rights of Third Parties) Act 1999 applies. Although the Act confers no rights on a third party in the case of a ontract on bill or note, the party, in the position of the drawer, may be able to rely upon a separate and independent contract between the acceptor and acceptor's bank, in order to enforce the term that the money was intended for his benefit.

creditor,[34] and where funds were remitted by a country banker to a London banker, who was instructed to meet certain acceptances, the London banker was held entitled, on the failure of the country banker, to retain them for a debt due to him from the sender on the ground that there was no appropriation.[35]

A statement by the drawer of the bill to the holder that there will be funds in the hands of the acceptor to meet it at maturity, or that it is drawn expressly against funds remitted to him, is not an appropriation of any funds in the acceptor's hands at maturity, nor is it an equitable assignment.[36]

Acceptor's benefit of guarantee

The acceptor's right to the benefit of a guarantee given to him is not transferred to a holder of the bill[37] unless the guarantee is given for the purpose of being exhibited to other parties.[38]   **34–32**

Bills discounted or held short

Bills remitted to an agent as a factor or banker, and entered short while unpaid, or paid in generally, for the amount to be received[39] by such banker, or for any other specific purpose, and not discounted or treated as cash,[40] are considered as still in the possession of the principal; and, therefore, in case of the insolvency of such agent, banker, or factor, they do not pass to the estate but must be returned to the principal, subject to such lien as the agent may have upon them. "Every man", says Lord Ellenborough, "who pays bills not then due into the hands of his banker, places them there, as in the hands of his agent, to obtain payment of them when due. If the banker discounts the bill or advances money upon the credit of it, that alters the case; he then acquires the entire property in it, or has a lien on it, *pro tanto*, for his advance."[41]   **34–33**

---

[34] *Re Barned's Banking Co., Massey's Case* (1870) 39 L.J.Ch. 635, distinguishing *Farley v. Turner, supra.*

[35] *Johnson v. Robarts* (1875) L.R. 10 Ch.App. 105.

[36] *Thomson v. Simpson* (1870) L.R. 5 Ch. 659; *Bank of Louisiana v. Bank of New Orleans* (1873) L.R. 6 H.L. 352.

[37] *Re Barned's Banking Co., ex p. Stephens* (1868) L.R. 3 Ch. 753.

[38] *Re Agra and Masterman's Bank, ex p. Asiatic Banking Co.* (1867) L.R. 2 Ch. 391. In *Re Hallett & Co.* [1894] 2 Q.B. 256, the guarantee of the maker's solvency ran in favour of the payee or holder.

[39] See *Jombart v. Woollett* (1837) 2 Myl. & Cr. 389; *Ex p. Edwards* (1842) 11 L.J. Bk. 36.

[40] See *Ex p. Sargeant* (1810) 1 Rose 153; *Carstairs v. Bates* (1812) 3 Camp. 301.

[41] *Giles v. Perkins* (1807) 9 East 12; see *Ex p. Dumas* (1754) 1 Atk. 232; *Zinck v. Walker* (1777) 2 W.Bl. 1154; *Bolton v. Puller* (1796) 1 B. & P. 539; *Ex p. Rowton* (1810) 77 Ves. 426; *Ex p. Sollers* (1811) 18 Ves. 229; *Ex p. Pease* (1812) 1 Rose 232; *Ex p. Wakefield Bank* (1812) 1 Rose 243; *Ex p. Leeds Bank* (1812) 1 Rose 254; *Ex p. Buchanan* (1812) 1 Rose 280; *Ex p. Burton Bank* (1814) 2 Rose 162; *Ex p. Waring* (1815) 19 Ves. 345; *Ex p. McGae* (1816) 2 Rose 376. Sums retained by the banker to meet acceptances, the "marginal notes" for which given by the banker had been transferred, are not within the order and disposition of customer if bankrupt (*Ex p. Kemp* (1874) L.R. 9 Ch. 383). Bills indorsed to a bank by its customer to enable the bank to get them discounted are debts due to the customer and pass under an assignment of "book debts" (*Dawson v. Isle* [1906] 1 Ch. 633).

The law was held to be the same though the amount of the bills was entered by the banker in the cash column of the ledger and pass-book, and though the banker paid them away or discounted them at his discretion.[42]

A customer was in the habit of indorsing and paying into his banker's hands bills not due, which, if approved, were immediately entered as bills to his credit, to the full amount; and he was then at liberty to draw for that amount by cheques on the bank. The customer was charged with interest upon all cash payments to him from the time when made, and upon all payments by bills from the time when they were due and paid, and had credit for interest upon cash paid into the bank from the time of the payment, and upon bills paid in from the time when the amount of them was received. The bankers paid away such bills to their customers as they thought fit. The bankers having become insolvent, it was held that the customer might maintain trover against their assignees for bills paid in by him, and remaining *in specie* in their hands, the cash balance, independently of the bills, being in favour of the customer at the time of the insolvency, Bayley J. observing "It has been argued for the defendants that we must infer an agreement to have been made between the banker and his customer that as soon as bills reached the hands of the former, the property should be changed. Undoubtedly, if there were any such bargain, the defendants would be entitled to our judgment; but if there be no such bargain, then the case of customer and banker resembles that of principal and factor; and the bills, remaining *in specie*, will, notwithstanding the insolvency, continue the property of the customer." Though the amount of the bills was carried into the cash column, it does not follow that the customer consented to their being considered as cash.[43] The trustee may be restrained by injunction from negotiating the bills.[44]

Position of insolvent before the conclusion of the insolvency

34–34   The position of companies and individuals is different to the extent that individuals will be discharged from bankruptcy whereas companies will ordinarily be dissolved at the conclusion of the liquidation.

---

[42] *cf. Thompson v. Giles* (1824) 2 B. & C. 422. But the crediting of a cheque as cash in the pass-book has been held to show that the banker took the cheque as holder, and received subsequent payment for himself (*Capital and Counties Bank v. Gordon* [1903] A.C. 240), and see *ante,* p. 437. The Bills of Exchange (Crossed Cheques) Act 1906, repealed by the Cheques Act 1957, did not affect this decision save as to the application of s.82 of the 1882 Act in such a case; but see *Underwood v. Bank of Liverpool; Underwood v. Barclays Bank Ltd* [1924] 1 K.B. 775; and Paget (11th ed.), pp. 413 *et seq.*

[43] *Thompson v. Giles* (1824) 21 B. & C. 422; *Ex p. Barkworth* (1858) 27 L.J. Bk. 5. In *Re Mills & Co., ex p. Stannard* (1893) 10 Morr. 193, it was held by Vaughan Williams J. that the inference of fact drawn by the court in *Thompson v. Giles, supra,* was largely grounded on the bills not being due, and the entry in the cash column of the bankers' book being for the full amount of the bills without any deduction for the time the bills had to run, which negatived the inference that the bankers intended to take the bills, and that the same reasoning had no application to the case of an instrument payable on demand, such as a cheque. On the other hand, it was later held, in *Gaden v. Newfoundland Savings Bank* [1899] A.C. 281, 287, that the decision in *Thompson v. Giles* would cover the case of a cheque charged to the customer's account in the ledger, and entered in the pass-book.

[44] *Ex p. Jombert,* Cor., V.–C., December 1836.

If the holder of a bill of exchange, in which he has a beneficial interest, becomes bankrupt, the property in the bill vests, from the commencement of the insolvency in the trustee in bankruptcy.[45] The property of a company does not vest in the liquidator, but he has extensive powers to take into his custody or control all property belonging to the company.[46] An indorsement by a bankrupt subsequent to the commencement of the bankruptcy will not confer title on the indorsee.[47]

As in general, property in which the insolvent has no interest is not part of the insolvency estate, the insolvent can indorse a bill accepted for his accommodation, so as to convey to his indorsee a right of action against the accommodation acceptor.[48]

Where a negotiable instrument is given to a bankrupt after his bankruptcy, the bankrupt has the property in it, unless the trustee chooses to interfere.[49] Until the trustee interferes by notice in writing, all transactions by a bankrupt after the commencement of his bankruptcy with any person dealing with or without knowledge of the bankruptcy, are valid as against the trustee.[50]

If a man already a bankrupt is payee of a negotiable bill or note, the acceptor or maker cannot dispute the payee's capacity to indorse.[51]

Effect of discharge

By section 281 of the Insolvency Act 1986, the discharge of the bankrupt releases the bankrupt, with certain exceptions, from all debts provable in the bankruptcy.[52]   **34–35**

---

[45] Insolvency Act 1986 ss.283, 306 to 314.

[46] Sections 144, 145, and 234 of the Insolvency Act 1986.

[47] *Pinkerton v. Marshall* (1794) 2 H.Bl. 334; *Thomason v. Frere* (1808) 10 East. 418, Insolvency Act 1986 s.284.

[48] *Arden v. Watkins* (1803) 3 East 317; *Wallace v. Hardacre* (1807) 1 Camp. at 46; *Ramosbotham v. Cator* (1816) 1 Stark 228.

[49] *Pinkerton v. Marshall* (1794) 2 H.Bl. 334; *Thomson v. Frere* (1808) 10 East. 418.

[50] Insolvency Act 1986 s.307. *Cohen v. Mitchell* (1890) 25 Q.B.D. 262, 267; *Re Rogers* (1891)8 Morr. 236.

[51] *Drayton v. Dale* (1823) 2 B. & C. 293; *Herbert v. Sayer* (1844) 5 Q.B. 965.

[52] Discharge will now ordinarily be granted automatically after two or three years: s.279 of the Insolvency Act 1986. In *Temple v. Pullen* (1853) 6 Exch. 389, the defendant had given a blank signature before the commencement of the bankruptcy, which was not converted into a promissory note until after his discharge, and, it having been found that the conversion had taken place within a reasonable time, it was held that the plaintiff, who was an innocent indorsee, was entitled to recover notwithstanding the discharge.

BILLS OF EXCHANGE ACT 1882

PART I

PRELIMINARY

Short title

1. This Act may be cited as the Bills of Exchange Act 1882.

Interpretation of terms

2. In this Act, unless the context otherwise requires—

"Acceptance" means an acceptance completed by delivery or notification.

"Action" includes counter claim and set off.

"Banker" includes a body of persons whether incorporated or not who carry on the business of banking.

"Bankrupt" includes any person whose estate is vested in a trustee or assignee under the law for the time being in force relating to bankruptcy.

"Bearer" means the person in possession of a bill or note which is payable to bearer.

"Bill" means bill of exchange, and "note" means promissory note.

"Delivery" means transfer of possession, actual or constructive, from one person to another.

"Holder" means the payee or indorsee of a bill or note who is in possession of it, or the bearer thereof.

"Indorsement" means an indorsement completed by delivery.

"Issue" means the first delivery of a bill of note, complete in form to a person who takes it as a holder.

"Person" includes a body of persons whether incorporated or not.

"postal operator" has the meaning given by *section 125(1)* of the *Postal Services Act 2000.*[1]

"Value" means valuable consideration.

"Written" includes printed, and "writing" includes print.

---

[1] Definition inserted by S.I. 2000 No. 1149 (The Postal Services Act 2000 (Consequential Modifications No. 1) Order 2001, Sched. 1, para. 4(2)).

PART II

BILLS OF EXCHANGE

Forms and Interpretation

Bill of exchange defined

3. (1) A bill of exchange is an unconditional order in writing, addressed by one person to another, signed by the person giving it, requiring the person to whom it is addressed to pay on demand or at a fixed or determinable future time a sum certain in money to or to the order of a specified person, or to bearer.

(2) An instrument which does not comply with these conditions, or which orders any act to be done in addition to the payment of money, is not a bill of exchange.

(3) An order to pay out of a particular fund is not unconditional within the meaning of this section; but an unqualified order to pay, coupled with (a) an indication of a particular fund out of which the drawee is to reimburse himself or a particular account to be debited with the amount, or (b) a statement of the transaction which gives rise to the bill, is unconditional.

(4) A bill is not valid by reason—

(a) That it is not dated;

(b) That it does not specify the value given, or that any value has been given therefor;

(c) That it does not specify the place where it is drawn or the place where it is payable.

NOTES

- Act amended by Consumer Credit Act 1974 (c. 39), s.125(2).

- Section 3 amended by Decimal Currency Act 1969 (c. 19), s.2.

Inland and foreign bills

4. (1) An inland bill is a bill which is or on the face of it purports to be (a) both drawn and payable within the British Islands, or (b) drawn within the British Islands upon some person resident therein. Any other bill is a foreign bill.

For the purposes of this Act "British Islands" mean any part of the United Kingdom of Great Britain and Ireland, the islands of Man, Guernsey, Jersey, Alderney, and Sark, and the islands adjacent to any of them being part of the dominions of Her Majesty.

(2) Unless the contrary appear on the face of the bill the holder may treat it as an inland bill.

Effect where different parties to bill are the same person

5. (1) A bill may be drawn payable to, or to the order of, the drawer, or it may be drawn payable to, or to the order of, the drawee.

(2) Where in a bill drawer and drawee are the same person, or where the drawee is a fictitious person or a person not having capacity to contract, the holder may treat the instrument, at his option, either as a bill of exchange or as a promissory note.

Address to drawee

6. (1) The drawee must be named or otherwise indicated in a bill with reasonable certainty.

(2) A bill may be addressed to two or more drawees whether they are partners or not, but an order addressed to two drawees in the alternative or to two or more drawees in succession is not a bill of exchange.

Certainty required as to payee

7. (1) Where a bill is not payable to bearer, the payee must be named or otherwise indicated therein with reasonable certainty.

(2) A bill may be made payable to two or more payees jointly, or it may be made payable in the alternative to one of two, or one of some of several payees. A bill may also be made payable to the holder of an office for the time being.

(3) Where the payee is a fictitious or non-existing person the bill may be treated as payable to bearer.

What bills are negotiable

8. (1) When a bill contains words prohibiting transfer, or indicating an intention that it should not be transferable, it is valid as between the parties thereto, but is not negotiable.

(2) A negotiable bill may be payable either to order or to bearer.

(3) A bill is payable to bearer which is expressed to be so payable, or on which the only or last indorsement is an indorsement in blank.

(4) A bill is payable to order which is expressed to be so payable, or which is expressed to be payable to a particular person, and does not contain words prohibiting transfer or indicating an intention that it should not be transferable.

(5) Where a bill, either originally or by indorsement, is expressed to be payable to the order of a specified person, and not to him or his order, it is nevertheless payable to him or his order at his option.

Sum payable

9. (1) The sum payable by a bill is a sum certain within the meaning of this Act, although it was required to be paid—

(a) With interest.

(b) By stated instalments.

(c) By stated instalments, with a provision that upon default in payment of any instalment the whole shall become due.

(d) According to an indicated rate of exchange or according to a rate of exchange to be ascertained as directed by the bill.

(2) Where the sum payable is expressed in words and also in figures, and there is a discrepancy between the two, the sum denoted by the words is the amount payable.

(3) Where a bill is expressed to be payable with interest, unless the instrument otherwise provides, interest runs from the date of the bill, and if the bill is undated from the issue thereof.

Bill payable on demand

10. (1) A bill is payable on demand—

(a) Which is expressed to be payable on demand, or at sight, or on presentation; or

(b) In which no time for payment is expressed.

(2) Where a bill is accepted or indorsed when it is overdue, it shall, as regards the acceptor who so accepts, or any indorser who so indorses it, be deemed a bill payable on demand.

Bill payable at a future time

11. A bill is payable at a determinable future time within the meaning of this Act which is expressed to be payable—

(1) At a fixed period after date or sight.

(2) On or at a fixed period after the occurrence of a specified event which is certain to happen, though the time of happening may be uncertain.

An instrument expressed to be payable on a contingency is not a bill, and the happening of the event does not cure the defect.

Omission of date in bill payable after date

12. Where a bill expressed to be payable at a fixed period after date is issued undated, or where the acceptance of a bill payable at a fixed period after sight is undated, any holder may insert therein the true date of issue or acceptance, and the bill shall be payable accordingly.

Provided that (1) where the holder in good faith and by mistake inserts a wrong date, and (2) in every case where a wrong date is inserted, if the bill subsequently comes into the hands of a holder in due course the bill shall not be avoided thereby, but shall operate and by payable as if the date so inserted had been the true date.

Ante-dating and post-dating

13. (1) Where a bill or an acceptance or any indorsement on a bill is dated, the date shall, unless the contrary be proved, be deemed to be the true date of the drawing, acceptance, or indorsement, as the case may be.

(2) A bill is not invalid by reason only that it is ante-dated or postdated, or that it bears date on a Sunday.

Computation of time of payment

14. Where a bill is not payable on demand the day on which it falls due is determined as follows:

[(1) The bill is due and payable in all cases on the last day of the time of payment as fixed by the bill or, if that is a non-business day, on the succeeding business day.][1]

---

[1] Section 14(1) substituted except in relation to bills drawn and notes made before 16.1.1972 by Banking and Financial Dealings Act 1971 (c. 80), s.3(2)(3).

(2) Where a bill is payable at a fixed period after date, after sight, or after the happening of a specified event, the time of payment is determined by excluding the day from which the time is to begin to run and by including the day of payment.

(3) Where a bill is payable at a fixed period after sight, the time begins to run from the date of the acceptance if the bill be accepted, and from the date of nothing or protest if the bill be noted or protested for non-acceptance, or for non-delivery.

(4) The term "month" in a bill means a calendar month.

Case of need

15. The drawer of a bill and any indorser may insert therein the name of a person to whom the holder may resort in case of need, that is to say, in case the bill is dishonoured by non-acceptance or non-payment. Such person is called the referee in case of need. It is in the option of the holder to resort to the referee in case of need or not as he may think fit.

Optional stipulations by drawer or indorser

16. The drawer of a bill, and any indorser, may insert therein an express stipulation—
(1) Negativing or limiting his own liability to the holder.
(2) Waiving as regards himself some or all of the holder's duties.

Definition and requisites of acceptance

17. (1) The acceptance of a bill is the signification by the drawee of his assent to the order of the drawer.

(2) An acceptance is invalid unless it complies with the following conditions, namely:

(a) It must be written on the bill and be signed by the drawee. The mere signature of the drawee without additional words is sufficient.

(b) It must not express that the drawee will perform his promise by any other means than the payment of money.

Time for acceptance

18. A bill may be accepted—
(1) Before it has been signed by the drawer, or while otherwise incomplete;
(2) When it is overdue, or after it has been dishonoured by a previous refusal to accept, or by non-payment;
(3) When a bill payable after sight is dishonoured by non-acceptance, and the drawee subsequently accepts it, the holder, in the absence of any different agreement, is entitled to have the bill accepted as of the date of first presentment to the drawee for acceptance.

General and qualified acceptances

19. (1) An acceptance is either (a) general or (b) qualified.

(2) A general acceptance assents without qualification to the order of the drawer. A qualified acceptance in expressed terms varies the effect of the bill as drawn.

In particular an acceptance is qualified which is—

(a) conditional, that is to say, which makes payment by the acceptor dependent on the fulfillment of a condition therein stated;

(b) partial, that is to say, an acceptance to pay part only of the amount for which the bill is drawn;

(c) local, that is to say, an acceptance to pay only at a particular specified place;

An acceptance to pay at a particular place is a general acceptance, unless it expressly states that the bill is to be paid there only and not elsewhere:

(d) qualified as to time;

(e) the acceptance of some one or more of the drawees, but not of all.

Inchoate instruments

20. (1) Where a simple signature on a blank [. . .][1] paper is delivered by the signer in order that it may be converted into a bill, it operates as a prima facie authority to fill it up as a complete bill for any amount [. . .],[2] using the signature for that of the drawer, or the acceptor, or an indorser; and, in like manner, when a bill is wanting in any material particular, the person in possession of it has a prima facie authority to fill up the omission in any way he thinks fit.

(2) In order that any such instrument when completed may be enforceable against any person who became a party thereto prior to its completion, it must be filled up within a reasonable time, and strictly in accordance with the authority given. Reasonable time for this purpose is a question of fact.

Provided that if any such instrument after completion is negotiated to a holder in due course it shall be valid and effectual for all purposes in his hands, and he may enforce it as if it had been filled up within a reasonable time and strictly in accordance with the authority given.

Delivery

21. (1) Every contract on a bill, whether it be the drawer's, the acceptor's, or an indorser's, is incomplete and revocable, until delivery of the instrument in order to give effect thereto.

Provided that where an acceptance is written on a bill, and the drawee gives notice to or according to the directions of the person entitled to the bill that he has accepted it, the acceptance then becomes complete and irrevocable.

(2) As between immediate parties, and as regards a remote party other than a holder in due course, the delivery—

(a) in order to be effectual must be made either by or under the authority of the party drawing, accepting, or indorsing, as the case may be;

(b) may be shown to have been conditional or for a special purpose only, and not for the purpose of transferring the property in the bill.

But if the bill be in the hands of a holder in due course a valid delivery of the bill by all parties prior to him so as to make them liable to him is conclusively presumed.

---

[1] Words repealed by Finance Act 1970 (c. 24), Sched. 8, Pt V and Finance Act (Northern Ireland) 1970 (c. 21), Sched. 3, Pt III.
[2] Words repealed by Finance Act 1970 (c. 24), Sched. 8, Pt V and Finance Act (Northern Ireland) 1970 (c. 21), Sched. 3, Pt III.

(3) Where a bill is no longer in the possession of a party who has signed it as drawer, acceptor, or indorser, a valid and unconditional delivery by him is presumed until the contrary is proved.

Capacity and Authority of Parties

Capacity of parties

22. (1) Capacity to incur liability as a party to a bill is coextensive with capacity to contract.

Provided that nothing in this section shall enable a corporation to make itself liable as drawer, acceptor, or indorser of a bill unless it is competent to it so to do under the law for the time being in force relating to corporations.

(2) Where a bill is drawn or indorsed by an infant, minor, or corporation having no capacity or power to incur liability on a bill, the drawing or indorsement entitles the holder to receive payment of the bill, and to enforce it against any other party thereto.

Signature essential to liability

23. No person is liable as drawer, indorser, or acceptor of a bill who has not signed it as such: Provided that

(1) Where a person signs a bill in a trade or assumed name, he is liable thereon as if he had signed it in his own name;

(2) The signature of the name of a firm is equivalent to the signature by the person so signing of the names of all persons liable as partners in that firm.

Forged or unauthorised signature

24. Subject to the provisions of this Act, where a signature on a bill is forged or placed thereon without the authority of the person whose signature it purports to be, the forged or unauthorised signature is wholly inoperative, and no right to retain the bill or to give a discharge therefor or to enforce payment thereof against any party thereto can be acquired through or under that signature, unless the party against whom it is sought to retain or enforce payment of the bill is precluded from setting up the forgery or want of authority.

Provided that nothing in this section shall affect the ratification of an unauthorised signature not amounting to a forgery.

Procuration signatures

25. A signature by procuration operates as notice that the agent has but a limited authority to sign, and the principal is only bound by such signature if the agent in so signing was acting within the actual limits of his authority.

Person signing as agent or in representative capacity

26. (1) Where a person signs a bill as drawer, indorser, or acceptor, and adds words to his signature, indicating that he signs for or on behalf of a principal, or in a representative character, he is not personally liable thereon; but the mere addition to his signature of words describing him as an agent, or as filling a representative character, does not exempt him from personal liability.

(2) In determining whether a signature on a bill is that of the principal or that of the agent by whose hand it is written, the construction most favourable to the validity of the instrument shall be adopted.

The Consideration for a Bill

Value and holder for value

27. (1) Valuable consideration for a bill may be constituted by,—

(a) Any consideration sufficient to support a simple contract;

(b) An antecedent debt or liability. Such a debt or liability is deemed valuable consideration whether the bill is payable on demand or at a future time.

(2) Where value has at any time been given for a bill the holder is deemed to be a holder for value as regards the acceptor and all parties to the bill who became parties prior to such time.

(3) Where the holder of a bill has a lien on it arising either from contract or by implication of law, he is deemed to be a holder for value to the extent of the sum for which he has a lien.

Accommodation bill or party

28. (1) An accommodation party to a bill is a person who has signed a bill as drawer, acceptor, or indorser, without receiving value therefor, and for the purpose of lending his name to some other person.

(2) An accommodation party is liable on the bill to a holder for value; and it is immaterial whether, when such holder took the bill, he knew such party to be an accommodation party or not.

Holder in due course

29. (1) A holder in due course is a holder who has taken a bill, complete and regular on the face of it, under the following conditions; namely,

(a) That he became the holder of it before it was overdue, and without notice that it had been previously dishonoured, if such was the fact;

(b) That he took the bill in good faith and for value, and that at the time the bill was negotiated to him he had no notice of any defect in the title of the person who negotiated it.

(2) In particular the title of a person who negotiates a bill is defective within the meaning of this Act when he obtained the bill, or the acceptance thereof, by fraud, duress, or force and fear, or other unlawful means, or an illegal consideration, or when he negotiates it in breach of faith, or under such circumstances as amount to a fraud.

(3) A holder (whether for value or not), who derives his title to a bill through a holder in due course, and who is not himself a party to any fraud or illegality affecting it, has all the rights of that holder in due course as regards the acceptor and all parties to the bill prior to that holder.

Presumption of value and good faith

30. (1) Every party whose signature appears on a bill is prima facie deemed to have become a party thereto for value.

(2) Every holder of a bill is prima facie deemed to be a holder in due course; but if in an action on a bill it is admitted or proved that the acceptance, issue, or subsequent negotiation of the bill is affected with fraud, duress, or force and fear, or illegality, the burden of proof is shifted, unless and until the holder proves that, subsequent to the alleged fraud or illegality, value has in good faith been given for the bill.

Negotiation of Bills

Negotiation of bill

31. (1) A bill is negotiated when it is transferred from one person to another in such a manner as to constitute the transferee the holder of the bill.

(2) A bill payable to bearer is negotiated by delivery.

(3) A bill payable to order is negotiated by the indorsement of the holder completed by delivery.

(4) Where the holder of a bill payable to his order transfers it for value without indorsing it, the transfer gives the transferee such title as the transferor had in the bill, and the transferee in addition acquires the right to have the indorsement of the transferor.

(5) Where any person is under obligation to indorse a bill in a representative capacity, he may indorse the bill in such terms as to negative personal liability.

Requisites of a valid indorsement

32. An indorsement in order to operate as a negotiation must comply with the following conditions, namely,—

(1) It must be written on the bill itself and be signed by the indorser. The simple signature of the indorser on the bill, without additional words, is sufficient.

An indorsement written on an allonge, or on a "copy" of a bill issued or negotiated in a country where "copies" are recognised, is deemed to be written on the bill itself.

(2) It must be an indorsement of the entire bill. A partial indorsement, that is to say, an indorsement which purports to transfer to the indorsee a part only of the amount payable, or which purports to transfer the bill to two or more indorsees severally, does not operate as a negotiation of the bill.

(3) Where a bill is payable to the order of two or more payees or indorsees who are not partners all must indorse, unless the one indorsing has authority to indorse for the others.

(4) Where, in a bill payable to order, the payee or indorsee is wrongly designated, or his name is mis-spelt, he may indorse the bill as therein described, adding, if he thinks fit, his proper signature.

(5) Where there are two or more indorsements on a bill, each indorsement is deemed to have been made in the order in which it appears on the bill, until the contrary is proved.

(6) An indorsement may be made in blank or special. It may also contain terms making it restrictive.

Conditional indorsement

33. Where a bill purports to be indorsed conditionally the condition may be disregarded by the payer, and payment to the indorsee is valid whether the condition has been fulfilled or not.

Indorsement in blank and special indorsement

34. (1) An indorsement in blank specifies no indorsee, and a bill so indorsed becomes payable to bearer.

(2) A special indorsement specifies the person to whom, or to whose order, the bill is to be payable.

(3) The provisions of this Act relating to a payee apply with the necessary modifications to an indorsee under a special indorsement.

(4) When a bill has been indorsed in blank, any holder may convert the blank indorsement into a special indorsement by writing above the indorser's signature a direction to pay the bill to or to the order of himself or some other person.

Restrictive indorsement

35. (1) An indorsement is restrictive which prohibits the further negotiation of the bill or which expresses that it is a mere authority to deal with the bill as thereby directed and not a transfer of the ownership thereof, as, for example, if a bill be indorsed "Pay D. only", or "Pay D. for the account of X", or "Pay D. or order for collection".

(2) A restrictive indorsement gives the indorsee the right to receive payment of the bill and to sue any party thereto that his indorser could have sued, but gives him no power to transfer his rights as indorsee unless it expressly authorise him to do so.

(3) Where a restrictive indorsement authorises further transfer, all subsequent indorsees take the bill with the same rights and subject to the same liabilities as the first indorsee under the restrictive indorsement.

Negotiation of overdue or dishonoured bill

36. (1) Where a bill is negotiable in its origin it continues to be negotiable until it has been (a) restrictively indorsed or (b) discharged by payment or otherwise.

(2) Where an overdue bill is negotiated, it can only be negotiated subject to any defect of title affecting it at its maturity, and thenceforward no person who takes it can acquire or give a better title than that which the person from whom he took it had.

(3) A bill payable on demand is deemed to be overdue within the meaning and for the purposes of this section, when it appears on the face of it to have been in circulation for an unreasonable length of time. What is an unreasonable length of time for this purpose is a question of fact.

(4) Except where an indorsement bears date after the maturity of the bill, every negotiation is prima facie deemed to have been effected before the bill was over-due.

(5) Where a bill which is not overdue has been dishonoured any person who takes it with notice of the dishonour takes it subject to any defect of title attaching thereto at the time of dishonour, but nothing in this sub-section shall affect the rights of a holder in due course.

Negotiation of bill to party already liable thereon

37. Where a bill is negotiated back to the drawer, or to a prior indorser or to the acceptor, such party may, subject to the provisions of this Act, re-issue and further negotiate the bill, but he is not entitled to enforce payment of the bill against any intervening party to whom he was previously liable.

Rights of the holder

38. The rights and powers of the holder of a bill are as follows:

(1) He may sue on the bill in his own name;

(2) Where he is a holder in due course, he holds the bill free from any defect of title of prior parties, as well as from mere personal defences available to prior parties among themselves, and may enforce payment against all parties liable on the bill;

(3) Where his title is defective (a) if he negotiates the bill to a holder in due course, that holder obtains a good and complete title to the bill, and (b) if he obtains payment of the bill the person who pays him in due course gets a valid discharge for the bill.

General Duties of the Holder

When presentment for acceptance is necessary

39. (1) Where a bill is payable after sight, presentment for acceptance is necessary in order to fix the maturity of the instrument.

(2) Where a bill expressly stipulates that it shall be presented for acceptance, or where a bill is drawn payable elsewhere than at the residence or place of business of the drawee, it must be presented for acceptance before it can be presented for payment.

(3) In no other case is presentment for acceptance necessary in order to render liable any party to the bill.

(4) Where the holder of a bill, drawn payable elsewhere than at the place of business or residence of the drawee, has not time, with the exercise of reasonable diligence, to present the bill for acceptance before presenting it for payment on the day that it falls due, the delay caused by presenting the bill for acceptance before presenting it for payment is excused, and does not discharge the drawer and indorsers.

Time for presenting bill payable after sight

40. (1) Subject to the provisions of this Act, when a bill payable after sight is negotiated, the holder must either present it for acceptance or negotiate it within a reasonable time.

(2) If he do not do so, the drawer and all indorsers prior to that holder are discharged.

(3) In determining what is a reasonable time within the meaning of this section, regard shall be had to the nature of the bill, the usage of trade with respect to similar bills, and the facts of the particular case.

Rules as to presentment for acceptance, and excuses for non-presentment

41. (1) A bill is duly presented for acceptance which is presented in accordance with the following rules:

(a) The presentment must be made by or on behalf of the holder to the drawee or to some person authorised to accept or refuse acceptance on his behalf at a reasonable hour on a business day and before the bill is overdue;

(b) Where a bill is addressed to two or more drawees, who are not partners, presentment must be made to them all, unless one has authority to accept for all, then presentment may be made to him only;

(c) Where the drawee is dead presentment may be made to his personal representative;

(d) Where the drawee is bankrupt, presentment may be made to him or to his trustee;

(e) Where authorised by agreement or usage, a presentment through [a postal operator][1] is sufficient.

(2) Presentment in accordance with these rules is excused, and a bill may be treated as dishonoured by non-acceptance—

(a) Where the drawee is dead or bankrupt, or is a fictitious person or a person not having capacity to contract by bill;

(b) Where, after the exercise of reasonable diligence, such presentment cannot be effected;

(c) Where, although the presentment has been irregular, acceptance has been refused on some other ground.

(3) The fact that the holder has reason to believe that the bill, on presentment, will be dishonoured does not excuse presentment.

Non-acceptance

42. When a bill is duly presented for acceptance and is not accepted within the customary time, the person presenting it must treat it as dishonoured by non-acceptance. If he do not, the holder shall lose his right of recourse against the drawer and indorsers.

Dishonour by non-acceptance and its consequences

43. (1) A bill is dishonoured by non-acceptance—

(a) when it is duly presented for acceptance, and such an acceptance as is prescribed by this Act is refused or cannot be obtained; or

(b) when presentment for acceptance is excused and the bill is not accepted.

(2) Subject to the provisions of this Act when a bill is dishonoured by non-acceptance, an immediate right of recourse against the drawer and indorsers accrues to the holder, and no presentment for payment is necessary.

Duties as to qualified acceptances

44. (1) The holder of a bill may refuse to take a qualified acceptance, and if he does not obtain an unqualified acceptance may treat the bill as dishonoured by non-acceptance.

(2) Where a qualified acceptance is taken, and the drawer or an indorser has not expressly or impliedly authorised the holder to take a qualified acceptance, or does not subsequently assent thereto, such drawer or indorsers is discharged from his liability on the bill.

---

[1] Words substituted by S.I. 2001 No. 1149 (The Postal Services Act 2000 (Consequential Modifications No. 1) Order 2001, Sched. 1, para. 4(3)).

The provisions of this sub-section do not apply to a partial acceptance, whereof due notice has been given. Where a foreign bill has been accepted as to part, it must be protested as to the balance.

(3) When the drawer or indorser of a bill receives notice of a qualified acceptance, and does not within a reasonable time express his dissent to the holder he shall be deemed to have assented thereto.

Rules as to presentment for payment

45. Subject to the provisions of this Act a bill must be duly presented for payment. If it be not so presented the drawer and indorsers shall be discharged.

A bill is duly presented for payment which is presented in accordance with the following rules:

(1) Where the bill is not payable on demand, presentment must be made on the day it falls due.

(2) Where the bill is payable on demand, then subject to the provisions of this Act, presentment must be made within a reasonable time after its issue in order to render the drawer liable, and within a reasonable time after its indorsement, in order to render the indorser liable.

In determining what is a reasonable time, regard shall be had to the nature of the bill, the usage of trade with regard to similar bills, and the facts of the particular case.

(3) Presentment must be made by the holder or by some person authorised to receive payment on his behalf at a reasonable hour on a business day, at the proper place as hereinafter defined, either to the person designated by the bill as payer, or to some person authorised to pay or refuse payment on his behalf if with the exercise of reasonable diligence such person can there be found.

(4) A bill is presented at the proper place—

(a) Where a place of payment is specified in the bill and the bill is there presented.

(b) Where no place of payment is specified, but the address of the drawee or acceptor is given in the bill, and the bill is there presented.

(c) Where no place of payment is specified and no address given, and the bill is presented at the drawee's or acceptor's place of business if known, and if not, at his ordinary residence if known.

(d) If any other case if presented to the drawee or acceptor wherever he can be found, or if presented at his last known place of business or residence.

(5) Where a bill is presented at the proper place, and after the exercise of reasonable diligence no person authorised to pay or refuse payment can be found there, no further presentment to the drawee or acceptor is required.

(6) Where a bill is drawn upon, or accepted by two or more persons who are not partners, and no place of payment is specified, presentment must be made to them all.

(7) Where the drawee or acceptor of a bill is dead, and no place of payment is specified, presentment must be made to a personal representative, if such there be, and with the exercise of reasonable diligence he can be found.

(8) Where authorised by agreement or usage a presentment through [a postal operator][1] is sufficient.

---

[1] Words substituted by S.I. 2001 No. 1149 (The Postal Services Act 2000 (Consequential Modifications No. 1) Order 2001, Sched. 1, para. 4(4)).

Excuses for delay or non-presentment for payment

46. (1) Delay in making presentment for payment is excused when the delay is caused by circumstances beyond the control of the holder, and not imputable to his default, misconduct, or negligence. When the cause of delay ceases to operate presentment must be made with reasonable diligence.

(2) Presentment for payment is dispensed with,—

(a) Where, after the exercise of reasonable diligence presentment, as required by this Act, cannot be effected.
The fact that the holder has reason to believe that the bill will, on presentment, be dishonoured, does not dispense with the necessity for presentment.

(b) Where the drawee is a fictitious person.

(c) As regards the drawer where the drawee or acceptor is not bound as between himself and the drawer, to accept or pay the bill, and the drawer has no reason to believe that the bill would be paid if presented.

(d) As regards an indorser, where the bill was accepted or made for the accommodation of that indorser, and he has no reason to expect that the bill would be paid if presented.

(e) By waiver of presentment, express or implied.

Dishonour by non-payment

47. (1) A bill is dishonoured by non-payment (a) when it is duly presented for payment and payment is refused or cannot be obtained, or (b) when presentment is excused and the bill is overdue and unpaid.

(2) Subject to the provisions of this Act, when a bill is dishonoured by non-payment, an immediate right of recourse against the drawer and indorsers accrues to the holder.

Notice of dishonour and effect of non-notice

48. Subject to the provisions of this Act, when a bill has been dishonoured by non-acceptance or by non-payment, notice of dishonour must be given to the drawer and each indorser, and any drawer or indorser to whom such notice is not given is discharged:
Provided that—

(1) Where a bill is dishonoured by non-acceptance, and notice of dishonour is not given, the rights of a holder in due course, subsequent to the omission, shall not be prejudiced by the omission.

(2) Where a bill is dishonoured by non-acceptance, and due notice of dishonour is given, it shall not be necessary to give notice of a subsequent dishonour by non-payment unless the bill shall in the meantime have been accepted.

Rules as to notice of dishonour

49. Notice of dishonour in order to be valid and effectual must be given in accordance with the following rules:

(1) The notice must be given by or on behalf of the holder, or by or on behalf of an indorser who, at the time of giving it, is himself liable on the bill.

(2) Notice of dishonour may be given by an agent either in his own name, or in the name of any party entitled to give notice whether that party be his principal or not.

(3) Where the notice is given by or on behalf of the holder, it ensures for the benefit of all subsequent holders and all prior indorsers who have a right of recourse against the party to whom it is given.

(4) Where notice is given by or on behalf of an indorser entitled to give notice as hereinbefore provided, it enures for the benefit of the holder and all indorsers subsequent to the party to whom notice is given.

(5) The notice may be given in writing or by personal communication, and may be given in any terms which sufficiently identify the bill, and intimate that the bill has been dishonoured by non-acceptance or non-payment.

(6) The return of a dishonoured bill to the drawer or an indorser is, in point of form, deemed a sufficient notice of dishonour.

(7) A written notice need not be signed, and an insufficient written notice may be supplemented and validated by verbal communication. A misdescription of the bill shall not vitiate the notice unless the party to whom the notice is given is in fact misled thereby.

(8) Where notice of dishonour is required to be given to any person, it may be given either to the party himself, or to his agent in that behalf.

(9) Where the drawer or indorser is dead, and the party giving notice knows it, the notice must be given to a personal representative if such there be, and with the exercise of reasonable diligence he can be found.

(10) Where the drawer or indorser is bankrupt, notice may be given either to the party himself or to the trustee.

(11) Where there are two or more drawers or indorsers who are not partners, notice must be given to each of them, unless one of them has authority to receive such notice for the others.

(12) The notice may be given as soon as the bill is dishonoured and must be given within a reasonable time thereafter.

In the absence of special circumstances notice is not deemed to have been given within a reasonable time, unless—

(a) where the person giving and the person to receive notice reside in the same place, the notice is given or sent off in time to reach the latter on the day after the dishonour of the bill.

(b) where the person giving and the person to receive notice reside in different places, the notice is sent off on the day after the dishonour of the bill, if there be a post at a convenient hour on that day, and if there be no such post on that day then by the next post thereafter.

(13) Where a bill when dishonoured is in the hands of an agent, he may either himself give notice to the parties liable on the bill, or he may give notice to his principal. If he give notice to his principal, he must do so within the same time as if he were the holder, and the principal upon receipt of such notice has himself the same time for giving notice as if the agent had been an independent holder.

(14) Where a party to a bill receives due notice of dishonour, he has after the receipt of such notice the same period of time for giving notice to antecedent parties that the holder has after the dishonour.

(15) Where a notice of dishonour is duly addressed and posted, the sender is deemed to have given due notice of dishonour, notwithstanding any miscarriage by the [postal operator concerned].[1]

Excuses for non-notice and delay

50. (1) Delay in giving notice of dishonour is excused where the delay is caused by circumstances beyond the control of the party giving notice, and not imputable to his

[1] Words substituted by S.I. 2001 No. 1149 (The Postal Services Act 2000 (Consequential Modifications No. 1) Order 2001, Sched. 1, para. 4(5)).

default, misconduct, or negligence. When the cause of delay ceases to operate the notice must be given with reasonable diligence.

(2) Notice of dishonour is dispensed with—

(a) When, after the exercise of reasonable diligence, notice as required by this Act cannot be given to or does not reach the drawer or indorser sought to be charged;

(b) By waiver express or implied. Notice of dishonour may be waived before the time of giving notice has arrived, or after the omission to give due notice;

(c) As regards the drawer in the following cases, namely, (1) where drawer and drawee are the same person, (2) where the drawee is a fictitious person or a person not having capacity to contract, (3) where the drawer is the person to whom the bill is presented for payment, (4) where the drawee or acceptor is as between himself and the drawer under no obligation to accept or pay the bill, (5) where the drawer has countermanded payment;

(d) As regards the indorser in the following cases, namely, (1) where the drawee is a fictitious person or a person not having capacity to contract, and the indorser was aware of the fact at the time he indorsed the bill, (2) where the indorser is the person to whom the bill is presented for payment, (3) where the bill was accepted or made for his accommodation.

Noting or protest of bill

51. (1) Where an inland bill has been dishonoured it may, if the holder think fit, be noted for non-acceptance or non-payment, as the case may be; but it shall not be necessary to note or protest any such bill in order to preserve the recourse against the drawer or indorser.

(2) Where a foreign bill, appearing on the face of it to be such, has been dishonoured by non-acceptance it must be duly protested for non-acceptance, and where such a bill, which has not been previously dishonoured by non-acceptance, is dishonoured by non-payment it must be duly protested for non-payment. If it be not so protested the drawer and indorsers are discharged. Where a bill does not appear on the face of it to be a foreign bill, protest thereof in case of dishonour is unnecessary.

(3) A bill which has been protested for non-acceptance may be subsequently protested for non-payment.

(4) Subject to the provisions of this Act, when a bill is noted or protested, it may be noted on the day of its dishonour and must be noted not later than the next succeeding business day. When a bill has been duly noted, the protest may be subsequently extended as of the date of the noting.

(5) Where the acceptor of a bill becomes bankrupt or insolvent or suspends payment before it matures, the holder may cause the bill to be protested for better security against the drawer and indorsers.

(6) A bill must be protested at the place where it is dishonoured:
Provided that—

(a) When a bill is presented through [a postal operator],[1] and returned by post dishonoured, it may be protested at the place to which it is returned and on the day of its return if received during business hours, and if not received during business hours, then not later than the next business day;

(b) When a bill drawn payable at the place of business or residence of some person other than the drawee has been dishonoured by non-acceptance, it must be

---

[1] Words substituted by S.I. 2001 No. 1149 (The Postal Services Act 2000 (Consequential Modifications No. 1) Order 2001, Sched. 1, para. 4(6)).

protested for non-payment at the place where it is expressed to be payable, and no further presentment for payment to, or demand on, the drawee is necessary.

(7) A protest must contain a copy of the bill, and must be signed by the notary making it, and must specify—

(a) The person at whose request the bill is protested;

(b) The place and date of protest, the cause or reason for protesting the bill, the demand made, and the answer given, if any, or the fact that the drawee or acceptor could not be found.

(8) Where a bill is lost or destroyed, or is wrongly detained from the person entitled to hold it, protest may be made on a copy or written particulars thereof.

(9) Protest is dispensed with by any circumstance which would dispense with notice of dishonour. Delay in noting or protesting is excused when the delay is caused by circumstances beyond the control of the holder, and not imputable to his default, misconduct, or negligence. When the cause of delay ceases to operate the bill must be noted or protested with reasonable diligence.

Duties of holder as regards drawee or acceptor

52. (1) When a bill is accepted generally presentment for payment is not necessary in order to render the acceptor liable.

(2) When by the terms of a qualified acceptance presentment for payment is required, the acceptor, in the absence of an express stipulation to that effect, is not discharged by the omission to present the bill for payment on the day that it matures.

(3) In order to render the acceptor of a bill liable it is not necessary to protest it, or that notice of dishonour should be given to him.

(4) Where the holder of a bill presents it for payment, he shall exhibit the bill to the person from whom he demands payment, and when a bill is paid the holder shall forthwith deliver it up to the party paying it.

Liabilities of Parties

Funds in hands of drawee

53. (1) A bill, of itself, does not operate as an assignment of funds in the hands of the drawee available for the payment thereof, and the drawee of a bill who does not accept as required by this Act is not liable on the instrument. This sub-section shall not extend to Scotland.

(2) [Subject to *section 75A* of this Act,][1] In Scotland, where the drawee of a bill has in his hands funds available for the payment thereof, the bill operates as an assignment of the sum for which it is drawn in favour of the holder, from the time when the bill is presented to the drawee.

Liability of acceptor

54. The acceptor of a bill, by accepting it—

(1) Engages that he will pay it according to the tenor of his acceptance;

[1] Words inserted by Law Reform (Miscellaneous Provisions) (Scotland) Act 1985 (c. 73), s. 11(a).

(2) Is precluded from denying to a holder in due course:

(a) The existence of the drawer, the genuineness of his signature, and his capacity and authority to draw the bill;

(b) In the case of a bill payable to drawer's order, the then capacity of the drawer to indorse, but not the genuineness or validity of his indorsement;

(c) In the case of a bill payable to the order of a third person, the existence of the payee and his then capacity to indorse, but not the genuineness or validity of his indorsement.

Liability of drawer or indorser

55. (1) The drawer of a bill by drawing it—

(a) Engages that on due presentment it shall be accepted and paid according to its tenor, and that if it be dishonoured he will compensate the holder or any indorser who is compelled to pay it, provided that the requisite proceedings on dishonour be duly taken;

(b) Is precluded from denying to a holder in due course the existence of the payee and his then capacity to indorse.

(2) The indorser of a bill by indorsing it—

(a) Engages that on due presentment it shall be accepted and paid according to its tenor, and that if it be dishonoured he will compensate the holder or a subsequent indorser who is compelled to pay it, provided that the requisite proceedings on dishonour be duly taken;

(b) Is precluded from denying to a holder in due course the genuineness and regularity in all respects of the drawer's signature and all previous indorsements;

(c) Is precluded from denying to his immediate or a subsequent indorsee that the bill was at the time of his indorsement a valid and subsisting bill, and that he had then a good title thereto.

Stranger signing bill liable as indorser

56. Where a person signs a bill otherwise than as drawer or acceptor, he thereby incurs the liabilities of an indorser to a holder in due course.

Measure of damages against parties to dishonoured bill

57. Where a bill is dishonoured, the measure of damages, which shall be deemed to be liquidated damages, shall be as follows:
(1) The holder may recover from any party liable on the bill, and the drawer who has been compelled to pay the bill may recover from the acceptor, and an indorser who has been compelled to pay the bill may recover from the acceptor or from the drawer, or from a prior indorser—

(a) The amount of the bill;

(b) Interest thereon from the time of presentment for payment if the bill is payable on demand, and from the maturity of the bill in any other case;

(c) The expenses of nothing, or, when protest is necessary, and the protest has been extended, the expenses of protest.

(2) [—]¹

(3) Where by this Act interest may be recovered as damages, such interest may, if justice require it, be withheld wholly or in part, and where a bill is expressed to be payable with interest at a given rate, interest as damages may or may not be given at the same rate as interest proper.

Transferor by delivery and transferee

58. (1) Where the holder of a bill payable to bearer negotiates it by delivery without indorsing it he is called a "transferor by delivery".

(2) A transferor by delivery is not liable on the instrument.

(3) A transferor by delivery who negotiates a bill thereby warrants to his immediate transferee being a holder for value that the bill is what it purports to be, that he has a right to transfer it, and that at the time of transfer he is not aware of any fact which renders it valueless.

Discharge of Bills

Payment in due course

59. (1) A bill is discharged by payment in due course by or on behalf of the drawee or acceptor.

"Payment in due course" means payment made at or after the maturity of the bill to the holder thereof in good faith and without notice that his title to the bill is defective.

(2) Subject to the provisions hereinafter contained, when a bill is paid by the drawer or an indorser it is not discharged; but

(a) Where a bill payable to, or to the order of, a third party is paid by the drawer, the drawer may enforce payment thereof against the acceptor, but may not re-issue the bill.

(b) Where a bill is paid by an indorser, or where a bill payable to drawer's order is paid by the drawer, the party paying it is remitted to his former rights as regards the acceptor or antecedent parties, and he may, if he thinks fit, strike out his own subsequent indorsements, and again negotiate the bill.

(3) Where an accommodation bill is paid in due course by the party accommodated the bill is discharged.

Banker paying demand draft whereon indorsement is forged

60. When a bill payable to order on demand is drawn on a banker, and the banker on whom it is drawn pays the bill in good faith and in the ordinary course of business, it is not incumbent on the banker to show that the indorsement of the payee or any subsequent indorsement was made by or under the authority of the person whose indorsement it purports to be, and the banker is deemed to have paid the bill in due course, although such indorsement has been forged or made without authority.

---

¹ Repealed by Administration of Justice Act 1977 (c. 38), s.4(2)(a)(3) with saving for bills drawn before 29.8.1977.

Acceptor the holder at maturity

61. When the acceptor of a bill is or becomes the holder of it at or after its maturity, in his own right, the bill is discharged.

Express waiver

62. (1) When the holder of a bill at or after its maturity absolutely and unconditionally renounces his rights against the acceptor the bill is discharged.

The renunciation must be in writing, unless the bill is delivered up to the acceptor.

(2) The liabilities of any party to a bill may in like manner be renounced by the holder before at, or after its maturity; but nothing in this section shall affect the rights of a holder in due course without notice of the renunciation.

Cancellation

63. (1) Where a bill is intentionally cancelled by the holder or his agent, and the cancellation is apparent thereon, the bill is discharged.

(2) In like manner any party liable on a bill may be discharged by the intentional cancellation of his signature by the holder or his agent. In such case any indorser who would have had a right of recourse against the party whose signature is cancelled is also discharged.

(3) A cancellation made unintentionally, or under a mistake, or without the authority of the holder is inoperative; but where a bill or any signature thereon appears to have been cancelled the burden of proof lies on the party who alleges that the cancellation was made unintentionally, or under a mistake, or without authority.

Alteration of bill

64. (1) Where a bill or acceptance is materially altered without the assent of all parties liable on the bill, the bill is avoided except as against a party who has himself made, authorised, or assented to the alteration, and subsequent indorsers.

Provided that,

Where a bill has been materially altered, but the alteration is not apparent, and the bill is in the hands of a holder in due course, such holder may avail himself of the bill as if it had not been altered, and may enforce payment of it according to its original tenor.

(2) In particular the following alterations are material, namely, any alteration of the date, the sum payable, the time of payment, the place of payment, and, where a bill has been accepted generally, the addition of a place of payment without the acceptor's assent.

Acceptance and Payment for Honour

Acceptance for honour supra protest

65. (1) Where a bill of exchange has been protested for dishonour by non-acceptance, or protested for better security, and is not overdue, any person, not being a party already liable thereon, may, with the consent of the holder, intervene and accept the bill supra protest, for the honour of any party liable thereon, or for the honour of the person for whose account the bill is drawn.

(2) A bill may be accepted for honour for part only of the sum for which it is drawn.

(3) An acceptance for honour supra protest in order to be valid must—

(a) be written on the bill, and indicate that it is an acceptance for honour;

(b) be signed by the acceptor for honour.

(4) Where an acceptance for honour does not expressly state for whose honour it is made, it is deemed to be an acceptance for the honour of the drawer.

(5) Where a bill payable after sight is accepted for honour, its maturity is calculated from the date of the noting for non-acceptance, and not from the date of the acceptance for honour.

Liability of acceptor for honour

66. (1) The acceptor for honour of a bill by accepting it engages that he will, on due presentment, pay the bill according to the tenor of his acceptance, if it is not paid by the drawee, provided it has been duly presented for payment, and protested for non-payment, and that he receives notice of these facts.

(2) The acceptor for honour is liable to the holder and to all parties to the bill subsequent to the party for whose honour he has accepted.

Presentment to acceptor for honour

67. (1) Where a dishonoured bill has been accepted for honour supra protest, or contains a reference in case of need, it must be protested for non-payment before it is presented for payment to the acceptor for honour, or referee in case of need.

(2) Where the address of the acceptor for honour is in the same place where the bill is protested for non-payment, the bill must be presented to him not later than the day following its maturity; and where the address of the acceptor for honour is in some place other than the place where it was protested for non-payment, the bill must be forwarded not later than the day following its maturity for presentment to him.

(3) Delay in presentment or non-presentment is excused by any circumstances which would excuse delay in presentment for payment or non-presentment for payment.

(4) When a bill of exchange is dishonoured by the acceptor for honour it must be protested for non-payment by him.

Payment for honour supra protest

68. (1) Where a bill has been protested for non-payment, any person may intervene and pay it supra protest for the honour of any party liable thereon, or for the honour of the person for whose account the bill is drawn.

(2) Where two or more persons offer to pay a bill for the honour of different parties, the person whose payment will discharge most parties to the bill shall have the preference.

(3) Payment for honour supra protest, in order to operate as such and not as a more voluntary payment, must be attested by a notarial act of honour which may be appended to the protest or form an extension of it.

(4) The notarial act of honour must be founded on a declaration made by the payer for honour, or his agent in that behalf, declaring his intention to pay the bill for honour, and for whose honour he pays.

(5) Where a bill has been paid for honour, all parties subsequent to the party for whose honour it is paid are discharged, but the payer for honour is subrogated for, and

succeeds to both the rights and duties of, the holder as regards the party for whose honour he pays, and all parties liable to that party.

(6) The payer for honour on paying to the holder the amount of the bill and the notarial expenses incidental to its dishonour is entitled to receive both the bill itself and the protest. If the holder do not on demand deliver them up he shall be liable to the payer for honour in damages.

(7) Where the holder of a bill refuses to receive payment supra protest he shall lose his right of recourse against any party who would have been discharged by such payment.

Lost Instruments

Holder's right to duplicate of lost bill

69. Where a bill has been lost before it is overdue the person who was the holder of it may apply to the drawer to give him another bill of the same tenor, giving security to the drawer if required to indemnify him against all persons whatever in case the bill alleged to have been lost shall be found again.

If the drawer on request as aforesaid refuses to give such duplicate bill he may be compelled to do so.

Action on lost bill

70. In any action or proceeding upon a bill, the court or a judge may order that the loss of the instrument shall not be set up, provided an indemnity be given to the satisfaction of the court or judge against the claims of any other person upon the instrument in question.

Bill in a Set

Rules as to sets

71. (1) Where a bill is drawn in a set, each part of the set being numbered, and containing a reference to the other parts the whole of the parts constitute one bill.

(2) Where the holder of a set indorses two or more parts to different persons, he is liable on every such part, and every indorser subsequent to him is liable on the part he has himself indorsed as if the said parts were separate bills.

(3) Where two or more parts of a set are negotiated to different holders in due course, the holder whose title first accrues is as between such holders deemed the true owner of the bill; but nothing in this sub-section shall affect the rights of a person who in due course accepts or pays the part first presented to him.

(4) The acceptance may be written on any part, and it must be written on one part only.

If the drawee accepts more than one part, and such accepted parts get into the hands of different holders in due course, he is liable on every such part as if it were a separate bill.

(5) When the acceptor of a bill drawn in a set pays it without requiring the part bearing his acceptance to be delivered up to him, and that part at maturity is outstanding in the hands of a holder in due course, he is liable to the holder thereof.

(6) Subject to the preceding rules, where any one part of a bill drawn in a set is discharged by payment or otherwise, the whole bill is discharged.

Conflict of Laws

Rules where laws conflict

72. Where a bill drawn in one country is negotiated, accepted, or payable in another, the rights, duties, and liabilities of the parties thereto are determined as follows:

(1) The validity of a bill as regards requisites in form is determined by the law of the place of issue, and the validity as regards requisites in form of the supervening contracts, such as acceptance, or indorsement, or acceptance supra protest, is determined by the law of the place where such contract was made.

Provided that—

(a) Where a bill is issued out of the United Kingdom it is not invalid by reason only that it is not stamped in accordance with the law of the place of issue;

(b) Where a bill, issued out of the United Kingdom, conforms, as regards requisites in form, to the law of the United Kingdom, it may, for the purpose of enforcing payment thereof, be treated as valid as between all persons who negotiate, hold, or become parties to it in the United Kingdom.

(2) Subject to the provisions of this Act, the interpretation of the drawing, indorsement, acceptance, or acceptance supra protest of a bill, is determined by the law of the place where such contract is made.

Provided that where an inland bill is indorsed in a foreign country the indorsement shall as regards the payer be interpreted according to the law of the United Kingdom.

(3) The duties of the holder with respect to presentment for acceptance or payment and the necessity for or sufficiency of a protest or notice of dishonour, or otherwise, are determined by the law of the place where the act is done or the bill is dishonoured.

(4) [—][1]

(5) Where a bill is drawn in one country and is payable in another, the due date thereof is determined according to the law of the place where it is payable.

PART III

CHEQUES ON A BANKER

Cheque defined

73. A cheque is a bill of exchange drawn on a banker payable on demand. Except as otherwise provided in this Part, the provisions of this Act applicable to a bill of exchange payable on demand apply to a cheque.

Presentment of cheque for payment

74. Subject to the provisions of this Act—

(1) Where a cheque is not presented for payment within a reasonable time of its issue, and the drawer or the person on whose account it is drawn had the right at the time of such presentment as between him and the banker to have the cheque paid and suffers actual damage through the delay, he is discharged to the extent of such damage,

---

[1] Repealed by Administration of Justice Act 1977 (c. 38), s.4(2)(a)(3) with saving for bills drawn before 29.8.1977.

that is to say, to the extent to which such drawer or person is a creditor of such banker to a larger amount than he would have been had such cheque been paid.

(2) In determining what is a reasonable time regard shall be had to the nature of the instrument, the usage of trade and of bankers, and the facts of the particular case.

(3) The holder of such cheque as to which such drawer or person is discharged shall be a creditor, in lieu of such drawer or person, of such banker to the extent of such discharge, and entitled to recover the amount from him.

Presentment of cheque for payment: alternative place of presentment

74A. Where the banker on whom a cheque is drawn—

(a) has by notice published in the London, Edinburgh and Belfast Gazettes specified an address at which cheques drawn on him may be presented, and

(b) has not by notice so published cancelled the specification of that address,

the cheque is also presented at the proper place if it is presented there.][1]

Presentment of cheque for payment: alternative means of presentment by banker

74B. (1) A banker may present a cheque for payment to the banker on whom it is drawn by notifying him of its essential features by electronic means or otherwise, instead of by presenting the cheque itself.

(2) If a cheque is presented for payment under this section, presentment need not be made at the proper place or at a reasonable hour on a business day.

(3) If, before the close of business on the next business day following presentment of a cheque under this section, the banker on whom the cheque is drawn requests the banker by whom the cheque was presented to present the cheque itself—

(a) the presentment under this section shall be disregarded, and

(b) this section shall not apply in relation to the subsequent presentment of the cheque.

(4) A request under subsection (3) above for the presentment of a cheque shall not constitute dishonour of the cheque by non-payment.

(5) Where presentment of a cheque is made under this section, the banker who presented the cheque and the banker on whom it is drawn shall be subject to the same duties in relation to the collection and payment of the cheque as if the cheque itself had been presented for payment.

(6) For the purposes of this section, the essential features of a cheque are—

(a) the serial number of the cheque,

(b) the code which identifies the banker on whom the cheque is drawn,

(c) the account number of the drawer of the cheque, and

(d) the amount of the cheque is entered by the drawer of the cheque.][2]

---

[1] Added by S.I. 1996 No. 2993 (Deregulation (Bills of Exchange) Order, Art. 3.
[2] Added by S.I. 1996 No. 2993 (Deregulation (Bills of Exchange) Order, Art. 4(1).

Cheques presented for payment under section 74B: disapplication of section 52(4)

[**74C.** Section 52(4) above—

(a) so far as relating to presenting a bill for payment, shall not apply to presenting a cheque for payment under section 74B above, and

(b) so far as relating to a bill which is paid, shall not apply to a cheque which is paid following presentment under that section.][1]

Revocation of banker's authority

75. The duty and authority of a banker to pay a cheque drawn on him by his customer are determined by—
(1) Countermand of payment;
(2) Notice of the customer's death.

[**75A.** (1) On the countermand of payment of a cheque, the banker shall be treated as having no funds available for the payment of the cheque.
(2) This section applies to Scotland only.][2]

Crossed cheques

General and special crossings defined

76. (1) Where a cheque bears across its face an addition of—

(a) The words "and company" or any abbreviation thereof between two parallel transverse lines, either with or without the words "not negotiable"; or

(b) Two parallel transverse lines simply, either with or without the words "not negotiable";

that addition constitutes a crossing, and the cheque is crossed generally.

(2) Where a cheque bears across its face an addition of the name of a banker, either with or without the words "not negotiable", that addition constitutes a crossing, and the cheque is crossed specially and to that banker.

Crossing by drawer or after issue

77. (1) A cheque may be crossed generally or specially by the drawer.
(2) Where a cheque is uncrossed, the holder may cross it generally or specially.
(3) Where a cheque is crossed generally the holder may cross it specially.
(4) Where a cheque is crossed generally or specially, the holder may add the words "not negotiable".
(5) Where a cheque is crossed specially, the banker to whom it is crossed may again cross it specially to another banker for collection.
(6) Where an uncrossed cheque, or a cheque crossed generally, is sent to a banker for collection, he may cross it specially to himself.

---

[1] Added by S.I. 1996 No. 2993 (Deregulation (Bills of Exchange) Order, Art. 4(1).
[2] Section 75A inserted by Law Reform (Miscellaneous Provisions) (Scotland) Act 1985 (c. 73), s.11(b).

Crossing a material part of cheque

78. A crossing authorised by this Act is a material part of the cheque; it shall not be lawful for any person to obliterate or, except as authorised by this Act, to add to or alter the crossing.

Duties of banker as to crossed cheques

79. (1) Where a cheque is crossed specially to more than one banker except when crossed to an agent for collection being a banker, the banker on whom it is drawn shall refuse payment thereof.

(2) Where the banker on whom a cheque is drawn which is so crossed nevertheless pays the same, or pays a cheque crossed generally otherwise than to a banker, or if crossed specially otherwise than to the banker to whom it is crossed, or his agent for collection being a banker, he is liable to the true owner of the cheque for any loss he may sustain owing to the cheque having been so paid.

Provided that where a cheque is presented for payment which does not at the time of presentment appear to be crossed, or to have had a crossing which has been obliterated, or to have been added to or altered otherwise than as authorised by this Act, the banker paying the cheque in good faith and without negligence shall not be responsible or incur any liability, nor shall the payment be questioned by reason of the cheque having been crossed, or of the crossing having been obliterated or having been added to or altered otherwise than as authorised by this Act, and of payment having been made otherwise than to a banker or to the banker to whom the cheque is or was crossed, or to his agent for collection being a banker, as the case may be.

Protection to banker and drawer where cheque is crossed

80. Where the banker, on whom a crossed cheque [(including a cheque which under *section 81A* below or otherwise is not transferable)][1] is drawn, in good faith and without negligence pays it, if crossed generally, to a banker, and if crossed specially, to the banker to whom it is crossed, or his agent for collection being a banker, the banker paying the cheque, and, if the cheque has come into the hands of the payee, the drawer, shall respectively be entitled to the same rights and be placed in the same position as if payment of the cheque had been made to the true owner thereof.

Effect of crossing on holder

81. Where a person takes a crossed cheque which bears on it the words "not negotiable", he shall not have and shall not be capable of giving a better title to the cheque than that which the person from whom he took it had.

Non-transferable cheques

[**81A.** (1) Where a cheque is crossed and bears across its face the words "account payee" or "a/c payee", either with or without the word "only", the cheque shall not be transferable, but shall only be valid as between the parties thereto.

---

[1] Words inserted by Cheques Act 1992 (c. 32), s.2.

(2) A banker is not to be treated for the purposes of section 80 above as having been negligent by reason only of his failure to concern himself with any purported indorsement of a cheque which under subsection (1) above or otherwise is not transferable.][1]

82. [—][2]

PART IV

Promissory Notes

Promissory note defined

83. (1) A promissory note is an unconditional promise in writing made by one person to another signed by the maker, engaging to pay, on demand or at a fixed or determinable future time, a sum certain in money, to, or to the order of, a specified person or to bearer.

(2) An instrument in the form of a note payable to maker's order is not a note within the meaning of this section unless and until it is indorsed by the maker.

(3) A note is not invalid by reason only that it contains also a pledge of collateral security with authority to sell or dispose thereof.

(4) A note which is, or on the face of it purports to be, both made and payable within the British Islands is an inland note. Any other note is a foreign note.

Delivery necessary

84. A promissory note is inchoate and incomplete until delivery thereof to the payee or bearer.

Joint and several notes

85. (1) A promissory note may be made by two or more makers, and they may be liable thereon jointly, or jointly and severally according to its tenor.

(2) Where a note runs "I promise to pay" and is signed by two or more persons it is deemed to be their joint and several note.

Note payable on demand

86. (1) Where a note payable on demand has been indorsed, it must be presented for payment within a reasonable time of the indorsement. If it be not so presented the indorser is discharged.

(2) In determining what is reasonable time, regard shall be had to the nature of the instrument, the usage of trade, and the facts of the particular case.

(3) Where a note payable on demand is negotiated, it is not deemed to be overdue, for the purpose of affecting the holder with defects of title of which he had no notice, by reason that it appears that a reasonable time for presenting it for payment has elapsed since its issue.

---

[1] Added by Cheques Act 1992 (c. 32), s.1.
[2] Repealed by Cheques Act 1957 (c. 36), Sched.

Presentment of note for payment

87. (1) Where a promissory note is in the body of it made payable at a particular place, it must be presented for payment at that place in order to render the maker liable. In any other case, presentment for payment is not necessary in order to render the market liable.

(2) Presentment for payment is necessary in order to render the indorser of a note liable.

(3) Where a note is in the body of it made payable at a particular place, presentment at that place is necessary in order to render an indorser liable; but when a place of payment is indicated by way of memorandum only, presentment at that place is sufficient to render the indorser liable, but a presentment to the maker elsewhere, if sufficient in other respects, shall also suffice.

Liability of maker

88. The maker of a promissory note by making it—

(1) Engages that he will pay it according to its tenor;

(2) Is precluded from denying to a holder in due course the existence of the payee and his then capacity to indorse.

Application of Part II to notes

89. (1) Subject to the provisions in this part, and except as by this section provided, the provisions of this Act relating to bills of exchange apply, with the necessary modifications, to promissory notes.

(2) In applying those provisions the maker of a note shall be deemed to correspond with the acceptor of a bill, and the first indorser of a note shall be deemed to correspond with the drawer of an accepted bill payable to drawer's order.

(3) The following provisions as to bills do not apply to notes; namely, provisions relating to—

(a) Presentment for acceptance;

(b) Acceptance;

(c) Acceptance supra protest;

(d) Bills in a set.

(4) Where a foreign note is dishonoured, protest thereof is unnecessary.

PART V

SUPPLEMENTARY

Good faith

90. A thing is deemed to be done in good faith, within the meaning of this Act, where it is in fact done honestly, whether it is done negligently or not.

Signature

91. (1) Where, by this Act, any instrument or writing is required to be signed by any person it is not necessary that he should sign it with his own hand, but it is sufficient if his signature is written thereon by some other person by or under his authority.

(2) In the case of a corporation, where, by this Act, any instrument or writing is required to be signed, it is sufficient if the instrument or writing be sealed with the corporate seal.

But nothing in this section shall be construed as requiring the bill or note of a corporation to be under seal.

Computation of time

92. Where, by this Act, the time limited for doing any act or thing is less than three days, in reckoning time, non-business days are excluded.

"Non-business days" for the purposes of this Act mean—

(a) [Saturday]¹ Sunday, Good Friday, Christmas Day;

(b) A bank holiday under [the *Banking and Financial Dealings Act 1971*]²

(c) A day appointed by Royal proclamation as a public fast or thanksgiving day.

[(d) A day declared by an order under *section 2* of the *Banking and Financial Dealings Act 1971* to be a non-business day.]³

Any other day is a business day.

When noting equivalent to protest

93. For the purposes of this Act, where a bill or note is required to be protested within a specified time or before some further proceeding is taken, it is sufficient that the bill has been noted for protest before the expiration of the specified time or the taking of the proceeding; and the formal protest may be extended at any time thereafter as of the date of the noting.

Protest when notary not accessible

94. Where a dishonoured bill or note is authorised or required to be protested, and the services of a notary cannot be obtained at the place where the bill is dishonoured, any householder or substantial resident of the place may, in the presence of two witnesses, give a certificate, signed by them, attesting the dishonour of the bill, and the certificate shall in all respects operate as if it were a formal protest of the bill.

The form given in *Schedule 1* to this Act may be used with necessary modifications, and if used shall be sufficient.

Dividend warrants may be crossed

95. The provisions of this Act as to crossed cheques shall apply to a warrant for payment of dividend.

96. [—]⁴

---

¹ Word inserted by Banking and Financial Dealings Act 1971 (c. 80), s.3(1)(3).
² Words substituted by Banking and Financial Dealings Act 1971 (c. 80), s.4(4).
³ Section 92(d) added by Banking and Financial Dealings Act 1971 (c. 80), s.4(4).
⁴ Repealed by Statute Law Revision Act 1898 (c. 22).

Savings

97. (1) The rules in bankruptcy relating to bills of exchange, promissory notes, and cheques, shall continue to apply thereto notwithstanding anything in this Act contained.

(2) The rules of common law including the law merchant, save in so far as they are inconsistent with the express provisions of this Act, shall continue to apply to bills of exchange, promissory notes, and cheques.

(3) Nothing in this Act or in any repeal effected thereby shall affect—

(a) [...]¹ any law or enactment for the time being in force relating to the revenue;

(b) The provisions of the *Companies Act 1862*, or Acts amending it, or any Act relating to joint stock banks or companies;

(c) The provisions of any Act relating to or confirming the privileges of the Bank of England or the Bank of Ireland respectively;

(d) The validity of any usage relating to dividend warrants, or the indorsements thereof.

Saving of summary diligence in Scotland

98. Nothing in this Act or in any repeal effected thereby shall extend or restrict, or in any way alter or affect the law and practice in Scotland in regard to summary diligence.

Construction with other Acts, etc

99. Where any Act or document refers to any enactment repealed by this Act, the Act or document shall be construed, and shall operate, as if it referred to the corresponding provisions of this Act.

Parole evidence allowed in certain judicial proceedings in Scotland

100. In any judicial proceeding in Scotland, any fact relating to a bill of exchange, bank cheque, or promissory note, which is relevant to any question of liability thereon, may be proved by parole evidence:

Provided that this enactment shall not in any way affect the existing law and practice whereby the party who is, according to the tenour of any bill of exchange, bank cheque, or promissory note, debtor to the holder in the amount thereof, may be required, as a condition of obtaining a sist of diligence, or suspension of a charge, or threatened charge, to make such consignation, or to find such caution as the court or judge before whom the cause is depending may require.

[...]²

¹ Words repealed by Statute Law Revision Act 1898 (c. 22).
² Words repealed by Prescription and Limitation (Scotland) Act 1973 (c. 52), s.16(2), Sched. 5, Pt I.

FIRST SCHEDULE

FORM OF PROTEST WHICH MAY BE USED WHEN THE SERVICES OF A NOTARY CANNOT BE
OBTAINED

Section 94

Know all men that I, A.B. [householder] of   , in the county of   , in
the United Kingdom, at the request of C.D., there being no notary public available, did
on the   day of   ,   , demand payment [*or* acceptance] of the bill
of exchange hereunder written, from E.F., to which demand he made answer [state
answer, if any] wherefore I now, in the presence of G.H. and J.K., do protest the said
bill of exchange.

> (Signed) *A.B.* }
>   *G.H.* } Witnesses
>   *J.K.* }

N.B.—The bill itself should be annexed, or a copy of the bill and all that is written
thereon should be underwritten.

BILLS OF EXCHANGE (TIME OF NOTING) ACT 1917

An Act to amend the Bills of Exchange Act 1882 with respect to the time for noting
Bills

[8th November 1917]

Time of noting

1. In subsection (4) of section fifty-one of the Bills of Exchange Act 1882 (which
relates to the time of noting a dishonoured bill), the words "it must be noted on the day
of its dishonour" shall be repealed, and the following words shall be substituted
therefor; namely, "it may be noted on the day of its dishonour and must be noted not
later than the next succeeding business day".

Short title and construction

2. This Act may be cited as the Bills of Exchange (Time of Noting) Act 1917 and
shall be construed as one with the Bills of Exchange Act, 1882, and the Bills of
Exchange Acts 1882 and 1906 and this Act may be cited together as the Bills of
Exchange Acts 1882 to 1917.

CHEQUES ACT 1957

AN Act to amend the law relating to cheques and certain other instruments.

Protection of bankers paying unindorsed or irregularly indorsed cheques, etc.

1. (1) Where a banker in good faith and in the ordinary course of business pays a
cheque drawn on him which is not indorsed or is irregularly indorsed, he does not, in
doing so, incur any liability by reason only of the absence of, or irregularity in,
indorsement, and he is deemed to have paid it in due course.

(2) Where a banker in good faith and in the ordinary course of business pays any such instrument as the following, namely,—

(a) a document issued by a customer of his which, though not a bill of exchange, is intended to enable a person to obtain payment from him of the sum mentioned in the document;

(b) a draft payable on demand drawn by him upon himself, whether payable at the head office or some other office of his bank;

he does not, in doing so, incur any liability by reason only of the absence of, or irregularity in, indorsement, and the payment discharges the instrument.

Rights of bankers collecting cheques not indorsed by holders

2. A banker who gives value for, or has a lien on, a cheque payable to order which the holder delivers to him for collection without indorsing it, has such (if any) rights as he would have had if, upon delivery, the holder had indorsed it in blank.

Unindorsed cheques as evidence of payment

3. [(1)] An unindorsed cheque which appears to have been paid by the banker on whom it is drawn is evidence of the receipt by the payee of the sum payable by the cheque.

[(2) For the purposes of subsection (1) above, a copy of a cheque to which that subsection applies is evidence of the cheque if—

(a) the copy is made by the banker in whose possession the cheque is after presentment and,

(b) it is certified by him to be a true copy of the original.]¹

Protection of bankers collecting payment of cheques, etc.

4. (1) Where a banker, in good faith and without negligence,—

(a) receives payment for a customer of an instrument to which this section applies; or

(b) having credited a customer's account with the amount of such an instrument, receives payment thereof for himself;

and the customer has no title, or a defective title, to the instrument, the banker does not incur any liability to the true owner of the instrument by reason only of having received payment thereof.

(2) This section applies to the following instruments, namely,—

(a) cheques [(including cheques which under section 81A(1) of the Bills of Exchange Act 1882 or otherwise are not transferable)]²

(b) any document issued by a customer of a banker which, though not a bill of exchange, is intended to enable a person to obtain payment from that banker of the sum mentioned in the document;

¹ Added by the Deregulation (Bills of Exchange) Order 1996 (S.I. 1996 No. 2993) Art. 5.
² Words inserted by Cheques Act 1992 (c. 32), s.3.

(c) any document issued by a public officer which is intended to enable a person to obtain payment from the Paymaster General or the Queen's and Lord Treasurer's Remembrancer of the sum mentioned in the document but is not a bill of exchange;

(d) any draft payable on demand drawn by a banker upon himself, whether payable at the head office or some other office of his bank.

(3) A banker is not to be treated for the purposes of this section as having been negligent by reason only of his failure to concern himself with absence of, or irregularity in, indorsement of an instrument.

Application of certain provisions of Bills of Exchange Act, 1882, to instruments not being bills of exchange

5. The provisions of the Bills of Exchange Act 1882 relating to crossed cheques shall, so far as applicable, have effect in relation to instruments (other than cheques) to which the last foregoing section applies as they have effect in relation to cheques.

Construction, saving and repeal

6. (1) This Act shall be construed as one with the Bills of Exchange Act 1882.
(2) The foregoing provisions of this Act do not make negotiable any instrument which, apart from them, is not negotiable.
(3) [—][1]

Provisions as to Northern Ireland

7. This Act extends to Northern Ireland,[...][2]

Short title and commencement

8. (1) This Act may be cited as the Cheques Act 1957.
(2) This Act shall come into operation at the expiration of a period of three months beginning with the day on which it is passed.

BANKING AND FINANCIAL DEALINGS ACT 1971

An Act to make new provision in place of the Bank Holidays Act 1871, to confer power to suspend financial and other dealings on bank holidays or other days, and to amend the law relating to bills of exchange and promissory notes with reference to the maturity of bills and notes and other matters affected by the closing of banks on Saturdays, and for purposes connected therewith.

[16th December 1971]

---

[1] Repealed by Statute Law (Repeals) Act 1974 (c. 22).
[2] Words repealed by Northern Ireland Constitution Act 1973 (c. 36) Sched. 6, Pt 1.

Bank holidays

1. (1) Subject to subsection (2) below, the days specified in Schedule 1 to this Act shall be bank holidays in England and Wales, in Scotland and in Northern Ireland as indicated in the Schedule.

(2) If it appears to Her Majesty that, in the special circumstances of any year, it is inexpedient that a day specified in Schedule 1 to this Act should be a bank holiday, Her Majesty may by proclamation declare that that day shall not in that year be a bank holiday and appoint another day in place of it; and the day appointed by the proclamation shall, in that year, be a bank holiday under this Act instead of the day specified in Schedule 1.

(3) Her Majesty may from time to time by proclamation appoint a special day to be, either throughout the United Kingdom or in any place or locality in the United Kingdom, a bank holiday under this Act.

(4) No person shall be compellable to make any payment or to do any act on a bank holiday under this Act which he would not be compellable to make or do on Christmas Day or Good Friday; and where a person would, apart from this subsection, be compellable to make any payment or to do any act on a bank holiday under this Act, his obligation to make the payment or to do the act shall be deemed to be complied with if he makes or does it on the next following day on which he is compellable to make or do it.

(5) The powers conferred on Her Majesty by subsection (2) and (3) above may, as respects Northern Ireland, be exercised by the [Secretary of State].[1]

(6) The provision made by this section for January 2nd or 3rd to be a bank holiday in Scotland shall have effect for the year 1973 and subsequent years.

Bills of exchange and promissory notes

3. (1) Section 92 of the Bills of Exchange Act 1882 (which, in a case in which the time limited by that Act for doing any act or thing is less than three days, excludes non-business days from the reckoning of that time, and defines such days for the purposes of the Act) shall have effect as if, in paragraph (a) of the definition of non-business days, "Saturday" were inserted immediately before "Sunday".

This subsection shall not operate to extend any period expiring at or before the time it comes into force.

(2) For section 14(1) of the Bills of Exchange Act 1882 (under or by virtue of which the date of maturity of a bill or promissory note that does not say otherwise is arrived at by adding three days of grace to the time of payment as fixed by the bill or note, but is advanced or postponed if the last day of grace is a non-business day) there shall be substituted, except in its application to bills drawn and notes made before this subsection comes into force, the following paragraph—

"(1) The bill is due and payable in all cases on the last day of the time of payment as fixed by the bill or, if that is a non-business day, on the succeeding business day."

(3) This section shall come into force at the expiration of one month beginning with the date on which this Act is passed.

Consequential and supplementary

4. (1) Except as otherwise provided by this Act, in any, enactment or instrument passed or made before the coming into force of this section (including an enactment of

[1] Words substituted by virtue of Northern Ireland Constitutions Act 1973 (c. 36), Sched. 5, para. 4(1).

the Parliament of Northern Ireland or instrument having effect under such an enactment) any reference to a bank holiday under the Bank Holidays Act 1871 or a holiday
under the Holidays Extension Act 1875 shall have effect as a reference to a bank
holiday under this Act.

(2) [—][1]

(3) An order under section 2 above may be made with respect to a bank holiday or
other day which is a non-business day for the purposes of the enactments relating to
bills of exchange and promissory notes or with respect to a business day; but if a day
specified under section 2(1) is otherwise a business day for those purposes, the order
may declare it a non-business day.

(4) [—][2]

(5) [—][3]

SCHEDULE 1

BANK HOLIDAYS

1. The following are to be bank holidays in England and Wales—

Easter Monday.

The last Monday in May.

The last Monday in August.

26th December, if it be not a Sunday.

27th December in a year in which 25th or 26th December is a Sunday.

2. The following are to be bank holidays in Scotland—

New Year's Day, if it be not a Sunday or, if it be a Sunday, 3rd January.

2nd January, if it be not a Sunday or, if it be a Sunday, 3rd January.

Good Friday.

The first Monday in May.

The first Monday in August.

Christmas Day, if it be not a Sunday or, if it be a Sunday, 26th December.

3. The following are to be bank holidays in Northern Ireland—

17th March, if it be not a Sunday or, if it be a Sunday, 18th March.

Easter Monday.

The last Monday in May.

The last Monday in August.

26th December, if it be not a Sunday.

27th December in a year in which 25th or 26th December is a Sunday.

---

[1] Repealed by Employment Act 1989 (c. 38), s.29(4), Sched. 7, Pt II.
[2] Textually amends Bills of Exchange Act 1882 (c. 61), s.92(b) and adds new s.92(d) to that
Act.
[3] Repeals enactments specified in Sched. 2.

THE GENEVA CONVENTIONS ON BILLS OF EXCHANGE OF 1932

ANNEXE I

LOI UNIFORME CONCERNANT LA LETTRE DE CHANGE ET LE BILLET A ORDRE

TITRE I

DE LA LETTRE DE CHANGE

CHAPITRE I.—DE LA CREATION ET DE LA FORME DE LA LETTRE DE CHANGE

Article premier

La lettre de change contient:

1. La dénomination de lettre de change insérée dans le texte meme du titre et exprimée dans la langue employée pour la rédaction de ce titre;
2. Le mandat pur et simple de payer une somme déterminée;
3. Le nom de celui qui doit payer (tiré);
4. L'indication de l'échéance;
5. Celle du lieu où paiement doit s'effectuer;
6. Le nom de celui auquel ou à l'ordre duquel le paiement doit être fait;
7. L'indication de la date et du lieu où la lettre est créée;
8. La signature de celui qui émet la lettre (tireur).

Article 2

Le titre dans lequel une des énonciations indiquées à l'article précédent fait défaut ne vaut pas comme lettre de change, sauf dans le cas déterminés par les alinéas suivants:

La lettre de change dont l'échéance n'est pas indiquée est considérée comme payable à vue.
A défaut d'indication spéciale, le lieu désigné à côté du nom due tiré est réputé être le lieu du paiement et, en même temps, le lieu due domicile due tiré.

La lettre de change n'indiquant pas le lieu de sa création est considérée comme souscrite dans le lieu désigné à côté du nom du tireur.

Article 3

La lettre de change peut être à l'ordre du tireur lui-même.
Elle peut être tirée sur le tireur lui-même.
Elle peut être tirée pour le compte d'un tiers.

Article 4

Une lettre de change peut être payable au domicile d'un tiers, soit dans la localité où le tiré a son domicile, soit dans une autre localité.

Article 5

Dans une lettre de change payable à vue ou à un certain délai de vue, il peut être stipulé par le tireur que la somme sera productive d'intérêts. Dans toute autre lettre de change, cette stipulation est réputée non écrite.

Le taux des intérêts doit être indiqué dans la lettre; à défaut de cette indication, la clause est réputée non écrite.

Les intérêts courent à partir de la date de la lettre de change, si une autre date n'est pas indiquée.

Article 6

La lettre de change dont le montant est écrit à la fois en toutes lettres et en chiffres vaut, en cas de différence, pour la somme écrite en toutes lettres.

La lettre de change dont le montant est écrit plusieurs fois, soit en toutes lettres, soit en chiffres, ne vaut, en cas de différence, que pour la moindre somme.

Article 7

Si la lettre de change porte des signatures de personnes incapables de s'obliger par lettre de change, des signatures fausses ou des signatures de personnes imaginaires, ou des signatures qui, pour toute autre raison, ne sauraient obliger les personnes qui ont signé la lettre de change, ou du nom desquelles elle a été signée, les obligations des autres signataires n'en sont pas moins valables.

Article 8

Quiconque appose sa signature sur une lettre de change, comme représentant d'une personne pour laquelle il n'avait pas le pouvoir d'agir, est obligé lui-même en vertu de la lettre et, s'il a payé, a les mêmes droits qu'aurait eu le prétendu représenté. Il en est de même du représentant qui a dépassé ses pouvoirs.

Article 9

Le tireur est garant de l'acceptation et du paiement.

Il peut s'exonérer de la garantie de l'acceptation; toute clause par laquelle il s'exonère de la garantie du paiement est réputée non écrite.

Article 10

Si une lettre de change, incomplète à l'émission, a été complétée contrairement aux accords intervenus, l'inobservation de ces accords ne peut être opposée au porteur, à moins qu'il n'ait acquis la lettre de change de mauvaise foi ou que, en l'acquérant, il n'ait commis une faute lourde.

Chapitre II—De l'endossement

Article 11

Toute lettre de change, même non expressément tirée à ordre, est transmissible par la voie de l'endossement.

Lorsque le tireur a inséré dans la lettre de change les mots "non à ordre" ou une expression équivalente, le titre n'est transmissible que dans la forme et avec les effets d'une cession ordinaire.

L'endossement peut être fait même au profit du tiré, accepteur ou non, du tireur ou de tout autre obligé. Ces personnes peuvent endosser la lettre à nouveau.

Article 12

L'endossement doit être pur et simple. Toute condition à laquelle il est subordonnée est réputée non écrite.

L'endossement partiel est nul.

L'endossement au porteur vaut comme endossement en blanc.

Article 13

L'endossement doit être inscrit sur la lettre de change ou sur une feuille qui y est attachée (allonge). Il doit être signé par l'endosseur.

L'endossement peut ne pas désigner le bénéficiaire ou consister simplement dans la signature de l'endosseur (endossement en blanc). Dans ce dernier cas, l'endossement, pour être valable, doit être inscrit au dos de la lettre de change ou sur l'allonge.

Article 14

L'endossement transmet tous les droits résultant de la lettre de change.

Si l'endossement est en blanc, le porteur peut:

1° Remplir le blanc, soit de son nom, soit du nom d'une autre personne;

2° Endosser la lettre de nouveau en blanc ou à une autre personne;

3° Remettre la lettre à un tiers, sans remplir le blanc et sans l'endosser.

Article 15

L'endosseur est, sauf clause contraire, garant de l'acceptation et du paiement.

Il peut interdire un nouvel endossement; dans ce cas, il n'est pas tenu à la garantie envers les personnes auxquelles la lettre est ultérieurement endossée.

Article 16

Le détenteur d'une lettre de change est considéré comme porteur légitime, s'il justifie de son droit par une suite ininterrompue d'endossements, même si le dernier endossement est en blanc. Les endossements biffés sont à cet égard réputés non écrits. Quand un endossement en blanc est suivi d'un autre endossement, le signataire de celui-ci est réputé avoir acquis la lettre par l'endossement en blanc.

Si une personne a été dépossédée d'une lettre de change par quelque événement que ce soit, le porteur, justifiant de son droit de la manière indiquée à l'alinéa précédent, n'est tenu de se dessaisir de la lettre que s'il l'a acquise de mauvaise foi ou si, en l'acquérant, il a commis une faute lourde.

Article 17

Les personnes actionées en vertu de la lettre de change ne peuvent pas opposer au porteur les exceptions fondées sur leurs rapports personnels avec le tireur ou avec les porteurs antérieurs à moins que le porteur, en acquérant la lettre, n'ait agi sciemment au détriment du débiteur.

Article 18

Lorsque l'endossement contient la mention "valeur en recouvrement", "pour encaissement", "par procuration" ou toute autre mention impliquant un simple man-dat, le porteur peut exercer tous les droits dérivant de la lettre de change, mais il ne peut endosser celle-ci qu'à titre de procuration.

Les obligés ne peuvent, dans ce cas, invoquer contre le porteur que les exceptions qui seraient opposables à l'endosseur.

Le mandat renfermé dans un endossement de procuration ne prend pas fin par le décès du mandant ou la survenance de son incapacité.

Article 19

Lorsque'un endossement contient la mention "valeur en garantie", "valeur en gage" ou toute autre mention impliquant un nantissement le porteur peut exercer tous les droits dérivant de la lettre de change, mais un endossement fait par lui ne vaut que comme un endossement à titre de procuration.

Les obligés ne peuvent invoquer contre le porteur les exceptions fondées sur leurs rapports personnels avec l'endosseur, à moins que le porteur, en recevant la lettre, n'ait agi sciemment au détriment du débiteur.

Article 20

L'endossement postérieur à l'échéance produit les mêmes effets qu'un endossement antérieur. Toutefois l'endossement postérieur au protêt faute de paiement, ou fait après l'expiration du délai fixé pour dresser le protêt, ne produit que les effets d'une cession ordinaire.

Sauf preuve contraire, l'endossement sans date est censé avoir été fait avant l'expiration du délai fixé pour dresser le protêt.

Chapitre III—De l'acceptation

Article 21

La lettre de change peut être, jusqu'à l'échéance, présentée à l'acceptation du tiré, au lieu de son domicile, par le porteur ou même par un simple détenteur.

Article 22

Dans toute lettre de change, le tireur peut stipuler qu'elle devra être présentée à l'acceptation, avec ou sans fixation de délai.

Il peut interdire dans lettre la présentation à l'acceptation, à moins qu'il ne s'agisse d'une lettre de change payable chez un tiers ou d'une lettre payable dans une localité autre que celle du domicile du tiré ou d'une lettre tirée à un certain délai de vue.

Il peut aussi stipuler que la présentation à l'acceptation ne pourra avoir lieu avant un terme indiqué.

Tout endosseur peut stipuler que la lettre devra être présentée à l'acceptation, avec ou sans fixation de délai, à moins, qu'elle n'ait été déclarée non acceptable par le tireur.

Article 23

Les lettres de change à un certain délai de vue doivent être présentées à l'acceptation dans le délai d'une an à partir de leur date.

Le tireur peut abréger ce dernier délai ou en stipuler un plus long.

Ces délais peuvent être abrégés par les endosseurs.

Article 24

Le tiré peut demander qu'une seconde présentation lui soit faite le lendemain de la première. Les intéressés en sont admis à prétendre qu'il n'a pas été fait droit à cette demande que si celle-ci est mentionée dans le protêt.

Le porteur n'est pas obligé de se dessaisir, entre les mains due tiré de la lettre présentée à l'acceptation.

Article 25

L'acceptation est écrite sur la lettre de change. Elle est exprimée par le mot "accepté" ou tout autre mot équivalent; elle est signée du tiré. La simple signature du tiré apposée au recto de la lettre vaut acceptation.

Quand la lettre est payable à un certain délai de vue ou lorsqu'elle doit être présentée á l'acceptation dans un délai déterminé en vertu d'une stipulation spéciale, l'acceptation doit être datée du joir où elle a été donnée, à moins que le porteur n'exige qu'elle soit datée du jour de la presentation. A défaut de date, le porteur, pour conserver ses droits de recours contre les endosseurs et contre le tireur fait constater cette omission par un protêt dressê en temps utile.

Article 26

L'acceptation est pure et simple, mais le tiré peut la restreindre à une partie de la somme.

Toute autre modification apportée par l'acceptation aux énonciations de la lettre de change équivaut à un refus d'acceptation. Toutefois, l'accepteur est tenu dans les termes de son acceptation.

Article 27

Quand le tireur a indiqué dans la lettre de change un lieu de paiement autre que celui du domicile du tiré, sans désigner un tiers chez qui le paiement doit être effectué, le tiré peut l'indiquer lors de l'acceptation. A défaut de cette indication, l'accepteur est réputé s'être obligé à payer lui-même au lieu du paiement.

Si la lettre est payable au domicile du tiré, celui-ci peut, dans l'acceptation, indiquer une addresse du même lieu où le paiement doit être effectué.

Article 28

Par l'acceptation, le tiré s'oblige à payer la lettre de change à l'échéance.

A défaut de paiement, le porteur, même s'il est le tireur, a contre l'accepteur une action directe résultant de la lettre de change pour tout ce qui peut étre exigé en vertu des articles 48 et 49.

Article 29

Si le tiré qui a revêtu la lettre de change de son acceptation a biffé celle-ci avant la restitution de la lettre, l'acceptation est censée refusée. Sauf preuve contraire, la radiation est réputée avoir été faite avant la restitution du titre.

Toutefois, si le tiré a fait connaître son acceptation par écrit au porteur ou à un signataire quelconque, il est tenu envers ceux-ci dans les termes de son acceptation.

CHAPITRE IV—DE L'AVAL

Article 30

Le paiement d'une lettre de change peut être garanti pour tout ou partie de son montant par un aval.

Cette garantie est fournie par un tiers ou même par un signataire de la lettre.

Article 31

L'aval est donné sur la lettre de change ou sur une allonge.

Il est exprimé par les mots "bon pour aval" ou par toute autre formule équivalente; il est signé par le donneur d'aval.

Il est considéré comme résultant de la seule signature du donneur d'aval, apposée au recto de la lettre de change, sauf quand il s'agit de la signature du tiré ou de celle du tireur.

L'aval doit indiquer pour le compte de qui il est donné. A défaut de cette indication, il est réputé donné pour le tireur.

Article 32

Le donneur d'aval est tenu de la même manière que celui dont il s'est porté garant.

Son engagement est valable, alors même que l'obligation qu'il a garantie serait nulle pour toute cause autre qu'un vice de forme.

Quand il paie la lettre de change, le donneur d'aval acquiert les droits résultant de la lettre de change contre le garanti et contre ceux qui sont tenus envers ce dernier en vertu de la lettre de change.

CHAPITRE V—DE L'ÉCHÉANCE

Article 33

Une lettre de change peut être tirée:

A vue;

A un certain délai de vue;
A un certain délai de date;
A jour fixe.

Les lettres de change, soit à d'autres échéances, soit à échéances successives, sont nulles.

Article 34

La lettre de change à vue est payable à sa présentation. Elle doit être présentée au paiement dans le délai d'un an à partir de sa date. Le tireur peut abréger ce délai ou en stipuler un plus long. Ces délais peuvent être abrégés par les endosseurs.

Le tireur peut prescrire qu'une lettre de change payable à vue ne doit pas être présentée au paiement avant un terme indiqué. Dans ce cas, le délai de présentation part de ce terme.

Article 35

L'échéance d'une lettre de change à un certain délai de vue est déterminée, soit par la date de l'acceptation, soit par celle due protêt.

En l'absence du protêt, l'acceptation non datée est réputée, à l'égard de l'accepteur, avoir été donnée le dernier jour du délai prévu pour la présentation à l'acceptation.

Article 36

L'échéance d'une lettre de change tirée à un ou plusieurs mois de date ou de vue à lieu à la date correspondante du mois où le paiement doit être effectué. A défaut de date correspondante, l'échéance a lieu le dernier jour de ce mois.

Quand une lettre de change est tirée à un ou plusieurs mois et demi de date ou de vue, on compte d'abord les mois entiers.

Si l'échéance est fixée au commencement, au milieu (mi-janvier, mi-février, etc.) ou à la fin du mois, on entend par ces termes le premier, le quinze ou le dernier jour du mois.

Les expressions "huit jours" ou "quinze jours" s'entendent, non d'une ou deux semaines, mais d'un délai de huit ou de quinze jours effectifs.

L'expression "demi-mois" indique un délai de quinze jours.

Article 37

Quand une lettre de change est payable à jour fixe dans un lieu où le calendrier est différent de celui du lieu de l'émission, la date de l'échéance est considérée comme fixée d'après le calendrier du lieu de paiement.

Quand une lettre de change tirée entre deux places ayant des calendriers différents est payable à une certain délai de date, le jour de l'émission est ramené au jour correspondant du calendrier du lieu de paiement et l'échéance est fixée on conséquence.

Les délais de présentation des lettres de change sont calculés conformément aux règles de l'alinéa précédent.

Ces règles ne sont pas applicable si une clause de la lettre de change, ou même les simple énonciations du titre, indiquent que l'intention a été d'adopter des règles différentes.

Chapitre VI—Du paiement

Article 38

Le porteur d'une lettre de change payable à jour fixe ou à certain délai de date ou de vue doit présenter la lettre de change au paiement, soit le jour où elle est payable, soit l'un des deux jours ouvrables qui suivent.

Le présentation d'une lettre de change à une Chambre de compensation équivaut à une présentation au paiement.

Article 39

Le tiré peut exiger, en payant la lettre de change, qu'elle lui soit remise acquittée par le porteur.

Le porteur ne peut refuser un paiement partiel.

En cas de paiement partiel, le tiré peut exiger que mention de ce paiement soit fait sur la lettre et que quittance lai en soit donnée.

Article 40

Le porteur d'une lettre de change ne peut être contraint d'en recevoir le paiement avant l'échéance.

Le tiré qui paie avant l'échéance le fait à ses risques et périls.

Celui qui paie à l'échéance est valablement libéré, à moins qu'il n'y ait de sa part une fraude ou une faute lourde. Il est obligé de vérifier la régularité de la suite des endossements mais non la signature des endosseurs.

Article 41

Lorsqu'une lettre de change est stipulée payable en une monnaie n'ayant pas cours au lieu du paiement, le montant peut en être payé dans la monnaie du pays d'après sa valeur au jour de l'échéance. Si le débiteur est en retard, le porteur peut à son choix, demander que le montant de la lettre de change soit payé dans la monnaire du pays d'après le cours, soit du jour de l'échéance, soit du jour de paiement.

Les usages du lieu du paiement servent à déterminer la valeur de la monnaie étrangère. Toutefois, le tireur peut stipuler que la somme à payer sera calculée d'après un cours déterminé dans la lettre.

Les régles ci-énoncées ne s'appliquent pas au cas où le tireur a stipulé que le paiement devra être fait dans une certaine monnaie indiquée (clause de paiement effectif en une monnaie étrangère).

Si le montant de la lettre de change est indiqué dans un monnaie ayant la même dénomination, mais une valeur différente dans le pays d'émission et dans celui du paiement, on est présumé s'être référé à la monnaie du lieu du paiement.

Article 42

A défaut de présentation de la lettre de change au paiement dans le délai fixé par l'article 38, tout débiteur a la faculté d'un remettre le montant en dépôt à l'autorité compétente, aux frais, risques et périls du porteur.

CHAPITRE VII—DES RECOURS FAUTE D'ACCEPTATION ET FAUTE DE PAIEMENT

Article 43

Le porteur peut exercer ses recours contre les endosseurs, le tireur et les autres obligés:
A l'échéance:

Si le paiement n'a pas eu lieu;

Même avant l'échéance;

1° S'il y a eu refus, total ou partiel, d'acceptation;

2° Dans les cas de faillite du tiré, accepteur ou non, de cessation de ses paiements, même non constatée par un jugement, ou de saisse de ses biens demurée infructueuse;

3° Dans les cas de faillite du tireur d'une lettre non acceptable.

Article 44

Le refus d'acceptation ou de paiement doit être constaté par un acte authentique (protêt faute d'acceptation ou faute de paiement).

Le protêt faute d'acceptation doit être fait dans les délais fixés pour la présentation à l'acceptation. Si, dans le cas prévu par l'article 24, premier alinéa, la première présentation a eu lieu le dernier jour du délai, protêt peut encore être dressé le lendemain.

Le protêt faute de paiement d'une lettre de change payable à jour fixe ou à un certain délai de date ou de vue doit être fait l'un des deux jours ouvrables qui suivent le jour où la lettre de change est payable. S'il s'agit d'une lettre payable à vue, le protêt doit être dressé dans les conditions indiquées à l'alinéa précédent pour dresser le protêt, faute d'acceptation.

Le protêt faute d'acceptation dispense de la présentation au paiement et du protêt faute de paiement.

En cas de cessation de paiement du tiré accepteur ou non, ou en cas de saisie de ses biens demeurée infructueuse, le porteur ne peut exercer ses recours qu'après présentation de la lettre au tiré pour le paiement et après confection d'un protêt.

En cas de faillite déclarée du tiré, accepteur ou non, ainsi qu'en cas de faillite déclarée du tireur d'une lettre non acceptable, la production du jugement déclaratif de la faillite suffit pour permettre au porteur d'exercer ses recours.

Article 45

Le porteur doit donner avis du défault d'acceptation ou de paiement à son endosseur et au tireur dans les quatre jours ouvrables qui suivent le jour du protêt ou celui de la présentation en cas de clause de retour sans frais. Chaque endosseur doit, dans les deux jours ouvrables qui suivent le jour où il a reçu l'avis, fair connaître à son endosseur l'avis qu'il a reçu, en indiquant les noms et les addresses de ceux qui ont donné les avis précédents, et ainsi de suite, en remontant jusqu'au tireur. Les délais ci-dessus indiqués courent de la réception de l'avis précédent.

Lorsque, en conformité de l'alinéa précédent, un avis est donné à un signataire de la lettre de change, le même avis doit être donné dans le même délai à son avaliseur.

Dans le cas où un endosseur n'a pas indiqué son adresse ou l'a indiquée d'une façon illisible, il suffit que l'avis soit donné à l'endosseur qui le précède.

Celui qui a un avis à donner peut le faire sous une forme quelconque, même par un simple renvoi de la lettre de change.

Il doit prouver qu'il a donné l'avis dans le délai imparti. Ce délai sera considéré comme observé si une lettre missive donnant l'avis a été mise à la poste dans ledit délai.

Celui qui ne donne pas l'avis dans le délai ci-dessus indiqué n'encourt pas de déchéance; il est responsable, s'il y a lieu, du préjudice causé par sa négligence, sans que les dommages-intérêts puissent dépasser le montant de la lettre de change.

Article 46

Le tireur, un endosseur ou un avaliseur peut, par la clause "retour sans frais", "sans protêt" ou toute autre clause équivalente, inscrite sur le titre et signée, dispenser le porteur de faire dresser, pour exercer ses recours, un protêt faute d'acceptation ou faute de paiement.

Cette clause ne dispense pas le porteur de la présentation de la lettre de change dans les délais prescrits ni des avis à donner. La preuve de l'inobservation des délais incombe à celui qui s'en prévaut contre le porteur.

Si la clause est inscrite par le tireur, elle produit ses effets à l'égard de tous les signataires; si elle est inscrite par un endosseur ou un avaliseur, elle produit ses effets seulement à l'égard de celui-ci. Si, malgré la clause inscrite par le tireur, le porteur fait dresser le protêt, les frais en restent à sa charge. Quand la clause émane d'un endosseur ou d'un avaliseur, les frais du protêt, s'il en est dressé un, peuvent être recouvrés contre tous les signataires.

Article 47

Tous ceux qui tiré, accepté, endossé ou avalisé une lettre de change sont tenus solidairement envers le porteur.

Le porteur a le droit d'agir contre toutes ces personnes, individuellement ou collectivement, sans être astreint à observer l'ordre dans lequel elles se sont obligées.

Le même droit appartient à tout signataire d'une lettre de change qui a remboursé celle-ci.

L'action intentée contre un des obligés n'empêche pas d'agir contre les autres, même postérieurs à celui qui a été d'abord poursuivi.

Article 48

Le porteur peut réclamer à celui contre lequel il exerce son recours:

1° Le montant de la lettre de change non acceptée ou non payée avec les intérêts, s'il en a été stipulé;

2° Les intérêts au taux de six pour cent à partir de l'échéance;

3° Les frais du protêt, ceux des avis donnés, ainsi que les autres frais.

Si le recours est exercé avant l'échéance, déduction sera faite d'un escompte sur le montant de la lettre. Cet escompte sera calculé, d'après le taux de l'escompte officiel (taux de la Banque), tel qu'il existe à la date du recours au lieu du domicile du porteur.

Article 49

Celui qui a remboursé la lettre de change peut réclamer à ses garants:

   1° La somme intégrale qu'il a payée;

   2° Les intérêts de ladite somme, calculés au taux de six pour cent, à partir du jour où il l'a déboursée;

   3° Les frais qu'il a faits.

Article 50

Toute obligé contre lequel un recours est exercé ou qui est exposé à un recours peut exiger, contre remboursement, la remise de la lettre de change avec le protêt et un compte acquitté.

Tout endosseur qui a remboursé la lettre de change peut biffer son endossement et ceux des endosseurs subséquents.

Article 51

En cas d'exercise d'un recours après une acceptation partielle, celui qui rembourse la somme pour laquelle la lettre n'a pas été acceptée peut exiger que ce remboursement soit mentionné sur la lettre et qu'il lui en soit donné quittance. Le porteur doit, en outre, lui remettre une copie certifée conforme de la lettre et le protêt pour permettre l'exercice des recours ultérieurs.

Article 52

Toute personne ayant le droit d'exercer un recours, peut, sauf stipulation contraire, se rembourser au moyen d'une nouvelle lettre (retraite) tirée à vue sur l'un de ses garants et payable au domicile de celui-ci.

La retraite comprend, outre les sommes indiquées dans les articles 48 et 49, un droit de courtage et le droit de timbre de la retraite.

Si la retraite est tirée par le porteur, le montant en est fixé d'après le cours d'une lettre de change à vue, tirée du lieu où la lettre primitive était payable sur le lieu du domicile du garant. Si la retraite est tirée par un endosseur, le montant en est fixé d'après le cours d'une lettre à vue tirée du lieu où le tireur de la retraite a son domicile sur le lieu du domicile du garant.

Article 53

Après l'expiration des délais fixés:

   Pour la présentation d'une lettre de change à vue ou à certain délai de vue;
   Pour la confection du protêt faute d'acception ou faute de paiement;
   Pour la présentation au paiement en cas de clause de retour sans frais;

le porteur est déchu de ses droits contre les endosseurs, contre le tireur et contre les autres obligés, à l'exception de l'accepteur.

A défaut de présentation à l'acceptation dans le délai stipulé par le tireur, le porteur est déchu de ses droits de recours, tant pour défaut de paiement que pour défaut d'acceptation, à moins qu'il ne résulte des termes de la stipulation que le tireur n'a entendu s'exonérer que de la garantie de l'acceptation.

Si la stipulation d'un délai pour la présentation est contenue dans un endossement, l'endosseur, seul, peut s'en prévaloir.

Article 54

Quand la présentation de la lettre de change ou la confection du protêt dans les délais prescrits est empêchée par un obstacle insurmontable (prescription légale d'un Etat quelconque ou autre cas de force majeure), ces délais sont prolongés.

Le porteur est tenu de donner, sans retard, avis du cas de force majeure à son endosseur et de mentionner cet avis, daté et signé de lui, sur la lettre de change ou sur une allonge: pour le surplus, les dispositions de l'article 45 sont applicables.

Après la cessation de la force majeure, le porteur doit, sans retard, présenter la lettre à l'acceptation ou au paiement et, s'il y a lieu, faire dresser le protêt.

Si la force majeure persiste au delà de trente jours à partir de l'échéance, les secours peuvent être exercés, sans que ni la présentation ni la confection d'un protêt soit nécessaire.

Pour les lettres de change à vue ou à certain délai de vue, le délai de trente jours court de la date à laquelle le porteur a, même avant l'expiration des délais de présentation, donné avis de la force majeure à son endosseur; pour les lettres de change à un certain délai de vue, le délai de trente jours s'augmente du délai de vue indiqué dans la lettre de change.

Ne sont point considérés comme constituant des cas de force majeure les faits purement personnels au porteur ou à celui qu'il a chargé de la présentation de la lettre ou de la confection du protêt.

CHAPITRE VIII—DE L'INTERVENTION

1. DISPOSITIONS GÉNÉRALES

Article 55

Le tireur, un endosseur ou un avaliseur peut indiquer une personne pour accepter ou payer au besoin.

Le lettre de change peut être, sous les conditions déterminées ci-après, acceptée ou payée par une personne intervenant pour un débiteur quelconque exposé au recours.

L'intervenant peut être un tiers, même le tiré, ou en personne déjà obligée en vertu de la lettre de change, sauf l'accepteur.

L'intervenant est tenu de donner, dans un délai de deux jour ouvrables, avis de son intervention à celui pour qui il est intervenu. En cas d'inobservation de ce délai, il est responsable, s'il y a lieu, du préjudice causé par sa négligence sans que les dommages-intérêts puissent dépasser le montant de la lettre de change.

2. ACCEPTATION PAR INTERVENTION

Article 56

L'acceptation par intervention peut avoir lieu dans tous les cas oú des recours sont ouverts, avant l'échéance, au porteur d'une lettre de change acceptable.

Lorsqu'il a été indiqué sur la lettre de change une personne pour l'accepter ou la payer au besoin au lieu du paiement, le porteur ne peut exercer avant l'échéance ses droits de recours contre celui qui a apposé l'indication et contre les signataires subséquents à moins qu'il n'ait présenté la lettre de change à la personne désignée et que, celle-ci ayant refusé l'acceptation, ce refus n'ait été constaté par un protêt.

Dans les autres cas d'intervention, le porteur peut refuser l'acceptation par intervention. Toutefois, s'il l'admet, il perd les recours qui lui appartiennent avant l'échéance contre pour qui l'acceptation a été donnée et contre les signataires subséquents.

Article 57

L'acceptation par intervention est mentionnée sur la lettre de change; elle est signée par l'intervenant. Elle indique pour le compte de qui elle a lieu; à defaut de cette indication, l'acceptance est réputée donnée pour le tireur.

Article 58

L'accepteur par intervention est obligé envers le porteur et envers les endosseurs postérieurs à celui pour le compte duquel il est intervenu, de la même manière que celui-ci.

Malgré l'acceptation par intervention, celui pour lequel elle a été faite et ses garants peuvent exiger du porteur, contre remboursement de la somme indiquée à l'article 48, la remise de la lettre de change, du protêt et d'un compte acquitté, s'il y a lieu.

3. PAIEMENT PAR INTERVENTION

Article 59

Le paiement par intervention peut avoir lieu dans tous les cas où, soit à l'échéance, soit avant l'échéance, des recours sont ouverts au porteur.

Le paiement doit comprendre toute la somme qu'aurait à acquitter celui pour lequel il a lieu.

Il doit être fait au plus tard le lendemain du dernier jour admis pour la confection du protêt faute de paiement.

Article 60

Si la lettre de change a été acceptée par des intervenants ayant leur domicile au lieu du paiement, ou si des personnes ayant leur domicile dans ce même lieu ont été indiquées pour payer au besoin, le porteur doit présenter la lettre à toutes ces personnes et faire dresser, s'il y a lieu, un protêt faute de paiement au plus tard le lendemain du dernier jour admis pour la confection du protêt.

A défaut de protêt dans ce délai, celui qui a indiqué le besoin ou pour le compte de qui la lettre a été acceptée et les endosseurs postérieurs cessent d'être obligés.

Article 61

Le porteur qui refuse le paiement par intervention perd ses recours contre ceux qui auraient été libérés.

Article 62

Le paiement par intervention doit être constaté par un acquit donné sur la lettre de change avec indication de celui pour qui il est fait. A défaut de cette indication, le paiement est considéré comme fait pour le tireur.

La lettre de change et le protét, s'il en été dressé un, doivent être remis au payeur par l'intervention.

Article 63

Le payeur par intervention acquiert les droit résultant de la lettre de change contre celui pour lequel il a payé et contre ceux qui sont tenus vis-à-vis de ce dernier en vertu de la lettre de change. Toutefois, il ne peut endosser la lettre de change à nouveau.

Les endosseurs postérieurs au signataire pour qui le paiement a eu lieu sont libérés.

En cas de concurrence pour le paiement par intervention, celui qui opère le plus de libération est préféré. Celui qui intervient, en connaissance de cause, contrairement à cette règle, perd ses recours contre ceux qui auraient été libérés.

Chapitre IX—De la pluralité d'exemplaires et des copies

1. Pluralité d'exemplaires

Article 64

La lettre de change peut être tirée en plusieurs exemplaires indentiques.

Ces exemplaires doivent être numérotés dans le texte même du titre; faute de quoi, chacun d'eux est considéré comme une lettre de change distincte.

Tout porteur d'une lettre n'indiquant pas qu'elle a été tirée en un exemplaire unique, peut exiger à ses frais la délivrance de plusieurs exemplaires. A cet effet, il doit s'adresser à son endosseur immédiat, qui est tenu de lui prêter ses soins pour agir contre son propre endosseur, et ainsi de suite, en remontant jusqu'au tireur. Les endosseurs sont tenus de reproduire les endossements sur les nouveaux exemplaires.

Article 65

Le paiement fait sur un des exemplaires est libératoire, alors même qu'il n'est pas stipulé que ce paiement annule l'effet des autres exemplaires. Toutefois, le tiré reste tenu à raison de chaque exemplaire accepté dont il n'a pas obtenu la restitution.

L'endosseur qui a transféré les exemplaires à différentes personnes, ainsi que les endosseurs subséquents, sont tenus à raison de tous les exemplaires portant leur signature et qui n'ont pas été restitués.

Article 66

Celui qui a envoyé un des exemplaires à l'acceptation doit indiquer sur les autres exemplaires le nom de la personne entre les mains de laquelle cet exemplaire se trouve. Celle-ci est tenue de la remettre au porteur légitime d'un autre exemplaire.

Si elle s'y refuse, le porteur ne peut exercer de recours qu'après avoir fait constater par un protêt:

1° Que l'exemplaire envoyé à l'acceptation ne lui a pas été remis sur sa demande;

2° Que l'acceptation ou le paiement n'a pu être obtenu sur un autre exemplaire.

2. Copies

Article 67

Tout porteur d'une lettre de change a le droit d'en faire des copies.

La copie doit reproduire exactment l'original avec les endossements et toutes les autres mentions qui y figurent. Elle doit indiquer où elle s'arrête.

Elle peut être endossée et avalisée de la même manière et avec les mêmes effets que l'original.

Article 68

La copie doit désigner la détenteur du titre original. Celui-ci est tenu de remettre le dit titre au porteur légitime de la copie.

S'il s'y refuse, le porteur ne peut exercer de recours contre les personnel qui ont endossé ou avalisé la copie qu'après avoir fait constater par un protêt que l'original ne lui a pas été remis sur sa demande.

Si le titre original, aprés le dernier endossement survenu avant que la copie ne soit fait, porte la clause: "à partir d'ici l'endossement ne vaut que sur la copie" ou toute autre formule équivalente, un endossement signé ultérieurement sur l'original est nul.

Chapitre X—Des altérations

Article 69

En cas d'altération du texte d'une lettre de change, les signataires postérieures à cette altération sont tenus dans les termes du texte altéré; les signataires antérieurs le sont dans les terms du texte originaire.

Chapitre XI—De la prescription

Article 70

Toutes actions résultant de la lettre de change contre l'accepteur se prescrivent par trois ans à compter de la date de l'échéance.

Les actions du porteur contre les endosseurs et contre le tireur se prescrivent par an à partir de la date du protêt dressé en temps utile ou de celle de l'échéance, en cas de clause de retour sans frais.

Les actions des endosseurs les uns contre les autres et contre le tireur se prescrivent par six mois à partir du jour oú l'endosseur a remboursé la lettre ou du jour où il a été lui-même actioné.

Article 71

L'interruption de la prescription n'a d'effet que contre celui a l'égard duquel l'acte interruptif a été fait.

Chapitre XII—Dispositions générales

Article 72

Le paiement d'une lettre de change dont l'échéance est à un jour férié légal ne peut être exigé que le premier jour ouvrable qui suit. De même, tous autres actes relatifs à la lettre de change notamment la présentation à l'acceptation et le protêt, ne peuvent être faits qu'un jour ouvrable.

Lorsqu'un de ces actes doit être accompli dans un certain délai dont le dernier jour est un férié légal, ce délai est prorogé jusqu'au premier jour ouvrable qui en suit l'expiration. Les jours fériés intermédiaires sont compris dans la computation du délai.

Article 73

Les délais légaux ou conventionnels ne comprennent pas le jour qui leur sert de point de départ.

Article 74

Aucun jour de grâce, ni légal ni judiciaire, n'est admis.

TITRE II

DU BILLET À ORDRE

Article 75

Le billet à ordre contient:

1° La dénomination du titre insérée dans le texte même et exprimée dans la langue employée pour la rédaction de ce titre;

2° La promesse pure et simple de payer une somme déterminée;

3° L'indication de l'échéance;

4° Celle du lieu où paiement doit s'effectuer;

5° Le nom de celui auquel ou à l'ordre duquel le paiement doit être fait;

6° L'indication de la date et du lieu où le billet est souscrit;

7° La signature de celui qui émet le titre (souscripteur).

Article 76

Le titre dans lequel une des énonciations indiquées à l'article précédent fait défaut ne vaut pas comme billet à ordre, sauf dans les cas déterminés par les alinéas suivants.

Le billet à ordre dont l'échéance n'est pas indiquée est considéré comme payable à vue.

A défaut d'indication spéciale, le lieu de création du titre est réputé être le lieu du paiement et, en même temps, le lieu du domicile du souscripteur.

Le billet à ordere n'indiquant pas le lieu de sa créaction est considéré comme souscrit dans le lieu désigné à côte du nom du souscripteur.

Article 77

Sont applicables au billet à ordre, en tant qu'elles ne sont pas incompatibles avec la nature de ce titre les dispositions relatives à la lettre de change et concernant:

L'endossement (articles 11–20);
L'échéance (articles 33–37);
Le paiement (articles 38–42);
Les recours faute de paiement (articles 43–50, 52–54);
Le paiement par intervention (articles 55, 59–63);
Les copies (articles 67 et 68);
Les altérations (article 69);
La prescription (articles 70–71);
Les jours fériés, la computation des délais et l'interdiction des jours de grâce (articles 72, 73 et 74).

Sont aussi applicable au billet à ordre les dispositions concernant la lettre de change payable chez un tiers ou dans une localité autre que celle du domicile du tiré (articles 4 et 27), la stipulation d'intérêts (article 5), les différences d'énonciation relatives à la somme à payer (article 6), les conséquences de l'apposition d'une signature dans les conditions visées à l'article 7, celles de la signature d'une personne qui agit sans pouvoirs ou en dépassant ses pouvoirs (article 8), et la lettre de change en blanc (article 10).

Sont également applicables au billet à ordere, les dispositions relatives à l'aval (articles 30 à 32); dans le cas prévu à l'article 31, dernier alinéa, si l'aval n'indique pas pour le compte de qui il a été donné, il est réputé l'avoir été pour le compte du souscripteur du billet à ordre.

Article 78

Le souscripteur d'un billet à ordre est obligé de la même manière que l'accepteur d'une lettre de change.

Les billets à ordre payables à un certain délai de vue doivent être présentés au visa du souscripteur dans les délais fixés à l'article 23. Le délai de vue court de la date du visa signé du souscripteur sur le billet. Le refus du souscripteur de donner son visa daté est constaté par un protêt (article 25) dont la date de point de départ au délai de vue.

ANNEXE I

LOI UNIFORME CONCERNANT LE CHEQUE

Chapitre I—De la creation et de la forme du chèque

Article premier

Le chèque contient:

1. La dénomination de chèque, insérée dans le texte même du titre est exprimée dans la langue employée pour la rédaction de ce titre;

2. Le mandat pur et simple de payer une somme déterminée;

3. Le nom de celui qui doit payer (tiré);

4. L'indication du lieu où le paiement doit s'effecteur;

5. L'indication de la date et du lieu où le chèque est créé;

6. La signature de celui qui émet le chèque (tireur).

Article 2

Le titre dans lequel une des énonciations indiquées à l'article précédent fait défaut ne vaut pas comme chèque, sauf dans les cas déterminés par les aliénas suivants.

A défaut d'indication spéciale, le lieu désigné à côté du nom du tiré est réputé être le lieu de paiement. Si plusieurs lieux sont indiqués à côté du nom du tiré, le chèque est payable au premier lieu indiqué.

A défaut de ces indications ou de toute autre indication, le chèque est payable au lieu où le tiré a son établissement principal.

Le chèque sans indication du lieu de sa création est considéré comme souscrit dans le lieu désigné à côté du nom du tireur.

Article 3

Le chèque est tiré sur un banquier ayant des fonds à la disposition du tireur et conformément à une convention, expresse ou tacite, d'après laquelle le tireur a le droit de disposer de ces fonds par chèque. Néanmoins, en cas d'inobservation de ces prescriptions, la validité du titre comme chèque n'est pas atteinte.

Article 4

Le chèque ne peut pas être accepté. Une mention d'acception portée sur le chèque est réputée non écrite.

Article 5

Le chèque peut être stipulé payable:
A une personne dénommée, avec ou sans clause expresse "à ordre";
A une personne dénommée, avec la clause "non à ordre" ou une clause équivalente;
Au porteur.
Le chèque au profit d'une personne dénommée, avec la mention "ou au porteur", ou un terme équivalent, vaut comme chèque au porteur.
Le chèque sans indication du bénéficiaire vaut comme chèque au porteur.

Article 6

Le chèque peut être à l'ordre du tireur lui-même.
Le chèque peut être tiré pour le compte d'un tiers.
Le chèque ne peut être tiré sur le tireur lui-même, sauf dans le cas où il s'agit d'un chèque tiré entire différents établissements d'un même tireur.

Article 7

Toute stipulation d'intérêts insérée dans le chèque est réputée non écrite.

Article 8

Le chèque peut être payable au domicile d'un tiers, soit dans la localité où le tiré a son domicile, soit dans une autre localité, à condition toutefois que le tiers soit banquier.

Article 9

Le chèque dont le montant est écrit à la fois en toutes lettres et en chiffres vaut, en cas de différence, pour la somme écrite en toutes lettres.

Le chèque dont le montant est écrit plusieurs fois, soit en toutes lettres, soit en chiffres, ne vaut, en cas de différence, que pour la moindre somme.

Article 10

Si le chèque porte des signatures de personnes incapables de s'obliger par chèque, des signatures fausses ou des signatures de personnes imaginaires, ou des signatures qui, pour toute autre raison, ne sauraient obliger les personnes qui ont signé le chèque, ou au nom desquelles il a été signé, les obligations des autres signataires n'en sont pas moins valables.

Article 11

Quiconque appose sa signature sur un chèque, comme représentant d'une personne pour laquelle il n'avait pas le pouvoir d'agir, est obligé lui-même en vertu du chèque, et s'il a payé, a les mêmes droits qu'aurait eu le prétendu représenté. Il en est de même du représentant qui a dépassé ses pourvoirs.

Article 12

Le tireur est garant du paiement. Toute clause par lequel le tireur s'exonère de cette garantie est réputée non écrite.

Article 13

Si un chèque incomplet à l'émission, a été complété contrairement aux accords intervenus, l'inobservation de ces accords ne peut pas être opposée au porteur, à moins qu'il n'ait acquis le chèque de mauvaise foi ou que, en l'acquérant, il n'ait commis une faute lourde.

CHAPITRE II—DE LA TRANSMISSION

Article 14

Le chèque stipulé payable au profit d'une personnel dénommée avec ou sans clause expresse "à ordre" est transmissible par la voie de l'endossement.

Le chèque stipulé payable au profit d'une personne dénommée avec la clause "non à ordre" ou une clause équivalente n'est transmissible que dans la forme et avec les effets d'une cession ordinaire.

L'endossement peut être fait même au profit du tireur ou de tout autre obligé. Ces personnes peuvent endosser le chèque à nouveau.

Article 15

L'endossement doit être pur et simple. Toute condition à laquelle il est subordonné est réputée non écrite.

L'endossement partiel est nul.

Est également nul l'endossement du tiré.

L'endossement au porteur vaut comme endossement en blanc.

L'endossement au tiré ne vaut que comme quittance, sauf dans le cas où le tiré a plusieurs établissements et où l'endossement est fait au bénéfice d'un établissement autre que celui sur lequel le chèque e été tiré.

Article 16

L'endossement doit être inscrit sur le chèque ou sur une feuille qui y est attachée (allonge). Il doit étre signé par l'endosseur.

L'endossement peut ne pas désigner le bénéficiaire ou consister simplement dans la signature de l'endosseur (endossement en blanc). Dans ce dernier cas, l'endossement, pour être valable, doit être inscrit au dos du chèque ou sur l'allonge.

Article 17

L'endossement transmet tous le droits résultant du chèque.

Si l'endossement est en blanc, le porteur peut:

    1° Remplir le blanc, soit de son nom, soit du nom d'une autre personne;

    2° Endosser le chèque de nouveau en blanc ou à une autre personne;
       Remettre le chèque à un tiers, sans remplir le blanc et sans l'endosser.

Article 18

L'endosseur est, sauf clause contraire, garante du paiement.

Il peut interdire un nouvel endossement; dans ce cas, il n'est pas tenu à la garantie envers les personnes auxquelles le chèque est ultérieurement endossé.

Article 19

Le détenteur d'un chèque endossable est considéré comme porteur légitime s'il justifie de son droit par une suite ininterrompue d'endossements, même si le dernier endossement est en blanc. Les endossements biffés sont, à cet égard, réputés non écrits. Quand un endossement en blanc est suivi d'un autre endossement, le signataire de celui-ci est réputé avoir acquis le chèque par l'endossement en blanc.

Article 20

Un endossement figurant sur un chèque au porteur rend l'endosseur responsable aux termes des dispositions qui régissent le recours; il ne convertit, d'ailleurs, pas le titre en un chèque à ordre.

Article 21

Lorsque'une personne a été dépossédée d'un chèque par quelque événement que ce soit, le porteur entre les mains duquel le chèque est parvenu—soit qu'il s'agisse d'un chèque au porteur, soit qu'il s'agisse d'un chèque endossable pour lequel le porteur justifie de son droit de la manière indiquée à l'article 19—n'est tenu de se dessaisir du chèque que s'il l'a acquis de mauvaise foi ou si, en l'acquérant, il a commis une faute lourde.

Article 22

Les personnes actionnées en vertu du chèque ne peuvent pas opposer au porteur les exceptions fondées sur leurs rapports personnels avec le tireur ou avec les porteurs antérieurs, à moins que le porteur, en acquérant le chèque, n'ait agi sciemment au détriment du débiteur.

Article 23

Lorsque l'endossement contient la mention "valeur en recouvrement", "pour encaissement", "par procuration" ou toute autre mention impliquant un simple mandat, le porteur peut exercer tous les droits découlant du chèque, mais il ne peut endosser celui-ci qu'à titre de procuration.

Les obligés ne peuvent, dans ce cas, invoquer contre le porteur que les exceptions qui saraient opposables à l'endosseur.

Le mandat renfermé dans un endossement de procuration ne prend pas fin par le décès du mandant ou la survenance de son incapacité.

Article 24

L'endossement fait après le protêt ou une constation équivalente, ou après l'expiration du délai de présentation, ne produit que les effets d'une cession ordinaire.

Sauf preuve contraire, l'endossement sans date est présumé avoir été fait avant le protêt ou les constatations équivalentes ou avant l'expiration du délai visé à l'alinéa précédent.

Chapitre III—De l'aval

Article 25

Le paiement d'un chèque peut être garanti pour tout ou partie de son montant par un aval.

Cette garantie est fournie par un tiers, sauf le tiré, ou même par un signataire du chèque.

Article 26

L'aval est donné sur le chèque our sur une allonge.

Il est exprime par le mots "bon pour aval" ou par toute autre formule équivalente; il est signé par le donneur d'aval.

Il est considéré comme résultant de la seule signature du donneur d'aval, apposée au recto du chèque, sauf quand il s'agit de la signature du tireur.

L'aval doit indiquer pour le compte de qui il est donné. A défaut de cette indication, il est réputé donné pour le tireur.

Article 27

Le donneur d'aval est tenu de la même manière que celui dont il s'est porté garant.

Son engagement est valable, alors même que l'obligation qu'il a garantie serait nulle pour toute cause autre qu'un vice de forme.

Quand il paie le chèque, le donneur d'aval acquiert les droits résultant du chèque contre le garanti et contre ceux qui sont tenus envers ce dernier en vertu du chèque.

CHAPITRE IV—DE LA PRÉSENTATION ET DU PAIEMENT

Article 28

Le chèque est payable à vue. Toute mention contraire est réputée non écrite.

Le chèque présenté eu paiement avant le jour indiqué comme date d'émission est payable le jour de la présentation.

Article 29

Le chèque émis et payable dans le même pays doit être présenté au paiement dans le délai de huit jours.

Le chèque émis dans un autre pays que celui où il est payable doit être présenté dans un délai, soit de vingt jours, soit de soixante-dix jours, selon que le lieu d'émission et le lieu de paiement se trouvent situés dans la même ou dans une autre partie du monde.

A cet égard, les chèques émis dans un pays de l'Europe et payables dans un pays riverain de la Méditerranée ou *vice versa* sont considérés comme émis et payables dans la même partie du monde.

Le point de départ de délais susindiqués est le jour porté sur le chèque comme date d'émission.

Article 30

Lorsqu'un chèue est tiré entre deux places ayant des calendriers différents, le jour de l'émission sera ramené au jour correspondant du calendrier du lieu du paiement.

Article 31

La présentation à une Chambre de compensation équivaut à la présentation au paiement.

Article 32

La révocation du chèque n'a d'effect qu'après l'expiration du délai de présentation.

S'il n'ye a pas de révocation, le tiré peut payer même après l'expiration du délai.

Article 33

Ni le décès du tireur ni son incapacité survenant après l'émission ne touchent aux effects du chèque.

Article 34

Le tiré peut exiger, en payant le chèque, qu'il lui soit remis acquitté par le porteur.

Le porteur ne peut pas refuser un paiment partiel.

En cas de paiment partiel, le tiré peut exiger que mention de ce paiement soit faite sur le chèque et qu'une quittance lui en soit donnée.

Article 35

Le tiré qui paie un chèque endossable est obligé de vérifier la régularité de la suite des endossements mains non la signature des endosseurs.

Article 36

Lorsqu'un chèque est stipulé payable en une monnaie n'ayant pas cours au lieu du paiement, le montant peut en être payé, dans le délai de présentation du chèque, en la monnaie du pays d'après sa valeur au jour du paiement. Si le paiment n'a pas été effectué à la présentation, le porteur peut, à son choix, demander que le montant du chèque soit payé dans la monnaie du pays d'après le cours, soit du jour de la présentation, soit du jour du paiement.

Les usages du lieu du paiment servent à déterminer la valeur de la monnaie étrangère. Toutefois, le tireur peut stipuler que la somme à payer sera calculée d'aprè un cours déterminé dans le chèque.

Les régles ci-énoncées ne s'appliquent pas au cas où le tireur a stipulé que le paiement devra être fait dans une certaine monnaie indiquée (cflause de paiement effectif en une monnaie étrangére).

Si le montant du chèque est indiqué dans une monnaie ayant le même dénomination, mais une valeur différente, dans le pays d'émission et dans celui du paiement, on est présumé s'être référé à la monnaie du lieu du paiement.

CHAPITRE V—DU CHÈQUE BARRÈ ET DU CHÈQUE A PORTER EN COMPTE

Article 37

Le tireur ou le porteur d'un chèque peut le barrer avec les effets indiqués dans l'article suivant.

Le barrement s'effectue au moyen de deux barres parallèles apposées au recto. Il peut être général ou spécial.

Le barrement est général s'il ne porte entre les deux barres aucune désignation ou la mention "banquier" ou un terme équivalent; il est spécial si le nom d'un banquier est inscrit entre les deux barres.

Le barrement général peut être transformé en barrement spécial, mais le barrement spécial ne peut être trnasformé en barrement général.

Le biffage du barrement ou du nom du banquier désigné est réputé non avenue.

Article 38

Un chèque à barrement général ne peut être payé par le tiré qu'à un banquier ou à un client du tiré.

Un chèque à barrement spécial ne peut être payé par le tiré qu'au banquier désigné ou, si celui-ci est le tiré, qu'à son client. Toutefois, le banquier désigné peut recourir pour l'encaissement à un autre banquier.

Un banquier ne peut acquérir un chèque barré d'un de ses clients ou d'un autre banquier. Il ne peut l'encaisser pour le compte d'autres personnes que celles-ci.

Un chèque portant plusieurs barrements spéciaux ne peut être payé par le tiré que dans le cas où il s'agit de deux barrements, dont l'un pour encaissement par une Chambre de compensation.

Le tiré ou le banquier qui n'observe pas le dispositions ci-dessus est responsable du préjudice jusqu'à concurrence du montant du chèque.

Article 39

Le tireur, ainsi que le porteur d'un chèque, peut défendre qu'on le paye en espèces, en insérant au recto la mention transversale "à porteur en compte" ou une expression équivalente.

Dans ce cas, le chèque ne peut donner lieu, de la part du tiré, qu'à un règlement par écritures (crédit en compte, virement ou compensation). Le règlement par écritures, vaut payement.

Le biffage de la mention "à porteur en compte" est réputé non avenu.

Le tiré qui n'observe pas les dispositions ci-dessus est responsable du préjudice jusqu'à concurrence du montant du chèque.

Article 40

Le porteur peut exercer ses recours contre les endosseurs, le tireur et les autres obligés, si le chèque, présenté on temps utile, n'est pas payé et si le refus de paiement est constaté:

1° Soit par un acte authentique (protêt);

2° Soit par une déclaration du tiré, datée et écrite sur le chèque avec l'indication du jour de la présentation;

3° Soit par une déclaration datée d'une Chambre de compensation constatant que le chèque a été remis en temps utile et qu'il n'a pas été payé.

Article 41

Le protêt ou la constatation équivalente doit être fait avant l'expiration du dèlai de présentation.

Si la présentation a lieu le dernier jour du délai, le protêt ou la constatation équivalente peut être établi le premier jour ouvrable suivant.

Article 42

Le porteur doit donner avis du défaut de paiement à son endosseur et au tireur dans le quatre jours ouvrables qui suivent le jour du protêt ou de la constatation équivalente, et, en cas de clause de retour sans frais, le jour de la présentation. Chaque endosseur doit, dans les deux jours ouvrables qui suivent le jour où il a reçu l'avis, faire connaître à son endosseur l'avis qu'il a reçu, en indiquant les nomes et les adresses de ceux qui ont donné les avis précédents, et ainsi de suite, en remontant jusqu'au tireur. Les délais ci-dessus indiqué courent de la réception de l'avis précédent.

Lorsque'en conformité de l'alinéa précédent, un avis est donné à un signataire du chèque, le même avis doit être donné dans le même délai à son avaliseur.

Dans le cas où un endosseur n'a pas indiqué son adresse ou l'a indiquée d'une façon illisible il suffit que l'avis soit donné à l'endosseur qui le précède.

Celui qui a un avis à donner peut le faire sous une forme quelconque, même par un simple renvoi du chèque.

Il doit prouver qu'il a donné l'avis dans le délai imparti. De délai sera considéré comme observé si une lettre-missive donnant l'avis a été mise à la poste dans ledit délai.

Celui qui ne donne pas l'avis dans le délai ci-dessus indiqué, n'encourt pas de déchéance; il est responsable, s'il y a lieu, du préjudice causé par sa négligence, sans que les dommages-intérêts puissent dépasser le montant du chèque.

Article 43

Le tireur, un endosseur ou un avaliseur peut, par la clause "retour sans frais", "sans protêt" ou toute autre clause équivalente, inscrite sur le titre et signée, dispenser le porteur, pour exercer ses recours, de faire établir un protêt ou une constatation équivalente.

Cette clause ne dispense pas le porteur de la présentation due chèque dans le délai prescrit ni des avis à donner. La preuve de l'inobservation du délai incombe à celui qui s'en prévaut contre le porteur.

Si la clause est inscrite par le tireur, elle produit ses effets à l'égard de tous les signataires; si elle est inscrite par un endosseur ou un avaliseur, elle produit ses effets seulement à l'égard de celui-ci. Si, malgré la clause inscrite par le tireur, le porteur fait établir le protêt ou la constatation équivalente, les frais en restent à sa charge. Quand la clause émane d'un endosseur ou d'un avaliseur, les frai du protêt ou de la constatation équivalente, s'il est dressé un acte de cette nature, peuvent être recouvrés contre tous les signataires.

Article 44

Toutes les personnes obligées en vertu d'un chèque sont tenues solidairement envers le porteur.

Le porteur a le droit d'agir contre toutes ces personnes, individuellement ou collectivement, sans être astreint à observer l'ordre dans lequel elles se sont obligées.

Le même droit appartient à tout signataire d'un chèque qui a remboursé celui-ci.

L'action intentée contre un des obligés n'empêche pas d'agir contre les autres, même postérieurs à celui qui a été d'abord poursuivi.

Article 45

Le porteur peut réclamer à celui contre lequel il exerce son recours;

   1° Le montant du chèque non payé;

   2° Les intérêts au taux de 6% à partir du jour de la présentation;

   3° Les frais du protêt ou de la constatation équivalente, ceux des avis donnés, ainsi que les autres frais.

Article 46

Celui qui a remboursé le chèque peut réclamer à ses garants:

   1° La somme intégrale qu'il a payée;

   2° Les intérêts de ladite somme, calculés au taux de 6%, à partir du jour où il l'a déboursée;

3° Les frais qu'il a faits.

Article 47

Tout obligé contre lequel un recours est exercé ou qui est exposé à un recours peut exiger, contre remboursement, la remise du chèque avec le protêt ou la constatation équivalente et un compte acquitté.

Tout endosseur qui a remboursé le chèque peut biffer son endossement et ceux des endosseurs subséquents.

Article 48

Quand la présentation de chèque, la confection du protêt ou la constatation équivalente dans les délais prescrits est empêchée par un obstacle insurmontable (prescription légale d'un Etat quelconque ou autre cas de force majeure), ces délais sont prolongés.

Le porteur est tenu de donner, sans retard, avis du cas de force majeure à son endosseur et de mentionner cet avis, daté et signé de lui, sur le chèque ou sur une allonge; pour le surplus, les dispositions de l'article 42 sont applicables.

Après la cessation de la force majeure, le porteur doit, sans retard, présenter le chèque au paiement et, s'il y a lieu, faire établir le protêt ou une constatation équivalente.

Si la force majeure persiste au delà de quinze jours à partir de la date à laquelle la porteur a, même avant l'expiration du délai de présentation, donné avis de la force majeure à son endosseur, les recours peuvent être exercés, sans que ni la présentation ni le protêt ou une constatation équivalente soit nécessaire.

Ne sont pas considérés comme constituant de cas de force majeure les faits purement personnels au porteur ou à celui qu'il a chargé de la présentation du chèque ou de l'établissement de protêt ou d'une constatation équivalente.

Chapitre VII—De la pluralité d'exemplaires

Article 49

Sauf les chèques au porteur, tout chèque émis dans un pays et payable dans un autre pays ou dans une partie d'outre-mer du même pays et *vice versa*, ou bien émis et payable dans la même partie ou dans diverses parties d'outre-mer du même pays, peut être tiré en plusieurs exemplaires indentiques. Lorsqu'un chèque est établi en plusieurs exemplaires, ces exemplaires doivent être numérotés dans le texte même du titre, faute de quoi chacun d'eux est considéré comme un chèque distinct.

Article 50

Le paiement fait sur un des exemplaires est libératoire, alors même qu'il n'est pas stipulé que ce paiement annule l'effect des autres exemplaires.

L'endosseur qui a transmis les exemplaires à différentes personnes, ainsi que les endosseurs subséquents, sont tenus à raison de tous les exemplaires portant leur signature qui n'ont pas été restitués.

Chapitre VIII—Des alterations

Article 51

En cas d'altération du texte d'un chèque, les signataires postérieurs à cette altération sont tenus dans les termes du texte altéré; les signataires antérieurs le sont dans les terms du texte originaire.

Chapitre IX—De la prescription

Article 52

Les actions en recours du porteur contre les endosseurs, le tireur et les autres obligés se prescrivent par six mois à partir de l'expiration de délai de présentation.

Les actions en recours des divers obligés au paiement d'un chèque les uns contre les autres se prescrivent par six mois à partir du jour où obligé a remboursé le chèque ou du jour où il a été lui-même actionné.

Article 53

L'interruption de la prescription n'a d'effet que contre celui à l'égard duquel l'acte interruptif a été fait.

Chapitre X—Dispositions generales

Article 54

Dans la présente loi, le mot "banquier" comprend aussi les personnes ou institutions assimillées par la loi aux banquiers.

Article 55

La présentation et le protêt d'un chèque ne peuvent être faits qu'un jour ouvrable.

Lorsque le dernier jour accordé du délai par la loi pour l'accomplissement des actes relatifs au chèque, et notamment pour la présentation ou pour l'etablissement du protêt ou d'un acte équivalent, est un jour férié légal, ce délai est prorogé jusqu'au premier jour ouvrable qui en suit l'expiration. Les jours fériés intermédiares sont compris dans la computation du délai.

Article 56

Les délais prévus par la présente loi ne comprennent pas le jour qui leur sert de point de départ.

Article 57

Aucun jour de grâce, ni légal ni judicaire, n'est admis.

ANNEX I

UNIFORM LAW ON BILLS OF EXCHANGE AND PROMISSORY NOTES

TITLE I

BILLS OF EXCHANGE

CHAPTER I—ISSUE AND FORM OF A BILL OF EXCHANGE

Article 1

A bill of exchange contains:

1. The term "bill of exchange" inserted in the body of the instrument and expressed in the language employed in drawing up the instrument;

2. An unconditional order to pay a determinate sum of money;

3. The name of the person who is to pay (drawee);

4. A statement of the time of payment;

5. A statement of the place where payment is to be made;

6. The name of the person to whom or to whose order payment is to be made;

7. A statement of the date and of the place where the bill is issued;

8. The signature of the person who issues the bill (drawer).

Article 2

An instrument in which any of the requirements mentioned in the preceding article is wanting is invalid as a bill of exchange, except in the cases specified in the following paragraphs:

A bill of exchange in which the time of payment is not specified is deemed to be payable at sight.

In default of special mention, the place specified beside the name of the drawee is deemed to be the place of payment, and at the same time the place of the domicile of the drawee.

A bill of exchange which does not mention the place of its issue is deemed to have been drawn in the place mentioned beside the name of the drawer.

Article 3

A bill of exchange may be drawn payable to drawer's order.
It may be drawn on the drawer himself.
It may be drawn for account of a third person.

Article 4

A bill of exchange may be payable at the domicile of a third person either in the locality where the drawee has his domicile or in another locality.

Article 5

When a bill of exchange is payable at sight, or at a fixed period after sight, the drawer may stipulate that the sum payable shall bear interest. In the case of any other bill of exchange, this stipulation is deemed not to be written (*non écrite*).

The rate of interest must be specified in the bill; in default of such specification, the stipulation shall be deemed not to be written (*non écrite*).

Interest runs from the date of the bill of exchange, unless some other date is specified.

Article 6

When the sum payable by a bill of exchange is expressed in words and also in figures, and there is a discrepancy between the two, the sum denoted by the words is the amount payable.

Where the sum payable by a bill of exchange is expressed more than once in words or more than once in figures, and there is a discrepancy, the smaller sum is the sum payable.

Article 7

If a bill of exchange bears signatures of persons incapable of binding themselves by a bill of exchange, or forged signatures, or signatures of fictitious persons, or signatures which for any other reason cannot bind the persons who signed the bill of exchange or on whose behalf it was signed, the obligations of the other persons who signed it are none the less valid.

Article 8

Whosoever puts his signature on a bill of exchange as representing a person for whom he had no power to act is bound himself as a party to the bill and, if he pays, has the same rights as the person for whom he purported to act. The same rule applies to a representative who has exceeded his powers.

Article 9

The drawer guarantees both acceptance and payment.

He may release himself from guaranteeing acceptance; every stipulation by which he releases himself from the guarantee of payment is deemed not to be written (*non écrite*).

Article 10

If a bill of exchange, which was incomplete when issued, has been completed otherwise than in accordance with the agreements entered into, the non-observance of such agreements may not be set up against the holder unless he has acquired the bill of exchange in bad faith or, in acquiring it, has been guilty of gross negligence.

CHAPTER II—ENDORSEMENT

Article 11

Every bill of exchange, even if not expressly drawn to order, may be transferred by means of endorsement.

When the drawer has inserted in a bill of exchange the words "not to order" or an equivalent expression, the instrument can only be transferred according to the form, and with the effects of an ordinary assignment.

The bill may be endorsed even in favour of the drawee, whether he has accepted or not, or of the drawer, or of any other party to the bill. These persons may re-endorse the bill.

Article 12

An endorsement must be unconditional. Any condition to which it is made subject is deemed not to be written (*non écrite*).

A partial endorsement is null and void.

An endorsement "to bearer" is equivalent to an endorsement in blank.

Article 13

An endorsement must be written on the bill of exchange or on a slip affixed thereto (*allonge*). It must be signed by the endorser.

The endorsement may leave the beneficiary unspecified or may consist simply of the signature of the endorser (endorsement in blank). In the latter case, the endorsement, to be valid, must be written on the back of the bill of exchange or on the slip attached thereto (*allonge*).

Article 14

An endorsement transfers all the rights arising out of a bill of exchange.

If the endorsement is in blank, the holder may:

(1) Fill up the blank either with his own name or with the name of some other person;

(2) Re-endorse the bill in blank, or to some other person;

(3) Transfer the bill to a third person without filling up the blank, and without endorsing it.

Article 15

In the absence of any contrary stipulation, the endorser guarantees acceptance and payment.

He may prohibit any further endorsement; in this case, he gives no guarantee to the persons to whom the bill is subsequently endorsed.

Article 16

The possessor of a bill of exchange is deemed to be the lawful holder if he establishes his title to the bill through an uninterrupted series of endorsements, even if the last endorsement is in blank. In this connection, cancelled endorsements are deemed not to be written (*non écrits*). When an endorsement in blank if followed by another endorsement, the person who signed this last endorsement is deemed to have acquired the bill by the endorsement in blank.

Where a person has been dispossessed of a bill of exchange, in any manner whatsoever, the holder who establishes his right thereto in the manner mentioned in the preceding paragraph is not bound to give up the bill unless he has acquired it in bad faith, or unless in acquiring it he has been guilty of gross negligence.

Article 17

Persons sued on a bill of exchange cannot set up against the holder defences founded on their personal relations with the drawer or with previous holders, unless the holder, in acquiring the bill, has knowingly acted to the detriment of the debtor.

Article 18

When an endorsement contains the statements "value in collection" ("*valeur en recouvrement*"), "for collection" ("*pour encaissement*"), "by procuration" ("*par procuration*") or any other phrase implying a simple mandate, the holder may exercise all rights arising out of the bill of exchange, but he can only endorse it in his capacity as agent.

In this case, the parties liable can only set up against the holder defences which could be set up against the endorser.

The mandate contained in an endorsement by procuration does not terminate by reason of the death of the party giving the mandate or by reason of his becoming legally incapable.

Article 19

When an endorsement contains the statements "value for security" ("*valeur en garantie*"), "value in pledge" ("*valeur en gage*"), or any other statement implying a pledge, the holder may exercise all the rights arising out of the bill of exchange, but an endorsement by him has the effects only of an endorsement by an agent.

The parties liable cannot set up against the holder defences founded on their personal relations with the endorser, unless the holder, in receiving the bill, has knowingly acted to the detriment of the debtor.

Article 20

An endorsement after maturity has the same effects as an endorsement before maturity. Nevertheless, an endorsement after protest for non-payment, or after the expiration of the limit of time fixed for drawing up the protest, operates only as an ordinary assignment.

Failing proof to the contrary, an endorsement without date is deemed to have been placed on the bill before the expiration of the limit of time fixed for drawing up the protest.

CHAPTER III—ACCEPTANCE

Article 21

Until maturity, a bill of exchange may be presented to the drawee for acceptance at his domicile, either by the holder or by a person who is merely in possession of the bill.

Article 22

In any bill of exchange, the drawer may stipulate that it shall be presented for acceptance with or without fixing a limit of time for presentment.

Except in the case of a bill payable at the address of a third party or in a locality other than that of the domicile of the drawee, or, except in the case of a bill drawn payable at a fixed period after sight, the drawer may prohibit presentment for acceptance.

He may also stipulate that presentment for acceptance shall not take place before a named date.

Unless the drawer has prohibited acceptance, every endorser may stipulate that the bill shall be presented for acceptance, with or without fixing a limit of time for presentment.

Article 23

Bills of exchange payable at a fixed period after sight must be presented for acceptance within one year of their date.

The drawer may abridge or extend this period.

These periods may be abridged by the endorsers.

Article 24

The drawee may demand that a bill shall be presented to him a second time on the day after the first presentment. Parties interested are not allowed to set up that this demand has not been complied with unless this request is mentioned in the protest.

The holder is not obliged to surrender to the drawee a bill presented for acceptance.

Article 25

An acceptance is written on the bill of exchange. It is expressed by the word "accepted" or any other equivalent term. It is signed by the drawee. The simple signature of the drawee on the face of the bill constitutes an acceptance.

When the bill is payable at a certain time after sight, or when it must be presented for acceptance within a certain limit of time in accordance with a special stipulation, the acceptance must be dated as of the day when the acceptance is given, unless the holder requires that it shall be dated as of the day of presentment. If it is undated, the holder, in order to preserve his right of recourse against the endorsers and the drawer, must authenticate the omission by a protest drawn up within the proper time.

Article 26

An acceptance is unconditional, but the drawee may restrict it to part of the sum payable.

Every other modification introduced by an acceptance into the tenor of the bill of exchange operates as a refusal to accept. Nevertheless, the acceptor is bound according to the terms of his acceptance.

Article 27

When the drawer of a bill has indicated a place of payment other than the domicile of the drawee without specifying a third party at whose address payment must be made, the drawee may name such third party at the time of acceptance. In default of this indication, the acceptor is deemed to have undertaken to pay the bill himself at the place of payment.

If a bill is payable at the domicile of the drawee, the latter may in his acceptance indicate an address in the same place where payment is to be made.

Article 28

By accepting, the drawee undertakes to pay the bill of exchange at its maturity.

In default of payment, the holder, even if he is the drawer, has a direct action on the bill of exchange against the acceptor for all that can be demanded in accordance with Articles 48 and 49.

Article 29

Where the drawee who has put his acceptance on a bill has cancelled it before restoring the bill, acceptance is deemed to be refused. Failing proof to the contrary, the cancellation is deemed to have taken place before the bill was restored.

Nevertheless, if the drawee has notified his acceptance in writing to the holder or to any party who has signed the bill, he is liable to such parties according to the terms of his acceptance.

CHAPTER IV—"AVALS"

Article 30

Payment of a bill of exchange may be guaranteed by an "aval" as to the whole or part of its amount.

This guarantee may be given by a third person or even by a person who has signed as a party to the bill.

Article 31

The "aval" is given either on the bill itself or on an "allonge".

It is expressed by the words "good as aval" (*"bon pour aval"*) or by any other equivalent formula. It is singed by the giver of the "aval".

It is deemed to be constituted by the mere signature of the giver of the "aval" placed on the face of the bill, except in the case of the signature of the drawee or of the drawer.

An "aval" must specify for whose account it is given. In default of this, it is deemed to be given for the drawer.

Article 32

The giver of an "aval" is bound in the same manner as the person for whom he has become guarantor.

His undertaking is valid even when the liability which he has guaranteed is inoperative for any reason other than defect of form.

He has, when he pays a bill of exchange, the rights arising out of the bill of exchange against the person guaranteed and against those who are liable to the latter on the bill of exchange.

CHAPTER V—MATURITY

Article 33

A bill of exchange may be drawn payable:

At sight;

At a fixed period after sight;
At a fixed period after date;
At a fixed date.

Bills of exchange at other maturities or payable by instalments are null and void.

Article 34

A bill of exchange at sight is payable on presentment. It must be presented for payment within a year of its date. The drawer may abridge or extend this period. These periods may be abridged by the endorsers.

The drawer may prescribe that a bill of exchange payable at sight must not be presented for payment before a named date. In this case, the period for presentment begins from the said date.

Article 35

The maturity of a bill of exchange payable at a fixed period after sight is determined either by the date of the acceptance or by the date of the protest.

In the absence of the protest, an undated acceptance is deemed, so far as regards the acceptor, to have been given on the last day of the limit of time for presentment for acceptance.

Article 36

Where a bill of exchange is drawn at one or more months after date or after sight, the bill matures on the corresponding date of the month when payment must be made. If there be no corresponding date, the bill matures on the last day of this month.

When a bill of exchange is drawn at one or more months and a half after date or sight, entire months must first be calculated.

If the maturity is fixed at the commencement, in the middle (mid-January or mid-February, etc.) or at the end of the month, the first, fifteenth or last day of the month is to be understood.

The expression "eight days" or "fifteen days" indicate not one or two weeks, but a period of eight or fifteen actual days.

The expression "half month" means a period of fifteen days.

Article 37

When a bill of exchange is payable on a fixed day in a place where the calendar is different from the calendar in the place of issue, the day of maturity is deemed to be fixed according to the calendar of the place of payment.

When a bill of exchange drawn between two places having different calendars is payable at a fixed period after date, the day of issue is referred to the corresponding day of the calendar in the place of payment, and the maturity is fixed accordingly.

The time for presenting bills of exchange is calculated in accordance with the rules of the preceding paragraph.

These rules do not apply if a stipulation in the bill or even the simple terms of the instrument indicate an intention to adopt some different rule.

Chapter VI—Payment

Article 38

The holder of a bill of exchange payable on a fixed day or at a fixed period after date or after sight must present the bill for payment either on the day on which it is payable or on one of the two business days which follow.

The presentment of a bill of exchange at a clearing-house is equivalent to a presentment for payment.

Article 39

The drawee who pays a bill of exchange may require that it shall be given up to him receipted by the holder.

The holder may not refuse partial payment.

In case of partial payment the drawee may require that mention of this payment shall be made on the bill, and that a receipt therefor shall be given to him.

Article 40

The holder of a bill of exchange cannot be compelled to receive payment thereof before maturity.

The drawee who pays before maturity does so at his own risk and peril.

He who pays at maturity is validly discharged, unless he has been guilty of fraud or gross negligence. He is bound to verify the regularity of the series of endorsements, but not the signature of the endorsers.

Article 41

When a bill of exchange is drawn payable in a currency which is not that of the place of payment, the sum payable may be paid in the currency of the country, according to its value on the date of maturity. If the debtor is in default, the holder may at his option demand that the amount of the bill be paid in the currency of the country according to the rate on the day of maturity or the day of payment.

The usages of the place of payment determine the value of foreign currency. Nevertheless, the drawer may stipulate that the sum payable shall be calculated according to a rate expressed in the bill.

The foregoing rules shall not apply to the case in which the drawer has stipulated that payment must be made in a certain specified currency (stipulation for effective payment in foreign currency).

If the amount of the bill of exchange is specified in a currency having the same denomination, but a different value in the country of issue and the country of payment, reference is deemed to be made to the currency of the place of payment.

Article 42

When a bill of exchange is not presented for payment within the limit of time fixed by Article 38, every debtor is authorised to deposit the amount with the competent authority at the charge, risk and peril of the holder.

CHAPTER VII—RECOURSE FOR NON-ACCEPTANCE OR NON-PAYMENT

Article 43

The holder may exercise his right of recourse against the endorsers, the drawer and the other parties liable:
At maturity:

If payment has not been made;

Even before maturity;

(1) If there has been total or partial refusal to accept;

(2) In the event of the bankruptcy (*faillite*) of the drawee, whether he has accepted or not, or in the event of a stoppage of payment on his part, even when not declared by a judgment, or where execution has been levied against his goods without result;

(3) In the event of the bankruptcy (*faillite*) of the drawer of a non-acceptable bill.

Article 44

Default of acceptance or of payment must be evidenced by an authentic act (protest for non-acceptance or non-payment).

Protest for non-acceptance must be made within the limit of time fixed for presentment for acceptance. If, in the case contemplated by Article 24, paragraph 1, the first presentment takes place on the last day of that time, the protest may nevertheless be drawn up on the next day.

Protest for non-payment of a bill of exchange payable on a fixed day or at a fixed period after date or sight must be made on one of the two business days following the day on which the bill is payable. In the case of a bill payable at sight, the protest must be drawn up under the conditions specified in the foregoing paragraph for the drawing up of a protest for non-acceptance.

Protest for non-acceptance dispenses with presentment for payment and protest for non-payment.

If there is a stoppage of payment on the part of the drawee, whether he has accepted or not, or if execution has been levied against his goods without result, the holder cannot exercise his right of recourse until after presentment of the bill to the drawee for payment and after the protest has been drawn up.

If the drawee, whether he has accepted or not, is declared bankrupt (*faillite déclarée*), or in the event of the declared bankruptcy of the drawer of a non-acceptable bill, the production of the judgment declaring the bankruptcy suffices to enable the holder to exercise his right of recourse.

Article 45

The holder must give notice of non-acceptance or non-payment to his endorser and to the drawer within the four business days which follow the day for protest or, in the case of a stipulation "*retour sans frais*", the day for presentment. Every endorser must, within the two business days following the day on which he receives notice, notify his endorser of the notice he has received, mentioning the names and addresses of those who have given the previous notices, and so on through the series until the drawer is reached. The periods mentioned above run from the receipt of the preceding notice.

When, in conformity with the preceding paragraph, notice is given to a person who has signed a bill of exchange, the same notice must be given within the same limit of time to his *avaliseur*.

Where an endorser either has not specified his address or has specified it in an illegible manner, it is sufficient that notice should be given to the preceding endorser.

A person who must give notice may give it in any form whatever, even by simply returning the bill of exchange.

He must prove that he has given notice within the time allowed. This time-limit shall be regarded as having been observed if a letter giving the notice has been posted within the prescribed time.

A person who does not give notice within the limit of time mentioned above does not forfeit his rights. He is responsible for the injury, if any, caused by his negligence, but the damages shall not exceed the amount of the bill of exchange.

Article 46

The drawer, an endorser, or a person guaranteeing payment by *aval (avaliseur)* may, by the stipulation *"retour sans frais"*, *"sans protêt"*, or any other equivalent expression written on the instrument and signed, release the holder from having a protest of non-acceptance or non-payment drawn up in order to exercise his right of recourse.

This stipulation does not release the holder from presenting the bill within the prescribed time, or from the notices he has to give. The burden of proving the non-observance of the limits of time lies on the person who seeks to set it up against the holder.

If the stipulation is written by the drawer, it is operative in respect of all persons who have signed the bill; if it written by an endorser or an *avaliseur*, it is operative only in respect of such endorser or *avaliseur*. If, in spite of the stipulation written by the drawer, the holder has the protest drawn up, he must bear the expenses thereof. When the stipulation emanates from an endorser or *avaliseur*, the costs of the protest, if one is drawn up, may be recovered from all the persons who have signed the bill.

Article 47

All drawers, acceptors, endorsers or guarantors by *aval* of a bill of exchange are jointly and severally liable to the holder.

The holder has the right of proceeding against all these persons individually or collectively without being required to observe the order in which they have become bound.

The same right is possessed by any person signing the bill who has taken it up and paid it.

Proceedings against one of the parties liable do not prevent proceedings against the others, even though they may be subsequent to the party first proceeded against.

Article 48

The holder may recover from the person against whom he exercises his right of recourse:

(1) The amount of the unaccepted or unpaid bill of exchange with interest, if interest has been stipulated for;

(2) Interest at the rate of 6 per cent, from the date of maturity;

(3) The expenses of protest and of the notice given as well as other expenses.

If the right of recourse is exercised before maturity, the amount of the bill shall be subject to discount. This discount shall be calculated according to the official rate of discount (bank-rate) ruling on the date when recourse is exercised at the place of domicile of the holder.

Article 49

A party who takes up and pays a bill of exchange can recover from the parties liable to him:

(1) The entire sum which he has paid;

(2) Interest on the said sum calculated at the rate of 6 per cent., starting from the day when he made payment;

(3) Any expenses which he has incurred.

Article 50

Every party liable against whom a right of recourse is or may be exercised, can require against payment that the bill shall be given up to him with the protest and a receipted account.

Every endorser who has taken up and paid a bill of exchange may cancel his own endorsement and those of subsequent endorsers.

Article 51

In the case of the exercise of the right of recourse after a partial acceptance, the party who pays the sum in respect of which the bill has not been accepted can require that this payment shall be specified on the bill and that he shall be given a receipt therefor. The holder must also give him a certified copy of the bill, together with the protest, in order to enable subsequent recourse to be exercised.

Article 52

Every person having the right of recourse may, in the absence of agreement to the contrary, reimburse himself by means of a fresh bill (redraft) to be drawn at sight on one of the parties liable to him and payable at the domicile of that party.

The redraft includes, in addition to the sums mentioned in Articles 48 and 49, brokerage and the cost of stamping the redraft.

If the redraft is drawn by the holder, the sum payable is fixed according to the rate for a sight bill drawn at the place where the original bill was payable upon the party liable at the place of his domicile. If the redraft is drawn by an endorser, the sum payable is fixed according to the rate for a sight bill drawn at the place where the drawer of the redraft is domiciled upon the place of domicile of the party liable.

Article 53

After the expiration of the limits of time fixed:

For the presentment of a bill of exchange drawn at sight or at a fixed period after sight;

For drawing up the protest for non-acceptance or non-payment;

For presentment for payment in the case of a stipulation *retour sans frais*, the holder loses his right of recourse against the endorsers, against the drawer and against the other parties liable, with the exception of the acceptor.

In default of presentment for acceptance within the limit of time stipulated by the drawer, the holder loses his right of recourse for non-payment, as well as for non-acceptance, unless it appears from the terms of the stipulation that the drawer only meant to release himself from the guarantee of acceptance.

If the stipulation for a limit of time for presentment is contained in an endorsement, the endorser alone can avail himself of it.

Article 54

Should the presentment of the bill of exchange or the drawing up of the protest within the prescribed limits of time be prevented by an insurmountable obstacle (legal prohibition (*prescription légale*) by any State or other case of *vis major*), these limits of time shall be extended.

The holder is bound to give notice without delay of the case of *vis major* to his endorser and to specify this notice, which he must date and sign, on the bill or on an *allonge*; in other respects the provisions of Article 45 shall apply.

When *vis major* has terminated, the holder must without delay present the bill of exchange for acceptance or payment and, if need be, draw up the protest.

If *vis major*, continues to operate beyond thirty days after maturity, recourse may be exercised, and neither presentment nor the drawing up of a protest shall be necessary.

In the case of bills of exchange drawn at sight or at a fixed period after sight, the time limit of thirty days shall run from the date on which the holder, even before the expiration of the time for presentment, has given notice of *vis major* to his endorser. In the case of bills of exchange drawn at a certain time after sight, the above time-limit of thirty days shall be added to the period after sight specified in the bill of exchange.

Facts which are purely personal to the holder or to the person whom he has entrusted with the presentment of the bill or drawing up of the protest are not deemed to constitute cases of *vis major*.

Chapter VIII—Intervention for Honour

1. General Provisions

Article 55

The drawer, an endorser, or a person giving an *aval* may specify a person who is to accept or pay in case of need.

A bill of exchange may, subject as hereinafter mentioned, be accepted or paid by a person who intervenes for the honour of any debtor against whom a right of recourse exists.

The person intervening may be a third party, even the drawee, or, save the acceptor, a party already liable on the bill of exchange.

The person intervening is bound to give, within two business days, notice of his intervention to the party for whose honour he has intervened. In default, he is responsible for the injury, if any, due to his negligence, but the damages shall not exceed the amount of the bill of exchange.

2. ACCEPTANCE BY INTERVENTION (FOR HONOUR)

Article 56

There may be acceptance by intervention in all cases where the holder has a right of recourse before maturity on a bill which is capable of acceptance.

When the bill of exchange indicates a person who is designated to accept or pay it in case of need at the place of payment, the holder may not exercise his rights of recourse before maturity against the person naming such referee in case of need and against subsequent signatories, unless he has presented the bill of exchange to the referee in case of need and until, if acceptance is refused by the latter, this refusal has been authenticated by a protest.

In other cases of intervention the holder may refuse an acceptance by intervention. Nevertheless, if he allows it, he loses his right of recourse before maturity against the person on whose behalf such acceptance was given and against subsequent signatories.

Article 57

Acceptance by intervention is specified on the bill of exchange. It is signed by the person intervening. It mentions the person for whose honour it has been given and, in default of such mention, the acceptance is deemed to have been given for the honour of the drawer.

Article 58

The acceptor by intervention is liable to the holder and to the endorsers subsequent to the party for whose honour he intervened, in the same manner as such party.

Notwithstanding an acceptance by intervention, the party for whose honour it has been given and the parties liable to him may require the holder, in exchange for payment of the sum mentioned in Article 48, to deliver the bill, the protest, and a receipted account, if any.

3. PAYMENT BY INTERVENTION

Article 59

Payment by intervention may take place in all cases where, either at maturity or before maturity, the holder has a right of recourse on the bill.

Payment must include the whole amount payable by the party for whose honour it is made.

It must be made at the latest on the day following the last day allowed for drawing up the protest for non-payment.

Article 60

If a bill of exchange has been accepted by persons intervening who are domiciled in the place of payment, or if persons domiciled there have been named as referees in case of need, the holder must present the bill to all these persons and, if necessary, have a protest for non-payment drawn up at the latest on the day following the last day allowed for drawing up the protest.

In default of protest within this limit of time, the party who has named the referee in case of need, or for whose account the bill has been accepted, and the subsequent endorsers, are discharged.

Article 61

The holder who refuses payment by intervention loses his right of recourse against any persons who would have been discharged thereby.

Article 62

Payment by intervention must be authenticated by a receipt given on the bill of exchange mentioning the person for whose honour payment has been made. In default of such mention, payment is deemed to have been made for the honour of the drawer.

The bill of exchange and the protest, if any, must be given up to the person paying by intervention.

Article 63

The person paying by intervention acquires the rights arising out of the bill of exchange against the party for whose honour he has paid and against persons who are liable to the latter on the bill of exchange. Nevertheless, he cannot re-endorse the bill of exchange.

Endorsers subsequent to the party for whose honour payment has been made are discharged.

In case of competition for payment by intervention, the payment which effects the greater number of releases has the preference. Any person who, with a knowledge of the facts, intervenes in a manner contrary to this rule, loses his right of recourse against those who would have been discharged.

CHAPTER IX—PARTS OF A SET, AND COPIES

1. PARTS OF A SET

Article 64

A bill of exchange can be drawn in a set of two or more identical parts.

These parts must be numbered in the body of the instrument itself; in default, each part is considered as a separate bill of exchange.

Every holder of a bill which does not specify that it has been drawn as a sole bill may, at his own expense, require the delivery of two or more parts. For this purpose he must apply to his immediate endorser, who is bound to assist him in proceeding against his own endorser, and so on in the series until the drawer is reached. The endorsers are bound to reproduce their endorsements on the new parts of the set.

Article 65

Payment made on one part of a set operates as a discharge, even though there is no stipulation that this payment annuls the effect of the other parts. Nevertheless, the drawee is liable on each accepted part which he has not recovered.

An endorser who has transferred parts of a set to different persons, as well as subsequent endorsers, are liable on all the parts bearing their signature which have not been restored.

Article 66

A party who has sent one part for acceptance must indicate on the other parts the name of the person in whose hands this part is to be found. That person is bound to give it up to the lawful holder of another part.

If he refuses, the holder cannot exercise his right of recourse until he has had a protest drawn up specifying:

(1) That the part sent for acceptance has not been given up to him on his demand;

(2) That acceptance or payment could not be obtained on another of the parts.

2. COPIES

Article 67

Every holder of a bill of exchange has the right to make copies of it.

A copy must reproduce the original exactly, with the endorsements and all other statements to be found therein. It must specify where the copy ends.

It may be endorsed and guaranteed by *aval* in the same manner and with the same effects as the original.

Article 68

A copy must specify the person in possession of the original instrument. The latter is bound to hand over the said instrument to the lawful holder of the copy.

If he refuses, the holder may not exercise his right of recourse against the persons who have endorsed the copy or guaranteed it by *aval* until he has had a protest drawn up specifying that the original has not been given up to him on his demand.

Where the original instrument, after the last endorsement before the making of the copy contains a clause "commencing from here an endorsement is only valid if made on the copy" or some equivalent formula, a subsequent endorsement on the original is null and void.

CHAPTER X—ALTERATIONS

Article 69

In case of alteration of the text of a bill of exchange, parties who have signed subsequent to the alteration are bound according to the terms of the altered text; parties who have signed before the alteration are bound according to the terms of the original text.

CHAPTER XI—LIMITATION OF ACTIONS

Article 70

All actions arising out of a bill of exchange against the acceptor are barred after three years, reckoned from the date of maturity.

Actions by the holder against the endorsers and against the drawer are barred after one year from the date of a protest drawn up within proper time, or from the date of maturity where there is a stipulation *retour sans frais*.

Actions by endorsers against each other and against the drawer are barred after six months, reckoned from the day when the endorser took up and paid the bill or from the day when he himself was sued.

Article 71

Interruption of the period of limitation is only effective against the person in respect of whom the period has been interrupted.

CHAPTER XII—GENERAL PROVISIONS

Article 72

Payment of a bill of exchange which falls due on a legal holiday (*jour férié légal*) cannot be demanded until the next business day. So, too, all other proceedings relating to a bill of exchange, in particular presentment for acceptance and protest, can only be taken on a business day.

Where any of these proceedings must be taken within a certain limit of time the last day of which is a legal holiday (*jour férié légal*), the limit of time is extended until the first business day which follows the expiration of that time. Intermediate holidays (*jours fériés*) are included in computing limits of time.

Article 73

Legal or contractual limits of time do not include the day on which the period commences.

Article 74

No days of grace, whether legal or judicial, are permitted.

TITLE II

PROMISSORY NOTES

Article 75

A promissory note contains:

(1) The term "promissory note" inserted in the body of the instrument and expressed in the language employed in drawing up the instrument;

(2) An unconditional promise to pay a determinate sum of money;

(3) A statement of the time of payment;

(4) A statement of the place where payment is to be made;

(5) The name of the person to whom or to whose order payment is to be made;

(6) A statement of the date and of the place where the promissory note is issued;

(7) The signature of the person who issues the instrument (maker).

Article 76

An instrument in which any of the requirements mentioned in the preceding article are wanting is invalid as a promissory note except in the cases specified in the following paragraphs;

A promissory note in which the time of payment is not specified is deemed to be payable at sight.

In default of special mention, the place where the instrument is made is deemed to be the place of payment and at the same time the place of the domicile of the maker.

A promissory note which does not mention the place of its issue is deemed to have been made in the place mentioned beside the name of the maker.

Article 77

The following provisions relating to bills of exchange apply to promissory notes so far as they are not inconsistent with the nature of these instruments, viz.:

Endorsement (Articles 11 to 20);
Time of payment (Articles 33 to 37);
Payment (Articles 38 to 42);
Recourse in case of non-payment (Articles 43–50, 52 to 54);
Payment by intervention (Articles 55, 59 to 63);
Copies (Articles 67 and 68);
Alterations (Article 69);
Limitation of actions (Articles 70 and 71);
Holidays, computation of limits of time and prohibition of days of grace (Articles 72, 73 and 74).

The following provisions are also applicable to a promissory note: The provisions concerning a bill of exchange payable at the address of a third party or in a locality other than that of the domicile of the drawee (Articles 4 and 27); stipulation for interest (Article 5); discrepancies as regards the sum payable (Article 6); the consequences of signature under the conditions mentioned in Article 7, the consequences of signature by a person who acts without authority or who exceeds his authority (Article 8); and provisions concerning a bill of exchange in blank (Article 10).

The following provisions are also applicable to a promissory note: Provisions relating to guarantee by *aval* (Articles 30–32); in the case provided for in Article 31, last paragraph, if the *aval* does not specify on whose behalf it has been given, it is deemed to have been given on behalf of the maker of the promissory note.

Article 78

The maker of a promissory note is bound in the same manner as an acceptor of a bill of exchange.

Promissory notes payable at a certain time after sight must be presented for the visa of the maker within the limits of time fixed by Article 23. The limit of time runs from the date of the visa signed by the maker on the note. The refusal of the maker to give his visa with the date thereon must be authenticated by a protest (Article 25), the date of which marks the commencement of the period of time after sight.

ANNEX I

UNIFORM LAW ON CHEQUES

Chapter I—The Drawing and Form of a Cheque

Article 1

A cheque contains:

1. The term "cheque" inserted in the body of the instrument and expressed in the language employed in drawing up the instrument;

2. An unconditional order to pay a determinate sum of money;

3. The name of the person who is to pay (drawee);

4. A statement of the place where payment is to be made;

5. A statement of the date when and the place where the cheque is drawn;

6. The signature of the person who draws the cheque (drawer).

Article 2

An instrument in which any of the requirements mentioned in the preceding article is wanting is invalid as a cheque, except in the cases specified in the following paragraphs:

In the absence of special mention, the place specified beside the name of the drawee is deemed to be the place of payment. If several places are named beside the name of the drawee, the cheque is payable at the first place named.

In the absence of these statements, and of any other indication, the cheque is payable at the place where the drawee has his principal establishment.

A cheque which does not specify the place at which it was drawn is deemed to have been drawn in the place specified beside the name of the drawer.

Article 3

A cheque must be drawn on a banker holding funds at the disposal of the drawer and in conformity with an agreement, express or implied, whereby the drawer is entitled to dispose of those funds by cheque. Nevertheless, if these provisions are not complied with the instrument is still valid as a cheque.

Article 4

A cheque cannot be accepted. A statement of acceptance on a cheque shall be disregarded.

Article 5

A cheque may be made payable:

To a specified person with or without the express clause "to order", or
To a specified person, with the words "not to order" or equivalent words, or
To bearer.

A cheque made payable to a specified person with the words "or to bearer", or any equivalent words, is deemed to be a cheque to bearer.

A cheque which does not specify the payee is deemed to be a cheque to bearer.

Article 6

A cheque may be drawn to the drawer's own order.

A cheque may be drawn for account of a third person.

A cheque may not be drawn on the drawer himself unless it is drawn by one establishment on another establishment belonging to the same drawer.

Article 7

Any stipulation concerning interest which may be embodied in the cheque shall be disregarded.

Article 8

A cheque may be payable at the domicile of a third person either in the locality where the drawee has his domicile or in another locality, provided always that such third person is a banker.

Article 9

Where the sum payable by a cheque is expressed in words and also in figures, and there is any discrepancy, the sum denoted by the words is the amount payable.

Where the sum payable by a cheque is expressed more than once in words or more than once in figures, and there is any discrepancy, the smaller sum is the sum payable.

Article 10

If a cheque bears signatures of persons incapable of binding themselves by a cheque, or forged signatures, or signatures of fictitious persons, or signatures which for any other reason cannot bind the persons who have signed the cheque or on whose behalf it was signed, the obligations of the other persons who have signed it are nonetheless valid.

Article 11

Whosoever puts his signature on a cheque as representing a person for whom he had no power to act is bound himself as a party to the cheque and, if he pays, has the same rights as the person for whom he purported to act. The same rule applies to a representative who has exceeded his powers.

Article 12

The drawer guarantees payment. Any stipulation by which the drawer releases himself from this guarantee shall be disregarded.

Article 13

If a cheque which was incomplete when issued has been completed otherwise than in accordance with the agreements entered into, the non-observance of such agreements may not be set up against the holder unless he has acquired the cheque in bad faith, or in acquiring it, has been guilty of gross negligence.

CHAPTER II—NEGOTIATIONS

Article 14

A cheque made payable to a specified person, with or without the express clause "to order", may be transferred by means of endorsement.

A cheque made payable to a specified person, in which the words "not to order" or any equivalent expression have been inserted, can only be transferred according to the form and with the effects of an ordinary assignment.

A cheque may be endorsed even to the drawer or to any other party to the cheque. These persons may re-endorse the cheque.

Article 15

An endorsement must be unconditional. Any condition to which it is made subject shall be disregarded.

A partial endorsement is null and void.

An endorsement by the drawee is also null and void.

An endorsement "to bearer" is equivalent to an endorsement in blank.

An endorsement to the drawee has the effect only of a receipt, except in the case where the drawee has several establishments and the endorsement is made in favour of an establishment other than that on which the cheque has been drawn.

Article 16

An endorsement must be written on the cheque or on a slip affixed thereto (*allonge*). It must be signed by the endorser.

The endorsement may leave the beneficiary unspecified or may consist simply of the signature of the endorser (endorsement in blank). In the latter case, the endorsement, to be valid, must be written on the back of the cheque or on the slip attached thereto (*allonge*).

Article 17

An endorsement transfers all the rights arising out of a cheque.

If the endorsement is in blank, the holder may:

(1) Fill up the blank either with his own name or with the name of some other person;

(2) Re-endorse the cheque in blank to some other person;

(3) Transfer the cheque to a third person without filling up the blank and without endorsing it.

Article 18

In the absence of any contrary stipulation, the endorser guarantees payment.

He may prohibit any further endorsement; in this case he gives no guarantee to the persons to whom the cheque is subsequently endorsed.

Article 19

The possessor of an endorseable cheque is deemed to be the lawful holder if he establishes his title to the cheque through an uninterrupted series of endorsements, even if the last endorsement is in blank. In this connection, cancelled endorsements shall be disregarded. When an endorsement in blank is followed by another endorsement, the person who signed this last endorsement is deemed to have acquired the cheque by the endorsement in blank.

Article 20

An endorsement on a cheque to bearer renders the endorser liable in accordance with the provisions governing the right of recourse; but it does not convert the instrument into a cheque to order.

Article 21

Where a person has, in any manner whatsoever, been dispossessed of a cheque (whether it is a cheque to bearer or an endorseable cheque to which the holder establishes his right in the manner mentioned in Article 19), the holder into whose possession the cheque has come is not bound to give up the cheque unless he has acquired it in bad faith or unless in acquiring it he has been guilty of gross negligence.

Article 22

Persons sued on a cheque cannot set up against the holder defences founded on their personal relations with the drawer or with previous holders, unless the holder in acquiring the cheque has knowingly acted to the detriment of the debtor.

Article 23

When an endorsement contains the statement "value in collection" (*"valeur en recouvrement"*), "for collection" (*"pour encaissement"*), "by procuration" (*"par procuration"*), or any other phrase implying a simple mandate, the holder may exercise all rights arising out of the cheque, but he can endorse it only in his capacity as agent.

In this case the parties liable can only set up against the holder defences which could be set up against the endorser.

The mandate contained in an endorsement by procuration does not terminate by reason of the death of the party giving the mandate or by reason of his becoming legally incapable.

Article 24

An endorsement after protest or after an equivalent declaration or after the expiration of the limit of time for presentment operates only as an ordinary assignment.

Failing proof to the contrary, an undated endorsement is deemed to have been placed on the cheque prior to the protest or equivalent declaration or prior to the expiration of the limit of time referred to in the preceding paragraph.

CHAPTER III—"AVALS"

Article 25

Payment of a cheque may be guaranteed by an "aval" as to the whole or part of its amount.

This guarantee may be given by a third person other than the drawee, or even by a person who has signed the cheque.

Article 26

An "aval" is given either on the cheque itself or on an "allonge".

It is expressed by the words "good as aval", or by any other equivalent formula. It is signed by the giver of the "aval".

It is deemed to be constituted by the mere signature of the giver of the "aval", placed on the face of the cheque, except in the case of the signature of the drawer.

An "aval" must specify for whose account it is given. In default of this, it is deemed to be given for the drawer.

Article 27

The giver of an "aval" is bound in the same manner as the person for whom he has become guarantor.

His undertaking is valid even when the liability which he has guaranteed is inoperative for any reason other than defect of form.

He has, when he pays the cheque, the rights arising out of the cheque against the person guaranteed and against those who are liable to the latter on the cheque.

CHAPTER IV—PRESENTMENT AND PAYMENT

Article 28

A cheque is payable at sight. Any contrary stipulation shall be disregarded.

A cheque presented for payment before the date stated as the date of issue is payable on the day of presentment.

Article 29

A cheque payable in the country in which it was issued must be presented for payment within eight days.

A cheque issued in a country other than that in which it is payable must be presented within a period of twenty days or of seventy days, according to as whether the place of issue and the place of payment are situated respectively in the same continent or in different continents.

For the purposes of this article cheques issued in a European country and payable in a country bordering on the Mediterranean or *vice versa* are regarded as issued and payable in the same continent.

The date from which the above-mentioned periods of time shall begin to run shall be the date stated on the cheque as the date of issue.

Article 30

Where a cheque is drawn in one place, and is payable in another, having a different calendar, the day of issue shall be construed as being the corresponding day of the calendar of the place of payment.

Article 31

Presentment of a cheque at a clearing-house is equivalent to presentment for payment.

Article 32

The countermand of a cheque only takes effect after the expiration of the limit of time for presentment.

If a cheque has not been countermanded, the drawee may pay it even after the expiration of the time-limit.

Article 33

Neither the death of the drawer or his incapacity taking place after the issue of the cheque shall have any effect as regards the cheque.

Article 34

The drawee who pays a cheque may require that it shall be given up to him receipted by the holder.

The holder may not refuse partial payment.

In case of partial payment the drawee may require that the partial payment shall be mentioned on the cheque and that a receipt shall be given to him.

Article 35

The drawee who pays an endorseable cheque is bound to verify the regularity of the series of endorsements, but not the signature of the endorsers.

Article 36

When a cheque is drawn payable in a currency which is not that of the place of payment, the sum payable may, within the limit of time for the presentment of the cheque, be paid in the currency of the country according to its value on the date of payment. If payment has not been made on presentment, the holder may at his option demand that payment of the amount of the cheque in the currency of the country shall be made according to the rate on the day of presentment or on the day of payment.

The usages of the place of payment shall be applied in determining the value of foreign currency. Nevertheless, the drawer may stipulate that the sum payable shall be calculated according to a rate expressed in the cheque.

The foregoing rules shall not apply to the case in which the drawer has stipulated that payment must be made in a certain specified currency (stipulation for effective payment in a foreign currency).

If the amount of the cheque is specified in a currency having the same denomination but a different value in the country of issue and the country of payment, reference is deemed to be made to the currency of the place of payment.

CHAPTER V—CROSSED CHEQUES AND CHEQUES PAYABLE IN ACCOUNT

Article 37

The drawer or holder of a cheque may cross it with the effects stated in the next article hereof.

A crossing takes the form of two parallel lines drawn on the face of the cheque. The crossing may be general or special.

The crossing is general if it consists of the two lines only or if between the lines the term "banker" or some equivalent is inserted; it is special if the name of a banker is written between the lines.

A general crossing may be converted into a special crossing, but a special crossing may not be converted into a general crossing.

The obliteration either of a crossing or of the name of the banker shall be regarded as not having taken place.

Article 38

A cheque which is crossed generally can be paid by the drawee only to a banker or to a customer of the drawee.

A cheque which is crossed specially can be paid by the drawee only to the named banker, or if the latter is the drawee, to his customer. Nevertheless, the named banker may procure the cheque to be collected by another banker.

A banker may not acquire a crossed cheque except from one of his customers or from another banker. He may not collect it for the account of other persons than the foregoing.

A cheque bearing several special crossings may not be paid by the drawee except in a case where there are two crossings, one of which is for collection through a clearing-house.

The drawee or banker who fails to observe the above provisions is liable for resulting damage up to the amount of the cheque.

Article 39

The drawer or the holder of a cheque may forbid its payment in cash by writing transversely across the face of the cheque the words "payable in account" ("*à porter en compte*") or a similar expression.

In such a case the cheque can only be settled by the drawee by means of book-entry (credit in account, transfer from one account to another, set off or clearing-house settlement). Settlement by book-entry is equivalent to payment.

Any obliteration of the words "payable in account" shall be deemed not to have taken place.

The drawee who does not observe the foregoing provisions is liable for resulting damage up to the amount of the cheque.

CHAPTER VI—RECOURSE FOR NON-PAYMENT

Article 40

The holder may exercise his right of recourse against the endorsers, the drawer and the other parties liable if the cheque on presentment in due time is not paid, and if the refusal to pay is evidenced:

(1) By a formal instrument (protest), or

(2) By a declaration dated and written by the drawee on the cheque and specifying the day of presentment, or

(3) By a dated declaration made by a clearing-house, stating that the cheque has been delivered in due time and has not been paid.

Article 41

The protest or equivalent declaration must be made before the expiration of the limit of time for presentment.

If the cheque is presented on the last day of the limit of time, the protest may be drawn up or the equivalent declaration made on the first business day following.

Article 42

The holder must give notice of non-payment to his endorser and to the drawer within the four business days which follow the day on which the protest is drawn up or the equivalent declaration is made or, in case of a stipulation (*retour sans frais*), the day of presentment. Every endorser must, within the two business days following the day on which he receives notice, inform his endorser of the notice which he has received, mentioning the names and addresses of those who have given the previous notices and so on through the series until the drawer is reached. The periods mentioned above run from the receipt of the preceding notice.

When, in conformity with the preceding paragraph, notice is given to a person who has signed a cheque, the same notice must be given within the same limit of time to his *avaliseur*.

When an endorser either has not specified his address or has specified it in an illegible manner, it is sufficient if notice is given to the endorser preceding him.

The person who must give notice may give it in any form whatever, even by simply returning the cheque.

He must prove that he has given notice within the limit of time prescribed. This time-limit shall be regarded as having been observed if a letter giving the notice has been posted within the said time.

A person who does not give notice within the limit of time prescribed above does not forfeit his rights. He is liable for the damage, if any, caused by his negligence, but the amount of his liability shall not exceed the amount of the cheque.

Article 43

The drawer, an endorser, or an *avaliseur* may, by the stipulation "*retour sans frais*", "*sans protêt*", or any other equivalent expression written on the instrument and signed, release the holder from having a protest drawn up or an equivalent declaration made in order to exercise his right of recourse.

This stipulation does not release the holder from presenting the cheque within the prescribed limit of time, or from giving the requisite notices. The burden of proving the non-observance of the limit of time lies on the person who seeks to set it up against the holder.

If the stipulation is written by the drawer, it is operative in respect of all persons who have signed the cheque; if it is written by an endorser or an *avaliseur*, it is operative only in respect of such endorser or *avaliseur*. If, in spite of the stipulation written by the drawer, the holder has the protest drawn up or the equivalent declaration made, he must bear the expenses thereof. When the stipulation emanates from an endorser or *avaliseur*, the costs of the protest or equivalent declaration, if drawn up or made, may be recovered from all the persons who have signed the cheque.

Article 44

All the persons liable on a cheque are jointly and severally bound to the holder.

The holder has the right to proceed against all these persons individually or collectively without being compelled to observe the order in which they have become bound.

The same right if possessed by any person signing the cheque who has taken it up and paid it.

Proceedings against one of the parties liable do not prevent proceedings against the others, even though such other parties may be subsequent to the party first proceeded against.

Article 45

The holder may claim from the party against whom he exercises his right of recourse:

(1) The unpaid amount of the cheque;

(2) Interest at the rate of 6% as from the date of presentment;

(3) The expenses of the protest or equivalent declaration, and of the notices given as well as other expenses.

Article 46

A party who takes up and pays a cheque can recover from the parties liable to him:

(1) The entire sum which he has paid;

(2) Interest on the said sum calculated at the rate of 6%, as from the day on which he made payment;

(3) Any expenses which he has incurred.

Article 47

Every party liable against whom a right of recourse is, or may be, exercised, can require against payment, that the cheque shall be given up to him with the protest or equivalent declaration and a receipted account.

Every endorser who has taken up and paid a cheque may cancel his own endorsement and those of subsequent endorsers.

Article 48

Should the presentment of the cheque or the drawing up of the protest or the making of the equivalent declaration within the prescribed limits of time be prevented by an insurmountable obstacle (legal prohibition (*prescription légale*) by any State or other case of *vis major*), these limits of time shall be extended.

The holder is bound to give notice without delay of the case of *vis major* to his endorser and to make a dated and signed declaration of this notice, on the cheque or on an *allonge*; in other respects, the provisions of Article 42 shall apply.

When *vis major* has terminated, the holder must without delay present the cheque for payment and, if need be, procure a protest to be drawn up or an equivalent declaration made.

If *vis major* continues to operate beyond fifteen days after the date on which the holder, even before the expiration of the time-limit for presentment, has given notice of *vis major* to his endorser, recourse may be exercised and neither presentment nor a protest nor an equivalent declaration shall be necessary.

Facts which are purely personal to the holder or to the person whom he has entrusted with the presentment of the cheque or the drawing up of the protest or the making of the equivalent declaration are not deemed to constitute cases of *vis major*.

CHAPTER VII—PARTS OF A SET

Article 49

With the exception of bearer cheques, any cheque issued in one country and payable in another or payable in a separate part overseas of the same country or *vice versa*, or issued and payable in the same or in different parts overseas of the same country, may be drawn in a set of identical parts. When a cheque is in a set of parts, each part must be numbered in the body of the instrument, failing which each part is deemed to be a separate cheque.

Article 50

Payment made on one part operates as a discharge, even though there is no stipulation that such payment shall render the other parts of no effect.

An endorser who has negotiated parts to different persons and also the endorsers subsequent to him are liable on all parts bearing their signatures, which have not been given up.

CHAPTER VIII—ALTERATIONS

Article 51

In case of alteration of the text of a cheque, parties who have signed subsequent to the alteration are bound according to the terms of the altered text; parties who have signed before the alteration are bound according to the terms of the original text.

CHAPTER IX—LIMITATION OF ACTIONS

Article 52

Actions of recourse by the holder against the endorsers, the drawer and the other parties liable are barred after six months as from the expiration of the limit of time fixed for presentment.

Actions of recourse by the different parties liable for the payment of a cheque against other such parties are barred after six months as from the day on which the party liable has paid the cheque or the day on which he was sued thereon.

Article 53

Interruption of the period of limitation is only effective against the person in respect of whom the period has been interrupted.

CHAPTER X—GENERAL PROVISIONS

Article 54

In the present law the word "banker" includes the persons or institutions assimilated by the law to bankers.

Article 55

The presentment or protest of a cheque may only take place on a business day.

When the last day of the limit of time prescribed by the law for performing any act relating to a cheque, and particularly for presentment or for the drawing up of a protest or the making of an equivalent declaration, is a legal holiday, the limit of time is extended until the first business day which follows the expiration of that time. Intermediate holidays are included in computing limits of time.

Article 56

The limits of time stipulated in the present law shall not include the day on which the period commences.

Article 57

No days of grace, whether legal or judicial, are permitted.

INDEX